D0931313

WASTE

WASTE

Consuming Postwar Japan

Eiko Maruko Siniawer

CORNELL UNIVERSITY PRESS   **ITHACA AND LONDON**

Cornell University Press gratefully acknowledges receipt of a subvention from Williams College that aided in the publication of this book.

First published 2018 by Cornell University Press

Printed in the United States of America

Library of Congress Cataloging-in-Publication Data

Names: Siniawer, Eiko Maruko, author.
Title: Waste : consuming postwar Japan / Eiko Maruko Siniawer.
Description: Ithaca : Cornell University Press, 2018. | Includes bibliographical references and index.
Identifiers: LCCN 2018000104 (print) | LCCN 2018000993 (ebook) | ISBN 9781501725852 (pdf) | ISBN 9781501725869 (epub/mobi) | ISBN 9781501725845 | ISBN 9781501725845 (cloth ; alk. paper)
Subjects: LCSH: Consumption (Economics)—Social aspects—Japan—History. | Waste minimization—Japan—History. | Refuse and refuse disposal—Social aspects—Japan—History. | Japan—Economic conditions—1945– | Japan—Social conditions—1945–
Classification: LCC HC465.C6 (ebook) | LCC HC465.C6 S745 2018 (print) | DDC 363.72/80952—dc23
LC record available at https://lccn.loc.gov/2018000104

To Pete

Contents

Acknowledgments

Many years before the topic of this book had taken shape, a faint curiosity about the history of rubbish was inspired by an unfortunate, if not grievous, faux pas I committed during my turn on garbage duty for our neighborhood in a residential area of Tokyo. What began as an inchoate notion of studying garbage has evolved and expanded into this book about waste, about the history of the idea of waste. All along the way, it has been nurtured by the generosity of many, to whom I am very grateful.

The book has benefited immeasurably from the thoughtful comments of those who read or heard work in progress. Magnus Bernhardsson, Jessica Chapman, Katarzyna Cwiertka, Charles Dew, Sara Dubow, Peter Frost, Sabine Frühstück, Ali Garbarini, Aparna Kapadia, Roger Kittleson, Eric Knibbs, Tom Kohut, Joel Lee, Karen Merrill, Steve Nafziger, Izumi Nakayama, Nakamura Naofumi, Scott North, Frank Oakley, Anne Reinhardt, Shawn Rosenheim, Franziska Seraphim, Charles Schencking, Jun Uchida, Bill Wagner, Scott Wong, and Jim Wood offered valuable feedback at key stages of the project. Obinata Sumio and Fujino Yūko created opportunities not just to do research but also to share ideas with colleagues in Japan. Many conversations informed my thinking about waste and sustained my work, through everything from a casual remark to a careful response to a particular question. It is a pleasure to be part of a community with Raja Adal, Dani Botsman, David Fedman, Andrew Gordon, Yoshikuni Igarashi, Jason Josephson Storm, Kyu Hyun Kim, Pia Kohler, Hiromu Nagahara, Emer O'Dwyer, Linda Saharczewski, Amy Stanley, and Mariko Tamanoi. For steady and candid support, my thanks to Christopher Bolton, Yoichi Nakano, Christopher Nugent, Mérida Rúa, and Hiraku Shimoda. When I first entertained the idea of this book, Chris Waters helped persuade me to take the topic seriously. And I am especially thankful to Kenda Mutongi for reading so many drafts of my writing, fostering a spirit of unpretentious intellectualism, and encouraging me to write history as I want to write it.

The staff and librarians at the Advertising Museum Tokyo Library, Harvard-Yenching Library, International Library of Children's Literature, Kokumin Seikatsu Sentā Jōhō Shiryōkan, Kyōkasho Kenkyū Sentā, Kyoto Prefectural Library, National Diet Library, NHK Archives, Osaka Municipal Library, Ōya Sōichi Bunko, Tokyo Metropolitan Library, and Waseda University libraries helped make sources available and accessible. Eric Van Slander at the National Archives at College Park as well as Shimada Ryōji and Kawakami Tsuneo of the PHP Institute in Kyoto were especially giving of their time and expertise. Tsuchida Takashi and Yamada Harumi of the Tsukaisute Jidai o Kangaeru Kai invited me to their offices, kindly agreed to talk about the history of the association, and provided many materials.

Two anonymous readers offered substantive and constructive reviews. Tentative ideas and draft chapters were inflicted on students, who responded with sharp and insightful questions. Special thanks are due to Cristina Florea, Sara Kang, Zoë Kline, Eilin Perez, Dave Samuelson, and Sungik Yang.

Roger Haydon of Cornell University Press has enabled my books to see the light of day; I am lucky that he has been interested in my work. Amin Ghadimi was thorough and efficient in securing copyright permissions for the reprinted images.

Generous funding for the research and writing of this book was provided by fellowships from the American Council of Learned Societies, National Endowment for the Humanities, American Historical Association, Association for Asian Studies, and Williams College. Material in chapter 9 was drawn from Eiko Maruko Siniawer, "'Affluence of the Heart': Wastefulness and the Search for Meaning in Millennial Japan," *Journal of Asian Studies* (2014), published by and reproduced with permission of Cambridge University Press.

Finally, extended family in Japan made me feel like I was never without a net, and Shūko-obasan and Mitsuo-ojisan in particular helped with the logistics of research stays. My parents are, as they always have been, steadfast in their support.

To Pete, who knows too well how inescapable waste can be in daily life, it is not possible to convey how extraordinarily fortunate I feel for his unwavering partnership in all things. I am deeply appreciative of the innumerable ways in which he has enriched this book and brought meaning and happiness to our life.

WASTE

MEANING AND VALUE
IN THE EVERYDAY

A teenage girl stands in a train on her morning commute to school, her eyes fixed impassively on the smartphone in her hands. In front of her sit two passengers, asleep, catching whatever rest they can. This sense of fatigue and weariness follows her as she goes through the day, at one point standing alone in a stairwell with her face buried in her hands and at another gasping, "I can't do this." A teenage boy in his work uniform slumps back against the shelf of a convenience store stockroom, staring blankly in front of him at a long row of brightly lit refrigerators filled with an array of bottled and canned drinks. When the words of a co-worker nudge him to sit up, the distant expression on his face shows a hint of resignation. These two youths were the creation of an animated public service announcement which inscribed on the screen one word that encapsulated its message: "wasteful," or in the original Japanese, *mottainai*.[1]

The ad, a high-quality production in the style of a movie trailer, promised nothing less than the potential of *mottainai* to transform melancholy about daily routines into contentedness with a life worth living. This theme was crafted jointly by the nonprofit Advertising Council Japan (AC Japan) and the national broadcaster NHK (Japan Broadcasting Corporation, or Nippon Hōsō Kyōkai), and was promoted through the television spot in the summer of 2015 and online for months thereafter.[2] Its ultimately hopeful note was expressed through the arc of the visuals, as the early scenes of youth dejected with school, sports practice, and work gave way in the second half to a montage of more heartening moments like playing at the beach with a friend and taking time for contemplation. This optimism, subdued and restrained, was underscored by the wistful soundtrack

1

FIGURE 0.1. Public Service Announcement about *Mottainai*. An early scene from the AC Japan and NHK public service announcement about *mottainai*.

From "AC Japan CM mottainai," https://www.youtube.com/watch?v=GXODCN6rfTc.

of piano and strings, joined in the second half by the sparkling of chimes. The motifs of promise and renewed search for purpose were emphasized by the intentional focus on young people with so much of their lives ahead of them. And they were well suited to a time when Japan, tested and tried by a series of challenges, was setting its sights ahead on recovery and revitalization. That the torpor of the present could somehow give way to a better life was explicitly expressed in a line presented over the closing scene: "With *mottainai*, the future will change."

Mottainai here meant more than just being wasteful. This was not an explicit definition or pedantic enumeration of practices that should be considered a waste; it was not that the teenage girl's absorption with her smartphone or the teenage boy's part-time job was being labeled wasteful.[3] Rather, what this take on *mottainai* urged was serious and purposeful reflection about what was wasteful in one's day-to-day life. Throughout the spot, the voice-over listed in a steady cadence all that could be realized just by being attentive to this single word: you could be rescued and revived; become courageous, serious, introspective, and kind; rediscover yourself; figure things out; feel at ease; embrace aspirations; and start moving forward. What the announcement encouraged was consideration of the motivations, purposes, and desires of one's daily life. It was the absence of such self-reflection, if anything, that rendered one's time and energy wasteful. This was a public service announcement not about a discrete social problem but about the idea of waste—about deliberately figuring out what is wasteful so as to discover what is meaningful.

This conception of wastefulness bore the marks of its time. In a long and shifting past reaching back many decades, waste had not always been understood this way. As we delve into the history of how waste and wastefulness have been thought about in Japan, from the immediate aftermath of devastating world war through the more recent past, we will see how malleable and capacious these ideas were and how deeply they were etched by the priorities and aspirations of their historical moment. What the announcement also illustrated so pointedly and elegantly was a fundamental quality of waste: its remarkable capacity to reveal what is valuable and meaningful. A historical examination of waste can thus be a story of people's many and ever-changing concerns, yearnings, disappointments, and hopes. This history of waste is at its heart a history of how people lived—how they made sense of, gave meaning to, and found value in the acts of the everyday in postwar Japan.

Waste and Everyday Life

To ask what has been considered waste and wasteful is to venture into various facets of day-to-day life, following the traces of people's expressions about what they do and do not value. When attuned to waste, we find its presence in so many questions asked in the course of modern living. Should this tired sweater be thrown away? How should all my stuff be organized? Can these old leftovers in the fridge be eaten? Is it justifiable to spend money on the latest smartphone? Is it possible to be more efficient and productive at work? Can this evening be spent playing video games or hanging out at the neighborhood bar? The ubiquity of waste comes into focus when its conception is broad and inclusive of its many manifestations.

Garbage, with all of its materiality, may be the most visible and tangible incarnation of waste. As many who study it have written, to categorize a thing as garbage, however mindlessly, is to implicitly reject it as valueless.[4] Once the tattered shirt, used plastic wrap, or paper coffee cup is discarded, it joins on the rubbish heap all of the detritus cast aside as useless. The amount and composition of trash itself is a mirror of the society responsible for its creation, and discussions about what to do with garbage and how to handle the afterlives of stuff suggest much about people's relationship to material things, what they want to own, how and what they choose to consume, and how they treat their possessions.

But waste need not be thought of just as discarded matter; it can also be understood more expansively as anything, material or not, that can be used and disused. Electricity, food, money, and time can all be wasted. Indeed, there is a parallel between deeming something garbage and deeming anything a waste, be it of energy or money or time. All are determinations of value. This wider conception of waste allows us to see a fuller swath of what might be considered wasteful. Rubbish, such as a broken refrigerator or outdated videocassette recorder, can tell us about the societal context in which the decision to discard was made, about opportunities for repair, attitudes toward disposability, or planned obsolescence. Other versions of this kind of judgment—to deem the use of a clothes dryer a waste of electricity or a lengthy meeting a waste of time—can further open the field of historical vision. They raise questions not just about clothes dryers or meetings but also about understandings of electricity and of time, household responsibilities and practices, and attitudes toward work. Thinking about waste writ large makes more evident the trade-offs in decisions about what to expend and what to save, like whether money and electricity should be spent on a washing machine to spare physical labor and time. Highlighted too is how a thing or action could be wasteful in more ways than one, how a television set could be a waste of money, electricity, space, and time.

Time is a purposeful inclusion, even though it is distinct in some ways from its material counterparts. Time cannot be accumulated like money or things; it cannot be reused or recycled like resources; it cannot be discarded; and it is always, continuously, and necessarily being expended, whether deliberately or not. Yet time is similar to things, resources, and money in its finite character, and in the linguistic possibility of its being "used," "saved," and "wasted." The categorical boundaries between waste of different sorts can also be porous, as time can be seen as a resource or converted into money. And it is interconnected with the material. Not depleting natural resources can extend time horizons, being efficient can translate into earning more money and buying more stuff, and throwing things away can mean mortgaging the future for the present. Precisely because the material is so bound up with modern, industrial, and capitalist notions of time, it should not be surprising that garbage, resources, money, and time have all been sites of anxiety about and hopes for daily life.

Across the various kinds of waste, the question of value remains central. And these determinations of value are not fixed: no object, use, or expenditure is inherently and unequivocally a waste.[5] To treat or describe something as a waste, be it pantyhose or buffets or long commutes, is to make a judgment or implication that is thoroughly subjective.[6] Because these categorizations are not stable or universal, something thrown away as garbage could, by a different person or at a different time, be recharacterized and repurposed as valuable. The washing machine, the disposable diaper, beer in a can, or golf club membership could be seen as indispensable, innocuous, or superfluous. It is because these determinations of value have been made in and shaped by a particular context that examining what has been considered waste and wasteful can reveal the social and cultural concerns of that historical moment. In addition, explicit conversations about what should be regarded as a waste, how to distinguish between undesirable stinginess and desirable frugality, how to draw the line between necessity and excess, and what should be thought of as a luxury have also reflected historical misgivings and desires. It is these historical, subjective definitions of waste that I am trying to capture, so my concern is not with what I (or you) might find wasteful in postwar Japan. That would be a very different book. This story is about how various Japanese people at various times thought about the waste they saw and experienced in the world around them.

Such ideas about waste were usually forged in and about the everyday, through the seemingly unremarkable regularity of the day-to-day that in postwar Japan as elsewhere was a principal domain of experience.[7] It was often in and about the mundane that people expressed their attitudes toward waste as workers, consumers, household managers, community members, and citizens. Questions of waste were embedded in the small decisions of daily life—about what you might do with a spare ten minutes between meetings; whether you should try to get the last bit of lotion out from the bottom of the container; how much effort you should put into fixing the toaster before you throw it away; how hot you need to feel before turning on the air conditioner; and when to upgrade to the latest computer model. For some, these questions elicited opinions, reflections on one's own behavior, and advice for curbing waste that were explicitly voiced. For others, it was their acts of the quotidian, intentional or not, that revealed how they wanted to spend their time, what they thought was worth purchasing, what material things they wanted around them, and what principles or causes they viewed as worthy of their dedication. What people needed and wanted was reflected in what they said about and what they did with their things, resources, money, and time. That people respond to larger existential questions in the everyday was incisively expressed by the sociologist Anthony Giddens, who argued that "the question, 'How shall I live?' has to be answered in day-to-day decisions about how to behave, what to wear and what to eat—and many other things."[8] Or put another way, the assumptions, habits, and decisions about waste and wastefulness were fundamentally about what people found meaningful and valuable in their daily lives.

Given the centrality of the everyday to shifting constructions of waste and wastefulness, the various kinds of physical waste that did not intersect visibly and regularly with day-to-day life appear little in the pages that follow. Industrial and nuclear waste, for example, were not only categorized differently from household rubbish by professional managers of waste, but also were not terribly relevant to understandings of waste, as pressing an issue as they were to certain people and communities. For most of the postwar period, their meanings were fairly consistent in popular imaginations as dangerous and undesirable substances that required containment. Human excrement also said little about the individual decisions of the day-to-day and, unlike with household garbage, its per capita volume neither changed significantly nor could be controlled much. The relatively straightforward challenge posed by the feces of increasing urban populations was one that could be addressed with the development of sewer systems. So it is touched upon only in the context of modernizing efforts around sanitation, health, and hygiene.[9] That these kinds of refuse receive scant attention should indicate that this book is not centrally about physical waste. Issues of garbage, or municipal solid waste, will certainly be discussed at length because it was understood as a by-product of a mass-consuming society and of a culture of disposability, and as a barometer of economic growth, views of material things, attitudes toward the environment, and more. But there will not be a march through the history of various categories of waste, be it medical, chemical, radioactive, or otherwise. What is of interest is the idea of waste more than physical waste itself.

To write a social and cultural history of waste requires creating one's own eclectic archive of sources and drawing from them attitudes and sentiments about wastage. A wide range of materials about the everyday forms the basis of this volume, revealing how day-to-day life has been at the crux of different and shifting thoughts about waste and wastefulness. Some of these sources could be characterized as mass-market, popular, even lowbrow, be they television programs, newspapers, weeklies that border on the tabloid, women's magazines, and so on. These kinds of materials are quite prominent in the pages that follow; they are usually named to make clear who was presenting certain ideas about waste.

Ideals of waste consciousness have often been articulated in the form of advice, doled out in newspapers, magazines, and mass-market books, about topics ranging from time management to electricity conservation to decluttering. Such advice literature has presented conceptions of waste and wastefulness more than it has described actual acts of waste consciousness. Advice manuals and books are articulations of aspirations, consumed by those whose lived experiences can be quite distant from what is depicted in their pages. As observed by the historian Catriona Kelly, "the relationship of behaviour books to real-life behaviour is complex and oblique."[10] The connections between the constructed ideal and actual practice have thus been probed carefully and skeptically, with no assumption that the world of the reader mirrored the world of the advice literature.

Fictional literature has served, depending on the work, as social commentary, an artifact marked by the economic and societal concerns of its time, or an articulation, sometimes fairly opaque, of an author's views of waste. Whenever possible, information has been presented about how a work circulated and by whom it was read so as to situate it in the social and cultural landscape of its time. And, following Michel de Certeau's urging, some attention is given to the ways in which ideas in texts were consumed and used.[11] In fact, one chapter is dedicated entirely to the themes of, and responses to, a single work of fiction so as to examine the contours of discussions about waste and to explore how ideas could assume different shades of meaning in different hands. Fictional stories have also been told through various media, with some manga taking up the topic of waste. The translation of *manga* as "comic books" or even "graphic novels" does not adequately convey their scope, richness, or artistic and literary depth. Manga have been written in many genres, enjoyed a readership of all ages, and constituted a lucrative industry. They are approached here like other works of fiction, but with due attention to and analysis of their visual element.

Children's stories and books have offered clear, didactic lessons about how not to waste. Most that have taken up this topic are nonfiction, and their numbers and popularity have swelled in the 2000s. Such works have defined aspirational values for and attempted to shape the behavior of children, though their parents have been secondary targets. Because most of their attention has been focused on influencing the values and lifestyles of adult generations to come, they have been by their very nature oriented more toward the future than to the past or the present. The same could be said of junior high and high school textbooks that address issues of waste for a slightly older readership of teenagers. Typically assigned in home economics or sociology classes, these course materials explain how and why young people should think about waste. And these messages have had an official quality to them, presented as they were in textbooks approved by the Ministry of Education.

The interests of the government have been patently apparent in its many large surveys that were dedicated to, or asked about, waste and everyday life. There were questionnaires about free time, daily life, resources, a culture of things, consumer issues, environmental problems, energy saving, and garbage. In addition to those conducted by the government, others were administered by citizens' groups, corporations, marketing firms, and research associations about environmental consciousness, attitudes toward saving, time use, energy consumption, recycling habits, and garbage management.[12] That there were surveys and survey questions about waste reflects the significance of the topic. Even more revealing is the wording of questions and options for multiple-choice answers, which illustrates the extent to which the surveys were exercises in moral suasion, consciousness raising, and the dissemination of information. When it comes to the survey results, in some cases they indicate what respondents thought the appropriate answer might be, while in other cases they suggest how survey takers wanted to see themselves. Responses that flagrantly buck the slant of the question or contradict the initiatives of the group administering the survey give a possible hint into how actual attitudes and behaviors deviated from the ideal. From surveys to children's books, advice literature to newspaper editorials, these varied and sundry materials forged the many meanings—the norms, aspirations, purposes, and practices—of waste in everyday life.

Waste Consciousness in Japan

It may be tempting to assume at the outset that the history of attention to waste is unique to Japan, that there has existed a uniquely Japanese culture of frugality. Such a presumption would be understandable given American media stories and mass-market literature on efficiency in Japanese manufacturing, especially in the 1980s, when there was much fascination with the country's successes in the automotive industry. More recently, there has been journalistic coverage of exacting systems for recycling that require residents to sort their trash into numerous categories, and popular enthusiasm for a decluttering method expertly promoted as being Japanese.[13] Some of these examples of minimizing waste resonate, I suspect, with vague impressions of Zen and its association with clean aesthetics and simplicity. In scholarly circles, research on generally high rates of monetary saving relative to the United States has encouraged a focus on Japanese thrift.[14] These characterizations have been perpetuated by various Japanese themselves who have suggested, with heightened enthusiasm since the early 2000s, that waste consciousness is a distinctively Japanese trait.

Yet waste consciousness in postwar Japan was forged largely and primarily by the logics of phenomena—mass production, mass consumption, economic growth, affluence, material abundance, and environmentalism—that assumed certain forms but were not unique to Japan. The equation of waste management with modern civilization; the importance of productivity, efficiency, rationalization, and profit; and the indispensability of natural resources have been assumed and experienced globally and with shared intensity in the developed world. Ideas and practices like Taylorism, planned obsolescence, recycling, reuse, and decluttering have circulated widely, through and beyond national borders. Attention to waste in Japan was not singular, even if configured and expressed in particular ways.

The simplistic notion of an inherent and enduring waste consciousness and frugality also collapses when we consider that there has been no such thing as a "Japanese conception of waste." What becomes apparent when we think about waste more capaciously, when the focus is not solely on the shop floor or the Zen temple or monetary savings, is that different and often contradictory understandings of waste and wastefulness have existed in Japan at the same time.

Furthermore, the postwar history of waste is one of change more than continuity. It is about how waste consciousness waxed and waned; how what was considered wasteful sometimes endured and sometimes shifted; how individuals, groups of people, and governments attempted to establish new norms and practices around waste for many and diverse reasons; and how waste assumed different meanings, be they practical, didactic, economic, psychological, moral, spiritual, or emotional.

However complex and familiar, the history of waste in Japan also has its particularities. Certain kinds of waste were the object of especially acute attention. The disposal of material waste was one such issue of special concern, in part because of the country's relatively small geographic area. Discussions of household garbage gained an urgency as space in landfills was depleted and the need to build incinerators intensified. Of relevance too has been the scant use of limited domestic natural energy resources, especially after the decline of the domestic coal industry and the demonstrated insufficiency of hydroelectricity in the 1950s. Over that decade and in the 1960s, reliance on foreign oil surged such that by the time of the global oil crisis in 1973, the country was the world's largest petroleum importer.[15] With comparatively little domestic coal, oil, and natural gas, and the oft-repeated mantra of Japan as a "resource-poor country," a sense of insecurity informed experiences of shortages and emergencies, and calls to not waste resources and energy could be especially insistent. These two aspects of the physical landscape go some way toward explaining why concerns about the waste of material things, resources, and energy became so tightly interwoven at formative moments in the construction of waste consciousness.[16]

Who took up the mantle of promoting waste consciousness, and whose behavior was the target of waste awareness efforts, were informed by postwar Japanese understandings of gender roles. Gendered responsibilities and expectations often gave waste consciousness different meanings for women and men. The figure of the housewife loomed large when it came to the management of waste in the household. When advice was offered and entreaties were made about minimizing household waste, the targeted readership was typically housewives. But the boundaries of who was considered a housewife were flexible. Forming the backbone of this category were full-time housewives, but they were rarely the sole intended audience for messages about waste, which tended to be quite inclusive and sought to establish widely accepted norms. To have addressed only full-time housewives would have been limiting because of their small numbers, especially in rural areas, in the 1950s. And in the entirety of the postwar period, the full-time housewife married to a salaryman was an idealized norm but never constituted, as actual lived experience, a majority among married women.[17] The implied definition was thus usually broader, with "housewife" referring to a married woman who ran the home.[18] It was the status of marriage, more than that of part-time or full-time employment, that defined a woman as a housewife.

Expectations that a housewife run the household persisted even as the percentage of women in the workforce increased from the late 1970s onward. A wife continued to be considered, and to assume the role of, the primary manager of the home.[19] Part and parcel of keeping the household humming along, it was usually wives who dealt with household waste in its various incarnations, be it the scheduling of time, household finances, garbage and recycling, or electricity use.[20] This gendering of the household as a female responsibility was reinforced by the sheer volume of suggestions and expectations about waste management in one's family, home, and nonworking life geared toward women. Additionally, the realm of the household often extended beyond the home to include the local community. The neighborhood or residents' associations, consumer organizations, parent-teacher associations, and citizens' groups that took up questions of waste usually consisted mainly of women.[21] A good number of these organizations had connections to or had the ear of municipal government officials, and served as sites of citizen activism around issues of waste.[22]

Juxtaposed with the construction of the household as the domain of women was that of the workplace as the domain of men. When advice was offered and entreaties were made about minimizing waste in the workplace, the intended readership was typically male managers or white-collar workers, especially through the 1980s. Expectations of waste management for men assumed the predominance of work in their daily lives and tended to superimpose the goals of the workplace on the male worker. Office supplies were to be used thoroughly, electricity was to be conserved, and time was to be spent efficiently for the sake of the financial bottom line. Gender was thus salient in differentiating not just realms of waste consciousness but also the purposes of attention to waste.

The centrality of the housewife, business manager, and white-collar worker in ideas about waste created normative conceptions of gender and waste consciousness that did not acknowledge diversity in lived experiences of the home or of work. The same could be said of the related construction of the middle class. Much of the discussion regarding waste and wastefulness, be it about work, leisure, or consumption, imagined a virtually universal and relatively homogeneous middle class. In some ways, this was not without basis. What could be called a middle-class life started to become a majority experience in the late 1950s as urban and suburban areas expanded, metropolitanism reached the countryside, employment in agriculture declined markedly, the number of nuclear families ticked up, and high school graduation rates rose.[23] These developments helped reinforce the notion that almost everyone was part of a fairly undifferentiated middle class. Much has been made of the question, posed annually since 1958 by the Prime Minister's Office in its survey of people's lifestyles, about the social stratum in which respondents would place themselves. Roughly 90 percent of people have identified themselves with three of the five options, as being in the lower-middle, middle, or upper-middle class. This consistent result has fed the presumption that there has existed a large *chūryū*, usually translated as "middle class," though it could mean something more like "mainstream." As the anthropologist William Kelly has argued, this image of the middle class or mainstream has elided socioeconomic difference and "does not refer to a class category but to a category that works to transcend class."[24] It also does not posit the existence of a lower or working class against which the middle is defined.[25] Even with increasing concern in the 2000s about Japan becoming an "unequal society" or "society of disparities" (*kakusa shakai*), self-identification with the middle has persisted such that worries about societal and economic gaps might be interpreted as those of and about the middle class.[26]

Discussions about waste and wastefulness for much of the postwar period have been predicated on this vision of Japan as a middle-class society and have perpetuated this assumption through the definition of practices, values, and aspirations of a middle-class life. Most people who concerned themselves with waste did so as middle-class women and men, appealing to an audience of the same. Those outside the imagined mainstream and those on the socioeconomic margins have made few appearances in the construction of waste and wastefulness and thus also in this book. This relative absence is certainly not to suggest that socioeconomic disparities have been historically unimportant, nor is it intended to perpetuate their erasure. It speaks instead to how tightly ideas about waste and wastefulness were interwoven with middle-class hopes and expectations, such that it would be only a slight exaggeration to contend that waste consciousness was constitutive of middle-classness in postwar Japan.

A History of Postwar Japan

This book is at once a history of waste and a history of postwar Japan. By the very definition of its chronological scope, it makes a case for thinking about the entirety of postwar Japan as one coherent and cohesive period. This is not to downplay the premodern history of concerns about waste, consumption, and luxury. Nor is it to diminish the importance of prewar precursors for many postwar approaches to waste and wastefulness. Continuities and persistence in what some historians have come to call "transwar Japan" are acknowledged, and historical debts to the late nineteenth and early twentieth centuries are given their due.[27] But the postwar period is now longer than the one that stretched from the Meiji Restoration to the outbreak of the Pacific War. And it can be distinguished not just by the longevity of conservative political rule and an international position at once weighty and subordinate, but also by a level of affluence that was previously unimaginable and a society of mass consumption that was virtually inescapable, both of which are so central to a history of waste.[28] Historians of Japan have not yet offered many narratives of the postwar as a whole, especially apart from some notable edited volumes, even after the groundbreaking call in the early 1990s to treat "postwar Japan as history."[29] Only by examining the entirety of this period might we have more productive debates about its persistent challenges, moments of fracture, and defining qualities. As one step in this direction, this book offers a history of the long postwar with its enduring continuities, relentless struggles, and pronounced shifts.

In the years after war's end, in the late 1940s and 1950s, the country embarked on a project of re-civilization and re-enlightenment, the postwar version of modernizing efforts past. Language familiar from the late nineteenth and early twentieth centuries about health, hygiene, efficiency, and rationalization was used to urge waste consciousness in the workplace and the home. And waste was to be managed not only to tackle the challenges of survival just after the war, but also to make Japan civilized and modern once again.

When economic recovery shifted gears into rapid growth in the latter half of the 1950s and the 1960s, societal and cultural adjustments were profound but not sudden or smooth in these years of transition into an era of unremitting mass consumption. In the late 1950s, as the financial and material exigencies of the immediate postwar began to ease, there was both discomfort and excitement about a burgeoning society of consumers. Different attitudes toward wastefulness took shape as people considered what was acceptable to purchase, which consumer desires were appropriate, and how tightly to embrace a more convenient and more comfortable life.

The achievements and changes spurred by high growth were brought into immediate question in the early 1970s, a sharp pivot point in the postwar period which sparked ambivalence about affluence, reflection about national goals, and diversification of individual values and commitments. Concerns about waste became acute as worries about garbage and resources inspired responses to the costs and consequences of mass production, mass consumption, and preoccupation with gross national product. With questions about whether the country had overextended itself, waste came to be equated not with civilizational backwardness but with excess. At the same time, the desirability of a middle-class life had become so deeply fixed that its conveniences and comforts were not to be sacrificed but defended. The prospect of scrimping or going without came to be considered anathema to the better lives that people had come to expect. Consciousness of waste was thus both to change priorities and practices and to preserve the hard-won gains and pleasures of daily life.

The 1980s, often excised from a longer history as an aberration because of the singularity of the bubble economy, should rather be treated as inextricable from the tapestry of the postwar. The need for the defensive posture of the previous decade did ebb, waste consciousness was muted, and what in years not so long past would have been considered luxuries became normalized as markers of the middle class. At the same time, the 1980s stoked not just exuberance but also dissatisfaction and unfulfilled desires. Questions were asked about what life should be about in a Japan of financial and material plenty, about the place of both things and time in a better life. Sometimes coupled with these reflections, waste consciousness came to be conceived in new terms of psychological, spiritual, and emotional satisfaction.

The convention of characterizing all of the years from the early 1990s onward as "lost" is intellectually inadequate, given the languorous shift into economic malaise over the course of the 1990s and the distinctive notes of optimism in the 2000s. As societal architecture was strained to reveal and create precarity of various kinds, there was a pervading and disorienting sense of retrogression and loss.[30] Yet moored by the endurance of relative affluence and mass consumption, there gradually opened a space for more expansive and variegated hopes for individual and societal futures. A more global environmentalism took firmer hold, and the broader conception of waste and meaning that had emerged in a previous time of economic confidence carried over into subsequent decades of economic malaise. In the 2000s, a broad definition of *mottainai* captured imaginations, supplementing more prosaic terms that meant waste or wasteful. The word *mottainai,* with its alleged Buddhist origins, became an umbrella term for waste of many different kinds, and came to appear with greater regularity than *rōhi* (which implied a criticism of extravagance and had declined in use since the early postwar decades) and as frequently as *muda* (which connoted uselessness and was a conventional way to express wastefulness). At the same time, challenges to the purported virtue of *mottainai* began to appear as people reconceived their attachments to material things and their very sense of self. In twenty-first-century Japan, the idea of waste expanded to encompass environmental commitments, a search for individual and national identities, and attempts to define anew relationships with things and with time in continued pursuit of an affluence of the heart, mind, and spirit (*kokoro no yutakasa*). This constructive and forward-looking orientation should expose the laziness of continuing to extend with each passing year the chronological reach of the so-called "lost decades." In time, we may come to better understand millennial Japan in terms of its various attempts at redefinition and at finding itself anew in a world of stagnant affluence.

Bringing this history as far up to the present as possible is intended to illustrate the persistence of postwar Japan as a historical phenomenon and an analytical apparatus, but there are real challenges with writing such a contemporary history. It is not clear what the implications and impacts of the disasters of March 2011 will be, and how they will fit into the narrative arc of millennial Japan. Without the benefit of hindsight, it is not evident whether something like the new minimalism will prove to be a quickly passing trend or a phenomenon with lasting influence. That politicians and scholars have repeatedly declared the postwar over has indicated instead that there has been no unequivocal point of closure, and it is hard to tell a story with no apparent end. History keeps unfolding, sometimes in ways that contradict what was written not long ago.[31] But I would suggest that histories, perhaps especially of the modern, never really end and that hindsight can erase the important contingencies and ephemera of the past. In the case of postwar Japan, we cannot artificially truncate the period and claim its end because we continue to live in the postwar; there has been no resolution to the complicated legacies of war, defeat, and occupation; and there has not been a catastrophic experience on the scale of another world war to mark unambiguously the period's conclusion. Nor can we wait until the period seems somehow over before we attempt to understand the larger stories of postwar Japan.

At this present moment, many people—not unlike the fictional teenagers in the public service announcement about *mottainai*—are grappling with how to live in, and make sense of, a postwar Japan built on the pillars of economic growth, financial affluence, and mass consumption.[32] This has been a struggle familiar in some form since the late 1950s and a defining characteristic of these many decades. Even as people came to marvel at the astonishing availability of products to consume and new amusements to pursue, they considered the disappointments, challenges, and unfulfilled promises of economic growth. Even as the country's wealth reached levels unrivaled by most in the world, there were ways in which it was seen to have fallen short in the ways people lived and in their sense of security and fulfillment. Desires to achieve and defend the privileges of middle-class lifestyles made possible by affluence have existed right alongside discomfort and dissatisfaction with the logics, costs, and consequences of that very prosperity. This tension has long endured in postwar Japan, as utterly inconceivable as it would have been to people in late 1945, who could imagine little beyond the exigencies of daily life in the aftermath of war.

Part I

RE-CIVILIZATION AND RE-ENLIGHTENMENT

Transitions of the Early Postwar
Period, 1945–1971

THE IMPERATIVES OF WASTE

Amid the devastation and disorientation of late August 1945, only weeks into an uncertain time suddenly without war, the popular women's magazine *Fujin kurabu* (Women's Club) managed to print an issue and used its precious supply of paper to address the urgent concerns of daily life in a defeated Japan. Finding and preparing food was the main subject, in response to one of the most immediate and dire challenges facing those who had survived the war. Anticipating hardships yet to come, with winter just around the corner, a member of the Japan Home Cooking Research Association (Nihon Katei Ryōri Kenkyūkai) instructed readers on how to preserve and cook what they had been summarily and habitually discarding. Even corncobs, spent tea leaves, and tangerine peels were not to be thrown out but thoroughly used for much-needed sustenance.[1]

To waste was unthinkable in the years just after the war, when many people were consumed by the pressing need to make the most of what little they had. Large swaths of more than sixty cities throughout the country had been destroyed by bombing, almost a third of people in urban areas were homeless, over half of Tokyo residences lay in ruins, and thousands of children had been orphaned.[2] In a time of widespread poverty and scarcity, wasting could be an existential threat, especially when it came to food. People were taught how the seemingly inedible could be made palatable and how to secure vital nutrients from whatever could be procured. When wasting could endanger health and even subsistence, such education about waste had gravity, and wastefulness could be conceived of as little more than an unaffordable luxury.

The idea that waste was dangerous and waste consciousness a necessity extended beyond food to garbage and human excrement, which garnered concern as filthy breeding grounds for pests, stench, and infectious diseases. As such, they were to be dealt with properly for the sake of basic health and hygiene. In these lean years when people discarded little, rubbish was not about abundance, excess, or a worrisome societal proclivity toward disposal. It was instead an issue of sanitation, something to be contained so as to mitigate threats to public health. Whether about food or garbage, waste consciousness focused on the acute challenges of day-to-day life and was, in fact, imperative in ways that it would never be again in the decades that followed.

Waste of various kinds was understood not just as perilous but also as backward and uncivilized. As the country sought to recover from its wartime destruction and establish itself once again as modern, there were clear parallels to ways of thinking that dated as far back as the late 1800s, when "civilization and enlightenment" had been the slogan of the day. Waste, as an impediment to the project of reconstruction and remodernization, was to be minimized or eliminated. Garbage did not just imperil health and hygiene but was also a marker of regression. The waste of money, effort, labor, and time were similarly viewed as both symptoms and symbols of civilizational inadequacy which were to be eradicated through the promotion of efficiency and rationalization. The impetus to do away with waste was partially pragmatic, to remove the inefficiency and irrationality that were considered obstacles to progress. It was also partially performative, to be rid of signs that Japan had not yet rejoined the countries of the modern and civilized world.

In the immediate postwar, what was imagined as progress was liberation from the fear of waste and wasting. A better life would be free from the exigencies of survival and would be characterized instead by a safety and security brought about by economic recovery. Sparked too in these years was a glimmer of what an ideal life might look like. In the context of occupation, rosy visions of an American middle-class lifestyle of abundance and prosperity began to capture imaginations even at a time when most Japanese could barely dream of much beyond the struggles of the day-to-day.

Perils and Prescriptions

The shortage of food was a wartime condition that persisted into the peace. Rationing had been a practice for years, starting with sugar in 1940 and rice in the six largest urban areas in 1941. With the Food Management Law (Shokuryō Kanri Hō) of 1942, the government sought to control the consumption of grains, beans, potatoes, fruits, vegetables, soy sauce, miso (fermented soybean paste), and fish, though staple foodstuffs were available on the black market.[3] By the last two years of the war, the lack of food had become severe, especially in major metropolitan areas and those provincial cities and towns struck by Allied bombing.[4] The situation in these most desperate months was described by one food scholar, who recalled of his childhood: "From 1944 on, even in the countryside, the athletic grounds of local schools were converted into sweet potato fields. And we ate every part of the sweet potato plant, from the leaf to the tip of the root. We also ate every part of the *kabocha* [winter squash] we grew, including the seeds and skin."[5] Such memories, common among the wartime generation, suggest that food may have been consumed thoroughly and completely less because of moral suasion or instruction about waste consciousness than out of the sheer need for subsistence.

This food crisis was exacerbated in the immediate postwar years by the halt to rice imports from the now former colonies of Taiwan and Korea, the sharp increase in mouths to feed with the return of millions of demobilized soldiers and civilians from across the collapsed empire, and the typhoons and floods in September 1945 which depressed an annual rice yield that was the lowest in over thirty years.[6] For those outside of the fortunate minority who averted hunger, "leftovers from restaurants, even the garbage of places where the more privileged dined, became depended-on sources of sustenance."[7] In the three months following the surrender, it was estimated that more than one thousand people in Tokyo, and over seven hundred in five other major cities, died from malnutrition. In the spring of 1946, the situation was so grave that hundreds of thousands of Japanese people protested against the lean food rations and corrupt black markets, and General Dwight Eisenhower, the U.S. Army chief of staff, asked President Harry Truman for emergency food shipments to avoid violent rebellion against Allied troops in both Germany and Japan. This importation of food, provided as a loan, helped avert the mass starvation that had been feared as imminent. Even so, for many people, hunger was an enduring and perpetual condition.[8]

Making the most of scant foodstuffs was thus a common topic of advice in magazines and newspapers. Aimed primarily at women in urban areas where food could not easily be grown, articles attempted to help readers subsist on meager rations that provided roughly half of the necessary daily caloric intake and whatever food they could afford to buy for exorbitant prices at mafia-run black markets.[9]

Suggested techniques for not wasting food were often about not wasting nutritional value, about extracting as many nutrients as possible from whatever foodstuffs could be procured. One commonly suggested method of eliminating the waste of food was to consume all of its parts, including those that, in better circumstances, would not have been considered palatable or edible. This included the leaves and stems of a sweet potato, the calyx at the top of an eggplant, the skin of persimmons, the core of cabbage, and the green leaves of the carrot and daikon radish. Tangerine peels were touted for being high in vitamin C. They could be dried for preservation and, before use, softened in water, minced, and added to simmered, vinegared, or dressed dishes. The dehydrated peels could also be sliced thinly or diced, roasted, and ground into a flour for use in steamed buns or dumplings. Corncobs could be chopped finely, dried, and then boiled in water for about ten minutes to create a liquid sweetener.[10]

In addition to maximizing the nutritional value of foodstuffs through proper preparation and consumption, attention to the measurement of amounts was recommended to make as much food as possible without wasting ingredients. An article in the April 1948 issue of *Fujin no tomo* (Woman's Companion) provided recipes that specified how many rolls of sushi, of particular sizes, could be made from one *gō* (0.18 liters, or 6.09 ounces) of rice; how much tempura could be prepared from one cup of flour; and how many *ohagi*, or rice balls coated with sweetened red bean paste, could be eked out of one *gō* of adzuki beans. Outlined too were the portions of various dishes that could be made with one egg, calculated as equivalent to three *shaku* (0.054 liters, or 1.83 ounces) of liquid.[11]

Such advice was offered in the hopes that education would heighten vital attention to the waste of food. The advised culinary practices were likely not new, given the food shortages of the later wartime years, when people were harvesting wild plants like bracken and mugwort for sustenance. But there was a sense in these articles that more didactic work could be done.[12] According to a book on nutrition published in August 1946, with multiple printings shortly thereafter, Japanese housewives were continuing to discard fruit and vegetable peels as well as the bones and liver of fish despite the scarcity of food. A contrast was drawn with Germany, where, reportedly, housewives who threw away vegetable skins were criticized as uneducated, children ate all parts of fruit including the core, and inedible peels such as those of bananas were used as fertilizer. Unlike their German counterparts, many Japanese housewives were allegedly treating such food as "garbage."[13] Instruction was thus required to enlighten women about their uninformed and injurious waste.

Such guidance in books, magazines, and newspapers about how to prepare nutritious and economical meals drew on several decades of literature about home management geared toward housewives. In the 1910s and 1920s, cookbooks had increasingly stressed practicality and frugality to appeal to a new kind of housewife, one who was less likely to hire people to do the household cooking. At a time when becoming a servant was increasingly unappealing as other opportunities opened up for women in the workforce, the housewife came to assume more of the responsibility of cooking for herself and her family. Earlier cookbooks about how to supervise domestic workers and entertain guests with special meals became less relevant, and the target readership expanded beyond upper-class women to include younger housewives and unmarried women. And in the context of the economic hardship of the late 1910s and 1920s, "domestic cookbooks placed more and more emphasis on economical cookery and useful recycling of waste."[14] During the wartime years, women's magazines geared toward an urban audience published articles about how to make the most of rationed foods and how to create substitutes for items that had become hard to acquire.[15]

The early postwar emphasis on nutrition as well as a more rational and scientific approach to food preparation were also an extension of "daily life improvement campaigns" from the 1920s and 1930s. The elimination of waste that had been promoted by government ministries, home economists, and others in those prewar decades remained relevant in the economic and social context of the immediate postwar.[16]

While the advice literature of the early postwar years continued to stress the importance of good nutrition, making do with little, and not wasting, it did not display the emphatically nationalist orientation of its prewar and wartime predecessors. Housewives of the 1910s and 1920s were to minimize waste and to be frugal so as to do their part in reducing the national debt and hastening an end to national economic woes.[17] Housewives of the wartime period were to eradicate waste for the sake of the nation's victory. The slogan "Luxury Is the Enemy!" was a common sight starting in the summer of 1940, appearing on signs and in magazines and newspapers to induce citizens to curb consumption and boost household saving.[18] The Meiji Confectionery Company (Meiji Seika), the country's largest candy maker, did its part for the war effort, sponsoring an advertising campaign in 1940 that urged people to refrain from purchasing luxury items and to buy war bonds instead. And throughout the wartime years, advice literature about food and cookery was infused with patriotic messages about the war effort.[19]

After the war's end, and especially in the earliest years of the postwar, references to nationwide concerns were more subdued than they had been in the prewar decades. Housewives were still to be skilled, knowledgeable, and resourceful, but the purposes of their waste minimization were more intimately connected to improving their own daily lives. These articles of the immediate postwar focused largely on the pressing needs of individual readers and responded to the challenges of day-to-day life. In squarely confronting the realities of the time, the advice literature of these years was markedly different from its later incarnation as a purveyor of aspirations for an idealized life. The gap between didactic discourse and lived experience was smaller than it would be in future decades, as both those who gave and those who sought advice shared an acute understanding of waste consciousness as a matter of sheer necessity in dire economic and material circumstances.

One Person's Trash . . .

Experiences of hunger, and of the need to make the most of what little there was without waste, were lived in the presence of American occupiers. In a defeated Japan, the United States loomed large as victor and occupier which, for over six years from the fall of 1945 to the spring of 1952, was "a reality encountered in everyday life."[20] The nature and extent of interactions with Americans varied, and as the historian Yoshimi Shun'ya has pointed out, different Japanese people had different understandings of and feelings about the United States. But one image of the United States that took substantial shape during these years was of a wealthy country. Indeed, however American prosperity was viewed, the occupation years were formative for the widespread consideration of the United States as the embodiment of affluence and abundance. In Japanese imaginations, the United States became a "reference culture," which, whether admired or criticized, served in the early postwar decades as a counterpoint for self-reflection about the status and future of Japan's own society.[21]

The notion of the United States as a model of affluence was fueled by the visible chasm between the financial and material lives of the occupier and the occupied. Disparity in the food available to victor and vanquished, for example, was stark. And in the eyes of at least some hungry Japanese, the relative bounty of American provisions was not excessive or wasteful but enviable and desirable. In the recollection of the policeman Harada Hiroshi, the meal he was given while on duty was one rice ball and some plain miso soup. At one point an American bakery opened nearby, but its prices were prohibitively expensive. More affordable was a local Japanese store called Inageya that sold left-over stew from the American military barracks. Harada described gratefully this nutritious meal without noting that something of value to him was unwanted or unneeded by the Americans.[22] A feeling of gratitude was also the predominant sentiment toward the emergency American food shipments, welcomed "like a merciful rain during a drought," which reinforced the image of the occupiers as generous and wealthy.[23] Even in early 1952, when the food crisis had eased considerably, Harada was surprised by the sheer amount and variety of food he encountered in an American mess hall. Allowed to eat with the American military police, he and his fellow Japanese policemen were astounded to see bread, butter, cornflakes, coffee, milk, oatmeal, bacon, celery, lemons, carrots, and eggs. On several occasions, Harada enjoyed being treated by his American military police friends to a drive-in movie at one of the handful of theaters in Tokyo, otherwise off limits to Japanese, complete with hamburgers, French fries, and a Coke.[24]

The profusion of not just food but other things available to the American occupiers was on full display. For many Japanese, the food shortage was accompanied by the scarcity of things in daily life because of the decline in factory production and skyrocketing prices driven upward by rampant inflation.[25] In contrast, occupation personnel and their families shopped at well-stocked PXs and commissaries. In the bustling Ginza district of Tokyo, the buildings of the watch and jewelry store Hattori Tokeiten (later Seikō) as well as the Matsuya department store were requisitioned in April 1946 for use as a PX. Although the occupied were not permitted inside, a few Japanese people, like the well-known beautician Yamano Chieko, did have the opportunity to enter. Yamano marveled at the availability of food, clothes, and daily necessities as well as the sparkle of the jewels on display under a chandelier. Along with the PXs, there were special stores managed by foreigners in Japan which carried the likes of menswear from England and electric washing machines which could be purchased only with American dollars. Japanese people were allowed into these establishments but generally could not afford to buy any of the merchandise. More tailored to the Japanese customer was Matsuya's two-story wood building, built behind its requisitioned original store, which operated from November 1946 until September 1952 and carried a few cosmetics, toys, and some popular foods.[26]

From the perspective of Americans in Japan, the material affluence of the occupiers inspired wonder for those Japanese who witnessed it. The wife of an American colonel noticed that "there was always a crowd of Japanese outside the PX . . . watching the customers come in and out, flattening their noses against the show windows, gazing in silent awe at the display of merchandise: the souvenirs, candy bars, cameras, milk shakes, shoes, wool sweaters, silk kimonos and guaranteed curios of the Orient."[27] A similar, if more self-aware, observation was made by one Lucy Herndon Crockett, who worked with the American Red Cross: "To the Japanese shuffling past, the six-storied Post Exchange is like a horn of plenty crammed with all the wondrous things they crave and others their imaginations cannot fathom. While waiting for a bus one day I watched their expressions as they passed its entrance. They would slow down almost to a stop, peer into its magic depths, gape at the unconsciously arrogant GIs and American women who flocked out with arms laden, munching freshly made popcorn or hot doughnuts."[28] We cannot know what sentiments were reflected in the perceived expressions of awe and amazement, but at the very least, the material life of the occupiers was prosperous enough to compel some Japanese passersby to stop and look.

The different values that occupied and occupier ascribed to material things, and their divergent views on what constituted useless waste, were clearly evident in their treatment of damaged goods from PXs. In June 1947, occupation authorities agreed to an arrangement whereby deteriorated products from American military exchanges could be purchased by the Japanese government for resale to Japanese people. This category of goods was defined as "all damaged merchandise that has salvage value but is unsaleable to U.S. personnel after drastic mark-downs have failed to liquidate the item or items; and including sub-standard foodstuff that is not saleable to U.S. personnel but has food value for the Japanese, such as moldy cheese, crackers that have no container protection, candy that has deteriorated with age, heat or water damage, and tobacco products which are moldy, infested or water damaged."[29] The list of such items no longer wanted by the main exchange in Yokohama in late October 1947 included smashed kipper snacks, moldy shoestring potatoes, damaged cookies, and moldy Baby Ruths, Milky Ways, and Clark Bars.[30] These goods required a medical certificate in the unlikely event that "the quantity of foodstuff listed on the spoiled and damaged report is greater than twenty-five dollars" and were typically delivered to the Industrial Reconstruction Agency (Sangyō Fukkō Kōdan), the Japanese government corporation tasked with the implementation of industrial policies to facilitate economic stabilization.[31] In 1949, the Eighth Army Central Exchange, which served the Tokyo-Yokohama area, was granted permission by occupation authorities to sell not just damaged but surplus and excess goods. Items from candy and vegetable shortening to shoe polish and razors were purchased by the Industrial Reconstruction Agency and sold at special bazaars held at department stores to raise money for the Boy Scout movement.[32] By September 1950, the sale of "damaged and spoiled merchandise," not in as much demand as the surplus goods, was transferred from the Industrial Reconstruction Agency to private commercial channels.[33]

The castoffs of the occupier could also be of value to the occupied when it came to another form of waste: rubbish. In late February 1947, the Supreme Commander for the Allied Powers declared that in thirty days' time, the Japanese government would be "responsible for the collection and disposition of garbage and waste materials from occupation force installations and housing in Japan." The fundamental assumption was that the value of this garbage and waste would be equal to or greater than the expense of collection and disposal.[34] In the Tokyo metropolitan area, the municipal government contracted with selected collection agencies to service designated districts; these contractors paid a levy to the government and hoped to make money by selling what they salvaged, be it empty bottles, cardboard, wastepaper, scrap wood, and the like.[35]

In its early months, the profitability of the arrangement was somewhat compromised by the collection of garbage by unauthorized people or agencies, a problem that was at least partially addressed in Tokyo by painting authorized trucks a canary color and outfitting them with a signboard for display.[36] By 1951, several of the contractors petitioned occupation authorities to discourage occupation establishments from removing valuable items from their waste. One Fukuyama Noriharu, the president of a waste disposal company in Tachikawa district, noted that the salvage section of the American base was taking out of its garbage marketable items, leaving his company with "the refuse which has no economic valuation."[37] Similarly, the director of another garbage collection contractor noted that the value of the waste produced by different military installations varied considerably. And the American salvage section was extending its reach to those establishments that were more profitable, like the bakery. As a result, his company was struggling financially, "left to clean up and carry away only worthless garbage at tremendous expense."[38] For such Japanese contractors, this distinction between discards that still had value and rubbish that was utterly without value was crucial for their financial bottom line.

Negotiations about garbage, different views of waste, and what was considered waste reflected the different economic positions of the occupier and the occupied. Whether interactions were understood in terms of generosity or pragmatism, compassion or expediency, the subjectivity and contingency of waste illustrated sharply the relative prosperity of the American occupiers and the relative poverty of the Japanese occupied.

The (Re)civilizing Project

At the same time that waste was viewed as an obstruction to physical and even financial survival, it was also increasingly associated with a backwardness unbefitting a country trying to reclaim its status as modern. Both a symptom and an emblem of civilizational inadequacy, waste was to be contained, minimized, or eliminated in a remodernizing Japan. As one kind of such waste, garbage was seen as vulgar and retrograde, in need of management both practically, for the sake of health and hygiene, and symbolically, so the country could perceive of and portray itself as healthy, hygienic, and therefore civilized and modern.

The conception of garbage as filth and as a health risk that needed to be contained or eradicated dated back to the late 1870s and mid-1880s, when cholera epidemics gave birth to the very concept of public health in Japan.[39] State and local governments issued a flurry of regulations about cleanliness, and the dump became one characteristic of a civilized society.[40] The Filth Cleaning Law (Obutsu Sōji Hō) of 1900, the legal foundation of Japan's administration of waste until 1954, specified what was considered filth (garbage, sludge, dirty water, and human excrement) and placed a fair amount of responsibility on municipalities to maintain systems of waste collection and transport that would ensure good hygiene.[41]

During and just after the war, the management of garbage was a challenge not because of volume, for people had little to throw out, but because gasoline and labor shortages along with wartime bombing crippled the physical infrastructure and systems that had been constructed to collect and dispose of waste in the decades before the war. In prewar Kyoto, about two hundred employees had used twenty motorcars, one horse-drawn cart, and twenty handcarts to collect the household garbage discarded in wooden boxes. The trash was picked up every five days in winter and every two days in summer, then burned at one of the city's two incineration plants and buried at one of two dumps. But by around 1941, people could not rely on municipal trash collection and instead disposed of their garbage themselves in shallow pits. Just after the war, the frequency of pickup was down to once every two weeks in the winter and summer, and the one functioning incinerator was used to burn the rubbish of the U.S. Sixth Army.[42] In prewar Yokohama, garbage had been collected in trucks and carts, then incinerated. After the war, municipal pickup was discontinued, and each household either burned its garbage or buried it in pits. This lack of municipal collection was not as much of a problem as it otherwise might have been because, as noted by two men from the city's Water Purification Section, there was in late 1945 "very little garbage."[43] In Hiroshima and Nagasaki, the atomic bombings decimated collection systems. There was no garbage pickup in post-bombing Hiroshima, and the portion of the population served by the sewer system dropped from 80 to 20 percent.[44] And in Nagasaki, collection had to be halted because forty-four vehicles were destroyed and the workforce was reduced by two-thirds to about twenty men. Households managed their own waste by burning it in open areas.[45] Most people across the country were by the last year of the war handling by themselves the disposal of what little household waste they generated, perhaps having heard entreaties to limit as much as possible their output of rubbish and having been affected by the breakdown of the sanitation infrastructure. The deterioration of municipal waste management over the course of the war was evident in the sharp decline in the amount of garbage collected countrywide, from about 3,150,000 tons in 1941 to 220,000 tons in 1945.[46] Having ground to a halt in many wards by the last months of the war, garbage collection did not resume in Tokyo until April 1946.[47]

Concerns about garbage and human waste disposal started to be voiced with greater frequency around 1948 and 1949, and had to do primarily with hygiene and sanitation. This was a response to the rampant spread of infectious diseases after the war. According to official records, almost 100,000 people died of communicable diseases between 1945 and 1948, and more than six times as many contracted such maladies as cholera, dysentery, typhoid fever, and diphtheria.[48] To stem this plague, both American and Japanese authorities sought to educate people about proper methods of disposal and the dangers of poor sanitation. At a press conference held by occupation personnel in August 1948, Japanese newspapers were urged to disseminate information about how to fly-proof bathrooms and garbage bins, and to explain that DDT, not yet recognized as hazardous, should be sprayed to kill insects as necessary. The case was made that "good health means better living and greater prosperity."[49] In November 1948, a representative of the occupation's Public Health Section spoke at a general meeting of a school sanitation association and explained that the fecal matter on the floor of school latrines that he had observed was covered with maggots, which would develop into flies that would contaminate the food served in schools and infect students with typhoid fever, dysentery, and other diseases. The trash piles in school yards, he said, also had to go.[50]

In Japanese newspapers, articles about the health dangers of filth were published with some regularity. In late August 1948, a regional newspaper in the northeast Tōhoku region described an inspection tour of three housing areas in the city of Sendai conducted by members of the occupation's Health Section, two men from the prefectural government, and journalists. The article concluded that people had not complied with municipal requests to maintain good sanitary conditions, the inspectors having found improperly installed sewage systems and piles of garbage all around the residences.[51] In April 1949, an article in the *Kyoto shinbun* newspaper instructed readers to dispose of their household trash in garbage boxes, to refrain from putting those boxes in the road or exposing them to rain, and to secure the lid to keep out flies and mice. On nice days, it was advised, the trash could be dried out in the containers.[52] Much farther north, in Hokkaidō, readers were told of "thoughtless and inconsiderate" people who were illegally dumping refuse at the end of narrow streets, causing outbreaks of flies even though the designated dumpsite itself was clean.[53] Put pointedly in an informative book by the public health specialist Ishikawa Tomoyoshi, outbreaks of diseases like dysentery and typhus were disgraceful in a civilized country.[54]

Garbage was frequently associated with pests and stench by Japanese and Americans alike, despite general satisfaction with the methods of waste disposal. In an October 1948 survey of 2,706 Japanese households in twenty-eight cities throughout the country, 82 percent reported that they were satisfied with the way their garbage was managed, which was largely either self-disposal at home (49 percent) or collection (46 percent). Satisfaction with human excreta disposal was even higher, at 89 percent; for the majority of households (66 percent), this took the form of pickup by a private night soil collector who would repurpose the waste as fertilizer.[55] Despite this affirmation for systems of waste management, there were smelly reminders that collection and disposal were not functioning effectively and consistently. Residents of the Minamishinagawa area of Tokyo, for example, expressed to occupation personnel that they were "troubled with flies" coming from the nearby dump and that requests made to the Shinagawa ward office to clean up the site had gone unanswered.[56] A more modest inquiry about the lack of a regular collection schedule came from a housewife who asked in the *Kyoto shinbun* newspaper whether it would be possible to know in advance, even at the end of narrow roads, when the garbage collector would be coming through the neighborhood. In a response from the city's Public Health Section, it was explained that cars could reach only wider roads, but an effort would be made to amplify the collection vehicle's bell, which was audible about ten minutes before the vehicle's arrival. The housewife was instructed to listen for the ring and then go out and wait for the collector.[57]

On the occupation's part, a register was kept of similar complaints lodged by Japanese and, more often, American residents within close proximity to reportedly stinky and filthy garbage. On April 18, 1949, the inhabitant of U.S. House no. 373 in Setagaya ward informed the authorities about "accumulated garbage in neighboring Jap houses," and months later, on February 6, 1950, a Mrs. Walker commented that the contents of the "Jap garbage box behind the house" had not been disposed of in the past week.[58] Most of the communications were requests for immediate or more frequent collection and disposal. For other American observers, the inadequate handling of garbage was part and parcel of Japanese filth. As Lucy Herndon Crockett described it, "the average Jap home, despite its dainty appearance, is filthy . . . Their ideas of sanitation and garbage disposal don't bear going into."[59] And in the experience of Hugh Smythe, a professor working at a Japanese university, "you have not seen filth until you travel on a Japanese train . . . [T]he people throw all kinds of trash on the floor and spit and carry on, with lots of germs circulating freely."[60]

In the Japanese media, too, the smell and disruption of garbage were of concern. In November 1951, the *Yomiuri* newspaper reported on a mountain of trash in front of the Shinbashi train station, considered the gateway to greater Tokyo, which was bringing the traffic of people and cars to a standstill. Without proper dumpsites, people were throwing filth in the road despite signs prohibiting such behavior. As the garbage accumulated, people had to plug their noses as they passed by what was not just an olfactory offense but a problem of hygiene, traffic, and appearance.[61]

The need to improve appearances, to beautify the everyday landscape, was occasionally evoked to explain the need to remove garbage from sight. In the city of Saga on the island of Kyūshū, in the summer of 1948 the municipal government, local newspaper, and city sanitation association spearheaded a Saga Beautification Campaign (Saga-shi Bika Undō). As part of this effort, the campaign solicited suggestions for slogans and posters from schools as well as the general public. The winning campaign motto from a high school student was "Expel and Sweep Out Garbage and Dirt" and, from the general public, "Toward a Beautiful and Sincere Saga."[62] Beyond this one city, others were described as needing similar aesthetic cleansing. In the assessment of the *Jiji shinbun* newspaper, the beauty of towns was being sullied by the shortage of garbage boxes. And when the Ministry of Health and Welfare (Kōseishō) announced a plan to make 800,000 bins for the entire country over the next five years, and 80,000 in the following year, it was presented as a step toward creating beautiful neighborhoods and towns.[63]

The desire to remove the unsightly and malodorous presence of refuse, and to contain its very real risks to public health, was simultaneously about improving the physical conditions of everyday life and re-creating the markers of a civilized society. As the anthropologist Mary Douglas has argued about dirt and uncleanliness, the elimination of refuse was about the restoration of order.[64] But this was not just order for its own sake, but one that signified control over physical, aesthetic, and symbolic threats and confirmed the reemergence of a civilized Japan.

The Scientification of Daily Life

Garbage was but one manifestation of waste to be disciplined as part of the larger postwar effort to resuscitate the country's lapsed modernity. While the physicality of rubbish helped make its perils visible, the dangers of other kinds of waste, from unproductive time to underutilized labor, were also considered obstacles to the recivilizing and remodernizing project. What was prescribed for the eradication of such waste in both the workplace and the home was efficiency and rationalization. Only through painstaking and exhaustive attention to waste could it be seen and eliminated, and only then could there be progress not just toward economic recovery but also toward lives and lifestyles that were somehow improved.

Attention to efficiency and rationalization dated back to the 1910s, when there emerged vocal proponents of scientific management, or the "scientific quest for efficiency in the production process," as conceived by the American mechanical engineer Frederick Winslow Taylor. By the 1920s, the adaptation of Taylorism in Japan had taken off and spread, paralleling its popularity in Europe and the United States. The basic tenets of Taylorism remained fairly consistent in their postwar incarnation when it came to the pursuit of efficiency and rationalization: each part of the production process was to be approached scientifically, scrutinized, and measured to maximize labor productivity, profit, and efficiency. More specifically, this entailed meticulous analyses of work processes, time-and-motion studies, standardization of material and procedures, and the entrusting of preparation and planning to managerial experts.[65]

The Taylorite concepts and strategies of waste elimination that had originated out of interest in the assembly line were increasingly applied in the postwar to the white-collar office, enshrining principles of efficiency and rationalization that would endure in some form until the present day. In its May 1949 issue, the magazine *Jitsumu techō* (Business Practice Notebook) offered specific suggestions for both the factory and the office. These techniques were applicable to workers, materials, and procedures, and were based on the premise that people and things should be used fully, that anything extraneous should be dispensed with, and that anything which impeded full functioning and productivity needed to be removed. For example: orders from management need not be issued in duplicate or triplicate; there should always be a work plan; the right job should be delegated to the right person; machines should be positioned according to the sequence of the work being done; an old, used item should be presented when being exchanged for a new one; unused lights should be turned off; lightbulbs and shades should be dusted; and anything that could still be of use should not be thrown away. More specific to an office environment, the article recommended using the reverse side of sheets of paper; always putting the caps back on pens; and displaying a board that indicated everyone's location, so no time would be spent searching for people when they were needed. All of these strategies for rationalization, which required a mindset of planning and investigation, were offered as antidotes to the idle habits and aimlessness that spawned waste.[66]

Such adaptations to the office of Taylorite efforts to minimize unnecessary movement, reduce misused time, and maximize labor productivity became fairly commonplace in publications about management and efficiency. One such magazine was *Jimu nōritsu* (Office Efficiency), of the Japan Management Association (Nihon Nōritsu Kyōkai, literally the Japan Efficiency Association). From the spring to the fall of 1949, it ran a series of six articles that listed eighty points about ridding the office of waste. These included point number 27, which offered one concrete way in which efficiency and rationalization could yield good results with less labor: workers should make use of office machines like an adding machine or slide rule rather than an abacus. Point number 36 recommended an American-style placement of desks, whereby executives were located closer to the door because they had to leave the office most often. And point number 39 suggested that shared items be kept in designated places, so people would not spend time looking for them.[67]

The purposes of applying such principles and methods of waste elimination to the factory and the office were primarily, but not solely, about rebuilding Japanese industry and the economy. The indisputable need to boost productivity and profit was accompanied by rhetoric about progress more broadly defined. For Matsushita Kōnosuke, founder of Matsushita Electric Industrial (Matsushita Denki Sangyō, later Panasonic), the eradication of waste was essential for the realization of a wealthy society, which in turn would somehow secure better lives. This idea was reflected in the name of the research institute established by Matsushita in 1946: PHP, or Peace and Happiness through Prosperity. Positing that there was too much waste (*muda*) in the country's institutions, work, and social life, the institute declared that one of its aims was to research specific methods of discovering and extirpating waste in unexpected places, because "the road to prosperity must start with the elimination of waste."[68] Matsushita would later explain that the PHP movement was not just about wealth but also about the oneness of matter and mind and the affluence of the heart and body.[69]

For one of the dons of scientific management, Ueno Yōichi, efficiency and rationalization were not just a way of working but also a way of living and being. In a lecture to workers in one office, Ueno gave the following advice. First, things were to be properly cleaned and tidied: anything that was unnecessary, including documents after a designated period of time, should be thrown out; the tops of desks should be free of clutter so that there would be plenty of space to work; and office supplies like pens, paper clips, pins, and such should be kept in drawers. Such advice was purely technical and mechanical. Second, bodies were to be properly cleaned and tidied: eye mucus or dirty fingernails resulting from insufficient washing only advertised one's messiness, and while it was difficult to take a bath in those times, bodies could be sponged down. Such rudimentary ablutions were not about enhancing productivity but about demonstrating a cleanliness synonymous with civilization and modernity. Third, hearts and minds (*kokoro*) were to be properly cleaned and tidied: one should not lie or deceive and should always walk a straight path.[70] For Ueno, eliminating waste was as relevant to a person's character as to the assembly line or desktop.

In other instances, the cold rationality of stamping out waste—decreasing expenses so as to maximize profit—was imbued with an almost spiritual meaning. In a special June 1949 issue of *Jitsumu techō* about saving on costs, there were plenty of concrete examples of how to cut spending, be it devising a way for employees to use a pencil for fifty days rather than forty, acquiring items at a lower per unit price, or making posters with lower-quality paper or with two colors instead of three. At the same time, saving was described not just as a matter of calculation but as a practice that welled up from a consciousness of waste and a sincerity of heart. Things were to be valued because they were in limited supply, irretrievable once lost, and foundational for the country's wealth. What is more, to not waste was said to have a spiritual dimension, whereby even one sheet of paper was to be used until there was nothing left of the mission for which it was born. Only through such exhaustive use could the sheet of paper be happy and pass away in contentment, and could the person discarding it avoid incurring punishment for being wasteful. The saving of things was thus endowed with a vaguely spiritual purpose along with the more concrete aim of rebuilding the postwar economy.[71]

Parallel to advice about efficiency and rationalization for the workplace was that for the home, where waste was to be eliminated by the housewife as its manager. The idea that scientific management was as important to the home as to the workplace was articulated emphatically by Ueno Yōichi, who believed that "the principles of Scientific Management should be spread widely, into individual households and through all areas of national society."[72] In this vein, the professor Ishimori Chiyo penned an article in 1949 to help busy women find more time in their day. To demonstrate how waste could be revealed and minimized through scientific examination and management of everyday life, Ishimori analyzed the daily schedule of a prototypical harried woman. Time spent on cleaning could be reduced by eleven minutes and thirty seconds, it was determined, if more than one cleaning cloth were on hand to obviate the need for multiple trips up and down the stairs to rinse one out. Time could also be saved by doing two or three things simultaneously, such as cleaning while making rice or doing laundry while cooking a stewed dish. Ishimori had clearly applied Taylorite time-and-motion study to the home, with the idea that efficiency and rationalization would give women more time to pursue whatever they would like, such as self-improvement through reading and studying.[73]

Inadequate time for reading, apparently a complaint lodged frequently enough by housewives to garner the attention of women's magazines, also inspired a time analysis conducted by the editorial division of the magazine *Seikatsu kagaku* (Lifestyle Science). The article's explicit premise was that the eradication of waste would improve the lives of women, that it would create more time for women to do what they wanted and make possible a brighter life. More implicit was a seeming response to readers' concerns that life would somehow be harder in a more democratic era, with its new constitutional guarantee of gender equality. The editors defensively insisted that while women could not lead lives of ease, careful examination of their time use would create opportunities for enjoyable pastimes. That is, a busy and well-managed life would also be a pleasant and bright life. To model the rigorous examination of daily life that it recommended for housewives, an investigation was conducted in December 1947 of how thirty households in Suge, a small hamlet in Kanagawa prefecture, spent their time. The article concluded that too much time was consumed by laundry, cleaning, and the preparation of meals. Although it was short on specific ideas, the suggestion was made that the amount of time spent on sewing (four hours a day in the households of salaried employees, and two hours and thirty minutes in the households of farmers and merchants) was too great and that even just half an hour could be reallocated for pleasure.[74]

More critical of what he considered the enormity of unplanned time and waste in the household was Ōmoto Moichirō, the author of *Katei seikatsu no kagakuka* (The Scientification of Home Life), published in 1949. To combat such wastefulness, Ōmoto explicitly evoked the principles of Ueno Yōichi and adapted them for the home. Ineffectual movement was to be minimized, which meant doing away with excessive walking, bending, stretching, standing, squatting, sitting, and climbing stairs. And standardization was to be sought with household furniture and goods, for example, having bowls of the same size. The housewife was to be the manager of the home, and was to delegate work in order to achieve the democratization of the family and the proper division of labor in the household. Wasted time was to be reduced through proper planning and organization: household events should be scheduled ahead for the day, the week, and the month; things should have a designated place in the home, and containers such as boxes or cans should be clearly labeled with a description of their contents; and a chest of drawers should contain only clothes appropriate for the season, so they could be accessed easily. Goods were also to be utilized skillfully. Laundry soap, for example, was not to be used with hard water because the interaction of the water's calcium, magnesium, and iron with the soap would just create scum. Electricity was also discussed by Ōmoto as a kind of material good, or input, as it was in the context of the factory or the office. Electricity should be conserved (*setsuden*) by using good-quality lightbulbs that did not consume too much electricity, keeping bulbs and lampshades clean so that the light was not dimmed by dust, and turning off lights when not in use. Ōmoto also eschewed ineffective and counterproductive methods for saving electricity. Replacing bulbs with those of lower wattage, for example, did not make sense because it only tired out one's eyes, impeded the ability to do work, and darkened moods. Ōmoto conceded that saving electricity might seem rather trivial, since household electricity consumption was less than one-fifth of total use. But electricity conservation was to be taken seriously, he argued, because the elimination of wasteful electricity use in the home would make more electricity available for factories, which would benefit production.[75]

Ueno Yōichi's version of scientific management for work and life in the home was propagated not just by efficiency and lifestyle experts and publications geared toward women but also by Ueno's own initiatives, such as his wartime brainchild, the Japan Efficiency School (Nihon Nōritsu Gakkō). In a February 1949 article, a member of the Japan Efficiency School clearly and succinctly proposed questions that housewives should be asking themselves about their daily lives. As in other publications, readers were prompted to consider whether they had a fixed place to put things, and whether they were multitasking. They were also asked if they were conserving their time: Did they become too engrossed in gossiping; did they unthinkingly spend more time than planned visiting people; did they continue to socialize even though wash was waiting to be done; and did they stop to read magazines while cleaning? Time could also be lost by not using one's head—by going to the ward office but forgetting to stamp the correct seal on the papers or failing to remember the documents altogether; by choosing the same size pot for making tea regardless of how many guests had to be served; or by doing laundry on cloudy days or major cleaning on dusty and windy ones. Housewives were to examine not just the waste of time but the waste of things as well. Were they planning a menu that called for an egg yolk but not the egg white; were they throwing out human excrement rather than applying it in the garden as fertilizer; and were they using too much soap to wash small items like handkerchiefs?[76]

Advice literature about efficiency and rationalization promoted the Taylorization of daily life with its values of waste elimination, the thorough use of things, and rigorous analysis, planning, and management. What was constructed by experts, publications, and institutions through their advancement of efficiency and rationalization was an ideal of freedom from the obstructionism of waste.

Admiring American Affluence

The appeal of prosperity held up by proponents of Taylorite rationalization was underscored by idealized depictions of affluence and efficiency in the United States. Starting in February 1948, a popular radio program from the public broadcaster NHK (Nippon Hōsō Kyōkai) consisted of an announcer reading articles sent from Washington, DC, by the newspaper reporter Sakai Yoneo, who shared his impressions and thoughts about life in the United States. The program originally aired on Saturday nights, then moved to Sunday evenings at 7:15 pm with a rebroadcast on Tuesday nights. Topics included "extremely rational" and "efficiency and kindness."[77] Sakai collected some of his observations in a book, published in 1949, in which he expressed optimism about Japan's future. Implicit was the suggestion that adopting certain American practices would improve life in his own country. When it came to efficiency, for example, Sakai praised American government offices, where people were not made to wait. Telegrams could simply be dictated over the phone, typed up, and sent, with the expense auto-matically added to the monthly phone bill. At large libraries, an assigned num-ber was electronically lit to inform you when your requested book had arrived. In general, Sakai admired how unnecessary processes were minimized or elimi-nated and work was made efficient with planning.[78] Like Sakai, the journalist and social commentator Nakano Gorō held American efficiency and practicality in great esteem. In his book *Amerika ni manabu* (Learn from America), published in 1949, Nakano observed that American women had devised strategies to mini-mize waste in the home and thus led efficient and enjoyable lives. Women from households both rich and poor had allegedly done away with ostentation and prioritized practicality. In Nakano's assessment, efficiency and practicality were not just great qualities of American women. They also constituted a sound atti-tude toward life that both put the brakes on the limitless pursuit of luxury and helped make possible a prosperity in which one in every four people had a car and every household owned two radios and an electric refrigerator.[79]

Like such accounts, the comic strip "Blondie" made available to Japanese readers a representation of American affluence. Published in the mass circula-tion *Asahi* newspaper from January 1949 to April 1951, the very popular comic became an icon of American culture with its portrayal of the daily lives of the middle-class Bumstead family.[80] Husband and father Dagwood was known for making very tall multilayered sandwiches, as he did in a strip published on March 7, 1949.[81] With the various ingredients for his late-night snack running down both of his outstretched arms, and the well-stocked electric refrigerator open behind him, his was not a life of want. He had time for leisure—to play golf, or to sit around reading the newspaper with the family dog, Daisy, at his feet while his wife, Blondie, chatted with a friend on the phone.[82] But the Bumsteads' comfortable life was not portrayed as extravagant, frivolous, or irrational. In one strip from November 1950, Dagwood informed his wife that they could afford to go out to a restaurant called Pierre's if they order the $1.25 dinner. Blondie, in excited anticipation, promptly went out to buy a $12.95 dress and a $5.55 hat. In the last cel, a stunned Dagwood uttered to the waiter at the restaurant, "We'll have the $21.00 dinner."[83] The Bumsteads could afford a meal at a restaurant and a nice outfit, but they were also clearly on a budget that should not, though could, allow for an impulsive and expensive purchase. In a flip of gender and family roles, Dagwood was the rational Japanese housewife who deemed his spouse's irrational consumption to be wasteful. The Bumsteads' middle-class life with its luxuries and occasional splurges was, the strip implied, made affordable by atten-tion to wastefulness and rational spending.

For Matsushita Kōnosuke, a trip to the United States impressed upon him the effectiveness of American-style management and the desirability of the

FIGURE 1.1. American Middle-Class Consumption in "Blondie." A waste-conscious response to an irrational splurge, depicted in the American comic strip "Blondie."

American-style affluence it had helped create. This idea was not new to Matsu-shita, who had spoken in the past about the lessons that his country could learn from the United States. In a speech before the Japan Society for the Promotion of Science (Nihon Gakujutsu Shinkōkai) in 1947, for example, he had argued that poor Japan needed to shed its feudal habits and become more like the prosper-ous United States by valuing practicality over appearance and eliminating the wasteful expenditure of time, money, and effort.[84] In 1951 the business executive traveled to the United States to research firsthand "what were then the world's most advanced management philosophies and practices."[85] Reflecting back on his trip in his autobiography, he revealed a slight hint of hesitation about the extent of American affluence: "The New York City I saw was extremely prosper-ous; in the eyes of us Japanese, it seemed extravagant to the point of wasteful-ness." But this was less a criticism than a reflection of the gap between American prosperity and Japanese poverty, as Matsushita went on to note: "The lights in Times Square were not turned off even during the day. Back in Japan, there was a chronic shortage of power and, indeed, the supply was turned off every night for one hour at 7:00 p.m. in Tokyo." Overall, Matsushita was struck by the "material abundance in the United States" and resolved "to bring that good life to Japan as well. Upon returning, I enjoined my staff members to dedicate themselves to the task of bringing to Japan the affluence I had seen in the United States."[86] As the historian Simon Partner has argued, "By the end of his visit, he had formed a vision of Japan's future: a middle-class, consuming society structured along American lines."[87]

"Is Luxury Really the Enemy?"

As reflected in Matsushita's impressions of American affluence and ambitions for his own country, in 1951 Japan could not have been described as a middle-class, mass consumption society. At the same time, there were hints that the worst economic hardships of the immediate postwar years might just be in the past. In the early 1950s, the economy was jolted out of stagnation by the outbreak of the Korean War, which stimulated Japanese industry through U.S. procurements. We now know that this would be the beginning of a general upswing in the Japa-nese economy, but the situation as experienced at the time was more mixed and uncertain. The economy had seemed to be on the brink of depression as recently as the spring of 1950, and the sense that the economy needed to grow much fur-ther remained acute. Yet daily life for many people was not as desperate as it had been, with clothing and basic household items more available. Dependence on the black market had abated, food rationing came to an end, and food consump-tion rebounded to prewar levels.[88]

In the early 1950s, advice literature about avoiding food waste continued to emphasize the importance of consuming as many nutrients as possible but was not framed as imperative for survival. In 1953, the food and nutrition specialist Okuda Junko commented that until a few years ago, people were living "base" and "primitive" lives, subsisting on wild plants and pieces of trees in a time of extreme food shortages. In many ways, Okuda's techniques for maximizing nutritional value and using parts of foods normally thrown away could have been written in the 1940s. She informed readers how tangerine peels could be cut thinly and put in a vinegared dish; fish bones could be braised or grilled and ground into a flour; and the cartilage from the head of salted salmon could be pickled. But Okuda also included suggestions that would likely have seemed superfluous to readers of even three or four years earlier. Most advice about tangerine peels, for example, had previously been about their consumption as food, and this article too described them as rich in carotene and vitamins A and C, and observed that they had been used in Chinese herbal medicine. At the same time, Okuda suggested applications unrelated to dietary needs, noting that they could serve as a mosquito fumigator or a deodorizer for the bathroom. And she even made mention of a use that would be oft repeated in later postwar decades: putting the tangerine peels in one's bath.[89]

An urgency of tone was likewise absent from a roundtable discussion with five participants that was published in the April 1953 issue of *Shufu to seikatsu* (The Housewife and Daily Life) titled "How to Eat Skillfully and without Waste." This article was the first in a new section of the magazine called "The Housewife's Research Seminar," in which an expert would be invited to educate young housewives about handling things like food, clothes, and child rearing with an approach that was scientific, efficient, and rational. In this inaugural installment, the moderator opened the discussion by calling for a reexamination of dietary practices at this moment when there was finally starting to be enough food to eat. The expert in this conversation, a professor from the National Institute of Nutrition (Kokuritsu Eiyō Kenkyūjo), instructed the other participants and readers about how to shop for food to stretch their money as far as possible, what foods were both economical and nutritious, and how an "extravagant" diet of too many eggs and too much milk, meat, and fish would make the blood overly acidic. Waste consciousness and frugality were valued, but nutrition was now less about how to consume enough calories to subsist and much more about achieving a nutritional balance and getting enough calcium and protein. Not wasting was understood in the context of better health more than sheer subsistence.[90]

As the strains of daily life eased, however modestly, it became possible to imagine or desire luxury (*zeitaku*) even as it remained elusive for most as an experience. In the late 1940s, there had been occasional renunciations of the wartime era proscriptions on extravagance, but encouragement of luxury was rare. And any affirmation was framed in terms not of material gratification for its own sake but of service to some greater purpose or ideal beyond oneself. A short piece in a women's magazine in June 1946 did turn the wartime slogan on its head, arguing that luxury should be not an enemy but a "friend." This was not just because it would mean the realization of material abundance and a convenient life, but also because it would signify a generosity of spirit. Because it was "sadistic" to think about such generosity while living in poverty, material luxury would have to be the steppingstone to what was ultimately desired: spiritual, emotional, or mental luxury (*seishinteki zeitaku*). Luxury was something to be sought actively and purposefully, but this was not about extravagance or excess but about being free of the psychological constraints of the wartime period.[91] Taking a slightly different tack, a 1948 article titled "Is Luxury Really the Enemy?" made a case for the importance of luxury in the creation of scientific culture. A luxurious, or desirous, heart was what spurred industries to research and develop, inspiring such innovations as the elevator, sleeping car, airplane, refrigerator, and heater. This too was a luxury not of overabundance or opulence, but of a healthy yearning that fed scientific progress.[92]

By the early 1950s, the idea of luxury could evoke not just discomfort but also desire, however modest or qualified. In a roundtable discussion published in 1951, the three participants agreed that few people at the time could actually afford to live a luxurious life, and that what might seem like aspirations to luxury in Japan would be considered common and ordinary in other countries like France or the United States. Their compatriots would not know how to pursue luxury, they claimed, in a country that was characterized as behind many others in the diffusion of goods like electric stoves, electric refrigerators, electric washing machines, and cars. But for them, luxury was not about the acquisition of particular material things but about the appreciation of pleasure. This might be sleeping in late, driving the family around in a car, or working in a warm place. And for participants Fukushima Keiko and Hanamori Yasuji, luxury would be finding joy in waste. Or to put this another way, a luxurious time would be one in which people did not have to be so attentive to wastefulness and had the latitude to enjoy wasting. Fukushima admitted that "it would be fun to be able to waste." Hanamori, who had founded the women's cultural magazine *Kurashi no techō* (Notebook of Everyday Life) a few years earlier, imagined a more specific example. The luxurious thing Hanamori most wanted to do at that moment? Smoke a cigarette for five minutes, and then just throw it away. With memories still very fresh of makeshift cigarettes rolled with such things as pine needles, Japanese knotweed, or corn silk, to dispose of a cigarette without smoking it completely was considered an almost shameful indulgence. The unapologetic desire to waste expressed by Fukushima seemed too enthusiastic for the other two participants; the artist Inokuma Gen'ichirō, for one, was more comfortable with the embrace of waste when using one word (*muda*) rather than another that had more of a connotation of extravagance (*rōhi*). But while waste was considered a luxury, it was also an acceptable and desirable one that could be beautiful, important for the development of culture, and just plain fun.[93]

Legacies of the Early Postwar

In the ten years after war's end, people in a defeated Japan experienced the uncertainties and dislocations of adjusting to life in a postwar era. In both the metaphorical and literal senses, the occupation was a large-scale exercise in disposing of the tools, possessions, ideologies, and symbols of empire and war. Munitions, textbooks, imperialist ambitions, colonies, militarists, and the bodies of the deceased were among the now useless artifacts of war that were to be discarded. And there were difficult questions about whether lives had been wasted, about whether the war itself had been a waste. But of immediate concern to most people was how to survive the physical and material devastation of the war, how to secure for themselves shelter, clothing, and food. In a different register, the country struggled to recover its economic footing and to reestablish itself as a modern and civilized society. It was this context of discard and reconstruction that shaped the postwar development of several strands of waste consciousness—some of which were unique to this moment and some of which would endure, revised and remade, well into the next century.

To not waste out of the imperatives of survival was an idea and a practice particular to the most desperate years just after the war; it would not resonate with the experiences of many people after the late 1940s and most people in the decades thereafter. As the economy grew, there would simply not be an analog to the widespread, extreme poverty of this time. Yet it would be evoked long after the worst hardships had passed by those who would claim that the wartime generation was endowed with the virtues of frugality or an inherently Japanese appreciation of waste consciousness. Forgotten in this romanticized nostalgia would be the context of scarcity and poverty which made not wasting a matter of sheer necessity.

The conception of waste as backward persisted, even though the idea became less explicit and less urgent over time. As Japan became more secure as a country rehabilitated and rebuilt, and more secure in its place among the advanced nations of the world, waste was less often discussed as a civilizational threat. When waste pushed back and seemed to flaunt control, there was little fear that it would drag the thoroughly remodernized country back into an uncivilized state. But even as anxieties about the status of Japan as a modern country abated, many of the calls to minimize or eradicate waste still presumed that it had a retrogressive force, that it acted against progress.

This notion of waste as an impediment to advancement fed into the logics of efficiency and rationalization which proved remarkably tenacious in the postwar period. That waste was something to be measured, studied, and explained so as to be eliminated became one of the pillars of thinking about postwar work and lifestyles. The association of efficiency and rationalization with maximizing profit and enhancing productivity also endured, as did their casting of both time and things as resources whose value was to be measured by their usefulness. The desirability of prioritizing financial goals, productivity, and utility would be questioned, and the goals of waste elimination would be complicated, as the economic story of the postwar unfolded. But the close relationship between waste and profit, productivity, and utility would be a persistent strain in understandings of wastefulness for many decades to come.

These conceptions of waste were not new to postwar Japan, derived as many of them were from civilizing and modernizing projects that reached back to well before the fall of 1945. But they established a vocabulary for thinking about waste in the postwar and became the foundational understandings of the era to come—the ideas and assumptions that would be evoked, revisited, distorted, revised, and supplemented in ever-shifting contexts.

Even in the early 1950s, to anyone looking back at the handful of years just passed, the bare subsistence of the 1940s seemed to be giving way, slowly and uneasily, to a life in which one might be able to desire something more and to imagine what luxury might be. The question was what would happen to wasting and wastefulness as the declarations of waste as the enemy and the deprivations of the immediate postwar years slipped into a more distant past.

BETTER LIVING THROUGH CONSUMPTION

As the economic and material constrictions on daily life began to ease, the president and founder of Sanyō Electric (Sanyō Denki) took to the pages of the prominent cultural magazine *Bungei shunjū* (Literary Times) to gently but firmly challenge resistance to purchasing goods that were widely dismissed as luxuries. In an article published in June 1955, Iue Toshio opened disarmingly enough by telling the story of his own interest in buying an electric washing machine, which led him to explore the domestic and foreign models then available on the market. Careful not to overstate the economic conditions of his country, he spoke of "us poor people in Japan" who should not be using the inefficient agitation-type machine popular in the United States. American life was so affluent, Iue explained, that clothes were considered unclean after being worn for only one day. In Japan, where clothes were not abundant and were not laundered until they were truly dirty, what was needed was a more effective washer that required less electricity. In an obvious promotion of Sanyō's jet-type electric washing machine, Iue attempted to make a case for the labor-saving utility and efficiency of a product that was found in very few households at the time. He specifically pushed back against older Japanese and those in rural areas, especially in the northeast Tōhoku region, whom he described as particularly inclined to consider such a device a luxury, to believe that the burden of laundry was a given, and to think that young wives who wanted to lessen their labor were simply trying to take it easy. Iue also made a case for the practicality of the electric mixer which, while perhaps unnecessary if thought of as only for juicing, could actually minimize waste if put to such uses as making tofu out of soybeans. But Iue did more than suggest that the products his company was selling were not luxuries. He also shifted the definition of what constituted a luxury by implying that it was mistaken to think of anything that provided convenience, ease, and comfort as an extravagance. Blurring the boundaries of this category of goods, Iue ended the article with his punch line: the wartime mindset that "luxury is the enemy" was itself a "great enemy" that needed to be quickly expelled. Today, argued Iue, antagonism to luxury constituted antagonism to the economy. It was time to move forward in pursuit of a cultured lifestyle, a comfortable life, and a bright home.[1]

At the time when Iue was making his pitch, many people could begin to imagine a better life. In the earlier postwar years, there had been much rhetoric about "brightness" and "newness" to promote peace, democracy, and a turn away from the past and toward the future.[2] But the dire economic and material circumstances made it difficult if not impossible to think much beyond the day-to-day. It was not until the mid-1950s, a decade or so after the war and several years after the American occupation of mainland Japan, that the country was really in a position to envision life in the future and to look further than the discrete goal of economic recovery. In 1955, gross national product was higher than it had ever been in the prewar period, and in July 1956, the Economic Planning Agency (Keizai Kikakuchō) released the most positive report on the state of the Japanese economy since the end of the war. Industrial production was up, growth in national income exceeded 10 percent, the international balance of payments was greatly improved, and the economy had expanded without inflation. Based on its assessment of the country's economy, the white paper famously determined that the "'postwar' is now over." But the impulse to forge ahead into the post-recovery era was tempered by uncertainty—about the stability of the country's economic future and about the values of an inchoate better life. The oft-quoted sentence about the end of the postwar was not a triumphant exclamation that figured prominently in the report. It was one line buried in a paragraph in the concluding section of the first of two parts of a lengthy and dry bureaucratic document. There was no tone of exuberance from a country that we now know was on the cusp of two decades of high economic growth; instead the report simply noted that Japan had managed to climb its way out of the "deep valley" into which it had been thrown by defeat.[3] Echoing this understated view, the mass circulation *Yomiuri* newspaper explained that the economic recovery was due largely to circumstance and good fortune.[4]

At a time when it was still unclear what a better life might and should be, there were those who encouraged consumption as an engine for and measure of improvement in both the economy and lifestyle. The Economic Planning Agency, for one, noted in its report that the increase in consumption was less than that in exports, production, and national income. As individual incomes grow, it urged, people should save the same amount as they have before but spend more.[5] Consumption was advocated by economists at the agency such as the influential Gotō Yonosuke, who posited a significant relationship between mass consumption and economic growth. For Gotō, this belief was solidified by the ten months he spent in the United States from late 1954 to the fall of 1955 interviewing fellow economists and government officials. In his book *Amerika keizai han'ei no kōzō* (The Structure of American Economic Prosperity), published in 1956 just before the Economic Planning Agency's white paper, Gotō "argued that the American experience showed that material prosperity in this new era was largely driven by the motor of consumption."[6] And this idea resonated at a time when a middle-class society that valued the consumer was increasingly viewed as the engine of future affluence.[7] For someone like Iue Toshio, the challenge was how to create consumer desire, how to convince people that it was not wasteful to purchase goods the likes of which they had never owned before, and that they did not know they wanted or needed.

The late 1950s and 1960s were a period of significant transition as consumption assumed an ever more significant place in conceptions of a better life, more people began to think of themselves as consumers, and daily lives changed in substantial ways. Over these years, a society of mass consumption developed from an idea into a reality lived by many. But the new opportunities created and fueled by affluence, material plenty, and consumerism were met by caution as well as anticipation, unease as well as excitement. Amidst the conflicted feelings about the changes of these years, different attitudes toward waste and wastefulness came to exist alongside one another. Some people continued to stress the need for rationalization and efficiency in daily life, very much in the mold of earlier efforts to modernize the workplace and the home. Waste was something to be eliminated for the sake of progress toward a "new" and "bright" Japan. Others took such values as rationalization and efficiency and remolded them to fit and justify the burgeoning of material consumption. Ideals of waste reduction proved flexible as they came to allow for the purchase of everything from expensive electric appliances to instant foods in the name of not wasting time, effort, and labor. Such products and their promotion of convenience and comfort would, in later years, be deemed the epitome of wastefulness. But at this moment, there were those like Iue Toshio who deliberately tested, expanded, and redrew the lines that had distinguished need from excess, waste from luxury.

As the "consumption revolution" gained momentum in the 1960s, it provoked discussions about the relationship between wastefulness and mass consumption. Waste, some began to suggest, was encouraged by and might even be endemic to the marketing, advertising, selling, and consuming that had become synonymous with progress. And it was feared that the desire to buy might be eroding waste consciousness. Garbage also assumed new meanings in an era of flourishing consumption. While its management was still very much a civilizational imperative, rubbish also started to be seen as a by-product of abundance and of increasingly voracious appetites for material things. Yet even as consumption inspired some reactionary rethinking about waste and wastefulness, such emergent concerns were restrained in these years when consumers were ever more captivated by the prospects and promises of the middle-class life.

"Eliminate Waste for Better Living"

Calls for the elimination of waste through rationalization and efficiency sounded very familiar notes in the 1950s, as a motley chorus of recognizable voices from years and even decades past continued to expound the importance of frugality for modernizing daily life. In 1955 they gained some momentum when Prime Minister Hatoyama Ichirō inaugurated the New Life Movement (Shin Seikatsu Undō). Having campaigned under the banner of constructing a "bright Japan," Hatoyama took a step in this direction by establishing the New Life Movement Association (Shin Seikatsu Undō Kyōkai) and endowing it with 50 million yen in government funds. The creation of the association had been recommended by the Ministry of Education (Monbushō), which sought to harness and coordinate the various "new life" initiatives of government bureaus, women's organizations, and corporations that had sprung up in the late 1940s. Emblematic of its nongovernmental and governmental ties, the association was headed by Maeda Tamon, a former minister of education and the president of Tokyo Telecommunications Engineering Corporation (Tokyo Tsūshin Kōgyō, later Sony). In November 1955, the group outlined its agenda at the first National Conference on the New Life Movement. The priorities included improvement of food, clothing, and shelter as well as health and hygiene; elimination of mosquitoes and flies; simplification of ceremonial occasions; rationalization of savings and household finances; strict observance of time; elimination of waste; elevation of public morality; and improvement of the activities and habits of daily life.[8]

Reflected in this list of concerns was the movement's blend of modernizing reformism and moralizing conservatism that had also characterized earlier efforts at what was termed "social education." In the 1920s, campaigns for "lifestyle improvement" sought to modernize daily life and elevate morality through simplifying and rationalizing ways of living. In the immediate postwar years, a predecessor to the New Life Movement was launched by the left-center coalition cabinet of the socialist prime minister Katayama Tetsu. In June 1947,

Katayama christened the National Movement to Construct a New Japan (Shin Nihon Kensetsu Kokumin Undō), which supplemented the rhetoric of rationalization with language about democratization. One of the central aims of Katayama's movement was the "establishment of rational and democratic customs in daily life," which entailed "cultivating an attitude of eliminating waste from daily life, abstaining from luxury, always thinking rationally, and handling matters efficiently."[9] But Katayama's administration was short-lived, and his message about a "new Japan" rang hollow, given the bleak economic circumstances of the mid-1940s. By the time Hatoyama took up the mantle, the conservative prime minister of what would be established in November 1955 as the Liberal Democratic Party (Jiyū Minshutō) could promote both modernization and a moral retrenchment in response to the perceived materialism, "irresponsible freedom," and "trend toward negativity" that modernization had allegedly wrought.[10] Between the tensions and contradictions of the movement, the flexibility and multiplicity of meaning of such ideas as "rationalization" and a "new life," and lack of direction from Hatoyama, the New Life Movement became a large umbrella for a loose assortment of initiatives related to daily life.

One of the issues taken up by the New Life Movement Association was the elimination of waste through the simplification of formalities such as wedding ceremonies. Pared-down weddings had been encouraged by local organizations and governments even before the formation of the national association. From 1949 to 1952, the Ministry of Agriculture and Forestry (Nōrinshō) encouraged "frugality in weddings and funerals: rent kimonos, hold modest parties, use inexpensive public halls."[11] In the Shinjuku ward of Tokyo, a modest wedding hall was opened in a municipal services building in October 1952 and was the site of over six hundred marriage ceremonies in the subsequent four months or so. The cost of renting the space was 300 yen, tea and pastries were about 100 yen per person, any sake brought onto the premises was limited to a little over one ounce a guest, the ceremony lasted roughly forty minutes, and the reception was kept under an hour. At a gathering in January 1953 of fifty couples who had been married in that wedding hall, one spoke about how their skeptical parents from the countryside had been won over by the simplified ceremony. And another thought that the event could be even more frugal if the ritual exchange of nuptial sake cups was not required but made optional. In keeping with this theme, the meeting ended with the pronouncement that "waste still remained"—that there was more work to be done to stamp out wastefulness.[12]

The promotion of unadorned weddings continued even as the economy improved, with an editorial in the mass circulation *Mainichi* newspaper supporting those young people who chose more modest events. A wedding was the most significant ceremony of one's life, the editors proclaimed, and also the one with the most meaningless waste. Critical of coercive consumption and the strain it put on parents, the newspaper touted waste-free celebrations that were held in the afternoon rather than the evening, or organized by friends, or paid for by contributions from guests. The current generation of young people was praised for understanding that marriage should be not about their parents but about their new life, and that waste was a societal vice.[13]

Also a target for streamlining were other rituals and formalities of daily life, such as gift giving, funerals, Christmas trees, and New Year's cards and decorations.[14] Toward the end of 1955, the New Life Movement Association peppered the airwaves with spots and dotted public places with color posters that read, "Let's exercise self-restraint from wasteful year-end and new-year parties"; "Let's stop sending formal gifts and New Year's cards"; and "Let's celebrate Christmas quietly."[15] In a similar vein, the *Mainichi* newspaper took aim in June 1956 at the upcoming midsummer gift exchange (*ochūgen*), deeming it a waste that needed to be stopped immediately. In the editorial's view, the rationalization of lifestyles had to start with the discarding of such conventions which, in the case of this particular practice, not only were wasteful but also greased the wheels of corruption and favoritism. Bestowing on the New Life Movement Association an authority it did not have, the editors called upon the organization as well as governments and public offices to prohibit such gift giving.[16] Periodically the newspaper also ran small pieces about waste consciousness, such as a letter from a high school student in Ibaraki prefecture who found the continual exchange of souvenirs from trips a costly, burdensome, and wasteful custom.[17] Given such coverage in mass circulation newspapers, it is not terribly surprising that a nationwide survey of three thousand people conducted by the association in 1957 found that for the 73.9 percent of respondents who knew of the New Life Movement, the issue with which it was most associated was the "simplification of ceremonial occasions."[18]

"New life" campaigns were also created by corporations that sought to rationalize both the workplace and the home. As the historian Andrew Gordon has described, four large business federations started their own New Life Movement in December 1953, well before Hatoyama's had taken shape. Initially concerned about frivolous corporate spending on entertainment, the movement advocated "self-restraint" when it came to such expenses as well as those for "company-sponsored funerals, New Year and midyear gift giving, and dress."[19] This corporate New Life Movement Association (Shin Seikatsu Undō no Kai), organized by the Japan Industrial Club (Nihon Kōgyō Kurabu), began with a membership of two hundred, which doubled during its first year. By 1959, a survey conducted by the Ministry of Health and Welfare (Kōseishō) found that forty-nine companies, with their 1.16 million workers, had New Life programs.[20]

Business literature about minimizing waste, though not directly connected to the corporate New Life Movement, dovetailed with its goals of maximizing productivity and profit through the rationalization of the workplace. Continuing in the vein of such advice from the immediate postwar years, publications geared toward managers offered detailed instructions about how to trim the perceived fat from offices and factories. A piece in the June 1954 issue of the magazine *Nōritsu* (Efficiency), published by the Tokyo Metropolitan Government's Efficiency Section (Tokyo-to Sōmukyoku Kikakubu Nōritsuka), made such suggestions as keeping the lid on the ink bottle to prevent the contents from evaporating (which would result in the loss of 63 percent of the ink); adding water to hardened glue so all of it could be used; putting down pencils and pens with the top facing you to save time when picking them back up; and choosing the appropriately sized staple for the job at hand.[21] Less fastidious but similarly pragmatic, the president of Hitachi advised readers of *Jimu to keiei* (Business and Management), a magazine of the Nippon Omni-Management Association (Nippon Keiei Kyōkai), about the four main categories of waste: materials, people, time, and money. Kurata Chikara laid out problems in the corporate workplace such as people not assembling at the appointed time for a meeting, too many meetings, an excess of gatherings with food and drink, and hiring more employees than a firm needed. At Hitachi, the vice president was put in charge of discovering and eliminating waste through controlling purchases at each office and examining everything from the use of a single pencil to the way letters were written.[22]

In a book titled *Muda monogatari* (Tales of Waste), released in 1954 by the economics and business publisher Daiyamondosha, the president of the Taiyū Company regaled readers with stories about eliminating waste drawn from what he had seen and heard in the business world. An executive of a relatively small industrial equipment and supply company, Miyanaga Susumu wrote in a casual and entertaining style about where to find waste and how to cut expenses. One case study started with a puzzle about two competent office workers who found themselves unusually busy, working overtime and feeling exhausted. These two women, it turned out, spent an inordinate amount of their time serving tea to colleagues and visitors to the office—anywhere between 100 to 150 cups depending on the day. The company then decided to experiment with self-service tea, asking workers and guests alike to help themselves from a thermos flask. The result was an increase in the efficiency of the two women employees, a reduction in the cost of tea by one-third because people could control the amount they wanted, and a decrease in the gas bill by two-thirds because the thermos flask obviated the need to constantly boil water. Although self-service tea did not catch on as a common practice in offices, this innovation was held up by Miyanaga as one that yielded savings of time, energy, and money. Another somewhat idiosyncratic initiative was spearheaded by a "Mr. M," or M-kun, who was in charge of cutting down on stationery expenses at his office. Costs were considered high, at a little over 1,000 yen per person for a company of about a thousand employees. So M-kun decided to become a "ragpicker" (*batayasan*), outfitting himself with a mask and gloves and sorting through the contents of office trash cans to determine if there was wastefulness in the use of stationery items. Surprised and dismayed by what he found, such as discarded paper with only one or two things written on it, he decided to open a "Wastepaper Exhibition." Displayed were the scraps he had collected as well as models of ideal waste consciousness: a thoroughly spent pencil, used writing paper and envelopes given a second life for memos, and useless catalogs repurposed for labels on files. Around the exhibition room were posted the unit prices of items, monthly costs, and amount consumed per person. In the month after the "Wastepaper Exhibition," consumption of stationery dropped by 10 to 15 percent, or over 100,000 yen.[23] While these particular strategies for cutting waste presented by Miyanaga were fairly unorthodox, the overarching view of and approach to waste—as something that needed to be eradicated through deliberate and thorough examination of practices—were very much in keeping with the decades-old management philosophy of rationalizing the workplace.

Efforts at eliminating waste in the office had their parallel in the factory, as corporations that had survived the worst of the immediate postwar years continued to feel an acute need to boost efficiency and productivity. At the Toyota Motor Company (Toyota Jidōsha), the assumptions of scientific management and Taylorism shaped the pillars of what would be widely celebrated in later decades as "lean production," or the so-called Toyota production system. In the 1950s, one key piece of the system, increased labor productivity, fell into place through the efforts of the engineer Ōno Tai'ichi. Ōno's aim was to "eliminate all unnecessary movements and allow no idle time, for machines or workers," by "altering workshop layouts, imposing more rigorous job routines, and installing new jigs and automatic devices to simplify procedures."[24] Having developed methods for one worker to operate multiple machines at the same time, Ōno was able to maximize labor potential and contribute to the company's efficient growth; during the 1950s, when the number of employees increased by a mere 10 percent, Toyota's production of automobiles grew by 1,000 percent.[25] The Ōno Tai'ichi of the steel industry was Orii Hyūga, who managed the labor division of NKK (Nippon Kōkan). In the late 1940s and early 1950s, Orii initiated an examination of "machine operating rates, calories expended per task, break time, and idle time for every job in the mill" as part of his larger project of adopting scientific approaches to manage labor.[26]

Consistent with earlier efforts to extend scientific management beyond the assembly line, rationalization of the workplace was to entail rationalization of the home, for NKK as for other companies that embraced the New Life Movement. The home was both the place that nurtured and supported the male employee, and the domestic counterpart to the workplace which was to be run rationally and efficiently by a housewife. At NKK, the first private company that became part of the movement, the expansive reach and vision of the corporation was articulated by Orii Hyūga, who observed that "workplace and home are intimately related parts of any person's life," and thus a skillful housewife was "the foundation for a bright, cheerful home, a bright society, and beyond that, a bright, cheerful workplace."[27] Also merging workplace and home under the corporate umbrella was Hongō Takanobu of the Welfare Section of Tōshiba (Tokyo Shibaura Electric, or Tokyo Shibaura Denki). Hongō espoused the view that labor management was too limited if confined just to the workplace, because the home was the source of energy and motivation for an employee and thus important for his health, safety, and efficiency. In December 1957, Hongō committed to extending the New Life Movement to housewives, which had not yet happened with much success in the more than two years of its existence at Tōshiba. Proposed recruitment strategies included promoting the movement through company news, first educating the husbands during afternoon breaks, sending invitations directly to housewives, and organizing casual events.[28] The New Life Movement did become well rooted in corporations like Tōshiba, NKK, and Hitachi, all of which housed a movement office at corporate headquarters, designated an official at each plant who served as a point person, and mobilized company employees as well as non-company counselors who organized housewives into small groups for discussions, lectures, and lessons. With the broad aim of creating rational and efficient households, the specific issues taken up varied and changed over time, but included hygiene, nutrition, child rearing, sewing, knitting, flower arranging, family planning, beauty and exercise, rational shopping, home improvement, and household accounts.[29]

Initiatives of the New Life Movement to rationalize households harmonized with published advice for housewives about how to reduce waste in the home, a gendered parallel to the business literature for corporate managers about how to reduce waste in the workplace. In newspapers, women's magazines, and business journals, practical strategies were doled out about how to run a streamlined household. One of the familiar advocates of efficiency in the home was the scientific management pioneer Ueno Yōichi, who continued to offer techniques for rationalizing housework, as he did on a program that aired on national broadcaster NHK in September 1955. Unnecessary movement should be reduced by putting things in their appropriate place (e.g., lining up kitchen utensils along one's workspace in the order in which they would be used); wasted time could be eliminated through multitasking (e.g., sewing, cooking beans, listening to the radio, and pressing pants under your floor cushion all at once); and idle moments should be spent planning (e.g., thinking ahead about the day if you stay in bed an extra five minutes in the morning).[30]

For rural households, such efforts at rationalization were part of lifestyle improvement campaigns which had been working to modernize farming life since the prewar period.[31] Along with initiatives to build infrastructure and mechanize agriculture, these campaigns, driven by the Ministry of Agriculture and Forestry, taught rural housewives how the inefficient layout of their kitchens was wasting their time and labor, and how remodeling or upgrading their cooking stoves would cut down on the waste of energy. Western-style clothes were also promoted as more efficient to sew, and proper organization of storage areas was recommended to create more space. Excess food currently being thrown out could instead be saved with the use of preservation methods, and even fruit fallen from trees could be turned into jam for later consumption.[32]

Outside of this campaign targeted at rural lifestyle improvement, most advice about eliminating waste was directed at housewives broadly defined. To this audience, the importance of planning was expressed time and again. In an *Asahi* newspaper article, to take but one example, the head of the Ministry of

FIGURE 2.1. Rationalizing Rural Life. Examples of how to rationalize and eliminate waste from rural life, explained in a book written by the Ministry of Agriculture and Forestry's Lifestyle Improvement Section.

Reproduced by permission from Nōrinshō Nōgyō Kairyōkyoku Seikatsu Kaizenka, ed., *Zusetsu nōka no seikatsu kaizen* (Tokyo: Asakura Shoten, 1954).

Agriculture and Forestry's Lifestyle Improvement Section (Nōrinshō Seikatsu Kaizenka) reiterated the principle that a brighter life started with planning. Yamamoto Matsuyo went on to recommend that women, like men in the workplace, should think about the day as consisting of eight hours of work in order to raise their labor efficiency. Housewives were to develop a detailed plan of household finances by calling a family meeting to determine for which upcoming expenditures, such as children's educational expenses, they should save. Time was to be thought of like money and apportioned for tasks such as cleaning, making rice, and doing laundry as well as some form of recreation.[33] Researcher Masuda Kinroku offered specific suggestions in a piece for the women's magazine *Fujin kurabu* (Women's Club), advocating the creation of a schedule and a to-do list so as to eliminate the waste of time.[34]

In addition to planning, careful measurement was also regularly extolled. A booklet titled *Korekara no kurashi* (Tomorrow's Daily Living), written by professors at Japan Women's University (Nihon Joshi Daigaku), outlined how housewives should scientize their lifestyle. Every kitchen was to be equipped with measuring cups, measuring spoons, a spring scale, and, if possible, a thermometer. Housewives were to get into the habit of using these tools, for example, when they measured water for making rice. Some fifty thousand copies of the publication were distributed to local youth and women's groups by the Central Council for Savings Promotion (Chochiku Zōkyō Chūō Iinkai) in the summer of 1956.[35] In addition to cooking, another household task that required measuring was laundry. As the *Asahi* newspaper instructed, there would be no waste if the ratio of detergent, water, and clothes was calculated properly: 800 grams of clothes required three level teaspoons of powdered detergent or six level teaspoons of so-called soapless soap.[36]

Housewives were also taught how to shop rationally. In a supplementary issue of the business magazine *Jitsugyō no Nihon* (Business Japan), readers were warned not to buy items for the house, such as furniture, without careful consideration. What should be done if you owned only five floor cushions and realized one day that you were expecting six guests? The temptation might be to run out to the Mitsukoshi department store and purchase another cushion on which the additional guest could sit. That, instructed the author, would not be prudent if you seldom entertained six people. The appropriate course of action would be to think about whether so many cushions would be required regularly, and then to discuss the matter as a couple before making any purchases.[37] In the pages of the same magazine, readers were told about comparison shopping. Housewives should know that the price of one daikon radish could vary by greengrocer.[38] Researching price differences was particularly important for more expensive goods. In the book *Kakei to seikatsu* (Household Finances and Daily Life), the three authors (including future Tokyo governor Minobe Ryōkichi) specified that for items like clothes, furniture, or a radio, the consumer should go to two or three stores to compare both price and quality. Attention was also to be paid to unit price. Yet another suggested strategy for maximizing purchasing power on a limited income was to examine one's motivations for buying, to distinguish between the rational (reflecting on why you want to purchase something) and the emotional (purchasing impulsively).[39]

The proximate goal of waste elimination for the household was saving money, or especially later in the 1950s, saving money in order to afford a large purchase like a washing machine, electric refrigerator, or television set.[40] For the corporations that participated in the New Life Movement, rationalizing the home was a potential way to create healthier, happier, more productive, and more loyal workers. But beyond these aims were others that were more vague. Unlike in the workplace, where the objectives of corporate productivity and profit were clear and calculable, eliminating waste in the household had murkier and broader purposes. The most frequently articulated aspiration in advice literature about household waste was for a somehow better and brighter daily life. Put romantically by the researcher Masuda Kinroku, eliminating the six main kinds of waste (in the areas of money, things, energy, nerves, time, and personal relationships) would lead to "paradise" within both one's heart and one's home.[41] Or put succinctly by the New Life Movement Association on its posters that decorated the country, "New Life, Eliminate Waste for Better Living."[42] Between the rather nebulous connection between waste consciousness and a brighter life, the mutability of the conception of a better daily life, and the vague equation of waste reduction with lifestyle improvement, there was a way in which jettisoning wastefulness from the household became an end in and of itself. A waste-free household was inherently better and brighter, and a waste-conscious housewife was necessarily a more skillful manager.

Waste consciousness was a virtue in the eyes of those who wrote admiringly of American households and workplaces, whose rationalization and efficiency were credited with promoting the country's prosperity. In an article written for the magazine *Ōru seikatsu* (All Life), from the publishing company Business Japan (Jitsugyō no Nihonsha), the journalist and social commentator Nakano Gorō was not blind to problems in the United States such as increases in the crime rate. But he highlighted what he saw as the successes of American society, namely, its affluence and rising standards of living, which he attributed to a practical and realistic way of living. Every American, wealthy or poor, was allegedly leading a "waste-free social life" and a "reasonable economic life." And it was simply a given that waste and immoderation were entirely forbidden in the workplace. In contrast, life in Japan was illogical and irrational as the country and the people overreached with their national and household finances. To illustrate this point, Nakano gave the example of an American named "Mr. U," a middle-aged vice president of a trading company. In Tokyo on business, Mr. U wanted to buy a handkerchief and was astonished when he was presented with the first option: one made of linen with a price tag of several thousand yen. He ultimately bought a much less expensive handkerchief for 40 yen, which was closer to what he had expected, given prices in the United States. While the comparison in this story was simplified, juxtaposing as it did an upscale store in the Nihonbashi area of Tokyo with a drugstore in New York City, it was drawn to underscore his argument about unreasonable consumption in Japan. Nakano viewed his country, which did not enjoy the affluence of the United States, as one of irrational spending, superfluous formalities, and a myopia about wastefulness.[43]

The characterization of life in the United States as more rational and reasonable than in Japan was also promoted by Katō Yoshio, the economics division chief and former New York City correspondent of the Jiji Tsūshin news agency. In a May 1955 article in *Jitsugyō no Nihon*, Katō listed what he saw as the numerous ways in which American life exhibited simplification and rationalization, including the supermarket, the drugstore, and one-man, or conductor-less, buses. And his exemplary product was not the handkerchief but coffee. American coffee was bad, he admitted, but the price point of around ten cents was much more rational than the comparatively expensive cup in Japan. For Katō, the rationalization of industry and households was not just a matter of money, of being able to afford more efficient equipment for the factory or an electric washing machine for the home, but about mindset. Although he did not mention the New Life Movement by name, his view that ways of thinking had not been adequately reformed in Japan would not have been at odds with its assumptions.[44]

Even as the reduction of waste in the household and workplace was typically discussed as desirable, there were faint criticisms of how the New Life Movement in particular went about promoting the virtues of waste consciousness. To some, there was a heavy-handed, cold, and rigid quality to the continued promotion of efficiency and rationalization which was not in keeping with the times. An article in the prominent left-leaning journal *Sekai* (The World) in February 1956 expressed discomfort with government involvement, pointing out that the funds for the New Life Movement Association were drawn entirely from the Ministry of Education's budget. Likening its ideas to those of youth groups from the prewar period, the article characterized the movement as the voice of the government and described its agenda bitingly as "disgustingly proper."[45] Aware of such negative reactions, Toshiba named its version the Movement for Skillful Living (Jōzu na Kurashi no Undō) so as to avoid the New Life Movement's "bureaucratic stench." The company also sought to distance its initiatives from the movement's stiffness and spirit of prohibition (*bekarazu shugi*).[46]

The man who directed Tōshiba's campaign, Hongō Takanobu, acknowledged one particular source of resistance to the New Life Movement: unions. In a 1957 report, Hongō spoke of the "surprisingly large" number of unions that were taking an oppositional stance to the movement based on concerns about overreach by the government, objections to undue intervention into private life, and suspicions that management was attempting to win over families in preparation for future labor disputes. While he deliberately and predictably refuted such claims, Hongō's language of nurturing employee trust and affinity for the company was less than selfless.[47] Indeed, Hongō was writing in the context of opposition by the left wing of the labor movement to efforts at boosting productivity in workplaces, upset about what that would entail for the pace of work and the cutting of jobs. Such apprehensions extended to the rationalization of the home. Although the intensity of union opposition to the New Life Movement varied, the historian Andrew Gordon described one particular union activist who "blasted the New Life Movement as an austerity campaign cast in the wartime mold, a household version of the newly launched industrial productivity campaign." What this worker sought instead was the improvement of productivity and standards of living through "higher wages, better working conditions, and shorter work hours."[48] Similar sentiments were expressed by a leader of the left-leaning General Council of Trade Unions of Japan (Nihon Rōdō Kumiai Sōhyō Gikai, or Sōhyō), who was quoted in an *Asahi* newspaper article as worrying that the New Life Movement "will be used as a tool for lowering already low wages, and restructuring by firing workers."[49]

In the view of Kaneko Hiroshi, a social psychologist and former head of the National Personnel Authority's Efficiency Section (Jinjiin Nōritsukyoku), movements for rationalization and efficiency were too rigidly focused on the "conquest of waste." Kaneko illustrated the inflexibility of this approach by contrasting it with the subjectivity of determining what should be considered a waste. In the magazine *Seikai ōrai* (Political World Correspondence), he juxtaposed the United States with Japan to highlight this point. One might, he said, look at American lifestyles and determine that they were replete with wastefulness: dishwashers that gobbled up hot water; wastepaper, wooden boxes, cans, and bottles that came out of kitchens; parking lots filled with idle cars; and paper towels in public restrooms. Dishwasher use was uncommon in Japan; recyclables from the kitchen were picked up by a ragman; parking lots were not so large; and people used their own handkerchiefs to dry their hands. But, noted Kaneko, one could also look at Japanese lifestyles and determine that they were replete with wastefulness: fragile homes were made out of wood and paper; conductresses on buses provided an annoying service; housewives spent too much time futilely dusting their homes; and multiple trips were made to the greengrocer and fishmonger when one would suffice. The thrust of Kaneko's argument was that different ways of understanding waste were not acknowledged, and were indeed smothered, by the push for rationalization and efficiency.

When he had been with the National Personnel Authority, Kaneko himself had embraced the philosophies of Ueno Yōichi and applied the principles of eliminating the "three *mu*"—*muda* (waste), *muri* (unreasonableness), and *mura* (inconsistency)—or the three manifestations of waste. Yet he had come to think that this approach was too much about minute details, too trivial. Making sure that ink bottles were capped and that the proper number of staples were used might not increase the vitality and output of the workplace. Moreover, implied Kaneko, the hatred and intolerance for the existence of waste jibed with a kind of totalitarianism. What he proposed instead was the development of techniques to make the best use of waste. Short on concrete examples, he encouraged his readers to overcome a miserly state of mind that worried about not wasting even one grain of rice and to nurture instead a spirit that could freely enjoy waste. The essence of democracy, contended Kaneko, was recognizing that all people have the "right to waste."[50]

In Kaneko's exhortation to take pleasure from waste, as with some of the unease with the New Life Movement and the skepticism of labor unions about the rationalization of the workplace and home, there were strains of resistance to the fundamental conception of waste as something that needed to be eliminated. But these views were relatively faint, muffled by the more prevalent view in the early and mid-1950s of the undesirability of waste. As exemplified by the advocates of the New Life Movement and the champions of scientific management, the established ambition of eradicating waste endured for the sake of ensuring a civilized, modern, and economically sound future—for a bright life in a bright Japan.

Rationalizing Consumption

The ideal of daily life in workplaces and homes purged of waste and wastefulness took shape in the process of redevelopment and remodernization. To eliminate wasting was to move ever closer to financial and material security, and to begin to reach toward the romanticized lifestyles of the American middle class. The pursuit of rationalization and efficiency, health and hygiene was intimately associated with ideas of civilization and progress. Yet ironically, these very aspirations and values that undergirded waste consciousness provided the rhetorical and conceptual building blocks for a surge in consumption. Ideals of waste reduction were shown to be flexible as they were adapted to revolutionary changes in society and lifestyles, many of which would be criticized in years to come as the font of rampant wastefulness.

To encourage people to consume and to think of themselves as consumers, companies along with marketers and advertisers tapped into nascent desires for a better life, offering their own version of what the new and bright should be and rationalizing the spending of money with their own twist on existing values. Especially in the early 1950s, advertisers strategically associated their products with the United States, thereby offering the subtle but pointed reminder that consumption of material goods was part of the appeal of American lifestyles. Advertisements for the Lion brand toothbrush emphasized that the nylon for the bristles was made by an American company, DuPont; the National brand interphone spoke of its "American-style speed"; and the manufacturer YKK heralded its zipper as a strong, elegant, and top-quality product because of its new "American-style" production method. Indeed, one of the ways to increase sales of a product was to describe it with the slogan *bunkateki, Amerikateki*, or "cultured and American-like."[51] In the mid-1950s, electric goods companies picked up on Prime Minister Hatoyama's slogan of a "bright Japan" to make the case that their products, from rice cookers to lightbulbs, could, metaphorically and sometimes quite literally, bring brightness into the home. Sanyō advertised "Sanyō Electrical Products for a Bright Life," and the National brand marketed itself as "Bright National."[52]

Electric goods companies also took care to present the purchase of an expensive washing machine or even a television set as rational, as the historian Simon Partner has compellingly illustrated. The rationale offered for significant financial outlays typically had to do with the "benefits of health and welfare, and economic benefits based on the saving of labor."[53] Such justifications would have sounded familiar to potential consumers who had previously learned about the civilizing virtues of health and hygiene, the folly of wasting money, and the importance of maximizing labor efficiency. Attempting to link its products with the rationalization of the household, Matsushita Electric Industrial (Matsushita Denki Sangyō, later Panasonic) described how food kept fresh in a refrigerator promoted good health and advertised its National brand washing machine as relieving housewives from the hard labor of having to do laundry by hand. To quantify the saving of both labor and money, Hitachi compared the cost of electricity for its washing machine (1 to 1.6 yen an hour) with the cost of food for a housewife who did laundry by hand (20 to 25 yen an hour). When it came to the television set, it might have seemed a harder task to justify the purchase of a good that cost about three times more than a washing machine without the labor-saving utility.

The Sharp Corporation made an attempt by appealing to people's desire to watch sports, calculating the price tag for actually attending all of the sporting and cultural events televised on NHK at 300,000 yen per person. In contrast, a television set (at a still whopping 84,500 yen) was, claimed Sharp, "very economical."[54] Such appeals to rationality meant that consumption did not have to come into tension with the idea of managing household finances. That more households in 1960 owned a television set (9 million) than a washing machine (6 million) or a refrigerator (2 million) spoke more than anything else to the flexibility of rationalization, to the way that large expenditures on what might be considered luxury goods could be understood as not the least bit wasteful.[55]

Spotlighting the excitement of the new while disarming it through association with familiar values was a strategy also employed by the food industry as it introduced one instant product after another to the market. In 1958, instant ramen made its debut, and in 1960, Morinaga unveiled its domestic brand instant coffee.[56] When Nissin Foods began to advertise its instant ramen on television in 1960, it tried to demonstrate "how convenient life could be with Chikin Rāmen" and underscored its "healthfulness, hygienic quality, novelty, and vitality."[57] At least some of this message seems to have resonated with consumers, who, according to a survey conducted in 1960, appreciated that instant foods saved time and trouble, could be made easily, and were inexpensive and convenient.[58] The idea of convenience had overtones of efficiency, evoking as it did the saving of time and labor. For the ostensible purpose of eliminating wastefulness, instant goods implicitly devalued and deemed wasteful what had been seen as necessary only a short time ago—the effort required to make one's own juice or soup or curry. That is, the embrace of new types of goods like instant foods and electric appliances had the consequence of redrawing the lines that defined what routines and practices in everyday life might be considered a waste.

There were other ways in which enduring values had unexpected implications for how people lived and for what was thought of as waste. Appreciation of hygiene and convenience, for example, encouraged the consumption of products that were packaged or intended to be thrown away, inaugurating an age of unprecedented disposability. The institution of the supermarket hastened this development. The first self-service food store, and arguably the first supermarket in Japan, was the Kinokuniya which opened in the Aoyama area of Tokyo in 1953. By 1962 there were over seven hundred supermarkets countrywide.[59] As they proliferated, there developed a need to establish systems for distributing, managing, and selling a large amount of product at numerous stores. The standardization of product shape and form helped facilitate mass distribution and uniformity across locations. This meant that produce like potatoes or onions was premeasured and packaged, fish was precut, and tofu could no longer be scooped by hand in the amount desired. The practice of bringing empty bowls and bottles from home to fill with miso or soy sauce disappeared, and home delivery of milk was eventually replaced by milk in a carton. It became standard for products to be prewrapped, priced, and, after passing through the register, placed in a paper bag. Opportunities for convenient consumption were also created by the spread of vending machines, which made packaged food, beverages, and other products available at all hours of the day. In 1962, there were roughly 10,000 machines across the country; by 1965, this number was about 290,000. And there also emerged the "auto parlor" (ōto pārā), or Automat, at which consumers could purchase food and drink from a row of vending machines.

Scientific and technological developments, especially in the manufacturing of plastics, also contributed to the proliferation of disposable goods. Plastic wrap started to be sold by Kureha Chemical (Kureha Kagaku Kōgyō) as kure rappu in 1961, and by Asahi Kasei as saran rappu in 1962.[60] By the late 1960s, pantyhose had caught on, thanks in part to the miniskirt, which made the one-piece combination of panties and stockings more desirable than the girdle or garter. This nylon product, developed by DuPont in the 1930s to replace silk imports from a militarist Japan, became widely used in postwar Japan as a disposable accessory.[61]

Be it disposability or convenience, ideas laced with established values such as rationalization, efficiency, health, and hygiene eased the transition into a new era of consumerism. Neither spending money on consumer goods nor discarding those products as garbage was considered wasteful, as long as the ways in which and reasons why one consumed bore some resemblance to such familiar, albeit malleable, ideals. The growing comfort with consuming, desire for convenience, and normalization of disposability raised some eyebrows at the time, but it would not be until later years that they would take on different meanings as perceived engines of mass waste.

"Stinginess Is a Virtue, Wasting Money Is Fun"

There was recognition at the time, in the late 1950s and early 1960s, of the transformations then unfolding. The groundswell of consumerism was officially characterized as a "consumption revolution" in 1960 by the Economic Planning Agency, which also detailed the "lifestyle revolution" it entailed.[62] The allure and pursuit of consumption were not without precedent. In the prewar period, department stores like Mitsukoshi sold consumer goods, large advertising firms like Dentsū promoted new products, and the print media as well as radio circulated ads and information about how to consume. But at its prewar height in the 1920s, such consumption remained a largely urban phenomenon restricted to a small middle class.[63] By the late 1950s, consumption was uneven across urban and rural areas, income, and occupation, but it was becoming normalized as an ideal if not yet a mass experience.[64] In 1960, individual consumption was growing at a rate of roughly 7 percent, and the proportion of urban households that owned a black-and-white television set had jumped from 23.6 percent in the previous year to around 40 percent, and for rural households from 4.3 to around 11 percent. Increases in spending on consumer durables and passenger cars was remarkable, noted the Economic Planning Agency, considering that incomes were one-ninth those in the United States.[65] And by the end of 1960, 78 percent of respondents in a survey reported that they had consumed instant ramen.[66] In 1960, Prime Minister Ikeda Hayato sought to accelerate, equalize, and extend the upward trajectory in people's living standards, announcing an ambitious plan to double gross national product and average household income in ten years. Between 1960 and 1965, the percentage of nonfarm households that owned a black-and-white television set jumped from 44.7 to 95 percent, an electric or gas refrigerator from 10.1 to 68.7 percent, and an electric washing machine from 49.6 to 78.1 percent.[67] Opening their pocketbooks, many people were participating in and propelling the revolution in material consumption.

As consumerism became "a new ethos, a way of living, a dominant social practice," what might have been considered extravagant spending in earlier years was normalized.[68] And the kinds of products that might previously have been categorized as luxury goods were becoming the necessities of more affluent lifestyles. Consumers who had imagined owning the "three treasures" (washing machine, vacuum cleaner, and refrigerator), or the "three S's" (senpūki, or electric fan; sentakki, or washing machine; and suihanki, or electric rice cooker) in the late 1950s aspired to the "three C's" (car, color television set, and kūrā, or air conditioner) by the mid-1960s.[69] Enabling the expansion of consumer desires was high economic growth, as the goal of doubling national income set by Prime Minister Ikeda in 1960 met its target in 1968, two years ahead of schedule. As the economy grew and consumer desires expanded, ideas about wastefulness mutated as different people attempted to make sense of, and decide how to live in, a mass consumption society. Among them were many who relaxed definitions of stinginess and wastefulness as they became more accustomed to spending money in pursuit of comfort, enjoyment, and pleasure.

Participants in a discussion published in the popular women's magazine *Shufu to seikatsu* (The Housewife and Daily Life) in 1961 were relatively liberal about what constituted wasteful spending. Titled "Stinginess Is a Virtue, Wasting Money Is Fun," the roundtable was not draconian in its definition of stinginess. Tomiko Katsuhisa, a division chief at Mitsubishi Trust (Mitsubishi Shintaku), reinterpreted the meaning of saving in the early modern Tokugawa period (1600–1868) to justify certain purchases. According to Tomiko, saving money as an end in itself was considered in Tokugawa Japan an undesirable form of stinginess, and the spending of money could be a virtue depending on what was purchased. Bringing this take on early modern thrift into contemporary times, the social commentator Togaeri Chizuko deemed it perfectly appropriate to save money for the sake of buying something or enjoying oneself. Or put in a more specific way, it was fine for a housewife to squirrel away savings unbeknownst to her husband to spend as she liked. Togaeri and Nakamura Takeshi, a writer and employee of Japan National Railways (Nihon Kokuyū Tetsudō), encouraged young people to enjoy themselves up until the age of thirty-five by spending money on a car, going skiing, and eating good food. Men were forgiven, too, for their wasteful spending on such expenses as taxi rides. So, agreed the participants, some wasteful spending on the part of housewives should also be overlooked. After all, said Tomiko, a human being's sense of freedom was created from wasteful spending.[70]

That a rigid and excessive concern about wastefulness could lead to an unnecessary and unbecoming stinginess was echoed in the advice given to a "Mrs. S," or S-kosan, in the *Mainichi* newspaper. S-kosan of Saitama prefecture had written in to complain about her husband, who did not understand how much enjoyment she found in remaking and reusing things, in embodying the virtue of frugality. When she made a diaper cover out of leftover wool cloth, he remarked that one could be bought for 200 to 300 yen. When she advised him to buy an overcoat in the summer, when it was less expensive, he laughed and said that was stupid. When she unraveled an old sweater to reuse the yarn, he wondered why she kept doing that. To S-kosan, her husband was like all men in his propensity to consume meaninglessly. So, she asked, how could women make men understand a mindset of frugality? The responses to this question were probably not what S-kosan expected. Yes, a thirty-six-year-old reader from Ibaraki prefecture agreed that men spend 300 to 400 yen on socks that they could buy for 150 yen, and a forty-eight-year-old woman from Tokyo observed that the habit of valuing things was disappearing as people were increasingly inclined to throw away things like clothes and shoes. But a thirty-one-year-old woman from Tokyo commented that the definition of frugality was changing and that it was time to rethink and reexamine a waste consciousness (*mottainai seishin*) that meant stuffing useless things into the closet just because it felt wasteful to throw them out. And buying an overcoat in the summer just because it was cheaper did not make sense; it would be preferable to choose the style one wanted, even if it meant spending more. Most critical was the formal advice given by the social commentator Akiyama Chieko, who encouraged S-kosan to continue saving but also told her to spend. Once every week or ten days she should not do anything or eat out with her husband, or enjoy any form of leisure. An overcoat was not to be considered expensive if it gave her husband a purpose for living. And most of all, S-kosan was to cut by one-third the number of times she told her husband she was saving. She was not to speak too much about "saving, saving" and was not to become miserly (*rinshoku*).[71]

The appeal of both moderate waste consciousness and purposeful consumption was also expounded by the well-known architect, designer, and professor Kon Wajirō. Kon was attentive to wastefulness but also justified large financial expenditures. On the one hand, consumption that was influenced by fashions and societal habits was a waste. He thus wore a jacket and canvas shoes, even to weddings if permitted, and had not sent out New Year's cards since the end of the war because they wasted money and the labor of the delivery person. Money could be spent freely, however, if it was an act of creation, if it had to do with the creation of the individual. Kon, for example, found it perfectly acceptable to expand his landholdings over the years so that his house would feel good to him.[72]

A small warning about what could be missed if one was too preoccupied with not being wasteful was conveyed in a children's story published in the parenting magazine *Haha no tomo* (Mothers' Friend). Titled "Mottainai, mottainai" ("Wasteful, Wasteful"), the tale chronicled the adventures of a rabbit named Hanapiku who transformed himself into a human child in order to rescue his rabbit friend Higepiku from captivity by a hunter who was preparing a stew. Hanapiku-as-child talked his way into the hunter's house, and every time the hunter became suspicious about Hanapiku's identity, he was sidetracked by his desire to not waste food. Just when the hunter noticed that "Hanapiku" sounded suspiciously like a rabbit's name, a piece of potato fell on the floor, prompting him to exclaim, "*Mottainai mottainai. Mottainai how mottainai*," and forget his line of questioning. When Hanapiku let slip that he lived in a hole on the edge of a forest and twitched his nose like a rabbit, the hunter's attention was again turned away from Hanapiku's real identity by his desire to not waste food fallen on the floor. Recognizing the hunter's preoccupation with wastefulness as a vice, Hanapiku ultimately saved himself and his friend Higepiku by intentionally dropping a biscuit on the ground. Saying again, "*Mottainai mottainai. Mottainai how mottainai*," the hunter put down his ax to pick up and eat the biscuit, which turned him into a rabbit. In this story intended for the ears of young children, consciousness of waste was an unhealthy obsession of a predatory character who, in the end, lost not only what he desired but also his human form.[73]

As conceptions of what constituted appropriate spending were broadened, expenditures of time or money on leisure were generally not considered a waste. Like household electric appliances, free time and leisure were understood as purposeful and as markers of improving lifestyles. In the early 1960s, the desirability of "free time" (*jiyū jikan*) was assumed in predictions that it would only increase in the coming years. The Ministry of Labor (Rōdōshō) posited that a declining birth rate would mean less child rearing and housework for women.[74] Household electric appliances were also assumed to lighten and shorten the labor of housewives.[75] When it came to the typical day of a (male) worker, the Vision Council of the Japan Recreation Association (Nihon Rekuriēshon Kyōkai Bijon Iinkai) optimistically projected that free time would increase from a little over two hours a day in 1965 to an astonishing eight and a half hours a day by the late 1980s.[76] Among those with less lofty and more immediate ambitions, there was hope for a regular day off, even a two-day weekend, across industries.[77] While there does not seem to have been a marked decline in actual hours worked in the early 1960s, what was more clear was an upward trajectory in the amount of money households spent on nonessentials.[78] By various measures, household expenditures on leisure appeared to be on a steady upswing.[79] Indeed, leisure became another commodity to be consumed. According to a study conducted in 1965 by the Nomura Research Institute (Nomura Sōgō Kenkyūjo), the areas of leisure in which consumers spent the most money were liquor (821.8 billion yen); trips (566.1 billion); gambling (532.4 billion); tobacco (364.7 billion); television and radio (347.1 billion); and publications such as books, newspapers, and magazines (306.3 billion).[80]

It was such expenditures on leisure, along with the expectation and hope of more free time, that fueled the idea that there was a "leisure boom" in the 1960s. Epitomized by photographs of crowded beaches and inviting ski slopes, leisure was to be desired, its newness underscored by the eclipse of the older term for leisure (*yoka*) by the romanized English word (*rejā*).[81] As leisure garnered more attention, it became almost interchangeable with the idea of free time—and neither leisure nor free time was considered wasteful. They both designated a category of time that was to be put to some particular use, be it enjoyment, fun, rest, or cultural enrichment. And this was congruent with the conception of time as a resource to be well managed for productive ends however defined. Some thought of free time not as liberation from labor but as a chance for restoration and recuperation which enhanced labor. Others, especially those who were critical of the homogenization and commodification of leisure activities, preferred to view free time as an opportunity for the pursuit of individualism and freedom.[82] In all of these various ways, time away from work was not a luxury, was not time wasted.

"Is Consumption a Virtue?"

At a time when the allure of economic growth and changing lifestyles was powerful, there emerged new concerns about what the burgeoning phenomenon of mass consumption might mean for wastefulness. Some voiced unease about how and why consumers wanted to spend their money. And some began to consider whether wasting was stoked by marketing and advertising, and bred by consuming. Wastefulness, it seemed, might be intrinsic to what was largely viewed as progress. Yet such criticisms were tepid in the 1960s, their message and reception blunted by heightened and widespread exuberance about the pursuit of wealth and material abundance.

Ambivalence about the possible wastefulness of mass consumption was evident in the response of various Japanese readers to the publication of books by social critics in the United States who complicated the rosy picture of American prosperity. These translated works, popular in Japan, provided a vocabulary for considering how mass consumption might be wasteful and raised questions about how the mechanisms of consumerism might encourage wastefulness. Put before a Japanese audience was the provocative issue of whether consumer desire was intentionally manipulated to create waste. At the time of their publication, these works did garner a fair amount of reader attention, but they stopped well short of igniting the kind of impassioned criticism of affluence and waste expressed by their authors.

One such book was *Yutaka na shakai*, published in 1960 as the Japanese translation of *The Affluent Society* by the Harvard economist John Kenneth Galbraith. In the preface to the Japanese edition, Galbraith underscored his argument that after production surpassed a certain level, it was as much about creating as satisfying desire.[83] As he contended in the book, consumer demand was trumped up by producers and manipulated by advertisers. Such artificially constructed consumption was, he implied, wasteful: "Consumer wants can have bizarre, frivolous, or even immoral origins, and an admirable case can still be made for a society that seeks to satisfy them. But the case cannot stand if it is the process of satisfying wants that creates the wants."[84] Addressing his Japanese readers, Galbraith encouraged them to consider the extent to which the book was pertinent to their own country, but also offered his view that it was at least somewhat relevant, that it would be mistaken to think of Americans as uniquely affluent.[85]

In Japan, Galbraith's book did not become part of a spirited debate about mass production, mass consumption, and the jobs of the marketer and the advertiser. Rather, his ideas were inflected in ways that dulled their incisiveness. There were those like Shinozaki Hiromi who did cite Galbraith when posing the question of whether the phrase "waste is a virtue" might capture the prevailing sentiment of the coming decade.[86] And a short review of *Yutaka na shakai* published in the *Yomiuri* newspaper did agree that much of what the book said could apply to Japan as a "little America" one step behind its model. Yet what was highlighted by this reviewer was not Galbraith's social critique or challenge to Keynesian economics, but a misleadingly positive understanding of the book's central subject: that an "affluent society" was one that had eliminated poverty.[87] The phrase *yutaka na shakai* was thus endowed with a favorable connotation, and the term gained currency as a desirable aspiration. Indeed, a few years later, in 1964, a *Yomiuri* newspaper article observed that the words were catching on "like a rosy dream" because of the fame of Galbraith's book, while the issues and concerns he had raised had been forgotten.[88]

This positive recasting and defusing of Galbraith's arguments lent weight to the claims of his critics, like George Katona, who did not think there was a relationship between the mechanisms of consumerism and waste. Katona's book *The Mass Consumption Society* was made available in Japan as *Taishū shōhi shakai* by the economics and business publisher Daiyamondosha in 1966. Katona, a psychologist who became known as the "dean of behavioral economists," argued that the consumer was a valued contributor to the stabilization of the economy and was not prone to excess.[89] He took issue with books such as *The Affluent Society*, in which "the wealth of consumer goods is equated, not with the high American standard of living, but with gadgetry and waste."[90] Defending American affluence as well as the society and life that it helped create, Katona reassured his readers that "the new ability to satisfy wants ... makes life easier but does not necessarily result in soft living and waste."[91] In his preface to *Taishū shōhi shakai*, the social psychologist Minami Hiroshi of Hitotsubashi University and the Social Behavior Research Institute (Shakai Kōdō Kenkyūjo) did not address the ways in which Katona's perspective was at odds with that of someone like Galbraith; instead he commented blandly on the spread of consumer goods and leisure in Japan.[92] And Katona's defense of consumption in the name of economic growth and improved lifestyles was very much in line with the stances of many in Japan at the time, including the Economic Planning Agency and those like Ishii Kinnosuke, author of the book *Shōhi wa bitoku de aru* (Consumption Is a Virtue).[93] In the absence of vigorous debate about wasteful consumerism, reservations such as those expressed by Galbraith about the future of affluent mass consumption societies were deflated.

More provocative was the work of Vance Packard, whose blunt and direct attacks on the waste inherent in mass consumption did invite and elicit a somewhat broader range of reactions in Japan. A journalist turned freelance writer, Packard published in quick succession three nonfiction best sellers intended for a general audience, each of which was translated into Japanese shortly after its American release: *Kakureta settokusha* in 1958 (*The Hidden Persuaders*, 1957); *Chi'i o motomeru hitobito* in 1960 (*The Status Seekers*, 1959); and *Rōhi o tsukuridasu hitobito* in 1961 (*The Waste Makers*, 1960).[94] In *The Hidden Persuaders*, Packard excoriated marketers and advertisers who employed the strategies of motivational research, a relatively new field in which psychology was used to determine why people act the way they do and then persuade them to make particular purchasing decisions. He also remarked on the wasteful consumption encouraged by marketers through "planned obsolescence," whereby goods were intentionally made obsolete so as to promote repetitive consumption. The specific variant discussed was "psychological obsolescence" or "style obsolescence": frequently creating goods in a new style so that consumers would become dissatisfied with their older model and want to purchase the most recent one. Asked Packard, "What is the morality of developing in the public an attitude of wastefulness toward natural resources by encouraging the 'psychological obsolescence' of products already in use?"[95]

These themes were developed more fully in *Rōhi o tsukuridasu hitobito*, a best seller in Japan, which brought attention to wastefulness but was also read and used in thoroughly unanticipated ways. Criticism of wasteful consumption was at the heart of *The Waste Makers*, which Packard dedicated "To my Mother and Father who have never confused the possession of goods with the good life." When he spoke of the "waste makers," Packard was referring to the marketers, advertisers, and business executives "who are seeking to make their fellow citizens more prodigal in their daily lives" as well as "most Americans" who were complicit in encouraging this prodigal spirit in what Packard thought would come to be understood by historians as the "Throwaway Age."[96] Packard asserted that "wastefulness has become a part of the American way of life," and this concerned him because of the effect it would have on the so-called American character and spirit. He worried that Americans, pressured to consume and encouraged to find satisfaction more in consumption than in production, were starting to exhibit characteristics such as "pleasure-mindedness, self-indulgence, materialism, and passivity."[97]

Wasteful consumers were being created, Packard asserted, by nine strategies used by marketers to encourage ever-increasing levels of consumption. These nine techniques included persuading people to purchase more of a good (multiple telephones or pairs of eyeglasses to match the color and style of every room or outfit, or a wedding ring for the groom as well as the bride).[98] More pertinent to waste was the selling of disposable goods (aluminum frying pans, food in aerosol cans or boil-in bags, or plastic razors).[99] The epitome of this "throwaway spirit" was the psychological obsolescence that Packard had touched on in *The Hidden Persuaders*, or what he called here the "planned obsolescence of desirability": a way for companies to encourage the purchase of the newest version or latest model of a product through changes in style and design. By altering color, ornamentation, profile, and the like, manufacturers could market women's shoes with pointed toes, cars with smaller tailfins, and slimmer television sets as alluring for consumers whose current shoes, cars, and television sets were still perfectly functional.[100]

Quite contrary to Packard's intent, in Japan these techniques and management strategies seem to have been adopted as a model by marketers who read *Rōhi o tsukuridasu hitobito*. This observation was made multiple times by Ishikawa Hiroyoshi, a social psychologist, professor at Seijō University, and translator who published part of Packard's book in the prominent highbrow magazine *Chūō kōron* (the Central Review) in April 1961. In a foreword to the translated excerpt, Ishikawa felt it necessary to explain that the book was a criticism of consumerism and that those in Japan who were reading it as a playbook for marketing and advertising were doing so contrary to Packard's original aim in writing it.[101] That Packard was being received most enthusiastically by managers was also noted in a review of the book and by an article in the *Yomiuri* newspaper.[102] And the economist Katō Hiroshi lamented that Packard was popular in Japan because of his talent for writing best sellers and for providing an analysis of selling strategies from which people could learn business methods for a consumer society.[103] By 1964, a *Yomiuri* article could claim that the methods of motivational research, so objectionable to Packard, were popularized in Japan by his books.[104]

The psychologist and translator Ishikawa elaborated on this unintended influence of *Rōhi o tsukuridasu hitobito*, explaining those specific strategies that were inspired by Packard and advocated by Japanese marketing consultants. Some of these techniques were wasteful in the sense that they encouraged the consumption of goods that were not previously considered necessities: making people think of certain products as gifts to buy for others, be they vitamin pills or cologne; encouraging the purchase of a "second" good, such as a second car, house, or camera; and introducing increasingly differentiated versions of the same product, like special vitamins for people of different ages or underwear in a different color for each day of the week. There was also the creation of physical waste through the development of disposable goods like 1,000 yen watches or 100 yen panties, and the waste of the product itself, as with aerosol containers that released more than one wanted. And there was planned obsolescence of desirability, convincing people that their version of a good was out of style and outdated so that they would replace it by purchasing a new one.[105] It would be too simplistic to draw a single direct line from Packard to the selling practices of Japanese manufacturers, who were already familiar with motivational research pioneers like Ernest Dichter and with the books of the marketing consultant Hayashi Shūji.[106] But it can be said that the unintended reading of *Rōhi o tsukuridasu hitobito* by marketers and managers coincided with and likely informed contemporary trends in Japanese industry like regularly changing models in electronics and automobiles, and paying greater attention to color choice and package design.[107]

To some extent, the publication of *Rōhi o tsukuridasu hitobito* did shed light on the wastefulness of mass consumption. The book was clearly advertised by its Japanese publisher as a criticism of a "consumption culture" created by the artifice of firms that made people waste. Described as removing the mask from the "affluent society," the ad evoked the mistakenly positive understanding of Galbraith's phrase and set up Packard's stance as its critical opposite.[108] The book was presented in a less catchy but still earnest fashion in the pages of *Jitsugyō no Nihon* by the Waseda University professor Uno Masao, who took seriously its characterization of American society as a cautionary tale and suggested its applicability to Japanese attitudes toward daily life.[109] Also, in a completely different field, the textile executive and art connoisseur Ōhara Sōichiro was inspired by Packard to consider what kind of society mass production was creating and what that might mean for the future of *mingei*, Japanese folk art. In a twelve-part series titled "Rōhi o tsukuridasu hitobito," Ōhara contemplated the place of *mingei* in a capitalist, ostensibly prosperous American-style society that mass-produced goods.[110]

A case for the relevance of *The Waste Makers* to Japan was made concretely and explicitly by Packard himself in December 1962, when he visited the country on the invitation of the government-affiliated Japan External Trade Organization and observed firsthand various practices he considered shockingly wasteful. In a conversation with the professor Daimon Ichiju that was published in the *Yomiuri* newspaper, Packard commented on his surprise at traveling through the south-central Kansai region on a train and sighting through the window a billboard advertisement for an electronics maker in the middle of a rice paddy. Such a thing was not even seen in the United States, he remarked. Packard also noted that the belongings of some people walking around the Ginza district of Tokyo were more luxurious than those of Americans, and criticized what he understood as the Japanese habit of spending one's bonus in a single shot. He remarked that there was no bonus system in the United States, but if there were, Americans would not use it all at once but would purchase things gradually over a period of six months. Japanese consumers needed to buy more rationally, like American consumers, he urged, for only with such planning and rational spending would there be real affluence.[111] Not only were Japanese practices wasteful and Japanese affluence shallow, but also, Japan's attempt to imitate the United States was unbecoming to the country's pride. In Packard's estimation, Japan was a wasteful society even as it lagged behind the United States in certain measures of civilizational maturity.[112]

For some Japanese commentators, the encounter with Packard's ideas about waste provoked insight and reflection but did not inspire impassioned social criticism of fundamental aspects of a mass consumption society. In the afterword to the book itself, the translators Minami Hiroshi and Ishikawa Hiroyoshi deemed relevant to Japan the question of how to transform an economy of waste into a healthy economy of consumption. At the same time, they made no explicit statements about whether a "wasteful lifestyle" had arrived in Japan.[113] Similarly, the Waseda University professor Uno Masao described Japan as being in the infancy of its "consumption revolution" (*shōhi kakumei*) such that the country was still some distance from and could, Uno hoped, avoid the "waste revolution" (*rōhi kakumei*) then embroiling the United States.[114] In a 1962 article in the *Yomiuri* newspaper, it was suggested that many examples of wastefulness in Packard's book would seem familiar to Japanese readers (such as the lipstick tube or paint can intentionally designed so that not all of the product could be used), even though the level of consumption in Japan was only one-tenth that of the United States. But again, there was no examination of the ways in which Packard's arguments might apply to Japanese consumption and waste, no probing questions about material prosperity or affluence, and no call for any kind of change in behavior. One of a fifty-one-part series titled "Let's Become Kings, Smart Consumer," this article played on the marketing slogan "The Consumer Is King" to contend that the real king was the smart consumer. After reading this installment, the Japanese consumer might have become smarter through sheer awareness of wasteful consumption, but it was not clear how they could actually become less wasteful.[115]

Several months later, in the pages of the same newspaper, the economist and Keio University professor Katō Hiroshi offered his own variation of "The Consumer Is King" by describing deceived consumers as "naked kings." Like the naked emperor who only imagined his sartorial splendor, the article observed, consumers were being deluded by salesmen and producers. In some ways, Katō was quite critical of this state of affairs: he wished that people were more concerned with society as a whole than with selling strategies, and argued that if prosperity did not turn consumers into real kings, they might as well be living in the Stalin-era Soviet Union where there was only pride in growth through investment. In other ways, Katō blunted Packard's critical stance by not painting salesmen and producers as intentionally duplicitous. He suggested instead that government policies had created an environment of excessive competition in which producers had no choice but to adopt strategies that encouraged people to throw things away.[116]

Although the social critiques of Galbraith and Packard did not carry the full weight of their intentions in Japan, the response to their books helped turn the relationship between mass consumption and waste into a substantive issue worthy of discussion. The relatively circumscribed contours of this conversation

were due at least in part to the incipience of the phenomenon of mass consumption in the late 1950s and early 1960s. Those who were reflecting on the
connections between consumption and waste were doing so in the throes of the
"consumption revolution," trying to anticipate its ramifications in Japan. And
the terrain they were navigating was shifting, characterized by rising expectations of economic and material security and the increasing appeal of comfort
and convenience.

Some witnesses to these changes taking place around them did offer variations
on the themes of Packard's social criticism, expressing the concern that attitudes
toward consumption could go too far and result in waste. In an editorial titled
"Can Consumption Be Called a Virtue?," the *Mainichi* newspaper acknowledged
that being "excessively stingy" (*muyami ni kechikechi suru*) was probably not
suitable given contemporary economic structures, and that consumption, even
repetitive consumption in moderation, was important for stimulating production and preventing economic decline. The editors were worried, however, that
people were so taken with consumption as a virtue that the logics of daily life
were changing. Clever advertising was whipping up people's unthinking desire
to buy things (like a car) or to purchase something that would entail even more
consumption (like skis), and was causing them to forget acquiring things that
they actually did need. Like people taking medicine when they were not really
sick, consumers were buying things that were unnecessary. The editorial closed
by urging self-awareness about the intentions behind one's own purchasing decisions as an antidote to manipulation by advertising and the trend toward engaging in thoughtless and wasteful consumption.[117]

The concern that consumer preferences were encouraging waste was also
expressed about food. A *Yomiuri* newspaper article reported in 1961 that there
was an increasing tendency for shoppers to request that the leaves of the daikon
root be cut off and thrown away, to the point where one particular greengrocer in the Yamanote area of Tokyo had taken to asking his customers whether
they would like the greens removed. Recognizing this trend, the Tokyo Central
Wholesale Market (Tokyo-to Chūō Orishiuri Shijō) had started asking producers
to trim the daikon so that only two-thirds of the leaves were left, cut carrots and
burdock just above the root, and make sure that the green top part of a leek was
only one-third the length of the white bottom section. From the perspective of
the market, it was wasteful to spend money on transporting and discarding food
that consumers were not inclined to want. As it was, about 42 to 43 million yen
was spent each year to dispose of the 45,000 tons of garbage created by the market,
most of which consisted of scrap leaves which were hard to incinerate because of
their high moisture content. But to make the market more efficient, hygienic, and
bright, lamented the specialists interviewed in the article, nutrition was being

wasted. Housewives were throwing out nutrient-rich parts of vegetables, thereby exacerbating deficiencies in vitamins B_1 and C. And the responsibility was placed on greengrocers to encourage housewives to eat the discarded leaves.[118]

Some who worried about what they saw as changes in attitudes toward wastefulness framed their anxieties in terms of loss, particularly the loss of past values. A *Yomiuri* newspaper reporter illustrated the contemporary lessening of waste consciousness (*mottainai*) by describing how in some indeterminate past, mothers-in-law instructed their daughters-in-law to pull up the cuffs of their kimono when eating boiled beans or rice in hot tea (*ochazuke*) so that the brisk movement of the chopsticks would not fray the fabric. That such mothers-in-law no longer existed exemplified the waning of the desire to not waste things. Instead, things were used only as much as one wanted and then replaced with a new item because such behavior was considered economical and convenient.[119] Some years later in the same newspaper, one Ogata Noboru reprinted and interpreted a work by the well-known nineteenth-century poet Masaoka Shiki. In this poem, Masaoka famously spoke about a gift, a fish from the Kinugawa River, sent to him by a beloved disciple. But in transit, the fish rotted. In Ogata's gloss, Masaoka cooked and happily ate the fish nonetheless, not just because he did not want it go to waste, but also because he deeply appreciated the feelings of his student. Such a sentiment, observed Ogata, was fading in an era abundant in things, at a time when young children did not know the meaning of the word *mottainai*.[120]

Expressing a similar sentiment in a more intellectual outlet was Terai Minako, who in 1965 wrote an article on wastefulness for the journal *Shisō no kagaku* (The Science of Thought), a publication of the Research Group on the Science of Thought (Shisō no Kagaku Kenkyūkai), founded by the leftist historian and philosopher Tsurumi Shunsuke. In Terai's depiction, the time in which she was writing could be characterized by the popularization of the slogan "The Consumer Is King," the making and marketing of one new thing after another, and the loosening of people's purse strings as they became accustomed to this faster pace of production and consumption. Goods were ready-made and, when they came to the end of their lifespan, went into a garbage can. What was being lost, Terai regretted, was an appreciation for the value of an object, and with it a respect for the effort, labor, and love of the person who made it. To illustrate her point, Terai recounted a story about an acquaintance who was turning the fabric from an old kimono into a cushion so that she could continue to enjoy in a different form an article of clothing that she had worn for many years. She was shocked when her daughter, nearly twenty years old, told her that this was *mottainai*, a waste of time and effort. In the daughter's eyes, it would have been preferable for her mother to buy fabric in a pretty new print and save herself the work of repurposing the kimono. To Terai, what was disappearing was an understanding of value that was not purely monetary or material.[121]

A more ideological variation on this theme was spun by the Confucian nationalist Yasuoka Masahiro. Yasuoka did not draw an explicit connection between wastefulness and mass consumption, did not think that morality and business were incompatible, and was not critical of government or corporations. Quite to the contrary, he served as an adviser and mentor to high-ranking politicians, from those in Prime Minister Ikeda Hayato's political faction to Prime Minister Satō Eisaku. He also had ties with executives at some of the country's largest companies and wrote books and articles on moral cultivation for managers. At the same time, what Yasuoka attempted to do was reinforce understandings of waste with moral underpinnings. In a piece on wastefulness, Yasuoka quoted Ninomiya Sontoku, the nineteenth-century agriculturalist and ethicist often invoked as a paragon of thrift, and infused the idea of value with a premodern sensibility, equating it with that which was elemental, natural, and vaguely spiritual. He went on at some length about nature, be it an orange or the soil or an earthworm or kudzu; and he extolled the importance of knowing things deeply, rather than thinking wastefully, which was the starting point for scholarship, art, religion, and morality.[122] A premodern morality, Yasuoka seemed to be saying, was what was needed to stave off the thoughtless wasting of things in the contemporary era.

Harking back to the values of an idealized and imagined past, those who wanted to defend and fortify a supposedly long-held, fixed conception of wastefulness were actually engaging in a practice not yet seen in the postwar period: the redefinition of waste in reaction to societal and cultural shifts. In the 1940s and 1950s, there were those who thought that people should be more conscious of wastefulness in order to realize certain goals and aspirations. What was new in the 1960s was the construction of a given understanding of wastefulness in response to anxieties about a perceived erosion of values, or put more concretely, the promotion of waste consciousness as a bulwark against the seeming threats of mass consumption.

The greater financial and material prosperity of the 1960s also raised questions, not yet asked in the postwar period, about what constituted a wastefulness of excess—about what was superfluous overabundance, exorbitant luxury, or flagrant extravagance. In the immediate postwar years, poverty and scarcity had rendered such concerns moot. But by December 1960, an article in the *Yomiuri* newspaper could ask: "Is consumption a virtue? Is luxury a virtue?" The answer, it seemed, was that the cost, availability, and pretentiousness of luxury goods was excessive. The photographs of a 200,000 yen mink stole and a 21,000 yen ashtray exemplified this absurdity, as did the various other products described in the article: the 360,000 yen overcoat for men, the 45,000 yen decorative figurine from Germany, the 130,000 yen crocodile handbag from Italy, and so on. At a time when the vast majority of readers could not have afforded such items, these luxury goods encapsulated doubts about the trend toward "deluxification" (*derakkusuka*) and the "innocent enjoyment" of the consumption boom. An explicit answer to the article's questions was given in closing by Hanamori Yasuji, founder of the women's cultural magazine *Kurashi no techō* (Notebook of Everyday Life). The thinking that "luxury is the enemy" was mistaken, Hanamori concluded, because it was the sentiment of a time when not buying even those things that one needed was admirable. But wrongheaded too was the idea of "consumption is a virtue," because there was nothing virtuous about buying things you did not need simply because you had the money to do so.[123]

Later in the 1960s, criticism of those who had clearly crossed the line between responsible consumption and a wasteful consumption of excess became more pointed. Quoting an *Asahi* newspaper article which suggested that the consumption boom was becoming more about waste than lifestyle improvement, the popular if journalistically questionable *Shūkan shinchō* (Weekly Shinchō) gave examples of what was intended to be understood as wasteful spending. There was the story of "Mr. P," or P-shi, who worked for a department store headquartered on the northern island of Hokkaidō. In Tokyo on business, P-shi went out to a fancy Japanese restaurant with two old friends, where they drank—a lot. Around midnight, they decided that they wanted to eat Sapporo ramen, and rather than finding a shop nearby that specialized in this kind of miso ramen, they hopped on a late-night flight from Haneda Airport to Sapporo. Back at the Tokyo restaurant the next night, they marveled at how delicious their 20,000 yen-a-bowl ramen had been. There was also the story of the housewife in the Jiyūgaoka neighborhood of Tokyo who flew roughly six hundred miles at a cost of 24,200 yen to shop at a market in Fukuoka, on the southern island of Kyūshū. Haneda Airport was closer to her house by car than the Ginza district, she explained. Plus the pickles in Fukuoka were delicious. Slightly more ambiguous were the lessons about wastefulness to be drawn from the description of trips taken abroad by college students and young salarymen with special price tags for younger travelers of 210,000 yen for five nights in Hawaii or 490,000 yen for three weeks in Europe.[124]

For the Kantō Gakuin University professor Daimon Ichiju, there was no doubt that he was living in an era of luxury, with the splendor of department stores at which consumers could buy expensive high-end goods and of "deluxe" buildings from which well-dressed people came and went. He readily adopted a term reportedly coined by Fukuda Takeo, a future prime minister, to describe this time: "Shōwa Genroku," a combination of the current era name (Shōwa) and one from the early modern period (Genroku, 1688–1704) known for its flourishing commercial economy and urban culture, and often associated with idleness and luxury. To Daimon, the times were so extravagant that even Europeans and Americans were surprised. What, then, was to distinguish luxury from waste? To Daimon, there were two kinds of luxury. One was about enjoyment of an affluent life. The other was the wasteful incarnation, unconnected to an affluent life and about the mere satisfaction of desire. Examples of wasteful luxury included purchasing cosmetics that were worth 100 yen but that sold for 1,000 because of their "deluxe" appearance and branding; eating at fancy hotel restaurants without caring anything about the taste of the food; and acquiring extravagant and showy items but being irresponsible when it came to purchasing necessities. In a luxurious era of overstimulated desire, be it for goods, alcohol, sex, or gambling, the masses who overextended themselves were, Daimon feared, falling into wastefulness.[125]

A Fragile Modernity

While marketers and advertisers polished the sheen on the "bright life" and more consumers bought shiny new washing machines, refrigerators, and televisions, Tokyo stank. The Sumida River was black, threw off a stench, and emitted methane gas from the human waste flushed into its waters; the Tama and Arakawa rivers were polluted by raw liquid industrial waste from nearby factories; the Kanda and Meguro rivers were used as dumps for kitchen garbage; the increasing number of cars on the road emitted exhaust fumes; garbage was scattered in the streets; and wooden garbage boxes could not contain the smell of the rubbish within, attracting mosquitoes and flies in droves.[126]

Using language that dated back to the late 1800s and was resurrected in the late 1940s, critics construed such physical waste as a threat to civilization and modernity. Superimposed upon this familiar rhetoric was the idea of a bright life that was supposed to be cleansed of filth along with any other manifestations of backwardness. The challenges posed by rubbish were thus to be met by continued modernization of sanitation infrastructure coupled with the improvement of daily sanitary practices. But in the 1960s, garbage also assumed new meaning as a by-product of a mass-consuming society. No longer was rubbish simply emblematic of retrogression; rather it was becoming a problem fed by thoroughly modern patterns of consumption that threatened to expose the fragility and superficiality of that very modernity. Even as consumption suggested civilizational achievement, it created in garbage a force that seemed to flaunt the civilizing project. Infrastructure was now insufficient not because of wartime damage but because it did not have the capacity to handle the ever-increasing amount of stuff thrown out by consumers.

That changes in daily life were creating waste was explained with some regularity to the residents of Tokyo by its Sanitation Bureau (Seisōkyoku). In a ten-minute news segment that aired in May 1954, viewers were bombarded by image after image of garbage—being scooped up from rivers, collected from garbage boxes, piled high on boats, carried by truck to incinerators, and heaped in landfills. Describing rubbish as the "leftovers of life," the program provided data about the threefold surge in trash since just after the war. This trend was attributed not just to the growing population of the metropolis but also to the greater abundance of goods and the increase in individual consumption. Families were also taken to task for their wastefulness, for discarding things that still had value. A scene of a housewife throwing out scraps of a vegetable and the paper in which it had been wrapped was accompanied by a voice-over in which the narrator commented on how everyone was discarding such things so casually. A shot of a garbage box containing kitchen waste mixed with empty cans and bottles was accompanied by information about how it would be more effective to separate rubbish for recycling. The Sanitation Bureau seemed to be suggesting that it was overwhelmed by trash created by forces beyond its control, and it attempted to place some of the responsibility for handling waste on the shoulders of residents. But this video was not clear about what exactly people were supposed to do with their garbage, given the lack of established municipal systems for composting or recycling. Shortcomings in municipal collection systems and infrastructure were acknowledged, at least when it came to the lack of incinerators. It was admitted that only 5 percent of garbage was disposed of by the ideal method of burning because incinerators were expensive to build. As a result, most of Tokyo's rubbish was ending up in one of twenty or so landfills.[127]

Landfills were a prime breeding ground for mosquitoes and flies—pests that were emblematic of the inability of municipalities and residents alike to control waste and to create modern and bright daily lives. In 1955 the Ministry of Health and Welfare launched a nationwide three-year Movement to Get Rid of Mosquitoes and Flies (Ka to Hae o Nakusu Undō), and the New Life Movement included among its priorities the elimination of these insects. Not long thereafter, in June 1956, an editorial in the Yomiuri newspaper defined a "cultured nation" (bunka kokka) as one without mosquitoes and flies, and declared that all of the talk at the time about Japan being a nation of culture was nonsense so long as the pests continued to fly about. The newspaper criticized the government for the movement's inadequate budget of 1.4 million yen and cast aspersions on the Hatoyama cabinet and the New Life Movement alike. What people did not adequately understand, according to the editors, was how serious efforts needed to be for ensuring good hygiene and raising the productivity and efficiency of laborers and farmers, who should be able to sleep without worrying about these insects.[128] The *Yomiuri* newspaper continued its coverage of this issue for years, reporting on the unevenness and limitations of the movement. Some towns and villages were freed of mosquitoes and flies while others were not, and although the number of the insects had seemingly decreased by June 1957, they had not been eradicated.[129] On the three-year anniversary of the movement's inauguration, in April 1958, flies were still making their presence known with all their stubbornness and impudence.[130]

Disgust with such infestations reinforced the idea that garbage, offensive and repellent, sullied anything it touched. Rubbish was thus quarantined to the edges of societal acceptability, residing there with marginalized people, who counted among their numbers those who worked with refuse. The scholar and commentator Kang Sangjung grew up in the 1950s as a second-generation *zainichi* (Korean living in Japan) and son of a semiliterate father and an illiterate mother who ran a scrap business. The world of Kang and his family was inhabited by people who were "driven to the bottom of society." His parents made their living by collecting and recycling the castoffs of others, including the garbage from a local leprosarium. Like the patients, Kang's *zainichi* family and friends had a sense of themselves as unfortunates and were not afraid to come into contact with what was considered "unclean" or "unsightly."[131]

The low social status of those who worked with rubbish was also described by the sanitation industry expert Shibata Tokue. In his book about the "sanitation problem" published in 1961, he exposed the "discrimination" and "prejudice" experienced by garbage collectors, particularly outside the big cities. Workers who were young worried about their marriage prospects, and many had personal stories about cold treatment by residents. One man recalled an encounter with an elementary school teacher and her students. As he passed them, pulling a heavy garbage cart, the teacher pointed at him and warned her students, "If you don't listen well to what I say and don't do your homework, you'll become that kind of person." Even those who worked in the Sanitation Bureau offices in Tokyo, reported Shibata, answered the telephone with a generic and unidentifiable salutation like "Tokyo Metropolitan Government offices" or "city hall." In Shibata's assessment, discrimination toward sanitation workers and toward the Buraku minority had much in common and, in the cities of western Japan, even overlapped.[132] The marginalization of people seen as tainted, some doubly so by identity and by occupation, would ease somewhat in the 1970s as the demand for "ragpickers" abated and the societal profile of sanitation workers received a governmental boost. But in these years, the reach of the contaminating potential of waste was insidiously long.

The repulsiveness of waste underscored the pressing need to contain garbage, and this push to clean and beautify the country became all the more urgent with the announcement in May 1959 that Tokyo was to host the 1964 Summer Olympics. To prove that Japan was rehabilitated from its wartime misadventures and had recovered from wartime destruction, the country needed to display itself before an international audience as thoroughly civilized and modern. Just days after Japan's selection as the host country was made public, the Ministry of Health and Welfare kicked off a nationwide Environmental Cleanup Movement (Kankyō Jōka Undō). Concerned that the Olympics would be taking place during the peak months for infectious diseases like Japanese encephalitis and dysentery, the ministry urged that preparations begin immediately to prevent creating an international incident by infecting the country's foreign guests. First and foremost on the agenda was improving the disposal of garbage and human waste. As the *Yomiuri* newspaper asserted, while Japan might boast of being a modern and international nation, when it came to garbage and human waste, it was "utterly of a previous era."[133]

Part of the Environmental Cleanup Movement's tackling of garbage and human waste was an attempt to better manage the problems they spawned, which included the intensification of efforts to eliminate mosquitoes and flies.[134] In Tokyo, the distribution and spraying of insecticide was stepped up, the number of groups working to exterminate pests from public places and facilities was increased, efforts were made to dispose of accumulated garbage and mud, and posters and leaflets were printed to promote towns freed from mosquitoes and flies.[135] In August 1963, the Sanitation Bureau designated two days on which light traps were set up in various places around the city to investigate the severity of the mosquito situation, and cages were placed at fifty-nine different public health centers to assess the prevalence of flies. And on four days in the middle of the month, at four places each in the areas of Asakusa and Shibuya, counseling centers were set up to coach people about how and where to spray insecticide.[136] The New Life Movement Association also threw its weight behind these efforts, which included printing instructional material. In one issue of its published series, the association explained that flies were generated by the decomposition of waste, particularly kitchen waste, in garbage boxes, which bred maggots with the slightest inattention. Readers were advised to ask for the head and tail to be cut off when buying fish, and the leaves of carrots to be removed, so that they would not end up in the garbage as fodder for pests. It also encouraged people to reduce the amount of garbage they were producing.[137]

Another strategy implemented by the Tokyo Metropolitan Government was the removal of wooden garbage boxes and the introduction of scheduled trash collection. Wooden garbage boxes had been the source of much frustration throughout the 1950s, prone as they were to catching fire, smelling, and attracting pests. Housewives fought to keep them clean and were instructed to spray

FIGURE 2.2. Trash Collection. Before the advent of scheduled collection, residents kept an ear out for the tinkling bell of an approaching garbage truck to know when to meet it with their rubbish.

From Shibata Tokue, *Gomi* (Osaka: Rokugatsusha, 1964).

them with DDT to exterminate mosquitoes and flies.[138] Dealing with the dirty garbage boxes was a particular challenge in business districts like Ginza, where the beauty of the fashionable windows and spectacular neon was marred by the garbage and filthy water spilling out into the street. Producing a tremendous amount of physical waste and lacking the social structure of residential areas to assign responsibility for cleaning and maintenance, Ginza was singled out early for its broken and filthy garbage boxes and its dire need for beautification.[139]

The question was what might replace the wooden garbage boxes. In the spring of 1960, two trial areas comprising 5,360 homes were given a budget of 3.2 million yen to ban the wooden garbage boxes and try sharing a communal garbage container among four to five residences. It had not yet been decided what the containers would be made of, but housewives were assured that they would have a bright and modern design.[140] In the summer of 1961, five trial areas (Kanda, Kōjimachi, Nihonbashi, Kyōbashi, and Shiba) were designated in which residents would replace the wooden garbage boxes with garbage containers made of plastic. And there would be a scheduled garbage collection system, whereby each household would bring its plastic garbage container to a specific place at a predetermined date and time to meet the garbage truck. This would do away with the inefficiency of the existing practice, which required the sanitation worker to go to each individual home, transfer the refuse from the garbage box into his garbage basket, and then throw the contents of the basket into the truck. The new trial process was presented as a marked improvement because it did away with the filthy garbage box and garbage basket and, because of the more efficient use of the sanitation worker's time, promised more frequent garbage collection.[141] By the summer of 1962, the system had been implemented in the center of Tokyo and some surrounding wards by some 530,000 homes.[142] By 1963, all of the twenty-three wards that constituted the core of the metropolis had scheduled garbage collection.[143]

A symbol of this new system of garbage pickup was the plastic garbage container, which was advertised to consumers as a modern and innovative product, made by modern and innovative companies, for the control of uncivilized rubbish. Newspaper advertisements were regularly run by Sekisui Chemical (Sekisui Kagaku), which dubbed itself "Sekisui Chemical of Plastics" (Purasuchikku no Sekisui Kagaku). Describing itself as "serving society through plastics" and as a "supporter of creating beautiful towns," the company attempted to brand itself as a modern, cutting-edge company that used scientific development for desirable societal ends. One newspaper advertisement printed in July 1962 was titled "Olympics in a Clean Tokyo." The substantial amount of text in the ad included a countdown of days until the Games, when people from ninety countries around the world would come to the capital. Before then, it explained, the "garbage problem" must be solved: the 7,000 tons of garbage being produced each day must be properly disposed of, and unhygienic garbage boxes must be replaced by polyethylene garbage containers. Then the disgraceful "Dirty Tokyo" of smells and flies would be transformed, so that there could be an "Olympics in a town without garbage boxes, in a pretty Tokyo!"[144] Pictured in the advertisement was a neat row of garbage containers, with one being placed in the line by a young apron-clad girl. Through this image, Sekisui depicted the garbage containers as sanitary, hygienic, and convenient; in other versions of the advertisement, the light polyethylene containers were explicitly contrasted with the heavy garbage boxes that were difficult to move.[145] And the widely used image of a young girl or woman in these Sekisui ads unequivocally gendered household waste as the housewife's responsibility.[146]

Several months later, at the end of December, a Sekisui advertisement announced that Japan's towns had become clean but commented, in a smaller font, that the battle against garbage had just begun. Included was the recent history of this fight: Sekisui's decision back in March to support the movement to clean up towns; the disappearance of garbage boxes from Ginza in April; and the notification from the Ministry of Construction (Kensetsushō) in March about

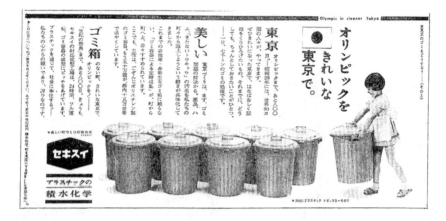

FIGURE 2.3. Advertisement for Plastic Garbage Containers. An advertisement by Sekisui Chemical for its plastic garbage containers.

From *Yomiuri shinbun*, July 12, 1962.

the countrywide effort to rid streets of garbage boxes. According to Sekisui, 1 million polyethylene containers were being used in 150 cities across the country from Hokkaidō in the north to Kagoshima in the south. Stressed again was the contribution that strong molded plastic was making to this "garbage war"; even tonight, said the ad, Sekisui's injection molding machines were humming away, casting garbage containers.[147] By the summer of 1963, plastic garbage bags were also being touted as a way to contain the smell of wet garbage and were marketed as exemplifying the wonders of mass molding to produce strong, inexpensive, and convenient polyethylene.[148]

Preparations were also made for dealing with waste during the Olympics themselves, when the flood of people would strain waste collection structures and systems. It was said that a special telephone number, like the emergency number 110 to reach the police, would be established so that people could call and request the quick dispatch of a "cleaning patrol car" to dispose of waste. The suggested number for this service was 5-3-7-4, or *go-mi-na-shi*, meaning "no garbage."[149] Arrangements were made for special disposal of night soil in the five days before and after the Olympics, so that dipping of human waste could be kept at a minimum during the games. And from October 1 to 25, garbage collection would occur early in the morning at 8:00 am. These measures were all intended to keep Olympic tourists, foreign and domestic, from witnessing night soil and garbage collection.[150] After all, to see waste would be to reveal that Japan had not thoroughly recovered from defeat and was not deserving of taking a place among the modern nations of the civilized world.

Attempts to remove human waste from sight included the repair and construction of sewers. For the years 1957 to 1966, a total of 127.6 billion yen was budgeted for the sewer system, of which almost 71.6 billion had been spent by 1964.[151] This effort was intended to address the acknowledged shortcomings in sewage infrastructure: as of 1962, the usage rate of sewers in Japan's urban areas was 10 percent, compared to 70 to 90 percent in Western countries. Even at the end of 1963, 45 percent of human waste was being dumped into Tokyo Bay.[152] With the prioritization of improving the sewage system in the areas of Tokyo central to the Olympics, the diffusion rate was up to 60 percent, at least in Shibuya ward.[153]

Management of human waste and rubbish was part of a broader, multifaceted campaign to clean and beautify the country. In Tokyo, such efforts were coordinated under the umbrella of a movement to beautify the capital. The Metropolitan Beautification Council (Shuto Bika Shingikai) presented in August 1962 a draft of a report that included calls for the discouragement of public urination; the cessation of spitting phlegm and saliva; the construction of small pay toilets; and the designation of one day a month when households, public offices, companies, and factories in the city would all clean.[154] The Headquarters for the Promotion of Metropolitan Beautification (Shuto Bika Suishin Honbu) was established in December, and it promptly designated the tenth of every month Metropolitan Beautification Day, on which people all across Tokyo were to clean the city. Instructions included: do not throw away wastepaper or cigarette ash; do not spit phlegm or saliva; do not dump garbage illegally; clean in front of and around your house; pick up dog shit; take care of lawns and plants; get rid of the sources of mosquitoes and flies in and around your house; and exterminate mice and cockroaches.[155] On one such Metropolitan Beautification Day in January 1964, between town assemblies, women's associations, and students, about 2 million people were mobilized.[156] Efforts at beautification were not confined to the capital. In February 1962, opening ceremonies were held for the Movement to Beautify the Country (Kokudo o Utsukushikusuru Undō), which spread well beyond Tokyo through the efforts of organizations like the New Life Movement Association and the Japan Tourist Association (Nihon Kankō Kyōkai). According to an editorial in the Yomiuri newspaper that was supportive of the movement, there was no opposition because cleaning up the country seemed like a natural thing to do when it was so dirty.[157]

Yet for some, beautification campaigns were a superficial effort to present a sanitized image of the country to the outside world. When the governor of Tokyo picked up a broom and swept in front of the Tokyo Metropolitan Government Office on one Metropolitan Beautification Day, his actions were criticized as grandstanding. Did the governor not have anything better to do, some wondered.[158] A more deliberate critique was staged in October 1964 by the members of the Hi Red Center, an avant-garde collective founded by the artists Akasegawa Genpei, Nakanishi Natsuyuki, and Takamatsu Jirō. Characteristic of their work was a descent to the mundane, the use of ordinary objects and waste to provoke engagement with changes in everyday life.[159] On October 16, a week into the Olympics, members of the center took to the streets of the Ginza district in one of their "happenings" called "Cleaning Event." In Akasegawa's recollection, the center felt compelled to address the flurry to clean Tokyo, to make presentable what could be seen from the outside. So the artists decided to clean like everyone else, but to do it "properly, conscientiously, thoroughly."[160] Through the performance of earnestness, the group sought to prompt reflection about the shallowness of beautification. Akasegawa put effort into creating signs mimicking the style of official ones that read "Cleaning in Progress," taking on the appearances of the beautification movement while also suggesting its hollowness. The artists also donned white coats and white face masks, suggesting the absurdity of the cleaning enterprise by taking it to its extreme. In that vein, they scrubbed the cement sidewalk with sponges, meticulously scoured manhole covers, and even cleansed a tree, from which they hung deodorizers and a strip of tape with the character for "done." Continuing their event at night, they held up traffic to the point where one taxi driver complained that cleaning for the Olympics was fine, but they should hurry it up. Most passersby paid the artists little attention, with some casting a suspicious look in their direction and others mistaking them for participants in the official cleaning campaign.[161] Although the men wore armbands with the Hi Red Center's logo of a red exclamation point, they carried out their disturbance with relative subtlety, their acerbic commentary so enmeshed in the everyday that it was minimally visible. While their happening hinted at the existence of different attitudes toward the sanitization of the city, their circumscribed disruption also spoke to the predominance of efforts to clean.

As the Hi Red Center's "Cleaning Event" implied, initiatives to beautify the country in advance of the Olympics did not fully address nor solve enduring problems of infrastructure and waste management. Although the Games provided a strong impetus to reform practices and systems for controlling garbage, human waste, and filth, certain issues persisted beyond the fall of 1964. The city continued its battle against pests, which at various times it seemed to be losing. In the summer of 1965, the large landfill in Tokyo Bay called the Island of Dreams (Yume no Shima) spurned its utopian name by spawning an army of flies that infested nearby residential neighborhoods in what was dubbed the "fly riot" (hae sōdō). In mid-July, hundreds of personnel from the fire department, Coast Guard, Ground Self-Defense Force (Rikujō Jieitai), and Metropolitan Police Department (Keishichō) as well as public health centers were mobilized as part of a scorched-earth strategy whereby parts of the artificial island made of trash were doused in oil and set on fire to eradicate the pests.[162] The portrayal of the Island of Dreams as a frightening dystopia was common, with the vocabulary and metaphors of war often invoked in this civilizational struggle. A half-hour television program that aired on NHK titled *Gendai no eizō: Jinkai toshi* (Images of Modern Times: Trash City) opened with a shot of a lone helicopter dropping what was presumably insecticide on a landscape of endless garbage, to a score of dramatic music befitting a war film.[163] When the flies subsided in late July, a newspaper article worried that this was a "short-lived peace" and described the residents of Kōtō ward, which housed the landfill, as wondering when the hordes would return.[164]

Several months later, in the fall, the site of the fly riot became "heaven for rats." The Island of Dreams had been used as a landfill since 1957, and the older areas of the dump provided welcome heat for pests as the trash decomposed. In October 1965, the Edagawa Sanitation Office estimated that the landfill was teeming with some 140,000 to 150,000 rats. So bold were these rodents that they did not run away from the newspaper photographers who came to take their picture and even "chase[d] away any cats invading their territories."[165] The infestation was not a cause for much immediate concern as long as the rats stayed within the confines of the landfill, but the question was what they would do and where they would go upon the closing of the Island of Dreams to new dumping. Given the rate of disposal, it was anticipated that the site would completely fill up with garbage within the next few years, at which point the rats might move to a nearby landfill or into residential areas like Minami Sunamachi and Edagawa. As a precautionary measure, in November 1965, sanitation workers made 200,000 small dumplings out of flour, curry, cooking oil, and poison. The hope was that the dumplings would eliminate about twenty thousand rats from the island.[166]

In addition to these reactionary countermeasures, more deliberate and systematic approaches to waste management were taken as well. In 1965 and 1966, the Ministry of Health and Welfare placed traps in various locations to study the number and type of flies around the city. While the frequency of most infectious disease outbreaks was declining, the increase in cases of dysentery and its possible link to flies were of particular concern.[167] Also at the national level, the cabinet put its weight behind a five-year plan for the improvement of public sanitation and the "living environment" through significant investment in infrastructure for the disposal and management of human waste and garbage.[168] This was followed by a five-year plan from the Ministry of Health and Welfare to invest further in sanitation facilities starting in 1967, with the goal of incinerating 75 percent of garbage by 1971.[169]

In anticipation of the one-year anniversary of the fly riot, care was taken to avoid another infestation. Twice in April 1966 the Island of Dreams was doused with insecticide sprayed from planes, and in the following month this became a thrice-weekly practice.[170] Toward the end of the summer, on August 4, 1966, at 3:00 pm, the governor of Tokyo along with other high-ranking officials and sanitation specialists inspected the landfill. In a confident declaration of mission accomplished, Governor Azuma Ryōtarō assured residents, "There is no need to worry anymore about flies."[171]

While there was a familiar strand in waste management discussions about ensuring civilization and modernity, there emerged in this decade new rhetorical and conceptual vocabularies about the dangers of rubbish. Especially in the second half of the 1960s, when there was increasing attention to the environmental and human costs of rapid economic growth, the problems posed by garbage came to be described as their own kind of *kōgai*. Meaning pollution or contamination, *kōgai* was already part of the lexicon used to talk about the health and environmental disasters caused by the dumping of industrial waste. The publication in 1964 of the pathbreaking book *Osorubeki kōgai* (Fearsome Pollution) by the engineer Shōji Hikaru and the economist Miyamoto Ken'ichi had brought attention to the term *kōgai* and raised awareness about various forms of industrial pollution.[172] As the difficulties of managing rubbish endured, the word began to appear in discussions about household waste. In the NHK program that aired in the summer of 1965, the flies that swarmed around Tokyo were characterized as the "*kōgai* of garbage," and those residents who were aggressively resisting the construction of incinerators in their neighborhood demanded from the Sanitation Bureau its assurance that there would be no associated pollution of their neighborhood. In newspaper articles, too, various problems related to rubbish were described as kinds of *kōgai*, from garbage management issues in the United States to the filth and bad smells emanating from improperly handled plastic garbage containers.[173]

Garbage was also increasingly considered a reflection of changes in daily lives. Greater attention was paid to the rise in the amount of garbage produced, especially by sanitation experts like Shibata Tokue. In 1964 Shibata published a book about garbage, accessible to a popular readership, in which he highlighted how it was proliferating and the challenges that posed for disposal. And he connected the growing mountains of rubbish with practices of consumption, such as the approximately 1 million sheets of wrapping paper used every month by department stores in the Nihonbashi area of Tokyo, the roughly 300 million advertising inserts distributed every month in the capital, and the 2.6 billion or so direct mailings sent out in one year.[174]

Shibata was at the vanguard of rubbish issues and so was somewhat unusual in his level of concern; most observations about the accumulation of garbage were more prosaic. As rubbish roughly doubled in Tokyo to 8,000 tons a day between 1960 and 1965, this was evidence, at least in the view of the *Yomiuri* newspaper, of welcome improvement in the lives of city residents. When Governor Azuma visited the Island of Dreams on that day in August 1966, he observed that whatever was at the department store was also here at the landfill. In what seems from a written account like a rather matter-of-fact tone, Azuma commented that before him was "a mountain of garbage that would become luxurious," that would consist of more and more luxurious items as those consumer products recently purchased increasingly appeared on trash heaps.[175] In the later years of the decade, the amount of garbage produced by the country as a whole continued to grow; between 1968 and 1970, rubbish output rose from 62,005 tons a day, or 815 grams per person per day, to 76,998 tons a day, or 909 grams per person per day.[176] And one oft-noted trend in these years was the increasing disposal of "large garbage" (*ōgata gomi*) such as television sets, washing machines, refrigerators, and cars. Many a newspaper article commented on how the discarding of these consumer goods reflected the practice of replacing older items with newer versions and models, the increase in the production of consumer durables, a rising standard of living, the Westernization of homes, the quickening pace of trends, and the celebration of high economic growth.[177]

Viewed largely as an inconvenient by-product of the consumer revolution, garbage was seen to require the attention of households but was mainly considered the responsibility of municipalities. Large consumer durables posed a problem because they could not be easily handled by ragpickers; nor did most municipalities have established systems of collection for rubbish of that size. There were calls for manufacturers to assume responsibility for the disposal of the products they sold, picking up those items that could no longer be used or were no longer wanted.[178] More common was the expectation that municipalities should better manage the collection of large garbage, following the example of a place like Kawasaki city in Kanagawa prefecture which instituted twice-monthly collection of "consumer durable garbage."[179] That such demands were made of municipal governments was not surprising, consistent as they were with the fundamental assumptions of the Cleaning Law (Seisō Hō) of 1954, which had clearly placed the lion's share of responsibility for the management of "filth" on their shoulders.[180] In this vein, a *Mainichi* newspaper editorial of April 1969 called for municipalities to examine the frequency and method of pickup, their collection trucks, their disposal facilities, and so on. In the 1960s, and especially by the decade's end, a society thoroughly remade into one of mass consumption was expected to be civilized and modern enough to contain the very garbage it created and to disarm this "troublesome by-product of affluence."[181]

Waste and the Consumption Revolution

Despite the formidable challenges posed by the detritus of an increasingly affluent society, consumers were not encouraged to consume less or to consume differently—to not purchase an electric washing machine, to hold off on replacing their black-and-white television set with the new color model, to make do with shoes from several seasons ago, to not try instant ramen or beer in a can, or to refrain from wearing pantyhose. For to abstain from such consumption would be to forgo the gains of economic growth and the improvements in lifestyle promised by the new consumer goods that had become available on the mass market.

The allure of economic growth and the bright sheen of mass consumption were powerful and shaped the many ways in which waste came to be understood. The meanings of waste became more flexible and open, and the definitions of wastefulness more up for grabs than they had ever been in the postwar. In the years of the consumption revolution, many different and conflicting thoughts about waste came to exist at one and the same time. The continued emphasis on mass production with its logics of efficiency, rationalization, and waste elimination was coupled with new patterns of consumption that inspired many to draw on, alter, and supplement those ideas with others. Spending money could be rational, stinginess could be undesirable, enjoyment and pleasure could have their own kind of utility, and luxury could no longer be the enemy. With all of its mutability, waste consciousness could still be evoked as a desirable value, but one that was no longer bound up with subsistence as it once had been. Instead, waste was generally framed in terms of maximizing production and productivity, or reconfigured to jibe with the values at the heart of mass consumerism—comfort, convenience, ease, and enjoyment.

To some degree, waste also became a site of reflection about the consumption revolution and the mass consumption society. Questions were raised about whether marketing and advertising encouraged wastefulness, what distinguished luxury from waste, and what might be lost in the throes of this societal shift. But concerns about wastefulness were relatively muted and did not yet offer either impassioned criticism of fundamental aspects of affluence and mass consumption or prescriptions for how to live in or change a wasteful society. Garbage was something to be tamed mainly for the sake of health, hygiene, and the appearance of civilization; it was not yet treated as a physical manifestation of wastefulness.

Greater temptations and opportunities to waste were something to be managed in the eyes of those who advocated household thrift and frugality but were not to be rejected outright. And the alleged promotion of waste by marketers and advertisers was something to be aware of, not a wastefulness inherent in consumer capitalism. Critical conversations about waste and wastefulness thus served as mere friction to what seemed like inevitable progress toward a financially affluent and materially abundant good life.

The emergence of mass consumption in tandem with mass production did indeed constitute a societal revolution. An orientation toward the mass creation and acquisition of things; the idea that time, even free time, not only should have utility but also could be commodified; and the treatment of rubbish as an inconvenient by-product of mass production and mass consumption took root in these years. To different extents and in varying ways, they would endure in a Japan that had become, and continues to be, a mass consumption society.

Yet, at the very end of the 1960s, there were voices that were beginning to raise strong doubts about the negative costs of economic growth and to wonder about the desirability of rampant consumerism. Such concerns together with unanticipated jolts reverberated through the next decade, destabilizing understandings of waste and wastefulness even as the appeal of middle-class lifestyles proved persistent.

Part II

SHOCKS, SHIFTS, AND SAFEGUARDS

Defending Middle-Class Lifestyles,
1971–1981

WARS AGAINST WASTE

On September 28, 1971, the governor of Tokyo declared war against garbage. In a speech to the Tokyo Metropolitan Assembly, Governor Minobe Ryōkichi officially launched what he called the Garbage War (*gomi sensō*)—a frontal assault on material, physical waste. In his opening rhetorical salvo, Minobe took aim at the alarmingly rapid rate at which trash had been proliferating. The amount of garbage created in the twenty-three wards of Tokyo had increased 2.3 times over the past decade, he explained.[1] And the challenge of managing this volume of waste was exacerbated by three substantial changes in its composition. First, plastic as a percentage of garbage was surging, such that it came to exceed 10 percent of what was sent to incineration plants, causing the overheating and rapid corrosion of furnaces.[2] Second, there had been an almost fivefold increase in the disposal of large refuse such as cars and electric home appliances, from 41,000 tons in 1961 to 192,000 tons in 1970. And third, there had been a rise in the amount of dangerous industrial waste such as used acids and oil, cyanogen, and heavy metals. With its threat of overrunning and endangering the lives of Tokyo residents, the enemy in this war was identified as garbage itself.[3]

In some ways, the scope of the Garbage War was circumscribed, especially as Minobe presented it on this inaugural day.[4] Having targeted an inanimate enemy, he planned to wield the weapon of urban infrastructure. Garbage was to be eliminated through the construction of more incinerators and landfills, the shortage of which he diagnosed as the fundamental cause of the "garbage problem." The progressive Minobe also demanded that government and industry assume a greater role in mitigating the production of waste. He called on the government to snap out of its indifference to sanitation challenges, hold manufacturers responsible for the collection and recycling of their waste, establish limits on products with undetermined disposal methods, and regulate industry, which discharged ten times as much waste as households. Minobe's publicly stated approach to garbage was less moral or even social, more technical and administrative. The war against discarded stuff was to be fought with infrastructure development, government action, and industrial accountability.[5]

Yet in other ways, the Garbage War had expansive and transformative reverberations. Most plainly and intentionally, the governor thrust garbage into the public's attention with his very declaration and with his use of the language of war, provocative and significant even more than two decades after what most people still thought of as "the war."[6] The Garbage War received substantial media coverage and encouraged discussions about rubbish not just in Tokyo but across the country. Moreover, the way in which Minobe framed the war contributed to a fundamental shift in how garbage was viewed. The garbage problem, he argued, was a "strain" or "distortion" caused by the policies of high economic growth.[7] That is, the struggle to manage waste was not to be understood as a shortcoming of civilization, and the dearth of incinerators and landfills was not to be considered a reflection of civilizational inadequacy as it had been not too many years earlier. This was not the urgent call for shoring up modern systems of waste management which preceded the 1964 Olympics, driven by the fear that Japan would be exposed before an international audience as backward. Rather, the now prevalent view was that the achievement of civilization, defined in terms of rapid economic growth and relatively affluent, mass-consuming lifestyles, had created the problem of unmanageable waste.[8] Rubbish was to be considered a manifestation of postwar modernity which could be managed largely by modern technology.

Together with the Garbage War, another jolt that thrust waste and wastefulness into the public eye was the oil crisis of 1973. In mid-October of that year, the Arab members of the Organization of Petroleum Exporting Countries (OPEC) placed an embargo on the export of oil to countries, including Japan, that were supportive of Israel in the Yom Kippur War. While the Japanese government promptly backed away from Israel in order to reopen the spigot on a much-needed supply of oil, OPEC continued to raise the price of this vital commodity. Between October 1973 and January 1974, the price of oil almost quadrupled from $3 to more than $11 a barrel.[9] In Japan, the economic consequences of what was experienced as the "Oil Shock" were stunning: in 1973, inflation was hovering around 29 percent; in early 1974, the wholesale price index was up 37 percent and the consumer price index up more than 26 percent over the previous year.[10] In 1974, the economic growth rate was negative and the economy fell into a recession.

A real sense of vulnerability set in as the Oil Shock revealed the extent to which economic growth, and people's lifestyles, had been fueled by a ready supply of cheap oil. Recent economic achievements seemed fragile as high oil prices accentuated how dependent Japan was on foreign sources of energy, that the country relied on petroleum imports for three-quarters of its energy needs. And there was, domestically as well as globally, much concern about the depletion of resources.[11] A feeling of insecurity about resources and energy was not new to Japan in 1973; the idea of a "resource-poor Japan" had a long history that stretched back well before the Pacific War.[12] But the Oil Shock shaped a particular variation on the theme, which in its 1970s iteration reinforced the realization that resources and energy were finite and could act as a limit to economic growth.

The near concurrence of the Garbage War and the Oil Shock catapulted issues of waste into a place of visibility unprecedented in the postwar period, fueling discussions about the sources of its creation. Waste was found to have insinuated itself into the values, priorities, and habits of the high-growth, mass-consuming society as people asked themselves various interconnected questions about what kinds of products they purchased, why consumers had the preferences they did, how people treated and discarded their stuff, and how they determined what was no longer of any use. The waste of things, resources, and energy came to be seen as tightly interrelated, with each and all strands of such waste viewed from the vantage point of a world changed from the one of high-speed growth that had just met an abrupt end.

The multiple shocks of the early 1970s precipitated significant shifts in ideas and practices involving waste, such that the undesirability of waste was framed in ways that differed from those of postwar decades past. In addition to the more somber economic mood, environmental considerations came to figure more substantially in how waste was understood. While some had started to talk about garbage as a kind of pollution (*kōgai*) in the previous decade, there was wider recognition in the 1970s of the negative environmental impacts of disposal and greater acknowledgment of the need for environmental protection. The startling message delivered by the oil crisis about the scarcity of resources and energy also highlighted how the extraction and depletion of natural resources taxed the environment. Environmental concerns at this time were rather anthropocentric, focused on people's lifestyles, and were not as prominent as they would become in later decades. Nonetheless, an environmental consciousness helped inform the ways in which various and interwoven manifestations of waste (of things, resources, and energy) were understood as exemplifying the costs and consequences of rapid economic growth.

As the warts of recent achievements were laid bare, waste became a site of reflection about the values and priorities of the society that high growth had created. The recognition dawned that a society of mass production and mass consumption might also be one of mass waste. Japan was declared by many to be a "throwaway society" with a "culture of disposability" epitomized by wasteful attitudes toward things, resources, and energy. And there was more serious engagement with the possibility, only casually considered in the past, that wastefulness was inherent in consumption. In the wake of the Garbage War and Oil Shock, waste and wastefulness were increasingly viewed as societal symptoms of problems endemic to high economic growth and mass consumption.

To be aware of waste was thus to adjust to a world in which the environment was not invulnerable, resources were not infinite, and economic growth would not proceed at a breakneck pace. Contemporary waste consciousness implied a sensitivity to limits in behavior appropriate to the limits of a post–oil crisis Japan. It also took shape in a context of continued affluence and consumption quite different from the poverty of the wartime period or the transitions of the 1950s and 1960s. Waste consciousness in these years was thus not about subsistence nor about friction to societal changes, but was rather a way to defend the middle-class lifestyles that had already been achieved and to ensure their longevity well into the future.

In terms of practice, this meant initiating or accelerating waste reduction campaigns of various kinds. The early 1970s saw the genesis of concerted movements spearheaded by governments, corporations, and social groups to reuse and recycle things and to "save resources" (*shōshigen*) and "save energy" (*shōenerugī*, or *shōene*). Swap meets and repair centers got off the ground, as did the separation of garbage into categories and the recycling of so-called "resource garbage" (*shigen gomi*) first by local organizations and then by municipalities.

Despite these many changes in conceptions of waste and wastefulness, there did persist an expectation of maintaining affluent middle-class lifestyles. And while economic growth might no longer be of the high-speed variety, it was presumed that there would be growth. When Governor Minobe inaugurated the war on garbage, he did not name among his adversaries the residents of Tokyo, who notably escaped his disfavor. He seemed instead to be fighting the war to protect their lives and preserve their lifestyles. Not just with the Garbage War but in the various battles waged against waste, there were hints that many people were neither changing nor wanting to change substantially their consuming and disposing ways. In the face of the Garbage War and Oil Shock, there were calls for a rethinking of values and practices that had been defined over the past decade and a half, even as there was an abiding desire to sustain lifestyles that had been made possible by economic growth, the development of a mass consumption society, and affluence.

Garbage on Display

"I intend to become a clean-up man for Tokyo," announced Minobe Ryōkichi in a speech after winning the governorship in April 1967. Speaking both literally and figuratively, he went on to lay the philosophical groundwork for what would become the Garbage War. He articulated his commitment to addressing "some of the biggest distortions of high-speed growth," to raising the quality of living in the metropolis, and to keeping his campaign promise of "correct[ing], if even only slightly, the inequities, the foulness, the inequality and the ill treatment of the weak by society."[13] In terms of concrete priorities, sanitation and environmental pollution were high on the list. Demonstrating that his words were not empty, he appointed as his chief economic planner Shibata Tokue, a professor at Tokyo Metropolitan University and an expert on matters sanitary. Shibata was the author of several books, including *Nihon no seisō mondai* (Japan's Sanitation Problem), which was published a full decade earlier and was well ahead of its time in considering the relationship between economic changes, societal shifts, and waste.[14]

What Minobe hoped to do was build incinerators in wards throughout the metropolis, so that each area of the capital would become more directly responsible for its own garbage, and the disproportionate onus for disposal then placed on one particular ward, Kōtō, would be alleviated. At a pragmatic and strategic level, the Garbage War was a campaign to convince residents that ensuring their standard of living might very well require assenting to an incinerator in their backyard. The declaration of war in September 1971 was thus an appeal to Tokyoites: that the dire state of the garbage problem would have to be addressed to preserve their lives and lifestyle, and the most effective weapon in this battle would be the modern incinerator.[15] On a societal and political level, the Garbage War was about how to apportion more fairly the responsibility for disposing of the undesirable by-products of modern civilization.

In many ways, Minobe's offensive sought to thoroughly modernize waste. Rubbish was to be treated as the creation of a modern and civilized society, and was to be managed with technology so advanced that incinerators could stand and be seen in the heart of metropolitan neighborhoods as symbols of their capacity to tame waste. What Minobe was fighting was the enduring view of garbage as, to borrow the historian David Howell's description of human shit, yucky.[16] And not just yucky but potentially dangerous, so that it should be kept at the city's margins or, at the very least, outside of one's own backyard.

Even before the fall of 1971, it was clear that many residents would resist the construction of new incinerators for various reasons having to do with environmental impact, health, and safety as well as financial costs and the inter-vention of the metropolitan government into ward affairs. A prime case was the refusal of Suginami ward to house an incinerator on its soil, a position that rendered it a combatant in an eight-year war of its own. Plans for a facility in Suginami had been in the works since 1939, were put on hold in the war-torn 1940s, and were resuscitated as part of the metropolitan government's (unkept) promise in 1964 to be incinerating all garbage by 1970. Understanding that facili-ties would have to be built in various wards throughout Tokyo, the residents of Suginami began to discuss the prospect for their ward. But in November 1966, they were abruptly informed by the metropolitan government of the specific site that had been chosen, one that was located near an elementary school and a train station and would require the sale of privately owned land. Stunned by this unexpected decision, ward residents organized a resistance movement that was still holding its oppositional stance in the fall of 1971.[17]

Parallel to Suginami's battle against the introduction of an incinerator into its ward, Kōtō had been defending itself against an onslaught of garbage for years.[18] Kōtō was located on the shores of Tokyo Bay and was home to two-thirds of the capital's landfills. Garbage trucks transported waste from all across Tokyo, converging in a daily parade of noise and odor in the ward's congested streets. Official figures put at five thousand the number of trucks that passed through each day, with the area of Edagawa near the landfills most affected. There were regular outbreaks of flies, and rubbish whirling through the air on windy days. Long frustrated by its inordinate obligation to dispose of the capital's waste, the ward resisted stridently when it was asked by the metropolitan government in mid-August 1971 to support extending the life of Landfill Number Fifteen (the infamous Island of Dreams, or Yume no Shima, and technically the new, or sec-ond, Island of Dreams).[19] Over the next month, the ward formally expressed its opposition to the government's plan, and on September 27, one day before Minobe's declaration of the Garbage War, the Kōtō ward assembly adopted ques-tions to be posed publicly to the metropolitan government and to the twenty-two other wards of the capital about the structures, assumptions, and unequal bur-dens of waste disposal.[20]

Particularly irksome to Kōtō residents was the irresponsibility of Suginami ward which, though wealthy and populous with roughly half a million residents, did not have its own sanitation plant and was entirely reliant on Kōtō ward for waste management. In the eyes of the frustrated citizens of Kōtō, Suginami's continued refusal to build an incinerator not only suggested its indifference to the inequities of the situation but also symbolized the unwillingness of other wards to take responsibility for their garbage. The conflict between the two wards grabbed significant public attention in late December 1971, when Kōtō ward

FIGURE 3.1.   Garbage War. During Kōtō ward's blockade of its Landfill Number Fifteen, the *Yomiuri* newspaper published a photograph of garbage, being sprayed with disinfectant, piled up in the streets of Suginami ward.

Reproduced by permission from *Yomiuri shimbun*, May 22, 1973.

decided to forcibly block trucks carrying Suginami's trash from entering Landfill Number Fifteen. Beginning early in the morning on December 22, all of the arriving trucks were checked and those from Suginami were turned away; as one sign read, "Take Back Suginami's Garbage." The ongoing showdown between the citizens of Kōtō and Suginami came for many to epitomize, and adopt the moniker of, the Garbage War.[21]

This dimension of the Garbage War, the confrontation between citizens of Kōtō and Suginami wards, heightened the visibility of the garbage problem even as it was about who should be obliged to render garbage invisible. In late May 1973, when Kōtō again refused to accept garbage from a Suginami that had not yet agreed to house its own incinerator, people opened their newspapers and turned on their televisions to witness members of the Kōtō ward assembly in helmets, physically barring entrance to Landfill Number Fifteen. And for at least the few days when collection was suspended, denizens of Suginami ward encountered piles of garbage spreading across their sidewalks.[22] The presence of rubbish, made inescapable by Kōtō's actions, helped force an intervention by Minobe, who persuaded Kōtō to end its blockade and resumed negotiations with a Suginami ward more committed to figuring out a site for construction of its incinerator.[23]

The political conflicts about the construction of incinerators shone a light on the sheer volume and unceasing accumulation of garbage, as well as on the desire of many Tokyoites not to have to see or deal with that garbage in their daily lives. Insofar as Minobe had hoped to draw attention to the garbage problem, he succeeded; but his aim of urban infrastructure development bumped up against the understanding, even the visceral feeling, that garbage was filthy, that it was to be carted away and kept at a distance. This conception of rubbish was implicit in the stances of Suginami ward and others that resisted Minobe's sanitation plans. A documentary aired by the national broadcaster NHK in October 1973 highlighted and exemplified the ways in which concerns about visibility and invisibility were inherent in the clashes over garbage. The very title of the half-hour program, *Gomi to tokonoma* (Garbage and the Alcove), alluded to the question of how garbage should be seen with its evocation of the *tokonoma*, a raised and recessed space in a Japanese-style room in which an object (typically art, a scroll, or flowers) was displayed. The specific issue taken up in the documentary was the proposed construction of a sanitation plant in the heart of Shinjuku ward, a major hub of business, entertainment, and government administration. Minobe's plan, announced in September 1973, was to build a forty-eight-story facility in a location that was highly visible, purposely and purposefully not hidden.[24] Residents of Shinjuku responded with indignation, and the local neighborhood association (*chōnaikai*) collected ten thousand signatures from those who opposed the construction of the facility. At one boisterous meeting of residents with representatives of the Minobe administration, many opponents succinctly broadcast their position by wearing headbands emblazoned in red with "Down with Garbage" or "No to Garbage" (*Gomi hantai*). Shouting at the government administrators, they expressed their concern that Shinjuku would become a "toilet neighborhood" (*benjo no machi*)—both a place where shit resided and a shitty place. The government representatives tried to assure the residents that the image of Shinjuku would not be damaged, that the facility would be a model of new town planning which mitigated the dangers of pollution and traffic, and that the ward would become a *tokonoma*, a space that displayed a state-of-the-art sanitation facility. In interviews with men and women on the streets of Kōtō, many found it unfair that all of Shinjuku's garbage was brought into their ward, that Shinjuku, like Suginami, did not have to deal with its own waste, and that two years into the Garbage War, not a single incinerator had yet been built. In the words of one resident, Kōtō would also like to be a *tokonoma*. Although the documentary itself did not explicitly stake out a position in this conflict, it did use images to suggest impatience with Shinjuku's resistance. After it was stated that the planned incinerator would handle the 500 tons of garbage thrown out per day in Shinjuku, there was a lingering shot of a discarded McDonald's paper cup surrounded by other rubbish in a garbage can. After Minobe explained his plan for each area of the metropolis to dispose of its own trash, the camera panned slowly over empty metal cans and other litter, giving weight to his argument that the garbage problem needed to be addressed. And in the closing scenes of the documentary, the loud voices of opponents in Shinjuku were juxtaposed with a final image, in foreboding silence, of garbage being dumped.[25]

Minobe was ultimately victorious in his war, winning the assent of residents to the construction of inescapably conspicuous facilities in more areas of the capital. In November 1974, all parties on the Suginami side agreed to have an incineration plant built in the Takaido area of the ward, having secured concessions to mitigate its visibility, risk of pollution, and disruption to the lives of residents. The plant itself was to use cutting-edge technology to control any possible pollution; underground tunnels were to be constructed for garbage trucks; and the trucks themselves were to be redesigned to contain as much as possible their smells and rubbish. And the incinerator also provided amenities for the area: the heat generated was to warm the water for a nearby swimming pool and senior citizens' home, and new community spaces and facilities were to be constructed, such as a large plaza and a library. After several hundred local meetings, many rounds of negotiations, and legal action, construction started in 1979 on the Takaido plant, which came online in 1982.[26] Minobe and his allies had managed to usher in the era of the modern incinerator. And though a facility in Shinjuku never came to pass, other wards did accede, as ground was broken in Adachi in 1974 and Hikarigaoka in 1980. Over the next twenty or so years, more than a dozen incinerators would be built.[27]

Through the waging of the Garbage War, views of rubbish were modified. It would be too simplistic to reduce the various and numerous conflicts down to just the meaning of waste, given the many interests involved concerning the health and safety of communities, equity, land-ownership, and the democratic process. Complicated too were the differences of opinion even within wards. But the eventual construction of incinerators suggests that, despite lingering concerns about its contaminating potential, there were shifts in ideas about garbage—that its danger and filth could be controlled; that with certain guarantees and proper incentives, a sanitation plant could be tolerated; and that waste could be made safe enough to be in your neighborhood.

There were other indications of a general softening in resistance to the idea of a sanitary treatment plant in one's neighborhood. The Tokyo Metropolitan Citizens' Office (Tokyo-to Tominshitsu) conducted multiple public opinion surveys about the garbage problem which included questions about views toward incinerators, a sign of how central their construction was to the Garbage War. In November 1971, when residents were asked how they would react if a sanitary treatment plant had to be built near their home, almost a quarter (24.3 percent) of the 1,080 respondents said that they would be absolutely opposed. Roughly three-quarters (75.1 percent) said that they could find it acceptable, either with or without conditions.[28] When the same question was asked two years later, in late November and early December 1973, the percentage of the 973 survey takers who would assent remained about the same (75.6 percent), but of those people, many more agreed without conditions. And the percentage who were opposed declined markedly (24.3 to 8.1 percent).[29] This downward trend was loosely corroborated by answers to other questions; it was, for example, consistent with a declining aversion to the principle that each area should dispose of its own garbage.[30] A qualification does need to be made. All of these responses were to questions about hypothetical situations or general ideas, which likely made survey participants seem more amenable to the building of new incinerators than they might actually have been. When asked about the specific, concrete issue of a facility in Suginami ward, almost a third (31 percent) of the respondents did not support its construction. This meant that more people objected to the real possibility of an incinerator in Suginami ward than to the abstract principle of each area taking responsibility for its own garbage.[31] But at least in the realm of the hypothetical, there was somewhat greater comfort with the ability of incinerators to manage distasteful and potentially harmful garbage.

There were also changes, more intentional and self-conscious, in the ways that the Tokyo Sanitation Bureau (Tokyo-to Seisōkyoku) conceived of garbage and its industry. Around 1971, the bureau came to think of its work as being less about the disposal of filth (obutsu) for the purpose of beautification or even cleaning and more about the creation of a comprehensive system for preserving the environment. The bureau started to speak not of filth but of waste (haikibutsu), which it saw as exceeding levels tolerable for the environment. The large amount of garbage produced by expanded economic activity as well as the dumping of waste where it did not belong breached the capacities of the environment. The bureau thus saw its responsibility as less about hygiene or sanitation, and more about restoration of the lost balance between waste and the environment.[32]

The Sanitation Bureau's view of waste as its own kind of pollution, or "the third kōgai" after that of air and water, was informed by greater acknowledgment in the late 1960s and early 1970s of the environmental costs of the country's rapid economic rise. Particularly hard to ignore was the human price extracted by the environmental degradation and disasters wrought by industrial pollution. Citizens' antipollution movements were especially active in these years, and victims aggressively sought redress in the courts. Most widely known were the so-called "big four" pollution lawsuits which brought national attention to the four major "pollution diseases" caused by the mishandling of industrial waste by corporations: Minamata disease from methylmercury dumped by the Chisso Corporation off the coast of Kyūshū; Niigata Minamata disease from methylmercury discarded by the chemical engineering company Shōwa Denkō; itai-itai disease from cadmium released by mining companies in Toyama prefecture; and Yokkaichi asthma from the sulfur oxide pollution of petrochemical processing facilities in Mie prefecture. All four of these cases resulted in legal victories that secured compensation for the victims and helped make pollution an issue of social and political prominence.[33] Such litigation and environmental protests were largely responsible for landmark legislation, including the passage by the so-called "pollution Diet" in November 1970 of fourteen new laws that established strict antipollution regulations. And in May 1971, Prime Minister Satō Eisaku established the Environment Agency (Kankyōchō).[34] It was in this context that the Tokyo Sanitation Bureau increasingly approached waste as an environmental matter that affected people's lives.

In addition to framing their work in terms of environmental protection, sanitation professionals used the subject of garbage to voice skepticism and pose questions about the society's direction and priorities. The Tokyo Sanitation Bureau, nodding toward the link between the garbage problem and environmental degradation, urged people to focus on what was being lost with the "immense profits of businesses" and the attainment of "an affluent, consuming lifestyle."[35] Expounded here was not just the implications of waste proliferation but also its understood causes of mass production and mass consumption. And both of these phenomena were connected to high economic growth, which was identified as the source of the abundance of things available for consumption and the production of large amounts of garbage. As was expressed in one pithy phrase: GNP is both gross national product and "garbage [gomi] national product."[36]

Garbage was viewed not just as a result of economic growth but also as evidence of the inability of gross national product (GNP) to effectively capture and measure progress. There was vocal criticism in the early 1970s of an obsession with GNP growth for its elision or even exacerbation of environmental degradation and social problems, and for its obfuscation or even obstruction of understanding what a high quality of life might be. In 1970, the *Asahi* newspaper published a long multipart series titled "Down with GNP!" (*Kutabare GNP!*) to examine one hundred years of Japan's history as a late-developing capitalist country as well as the "distortions" of postwar economic growth, and to look ahead toward stable and healthy economic growth for the sake of an affluent life that all Japanese people could enjoy. Its inaugural installment expressed doubt about whether GNP growth alone was sufficient, especially when it came to broader concerns about people's welfare, and asked whether there might be a better measure of societal affluence.[37] In one piece in the series that addressed rubbish, the economist John Kenneth Galbraith discussed "the external diseconomies of high level consumption" and listed as examples "disposable beer cans and bottles from the beverage industries, discarded containers from other consumers' food industries, [and] the garbage and sewage and other wastes of the high consumption household."[38] Among the other authors in the series was the economist Tsuru Shigeto, an adviser to Minobe, who wrote regularly about his skepticism toward GNP: "Numerical measures such as GNP will not automatically carry connotations as to the magnitude or extent of economic welfare. We shall have to question increasingly the meaningfulness of certain quantitative measures or indexes which in the past we have been conditioned to take for granted."[39] Like Tsuru, Minobe found GNP an inapplicable metric when it came to success in the Garbage War. It should be noted that none of these men, nor the editors of the *Asahi* newspaper series, were rejecting economic growth outright. Nor were they talking about pollution as having enabled high economic growth, as some did.[40] What they stressed were the costs of economic growth, the particular negative consequences of the high-speed variety, the shortcomings of GNP as an index of societal health, and the need for people to think beyond GNP to what their values and commitments should be.

Sharp criticisms of the mass consumption fanned by economic growth were presented in an exhibit about the garbage problem housed in the metropolitan government building just after Minobe's declaration of the Garbage War. Titled "Let's Shine a Light on Garbage," the display consisted of graphs, charts, and photographs as well as a pamphlet that identified the root cause of the garbage problem as "an economy of mass consumption that creates waste [*muda*]." Viewers were encouraged to confront the meanings of mass consumption and to ponder two sweeping, even existential, issues: What is truly important and of value in life, and what should modern civilization be?[41] Implicit in these questions was the belief that mass consumption should not define modern lives and modern civilization, and that the economic success it enabled was not all it had been hoped to be. In the view of the sanitation expert and chief economic planner Shibata Tokue, the optimistic logic that high levels of consumption and high economic growth would deliver high levels of happiness was being overturned. There was thus a need, he said, to reconsider modern economics and culture.[42]

Sanitation professionals strove to disseminate their conceptions of garbage to the public at large, to convince people that their rubbish could and should be managed in environmentally conscious ways and that what they threw out should be seen as a reflection of modern life. As part of the Garbage War, the Tokyo Sanitation Bureau took great pains to spread an understanding of incinerators as safe, clean, and modern. One arrow in the bureau's quiver was public tours of sanitation treatment plants, to challenge any images and preconceptions Tokyoites might have about dirty and filthy incinerators and to reduce the likelihood that they would oppose one in their own neighborhood. In 1972, the bureau conducted 173 such tours with a total of 7,635 participants. The bureau's outreach strategy also included meetings with neighborhood associations (of which it conducted 1,300 in 1973), panel discussions, symposia, and "summer schools," or multi-day instruction sessions about garbage matters. In 1974, responding to a particularly aggressive push that summer, 44,392 Tokyoites took part in a plant visit or symposium; in 1976, 60,000 people saw an incinerator and 11,000 a landfill.[43] The bureau also did some targeted outreach to the next generation of residents, and through them to their parents as well. Special parent-child tours of incinerators were organized. And the bureau sponsored an annual contest and exhibition of children's drawings on garbage-related themes, for which it received thousands of entries from elementary school students across the metropolis.[44]

It is hard to gauge the extent to which the bureau's programs and own thinking about garbage influenced the views and behaviors of Tokyo residents, but the Garbage War certainly brought the garbage problem to people's attention and garbage to their consciousness, even if results in terms of their knowledge and actions were mixed. Less than two months after Minobe's declaration of war, almost three-quarters of respondents (73.6 percent) in a survey of 1,080 Tokyoites reported that they were familiar with the term "Garbage War."[45] More than that, their sense that the production of garbage had been increasing in recent years was in line with the metropolitan government's description of the proliferation of trash. Asked how they would compare the amount of garbage in Tokyo to that of three or four years earlier, a full 95 percent observed that it had increased to some extent. And many survey takers did not exempt their own behavior from this trend, with 69.1 percent saying that the amount of garbage that their household threw out had increased over the same period. The sense of urgency that the metropolitan government projected about this trend was mirrored in the widespread belief that the streets of Tokyo would become "mountains of garbage" some years hence, with 62.3 percent of participants reporting that this was a possibility.[46]

Although there seems to have been familiarity with the contours of the garbage problem as the metropolitan government defined it, knowledge about specific systems and practices was murkier, suggesting a limit to residents' interest in and attention to matters of waste. During the ongoing conflict over a possible sanitation facility in Suginami, the Suginami Association of Consumers (Suginami Shōhisha no Kai) and daily life schools (seikatsu gakkō) conducted a survey of 493 housewives who lived in their ward. These groups had been spearheading trash reduction efforts even before the fall of 1971 and were curious about how housewives were thinking about garbage, especially in the context of the protracted struggles over the incinerator. While a member of the association spoke highly of the Garbage War as bringing to the surface an issue previously considered unsavory, she was dismayed about the lack of knowledge revealed by the survey. For instance, the ward had a particular system for the collection of large refuse according to which a resident had to contact the sanitation office three days before a designated date to schedule a pickup. Only 58 percent of respondents knew that this was how to dispose of such items; 37 percent thought that the method was the same for regular and large garbage, which likely meant that they were throwing out bulky objects for normal trash collection. A measly 4 percent of the participants knew the ultimate fate of Suginami's garbage—that roughly 60 percent was incinerated in other wards and that the rest was transported to Landfill Number Fifteen. Perhaps most alarming given the long-standing and vocal opposition to the construction of an incinerator in their ward, 19 percent of the housewives believed that their garbage was disposed of at a (then nonexistent) plant in Suginami.[47]

From the perspective of garbage collectors, there were different impressions about the influence of the Garbage War on residents' awareness of trash matters. In conversations with twenty garbage collectors from five different areas of the capital, some noticed that people had become more responsive to requests and directives from their office. Some observed that in certain places and among certain dedicated people, such as members of particular organizations, there was more recognition of the garbage problem. And one worker suggested that a higher level of interest in general could be attributed to newspaper and radio coverage of the Garbage War. But most said that people treated their garbage as they had before—that trash piled up again shortly after collection and that the level of knowledge about how to dispose of rubbish was low, especially among those who lived in large apartment buildings. One sanitation worker noted that many residents still did as they pleased with their garbage.[48]

On its own, the impact and legacies of the Garbage War on attitudes toward waste would have been significant, if not monumental. Waste was rendered visible—through the construction of incinerators and as the topic of discussions about the contemporary economy and society. Sanitation experts shifted their thinking about garbage (from a symptom of civilizational inadequacy to a product of civilizational excess), and about their industry (from beautification and cleanliness to environmental protection). And rubbish came to be viewed as a problem of postwar modernity to be tackled in new ways.

The Age of Limits

What amplified, extended, and expanded all of these developments was the Oil Shock. The global oil crisis in October 1973 was especially alarming to Japan, the world's largest petroleum importer, which relied on foreign countries for 99.7 percent of its oil, and the Middle East in particular for 80 percent.[49] This was the outcome of having transitioned in the decade and a half after the war from a heavy reliance on domestic coal and hydroelectricity to imported oil.[50] As prices rose and inflation spiked, there was an acute sense of the limits not just to oil but also to resources and energy more generally. Conversations about resources and energy drew in the subject of rubbish, as both the Garbage War and the Oil Shock struck the same anxious chord about the costs and consequences of high economic growth and the future of affluent middle-class lifestyles. As assumptions and goals of the recent past were destabilized, many attempted to navigate a new age of limits by calling for changes in values and behavior while holding dear the much-coveted gains of the high-growth years.

The realization that a shortage of resources could dampen economic growth was already starting to dawn on various people in Japan as elsewhere before the Oil Shock. A book that brought a good deal of global attention to resource limits on economic expansion was authored by the Club of Rome, a group of seventy individuals of twenty-five nationalities with no single ideological or political persuasion, which launched an initiative modestly titled the Project on the Predicament of Mankind. As part of this project, some members of the Club published in 1972 *The Limits to Growth*, which sought to "encourage each reader to think through the consequences of continuing to equate growth with progress." Widely known and translated into Japanese that same year, the book observed, "Nowadays, more than ever before, man tends toward continual, often accelerated growth—of population, land occupancy, production, consumption, waste, etc." Such expansion left unchecked would, the authors alarmingly claimed, spell the end to growth on earth within the next hundred years.[51] In Japan as in other economically advanced countries, *The Limits to Growth*, along with the economist E. F. Schumacher's *Small Is Beautiful* (translated into Japanese as *Ningen fukkō no keizai*, or An Economy for Human Revival, in 1976) and the works of the social scientist K. E. Boulding (translated into Japanese throughout the 1970s and 1980s), informed conversations about the relationship between the mass consumption of resources and energy and the viability of continued economic growth.[52]

In the more immediate aftermath of the oil crisis, nothing exemplified anxieties about resource shortages more than the "toilet paper riots," or more aptly the "toilet paper panic"—so much so that the urgent buying of toilet paper is still remembered by many as emblematic of the Oil Shock. It is hard to know precisely when and how the panic, stoked by rumor and media coverage, began. It might have started at the Daiei supermarket in Senri New Town (Senri Nyū Taun), a residential development of multistory apartment complexes near Osaka. The Daiei had been selling four rolls of toilet paper for the bargain basement price of 98 yen, but when the cost went up and the market could no longer stock the product, that shelf sat bare. This sight made customers uneasy, and word and worry spread through the apartments. Or it might have started at a supermarket in the district of Sannomiya in Kobe. Here, toilet paper had been on special sale, and when the store warned that the price was about to go up and urged customers to buy as soon as possible, the product sold out, which made people nervous.[53] Or it might have started with a housewife in Senri New Town who casually mentioned to a friend that she had been shopping in Osaka where no toilet paper was being sold. This turned into the rumor that housewives in Osaka were buying up toilet paper.[54] Then there was the media—an NHK television broadcast on October 31 that called for a movement to use paper rationally, and an *Asahi* newspaper story that same day about toilet paper disappearing from stores and a housewife in the city of Nara who bought two years' worth just in case.[55]

What does seem clear is that after rumors spread on October 31 about an impending shortage of toilet paper, hundreds of housewives began to swamp supermarkets the next day to secure the necessity, and mass media coverage helped turn the hoarding of toilet paper into a national story. On that morning of November 1, it has been said, a line of two hundred housewives formed outside a particular supermarket in Senri New Town even before it opened its doors. For four or five days, stores desperately tried to stock their shelves with emergency shipments of toilet paper and continued to sell out. Images of barren aisles, long lines, and women reaching for coveted rolls could be seen on television and in newspapers. Hoarding extended beyond toilet paper to detergent, kerosene, salt, and soy sauce.[56] And after the flurry of buying had calmed down in the Kansai region, the phenomenon struck the greater Tokyo area.[57] On November 18, on what usually would have been a sleepy Sunday morning, a Peacock store in the Minato ward of Tokyo sold out of toilet paper, salt, sugar, soap powder, and hygiene products within half an hour of opening. At another store, this one in Yokohama, a line of about a thousand housewives had formed two hours before its 10:00 am opening. The sale of toilet paper was limited to one package per customer, but the entire supply of five hundred was depleted within fifteen minutes. Similar stories were told about other locations, and many supermarkets displayed signs noting that they were sold out of daily necessities.[58]

Suggestive of the nature of the panic was the disjuncture between people's anxieties and the material situation. There was no actual shortage in the supply of toilet paper. The unexpected spurt of buying did denude supermarkets of their stock on hand, but within days, manufacturers dispatched emergency supplies. The only products that were truly scarce were salt and kerosene cans, the lack of cans making it seem as though the oil crisis had precipitated a shortfall of kerosene.[59] The government attempted to assuage people's concerns, with the Ministry of International Trade and Industry (Tsūshō Sangyōshō, or MITI) repeatedly assuring people that there was plenty of toilet paper. The ministry

FIGURE 3.2. Toilet Paper Panic. At this Daiei supermarket, packages of toilet paper were limited to one per customer during the toilet paper panic.

Reproduced by permission from *Yomiuri shimbun*, November 2, 1973.

launched a "don't worry campaign" and explained to the public that 122,000 tons of toilet paper had been manufactured between January and August, an increase of 16 percent over the previous year.[60] Yet consumers continued to buy up goods, most of which had little to almost nothing to do with petroleum. And consumers in the capital went to great lengths to purchase necessities even after panics in other parts of the country had subsided.

What the toilet paper panic illustrated so stunningly was how accustomed people had become to the goods and practices that brought them cleanliness, comfort, and convenience. To see supermarket shelves not full of such products was scary, and to think of an alternative to toilet paper was unpleasant. Those who engaged in the buying up of products tended to be, it seems, somewhat younger and better educated. In one survey of 182 Tokyoites conducted by a housewives' association, roughly a third (30 percent) said they had stocked up on goods. The average age of those who hoarded was forty; of those who did not, forty-six. The level of schooling of those who hoarded was somewhat higher, with a greater percentage having had at least some specialized education (23.6 percent compared to 11.8 percent).[61] Beyond this relatively small survey, one could also consider the demographics of a development like Senri New Town. It had been built in 1961 and most of its roughly 3,700 households were families of three to five who lived in apartments with a dining room, kitchen, and two other rooms. They also had easy access to the various stores that were part of this "new town," one of several such urban planning projects from the 1960s.[62] The housewives who crowded into the supermarkets around Senri New Town could afford to live in a complex designed to provide the amenities of a middle-class life. A reminder of the privileges of those like the residents of Senri New Town is provided by its counterpoint, a certain "Mr. A," or A-san, whose daily life was described in the *Asahi* newspaper. A-san was a forty-something employee of a taxi company who lived with his wife and three children in a tiny apartment, barely managing to make ends meet. They did not have the time to stand in line for hours, since both husband and wife worked full days. They did not have the money to buy more than they needed at the moment, nor did they have the space to store extra packages of toilet paper.[63]

Some judgments were made about those who did participate in the toilet paper panic. Notably, the housewives who bought up goods were rarely described unsympathetically as crazy or stupid, even by government officials or the media. Perhaps this was because of an understanding of the general mood of anxiety, or because it did not seem particularly irrational to buy necessities for oneself as supermarkets began to empty. But some observations, tinged with a negative tone, were made about these housewives by other women, by women who did not hoard. The commentator and magazine editor Saegusa Saeko, for example, reflected on how the housewives who did buy up goods were of a postwar generation—one that had not learned through the experience of war how to survive in an emergency and how to endure hardship. This generation of women did not have the skills to use things carefully or the heart to appreciate them. They had not been scolded when they were wasteful, nor were they communicating to their own children the value of things.[64] In her own subjective terms, Saegusa was responding to what the toilet paper panic represented: that it was distinctly characteristic of the economic and societal changes of the high-growth era; that it revealed how deeply the ability to consume, and the desire for cleanliness, comfort, and convenience, had taken root; that it was inflamed by the overconsumption of a thoroughly disposable good.

In responses to the toilet paper panic, there was a common call for the resurrection of a waste consciousness supposedly lost in the previous decade's flurry of consumption. In late November 1973, the chairman of the Japan Paper Association (Nihon Seishi Rengōkai) and president of the Jūjō Paper Company (Jūjō Seishi) was interviewed in the *Yomiuri* newspaper, presumably to calm nerves frayed by the perceived shortage of toilet paper. Kaneko Saichirō attempted to put readers' minds at ease, assuring them that every attempt would be made to avoid cuts in supplies of paper necessities like toilet paper and textbooks. But he did paint an honest picture of an unsettling situation, one in which an industry that needed oil in its production process was trying to adjust to reductions in supply. He noted that newspapers and publishers had already been asked to cut back, and seemed to concede that a rise in the price of paper goods was almost inevitable. When asked what consumers should do in the face of these challenges, Kaneko answered, "In the end, there is nothing else to do but stop wasting." When it came not just to paper but also to oil, plastic, and clothing, the "age of saving" had come. No longer was it an era when "consumption is a virtue"; now, he said, "saving is a virtue." But Kaneko himself acknowledged that he was extolling the need to save at a time that, though insecure, was also wealthy. He realized how difficult it might be to realize a substantive shift from a mindset of consumption to one of waste consciousness. It had been one thing to save in the past, when there was no money; it was another to eliminate waste in a time of affluence.[65]

The need for a shift from wasting to waste consciousness was made prominently by Prime Minister Tanaka Kakuei, who gave a televised speech before the Diet in December 1973 about the oil crisis. Tanaka identified this moment as a historical turning point which marked the end of increases in production and the expansion of employment spurred by plentiful and inexpensive oil, and the start of the pursuit of a "new affluence" amidst resource constraints. Industry was to adapt by saving resources and saving energy. And there had to be a reversal in the people's attitude toward daily life: the waste of resources was to be rejected, and the value of "saving is a virtue" was to be firmly established.[66] To some who were watching and wanting a more sincere and substantive response in a tumultuous time, these were empty words from a hypocritical messenger. The vice chair of the Housewives Association (Shufu Rengōkai, or Shufuren) wanted more substance and action, like the strict saving ordinances of other countries. The chairwoman of the Kobe League of Women Voters (Kobe Fujin Yūkensha Renmei) eviscerated Tanaka for having boasted about high growth, encouraging the country to build cars and highways, only to speak now of saving. This criticism was echoed by the executive director of the Japan Consumers' Co-operative Union (Nihon Seikatsu Kyōdō Kumiai Rengōkai), who was shocked that the ringleader of economic growth and cheerleader for "consumption is a virtue" was now extolling the virtues of saving.[67] The critics had a point, for perhaps no one epitomized public works projects more than Tanaka Kakuei, who as a Liberal Democratic Party (Jiyū Minshutō) politician had lobbied to build dams, roads, and highways. He published in June 1972, a month before he became prime minister, the best seller *Nihon rettō kaizō ron* (Remodeling the Japanese Archipelago), in which he argued that it was possible to promote economic growth and mitigate its negative consequences through construction, through the development and revitalization of rural Japan.[68]

Even as the language of a shift from waste to waste consciousness and from consumption to saving seemed like vapid rhetoric, especially from certain mouths to certain ears, it did become a fixture in the lexicon of the early 1970s. The Garbage War and the Oil Shock destabilized what had seemed so alluring to many, be it economic goals or unfettered consumption. The concerns they elicited were various, as some reconsidered the desirability of past ways of life and many others sought to preserve them. But there was a similar response to the general sense of instability and anxiety: the need to be more attentive to waste. Phrases such as "consumption is a virtue," "waste is a virtue," and "era of disposability" were associated with the period of high growth now past and were evoked far more often in hindsight, during the 1970s, than they had been at the time. In 1971, the Tokyo Sanitation Bureau looked back on the 1960s and characterized it as an era of mass consumption in which waste was considered a virtue, when people were made to throw things away and waste.[69] Major daily newspapers like the *Mainichi*, *Asahi*, and *Yomiuri* came to speak regularly of an age of consumption and disposability.[70] Marketers were blamed by some for pumping up the desires of consumers for goods they did not really need and for encouraging people to throw things away, and the criticisms of advertising, mass consumption, and affluence made by John Kenneth Galbraith and Vance Packard in the previous decade gained more traction.[71] It was commonly said that the Oil Shock blew the whistle on the falsely seductive nature of the phrase "consumption is a virtue," which had been so actively promoted in the previous decade, and that there was a complete turnabout in 1973 to a new era of saving.[72] Together, the Garbage War and the Oil Shock helped propel to public attention this language about a reversal in the virtues of consumption, disposability, waste, and saving. This rhetorical and conceptual vocabulary could then be used by the government, industry, and consumer groups alike to encourage behaviors and attitudes better aligned with ideals they considered more fit for an age of resource constraints, economic insecurity, and environmental fragility.

Disposability and Its Discontents

With the heightened visibility of waste in the wake of the Garbage War and the Oil Shock, the realization set in that the time in which people were living and the way in which people were living could be defined in terms not just of consumption but also of disposability. Heaps of discarded stuff were the incontrovertible evidence that objects once coveted were being thrown away, that production and consumption led inevitably to rubbish, that things still usable had been disposed of as valueless, that value might be saved or recaptured from the trash heap, and that the excretion of goods was also the excretion of resources. Emblematic of the newly christened "throwaway age" (*tsukaisute jidai*) was the waste of material things and resources, as well as the inattention to discarding and the very desire for disposability. For some, like the fifty-year-old housewife Inoue Yayoi of Nagoya, the casual throwing away of things was what had been punished by the crises in the fall of 1973; the Oil Shock was retaliation for the unthinking embrace of a wasteful culture of disposability.[73] If there was to be an end to this stubbornly enduring age, it was thought, people had to examine their relationship to things and what they valued in their daily lives. Necessary too was the implementation of concrete practices to stem the tide of the many incarnations of waste and wastefulness in the "culture of disposability."

Symptomatic of the throwaway age, it was readily observed, was not just the disposal of products but also the creation and proliferation of products intentionally designed to be disposable. An article titled "The Fearsome 'Throwaway Age'" ("Osorubeki 'tsukaisute jidai'"), published in a weekly report of the Headquarters for Tokyo Garbage War Countermeasures (Tokyo-to Gomi Sensō Taisaku Honbu), noted that paper cups, paper plates, and paper towels could be seen with regularity and that disposable diapers were becoming more popular. Even delivery orders from soba noodle shops were coming in paper or plastic, rather than lacquerware boxes and bowls that would have to be returned to the restaurant, in an illustration of "one-wayization," or the increasingly one-way flow in the distribution of goods from producer to consumer.[74] Such impressions corresponded with the results of a survey conducted in the spring of 1971 by the Lion Fat and Oil Company (Raion Yushi) of four hundred housewives in Osaka and Tokyo. Almost 85 percent of the respondents reported that they used, on a daily basis, between three to seven of the following disposable products: plastic bags, tissues, disposable chopsticks, straws, paper napkins, aluminum foil tableware, paper cups, paper towels, paper plates, and disposable diapers. Examining the survey data, the commentator Ishikawa Teizō concluded that this era was different from those past in having lost the virtue of finding value in old things. Making it a point to note that he was writing in the twenty-sixth year after the end of the war, Ishikawa attributed the embrace of disposable goods to the valuing of convenience and efficiency. He punctuated this claim with the statistic that approximately 73 percent of those respondents who thought that paper towel use would increase in the future cited as the reason its convenience and efficiency.[75] Even more biting in its assessment of this trend, the *Asahi* newspaper asserted that the purchase of disposable goods in the name of saving labor rendered lifestyles more and more "self-indulgent."[76]

So deep-seated was this culture of disposability, the criticism went, that even consumer durables were being treated like easily expendable goods. It was pointed out that cars, for example, were being thrown out more quickly in Japan than in other countries. In the United States and West Germany, the percentage of cars on the road which were over six years old was about 40 percent; in Japan, about 12 percent. Over half (55 percent) of cars in Japan were being used less than three years, the *Yomiuri* newspaper reported, citing this as a prime case of waste in a culture of disposability.[77] In the Tokyo Sanitation Bureau's assessment, the frequent introduction of new types of electric household appliances, like the color television set, was driving upward the quantity of large refuse. As mass production and mass consumption had extended to consumer durables, and with limited opportunities to reuse or trade in electric goods or furniture, they too were ending up on the ever-growing trash heap.[78]

This claim that the decisions of producers were encouraging the wasteful behavior of consumers was made more plainly and acerbically by others. The *Yomiuri* newspaper article about the large number of cars thrown away each year attributed this phenomenon to auto manufacturers who were in perpetual competition to develop new models. And when it came to color television sets, there had been sixteen model changes in the seven years that the product had been available to consumers.[79] This connection between disposability and the continual introduction of new goods to the market seemed fairly well recognized, as reflected in a nationwide survey conducted in December 1973 by the Japan Public Opinion Research Association (Nihon Seron Chōsakai). Of the 2,526 respondents, 90 percent thought that there had been a strong move in the past ten years toward throwing things away, and almost three-quarters of those surveyed (73.3 percent) attributed this disposability to changes in, and competition between, models of products such as household goods and cars.[80]

Some observers went further, accusing manufacturers of intentionally encouraging wasteful consumption. Evoked was the idea, popularized by the writer Vance Packard, of planned obsolescence—that producers intentionally made goods obsolete (through strategies like changing style and design) so as to promote repetitive consumption. Planned obsolescence had been discussed to some extent in the 1960s, but it gained traction in these years as a weapon of social critique. In remarks delivered at a "summer school" held by the Tokyo Sanitation Bureau in 1970, the vice chair of the Housewives Association told the seventy-some attendees that they did not have to be drawn into economic currents, that they could value things, make the most of garbage, and refrain from seeking even more convenience and purchasing every conceivable product. Haruno Tsuruko encouraged people to resist the trend toward disposability whipped up by the pursuit of economic gain, and to explain her point, she provided a quote from Packard about how American economic development and lifestyles caused people to waste, about how businesses and the growth of the national economy depended on waste.[81] Planned obsolescence was also criticized even when it was not explicitly named. In a roundtable discussion about the throwaway age which took place in May 1972, the vice president of the Consumer Association of Bunkyō Ward (Bunkyō-ku Shōhisha no Kai) joined a conversation about the poor quality of pantyhose to assert that goods were not just being made badly, but intentionally so.[82] Wakamori Tamae shared her understanding that research was now being done to make television sets that would break down after a certain number of years, putting consumers in a position of having to replace them by buying another, thereby shortening the time between purchases.[83] For people like Wakamori and others, there was much greater consideration given in the early 1970s than in years past to a connection between production, consumption, and waste, a causal link between the marketing practices of manufacturers and the disposing practices of consumers.

As much as the throwaway age and its culture of disposability were judged negatively, some of the practices that critics described as wasteful seemed to be enduring as people continued to make the lifestyle decisions to which they had grown accustomed. When it came to disposable products, large numbers of consumers seemed to be voting with their pocketbooks, spending money on such goods and thus encouraging their development. Products in disposable containers which could be consumed almost instantly continued to appear on the market; coffee in a can was introduced in 1969 and Cup Noodle, instant noodles in a Styrofoam cup, in 1971, to give but two iconic examples.[84]

In an effort to change such wasteful behavior, social organizations from neighborhood associations to consumer groups targeted the abiding values and practices of disposability. Attempting to capitalize on the familiarity with notions of the throwaway age and the culture of disposability, they promoted not just the virtues of waste consciousness but also concrete initiatives to reduce waste in daily life.

One specific issue of concern to such organizations was what they considered the wastefulness of packaging, often referred to as "excessive packaging," such as the polystyrene tray and plastic wrap that encased produce at the supermarket, cartons for eggs, and the boxes in which gifts from department stores were presented. In late 1971, coupled with trash reduction efforts under the umbrella of the Garbage War, social groups stepped up efforts to combat unnecessary or undesirable packing with a No Packaging Movement (Nō Hōsō Undō).[85] This movement involved facilitating and promoting the use of a consumer's own containers for goods, like a colander for eggs or a bowl for tofu; the reuse of egg cartons; the replacement of markets' disposable shopping bags with a wrapping cloth (*furoshiki*) or bag of one's own; and the substitution of paper or cardboard for plastic containers. Such efforts, organized by groups such as consumer associations, daily life schools, and the New Life Movement Association (Shin Seikatsu Undō Kyōkai), took root in various places across the country.[86]

As one example of how active these organizations could be, the Mitaka Association of Consumers (Mitaka-shi Shōhisha no Kai) tried to persuade supermarkets and other businesses to cut down on extraneous and disposable packaging. On November 2, 1971, the association invited about fifty people from the supermarket industry, public health center, incineration plant, and city hall to talk about the possibility of using paper containers instead of plastic ones, allowing housewives to use egg cartons multiple times, and instituting an egg carton buy-back program—all under the theme "Banishing Wasteful Packaging." And the governing council of a large apartment complex in the city educated residents about the garbage produced from packaging as well as the health dangers from incinerator smoke caused by burning vinyl and polyethylene.[87] One housewives' association in Ibaraki prefecture took a novel approach, sending cardboard boxes full of containers, emptied of the products they once held, back to the original manufacturers. The hope was that the surprise of opening a box overflowing with such detritus would induce producers to think more about the end of their goods' lives and reverse the one-way flow of disposable packaging.[88] Various groups also coordinated their No Packaging Movement efforts. Local branches of the Association of Consumers, the New Life Movement Association, Housewives Association, and daily life schools all came together for a meeting that took place on October 27, 1972, on the theme "Let's Do Away with Wasteful Packaging." The second of such gatherings that year, it was timed to anticipate the especially voluminous packaging of the year-end and New Year gift-giving season and brought together not just members of the different groups but also citizens with metropolitan administrators, including the head of the Tokyo Sanitation Bureau.[89] At the national level, the Ministry of Health and Welfare (Kōseishō) stepped in to request self-restraint with packaging from member businesses of the Japan Department Store Association (Nihon Hyakkaten Kyōkai) and other such industry organizations.[90]

These initiatives to curb wasteful packaging met with some notable successes. Various businesses agreed to buy back egg cartons for reuse; some stores allowed consumers to bring their own containers for tofu and eggs; and some fishmongers replaced plastic plates with ones made of paper. Hyōgo prefecture eventually did away with wrapping made of synthetic resins for vegetables, fruits, and fish. Department stores also made efforts toward cooperating with the No Packaging Movement. In the Nihonbashi area of Tokyo, department store customers could choose to have purchased goods marked with a sticker rather than placed in a shopping bag. The Seibu department store decided in October 1971 to prohibit the use of all polystyrene and vinyl packaging, using instead cardboard, cellophane, and thin paper. The Tōkyū department store also made similar moves, as did Marubutsu and Fujii Daimaru in Kyoto. Keio in Shinjuku announced that it would try to reduce polystyrene as much as possible and that it had banned plastic bags, about 200,000 of which it had used each month. And in November 1973, the department store ran newspaper ads asking for customers' understanding with its push to do away with excessive wrapping, given shortages of paper and resources.[91] In addition, the Japan Chain Store Association (Nihon Chēn Sutoa Kyōkai) established a Packaging Improvement Committee, which requested that manufacturers simplify packaging. And specific manufacturers, like the Calpis Company (Karupisu), began experimenting with changing their packaging from plastic to cardboard.[92] These moves were substantial enough to create the impression of a reduction in the use of packaging. Professor Hanayama Yuzuru and Terada Katsuko, the vice chair of the Suginami Association of Consumers, observed in the fall of 1974 that there was less packaging at department stores, and that the gift boxes for canned goods and for relatively inexpensive soaps had become smaller. And they appreciated new practices as well, such as one whereby the sending of wrapped presents like beer or ham from the department store was replaced by giving a ticket that could be redeemed by the receiver at a small shop.[93]

Still, there were limits to these achievements. Manufacturers did not readily embrace changes in packaging, especially in the absence of an alternative that was just as light, durable, protective, and inexpensive as plastic. Producers worried about having to pass on the cost to the consumer of, for example, a paper shopping bag, which was 1 or 2 yen more expensive than its plastic counterpart.[94] Some stores, too, did not want to spend the time and money to remove or replace the packaging in which goods came from wholesalers.[95] There were also the mixed signals sent by consumers themselves. As much as members of various social groups pushed for a reduction in wasteful and environmentally harmful packaging, reports of consumer behavior suggested different preferences. The main branch of the Mitsukoshi department store in Nihonbashi said that it was making efforts to respect the requests of the No Packaging Movement, but that customers were happier when the packing and wrapping were elegant. The manufacturers of Kewpie mayonnaise explained that while they would prefer the glass bottle to the plastic squeeze container because it interfered less with flavor, an overwhelming portion of their sales (95 percent) was of the tube variety because, they speculated, of its convenience, light weight, and lower price. And as much as supermarket customers said they objected to the packaging of everything from tomatoes to salmon on a polystyrene tray with plastic wrap, not just because of the environmental effects but also because it prevented them from examining the quality of the food, at least one article in the *Asahi* newspaper suggested otherwise. When the same goods were displayed with and without such packaging, the packaged goods sold better. Touching on the contradictions between consumers' stated desires and actual behavior, or between some consumers' preferences and those of others, this particular article hinted at why there had been no sea change in people's attitudes toward, or practices regarding, packaging.[96]

In addition to movements against excessive packaging, many groups organized swap meets to raise consciousness about the unused stuff sitting in purgatory in people's homes and to forestall their inevitable condemnation to the rubbish pile. Especially during the Oil Shock, when consumer and women's groups were very active, the two most common initiatives they took up were doing away with unnecessary packaging and organizing swap meets.[97] Typically, swap meets were widely publicized through published notices that invited people to drop off their unwanted items like furniture, clothes, and gifts at a given time and explained what commissions they would receive if their stuff was purchased. Organizations such as the Japan League of Women Voters, the Housewives Association's Consumer Cooperative, affiliates of the New Life Movement Association, regional housewives' associations, youth organizations, PTAs, and women's associations, along with local governments and major newspapers, sponsored these swap meets, which were usually one- or two-day affairs held in large halls.[98] Over the course of the 1970s, groups everywhere from Tokyo to the prefectures of Akita, Gifu, Hyōgo, Miyazaki, and Ehime held such events.[99]

Akin to the swap meet, a way to buy and sell used goods on a more regular basis was established by the Recycling Movement Citizens' Association (Risaikuru Undō Shimin no Kai), a group that was formally established in January 1977 through the efforts of college students in Kobe. In May of that year, the association set up a database to facilitate the circulation of used goods. People with something to sell would call in with a description of the item, how many years it had been used, and the desired price; and people who were looking to buy something would call in and receive information about articles of potential interest and the phone number of the sellers. The purpose of the database, explained the association, was to prevent people from being manipulated into consuming wastefully. They could then pursue a more rational lifestyle and contribute to the saving of resources. To these ends, the association also held garage sales, organized recycling fairs for toys and books, and maintained a used goods information board.[100]

A variation on the swap meet was the exhibition of still usable items pulled from the trash, which were given away by lottery. Such displays were intended to educate people about the number and kind of perfectly good possessions that were being discarded, to encourage them to think about what they were throwing away, and to give objects a second life. As part of an exhibit on consuming lifestyles, Suginami ward presented furniture like dressers and sofas, color television sets, refrigerators, washing machines, and children's toys—all of which had been collected by the sanitation offices of Setagaya, Suginami, and Shinjuku wards. Over 350 housewives came on the first day, with one woman expressing surprise at what was being thrown away even during a recession. An article on the event in the *Yomiuri* newspaper presented her reflections about how much people had grown accustomed to an "age of disposability."[101] Another exhibition, this one in the city of Nagoya, focused on large refuse and gave away to residents resuscitated bicycles, typewriters, vacuum cleaners, clocks, and television sets.[102] At yet another fair, attended by a few thousand housewives, there was a display of about eighty "recycled works," including a chandelier made out of used multicolored soft drink bottles.[103]

In the same vein of promoting reuse, municipalities experimented with setting up public repair centers, typically in government buildings, where residents could bring used items like electric goods and furniture that needed fixing. In the city of Funabashi, in Chiba prefecture, a center was established with the intention of killing two birds with one stone: reducing garbage and fostering a "mood of saving."[104] In the ward of Itabashi, a "repair corner," reportedly the first in the Tokyo area, was set up in the municipal welfare services building and mended everything from umbrellas to shoes to pots. The ward hoped that this would help "rationalize" consuming lifestyles and change the tide of the times from disposability to saving.[105] Such repair corners were not as regular or as popular as swap meets and garbage exhibitions, still remaining relatively uncommon by the middle of the decade. When asked about a variation on the public repair center, a repair area in a department store, a majority of respondents in a survey of 1,291 Tokyo housewives did say that they knew of one, but only about one out of every seven had actually made use of it.[106]

Such repair corners, displays of resurrected garbage, and swap meets were occasionally incorporated into even larger events designed to promote reuse. In December 1977, the national and local branches of the New Life Movement Association and the Asahi Newspaper Company (Asahi Shinbunsha), with support from such organizations as the Prime Minister's Office, MITI, the Tokyo Metropolitan Government, NHK, and TV Asahi (Terebi Asahi), organized a two-day event at the Kōrakuen Stadium exhibition center in Tokyo. Among the different sections were those on recycled products, energy saving, garbage and lifestyles, toy repair, selling used goods, and a garbage display that consisted of about one hundred previously discarded items, including television sets, radios, stereo systems, and stoves.[107]

Many of the social organizations that advanced these strategies for promoting the reuse of goods were well established, often had government ties, and consisted of women who wore multiple hats as consumers, housewives, and local residents. But there did emerge in the early 1970s a new, truly grassroots association that encapsulated many of the concerns of the time about daily lives of consumption and disposability, and engaged seriously with the meanings of a throwaway culture in ways that echoed and crystallized reflections about economic growth and affluence. The Association for Thinking about the Throwaway Age (Tsukaisute Jidai o Kangaeru Kai) began to take shape in the summer of 1973 and was formally inaugurated in September of that year. In a proposal written in July in anticipation of the group's establishment, a couple of dozen concerned citizens articulated their desire to be part of a movement that would examine disposability in their own lives by, for example, reducing as much as possible the amount of household garbage they threw out, holding swap meets, collecting wastepaper, repairing broken electronic goods, sharing books with one another, and donating their children's old clothes.[108] Disposability would be only one concern of many embraced by the association, which included in its official rules a commitment to fight all types of environmental pollution including dirty air, agricultural chemicals, and food additives.[109] The association went on to promote these causes by supplying safe soap powder at reasonable prices as an alternative to synthetic detergents; making available pesticide-free or reduced-pesticide produce including tangerines, apples, cabbage, strawberries, spinach, potatoes, tomatoes, watermelons, sweet potatoes, rice, leeks, and daikon; providing eggs from chickens raised in a natural environment; holding classes to teach people how to make their own miso; and establishing a supply center for safe agricultural products. By the time these activities were well off the ground, in 1975, the association had approximately six hundred members, published a quarterly newsletter, and had expanded from its base in Kyoto to Osaka as well as the prefectures of Shiga, Nagano, and northern Hyōgo.[110] Over the first decade of the association's life, its membership grew to roughly one thousand people.[111]

The throwaway age featured prominently in the association's name because it connected the various concerns of its members and captured its overarching philosophy. To think deeply and deliberately about the issues it took up was itself a central purpose of the intentionally named "association that thinks."[112] Its main concerns developed organically out of members' various interests, but the group's core principles have perhaps been articulated most cogently by Tsuchida Takashi, a founder who continues to be active in the association at this writing. Tsuchida had been an engineering professor at the prestigious Kyoto University when he began to doubt the value of training the next generation of engineers for Japanese industry, to feel distant from daily life, and to realize that he did not know what it meant to be a farmer, to work in the fields. Through the Waseda University professor Niijima Atsuyoshi, Tsuchida became involved in the commune movement and came to know people who belonged to the Yamagishikai (Yamagishi Association), a group of intentional agrarian communities that was headquartered in Mie prefecture. The Yamagishikai would be a source for many of the original members of the Association for Thinking about the Throwaway Age.[113] Tsuchida eventually gave up his professorship in 1979 because he felt as though he was "throwing himself away."[114] As this turn of phrase suggests, the association then, and Tsuchida over the years, have conceived of disposability in a multifaceted way. There was the disposal of things—the disregard for objects, the discarding of still usable items, and the increase in garbage. There was also the disposal of people—an indifference thought to be perpetuated by the habit in throwaway societies of determining what to keep and what to throw out on the basis of whether something (or someone) was useful or not. The association worried that the harm done to people's hearts through disposability had created a society that neglected children with disabilities and those who did not do well in school, and that shortchanged social welfare for the elderly. And Tsuchida included among the discarded anyone who was in a societally precarious position or who experienced prejudice and discrimination.[115] There was also a third kind of disposability, although in a conversation we had over forty years after the association's founding, Tsuchida had to reach deeper into the recesses of his memory to identify it. At first, he thought it was the disposal of the future—that wars and the plundering of natural resources for the sake of wealth threw away the promise of what was to come. Upon further reflection, he clarified that it was the disposal of the earth, though the worries about environmental harm and foreclosed opportunities were essentially the same as his conception of the disposal of the future.[116]

The Association for Thinking about the Throwaway Age stated in no uncertain terms that mass production and mass consumption fueled high economic growth and affluent lifestyles that encouraged disposability in all of its harmful incarnations. The pursuit of the new and the desire for ever greater convenience and ever greater wealth were to blame for the throwaway age. On handbills distributed in the summer of 1973, and on Tsuchida's own business card in 2015, were printed the phrase "For convenience, disposability even throws away the future." Problematic, too, said Tsuchida, was the attitude of "only money, only now, only oneself" which had become so prevalent.[117] In an expression of the ways in which disposability was central to its broader agenda, the nascent association in 1973 penned this poem:

> For convenience, disposability even throws away the heart;
> if affluent, the future is severed for the extravagant heart;
> convenient, affluent disposability consumes the future.[118]

Reflecting on the establishment of the association some thirty years later, an early member of the group described succinctly its constellation of values as having cast a stone against an era of "mass production, mass consumption, and mass waste."[119]

The Association for Thinking about the Throwaway Age was arguably a somewhat more progressive and deliberate incarnation of the many and various social groups that also promoted reuse, environmental awareness, and societal reflection in the 1970s. In aggregate, these organizations of concerned citizens made it much less tenable to talk or think about consumption uncoupled from disposability, to focus on the act of buying without considering the act of discarding. The idea of the "throwaway age" became a way for people to criticize practices of selling, purchasing, and disposing that had become second nature in the years of high growth. And it was in response to the perceived "culture of disposability" that they developed ways, some more effective, widespread, and enduring than others, to reduce and mitigate the creation of waste.

Resource Matters

When residents of Tokyo were asked their opinions on garbage in 1974, a full 93 percent of the 973 survey respondents agreed to at least some degree with the statement that "there must be reflection about a consumer culture in which things that could still be used are thrown away as garbage." And almost as many, 88.8 percent, answered similarly to the proposition that "the reuse of garbage must be advanced for the sake of conserving resources."[120] Reflected in both these questions and the responses was the assumption that the challenges of disposability and the shortage of resources were two sides of the same coin—that the thoughtless discarding of things wasted resources, that potential resources were sitting in the trash heap, and that the ways in which both goods and resources were treated had been shaped by the mass production and mass consumption of the high-growth years.

According to the prevailing diagnosis, the same societal developments that had given rise to the culture of disposability were to blame for the problem of resources. As the narrative went, high economic growth and mass consumption were perpetuated by the depletion of resources, and created a culture of disposability which wasted resources in the form of expelled rubbish. Or put a slightly different way, high economic growth created desires to consume that could be satisfied only through the wasteful depletion of resources, which accelerated the accumulation of garbage.[121] In a post–Oil Shock era of limited resources and energy, argued a *Yomiuri* newspaper editorial, it was simply not conceivable that double-digit economic growth could be maintained, nor should Japan ever have pursued the lifestyles of the large and wealthy United States. New ways of life had to be created that were based on values such as stability, deceleration, durability, and quality rather than convenience, efficiency, speed, things, money, and quantity.[122] Echoing this sentiment, others also thought that the values of convenience, comfort, and luxury fostered by mass consumption and the culture of disposability had to be reconsidered.[123]

This take on the country's contemporary situation and recent past was one that was articulated in some form by various municipal administrators, sanitation professionals, social groups, academics, and business leaders. In a book published by the Junior Chamber International Japan (Nihon Seinen Kaigisho), an international nonprofit organization of relatively young citizens oriented toward business and social change, a Chiba University professor observed that the planned obsolescence of goods and the luxurious tendency to throw them away had resulted in a lack of valuing things, which led to mountains of garbage and the waste of resources. He explained that real saving, unlike that of hollow slogans, meant picking up and fully using goods (like the disposable soap at hotels or disposable razors left at public baths) so as to save resources.[124] In the version articulated by Matsushita Kōnosuke, founder of Matsushita Electric Industrial (Matsushita Denki Sangyō, later Panasonic), the economy of high growth, or the economy of disposability, was no longer permissible. Before a meeting of producers organized by the Kansai Productivity Center (Kansai Seisansei Honbu), Matsushita argued that in present times, things had to be disposed of properly, money could not be used meaninglessly, and resources could not be wasted; both people and industry could no longer be wasteful.[125]

In the agendas of social organizations, issues having to do with disposability and resources became intertwined. When the National Federation of Regional Women's Associations (Zenkoku Chiiki Fujin Dantai Renraku Kyōgikai, or Chifuren), with roughly 6 million members, held a training session for its leadership in March 1973, it spoke of expanding their movement to reexamine the waste in daily lives. What this meant was thinking about the consumption around them, advocating for the development of products that last a long time, and using limited resources effectively.[126] For the Kansai Housewives Association (Kansai Shufuren), a nonpartisan group that was less tied to conservative and pro-business political forces, the Oil Shock was instrumental in melding together its formerly discrete movements for saving, effective utilization of garbage, and rational use of resources.[127] The Oil Shock also had an impact on the New Life Movement Association, which explicitly described it as a direct trigger for the organization's Movement to Value Resources. The era of high economic growth had ended, laid bare the shortage of resources, and ushered in an era of "saving resources." And so the association would promote recycling, which it defined as "the reuse of resources."[128]

Under the banner of shifting from a lifestyle of mass consumption to one of resource preservation, garbage was viewed in multiple ways—as a wasted potential resource, a symbol of an era of disposability that was frittering away resources, and a product of the mass consumption of resources and energy.[129] Certain items like wastepaper, empty glass bottles, and scrap metal became the target of rescue efforts, so that their residual utility would not be lost to the trash heap.

The realization that resources were being thrown away as garbage, that they still had value if separated out from the truly useless rubbish, propelled the recycling movements of this decade. Initially, social groups took it upon themselves to establish recycling practices. In the city of Ōgaki in Gifu prefecture, for example, the local women's association negotiated with city hall and a bottle maker to establish a system whereby households dropped off their glass bottles and other glass waste at one of many collection stations, from which they would be picked up and melted for reuse.[130] And in the Bunkyō ward of Tokyo, a group of about seventy housewives had kept their modest recycling system going for years. Twice a month, households were invited to bring their newspapers, magazines, cardboard, cans, and such to a designated location, from which a private waste collection firm would pick up the recyclables. The money earned from the transaction was donated to the local elementary school and senior citizens' center.[131] This was a common arrangement for the private management of recycling, with neighborhood or women's associations determining set days and places for pickup of wastepaper, scrap metal, and glass by a collection company. This practice started to become more structured in Tokyo in 1973, with the goodwill if not formal administrative support of the government, and was fairly well established by 1974. Reports vary, but in that year, anywhere between 711 and 1,007 groups and some 380,000 households in Tokyo were participating in these recycling efforts, which typically had slogans such as "Reduce Garbage" and "Let's Reexamine the Waste of Daily Life." On average, these recycling initiatives were together raising roughly 10 million yen a month.[132] In this early stage of recycling, there were still various challenges. Plastics were technologically difficult to recycle.[133] And the reliance on private collection and the needs of manufacturers were also liabilities as collection firms suffered from an aging of their workforce and insufficient labor power, and manufacturers increasingly purchased resources from abroad.[134]

Municipalities themselves began to establish in the 1970s what was called "separate collection" (bunbetsu shūshū), or the collection of garbage by category. The most rudimentary form of separate collection delineated two types of waste: combustible and noncombustible. Tokyo rushed to institute this system in 1973, which helped remove from the main waste stream those materials, like plastic and rubber, that could not be incinerated.[135] The more advanced form of separate collection incorporated recyclables, expanding the types of waste beyond just two. The model held up at the time, and mentioned still today, was the system established in the city of Numazu in Shizuoka prefecture, dubbed the "Numazu method." Its rationale and oft-repeated message was "If you separate waste it is a resource, if you mix it together it is garbage." This was an attractive notion in the early 1970s, when city administrators were embroiled in their own garbage war, faced with opposition to the continued use of an overflowing landfill and resistance to the construction of a new incinerator. When sanitation professionals took a closer look at the contents of Numazu's garbage, they realized that about 60 percent of it consisted of things, like bottles and cans, that were still of value. If those items were kept out of the waste stream, they could be reused, and the overall volume of waste sent to landfills would be reduced. After discussions about whether the city or its citizens should be responsible for separating the garbage, residents were convinced that they should take on the task in order to do their part in a resource-poor Japan, though the more practical reality was that the costs in labor and time were too high for sanitation workers to do the sorting. In December 1974, 120 out of 248 areas in the city were designated "models" for testing the system. And in April 1975, all of Numazu city began separate collection, by which waste was divided into three categories: combustible, noncombustible, and recyclables or "resource garbage."[136]

Over the ensuing years, the system of garbage collection by type spread to various municipalities across the country. In June 1976, for example, the city of Hiroshima began to separate its garbage into five categories: combustible, noncombustible, large refuse, hazardous waste, and "resource garbage." In these early years of separate collection, there were still kinks to be ironed out. With the pickup of certain kinds of waste not scheduled frequently enough, residents of small urban apartments found themselves short on space to keep various categories of garbage. Apartment buildings, which housed about a third of Tokyo's population in the early 1970s, struggled most with separate collection, especially if they did not have designated areas for the different kinds of garbage and a custodian responsible for separating them.[137] Nonetheless, incremental changes in how people dealt with their trash was seen as evidence that residents' consciousness of garbage disposal was increasing and that a daily war against garbage had become commonplace across the country.[138]

Much more modest and discrete recycling efforts also grabbed attention in the wake of the Oil Shock. A local consumer group in Sapporo was specifically interested in the waste of disposable chopsticks and launched a movement against their use. Propelling this movement was Ōkawara Shizue, a housewife who was appalled to learn that the amount of wood it took to make a year's worth of disposable chopsticks could instead be used to build twelve thousand two-bedroom residences. She began to carry her own personal chopsticks with her wherever she went. When she had first tried, in the late 1960s, to persuade friends to join her, they had laughed. But with increases in the price of wood, her consumer group of 140 to 160 or so housewives took up the charge in the early 1970s. They agreed not to use disposable chopsticks in their homes; guests would receive an explanation of the movement and be given for their use chopsticks designated for company.[139] In March 1974, responding to what they saw as the government's omission of disposable chopsticks from its list of resources to save and use effectively, the group's members took it upon themselves to begin collecting discarded chopsticks from the cafeterias of Hokkaido Electric (Hokkaidō Denryoku), the department store Kana'ichikan, and the Sapporo central police station. And they struck a deal with a building materials manufacturer that agreed to send a truck around to a handful of members' houses to pick up the chopsticks, which it would turn into high-density fiberboard. Repurposing used chopsticks seemed preferable to the alternatives, since employees in those offices thought that it would be unhygienic to bring their own chopsticks to work or to use bamboo or lacquered chopsticks provided by the cafeteria. The arrangement was not a profitable one for the building materials manufacturer, given the costs of transportation and liquefaction of the chopsticks. But, said a company representative, it wanted to "cooperate with a heart that values things." For her part, Ōkawara did not think her movement was a waste simply because the numbers did not add up. What would be a true waste was throwing away resources that could be reused. Imagine, she said, if the 10 billion pairs of disposable chopsticks manufactured each year could all be collected, they would make 40 million sheets of high-density fiberboard.[140]

While Ōkawara's dream was not fully realized, other disposal practices did gain traction, in part because of concerted and sustained efforts to bring attention to waste, recycling, and the reuse of resources. There were "recycling campaigns," such as the one organized by the *Asahi* newspaper and the New Life Movement Association with support from such public agencies as the Prime Minister's Office, MITI, and NHK. To publicize their cause, they sponsored an essay-writing contest, complete with monetary incentives, in 1974. Submissions were to address set themes, all of which had to do with strategies or proposals for recycling. And the seven prizewinning entries were published the following year in a book titled *Mono no seimei futatabi* (The Second Lives of Things). One of the essays, written by Imai Misako, a twenty-eight-year-old director of an atelier, described a lifestyle in which very little was purchased and very little was thrown away. She remade her children's clothes from hand-me-downs that had been given to her, and used for their toys odds and ends like the wooden board on which steamed fish paste (*kamaboko*) was packaged. The reason for her near abstention from consumption, explained Imai, was her desire to live a spiritually luxurious life. Another prizewinner, a twenty-nine-year-old housewife named Nakamura Mitsue, expounded on how the intentional wastefulness of manufacturers was characteristic of high growth. Without using the phrase "planned obsolescence," Nakamura described how objects like clocks, electric goods, cars, and kitchen items not only broke easily but also were difficult to repair, because parts were hard to come by for what quickly became outdated models. And shops that repaired goods like women's stockings were no more. That it was not much more expensive to buy a replacement anew than to fix what one already owned was a deliberate calculation by manufacturers, suggested Nakamura. The proliferation of disposable goods, too, should now be considered a frightening miscalculation, given the recent revelation about limited resources. True affluence, Nakamura opined, required a perspective that was less centered on people and assumed the point of view of the earth.[141] For Nakamura, as for all of the people who invested time, energy, and thought in writing and submitting an essay, the contest fulfilled its purpose of encouraging awareness about waste and recycling. And it may have, too, for those who read the winning submissions.

Similar to this essay contest was one sponsored by the *Yomiuri* newspaper as part of its nationwide Campaign to Value Resources. The submissions were to be about specific examples of waste in daily life and proposals for eliminating it, written by mothers along with their children of older elementary to middle school age. The winners, fifty pairs of mothers and children, were to be appointed "monitors" who would not only visit or "inspect" an incinerator and a landfill but also tour or "patrol" a ward looking for waste.[142] The essay contest seems to have had its intended effect on the prizewinners, who were shocked by the number of still usable items they saw among the voluminous garbage at the (third) Island of Dreams landfill and were surprised to see in Shinjuku the distribution of fliers that were not being read. A fifth-grader made the astute, and hoped-for, observation that adults, whose favorite phrase had changed suddenly from "consumption is a virtue" to "value things," were in actuality continuing to throw out usable things as garbage. Through the contest and its concomitant education efforts, the monitors became dedicated advocates of waste consciousness and fonts of information about the garbage problem, armed with specific strategies for eliminating waste and conserving resources in the school and in the home.[143]

In the campaigns and initiatives to reduce waste and save resources, the definition of a resource was relatively broad. Materials for production such as metal, wood, and glass were included in the category. So too were necessities of modern daily life that were, or could potentially be, in short supply. Food, for example, fit neatly into concerns about limited resources and reliance on imports. According to a book about "valuing food" which was published by the Better Home Association (Betā Hōmu Kyōkai) in 1976, food resources could very well become scarce in a world of increasing population. And Japan was considered to be in an especially precarious position, largely because of its low rate of food self-sufficiency.[144] When the Better Home Association spoke of food, it was not just referring to raw agricultural commodities like rice, wheat, and grain. There were certainly concerns about these goods; specialists noted that the country's grain self-sufficiency rate had dropped from about 83 percent in 1950 to roughly 37 percent by the 1970s. And an increase in the amount of oil it took to produce domestic rice exacerbated worries about this trend.[145] For non-experts, like the readers of the Better Home Association's book, it was not just such commodities but any and all foods that were to be valued and used completely. This encouragement was not like the advice for surviving the harshest years after the war, when food was scarce, but was instead an acknowledgment of possible limits to food resources and a strategy for preventing a future as desperate as the 1940s had been. Food was thus not to be casually discarded as it allegedly had been for the past twenty years, in an era when people bought lots of things. The association went so far as to say that there was "no wastefulness as great" as discarding food.[146]

Energy was another kind of resource that was to be valued and not wastefully consumed because of the insecurity of its supply, particularly in the wake of the Oil Shock. Indeed, "saving resources" and "saving energy" were often mentioned in the same breath as *shōshigen, shōenerugī*. At the government level, in September 1974 the cabinet established the Campaign to Value Resources and Energy Headquarters (Shigen to Enerugī o Taisetsu ni Suru Undō Honbu) to plan and oversee saving campaigns in companies and to promote saving in consumption among citizens.[147] For the national government as for others, energy was part of the narrative about the wastefulness and disposability of the high-growth years. To conserve resources and energy, lifestyles of mass consumption and disposability had to change into those of rational consumption and the efficient use of things. This was the argument of an interim report published by the Committee on Resource Conserving-Lifestyles (Shōshigen Seikatsu Iinkai), formed under the auspices of the Economic Planning Agency (Keizai Kikakuchō), which was chaired by a director from the Mitsubishi Research Institute (Mitsubishi Sōgō Kenkyūjo) and included among its members academics and journalists as well as representatives of housewives' and consumer organizations, the main business federation, agriculture, and various other industries. In the committee's diagnosis, the mass consumption of resources and energy was inextricably linked to the increase in garbage and environmental degradation, such that the continued expansion of material consumption and the continued trend toward disposability would only hasten the waste of resources and energy and the deterioration of the environment.[148] This promotion of limited consumption may have seemed surprising to those who associated the Economic Planning Agency and many of the committee members from business and industry with an earlier encouragement of mass consumption. And it is hard to glean motives or interests, be they profit, civic duty, or social responsibility, from a multifaceted report ostensibly about economic growth, environmental conservation, quality of life, and spiritual affluence. But broadly speaking, the members did seem to converge around the conviction that existing patterns of consumption and disposability had undesirable costs of various kinds that necessitated reexamination.

When it came to practices in daily life, there was a much more defined and finite conception of how to not waste energy as compared to things or resources. This was likely because energy was distinct from other resources in various ways. For one, its use and the impact of waste reduction measures could be more easily quantified, which made determinations about appropriate and excessive levels of consumption seem less arbitrary and subjective. These lines were more difficult to draw when it came to questions about how much gift packaging was too much, which disposable products were acceptable and which were not, and what kinds and amount of garbage production were tolerable. With energy, governments could and did make specific recommendations during the Oil Shock to mitigate its waste. The target of a 10 percent reduction in energy use was set, and the government requested in November 1973 that stores turn off their neon and display window lights at closing, lower the heat to no more than 20 degrees Celsius (68 degrees Fahrenheit), curtail the use of elevators and escalators, dim inside lights, and push back opening time by thirty minutes on all days except Sundays and holidays. Many of the stores that belonged to the Japan Department Store Association agreed to open later, and some of them decided to take many or all of the measures requested. All of the seventy-five companies, with nearly three thousand stores, that were part of the Japan Chain Store Association also agreed to comply.[149] In addition to these measures aimed at stores, the government also advised shortened hours for gas stations and self-restraint when it came to driving personal cars.[150] Offices and factories took similar steps to meet the 10 percent target, turning off lights during lunch breaks and dimming them during working hours. At Hitachi, for example, desks were lined up along the windows to take advantage of sunlight. And at Tōshiba (Tokyo Shibaura Electric, or Tokyo Shibaura Denki), a poster reminded employees, "Use natural light, don't waste lighting."[151] Government offices also took such measures as in Nagasaki, where city hall reduced the temperature, stopped running one of its elevators after 3:00 pm, and discouraged its workers from commuting by car.[152] General pleas to save energy and resources, be they electricity, gas, water, or paper, were also made by the Federation of Electric Power Companies (Denki Jigyō Rengōkai), Tokyo Gas (Tokyo Gasu), and Fuji Bank (Fuji Ginkō).[153]

Many of the efforts to reduce the waste of energy on the margins acknowledged that electricity in particular, more so than packaging or disposable products, had become central to people's sense of their standard of living. There were few categories of consumption in which serious reduction or even abstention could be realistically recommended. People could not be expected to go without their washing machine, lighting, or heating and cooling. Measures for saving energy thus specified how to moderate consumption. The Tokyo Electric Power Company (Tokyo Denryoku, or TEPCO) publicized information about specific ways to use the television set, electric *kotatsu* heater, refrigerator, and even the household car to save energy.[154] And the Toyota Motor Company (Toyota Jidōsha) ran ads about how to drive so as to conserve gasoline and eliminate the "three *mu*" of *muda* (waste), *muri* (unreasonableness), and *mura* (inconsistency). Advertisements also appeared for new designs of products that were touted as minimizing waste, such as a microwave oven from Sharp with a turntable to cut down on the three *mu* and the two-door top-freezer refrigerators from National and Tōshiba that saved electricity.[155] Concrete steps to reduce electricity consumption reportedly taken by housewives in Shikoku, Kyūshū, and the Kinki and Chūgoku regions included watching less television, lowering the heat, shortening the time that lights were on, changing to energy-saving lighting, reducing the frequency of baths, and curtailing use of the family car.[156] Trying to curb the time spent watching television was an approach taken by Fukushima prefecture, which organized a "no television campaign" whereby there was to be no television watching for one day a week. The effort, which was kicked off in December 1973 and eventually spread to 4,200 participating households, was intended not just to save electricity but also to nurture humane and affluent hearts and create a (figuratively) bright home life.[157]

The relative modesty of these initiatives implicitly recognized the challenge of persuading people to save energy, a presumption that seems to have been supported by a gap between people's ideals and their actual behavior. In a survey of 610 housewives conducted in the summer of 1974, an overwhelming percentage (90.5) said they felt the necessity of saving energy. But a substantially smaller percentage (69.2) reported that they actually practiced energy saving.[158] The move by manufacturers toward the development of energy-saving versions of products such as televisions, refrigerators, vacuum cleaners, and washing machines was thus strategic, for these products appealed to consumers who wanted to see themselves as energy conscious but did not want to make substantial changes to their daily lives.[159]

Energy was also distinct in that its wasteful use did not raise the same larger issues as the wasteful use of products and resources. After all, the main focus of household energy-saving efforts—electricity—was not material. It had a physical incarnation in the home only when mediated through an object like a lightbulb or a television set. So it did not touch on questions about how housewives should purchase and dispose of stuff, about people's relationship to material things, or about mass consumption, a culture of disposability, and reuse. This may explain why many more survey respondents blamed the energy crisis on the government than on large companies or individual consumers. Nonetheless, as the insecurity of energy resources resonated with the various anxieties of the early 1970s, calls to save electricity were folded into the broader sense at the time that waste consciousness might help secure a more stable, healthy, and desirable future.

In the Wake of High Growth

In 1971, the latest installment in the monster movie franchise—*Gojira tai hedora*, or *Godzilla vs. the Smog Monster*—was released for viewing by Japanese filmgoers. The opening shot was of the iconic Mount Fuji, framed by smokestacks spewing out grayish exhaust. As the title track "Return the Sun!" ("Kaese! Taiyō o") was sung, viewers heard lyrics about a polluted and potentially barren earth as the camera panned over seawater covered by a film of sludge, dead fish, and a stray discarded empty can. Scattered on the bay floor was a glass bottle here, an unwanted television set there, and on its surface, sewage and garbage—rubber tires, cardboard cartons, metal tins, and plastic bottles. The smog monster of the film's title, it was discovered, fed on society's detritus to become an ever-growing, vaguely octopus-shaped creature that oozed toxic slime. Protagonist Godzilla became an environmental crusader, so upset by the polluted water that he attempted to set it afire and burn the waste, with little effect. Ultimately, Godzilla stepped in during an electricity shortage to provide with his nuclear breath the vast amount of energy needed to power two large electrodes, which eventually incinerated the smog monster, turning him into ash. But the waste in the seas remained. This film, anomalous in the series for its unabashed dystopianism and psychedelic scenes, vividly illustrated the anxieties of its historical moment. And while it did not offer much social commentary beyond the obvious message of environmental preservation, it did quietly nod toward broader issues of the time through a question posed by one of its characters: "Who gave birth to the smog monster?"[160]

The resounding response to that question in the early 1970s was that waste and wasting were the result of the high-growth era then past and the enduring society of mass consumption and culture of disposability it had enabled and promoted. Garbage was no longer considered an inconvenient by-product of economic success, but a problem that required a rethinking of priorities and values. As depleting resources, purchasing, and discarding came to be seen as inextricably linked, waste assumed a place alongside production and consumption as a defining characteristic of modern postwar life.[161] It was often and widely

commented in mainstream outlets that a society characterized by mass production and mass consumption was almost inevitably one of mass waste—that the
creation of waste was inherent in producing and consuming at the pace and on
the scale to which postwar Japanese had become accustomed, and that wasting
was virtually inescapable in the ways of life they had come to expect.

With the Garbage War and the Oil Shock, waste became a site of critical reflection about the changes wrought by high economic growth. Unlike in the 1960s,
when social critiques around waste had been relatively tepid, the jolts of the early
1970s inspired pointed and probing conversations about the costs and consequences of high economic growth, the relationship between people and things,
the valuing of convenience and comfort fostered by mass consumption, and the
goals that should be pursued in the future. Put succinctly by the Industrial Planning Council (Sangyō Keikaku Kondankai) in its 1973 book about changes in citizens' views regarding the economy and society: the economy that had sung the
praises of consumption and disposability created garbage and wasted resources.
Economic growth was good, but not sufficient; it could no longer be assumed
that a rising GNP would deliver all that people needed and desired.[162]

The challenges embodied and posed by waste were to be mitigated by waste
consciousness, at least in the view of various social groups, media outlets, municipal governments, and national government agencies. Faced with the garbage
problem and the shortage of resources, waste consciousness lost some of its flexible and mutable quality from the transitional years of the 1960s and became
fairly well defined. People were to become more aware of what they were throwing out, resuscitate forgotten or forlorn possessions so as to reuse them, separate
resources from the waste stream so that they could be recycled, and curtail the
unnecessary consumption of energy. Slogans and campaigns as well as structures and systems were developed in an attempt to reduce waste. These ideas
and practices which emerged in the pivotal years of the early 1970s provided the
rhetorical, conceptual, and behavioral vocabulary that would inform discussions
of waste in the decades to come.

As much as the waste consciousness that was envisioned and encouraged challenged what was seen to be the wastefulness of mass consumption and a culture
of disposability, it did not overturn or subvert them in fundamental ways. It did
not even gesture toward, much less call for, a return to the kind of austerity that
had characterized wartime and immediate postwar hardship. Rather, the moderation and restraint encouraged in this decade were presented as a way to avoid
the desperation of those years when the country was starved of resources, and to
preserve all of the gains that had since been made. Over the course of the 1970s,
there appeared a tension between profound skepticism about the promises of
economic growth and the enduring allure of the ways of life that it afforded.

4

A BRIGHT STINGINESS

In January 1974, a roundtable discussion about stinginess—*kechi*—appeared in the pages of the popular women's magazine *Fujin kurabu* (Women's Club). The five participants were all women from Osaka in their thirties or forties who shared their strategies for managing waste in the home. They spoke about how to shop skillfully, make things oneself, save energy, control expenses, and extend the life of goods. Listening to the women's ideas was Suzuki Kenji, a television announcer for the public broadcaster NHK and the moderator of the discussion. Suzuki observed that the women's stinginess was not that of difficult times past, not a "miserable *kechi*," but a contemporary incarnation that he dubbed a "new spirit of *kechi*," a "bright *kechi*."[1] With a clever rhetorical twist, he appropriated the language of the "bright life"—the term of the 1950s and 1960s that had captured and promoted a middle-class standard of living with a modern home, a nuclear family with a housewife, and the ownership of electric goods—and superimposed it upon the idea of *kechi*. This stinginess was a pleasant, even cheery way to preserve middle-class aspirations and achievements.

The phrase "bright *kechi*" was an especially pithy expression of the remaking of stinginess amidst the uncertainties and hopes of the 1970s. There were aspects of this *kechi* that were new, as Suzuki suggested. The word had conventionally connoted the miserliness and cheapness of frugality taken too far, but came to be conceived in largely positive terms as a desirable consciousness of waste at a time when there was heightened attention to wastefulness of various kinds. Efforts to identify and reduce waste were commonly called "stinginess movements" (*kechikechi undō*). And in the wake of the Garbage War and Oil Shock, the waste of greatest concern was of things, resources, and energy. Folded into the stinginess movements, too, was an attention to reuse, recycling, and resource conservation characteristic of the 1970s.

Along with these newer dimensions of waste consciousness, there were also continuities in the bright *kechi*. Some of the specific strategies recommended for waste reduction in the home and in the workplace, be it about making the most of food or cutting expenses, were similar to those that had been advocated in advice literature since the early decades of the twentieth century. Certain logics of efficiency, rationalization, and profit maximization still very much applied to what still were modern, industrialized daily lives. The gendered ideals of a skilled housewife and a cost-conscious business manager also persisted, perpetuated by how-to publications, commentators, and various fonts of advice about home and work.

The bright *kechi* also revealed the extent to which the desires and values shaped by growing material and economic prosperity lived steadfastly on in the 1970s. Even the hallmarks of the new stinginess—that it should not mean going without, that it should not cause hardship—demonstrated how much people wanted to maintain the relatively high standards of living that many had attained. Suzuki's very language of brightness was a connection, in terms not just of rhetoric but also of expectations, to the late 1950s and 1960s. A *kechi* that was not to sacrifice comfort was distinctly different from the wartime and immediate postwar frugality born of the exigencies of survival in a difficult present, embodying instead aspirations of and for middle-class lifestyles that were to be secured and extended well into the future.

There were thus visible and meaningful shifts as well as an undercurrent of continuity when it came to waste and waste consciousness in the 1970s. On the one hand, the jolts early in the decade helped inspire the realization that there were limits and negative consequences to rapid economic growth, crystallized unease about preoccupation with financial and material success, and provoked challenges to values and practices that came to be seen as wasteful. Assumptions about high growth and the emphasis placed on mass consumption were reconsidered. And practices of reuse, recycling, and the saving of resources and energy were actively promoted, as was examined in the previous chapter.

On the other hand, the approaches and responses to the promotion of waste consciousness and reduction show how firmly rooted the desires of people in a wealthy and consumerist country had become. There was the bright *kechi* of moderation rather than abstention, of the preservation of middle-class lifestyles rather than subsistence. There was the encouragement of reducing waste without sacrificing standards of living. There was the continued emphasis on efficiency and productivity in the workplace for the sake of profit. And there were hints about a gap between ideals of waste consciousness and people's actual behavior, which suggested that the corner had not been turned on the so-called culture of disposability or the embrace of consumption. Many of the core assumptions and priorities that took shape as the postwar economy grew, individual incomes rose, and lifestyles changed stood firm as the country continued to be a modern, affluent, and mass-consuming society. The centrality of consumption to daily life, corporate focus on the maximization of profit, influence of marketing and advertising, and longing for convenience and comfort persisted. The ideal of waste consciousness was not a plea for, and did not result in, the reversal or rollback of these fundamental elements of recent decades. The calls to rein in excess, to appreciate what had been attained, and to preserve middle-class lifestyles revealed the depth and tenacity of the values and desires forged in the making of a wealthy Japan.

Enjoying Waste Consciousness

In the spring of 1974, the chair of the National Federation of Regional Women's Organizations (Zenkoku Chiiki Fujin Dantai Renraku Kyōgikai, or Chifuren) explained that the stinginess movements then under way were intended to safeguard standards of living against skyrocketing prices and material shortages. Or to use the language of the *Yomiuri* newspaper, they were a "line of defense" around people's lifestyles.[2] This stinginess, it was made clear, was fundamentally different from the wartime ideal of "desiring nothing until victory."[3] In this version of stinginess updated for the 1970s, luxury was not the enemy; quite to the contrary, the relative luxuries of middle-class life were to be secured. Rather than abstain from want, people were to moderate their appetites. Rather than refrain from all consumption, people were to consume intelligently. This insistence on securing the economic and material gains of recent years was a central thread in stinginess movements, which also attempted to paint frugality and waste consciousness as pleasurable and fun. Many of the ideas and strategies promoted were not particularly new, save for the greater attention to resources and energy. But they were reframed and rearticulated in various ways that stressed brightness and suffused advice with a positive hue.

As part of the refashioned *kechi*, the language of appreciating and valuing things affirmed the enjoyment to be found in one's relationship with material objects. Rather than emphasize abstention or restraint, the aims of reducing garbage and challenging a culture of disposability were to be sought through an appeal to feelings of affection and thankfulness. Such an approach to things would also enable and ensure a bright lifestyle, the argument often went.[4] One group that espoused this view was the Better Home Association (Betā Hōmu Kyōkai), which in September 1973 launched a nationwide campaign to value things. The organization, established a decade earlier primarily for the education of housewives, promoted this ideal through the publication of instructional books and a series of lectures around the country. Explained the head of the association's research office, "This is not a simple stinginess movement (*kechikechi undō*), but a movement to foster a heart that values the life of things." To help kick off its campaign, the association published *Mono o taisetsu ni suru dokuhon* (A Guidebook for Valuing Things). Dubbed a "stinginess guidebook" by the *Yomiuri* newspaper, the book compiled suggestions from its two thousand members about how to not waste when it came to garbage, clothes, paper, gas, electricity, and more.[5] Categories of things to be respected included food, which if used fully could make one's life more healthful and pleasurable.[6] In a less literal sense, objects of all kinds were seen as both making possible and enriching human life so that the thoughtless discarding of that which was just a little damaged or old both depleted resources and eroded the heart. If people had a heart that understood all things have a life to be nurtured and extended, then humanity would become truly affluent. In another instructional book, this one about how to repair various things from umbrellas to toilets and books to chairs, the Better Home Association seemed to be looking toward the past, even harking back to ancient times, when people allegedly did not have wasteful hearts and cared for things, and so did not destroy them without a sense of regret.[7] Yet the organization's movement was utterly of its moment. It was not encouraging the kind of rejection of things characteristic of the wartime years, and certainly was not advocating a return to the lifestyles of the ancient past. Rather, it was reinterpreting the past to construct lessons for the present. The idea of valuing things presumed consumption, suggesting an appreciation for all of the stuff that people were able to purchase and possess. To value things was to feel an immaterial sense of gratitude for the ownership of material goods.

A housewife who practiced and promoted waste consciousness with skill and deftness could also make stinginess bright. The ideal of a knowledgeable woman as the professional manager of a rationalized household reached back to before the war. In its 1970s version, the idea of a housewife in a middle-class home who was educated and dedicated enough to minimize waste and wastefulness was itself something positive and affirming that would, by extension, make waste consciousness bright. So closely associated was the woman with the management of waste in the home and with the moral value of not wasting that the discussion moderator Suzuki Kenji asked, "Couldn't it be said that women who are not *kechi* are not women?"[8] As embodiments of *kechi*, the middle-class housewives of this time were to teach their children how to value things in their everyday lives, and to master particular skills and bodies of knowledge.

Just as the middle-class housewife was cast in sunny tones if not redefined, familiar techniques for reviving, repurposing, and reusing things were presented as enjoyable. And it was implied that pleasure could be found in cultivating one's abilities of waste minimization. In a book titled *Kechi seikatsu no chie* (Advice for a Stingy Lifestyle), the reader could learn how to make toys out of paper cups, an insect cage out of an empty can, and a curtain out of twine.[9] Another book recommended stuffing the packing materials that came with an assortment of cakes or canned goods into cushions; indexing the household account book with parts of the remaining frame from a sheet of stamps; and cleaning bicycles and the fine crevices of tableware with a worn toothbrush.[10] Old clothes could be remade to fit children, and torn pantyhose could be separated at the crotch to somehow salvage the undamaged leg.[11] Tips were also given about how to extend the life of things, offered as "ideas for skillful stinginess" in the popular magazine *Fujin seikatsu* (Women's Life). A forty-six-year-old woman from Tokyo shared her strategy for making use of plain yogurt. By adding milk past its expiration date to it, she explained, one could make new plain yogurt. Another contributor, a thirty-five-year-old woman from Aichi prefecture, advised that small remnants of bar soap could be cut up finely, placed in a jar, and mixed with hot water to create a good liquid soap convenient for washing things like underwear. She added that pouring in soda water would strengthen the cleaning power of the concoction.[12]

Such advice about using things fully was not very new in content but was cast differently to serve the timely purposes of preserving resources and reducing garbage. Otherwise, specific tips about how to not waste food, for example, sounded quite familiar. One participant in the *Fujin kurabu* roundtable explained that daikon radish leaves were nutritious and that they could be fried in oil or made into pickles.[13] The daikon skin, another source advised, could be washed, cut finely, sautéed with sesame oil, sugar, and soy sauce, and finished with a seven-spice blend.[14] A book devoted to valuing food published by the Better Home Association instructed readers on what could be done with the bones of broiled fish, the green leaves of cauliflower, and tangerine peels.

Other suggestions had become common only recently, and reflected a contemporary condition of excess quite different from the scarcity of not so many years before, which had bred a miserable stinginess. With the proliferation in the sale and use of refrigerators, there was increased concern that people were buying more than they could eat and stuffing their fridge full of an inordinate amount of food which, hidden and forgotten, would rot.[15] Advice about mitigating other potential instances of waste also suggested that the fear of shortages was about a possible future or even a hypothetical situation more than it was about the actualities of the present. One woman told her children to write on a single sheet of paper until it was completely black, as if, she joked, it was the last sheet of paper in their lives.[16]

The frugality promoted in these years was not to mean abstention from consumption or the prioritization of saving above all else. Rather, housewives were to be wise consumers who knew how to shop and how to spend. They were to get the most for their money by doing such things as weighing at the grocery store anything like burdock root or squid that was priced per item. Daikon leaves, unwanted by most, could be purchased separately for little money. Housewives were also to hunt for economical alternatives, be it buying broken tofu at a low price or taking children to the library rather than purchasing books. And the financially sound option could also be a healthier one when it came to growing one's own food, if even just in a box on the balcony, or baking one's own bread.[17]

Advice literature of the early 1970s also featured, more prominently than in the past, strategies for not wasting energy and resources. To save gas, readers were advised to use an instantaneous gas water heater and to keep their stoves clean. To save electricity, lighting fixtures should be dusted and an electricity-saving clothes iron purchased. Methods for reducing water consumption were also often recommended. Reusing bathwater for laundry or cleaning was an oft-repeated piece of advice. Turning off the faucet while brushing one's teeth or washing one's face or hands and using the washing machine in certain ways would save water.[18] One housewife, Iguchi Keiko from Osaka, shared with readers of *Fujin seikatsu* a way to reduce water use, repurpose garbage, and save gas all at once. Iguchi had purchased a particular kind of bath, the water for which could be heated either with gas or by burning trash such as paper or boxes, thereby turning what would otherwise have been garbage into fuel. The family would also bathe in the same water for three days, after which the dirty water would be used to clean boots, the toilet, and the like.[19]

As much as *kechi* was stamped with the concerns and desires of the 1970s, it was not thoroughly cleansed of its wartime stench of poverty, scarcity, and hardship, of the kind of negativity associated with "cheap" or "cheapskate" in the United States.[20] But such unpleasant connotations came to be quite circumscribed. Conceptions of what was considered an undesirable *kechi* narrowed, opening up a wider swath of possibilities for desirable waste consciousness. As one commentator argued in the pages of the magazine *Shufu to seikatsu* (The Housewife and Daily Life), it was not *kechi* to save, value things, or buy long-lasting and durable goods.[21] Others expanded the meaning of saving beyond, and in tension with, simple penny-pinching. In a discussion between two housewives and a female commentator in the same *Shufu to seikatsu* series, it was agreed that the new saving was about buying higher-quality furniture even if it was more expensive and going to local stores rather than the supermarket even if it cost more. Saving was not just about money; it was also about subjective values and what would make one feel happier and richer in one's own life.[22]

When Ihara Ryūichi, vice president of the electronic medical equipment manufacturer Nihon Kohden, asked a television studio audience of housewives about *kechi*, a majority of them responded that they would not do it for anything. This aversion to the word *kechi* was also expressed by a fifty-eight-year-old housewife in Tokyo named Ogasawara Kinuko, who drew a sharp distinction between the desirability of saving and the undesirability of *kechi*. And yet women such as Ogasawara seemed to be acting in ways that fit perfectly the remade conception of stinginess. Ogasawara described how she saved fuel by wiping water off the bottom of pots, pans, and kettles before putting them on the range so that their contents would come to a boil faster. She saved gas by keeping her stove clean, and electricity by turning off lights in empty rooms. For his part, Ihara observed that at his neighborhood supermarket, women would try to weigh an egg in their palm to get the most for the per unit price, rifle through a pile of green onions to find the one with the shortest white section, and line up to buy products on sale. So while some still thought of the word *kechi* as connoting a miserliness necessitated by poverty, they might nevertheless have practiced a waste consciousness very much in keeping with the idea of a bright stinginess. What Ogasawara embraced was a kind of saving that did not trouble her family, that did not make them feel bad, and that did not mean scrimping when it came to food or education. In Ihara's view, too, stinginess was not about abstention from eating what one wanted or using what one wanted, but was about raising standards of living. And, he tentatively concluded, *kechi* should be seen as a virtue if it meant not spending money on unnecessary things in order to achieve some purpose. That is, *kechi* was about being frugal in certain ways so as to buy whatever might be desired, be it a new car or a mink coat.[23]

A Miserable Frugality

The first few pages of Bandō Eriko's graphic novel—*Āra mottainai!* (Ohhh, What a Waste!)—read like a scathing criticism of stinginess. Published in 1975, after the worst of price hikes and shortage scares had passed, the manga opened with a close-up on the face of a horrified young woman, mouth agape as she let out a scream and demanded to know why her mother had done something so wasteful. In the next frame, this central character, named Azuma Miyuki, was shown picking daikon leaves out of the trash can as proof of her mother's offense while explaining that they would be delicious if chopped and sautéed in sesame oil with some cayenne pepper. The use of daikon leaves was not being promoted here, as it often was in advice literature for housewives, but rather functioned as a representation of frugality to help illustrate Miyuki's particular (and problematic) understanding of waste consciousness. In this scene, Miyuki was not drawn sympathetically; she was hunched over the garbage can, half of her face darkened and her narrowed eyes glaring toward the other half of the cel, intruding on what otherwise would have been a peaceful domestic scene. At a kitchen table in front of a television, her father sat reading a newspaper while her aproned mother stood nearby. Interrupted by Miyuki's furious outburst, the father looked up from his paper and the mother cowered at her daughter's rebuke, frightened into stammering out a reactionary apology. Miyuki went on to admonish her mother for wasting too much at a time of high prices and food shortages, slammed her fist on the kitchen table while attacking her father for not smoking his cigarettes down to tiny butts, chastised her mother for letting a pot come to a furious boil when the price of gas had risen, and then punctuated her exit from the room with a resounding slam of the door behind her.[24]

This could be understood simply as a critique of stinginess, embodied in an unlikable and unsympathetic main character. As the story unfolds, however, it becomes clear that the manga took aim not at the very idea of stinginess but at Miyuki's version thereof. Her conception and enactment of waste consciousness was in the vein of "miserable *kechi*," devoid of pleasure and joy. In depicting Miyuki as creating hardship and unpleasantness for those around her, *Āra mottainai!* implicitly promoted instead the moderation and comfort of a bright stinginess, particularly for women and the home.

After Miyuki left the room in the first scene of the manga, her mother collapsed into a chair and her father dropped his head to the table in sheer exhaustion from their daughter's verbal abuse. Enjoyment of their comfortable middle-class life had been marred; the father could not read in peace, and the mother could not run the household smoothly and uneventfully as she might have wished. Miyuki's stinginess was not of the bright variety but, in disrupting the home, was unpalatably miserly. So fed up were the parents that they persuaded Miyuki to spend her winter break at a vacation resort in Shirakaba Kōgen, and as soon as she left, they danced around and sang about how they could now eat eel on rice, dine out in the Ginza area, and buy a diamond or a kimono.[25] That is, they could loosen their belts and enjoy some of the luxuries of their middle-class life.

Miyuki's stinginess was portrayed as especially objectionable because she was singularly and narrowly focused on being frugal to save and accumulate money purely for money's sake. She was excited about going to Shirakaba Kōgen not for the leisure activities like skiing that drew everyone else to the resort, but because

FIGURE 4.1. Miserable Stinginess. The miserable stinginess of Azuma Miyuki.

Reproduced by permission from Bandō Eriko, *Āra mottainai!* (Tokyo: Shūeisha, 1975) ©
Bandō Eriko.

it had appeared in a book about buried treasure. For Miyuki, the trip was an opportunity not to enjoy some free time but to search for a fortune. Her obsession with money was illustrated even on the bus ride to the resort. When a fellow passenger dropped something, she immediately identified it by sound as a 100 yen coin, pushed people aside to retrieve it, and triumphantly returned the coin to its owner, who turned out to be a former classmate named Suda Seiji. When he teasingly remembered her as "Miss Greedy," she proceeded to demonstrate the aptness of the moniker by demanding from him a 10 percent reward for finding his coin. Once at Shirakaba Kōgen, Miyuki was consumed with digging for the buried treasure. After various trials and tribulations, she eventually turned her attention to building a snow sculpture for the annual contest—not to have fun, for she initially deemed it a waste of time and effort, but to win what she had learned was a 100,000 yen prize.[26]

In all of these instances of Miyuki's moneygrubbing, it was not clear why she wanted to accumulate money. There was no mention of buying goods, living a certain kind of lifestyle, supporting a family, or attaining anything else with the money. What finally rescued Miyuki from her unreasonable stinginess was a romantic relationship that helped her realize that there was something more meaningful and important than money. In the predictable development of affection between Miyuki and Seiji, her obsession with money became the last barrier between them as Seiji confessed that she would otherwise be his perfect woman. And in the story's climactic moment, Miyuki finally demonstrated that she could feel affection greater than her love of money when she suggested that they literally burn cash to stay warm while trapped outdoors at the bottom of a deep hole. No more than one page after Miyuki's transformation did a marriage proposal follow. Miyuki's engagement to Seiji was a conventional validation of her awareness of, and attempt to renounce, her kind of stinginess and preoccupation with money.[27]

In *Ara mottainai!*, the saving and spending of money was acceptable as long as it had a purpose. Miyuki's parents could indulge in a nice meal, young people could vacation at a ski resort, and Miyuki's father could, as it was revealed, hire Seiji to cure his daughter of her unbecoming miserliness. The "waste" of the manga's title described the life devoid of joy and happiness that Miyuki had been living. Miyuki was ultimately rescued and redeemed not because she completely overcame her frugal instincts, but because she found meaning in her relationship with Seiji. This moderation of stinginess with the pursuit of pleasure and nonfinancial gratification was consistent with the conception of a bright *kechi*. Encountering the idea in both didactic publications and entertaining literature geared toward women, housewives were to understand, internalize, and embody this *kechi* so as to ensure the enjoyment of middle-class lives for themselves and their families.

Corporate Continuities

Parallel to the enduring desire for a comfortable middle-class home was the abiding pursuit by corporations for the profits that had secured their financial success and stoked the country's economic growth. Consciousness and elimination of waste were considered strategies for ensuring companies' financial futures, as there were familiar calls for rationalization, efficiency, and the reduction of expenses. As with the advice for the household, suggestions for the workplace were framed in new ways in the 1970s—in the language of *kechi*, and with more emphasis on the importance of saving resources and electricity. Unlike stinginess for the household, however, its counterpart for the office and the factory was not envisioned as particularly bright. Stinginess movements could be named so as to give a "bright impression," like the allegedly clever 10 UP Movement of Hitachi Kōki to cut its expenses by 10 percent. And in a nod to aims beyond the financial, some mention was made of encouraging a "spirit of stinginess."[28] But in stark contrast to the expectations placed on housewives, it was not incumbent on corporate managers to create a bright workplace, protect workers' psychological or spiritual well-being, encourage reflection about values, or instill virtues such as a heart that appreciates things. With the clear and quantifiable goal of defending and improving a company's financial health, there was less of a moral dimension to corporate stinginess movements. This difference between the more pragmatic and measurable goals of corporate *kechi* and the moralistic tenor of its household counterpart was expressed succinctly by Yoshida Sei, a former member of the Lower House of the Japanese Diet who, in a magazine published by the Japan Industrial Newspaper Company (Nihon Kōgyō Shinbunsha), recommended that businesses should be held responsible for their environmental transgressions. But he foregrounded the endless, irrational, and greedy consumption of "ordinary people" as necessitating stinginess movements; it was consumers, more than workers, who were to curtail wastefulness.[29] For Yoshida as for others, business executives did not have the same moral responsibilities as household executives, so women came to be associated with a bright *kechi* and the virtue of waste consciousness in ways that men were not. What was perpetuated by the corporate and household stinginess movements were gendered values and priorities intrinsic to the ideal middle-class life.

Corporate stinginess movements of the 1970s were instigated not by the oil crisis but by the financial climate in 1970 and 1971. The government's tight-money policy in response to increasing import and wholesale prices had worsened domestic business conditions, to the point where the manufacturing production growth rate was negative in the spring of 1971. And President Richard Nixon's decision in August to cancel the dollar's direct convertibility to gold and to institute an import surcharge constituted a "shock" for a domestic Japanese economy in recession.[30] In this financial environment, hortatory literature urged company managers to run a waste-free ship through the implementation of *kechi* policies to cut unnecessary spending in various areas. Entertainment was one target of scrutiny, with wasteful abuse of expense accounts a particular concern. To illustrate its point about bloat, an article in the monthly magazine *Keizai tenbō* (Outlook on the Economy) cited the calculation by the National Tax Agency (Kokuzeichō) that in 1969, a total of 915.5 billion yen was spent by businesses on expense accounts. With the growth rate of these accounts not accompanied by a concomitant increase in sales and profits, there were questions about what percentage of such funds was being frittered away on extravagant socializing over food and drink. The Sumitomo Corporation (Sumitomo Shōji), an enthusiastic participant in the stinginess movement, reported that entertainment constituted a large share of its total expenditures and formed a subcommittee to research ways of reducing such expenses by 20 percent. Nippon Steel (Shin Nippon Seitetsu, or Nittetsu), faced with cutbacks in crude steel production, aimed for a 10 percent cut.[31] According to one Nippon Steel section chief, even managers were now required to submit requests for entertainment funds, and there were unwritten rules about not using such moneys for first-class restaurants and bars or the extension of an evening of socializing to a second establishment. The Itōchū Corporation (Itōchū Shōji) also became more strict about expense account spending, which resulted in a decrease of roughly 15 percent. One suggestion made in the belt-tightening vein was that clients be courted at bowling alleys with several games and a meal at its restaurant. It seems that it was not just Itōchū that shifted venues from high-end bars to the more modest bowling alley. The manager of a 252-lane bowling alley in Tokyo limited to fifty reserved lanes this "entertainment bowling" so that demand from businessmen would not crowd out regular customers. And a counterpart in Osaka observed that since the fall of 1970, traffic from such corporate entertainment had increased with many businessmen bowling at his establishment then going to the buffet next door before heading home.[32]

In these years before the Oil Shock, stinginess movements were met with some resistance and skepticism. Employees of companies like the Sumitomo and Itōchū corporations were quoted as wondering how they could conduct business as effectively without the social lubrication and information gathering afforded by expense accounts.[33] Cost-cutting efforts that reduced services to consumers were also criticized. When the indebted Japanese National Railways (Nihon Kokuyū Tetsudō, or Kokutetsu) embarked on its stinginess movement and decided to remove as many lights as possible from stations, reduce the amount of toilet paper available in restrooms, and shorten the hours of its luggage storage service, it was raked over the coals by passengers and the *Yomiuri* newspaper for the nerve of pushing its financial woes onto customers.[34] One also has to wonder whether some efforts to save money created bureaucracy and wasted time. At TBS (Tokyo Broadcasting System, or Tokyo Hōsō), the earlier practice of simply signing a slip when having a meal or tea with a visitor was replaced by a process whereby an employee first had to secure the approval of a division chief and then receive the appropriate amount of cash from accounting.[35] To have to submit requests for entertainment funds presumably had a cost in paper, time, and labor.

Certain kinds of stinginess efforts were also dismissed at the time as extreme or trivial. Skepticism was voiced by *Keizai tenbō* about the mindset of "Many a little makes a mickle," and about the efficacy of measures like not replenishing toilet paper in employee restrooms and not turning on lights near windows.[36] Nippon Steel's encouragement of conveying one's point more quickly to shorten phone conversations was seen as exemplifying the "pretend saving" of large corporations.[37] Also in this category were taping over half the light switches in the restroom and turning off two out of every three ceiling lights in office corridors. And at Japanese National Railways, as at many companies, much attention was given to pencils. Here, employees in certain departments were to switch to mechanical pencils because of the lower cost of replacing only the lead.[38] One section chief at Japanese National Railways disparaged such efforts. What was needed to weather the recession was the management of production costs and the strengthening of the business's fundamentals—a "man's policy." Saving on pencils and such was belittled as a "woman's policy."[39]

Organized labor was critical of stinginess from a different perspective. Companies adopted *kechi* strategies in order to exaggerate their economic difficulties and the severity of the recession, and to justify restraining the spring labor offensive, they claimed. A bureau chief of the General Council of Trade Unions of Japan (Nihon Rōdō Kumiai Sōhyō Gikai, or Sōhyō) stated plainly that it would be a mistake for company management to think that they could deceive labor with such artifice.[40]

After the Oil Shock, there was much less doubt within the business world about the value of stinginess movements, even in the attention to cost-saving practices that might previously have been questioned as superficial or inconsequential. While Nippon Steel's *kechi* movement raised some eyebrows in 1971, in November 1973 it was noted in a monthly economics journal for its efficacy, with particular mention of the reduction in the company's telephone bill by 36 million yen.[41] By 1977, the business magazine *Shūkan daiyamondo* (Diamond Weekly) could observe in an article titled "Stingy Saving" ("Kechikechi setsuyaku") that such strategies as rationing pencils had become common sense. Everyone, it claimed, was economizing on office supplies: Maruzen Petroleum

(Maruzen Sekiyu) allowed each employee two pencils, one black pen, and one red pen; Daiwa House (Daiwa Hausu) supplied one pencil and a fraction of an eraser; and Sanyō Chemical Industries (San'yō Kasei) stopped purchasing office supplies altogether. At companies from Osaka Gas (Osaka Gasu) to the Honda Motor Company (Honda Giken Kōgyō), envelopes were reused and paper was used fully. Attempts were made to reduce the costs of phone calls and electricity, and the textile company Sankyō Seikō slashed entertainment allowances, ceasing to cover golf expenses for all employees from the president on down.[42]

Exhortations to pay attention to even the most minute instances of waste were normalized, such that advice about eliminating this kind of waste could be aimed at the management not just of major corporations but of all sizes. In an article geared toward managers of small- and medium-sized businesses, instructions were dispensed and a worksheet provided to help them scrutinize and eliminate waste in ten areas, from photocopying to transportation and from mail to business trips. Many of these recommendations were quite meticulous. In the category of office supplies, the establishment of a distribution or exchange system was suggested whereby, for example, an employee could get a new pencil only when the one being used became shorter than 7 centimeters. For meetings, instituting a fine for latecomers was recommended, along the lines of the 50 to 100 yen penalty imposed by Mitsubishi Heavy Industries (Mitsubishi Jūkōgyō). To conserve energy, women were to be discouraged from flushing the toilet twice. When it came to phone calls, one suggested strategy was putting usage meters on each phone, as the Taihō Industrial Corporation (Taihō Sangyō) had done. And in the area of entertainment costs, a certain publishing company's decision not to participate in the convention of midyear gift giving was offered as a potential idea.[43]

Along with the promotion of waste consciousness in the corporate office, production was to be streamlined in the factory. In the view of *Shūkan daiyamondo*, as much as stinginess movements reduced indirect costs and encouraged a spirit of saving, they were to play a supporting role in shoring up company financials. The lead role was to be the rationalization of production, such as decreasing the number of necessary parts, shortening the length of the line, and reducing stock.[44] One company that came to epitomize waste consciousness in production was the Toyota Motor Corporation (Toyota Jidōsha). Although it had been pursuing rationalization of its production processes for decades, informed by ideas of scientific management and Taylorism, the company's production system gained attention and popularity with the Oil Shock.[45] In 1978, company engineer Ōno Tai'ichi published a seminal book with Diamond Publishers (Daiyamondosha) titled *Toyota seisan hōshiki* (The Toyota Production System). The production management system was, at its core, about the "thorough elimination of various kinds of waste" in order to increase efficiency, decrease costs, and thus boost profits. In his book, Ōno exemplified a deep antipathy toward waste: "To make the Toyota production system your own, it is no good at all to understand waste only roughly. If you do not have the desire to get at it minutely and crush it, there will be little hope of success."[46]

Ōno explained to his readers that insufficient preparation and rationalization of poor operations would lead to *muda* (waste), *mura* (inconsistency), and *muri* (unreasonableness)—the "three *mu*"—in production methods and time. He laid out seven categories of waste that could and should be eradicated: overproduction; time on hand, or waiting; transportation; overprocessing, or too much machining; stock on hand, or inventory; movement; and the making of defective products. Specific suggestions about how to eliminate waste in these areas included scrutinizing efficiency at the level of the worker and the line. The example offered by Ōno was a line of ten people making one hundred things a day. One might be tempted to say that in a given day, each person was producing ten things and the line was producing one hundred things. But closer examination might reveal variations by hour and day, with wasteful overproduction or wasteful time on hand. Ōno suggested that in such a situation, two people could be removed so that eight people made the same target of one hundred things; alternatively, the two people could stay on the line but the output increased to 125 things. In this example, the two people and the products they made would both be considered the kind of non-value-added excess in need of purging. Ōno acknowledged the charge made by labor unions that the production system was a device for firing workers, like the two excess people in this case, but responded by saying that it was the responsibility of managers to use surplus personnel effectively and not to hire and fire employees according to business cycles.[47] Focused on how executives could eliminate waste in all of its guises, *Toyota seisan hōshiki* was a statement of management philosophy and a guidebook of practical strategies which set forth an unforgiving ideal of the waste-free workplace.[48]

In the context of the office and the factory, there were many more continuities than discontinuities with earlier efforts at waste elimination. The cutting of costs and the maximization of profits were the top priorities, familiar ideas of efficiency and rationalization garnered attention, and there was little room for moderation in the ideal model of waste consciousness. The results of the stinginess movement were also conceived and measured almost entirely in financial terms, a departure from the realm of the household, in which the word "saving" could apply to things, resources, and energy as readily as money, and the main tropes of waste consciousness were as much about valuing things and conserving resources and energy as economizing. In the realm of the workplace, *kechi* was neither especially bright nor especially new, but was an attempt to shore up corporate health and the financial backbone for a stable economy, with the defense of the middle-class lifestyle only an indirect goal and the enjoyment of its comforts distant from daily life in the workplace.

The Tenacity of Desire

Efforts to promote a bright stinginess and a sound waste consciousness reveal much about ideals and aspirations for daily life in the home and workplace, but they tell us relatively little about the extent to which consumers and workers changed their practices and routines—about whether people became less wasteful. For certain workplaces, where company policies dictated alterations in behavior, we can get a sense of the financial impact of stinginess measures. Toyota Motors, for example, did manage to reduce its costs by about 70 percent in the years following the Oil Shock.[49] But outside of the business world, and outside of those realms in which people's actions were prescribed by the policies and practices of governments or social groups, it is more difficult to discern whether the rhetoric of waste consciousness said more about how people wanted to see themselves than how they really were. When the spotlight is focused more directly on people's behavior, there is a mixed and hazy picture of the extent to which people became more waste conscious and actually acted in ways that pushed back against disposability and consumption.

People's understandings of waste consciousness did mirror the ways in which stinginess movements framed *kechi*, according to public surveys that shed light on both ideas and behavior. When asked by the Prime Minister's Office what it meant "to save," people most commonly replied "to value things," followed by "to eliminate waste" and "to use things efficiently." Not surprising, given the gendered conceptions of *kechi*, women were more likely than men to choose the valuing of things, and men were more likely than women to choose the efficient use of things. The idea that a bright *kechi* was not to entail hardship was reflected as well. Relatively few respondents defined saving as "restraint from what you want" and even fewer as "cutting back on one's lifestyle."[50] And in a survey of 3,427 people conducted by the Prime Minister's Office in 1974, a majority reported that their efforts at saving did not compromise improvements to their lifestyle (72 percent) or convenience in their lives (67 percent).[51] The Economic Planning Agency was pleased with this result indicating that the standard of living was such that saving would not impede progress in lifestyles.[52]

With this conception of *kechi* in mind, a substantial percentage of people at least presented themselves as being conscious of waste. In the Prime Minister's Office survey of 3,427 people, a majority (67 percent) said that they were regularly trying to save in their daily lives. When it came to particular saving behaviors, three-quarters (75 percent) said that they tolerated using old things as long as they were usable, and only a small fraction (10 percent) admitted to replacing old items with new ones.[53] In the same kind of survey conducted later that year, in 1974, respondents said that they were not wasting electricity, gas, and water (30.8 percent); were choosing to buy a more durable good even if it was slightly more expensive (26.9 percent); and were not buying goods that were fads (17.4 percent).[54]

Yet the extent of changes in behavior was unclear, and the connection between a consciousness of *kechi* and actual behavior could also be quite tenuous. In late 1973, the Tokyo Metropolitan Citizens' Office (Tokyo-to Tominshitsu) was concerned enough about people's unwillingness to alter aspects of their lives to ask residents what they thought of the following contention: "Once a civilized lifestyle has been experienced, it is hard to go back. If the current situation continues, there will be panic conditions with a buying up of food and a shortage of daily necessities." A majority (61.1 percent) of the 973 respondents agreed, and only a fairly small number (17.7 percent) disagreed.[55] While the phrase "civilized lifestyle" (*bunmei seikatsu*) could have been interpreted in different ways, survey takers seemed to be hesitant about the prospect of rolling back lifestyles. And although they could have been responding more to the second part of the question, about ensuing problems, than to the proposition suggested in the first part, the relatively high percentage of agreement to the statement as a whole can probably be read as moderate acceptance of a causal link from people's reluctance to sacrifice their standards of living to panic buying and shortages. As put succinctly by the sanitation expert and engineer Honda Atsuhiro, it was difficult if not impossible for people to sacrifice the enjoyment, convenience, and satisfaction that they had come to know. What could be expected was not a wartime mindset of "luxury is the enemy" but rather a moderate level of luxury.[56] And changes in people's actions might be quite modest. In a survey conducted by the Prime Minister's Office in 1975, fewer than a third of the respondents (29 percent) said that their attitude toward consumption was shifting from one of disposability to the valuing of things. Even more (35 percent) reported that they needed to be more mindful of saving, which hinted at a gap between expected and actual practice, and some (10 percent) even admitted that they were still in the mood of luxury, wastefulness, and disposability.[57]

That people's waste-conscious behavior seemed to wax and wane, even over the course of the 1970s, suggested that a spirit of *kechi* was not so indelible, and that the practices of consumption and disposability were deeply entrenched in middle-class life.[58] If we consider household garbage output to be a rough barometer of material consumption and attitudes toward physical waste, then the trend in the amount discarded reflected restraint and contraction as an immediate reaction to the Oil Shock, followed by gradual relaxation thereafter. The total amount of waste generated from daily life, which had been experiencing a steep upward trajectory, declined sharply in 1974. But it climbed back up during the rest of the decade. Similarly, waste generated from daily life per capita dropped over the previous year in 1971, 1973, and 1974, but increased in 1975 and remained relatively steady or grew thereafter.[59] These data seem to suggest that people were unusually aware of their disposal habits during and immediately after the Garbage War and the Oil Shock, but that this level of attention and constraint was difficult to maintain. Even mid-decade, the immediate post–Oil Shock decreases in garbage output were being characterized as only temporary by the likes of the sanitation expert Shibata Tokue.[60] And by 1977, the Economic Planning Agency concluded in its annual report on national lifestyles that a gap existed between waste consciousness and behavior. It noted that roughly one in five people had reported in a recent survey that they still had a feeling of wastefulness and disposability, and that they found it hard to save; at the same time, many respondents said that they were saving energy and resources. Frustrated by what they saw as contradictions, the report's authors also pointed out that while there had been a decrease in the amount of large refuse discarded, there had been a rapid diffusion of air conditioners, a consumer durable that consumed a great deal of electricity.[61]

The picture of waste consciousness was indeed muddy when it came to saving energy. According to the National Institute for Research Advancement (Sōgō Kenkyū Kaihatsu Kikō, or NIRA), an independent policy research organization, overall energy consumption declined in 1974 and 1975, but then rebounded in 1976. Moreover, the drop in the years immediately after the oil crisis was due to a decrease in consumption by industry; when it came to personal energy use, the amount consumed increased in each of these years.[62] This upward trend raises questions about the efficacy of moral suasion campaigns, and doubts about their influence are lent some weight by a peek into why people were conserving energy and resources. In a survey conducted in early 1978, the Prime Minister's Office asked those 6,789 respondents who said they were attempting to save energy and resources about their motives. A majority (53.3 percent) reported that they were trying to lessen the impact on household finances. Far fewer were trying to conserve because of limits to resources and energy (18.2 percent), concerns about environmental pollution and garbage (5.0 percent), or the virtue of saving (4.5 percent). Not only were the reasons given for saving energy and resources not aligned with the central themes of conservation campaigns, but also an overwhelming percentage (89.8) of the 8,032 respondents agreed to some extent that there were many ways that they could save more energy and resources in their day-to-day life.[63]

The stated explanations for not embracing energy-saving efforts could be quite mundane for some. One Satō Hideko, a forty-five-year-old housewife, said that she had tried to cut down on waste in her home after watching a television segment about stinginess. She asked her family who left the light on in the bathroom, who forgot to turn off the switch on the water heater, who kept the water running while washing their face, and so on. But everyone always responded, "Not me." Frustrated, she gave up.[64] In Satō's case, trying to change her family's behavior did not seem worth the annoyance and hassle. For others, according to NIRA's report, calculations about energy use did not figure into certain decisions, which were driven instead by the individualized pursuit of comfort and enjoyment. Trends in leisure, for example, were thought to have contributed to the increased consumption of energy. Multi-night long-distance vacations were expensive in energy terms: a three-night family ski trip to Hokkaidō from Tokyo required nine times more energy than a one-night tennis outing to Karuizawa. And sports consumed more energy than might have been expected, with playing tennis using twice as much indirect energy as watching a movie. The report was not suggesting that people should choose their recreational activities based on the amount of energy consumption alone, since the most important consideration was what would make them feel refreshed. But it was recommending greater awareness of the energy consequences of leisure choices, and offered the larger observation that the increasingly individualized decisions that people made in their affluent lives contributed to the increasing consumption of energy.[65]

A similar argument about the consequences of pursuing individual desires was made by the editorial board of the *Asahi* newspaper in 1976. By the mid-1970s, with an economy in recovery and summer bonuses a bit larger, the "mood of saving" was seen to be slackening. While consumers had reportedly learned from the Oil Shock to think more about the worth and price of goods, they were now making decisions not from an attitude of saving but, it was implied, from a sense of their own wants. These tastes and preferences could be seen in the unevenness in consumer spending, with sales of clothing, delivery of beer, and overnight trips down, but trips abroad up. And consumption-related industries attempted to capitalize on reinvigorated appetites, with some developing new products that allegedly tossed aside the importance of saving resources and saving energy. The editorial concluded that waste consciousness was not central to people's decision making, so the mood of saving, including the saving of resources and energy, had weakened.[66] The newspaper returned to a variation of this refrain in March 1978, when it commented in an editorial that the younger generation seemed more concerned with stylishness than with saving energy, and that advertisements and commercials for color television sets and refrigerators were highlighting their design and convenience.[67]

The tenacious appeal of consumption and its dampening of waste consciousness were brought into sharp relief by the second oil crisis, precipitated in 1979 by the Iranian Revolution and perpetuated by the outbreak of the Iran-Iraq War the following year. While these events led to a steep increase in the price of oil, Japanese fiscal authorities like the Bank of Japan were quicker to respond with policies of monetary restraint than they had been in 1973.[68] This helped soften the blow for Japan, relative both to the experience of other countries and to the first oil crisis. The second oil crisis also did not have the profound societal reverberations of the first, which had shaken assumptions about the availability of resources and the persistence of economic growth. Nonetheless, in the late 1970s, insecurity in the oil supply prompted the implementation of energy-saving measures reminiscent of those from earlier in the decade. In mid-June 1979, the Ministerial Council for Promoting a Comprehensive Energy Policy (Sōgō Enerugī Taisaku Suishin Kakuryō Kaigi), chaired by Prime Minister Ōhira Masayoshi, decided on countermeasures for saving oil and ways to achieve the target of a 5 percent reduction in its consumption. Self-restraint was recommended when it came to broadcasting television programs late at night, showing movies at theaters in the morning, and using neon and other lights for advertising.[69] The automotive industry also came out in 1979 with guidelines for gas-saving ways to drive, which it publicized through pamphlets and advertisements. In one particular newspaper ad, the Japan Automobile Industry Association (Nihon Jidōsha Kōgyōkai) educated readers about "seven methods for eliminating waste," such as avoiding sudden acceleration, idling, aimless driving, and carrying around extra stuff like a golf bag in the car.[70] Social groups like consumer organizations were also particularly active with their resource- and energy-saving efforts, such as promoting the reuse of bicycles abandoned around train stations and of disposable polyethylene shopping bags.[71]

Yet there was a tension between the encouragement of waste consciousness and the preservation of comfortable lifestyles. The home economist Shinozaki Etsuko dispensed advice about household energy saving in a *Mainichi* newspaper article, but she also acknowledged how hard it was for the slogan *shōenerugī* to be put into practice and to yield visible results. She suspected that the highly affluent lifestyles people were living were solely about the pursuit of convenience, and hoped that the oil crisis was an opportunity for them to reconsider, yet again, a heart that values things and the skills necessary for a relaxed and successful way of living.[72] Even in Shinozaki's own advocacy of waste consciousness, there was a friction between her criticism of fetishizing convenience and her promotion of a leisurely lifestyle. And she did not address why people would compromise their convenient and comfortable ways of living, which were fueled by energy consumption. Even a fifteen-year-old high school student who took the trouble

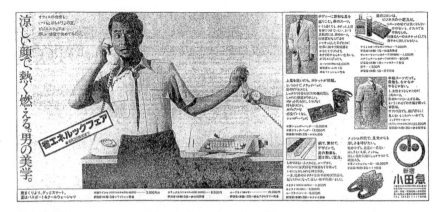

FIGURE 4.2.   The Energy-Saving Look. An advertisement by the Odakyū department store for the energy-saving look and related products.

Reproduced by permission from *Yomiuri shimbun*, May 24, 1979.

to write in to a newspaper about the waste of resources commented that it was hard to realize savings because the country's standard of living was fairly high.[73]

More critical of people wanting to hold on to affluent lifestyles was the well-known cartoonist Makino Kei'ichi, who portrayed such desires in the pages of the *Yomiuri* newspaper as almost hypocritical. In one cartoon, Makino drew a couple of parachutes carrying slogans about energy saving such as "Don't Use Wasteful Energy!" Also in the sky was Raijin, the demon-like god of thunder, lightning, and storms, hurling down thunderbolts from atop a cloud on the scene below—a large house and a golf course, from which men were fleeing in fright. The signs in the sky could be read as ephemeral, floating away in the wind, with only the threat of the god's destructive force scaring the men below. Makino seemed to suggest that it would take more than phrases but would require demonic fright to force men to give up their extravagant luxuries.[74]

That the appealing aspects of consumption could bump up against efforts to save energy was epitomized by the fate of the "energy-saving look" (*shōene rukku*) and its trademark "energy-saving suit" (*shōene sūtsu*), both of which were flops. The idea of energy-saving clothes was a response to the government's suggestion in mid-March 1979 that government offices and corporate buildings raise air conditioner settings from 25 to 28 degrees Celsius, or from about 77 to 82 degrees Fahrenheit. Recognizing that this temperature could be uncomfortable during the hot and humid summer, the Ministry of International Trade and Industry (Tsūshō Sangyōshō, or MITI) kicked off a "no jacket, no necktie campaign." Focusing on male office workers, the ministry attempted to convince them that it was acceptable to go to work in pants and a shirt, sans jacket and tie. To further promote the energy-saving look, the head of the Textile Products Section (Sen'i Seihinka) commissioned Toray Industries (Tōre) and clothes manufacturers to develop an outfit from fabrics appropriate for the campaign. What resulted was the energy-saving suit: a short-sleeved suit typically made of polyester and cotton, or linen. Soon, newspapers and magazines were running stories and photographs of Minister of International Trade and Industry Esaki Masumi and Prime Minister Ōhira Masayoshi donning the suits. On one particular morning, the prime minister appeared in the garden of his official residence for a fashion shoot wearing a short-sleeved beige jacket with matching pants, dress shirt, and necktie. He did not go so far as to wear the jacket "safari style," open and fully unbuttoned. And one could not help but notice that the aides in the background were in full formal business attire. Such staged photo ops were part of a marketing effort which included fashion shows at department stores like Odakyū in the Shinjuku area, designed to persuade customers to purchase energy-saving clothes.[75] Advertisements for the fashion shows and for the look also ran in major newspapers. In a large ad published in the *Asahi* newspaper in May 1979, the Textile Products Section chief, in conversation with a clothing and accessories critic, explained that the energy-saving look was intended to give men more summer fashion choices. Presented too were a photograph and sketches of some of the options: pants with a double-breasted short-sleeved shirt and necktie; the loose-fitting energy-saving suit with a wide-collared, four-pocket short-sleeved jacket and no necktie; and the energy-saving suit with necktie.[76]

The campaign was not a complete failure, with the general idea of lighter office wear catching on where there was more flexibility about what could be worn. The Kansai Electric Power Company (Kansai Denryoku) had already been discouraging its employees from wearing a jacket and tie, and had solicited ideas from its workers and their families for multiple shirt options for the summer. The Dai-Ichi Kangyo Bank (Dai-ichi Kangyō Ginkō) encouraged no neckties and alternatives to business shirts at all of their branches starting in June 1979. And going without a jacket and/or tie seems to have become somewhat acceptable.[77] Outside of the office, informal summer clothes for men, unconnected to the MITI initiative, do seem to have enjoyed a growth in sales.[78]

But overall, the energy-saving look did not catch on. The energy-saving suit did not sell well; some 20 to 30 percent of inventory languished into the next year, and it was declared by the *Yomiuri* newspaper to be "a dud."[79] The campaign for energy-saving office wear failed in part because of concerns about the look being too casual for the workplace, with some suspecting it would take time for the entrenched fashion habits of the business world to change.[80] The far more frequent criticism made about the energy-saving suit, in particular, was that it was ugly. The short-sleeved suit was described as boring, unappealing,

FIGURE 4.3.   Prime Minister Ōhira and the Energy-Saving Suit. Prime Minister Ōhira Masayoshi's photo op in an energy-saving suit.

Reproduced by permission from *Yomiuri shimbun*, June 6, 1979.

and unfashionable.[81] The lack of an energy-saving look for women parallel to those for men was a missed opportunity to loosen the purse strings of female consumers, both white-collar working women who needed outfits for the office and housewives, who might have been inclined to buy new clothes for both themselves and their husbands.[82] To make matters worse, the energy-saving look was poorly marketed. In an age when fashion sold because of the image it projected, parading out politicians as models was deemed a mistake.[83] The nakedly top-down nature of the campaign gave it a forced feeling, and photographs of smiling politicians made the look seem like mere pretense.[84] Antipathy toward politicians was captured in a cartoon by Makino Kei'ichi, who depicted a figure with the Diet building for its head wearing a short-sleeved energy-saving jacket and shaking politicians out of its clothes. The caption read, "Saving Energy: Let's Also Cut Back on Wasteful Diet Members."[85] The implication was that politicians, with their meaningless ideas about energy, should be discarded.

Critics of this energy-saving campaign's emptiness had a good point. The energy-saving suit did not curb the wasteful use of energy in particular or waste in general. These new suits required resources to be manufactured, encouraged consumption by people who already owned business wear, and required them to spend money. An energy-saving shirt, for example, cost somewhat more than its regular short-sleeved counterpart, and the suits were usually priced somewhere between 28,000 and 48,000 yen.[86] The idea of an energy-saving look was mainly a hollow symbol of energy saving, and was entirely about feeling good in a warmer office. In a purported attempt to reduce the use of wasteful energy, government officials were instead trying to encourage the consumption of a fashionable good intended to make life comfortable. And the look fizzled in large part because it did not become trendy enough, because it was not marketed in a way that made it seem cool and desirable, and was thus not purchased by unimpressed consumers. Some people seem to have shunned the look because it was not an effective way to conserve energy. But the failure of the energy-saving suit also suggests that moral suasion about saving energy was not in itself sufficient to shape behavior, and that it was competing with the power of marketing, fashion, and consumer desire.

Toward a New Affluence

On New Year's Day in 1979, the *Yomiuri* newspaper published an article about people's reflections on the past ten years and their aspirations for the decade to come. Subtitled "An Affluence of Things, Next Is Affluence of the Heart," the piece declared that Japanese people's lives had become wealthy in material terms and that the aim for the 1980s was to become wealthy in time and in heart, mind, and spirit. Noted were the trends over the previous ten years of valuing work less, and hobbies and leisure more, as people had begun to seek more relaxation and unconstricted time (*yutori*).[87] The sentiment that financial affluence had afforded people the opportunity to think more about how they wanted to enjoy their lives picked up on a growing sense of reflection in the late 1970s about what to desire. In 1977 the Economic Planning Agency had observed that with rising standards of living, people were looking beyond food and clothing, and even beyond the purchase of consumer durables, to education, sports, art, and travel. People seemed to be turning away from the acquisition of material consumer goods (*monobanare*) and toward the pursuit of pleasurable time.[88] As if to confirm this trend, in a survey of 8,239 people conducted by the Prime Minister's Office in May 1979, a substantial number (40.9 percent) said that they had become materially affluent to a certain extent, so that from here on in, they wanted to put more emphasis on affluence of the heart and a leisurely lifestyle. This question had been posed in the annual survey for some years, but 1979 was the first in which those who still wanted to place importance on making their lives materially wealthy (40.3 percent) were outnumbered, however slightly, by people who sought an "affluence of the heart" (*kokoro no yutakasa*).[89]

Such affirmation of the sense that people were leading financially and materially affluent lives is a reminder that despite the jolts, uncertainties, and challenges of the 1970s, many continued to see themselves as enjoying middle-class lifestyles that they wanted to preserve and improve. The larger economic story of the decade was mixed. On the one hand, the 1970s were marked by the end of rapid economic growth, the severe and acute financial shock precipitated by the oil crisis, rampant inflation, declines in operating profits, and increases in unemployment. On the other hand, economic growth rebounded from its low, and inflation was reined in after 1974 such that Japan avoided the prolonged "stagflation" that plagued countries like the United States. And the financial effects of the second oil crisis were mitigated as well.[90]

It seems understandable, then, that in the discussions of waste so bound up with these larger developments, there were two strands of waste consciousness. On the one hand, there came to be much greater attention to material waste, a vocabulary for talking and thinking about mass consumption and disposability, established practices for reuse and recycling, and the promotion of saving resources and energy. On the other hand, such substantial shifts were moderated, challenged, and perhaps even undermined by the abiding allure of the conveniences, comforts, and pleasures of affluent, mass-consuming middle-class lifestyles. On the cusp of the 1980s, it was not at all clear what would become of these two strands of waste consciousness at a time when people were expecting to pursue a new and nebulous kind of affluence—an affluence of the heart.

Part III

ABUNDANT DUALITIES

Wealth and Its Discontents in the 1980s
and Beyond

5

CONSUMING DESIRES

In 1984, the Isetan Shinjuku department store had no qualms about running a newspaper advertisement with the slogan "Luxury Is Splendid." An unmistakable inversion of the wartime sentiment that luxury was the "enemy" (*teki*), the declaration of indulgence as "splendid" (*suteki*) was unequivocal in its encouragement to purchase the advertised products, from Camembert cheese to pearl necklaces.[1] This, after all, was a decade emblematic of rampant consumerism and excessive materialism, inaugurated by the publication of the best-selling, award-winning novel *Nantonaku, kurisutaru* (Somehow, Crystal). Seeming to exemplify a naked desire to buy, its thin plot was littered with references to products, stores, and popular culture, all explained in the many footnotes. Mentioning the book as illustrative of its times became almost obligatory for Japanese cultural observers from the amateur to the sophisticated. And especially for youth who had disposable incomes to spend, the novel was popular as a guide for how and where to consume, despite the intentions of its author, Tanaka Yasuo, to examine life and identity in a materialistic society.[2]

It may be that such cultural episodes seem especially potent in hindsight, from the vantage point of the economic downturn that followed. But they did capture a Japan of the 1980s that was, by various quantitative measures, financially and materially affluent. The country's per capita gross domestic product (GDP) exceeded that of the United States in 1987 and would continue to rise through the early 1990s, and household financial consumption expenditure per capita ranked among the highest in the world.[3] The poverty rate of 7 to 8 percent was half what

FIGURE 5.1. Luxury Is Splendid. The Isetan Shinjuku department store advertisement with the slogan "Luxury Is Splendid."

Reproduced by permission from the Isetan Shinjuku department store, Studio Uni, Inc., and *Yomiuri shimbun*, March 21, 1984.

it would be in the late 1990s, and at least in the first half of the decade, wealth inequality as reflected in the Gini coefficient was substantially lower than in other advanced countries.[4] People also reported having a sense of material plenty, with almost 96 percent of several thousand respondents on a national survey feeling that theirs was an era abundant in things.[5]

A middle-class lifestyle with its mass consumption of conveniences, comforts, and pleasures had been defended in the insecure 1970s; in the more financially confident 1980s, the urgency of a defensive posture dissipated, waste of most kinds did not seem so immediately menacing to people's lifestyles, and consumer desires were amplified and expanded. The general idea and expectations of a middle-class life that were constructed in the 1960s and that were to be preserved through a bright stinginess in the 1970s persisted, but without the same degree of attention to wastefulness. In these years of increasing GDP, there was much less concern expressed about where the line might be drawn between frugality and stinginess, what it meant to consume skillfully, and when it might be wise to save and when it might be acceptable to indulge. With household saving rates relatively high as many people both consumed and saved, exhortations to not waste money were few and far between.[6] Waste consciousness in this decade was not so visible as attention and aspirations turned elsewhere in pursuit of an ever better life.

At a time when the desire to maintain a high standard of living was so strong, those who did advocate the curbing of wastefulness were careful to insist that waste consciousness would not disrupt daily life. This idea that the mitigation of waste should not entail hardship had been a basic tenet of bright stinginess in the 1970s; in the 1980s, it calcified into an assumption so fixed that it was hardly deserving of discussion. Those who promoted the saving of energy presumed that energy conservation should not compromise lifestyles, especially at a time when the compulsion to not waste energy was weakened by low crude oil prices. Those who championed decreases in garbage production, with their overwhelming focus on recycling, emphasized how pleasant and enjoyable such practices could be. This strategy of encouraging waste reduction as a negligible hassle, even as fun and entertaining, may have been the most appropriate and effective for its time, but it also narrowed the scope of those understandings about waste that did endure.

If there was one manifestation of waste that did manage to garner attention in the 1980s it was garbage, an ever-growing behemoth fed by unceasing consumption. Yet even as the problem of rubbish worsened as its volume increased, the responses were rather perfunctory. The challenges were presented largely in administrative and technical terms more than as reflections of societal practices. The promotion of reuse and recycling that had taken off in the previous decade did have momentum, but was incommensurate with the gravity of the "garbage problem." With the focus on physical waste, on the "ugly, shit end of capitalism," critical attention pivoted away from the consuming side of the equation.[7] Mass consumption, valued as a driver of economic growth and an intrinsic facet of middle-class life, was left relatively unscathed as garbage reduction campaigns gave implicit permission to consume as long as household trash was sorted, things were reused, and resources were recycled. There were people, invested in and dedicated to minimizing waste, who worried about the values and priorities of a society that expectorated so much and who criticized a culture of disposability, so we should hesitate to characterize this decade as one of unflinching consumption and unabashed materialism. But such probing considerations of waste were not prominent or mainstream. Especially compared to the wide-ranging, critical, and reflective conversations provoked by the Garbage War and Oil Shock in the early 1970s, discussions in this decade were quite circumscribed. Considerations of the connections between mass production, mass consumption, and mass waste waned, and the focus was on the management of rubbish and the promotion of recycling much more than on the societal, cultural, and economic forces that resulted in its creation.

Complacencies of Comfort

There was much to appreciate about a middle-class life with its physical possessions that offered comfort, convenience, and enjoyment. The material plenty enjoyed by salarymen and their families was made abundantly clear in a survey of 1,834 housewives in the Tokyo, Kyoto, Osaka, and Kobe metropolitan areas conducted from August 1982 to February 1983. On average, these families owned two television sets, one air conditioner, three heaters, and two cameras; the husband's wardrobe included twenty-one neckties and nine pairs of slacks, and the wife's contained fourteen one-piece dresses or suits and seven handbags.[8] Throughout the 1980s, the diffusion of consumer durables such as videocassette recorders, microwave ovens, air conditioners, and passenger cars trended sharply upward.[9] And in the latter half of the decade, during the bubble economy, consumption was observed becoming even more of a mass experience and even more luxurious in taste. "Excessive" consumption was becoming a general, widespread phenomenon, noted some critics.[10] Providing data on this trend, the *Asahi* newspaper reported that in 1988, consumption expenditures of all workers increased regardless of their income level, and the gap in ownership of consumer durables based on income narrowed. Department store sales were up, and high-priced items such as large television sets, luxury cars, and women's clothing were selling well.[11] Others pointed out that it was certain groups of people, namely those who invested in real estate or stocks as well as the young and single, who were regularly engaging in luxurious consumption. Nonetheless, it was asserted in the pages of the prominent monthly magazine *Sekai* (The World) that even "regular Japanese" could partake of some opulence and experience the feeling of being rich in this "luxuriously consuming society."[12] In November 1989, the *Nikkei ryūtsū shinbun* (Nikkei Marketing Journal) observed from survey data that while the majority of people did not think of their lives as luxurious, and many thought that (other) Japanese people were being too luxurious, they also sought an increasingly "comfortable" life in which they could do such things as ride in the first-class car of the train or hire someone to clean their house.[13] Implicit in these views and patterns of consumption was a shift in expectations of what it meant to lead a middle-class life, that it was not just about a minimal level of creature comforts or the acquisition of a certain home appliance, but also about being able to afford regular consumption of the latest goods as well as the occasional splurge or indulgence.

At the same time, self-reported perceptions of luxury and standards of living were not so secure that they could be compromised for waste consciousness. When asked in national surveys to compare their daily life with that of the previous year, a growing majority over the course of the 1980s responded that it was the same, that they were doing no worse and no better. This could reflect the various constituent elements of standard of living, which encompassed not just material well-being but also the nonmaterial, such as leisure time, with which there tended to be lower levels of satisfaction.[14] Nevertheless, the combination of higher expectations with little sense of improvement in daily living may help explain why waste consciousness was typically conceived as a minimal intrusion into the way people lived.

This tack was apparent in efforts to save energy, particularly as the second oil crisis faded into memory and crude oil prices remained low. In a 1981 report, the Research Group on Energy-Saving Lifestyles (Shōenerugī Seikatsu Kenkyūkai) made it a point to note that while the term "energy-saving" might connote economy and retrenchment, the energy saving that was currently being sought was consistent with improving the standard of living. The group, consisting of ten representatives from business, labor, consumer advocacy, and academia, took as a given that economizing had a negative association with the wartime years, when there was retrenchment out of clear necessity. What was being asked of people now was rational consumption of energy, meaning energy use without waste (e.g., not leaving lights on in unoccupied rooms or letting dust build up in the vacuum cleaner); improvement in energy efficiency (e.g., buying energy-efficient electronic goods or controlling room temperatures with curtains or carpet); and

attention to lifestyle measures (e.g., thinking about the tendency toward disposability and the prioritization of consumption over saving).[15]

A member of the group and vice president of the Mitsubishi Research Institute
(Mitsubishi Sōgō Kenkyūjo), Makino Noboru, was acutely aware of how difficult
it was to conserve energy without a decline in the standard of living—or without
making people feel as though there had been a decline in their standard of living.
Makino noted that the first question that came up with any proposed attempt
to implement energy saving was whether or not it would negatively impact one's
daily life, and he suggested that people would not be agreeable to any inconvenience or reduction in the consumption of goods. To illustrate the conundrum,
he offered the mundane example of no longer eating winter cucumbers, since it
took three cups of oil to grow just ten of them. One might think that not having
cucumbers in the winter would not constitute a decrease in standard of living,
but Makino's hunch was that there would be objections to not being able to enjoy
cucumbers whenever one would like, just as people would not feel as though
their standard of living was as high if they rode the bus or train rather than
driving their car. Congruent with this understanding of people's expectations,
Makino's proposed ideas about energy conservation (a technological revolution
and the proper allocation of energy use at the systemic level) avoided altogether
any meaningful changes in people's daily lives.[16] When Makino's research was
presented in an article in the *Asahi* newspaper, the key point conveyed to readers
was that energy use could be cut in households by 5 percent without a decline
in standard of living. The modest techniques for saving energy listed in the article were reducing the opening and closing of the refrigerator door; periodically
cleaning the burner of the gas stove; having family members take a bath one after
another; and running full loads of laundry in the washing machine.[17]

Specific suggestions for not wasting energy were also offered in the book
Shōenerugī no chie (Advice for Saving Energy), together with the reassurance
that energy saving did not mean the imposition of "unreasonable saving" because
life should be worthwhile and pleasant. The author and electrical engineering
specialist Hashimoto Takashi stressed at the end of his book, which went through
a second printing within a month of its original release in 1980, that leading an
energy-saving life was simply about changing one's viewpoint. He encouraged
readers to just look around them, ask why things were the way they were, and
imagine how they ought to be. When it came to changes in behavior, the solutions he provided for wasteful energy consumption entailed little disruption to
people's daily lives: shutting the doors of train cars if they sat at the platform for
some time, running escalators at train stations only when people needed to use
them, and trying to shift electricity use to off-peak hours. To those most resistant

to energy saving, he merely suggested trying not to use energy when and if that was possible.[18]

Little was also asked by a social studies textbook for high school students. After assuring its young readers that economic activity could be expanded without much of a rise in the use of resources and energy, it went on to define the saving of resources and energy modestly as stopping the increase in (not decreasing) their consumption. And rather than focus on what actions students might take to save resources and energy, the textbook shifted the responsibility to others by emphasizing efficiency in the industrial sector and technological innovation. It also simply informed students about how the proliferation of disposable goods and planned obsolescence promoted unnecessary consumption without suggesting specific alternative consumer behaviors. The central argument was that with due attention to constraints, it would be possible both to save resources and energy and to enhance standards of living.[19]

The preference for saving energy with minimal disruption to daily life was expressed by quite a few respondents in a survey conducted by the Mitsubishi Research Institute. Asked their thoughts about the relationship between energy consumption and standard of living, the largest number of respondents (48 percent) said that wasteful energy consumption should be curtailed while maintaining the current standard of living. A smaller group (28 percent) answered that energy consumption should be kept at current levels by cutting down on waste and such, while not simply maintaining but actually improving further the standard of living.[20]

Such surveys often had a didactic function, with the questions worded to provoke reflection and response options intended to suggest changes in behavior. With the clear aims of educating and influencing survey takers, the New Life Movement Association (Shin Seikatsu Undō Kyōkai) must have been frustrated by the fruits of its labor. In 1980 the association conducted an investigation into saving resources and energy in daily life in response to what it considered to be the dire energy situation in Japan. Even though crude oil was relatively inexpensive at the time, the association foresaw a collapse in the balance of global supply and demand for oil, an oil shortage, and an energy crisis. Part one of the investigation was a sweeping survey of 10,665 households in 143 different municipalities, which asked quite a few questions about how things were used, since things and energy were considered two sides of the same coin. Part two required participants to keep a daily diary for the entire month of July 1980 to record, for example, how many times the refrigerator door was opened, how many plastic containers were brought into the house, how many hours the air conditioning was on, how much wastepaper was created, and how much television was watched in any given day.

When participants were asked what they had learned from the experience, in an explicit attempt to change their daily habits around energy use, the two most common answers offered by the almost four thousand respondents was that they had become aware of the necessity of saving energy (11 percent) and that they had discovered waste in their home (10.9 percent). Given the purposes of the investigation, these numbers must have struck the association as disappointingly low. A mere 4.4 percent said that they would put effort into the movement to save resources, 4.3 percent thought that there were too many plastic containers, and 3.1 percent said they consumed a lot of electricity.[21] In that same year, the Tokyo Electric Power Company (Tokyo Denryoku, or TEPCO) and Energy Conservation Center (Shōenerugī Sentā) conducted a survey of 13,109 people from Hokkaidō to Okinawa and even expatriates in Taiwan about their energy-saving consciousness. While many were well informed about the relative amount of energy needed to run various electric household appliances, consumers did not much consider electricity use when deciding to purchase new electric goods, but weighed more heavily a product's price, quality, and ease of use.[22]

Around the same time, in 1981, the Furukawa Electric Company (Furukawa Denki Kōgyō) carried out a more modest survey of three hundred housewives in Tokyo and Osaka to prepare for its launch of a household solar energy product. The company found that while almost all respondents (99 percent) were familiar with the term "saving energy" (shōene), only 20 percent said that they were actively implementing energy-saving measures, and 64 percent claimed that they "tended to" carry out energy saving.[23] In the middle of the decade, when the Prime Minister's Office conducted a survey of nearly eight thousand people about resources and their everyday lives, respondents seemed to be making only small adjustments in their ways of living. When asked what in their daily life they endeavored to do to save energy, the most common answer (68.4 percent) by a large margin was diligently turning off lights when not in use. This was followed by not leaving the television or radio on and watching television less (49.8 percent). Almost 13 percent of men reported not making much effort at all to save energy.[24] By decade's end, the Economic Planning Agency's National Lifestyle Bureau (Keizai Kikakuchō Kokumin Seikatsukyoku) was lamenting that especially since 1985, both awareness and action regarding saving resources and energy had ebbed.[25]

The explanation offered by the National Lifestyle Bureau for the weak consciousness of waste was a common one: that a strong yen, the drop in crude oil prices, and economic expansion had sapped issues regarding resources, energy, and garbage of their urgency. In a variation on this theme, the economist Kishimoto Shigenobu surmised that for many people, to be affluent was to not have to be frugal. The idea of saving, stamped with a negative connotation through its association with both the war and the Oil Shock, was considered the polar opposite of affluence. The mistake, in Kishimoto's view, was forging a link from oil shortages to recycling and economizing, because waste consciousness would then wax and wane depending on how acute the oil supply problem was at any given time.[26]

The idea that comfortable times had lulled people into a false sense of complacency was also articulated by the Central Council of the National Movement to Value Resources and Energy (Shigen to Enerugī o Taisetsu ni Suru Kokumin Undō Chūō Kaigi), the New Life Movement Association, and the Association to Build the Japan of Tomorrow (Ashita no Nihon o Tsukuru Kyōkai). In a declaration published in 1983 by all who were present at their Nationwide Conference on the National Movement to Save Energy and Save Resources, the organizations tried to make a case for the importance of their movement, arguing that saving resources and energy remained critical for a resource-poor Japan that was 10 percent of the world's economy and a large consumer of resources and energy. But they also acknowledged that the price of oil was declining, oil dependency was at a relatively low 64 percent, and energy consumption was decreasing.[27]

These restrained calls to save energy and the dampened commitment to reduction in energy consumption mostly dated from the first half of the 1980s, when the second oil crisis had passed and overall energy use in the country was fairly flat.[28] By 1985, the *Asahi* newspaper reported that the "energy-saving boom" of the late 1970s was over and provided results from nationwide surveys about energy-conscious behaviors.[29] Comparing February 1980 to May 1985, it noted that the percentage of respondents who said they were engaged in various energy-saving strategies declined. Such specific practices included diligently turning off lights when they were not needed (80.9 to 68.4 percent); not leaving on, and reducing time spent with, television and radio (65.4 to 49.8 percent); making sure that cooling and heating were not excessive (54.2 to 32.6 percent); and refraining from use of the family car (22.8 to 11.7 percent).[30] It was not until the late 1980s, when an upward trend in residential energy use became clear and the burgeoning global environmental movement provided a new framework for talking about energy consumption, that waste consciousness about energy reclaimed a place in the mainstream.

Accommodating Rubbish

Whatever victories were won in the Garbage War of the early 1970s, they did not hold against the sheer proliferation of trash in the 1980s. According to government statistics, the total amount of municipal solid waste rose from 42.7 million tons in 1983 to 50.4 million tons in 1990. Over these same years, per capita municipal solid waste increased from 980 grams per person a day to 1,120 grams, with the upward trend particularly steep in the late 1980s during the bubble economy. Even if the period were shifted a bit from 1975 to 1985 to exclude the bubble years, there was still a combined rise in industrial and nonindustrial waste of 27.8 percent. And to take one year, 1988, as an example, the country threw away 48.4 million tons, or 869 pounds per person, of trash. This translated into 132,581 tons, or 66,300 garbage trucks full, a day.[31]

Concern about the garbage problem revolved around the challenges posed to the sanitation management system by the amount and kind of rubbish being discarded. This issue was familiar to the sanitation industry, if exacerbated as the consuming and disposing behavior of middle-class consumers proceeded apace. But rather than confronting this predicament with an expansive consideration of waste, discussions focused narrowly on the trash itself—more than on the practices, structures, and lifestyles responsible for its production. Much information was thus generated and circulated about the content and fate of discarded stuff. And the oft-discussed waste issues of the day were the large consumer durables, plastic, and paper that came to saturate daily life and threw a wrench into efforts at garbage reduction.

Large refuse (*sodai gomi*), a category that included everything from household furniture to automobiles, created dilemmas with its depletion of valuable landfill real estate and its constituent parts that rendered recycling difficult. An enduring refrain was that new types of household electric appliances and passenger cars were being treated as disposable goods. Indeed, according to estimates from the early 1980s, an increasing number of color television sets, refrigerators, washing machines, and vacuum cleaners were being discarded; in a comparison of 1978 with 1982, the increase in discarded color televisions, to take one example, was 2,183,000. And this at a time when television sets were bulky and weighed in at almost fifty pounds.[32] In Tokyo, the large refuse items collected increased almost 30 percent from about 1,850,000 in 1985 to 2,360,000 just two years later.[33] To bring attention to oversized refuse, the topic was featured prominently in a special aired by the public broadcaster NHK and covered by the *Yomiuri* newspaper, titled *Ōinaru muda* (Big Waste). The documentary provided viewers with an image of perfectly good refrigerators, washing machines, and televisions thrown away as useless trash. To underscore the point, the documentary staff assembled a nice living room set from discarded items they found at the Island of Dreams landfill (Yume no Shima). And at a car disposal site in Gunma prefecture, the producer Ishizawa Kiyoshi informed his audience that 3.7 million cars, with mostly imported parts, were discarded annually in Japan.[34]

Disposable containers and packaging also vexed sanitation professionals and waste reduction advocates alike. Despite efforts by the Ministry of International Trade and Industry (Tsūshō Sangyōshō, or MITI) to curtail what was criticized in the 1970s as "excessive packaging" by stipulating fill rates and expense ceilings, the amount of packaging material shipped per capita increased between 1980 and 1988.[35] Aggravating this problem was the introduction of the polyethylene terephthalate, or PET, bottle to consumers and the waste stream. Easy to mold, hard to break, and light, the PET bottle was approved as a container for beverages in 1982 by the Ministry of Health and Welfare (Kōseishō).[36] Consumers appreciated having easy access to just the amount of beverage they wanted, and producers and distributors welcomed the ease of handling the bottles. From 1983 through the end of the decade, the use of PET bottles increased dramatically.[37] Without a system in place for recycling the plastic bottles, there was concern about exacerbating the creation of litter and garbage. An editorial in the *Yomiuri* newspaper expressed concern that littering would rise and participation in local recycling movements would decline, overburdened by the obligation to deal with the plastic containers. Use of PET bottles should be banned, argued the editorial, until the beverage industry accepted its social responsibility to deal with the plastic containers and a route for recycling was established.[38] Reflecting back on almost a decade, in 1991 the Ministry of Health and Welfare acknowledged that the spread of PET bottles had caused failures in the recycling system.[39]

The proliferation of PET bottles was emblematic of the larger challenge of plastic, which most municipalities did not incinerate because of the amount of heat the process generated. Thus in 1985, 44.2 percent of municipalities were collecting plastic as noncombustible waste, and the majority of plastic ended up in landfills.[40] By the end of the decade, plastic constituted almost 20 percent of what was separated out from burnable garbage, and a majority of the country's municipalities were at a loss over what to do about plastic waste.[41] This as the production of plastics (like polyethylene, polystyrene, polypropylene, and polyvinyl chloride) continued to increase.[42] When it came to plastic packaging in particular, the amount shipped increased from 1,141,500 tons in 1980 to 2,106,800 tons in 1990.[43]

Also challenging for recycling systems was the decrease in the use of glass bottles of standard sizes that could be returned and reused. By the mid-1980s, the large 633 milliliter glass bottles in which most beer had been sold accounted for only about half of the market. And the 1.8 liter glass bottle, the so-called *isshōbin* for sake, had declined by about a third over ten years. Of the total bottles produced, the proportion that could be returned and reused fell from 70 to 25 percent. According to Yamamoto Isao, a member of the National Federation of Glass

Bottlers (Zenkoku Bin Shō Rengōkai), this trend was driven by the diversification of consumer preferences as well as fierce competition among beverage makers to create something new (such as the sports beverage Pocari Sweat, which hit the market in 1980; the flavored alcoholic drink *chūhai* in a can, which debuted in 1984; or the now iconic Asahi Super Dry beer, which was introduced in 1987).[44] Developing innovative drinks and putting them in different containers were strategies to attract consumer attention and boost consumption in what was already considered an "era of satiation." And Yamamoto warned that the collapse of the recycling system for bottles would have implications for environmental conservation, the war against garbage, saving resources, and saving energy.[45]

Increased disposal of paper also rendered more difficult the management of refuse and the attempt to minimize the waste of resources. With the spread of so-called office automation through the use of business machines like computers, printers, and photocopiers, the amount of paper thrown away by offices rose, contributing to a spike after 1985 in the disposal of garbage by businesses. To take some 133 office buildings in the Tokyo business district of Marunouchi as an example, almost half (49 percent) of their garbage consisted of paper. While systems for collecting paper were already in place, the surge in the consumption of copy paper tested its limits. For even as more paper was recycled through the mid-1980s, the increase in the amount of paper consumed meant that the recycling rate was practically flat.[46] In the country overall, the amount of paper and cardboard consumed rose from 19.2 million tons in 1984 to 25.6 million tons in 1988, so even though the amount of used paper collected increased during these years, the recycling rate dropped from 50.7 to 47.5 percent.[47] And between 1987 and the end of the decade, demand for printer and copier paper increased by over 30 percent.[48] The technical problem with more paper in the waste stream was that it caused incinerators to burn hotter and at less than maximum capability; the larger societal problem, as it was understood at the time, was the squandering of resources by a country that was a big importer of wood. The waste of paper prompted the organization of events such as the Earth Friendly Paper Recycling Exhibition (Chikyū ni Yasashī Kami Risaikuru Ten) in Osaka, and discussion at a meeting of nineteen government ministries and agencies. For even the Environment Agency (Kankyōchō) was said to be consuming 5 million sheets of copy paper a year, or ten thousand sheets per worker.[49]

In the face of a mounting garbage problem, the response was modest. In the telling words of Gotō Sukehiro of the Environment Agency, the biggest question to ask about the future was: To what extent could garbage be reduced while maintaining the standard of living?[50] The lifestyles that many people had come to expect were a given, not to be sacrificed. Rare was the person who dared suggest that waste reduction was important and desirable despite the possibility of negative economic implications. Ide Toshihiko was one such unusual voice, who served four terms as an assemblyman and five years as the mayor of Numazu city, in Shizuoka prefecture, and was a widely recognized innovator in garbage separation. Interviewed in the late 1980s about his thoughts on garbage disposal, Ide was quite active then in citizens' movements as the director of a consumer cooperative (Seikatsu Kurabu Seikyō) and a representative of the Citizens' Association for Thinking about Garbage (Haikibutsu o Kangaeru Shimin no Kai). Ide did not shy away from bold and implausible ideas, like turning a central park in large cities, such as Hibiya Park in Tokyo, into a dump so as to force people to experience firsthand the pain of garbage management. He also made no bones about the economic costs of reducing garbage. So entwined were systems of production and garbage disposal, and so great the dependency on mass production and mass consumption, that sincere efforts to reduce garbage would require slimming down production and lifestyles. If things were valued and kept for a long time, if disposability tapered, and if garbage were thus reduced, there would be, in Ide's blunt estimation, a sharp drop in GDP.[51] Such a view, expressed so unapologetically, was an aberration in this decade. Much more typical was the assumption that affluence and daily lives were not to be jeopardized, which encouraged the tendency to define the challenges posed by garbage in terms of sanitation management.

Quite often, garbage disposal was presented as an issue of sanitation administration with financial costs. In one *Yomiuri* newspaper article, readers were provided with calculations from the Ministry of Health and Welfare about the amount of garbage thrown out on a yearly and daily basis. The requisite expense was illustrated in a cartoon, framed centrally by the text, of garbage trucks dumping their loads on an island prominently marked with a price tag of 1.35 trillion yen. This was the rough estimated cost for disposing of the 50 million tons of trash to be landfilled on an island that Tokyo had been creating since 1977; this new island was drawn to dwarf the old Island of Dreams landfill in the background, with its much smaller price tag of 30 billion yen. With the caption "Nation Building, Modern Edition: If Garbage Accumulates, It Becomes an Island," the cartoon illustrated the absurdity of such large spending on waste and of the very idea of constructing a landmark out of trash. But to reduce the financial expenditure for processing garbage, readers were simply told not to discard "wasteful garbage" and to sort their garbage properly.[52]

The Ministry of Health and Welfare, the governmental body that oversaw sanitation, regularly emphasized the financial costs of citizens' lifestyles and economic activity. Katō Saburō of the ministry's Environmental Management Section (Kankyō Seibika) laid out in a newspaper article the four principles of trash: all human beings create trash, as they do excrement; no one likes it; garbage can be disposed of safely and cleanly if today's technology is used fully; and finally, disposal takes money, and is dependent on how much tax money is spent. The first principle ignored an important distinction between material and bodily waste: that the volume of garbage created can vary, and can be controlled to a much greater extent than human excrement. By eliding the ability of people to reduce their output of rubbish, Katō made the amount of stuff currently being thrown out seem perfectly natural. And the fourth principle implied that the garbage problem could be solved quite easily with the appropriate allocation of significant tax dollars.[53] In the same vein, the ministry enumerated in a white paper on public welfare the costs of a sanitation process that "made garbage vanish from before people's very eyes." In 1988, those figures were 1.2 trillion yen (an increase of 6.3 percent from the previous year), or 9,399 yen per person (an increase of 5.8 percent). The report also pointed out the hidden costs of garbage disposal to municipalities, the majority of which hauled away trash as a service without assessing a fee, and to consumers, who assumed the financial burden of disposal in the price they paid for a product. To make progress toward "real affluence," the ministry urged that the total cost of affluence be calculated more accurately and honestly by taking into account "social costs" like garbage disposal.[54]

Other responses to these garbage management challenges were much the same as they had been for over a decade, with great emphasis placed on recycling as a way to diminish the waste stream and recapture resources from the trash heap. The promotion of recycling had been jump-started by the Oil Shock in the early 1970s and remained vibrant in the 1980s, looming so large in waste consciousness that it seemed to be the primary answer to the garbage problem. And this answer was quite narrow in its preoccupation with preserving lifestyles of consumption: resources were to be valued because their depletion would spell the end of contemporary ways of life; proper separation of garbage and recyclables focused attention on practices of disposal rather than on consumption; and flea markets did not discourage the propensity to acquire material things.

One of the primary motivations for recycling continued to be saving resources, a rationale that had been shaped by the insecurities of the previous decade. A social studies textbook, approved for use in high schools through the 1980s by the Ministry of Education (Monbushō), offered a familiar narrative to another generation of students. The advanced countries of the world had fueled their affluence with oil and other resources, the textbook explained, but their societies of mass consumption and their cultures and economies of disposability were hastening the time when humankind would bump up against the limits to such resources, so there was no choice but to put effort into saving resources and energy. Specific mention was made of Japan's dependence on oil, which provided more than half of the country's energy, to perpetuate the understanding of Japan as a nation lacking in resources.[55]

The idea of a resource-poor Japan made objectionable the disregard for anything from metal and glass to oil that was considered a resource, and reinforced initiatives to save valuable resources from ending up as garbage. In terms of concrete actions, recycling (*risaikuru* or *saishigenka*, literally "turn into resources again") encompassed everything from taking large glass bottles back to stores for reuse to repairing appliances, from swapping used goods with others to composting. By the mid-1980s, roughly 90 percent of the more than three thousand municipalities in the country had recycling programs, the majority of which were run by private industry or civic groups.[56] While a similar percentage separated their garbage into at least two types, combustible and noncombustible, it is less clear how many went as far as Toyohashi city in Aichi prefecture, whose oft-mentioned collection system had five categories: combustible, noncombustible, oversized, toxic, and recyclable (*shigen gomi*, or "resource garbage").[57]

Citizens' groups such as consumer organizations, women's groups, neighborhood associations, and PTAs were largely responsible for the momentum behind recycling movements. They collected recyclables in places where municipalities had not yet assumed this responsibility; pushed for corporations to be responsible for collecting the used bottles and cans that littered the streets of cities like Kyoto; and facilitated the exchange of used goods like children's clothes and toys.[58] Such efforts could be on a small scale, as in Hakodate city in Hokkaidō, where the PTA of one elementary school decided to start collecting recyclables in 1980.[59] Or it could be on a larger scale, as in the twenty-three wards of Tokyo, where there were an estimated 1,700 to 1,900 recycling groups in 1980 with some 800,000 participating households; by 1982, there were 2,100 such groups with 890,000 participating households. A majority of these were already existing organizations that decided to take up recycling activities, but others formed for the specific purpose of collecting recyclables. There was a particular surge of attention in the early 1980s to aluminum cans, such that the estimated number of groups that collected them rose from ten in 1980 to five hundred the following year.[60]

By the middle of the decade, flea markets and garage sales, which had sprouted in the 1970s, seem to have gained a toehold as recycling phenomena. Responsible for some of the organizational momentum behind these events were regional branches of the Recycling Movement Citizens' Association (Risaikuru Undō Shimin no Kai), originally founded in the Kansai area in 1977. By the early 1980s, the Kansai group's monthly magazine *Risaikuru nyūsu* (Recycle News) had a circulation of 81,000 copies, the largest for any publication by a citizens' group. And the association had added more newly established branches in central Japan, focused on Nagoya, and in the Kantō area. A guiding principle behind their flea markets was that they should be fun and appeal to the playful mood of participants, especially the young people and housewives who constituted their core.[61] One association representative also noted that the efficacy of flea markets was in their embrace of an economic rationale in which things could be turned into money. Tapping into financial considerations, he thought, encouraged recycling more effectively than abstract appeals to appreciate things or value limited resources.[62]

Embracing the motivations of participants, the Recycling Movement Citizens' Association seems to have built a healthy interest in its events. One popular garage sale organized by the Kantō association was held regularly on the grounds of the Honganji Temple in the Tsukiji neighborhood of Tokyo. On one particular autumn Sunday, there were 230 vendors, half of whom set up shop in the back of their hatchbacks and station wagons to sell everything from clothes to furniture to home appliances in various conditions and at various prices to the fifty thousand or so people who came through between 10:00 am and 4:00 pm.[63] The Kantō group, which had about three thousand members in 1984, also held monthly flea markets in the city of Musashino.[64] One of the larger affairs organized jointly by multiple branches of the Recycling Movement Citizens' Association along with other groups and the municipal government was a two-day event in Hamamatsu city, Shizuoka prefecture, in August 1987. In a large public space alongside a lake, eight hundred stores were expected to pop up, along with a DJ corner and a teach-in area, to cater to some 100,000 attendees.[65] On occasion, the Recycling Movement Citizens' Association provided the initiative for the establishment of flea markets outside urban and suburban areas, which became locally self-sustaining, as with the "Alps flea market" in a hamlet of 2,600 people in Nagano prefecture.[66]

Overall, there is evidence to suggest that there was something of a boom in flea markets starting in the middle of the decade. According to a survey of one thousand people conducted by the Tokyo Metropolitan Government in 1987, 55 percent of households said that they had donated or sold used goods at a swap meet, bazaar, or garage sale, and 51 percent said that they had purchased such secondhand items. And 75 percent reported that they had participated in a swap meet or rummage sale.[67] In this vein of repurposing used things, there was also more interest, particularly among young people, in secondhand shops starting in the mid-1980s. It was estimated that there were a few hundred such shops in Tokyo, and approximately eight hundred nationwide. An early version of a genre that would become even more popular in the following decade, the weekly magazine *Asahi jānaru* (Asahi Journal) published a guide for readers, in manga style, to secondhand shops in the Tokyo, Nagoya, Osaka, Kyoto, and Kobe metropolitan areas.[68]

Recycling was also offered as an antidote to specific waste problems, be it large refuse or paper. The NHK producer Ishizawa Kiyoshi was optimistic, at least in the early 1980s, about technologies to sort large refuse and recover resources like platinum and cobalt.[69] In a more creative take on recycling, the city of Yokosuka in Kanagawa prefecture held a five-day event in mid-August 1980 called the Garbage and Living Exhibition (Gomi to Seikatsu Ten). City residents were to bring in empty metal cans to exchange for entry into a lottery for prizes such as a bed, kitchen set, refrigerator, washing machine, stereo, guitar, or bicycle. The twist was that the eight-hundred-some displayed objects had been picked out of collected large refuse and repaired by city officials. The purpose of the event was twofold: providing an incentive for people to pick up the used cans that littered city streets, and encouraging the reuse of large items that would otherwise be refuse.[70] When it came to paper as well, there were various efforts, on the part of corporations, to recycle and repurpose. Fuji Xerox and the Ōji Paper Company (Ōji Seishi) jointly developed a product for use in copy machines that was made from 70 percent recycled paper. And the Seibu department store (Seibu Hyakkaten), in cooperation with the West German paper company Steinbeis, created computer and copy paper made from 80 percent recycled newspaper. Somewhat more mundane than such product development, the Hiroshima-based Nichie supermarkets reused paper for shopping bags and wrapping paper. And the supermarket company Seiyū, together with Ōji Paper, established a recycling system whereby paper was reused within the company for printing and photocopying.[71]

To encourage recycling and discourage thoughtless disposal, one strategy from the 1970s that continued to be employed was the appeal for people to appreciate things. In Kyoto prefecture, a Council for the Promotion of the Movement to Value Things (Mono o Taisetsu ni Suru Undō Kyoto-fu Suishin Kaigi) was established to champion the saving of resources and energy. If the next generation was to inherit the affluent, happy, and comfortable way of living that had been realized, then things, resources, and energy could not be wasted. As part of its efforts, the council held a poster contest that solicited almost four hundred entries from elementary school and middle schools students, all of which were variations on the theme of appreciating things and resources.[72] Such attempts to educate young people could extend to high school students, as with a home economics textbook in which the authors urged readers to use things with care and to think about recycling in a section of the book titled "Garbage and Recycling: Things Also Have Life."[73]

Investing physical stuff with life (*inochi*) helped imbue the valuing of things with moral overtones and discourage their casual and callous disposal. In an editorial titled "Wasteful Purchase by a Careless Housewife," the *Yomiuri* newspaper castigated said thoughtless woman for ruining a new dress by throwing it into the washing machine. If she had paid more attention to the tag indicating that the dress had to be dry-cleaned, instructed the editorial, she might not have purchased it on impulse as she did and would not have put it in the washer and shrunk "the life of the thing."[74]

Occasionally the moral virtue of not wasting was expressed in vaguely religious terms. In an animated public service announcement produced by the advertising firm Dentsū Osaka, memorable to those who saw it at the time, four young children were invited to dinner at a Buddhist temple by its priest. There they made the grave mistake of being finicky and refusing to eat foods they did not like. Almost gleeful in their disregard for the food, they laughed while proclaiming their dislike for specific foods, with one boy even tossing aside a carrot, which bounced off a resting cat's head and onto the ground. That night, they were haunted in their nightmares by food—a carrot, daikon radish, eggplant, cucumber, bean, and stalk of rice—which encircled them and repeatedly chanted, "Wasteful, wasteful" (mottainai, mottainai). The next morning at breakfast, the priest explained that they had been visited by the "no waste ghost" (mottainai obake). Thoroughly frightened and chastised, the four children ate everything on their plates, to the approval of the priest, having demonstrated that they had learned the lesson that was explicitly and succinctly presented onscreen at the end of the announcement: "Cherish food."[75] The act of not turning food into garbage was imbued with moral and spiritual meaning by the setting of the Buddhist temple, the didacticism of the priest, and the supernatural haunting by the "no waste ghost."

Instruction about how to treat things could take other entertaining forms, as it did with "Risaikuru ondo" (The Recycling Song). This musical case for recycling was sung by the female artist Kashino Michi and was available on a record created by the city of Zentsūji in Kagawa prefecture. With a chorus that encouraged recycling resources by separating garbage, the song had three verses, each of which ended with a different version of a line about valuing things: "Cherish the life of things, if you throw it away, that's the end"; "Cherish the life of things, if you incinerate it, that's the end"; "Cherish the life of things, if you bury it, that's the end."[76] The evocation of incineration and burial made especially disturbing the song's equation of disposal with death.

In keeping with the vaguely spiritual overtones of valuing things, a connection was sometimes made between the treatment of material stuff and one's heart or soul (kokoro). The Asahi newspaper, in an article about large refuse published on the cusp of the 1980s, expressed fear about what would happen if waste consciousness and the valuing of things were to disappear, and warned that the bleakness of disposability would ruin the hearts of children and adults alike.[77] The valuing of things also served as a slogan for the encouragement of recycling, as it had in previous years. The Garbage and Living Exhibition organized by

Yokosuka city in 1980 was in part an advertisement for the sanitation bureau's campaign for "A Heart That Values Things."[78] And for the economist Kishimoto Shigenobu, it was not sufficient to value things; one had to be moved, touched by the life of things, as a fundamental condition for creating real affluence.[79]

With all the different shades of meaning that the appreciation of things could assume, it is not surprising that people had different understandings of the idea. In a survey conducted in 1985 by the Prime Minister's Office about lifestyles and resources, the very first question posed to the almost eight thousand respondents was about how they were valuing things in their daily lives. While the question nudged survey takers to consider the idea of valuing things as something more than pure rhetoric and in slightly more specific terms, the answer options were quite vague. Topping the list was "eliminating waste" at 58.4 percent, followed by "using things efficiently" at 38.4 percent. In a reflection of the financial and material affluence of the times, "abstaining from what you want," "scrimping on daily life," and "making do with inexpensive things" were the least popular responses. The second question on the survey followed up with an inquiry about the extent to which people were putting effort into valuing things in their daily lives. Given the moral tone of the question, it is not too surprising that the most common response was "always" at 53.2 percent. But it is worth noting that "sometimes" was the response chosen most often by people in their twenties and thirties.[80]

However flexible, the idea of appreciating things was part of the enthusiastic and almost singular focus on recycling as a corrective to the proliferation of physical waste. But there was occasional acknowledgment of the challenges, if not always the limits, to recycling. In a panel discussion about garbage hosted by the Tokyo Sanitation Bureau (Tokyo-to Seisōkyoku), one participant implied that there was a finite audience for such practices as swap meets because, he speculated, Japanese people were averse to used things, particularly other people's used things. To support his generalization, the film director Yamamoto Shin'ya spoke of funeral rites (kuyō) for inanimate objects like needles or clocks, at the end of which they were typically cremated (incinerated). This was evidence, he claimed, that Japanese people needed to get rid of something once it had been used, which rendered recycling or reuse very difficult. In more concrete and compelling terms, the waste management expert Tanaka Masaru touched on the economic disincentives to recycling as the stronger yen made it cheaper to simply import new materials from abroad.[81] And the producer Ishizawa Kiyoshi pointed to the technological hurdles, as his earlier optimism about recycling large refuse later gave way to disappointment that only the scrap iron and aluminum in cars were being recycled and that the increased use of plastic made fewer and fewer parts of a car recyclable. The revolution in materials was progressing apace without a concomitant revolution in recycling technology, he lamented.[82]

At the very end of the decade, any doubts about the efficacy of recycling were drowned out as heightened concerns about garbage reinforced convictions about the need to recycle. In 1989, attention to garbage and recycling intensified as the country, and especially its capital, struggled to deal with the problems created by the ever-increasing physical waste of the bubble economy. Even as lifestyles appeared to be more affluent than they had ever been in the postwar period, there were unpleasant and unavoidable reminders of the incivility of trash. In late September 1989, the language of "fly riots" (*hae sōdō*) made a comeback as the pests overran areas along Tokyo Bay, including the Shinagawa, Kōtō, Ōta, Edogawa, Chūō, and Minato wards. Public health centers and ward offices expressed concern as the flies laid their eggs in household garbage, and store owners, particularly food purveyors, who could not use insecticides, attempted to fend them off with swatters and flypaper. One fishmonger in Shinagawa testified that in a mere three hours, the flypaper strips he had hung in his shop became black with insects; and on one afternoon alone, some 230 complaints flooded in to ward offices. While the spraying of insecticide and use of flypaper brought the outbreak under control by mid-October, the uncertainty of its precise source even weeks later and suspicion about what was really happening at nearby garbage disposal sites unsettled those residents who had been shaken by what was dubbed the "fly panic."[83] Despite these concerns, in 1989 outbreaks of pests were not treated as a civilizational threat as they once had been, but were mere nuisances that should not inconvenience the routines of daily life.

In that same year, there were also comparatively cursory responses to what was called a Garbage War. Although this Garbage War highlighted the insufficiencies of sanitation management in Tokyo as its predecessor had done in 1971, it did not inspire prolonged conversations and extensive efforts to curtail the production of rubbish. The conflict erupted when it was revealed in May that the city of Chiba, a large commuter suburb of Tokyo, had transported to the faraway northern town of Takko in Aomori prefecture not just incinerator ash, as was claimed, but also a large amount of untreated garbage. What was transported to, and remained in, Takko-machi was equivalent to more than a year of its own refuse. The town's residents were upset that it was being treated as a dumping ground, and for their part, the people of Chiba were surprised to learn from the incident the severity of their garbage problem. In his response to the affront, the mayor of Takko-machi insisted that Tokyoites dispose of their own garbage and insinuated that there would be enough space to do so, even in crowded Chiba prefecture, if golf courses and seaside resorts were knocked down to make room for treatment plants. The obvious charge was that suburbanites were prioritizing leisure over sanitation infrastructure, pursuing luxury at the expense of what should be considered a necessity. The entire controversy left the impression of a privileged Tokyo that was being overwhelmed by its trash. And the situation with Aomori, together with examples of industrial waste disposal in other prefectures in the region like Yamagata and Miyagi, led critics to dub the situation the Tōhoku Garbage War (Tōhoku Gomi Sensō). While it seems misleading to characterize in aggregate the cases of waste transport from the Tokyo metropolitan area to the Tōhoku region, especially given the unclear and different extent of legal infraction and local complicity, there was a legitimate sense that a less wealthy area of the country was being made to assume an unfair burden for the wealth and extravagance of the capital. And extrapolating this injustice beyond Japan, the prominent and progressive monthly magazine *Sekai* saw Chiba's "dumping" of garbage on Takko-machi as a harbinger of what Japan as a whole would soon be doing to the countries of Southeast Asia.[84]

In response to the surge in garbage produced in the second half of the 1980s, and the faster than expected depletion of landfill space, the Tokyo Sanitation Bureau launched in June 1989 a campaign called TOKYO SLIM '89 to stress—in entertaining and enjoyable ways—the importance of recycling and garbage reduction. The campaign consisted of printing a thin magazine called *Gomi puresu* (Garbage Press), aimed at single women in their early twenties and housewives of the baby boom generation. The publication disseminated news about the sanitation industry and information about secondhand shops, PR tours, and the organization of various events, like displays and giveaways of perfectly good items rescued from the trash.[85] One of these affairs, in September 1989, was a combined concert and forum about garbage that had a talk show format. Rather than following the usual model of sanitation professionals and experts giving dense lectures, the campaign invited six panelists, including a comedian, an actress, and a movie director, who shared their own ideas about and personal experiences with garbage.[86] The campaign's largest event, in March 1990, was a "garbage festival" called "TOKYO SLIM IN DOME," held, as its name suggested, in the newly built Tokyo Dome stadium. With the aim of making recycling and waste reduction fun, the festival included concerts, a quiz show, the dome's first flea market, a museum with historical artifacts and information about the sanitation industry, and a garbage-themed playland for children and their parents. About 54,000 people were said to have participated in this event, which was designed, like the campaign itself, to disseminate information about garbage and recycling through pleasing and enjoyable media.[87]

Much of the marketing of the TOKYO SLIM '89 campaign seems to have been more about the evocation of feelings and aspirations than the nitty-gritty of garbage reduction. One of its frequently reproduced posters featured the campaign's name and slogan ("Wanting to Think Now about Tokyo's Garbage") against a backdrop of two photographs. One showed tall buildings, erect and with clean, straight lines. The other was a close-up on the face of a captivating foreign woman, head tilted slightly to the side, with a seductive look in her eyes. This photograph is puzzling in its beckoning of a male gaze and its presentation of a female beauty inherently unattainable to Japanese women in its non-Japaneseness, and at a time when women were the primary managers of household garbage. But considered together, the two images worked to capture the elements of the campaign—the buildings as "Tokyo," gendered male, and the face as "slim," gendered female. Without an explicit image or even a mention of garbage, save for the two *kana* characters for *gomi*, there was no indication that the campaign was about rubbish. What was being sold was beauty and even sexual allure.

If this poster free of garbage illustrated the aspirational feelings of the campaign, its mascot was both a visceral personification of muck and the embodiment of how to combat it. Created by the Sanitation Bureau, the squat monster had short arms, oversized feet, two antennae, a long tail, crooked teeth, and mischievous eyes. A contest was held to name it, and after eight thousand suggestions had been submitted and votes had been cast, the winning moniker was announced: Gomira, a pun on garbage (*gomi*) and Godzilla (Gojira). Said the monster: "My name is Gomira. I won't let slide those people who mishandle their garbage." It was explained that Gomira expressed its emotions easily (turning red when angry, pink when laughing, blue when crying) and liked children. More directly relevant to rubbish, he could separate garbage with his antennae and crush large refuse with his tail, and his hobby was participating in recycling movements. Like Godzilla, this monster seemed to have been created out of a human flaw and endowed with an enviable power. Gomira called upon a disgust with garbage, but also a desire to fight it; above all, the mascot gave the campaign a fun and playful feel.[88] This was not the gloomy approach to many waste reduction efforts of the early 1970s, with their apocalyptic images of overflowing garbage trucks and overwhelmed landfills intended to invoke fear of an immediate civilizational threat. Promoted instead were easy, fun, and modest measures to contain the problem and maintain a comfortable lifestyle.

Critiques from the Margins

The steep increase in municipal solid waste disposal in the second half of the 1980s seen in cities around the country (Yokohama, Kawasaki, Nagoya, Osaka, Hiroshima, and Kita Kyūshū) was particularly acute in Tokyo, such that efforts to curtail the rapid production of rubbish was dubbed by some the (second) Garbage War.[89] Although this Garbage War shared some concerns with the first in 1971, this one did not inspire sustained and probing discussions about the connections between economic growth, mass production, mass consumption, lifestyles of convenience and comfort, and the proliferation of rubbish. There were those who were critical of what they saw as a culture of disposability. Sanitation professionals and recycling proponents were among those who considered the volume and kind of Japan's "quotidian refuse" a reflection of the ease and frequency with which things were being deemed useless, and of lives replete with wasteful disposability.[90] But on the whole, these voices were not as common, prominent, or forceful as those of the previous decade.

The Ministry of Health and Welfare expressed a vague sense of discomfort with the values of a society that seemed to discard things so casually. Commenting on the seemingly inevitable pull toward disposability, the ministry appreciated that electric household appliances and disposable goods had lightened the burden of housework and child care, and that mass consumption and a culture of disposability were rational and necessary for increased demand and continued economic growth. And it conceded that the virtue of frugality that had been forged in the context of shortages could not be expected to fit the present and future. Only then was it suggested that the pursuit of economic growth had gone too far in making a virtue of disregard for disposal and the disposed, rendering it too easy to cast away and forget that which had been deemed useless.[91]

For some recycling advocates, especially leaders of the Recycling Movement Citizens' Association, the organization of flea markets was a direct and purposeful response to their concerns about the abundance and thoughtless disposal of things. Founder Takami Yūichi came to have doubts about a society that threw away so much and hoped for an era in which things were used, managed, and mastered. This treatment of things, he argued, was ultimately connected to living an enjoyable, individual lifestyle. What Takami was suggesting was not a rejection of the material or of material consumption, but a regard for things and their use. For Hagiwara Yoshiyuki, a representative of the central Japan group, what was especially concerning was how people's numbness toward things, brought on by high growth and mass consumption, translated into increasingly alienated and estranged human relationships. So for him, the exchange of used goods was also about establishing a connection between people—the passing down of baby clothes created an opportunity to talk about raising children, for example. Perhaps the boldest statement about the potential of flea markets to change people's behavior came from Ishige Takeshi, an original member of the group, who believed they encouraged people to reject shiny new things and famous brands. What Ishige seemed to be hinting at was the possibility for people to consume in a different way, one less shaped by trends, marketing, and advertising.[92]

Perhaps the most pointed and deliberate critique of disposability was articulated by Tsuchida Takashi, who had founded the Association for Thinking about the Throwaway Age (Tsukaisute Jidai o Kangaeru Kai) in 1973. At a symposium held to mark the tenth anniversary of the association, Tsuchida spoke frankly regarding the insufficiency of rhetoric about the valuing of things and the wastefulness of throwing things away. His comments about the emptiness of such slogans echoed the introductory remarks made by Yamada Kunihiro, who explicitly challenged the notion of recent shifts—from things to heart, from quantity to quality, and from high growth to stable growth—by pointing out the enduring allure and "sweet taste" of economic growth. Tsuchida went further to suggest that disposability was threatening humanity itself. Egoism and living only for the pleasures of the moment were the essence of present-day prosperity and civilization, and the ability to make things more easily and cheaply devalued the human labor that went into the creation of things, to the point where the disposal of stuff assumed the disposability of people.[93] Tsuchida's response in his own daily life was to challenge the standardization of products, resist expectation of the instantaneous, and appreciate human labor through such self-admittedly modest acts like eating additive-free foods, organic vegetables, and brown rice, and making his own miso. He taught this skill to others and encouraged people to grow their own produce, which could be done even in a city by repurposing a polystyrene box from the local fishmonger as a planter. What Tsuchida was attempting to do on a small scale was to distance himself from the logics and structures of industrialized food, and in the process he suggested that with the end of an industrial society would certainly come an era more materially poor but affluent of heart—more fun, symbiotic, peaceful, and protective of people and the earth.[94] Tsuchida's philosophy seems to have animated the work of the association as a whole, with some 1,700 member households, as he encouraged them to reflect on the relationship between consumers and producers and the meanings of convenience and affluence, and to pursue their own initiatives, whether eating organic foods, collecting used milk cartons, or disseminating information about garbage reduction.[95]

Much simpler messages about disposability were conveyed through the cartoons of Takatsuki Hiroshi, pen name High Moon, a professor with a doctorate in engineering and a waste management specialist. Straightforward in style, content, and didactic intention, his cartoons on the theme of garbage were originally published in the monthly magazine *Haikibutsu* (Waste) and then compiled in a seven-volume series, the first of which was published in 1986 and was in its eighth printing by the late 1990s. In one particular cartoon, an imagined scene from the near future, two vending machines stood side by side, one for canned beverages and one for umbrellas. Just after a rain, the ground was littered with discarded umbrellas and a garbage bin overflowed with both umbrellas and empty cans. The obvious point was that the practice of disposability, and mechanisms for the consumption of disposable goods, had become so accepted and common that even things not inherently disposable could be discarded with ease. Another of Takatsuki's cartoons pictured a baby with a contraption full of disposable diapers strapped to his back. When the baby wet his diaper, the electricity automatically turned on the machine, which ejected the dirty diaper packed in a plastic bag and replaced it with a clean one from the container on his back. The child's mother, talking with another woman over coffee, marveled at this "automatic diaper-changing machine" and decided, "Next, I want an automatic nursing machine." Below the cartoon were statistics about the increase in the production of disposable diapers, paper tissues, and paper towels.[96] Here Takatsuki was clearly criticizing how an absurd and unnatural desire for convenience resulted in the creation of physical waste.

In a much more irreverent way, the avant-garde artist and writer Akasegawa Genpei satirically described an entrenched "rhythm of life" by which things, from clothes to cars and homes, were regularly thrown out, to be replaced by the new. To Akasegawa, the disposability of postwar Japan was driven by a desire for convenience and comfort, and was thus different from the disposability of a "traditional" sort, which was about religion or aesthetics (talismans purchased annually at religious festivals, the rebuilding of the Ise Shrine every twenty years, easily torn *shōji* paper, the arrangement of flowers that would soon wither, and so on).[97] Akasegawa explored such issues of disposability through the Society for the Study of Disposability (Tsukaisute Kōgen Gakkai), which he helped establish in 1987 at the suggestion of the writer, editor, flea market organizer, and society chairman Ni'imi Yasuaki. Described as a "unique" group by the *Asahi* newspaper, it consisted at its founding of about fifty gallery owners, illustrators, and students. Akasegawa was inspired by his surprise that the country had become a "disposing superpower" and by his curiosity about how and why this had come to be.[98] In a book that seems to have grown out of the society's discussions, Akasegawa, together in conversation with the social critic Kure Tomofusa, listed items in postwar daily life that were disposable and wasteful, including cellophane tape, film canisters, the can for dried seaweed, the tin for Izumiya cookies, plastic wrap, aluminum foil, milk cartons, popcorn in its own pan, and disposable cameras.[99] To further illustrate how disposable goods permeated daily life, Akasegawa judged various household items in a contest of his own design, assigning each object points in three areas: level of convenience, wastefulness (*mottainai-do*), and fun. A high score, and a special "wastefulness" (*mottainai*) prize, were given to fancy packaging for high-end goods, such as the six layers of wrapping on sponge cakes sold by the store Fukusaya or the gift-wrapping of whisky. Bentō boxes, disposable hand and feet warmers, and the telephone card that could be used for public phones in place of coins were all part of the contest.

But the scoring itself had no meaning; because the three criteria were not treated as equivalent, morally or otherwise, the total score was not a measure of anything in particular. The lack of consideration of competing values (e.g., convenience, disposability, and good hygiene), the usefulness of things (e.g., condoms), and the arguable necessity of a product (e.g., medical syringes), combined with the impertinent tone, contributed to a sense of absurdity about both the game and the disposable items themselves. Following up the contest with a list of even more disposable goods, from toothpicks to lighters, and a discussion of disposable people, from athletes to salarymen and cabinet ministers, Akasegawa viscerally conveyed how saturated he found daily life to be with disposable commodities.[100]

In another, more thoughtful and rigorous way, Akasegawa highlighted the ubiquity of meaningless objects intentionally created by the desires of a commodified society by drawing attention to the rarity of their antithesis—objects that had seemingly outlived their use, that should have been discarded as waste, but that unintentionally and mysteriously continued to exist. Akasegawa stumbled upon such a thing in the early 1970s when he noticed an outdoor staircase in the Yotsuya neighborhood of Tokyo that could be ascended and descended from two opposite sides but led nowhere. Not only had the staircase not been destroyed and discarded, but also someone had made the effort to repair part of the banister. Mused Akasegawa: "Capitalism doesn't allow for this sort of uneconomical thing. Everything in our capitalist society has to have a purpose. So where does that leave this particular staircase?"[101] Artist Akasegawa considered the staircase an example of "hyperart," a work that is not created but comes into being unintentionally, through discovery. He then gave purposeless urban fragments like the staircase an afterlife as art, publishing a book in 1985 that dubbed such objects "Thomassons" (tomason).[102] The term was inspired by the American baseball player Gary Thomasson who, after a career in Major League Baseball, was hired by the Yomiuri Giants for what would turn out to be the final, and by all accounts disappointing, two years of his career. In Akasegawa's description: "He had a fully-formed body and yet served no purpose to the world . . . Seriously, I can't think of any way to describe Gary Thomasson but as 'living hyperart.'"[103] The search for Thomassons in urban Tokyo became a phenomenon in the 1980s, as the younger generation especially took to the streets to find and capture through photographs the beauty of these useless objects. Their hunt was organized by the satirically named Street Observation Science Society (Rojō Kansatsu Gakkai), which had been established in 1986 by Akasegawa and the architecture historian Fujimori Terunobu of the University of Tokyo, and was ignited by the release of the pocket edition of Akasegawa's book in 1987. In the recollection of the historian Jordan Sand, "all the kids in town" had the paperback in hand that year.[104]

FIGURE 5.2. The Original Thomasson. The staircase that inspired Akasegawa's search for Thomassons.

Reproduced by permission from Genpei Akasegawa, *Hyperart*, trans. Matthew Fargo (New York: Kaya Press, 2009).

Like Akasegawa, other commentators described aspects of seemingly entrenched structures of waste. For Miyajima Nobuo, it was the squandering of energy as well as things and resources that was systemic. Miyajima worked for most of his life at a foreign oil company, had a post-retirement career teaching at universities, and published numerous works on energy including *Tairyō rōhi shakai* (Mass Waste Society) in 1990. In his view, the increased use of plastic bottles, containers, and petroleum-based bags was evidence of the waste of energy. And then there was the selling of beverages in a growing number of vending machines—2.5 million, or one per every fifteen households, in 1988—which used electricity equivalent to 7 percent of total household electricity consumption. In an unusually wide-ranging critique, Miyajima took aim not just at consumers' expectations for convenience and disposability, but also at how an economic system built on the continual enlargement of productive power created garbage, threw away resources, and consumed large amounts of energy.[105]

Others emphasized the societal practices that made wasting virtually inescapable. Yorimoto Katsumi, a professor of government at Waseda University, pinned his hopes on consumers and businesses to "rein in the wasteful habits" that were the cause of the garbage problem, but he acknowledged the difficulty of what he was asking of consumers. Even those well-intentioned and savvy consumers who wanted to save resources found it hard to avoid waste, he observed, trapped as they were by the unavoidable wastefulness of a shopping excursion. A trip to the supermarket or convenience store would mean having to buy produce, meat, and fish packed on Styrofoam trays and wrapped in plastic.[106]

In the author and scientist Monna Kimiyuki's assessment, sustained use of a thing was made difficult by the disappearance of people willing or able to repair broken objects. In a survey he conducted of a few hundred housewives, the top two reasons why respondents threw away items as large refuse were the ineffectiveness and cost of repair.[107] The waning practice of repair was for Monna just an example of the larger problem of thinking about garbage as the output of a one-way path of producing, manufacturing, consuming, and disposing, rather than as part of a cycle. Using the language of "circulation" that would become more common in later decades, he argued that without a fundamental shift in thinking, the government's calls to save resources and energy would prove short-sighted and shallow.[108]

This kind of deep and expansive social criticism, characteristic of the previous decade, was given voice in the 1980s. Some people continued to express principles and convictions that had been forged in the years after the Oil Shock. Yet these concerns were dwarfed by moderate responses to the garbage problem and conventional efforts to sustain practices like recycling. More provocative ideas were usually articulated by specialists in waste matters or by those most dedicated to waste consciousness, and did not catch the public eye—at least, not for very long. And they were far from being the normative or hegemonic ways of thinking about waste. Without a more pressing sense of uncertainty, there was not much prospect of changing meaningfully the established assumptions, practices, and structures around waste.

Indulging Waste

For those who were attuned to waste in contemporary daily life, the Japan they saw in the 1980s was not just wasteful but more wasteful than its affluent counterparts. Having caught up economically with the United States and western Europe, Japan had somehow gone too far, so that it now needed to catch up in waste consciousness. In an anecdotal comparison to London, Japanese cities were said to remain lively much later into the night, using energy to fuel entertainment not just in the well-known Tokyo neighborhoods of Shinjuku and Ginza but in other localities as well. Commenting on both England and Europe as a whole, a *Yomiuri* newspaper article described a supposed European frugality and spirit of parsimony (*kechikechi seishin*). Not only were cities dark at night, but lighting in houses was also so dim that a Japanese person moving into an English person's house would have to swap out the lights for brighter ones. Japan was also no match for the English custom of carefully using things and valuing the old. While the article noted that what appeared to be a wasteful Japanese way of living might have been necessary for the country's remarkable progress, it suggested that Japan might now do well to foster a "stingy spirit" along the lines of the English.[109] Americans, too, were thought to be more waste conscious than Japanese. Reuse of large items was described as an "American sensibility," and mention was often made among recycling advocates of a model bottle deposit and recycling system in Oregon.[110] Gotō Sukehiro of the Environment Agency did not hesitate to assume that practices he had observed during his time in the United States decades earlier were still applicable. Americans, he claimed, comparison shopped for expensive items like household appliances; they looked carefully at their electricity bill at the end of the month, despite the abundance of resources; and at parties, they talked about money-saving strategies even if they were quite wealthy. All of this would seem very stingy to Japanese people, he concluded, who were capriciously wasting things and living beyond their means.[111]

To underscore these simplistic essentialisms about stinginess and wastefulness, some attention was given to the behaviors and attitudes of foreigners in Japan. In an era when foreigners taking up residence in the country could expect to find and equip their apartments with perfectly good furniture and appliances that had been shunted to the curb as garbage, there were reports of those from abroad commenting on Japan's wasteful habits.[112] There were the buyers from Hong Kong, Thailand, and other countries of Southeast Asia who came to automobile disposal sites, remarking how wasteful it was that virtually new cars were being discarded as they snatched them up.[113] There was the story about the two Americans who would scrounge through the trash in Kanagawa prefecture for finds to take back and sell at a junk shop in Los Angeles.[114] And then there was the meeting of almost two hundred housewives in Osaka, where a panel of foreign housewives living in Japan shared their observations about the wasteful aspects of daily life. The housewife from New Zealand found efforts to save energy to be insufficient; the housewife from Switzerland was surprised by how quickly it became difficult to find a spare part for something like a broken lamp; and the American housewife criticized the Japanese tendency to dispose of things, even cars and refrigerators. "The United States is called a country of disposability," she said, "but when it comes to large things, Japan is on top."[115]

Such observations by foreigners were presented by waste conscious Japanese as a mirror to shake their compatriots from their complacency about wastage. In connection with Earth Day in 1990, for example, an English theater group came to Japan and performed *The Whole World: How Much*, which humorously depicted a Japanese lifestyle of mass-consuming electricity and oil, and of discarding everyday items that could still be used. To introduce another moral dimension, the play portrayed lifestyles in comparatively poor Kenya, depicted as a place where things were carefully used and reused. As an audience member, the NHK producer Ishizawa Kiyoshi was embarrassed that things like disposability and excessive packaging, considered so normal in Japan, must look from the outside like an abnormal way of living.[116]

The critiques of a culture of disposability suggest that unfettered consumption and flagrant materialism were not unequivocally embraced in 1980s Japan. But in this decade, they were expressed by those most committed to energy saving, garbage reduction, and recycling, many of whom had taken up the mantle of waste consciousness in the 1970s and were trying to adjust their approach and message to the different economic context of the 1980s and of the bubble years. What they faced, and in some ways exemplified, were assumptions about and desires for comfortable and enjoyable lifestyles of consumption.

Indeed, the increase in the very amount of garbage produced suggests some attenuation in concern about the waste of material things and some indifference to the physical consequences of consumption. Suspicions that there was a lack of awareness about the connection between consumption decisions and garbage output were borne out, at least in one survey conducted in 1988 by the Prime Minister's Office. When the few thousand respondents were asked what they thought about when they shopped, only 16.7 percent said they considered whether the product would soon become useless, become garbage; 15.3 percent reported being sensitive to whether the product would make the amount of garbage too large; and a mere 7.1 percent claimed to consider whether or not what they were purchasing could be recycled. A majority (62 percent) said they had never thought about these or the three other garbage-related considerations listed. Likely reflecting who in the household was doing the shopping and the disposing, this blindness to garbage was more common among men (69 percent) than women (56.3 percent).[117]

The proliferation of rubbish, and the increase in disposable goods on the market, also reflected how any commitment to garbage reduction could conflict with other desires and values—for convenience, cleanliness, ease, and comfort. In an especially flagrant example of embracing the benefits of disposability, an article in the mass-market magazine _Shūkan hōseki_ (Weekly Jewel) asserted that if used well, disposable goods could help one lead a full life. Laziness, if that meant using a disposable item to save one's energy, physical strength, and time, was not bad. The article went on to profile various disposable goods, from paper slippers to wear on an airplane to wet wipes of various kinds for cleaning electric household appliances, toilets, or one's desk at work.[118] Hints of this appreciation of disposability could be found in the survey by the Prime Minister's Office. One question posited that garbage had been increasing recently because of disposable goods, then asked respondents what they thought about this phenomenon. About a fifth (21.5 percent) of respondents replied that disposable goods were convenient, so the rise in garbage was inevitable. Many more people (69.5 percent), some of whom might have been susceptible to the moral suasion in the wording of the question, said that it would be better if disposable goods did not appear on the market so that garbage would not increase; but this answer was qualified by the ambiguous phrase "to the extent possible" and placed the responsibility for changing behavior more on the shoulders of producers than consumers.[119] Even the representative of a campaign to boycott disposable diapers (*Sutoppu za kamiomutsu*), Suzuki Fumi of a consumer association in the city of Sendai, recognized that she was asking people, and young mothers in particular, to give up the convenience of disposability for the inconvenience of washing cloth diapers.[120]

In this era when many people seemed unwilling to make substantial changes to their ways of life, and without a sense of crisis to compel them to think differently, ideas about and responses to waste were relatively indulgent. Not wasting energy and not wasting material things were not to compromise standards of living, and practices of waste reduction were not to impose too much on daily life. Even the Recycling Movement Citizens' Association insisted that it was different from campaigns to save and from the stinginess movements of the 1970s, now considered, especially by young people, to be uncool and out of fashion. And it did not begrudge the material plenty that had been attained, suggesting only that attention could now be turned toward the achievement of a more individual way of living.[121]

There may also have been a way in which the expansion, regularization, and normalization of recycling practices blunted their potential to make people think about waste in their daily lives. When the separation of garbage and recyclables was introduced to a municipality, it forced residents to participate actively in the management of waste.[122] As the categorization of rubbish became more routine, it still required time and effort, but likely provoked less thought and reflection than when it was initially implemented.

Although recycling and garbage reduction movements began to be infused with new meanings in the late 1980s as a global environmental consciousness took root, for much of this decade their conceptions of waste and wastefulness were circumscribed. There was not much of a call to curtail material possession and scant interest in thinking about consumption in fundamentally different ways. And the suggested responses to waste were vague or limited. What implication was separating garbage supposed to have for deciding how and what to buy? How were flea markets to challenge the fetishization of material consumption? Was recycling an act of absolution for all sins of wastefulness in a mass-consuming society? So fixed were the assumptions of and desires for affluence, a high standard of living, material abundance, and consumption that aspirations were focused less on the costs and consequences of such a lifestyle than on its enhancement.

LIVING THE GOOD LIFE?

In late 1978, the infamous landfill known as the Island of Dreams (Yume no Shima) was reborn as a place of recreation, diversion, and amusement. The former Landfill Number Fourteen, having taken in over 10 million tons of trash from Tokyoites between 1957 and 1967, was covered over and transformed into a vast park of more than one hundred acres. The area housed, among other things, the Lucky Dragon Five Exhibition Hall (Dai Go Fukuryū Maru Tenjikan), which displayed the fishing boat that was contaminated, along with its crew of twenty-three men, by an American hydrogen bomb test at Bikini Atoll in 1954. The presence of the boat in the park was incongruous, a piece of resuscitated waste more dangerous and historic than the seemingly mundane rubbish buried below visitors' feet. It was the only hint that this was not just any park, even as the boat had been deemed safe to touch and experience, like the ground on which it rested. With only this small and rather inconspicuous nod to the unpleasant, the park was otherwise dedicated to the pursuit of fun, with its baseball diamond, soccer field, and large gymnasium with a pool heated by the nearby incineration plant and facilities for table tennis, martial arts, sumo, volleyball, basketball, tennis, and badminton.[1] There was something metaphorical about the Island of Dreams Park that presaged the decade to follow—that on a hidden foundation of material waste would rise a symbol of enjoyment and leisure in daily life.

There was in the 1980s an ever-increasing sense that the country had arrived: that it had picked itself up after the war, embarked on a project of reconstruction and economic growth, and weathered the energy challenges of the 1970s to become an economic superpower.[2] In the wake of such achievements, attention was newly focused on what, beyond financial wealth and material abundance, constituted an affluent life. For some, the issue was about what was next, about what more could be realized. For others, the problem was about what was lacking, what insufficiencies should be addressed and remedied. The fundamental question was what life should be about in a Japan of financial and material prosperity, and the language used was the pursuit of a "true affluence" (*shin no yutakasa*) or an "affluence of the heart" (*kokoro no yutakasa*). "True affluence" tended to connote deficiency in what had already been attained, while "affluence of the heart" was more hopeful, with *kokoro* used expansively to mean some hybrid of heart, mind, and spirit. While the specific definitions of these two flexible phrases varied, they conceived of affluence in psychological, spiritual, and emotional terms, with an attention to a well-being and self-fulfillment that extended beyond the purely financial. What was often being sought was *yutori*, a word difficult to translate that could mean something like leisure, relaxation, space, or unconstricted time.[3]

Despite some rhetoric and appearances to the contrary, such attempts to rethink what constituted an affluent life did not signal a turn away from valuing financial wealth, high standards of living, consumption, and material plenty. In fact, most presumed continued economic growth and the enhancement of comfort in daily life. Financial and material prosperity made possible, and created the privilege of, self-reflection about what a good life could and should be in an affluent society. As it was conceived in the 1980s, affluence of the heart was to supplement, not replace, financial and material affluence.

Desires for a true affluence or affluence of the heart were linked to conceptions of waste, which came to have a more psychological, spiritual, and emotional dimension than in decades past. Considerations of what should be defined as a waste of material objects and time did not fundamentally change, but were informed by and discussed with a more affective vocabulary. In some cases, the association between an affluent heart and waste was tenuous and superficial, deployed primarily as new rhetoric for the repackaging of existing ideas and practices. Marketers and retailers ironically heralded an era of a turn away from things and toward the heart, but in ways that encouraged mass consumption. Some literature about time management framed advice in terms that acknowledged the importance of a quality of life, but its assumptions and strategies were in the well-worn mold of improving productivity and efficiency. In other cases, the relationship forged between the heart and waste was more substantive. Some advocates of garbage reduction and recycling spoke of the waste of things not just as the squandering of resources but also as the erosion of a fundamental respect for life. Many, from the government to authors of advice literature, deemed time outside of work or "free time" not an unproductive waste but necessary for *yutori*. Drawing such connections, sometimes explicitly and often implicitly, endowed the idea of waste with a potential meaning that was not just moral or practical but spiritual, emotional, and psychological.

The Managed Heart

One variation of a turn toward the heart, which was ostensibly about a turn away from the material, was articulated by marketers and retailers who had a particular strategic take on what they described as a "detachment from things." In 1984, the Hakuhōdō Institute of Life and Living (Hakuhōdō Sōgō Kenkyūjo), the lifestyle research arm of the large advertising and public relations firm, coined the term "soft wave" to describe what it perceived as a significant change rippling through the economy and society. Soft wave was, in short, the move toward information and services that could be seen in the increasingly knowledge-intensive industrial structure, the rise of information-related business, and the shift away from the showcase to the service counter. According to Hakuhōdō, this was an era that was moving away from things and toward the heart.[4]

Closer to the decade's end, department stores expected the pursuit of an affluent heart to take the form of consuming not just physical objects but also experiences. It was predicted that consumers would no longer be satisfied by simply purchasing things, but would expect a shopping excursion to be memorable and have a luxurious feel. Department stores thus planned to incorporate museums or high-end restaurants into the shopping experience, or fashion themselves in the style of theme parks like Disneyland.[5] More generally, top executives of the country's major department stores like Tōkyū and Takashimaya spoke of inaugurating an era that was not about quantity and things but about quality and heart. Looking to the year ahead, the major advertising and public relations company Dentsū predicted that the key word for 1990 would be *yuirakuron*—a neologism that played on "materialism" (*yuibutsuron*) to mean something like "comfort-ism." In terms of consumption, *yuirakuron* was to take as the basis of value not money but the strings of one's heart. There was wordplay here too, as the characters for "money" and for "heartstrings" were homophones (*kinsen*).[6]

There was an irony in advertisers and retailers speaking about detachment from the material and affluence of the heart. After all, one of the reasons why they needed to think of new opportunities and ways to consume was that they were operating in an environment abundant with stuff in which there was heated competition for customers' attention. There also was, of course, their goal to sell things. For a retailer, the hope was that the yearning for an affluent heart would entail consumption, including the consumption of material goods. Indeed, emotional satisfaction and material consumption were not seen as antithetical, but were assumed to be perfectly complementary in various ways. The pursuit of *yutori*, after all, could very well require consumption, as many leisure activities from sports to various hobbies necessitated the purchase of equipment, clothing, and other physical accoutrements. The natural pairing of consumption with a true sense of meaning was described by one public-private group that examined consumer behavior. The National Council on Consumer Issues (Shōhisha Mondai Kokumin Kaigi) determined that a real affluence in people's lives could be fostered in part by greater freedom and diversity in consumer options and choice.[7] And consumption itself could bring joy: according to a planner at a department store, one of the ways in which customers were gratifying their hearts was by buying high-end jewelry.[8]

Another variation of an ostensible turn toward the psychological, spiritual, and emotional was expounded in advice literature for managers and salarymen about the elimination of waste, particularly the waste of time, from the workplace. Added to the conventional goals of waste reduction was seeking an affluent heart and creating more time outside of work for its cultivation. Such purposes did not even occur to earlier advocates of scientific management and would have sounded utterly strange to the pioneers of the Toyota Production System. But as new as this vocabulary of emotional satisfaction was, writers continued to call upon the assumptions and ideas at the core of the system with its elimination of the "three *mu*": *muda* (waste), *mura* (inconsistency), and *muri* (unreasonableness). In his book *Muda, mura, muri o nakuse* (Eliminate Muda, Mura, Muri), Kamada Masaru, with his background in industrial and management education, called for an increase in paid vacation, two-day weekends, and the pursuit of hobbies. He also resisted thinking about wasted spending or wasted things too strictly. Luxury could sometimes be "splendid" (*suteki*); things should not be considered wasteful if they made life richer and fuller; and money should not be saved or invested just for the sake of financial gain. Echoing calls for a different kind of affluence, Kamada advocated cultural affluence and conditions best for the heart. Yet those aims were to be met by applying the industrial logics of utility and productivity to time in the workplace. The first and foundational step for the elimination of waste was the elimination of wasted time, advised Kamada. It was a waste of time to watch all of the television news or read the entire newspaper in the morning; scanning the newspaper and reading in depth only those stories that grabbed your attention would suffice. Meetings were deemed a waste of time; the production of written documents was wasteful for the time they took to create and read, the space needed for storage, and as disposed paper; and commuting was a waste of time, money, and energy. While the purpose of such attention to wastefulness was taking more days off and thus living a more cultured life, Kamada perpetuated the mindset of scientific management whereby each minute was to be measured, scrutinized, and assessed for its value.[9]

Like Kamada, the lawyer and author Kurokawa Yasumasa defined both the management of one's work and the enjoyment of life as the purposes of using time effectively. To illustrate this point, Kurokawa listed everything he was able to do: he slept seven to eight hours every night, spent time with friends, read books, played Japanese chess, went on several long vacations abroad with his family every year, etcetera. And all of this in addition to his impressive résumé: he had published several dozen books, served as a consultant in various fields, made regular television appearances, given lectures, and written newspaper and magazine articles about time management strategies. Yet again, even though he spoke of a fulfilling and meaningful life, those desirable ends were dwarfed by the discipline required to account for all of one's time. Kurokawa advocated thinking about time as money, converting time saved or wasted into actual yen terms. He then outlined ways of making time, such as discovering various forms of hidden time. For example, on the JR Chūō rail line, one minute could pass between the announcement of the next train and the moment of boarding. If one were not to get up from the bench until the train actually opened its doors, one would have found a hidden minute. Or if the 3:00 meeting at your workplace regularly did not begin until 3:03, you could claim those three hidden minutes by not arriving until the actual start time. He also recommended multitasking, like listening to a tape while brushing your teeth or walking; setting deadlines more effectively; figuring out a commuting route based not on the shortest distance but on the most usable time; and recording television programs so as to control the pace and watch only those segments of interest to you. Even time in the bath was designated for purposeful relaxing, so that new ideas might come to mind.[10]

Some professed advocates of a truly affluent society with more leisurely lifestyles also could not escape the assumption that time had to be put to effective use, be it for workplace productivity or rest and relaxation. Suda Hiroshi, the president of the Central Japan Railway Company (Tōkai Ryokaku Tetsudō, or JR Tōkai), argued that Japan needed to shorten working hours and increase leisure time. But shorter working hours needed to be offset by efforts to increase productivity through greater efficiency, doing away with wasteful and excessive packaging or services. For the Central Japan Railway Company, this meant additional automatic turnstiles and trains operated by one person. In Suda's view, people also needed to become more skilled in their use of leisure time, not simply golfing or lounging around at home or going on trips at the same times of year as everyone else. In 1991, the Central Japan Railway began a campaign called "Let's Give Japan a Break" (Nihon o Yasumō), which Suda hoped would encourage people to disperse their travel throughout the year and make more use of their leisure time.[11]

Other advice literature mentioned an affluent heart as mere window dressing for careerist ambition. In a book specifically about strategies for managing time, Kanba Wataru acknowledged that one of the two main reasons why people sought such advice was to do their job efficiently so as to have time left over for hobbies and leisure, for the enjoyment of life. But the book put much more emphasis on job performance and career advancement, encapsulated by the eye-catching hook slapped on its cover: "Winning business and learning strategies to defeat your rivals." Then there was the book's subtitle, *24 jikan no tsukaikata ga subete o kimeru* (How You Use 24 Hours Determines Everything). In the first section of the book, Kanba explained that Toyota's "just in time" production system offered lessons for how to think about time and the thorough elimination of waste, and declared that how people managed their time would determine their success in life. Kanba, who taught management and law courses at the Industrial Efficiency Junior College (Sangyō Nōritsu Tanki Daigaku), enumerated various techniques for making good use of even scraps of time, those ten to fifteen minutes that might seem like garbage. Suggestions included reading a book during your commute, refraining from long phone calls, shortening meeting times, getting rid of wasteful meetings entirely, multitasking, writing down the schedule for the next day before you go to sleep, and so on.[12] The premise of most of the time-saving techniques suggested in this genre of advice literature was to put every minute to productive use of some kind; no time was to be wasted as purposeless or useless. Be it the embrace of productivity and efficiency in work, of utility in leisure, or of consumption in play, the language of an affluent heart or a turn away from the material was in certain hands a notable shift in rhetoric but not in substance.

The Poverty of Affluence

While the association of waste with an affluent heart could sometimes be rather tenuous and superficial, in other cases the relationship was described in more sincere and substantive ways. For advocates of recycling and garbage reduction, a broader conception of affluence jibed with arguments they had been marshaling for their cause and with the hope that their concerns might gain more traction. As explained by the economist Kishimoto Shigenobu, the very act of recycling was so inextricably bound up with the valuing of things that an economy and a society that could not recycle could not be truly affluent. Or to put it another way, a society had to appreciate the life of things and recycle to be genuinely wealthy.[13] Like Kishimoto, others used the idea of a true affluence or affluence of the heart to give more weight and a greater psychological or spiritual meaning to their standard calls to appreciate and value things. Ishizawa Kiyoshi, a producer with public broadcaster NHK, determined that a society with a garbage problem had more thinking to do about its attitude toward things and its philosophy of living. Only after such reflection, he implied, could it become a truly affluent society that valued things and respected life.[14]

At least one local government, attempting to promote the saving of resources and energy, also spoke of a real affluence that required the reexamination of societal values. In Shimane prefecture, in southwestern Japan, the Social Welfare Division's Lifestyle Section (Shimane-ken Shakai Fukushibu Kenmin Seikatsuka) sought to realize a "humble life" that balanced things and heart, or the material and the spiritual. The ideals of a materially frugal, spiritually modest, and affluent lifestyle were vague, beyond the hope that they would result in a greater commitment to not wasting resources and energy. In this instance, the language of a new lifestyle and new values attempted to rid "saving" (*setsuyaku*) of its negative connotations and helped to reintroduce and rebrand the idea. The reconceived affluence became the rhetorical umbrella for a movement that included the solicitation of essays and posters about saving resources and energy, the inclusion of illustrations about saving energy in the visitors' guide distributed at the prefectural office, and the airing of *Chīsa na muda* (Small Waste) on radio and television during energy-saving month.[15] In such instances, it was subtly implied that lifestyles overflowing with material consumption and material waste were somehow lacking in psychological, spiritual, or emotional meaning.

What waste reduction advocates were trying to tap into, and bring to discussions about waste, were the explicit and energetic critiques leveled at that time about the insufficiencies of financially and materially affluent lives. In her book *Yutakasa to wa nani ka* (What Is Affluence?), the economist and social commentator Teruoka Itsuko expressed more forcefully than most the superficiality of Japan's affluence. And her book hit the shelves around the same time as others in a similar vein, like *Yutakasa no seishin byōri* (The Psychopathology of Affluence) and *Hontō no yutakasa to wa* (What Is Real Affluence?), the transactions of an academic symposium held on that theme in 1990. These were also the years when a government-approved home economics textbook prodded students to consider as a central theme what affluence really was.[16] For Teruoka's part, she observed that many people secretly felt in their hearts a foreboding that their luxury was supported by a fragile castle built of sand that would collapse and disappear. Symptomatic of this wealth were the wastebaskets that kept filling up quickly no matter how often you dumped them out, and the furniture and electric products thrown out as large refuse. Punctuating her point, Teruoka asserted that nature was being polluted by industrial waste and discarded garbage, and people were being frozen by fear of nuclear weapons and washed away by the waste of energy. Embracing the arguments of John Kenneth Galbraith's *The Affluent Society* in a way that they were not when the book's Japanese translation was first published in 1960, Teruoka thought they fit her present perfectly because Japanese society had no philosophy of affluence and no happiness outside of the pleasure of economic growth.[17]

A more pointed critique, in the more entertaining form of a manga, was offered by *Dai Tokyo binbō seikatsu manyuaru* (Manual for Poor Living in Greater Tokyo), originally serialized by the publisher Kōdansha in its weekly magazine *Mōningu* (Morning) from 1986 to 1989 and popular enough to be later released and re-released as a multivolume collection. Written and illustrated by Maekawa Tsukasa, the comic did not just suggest that financially and materially affluent lifestyles were somehow unsatisfactory or insufficient. It went further, implying that they were wasteful in their saturation with unnecessary things. Psychological, spiritual, and emotional wealth, argued Maekawa, could be found in financial and material poverty. In the manga, Maekawa offered a way of living that transposed the frugality and waste consciousness of the wartime years onto the more peaceful and comfortable present. The first image of the first chapter was of people in wartime, holding flags reading "Poverty is in fashion," "Poverty is an ideology, it is life itself," and, in large font, the well-known "Luxury is the enemy!!" It would be simplistic to interpret these ideas as the central contention of the comic, for nothing in the image conveyed desirability; the expressions on the characters' faces were grim, and the uniformity of everyone's rigid stance, with ankles together and flag-waving arm raised in the air, exuded coercion.[18] In contrast, the cover adopted the composition of the wartime cel and thoroughly remade its spirit by rendering the image in full color, putting smiles and pleasant expressions of all different sorts on people's faces, and interspersing throughout the scene joyful things from everyday life, like a bicycle, a pet dog, and even a bentō in a plastic bag. At the center of it all was the slightly rumpled but rosy-cheeked Kōsuke, the main character, who led a life of financial and material modesty but psychological and spiritual richness. A university graduate who worked odd jobs rather than seek full-time employment, he represented a kind of "freeter" (*furītā*) at a time when the term was just coming into use to describe those who could and did make the decision to do temporary or part-time work and pursue enjoyment rather than a salaryman-like lifestyle.[19] Kōsuke's was a financial poverty of choice, in which waste consciousness was not about restraint or doing without but about appreciating money, time, and things as making possible the true pleasures of everyday life.

The character Kōsuke had answered for himself the question of what was necessary, and what was extraneous, to living happily. Without waste or excess, Kōsuke's daily life was one of material sparseness and deep contentedness. His

FIGURE 6.1.   Undesirable Poverty. The undesirability of wartime poverty, depicted to contrast with the version embraced by the main character Kōsuke in *Dai Tokyo binbō seikatsu manyuaru*.

Reproduced by permission from Maekawa Tsukasa, *Dai Tokyo binbō seikatsu manyuaru*, vol. 1 (Tokyo: Kōdansha, 1988).

small apartment of roughly one hundred square feet contained six "poverty goods": a newspaper picked out of the trash at the train station to use as a desk; an empty aluminum can to serve as an ashtray; an electric pot, necessary because his apartment did not have gas; disposable chopsticks; a paper bag; and a pair of leather shoes bought wholesale.[20] He reused disposed of or disposable things, and not just as one of his six staple possessions. He made use of empty bentō boxes, and soap and shampoo left by someone at the public bath, repurposed an empty milk carton as a flower vase, and repaired objects that were broken.[21] Kōsuke also did not waste money on excessive consumption, highlighted by the naming of brands and prices of some of the few things Kōsuke purchased in what was almost surely and consciously a poor man's version of *Nantonaku, kurisutaru* (Somehow, Crystal). Instead of luxury handbags from high-end boutiques, the advertised goods were Nabisco potato chips (at 178 yen, they tasted like real potatoes when added to instant miso soup); the Sapporo fried potatoes from the chain pub Tengū (at 250 yen, they were popular); and the Yukijirushi vanilla bar (at 30 yen, it made for a refreshing snack).[22] There was no wasting energy in what Kōsuke at one point called his "energy-saving poor life," in which he paid no gas bill and had no stove, refrigerator, or other electric appliance save a *kotatsu* heater.[23] The very notion of wasting time did not exist for Kōsuke, who had liberated himself from the logic of productivity. He enjoyed reading, sleeping, eating, or just lying around.

That financially and materially affluent lifestyles bred waste was an assumption of the manga, and it took direct aim at the equation of money with value and happiness. Ultimately, the comic was a manual less about how to get by on a small budget and much more about how to engage intentionally with structures of labor, money, and consumption in order to lead a full life. Kōsuke's seemingly extreme lifestyle, though informed by Maekawa's own experience and those of his friends, was likely unimaginable for most adult readers and was made accessible in various ways.[24] Maekawa acknowledged that Kōsuke needed the generosity and support of friends, neighbors, and a very understanding girlfriend. More important, Maekawa created a sympathetic character who was somehow not a self-centered mooch and not pedantic. When it came to waste, for example, Maekawa stopped short of criticizing or challenging disposable goods or a culture of disposability. Kōsuke did on occasion make his own pickles or buy tofu from an itinerant merchant, but he regularly enjoyed his instant coffee, cup of ramen, and bentō.[25] No comment was made about convenience stores, chain restaurants, or prepared foods. This less than radical criticism of consumption may be due to Maekawa's blindness or the inescapability of waste in consumption. But this moderation did help convey a sense that one need not live like Kōsuke to feel happy and fulfilled, for even with his unconventional lifestyle, he had not completely opted out of and divorced himself from social systems and practices. One could intentionally choose the nature of one's engagement with societal structures, and the extent of waste that entailed, to live a psychologically, spiritually, and emotionally affluent life.

In Pursuit of *Yutori*

What Maekawa Tsukasa created in the character of Kōsuke was an answer and an alternative, however unrealistic, to a fairly pervasive sense of dissatisfaction with daily lives at a time of financial wealth and material plenty.[26] Much of this malaise was expressed as a desire for *yutori*—for the time and space to breathe, to appreciate the fruits of one's labor, and to enjoy hard-won lifestyles. What was experienced as the lack of *yutori* fed the creation of a new identity: being "poor." This was not a poverty of dire financial need but a neologism intended to highlight privation of a different sort. The emergence of the "new poor" (*nyū pua*) was heralded in the mid-1980s by the Hakuhōdō Institute of Life and Living, which explained that this group of people felt as though they did not have *yutori* and so examined what they wanted and how they might be wasting in their lives. There was a financial dimension to this sentiment, as interviews with salarymen and housewives revealed a sense that the discretionary part of household budgets was decreasing as the pressures of educational expenses and home loan repayment were increasing. As a result, funds for leisure and cultural activities felt squeezed. Because such discretionary spending for the enjoyment of life had come to be considered a necessity, observed Hakuhōdō, any possible or actual reduction in such expenditures became a source of stress. And it was this shortage of *yutori* that defined this group. In a survey of two thousand people conducted in Tokyo, Osaka, and Kobe in 1988, 48 percent of respondents identified themselves as "new poor"—as not being financially poor but not having *yutori*.[27]

As consumers, the new poor sought *yutori* by considering not just whether a purchase was necessary or not but whether it would help them enjoy life and express themselves, whether it would bring pleasure and joy to their heart. In making these individual judgments, the new poor were considered the vanguard of the "fragmented masses" (*bunshū*), yet another neologism from Hakuhōdō, which evinced an era of the post-mass society in which consumers no longer desired the same products as in the past, like the three sacred treasures (television set, washing machine, and refrigerator) of the 1950s or the three Cs (car, cooler, and color television set) of the 1960s. They instead wanted to choose from a variety of products those that fit their specific taste, be it ice cream or cars. The new poor in particular would not be frugal by refraining from purchases such as the coffee they liked in order to save for one luxury good, for that would be joyless.[28] For the new poor, bereft of *yutori*, consumption was meaningful and thus not wasteful if it was in the pursuit of enjoyment and satisfaction.

At the center of the desire for *yutori* was a desire for time, as many people felt that their lives did not have "the mood of an affluent society," because while abundant with things, their lives seemed impoverished of time. Lifestyles were not experienced as leisurely in ways befitting the second-largest economy in the world, as exemplified by the shortage of free time.[29] Over four thousand people were asked by the Prime Minister's Office in 1982 if they were at their limit with their job, housework, and studies, or if they could do what they liked and had time to rest. The largest percentage of respondents (43.7 percent) said they tended not to have time to spare, with the squeeze felt most acutely (54 percent) by people in their forties. Of those who said that they did not have time (*yutori*), a substantial majority (81.7 percent) expressed a desire for it.[30] The economist Ōkita Saburō, well known for helping craft Prime Minister Ikeda Hayato's income-doubling plan of 1960 and for editing and translating the Club of Rome's 1972 report *The Limits to Growth*, observed that the more affluent a society became, the less inclined people were to work an additional hour to increase income. The desire to enjoy that hour was part of the greater attention to quality of life in a materially affluent society.[31] Speaking in a more imperative tone, the psychologist Akuto Hiroshi urged Japan to take a rest now that it had caught up to the United States and to realize a Japanese-style affluence and leisurely life not just through taking longer vacations but also by revolutionizing ways of thinking about lifestyles and values.[32]

Empirically, working hours for the employed did tick upward from the mid-1970s through at least the mid-1980s. According to a survey of over fourteen thousand people conducted by the public opinion polling division of NHK, the amount of time worked on a weekday was seven hours and twenty-seven minutes in 1975, seven hours and thirty minutes in 1980, and seven hours and forty-nine minutes in 1985. That number also increased in 1985 for Saturdays and Sundays.[33] Particularly notable was the ever greater percentage of people who worked more than ten hours a day (11 percent in 1975, 13 percent in 1980, and 19 percent in 1985).[34] There is evidence from the quasi-governmental Japan Institute of Labor (Nihon Rōdō Kenkyū Kikō) that working hours decreased after 1988, but the common phenomenon of unpaid and unreported overtime casts some doubt on the official statistics.[35] Across the three NHK surveys, free time (*jiyū jikan*) remained relatively flat or decreased slightly on weekdays (three hours and fifty-two minutes, three hours and fifty-one minutes, three hours and fifty-one minutes), Saturdays (four hours and forty-one minutes, four hours and thirty-six minutes, four hours and thirty-nine minutes), and Sundays (six hours and thirteen minutes, six hours and five minutes, six hours and eight minutes).[36]

More than these numbers might suggest, there was a widespread sense that people were working too much, that spending so many hours on the job was a waste of time and perhaps of one's life. The term "company slave" (*shachiku*) started to be used in the 1980s, and in the latter half of the decade, during the heyday of the bubble economy, attention was demanded by "death from overwork" (*karōshi*). In what was largely a white-collar phenomenon, people were dying suddenly from such medical causes as heart attacks and strokes brought on by stress, starvation, and other aspects of overwork. Though such deaths likely dated back to the 1970s, they were made into a societal problem of national concern in the late 1980s. In 1988, seven areas (Sapporo, Sendai, Tokyo, Kyoto, Osaka, Kobe, and Fukuoka) started a *karōshi* telephone hotline, and in November of that year, a front-page article in the *Chicago Tribune* introduced *karōshi* into the global lexicon.[37] This story was one of many that characterized Japan from the outside as overworked, a perception that had been vividly expressed in 1979 at a European Community meeting on trade by a French delegate who described Japan as "a nation of workaholics living in rabbit hutches." As has been noted by the political scientist David Leheny, this phrase "has been used in practically every Japanese-language work on leisure and lifestyle issues since it was originally uttered."[38] While some Japanese commentators pushed back against the description, most mentioned it at least in passing as resonant with their own view that their compatriots were working too many hours.[39]

The international spotlight on Japanese economic practices contributed to the increased attention to working hours, particularly on the part of the government. In the mid-1980s, when Japan's trade surplus hit a record high, criticisms of the export-centric strategy of Japanese manufacturers as well as economic and societal structures became especially heated. In response, Prime Minister Nakasone Yasuhiro established the Research Group on Economic Structural Adjustment for International Cooperation (Kokusai Kyōchō no Tame no Keizai Kōzō Chōsei Kenkyūkai), which in April 1986 released the so-called Maekawa Report. The report's central recommendation was a shift toward an economy driven by domestic demand. As part of this move, the report called for the implementation of a five-day workweek and working hours more in line with those in Europe and the United States. With the government, labor, and management each having its own reasons for supporting reduction in work hours, in 1987 the Diet passed an amendment to the Labor Standards Law, which gradually implemented a forty-hour workweek. The Ministry of Labor (Rōdōshō) and other government organizations then launched campaigns to help realize reduced hours in practice. The ministry published handbooks geared toward businesses and provided support to "model cities" that enthusiastically took up the cause, and the Tokyo Metropolitan Labor and Economy Bureau (Tokyo-to Rōdō Keizaikyoku) came up with the slogan "For Greater Leisure [*yutori*], Enjoy Life."[40]

There were critics of the Maekawa Report who feared that the reduction in work hours would cause the contemporary trend toward laziness and idleness to spread and the spirit of diligence to atrophy. In 1987 Toyama Shigeru, the head of the Central Council for Savings Promotion (Chochiku Zōkyō Chūō Iinkai), published a best-selling book in which he worried that monetary saving would wane and that the propensity toward luxury and waste would increase with government encouragement of domestic consumption. He outlined a history of advanced industrialized countries of the West in which work had become a mere servant to its master, leisure. Some new ethos of diligence and saving was necessary, Toyama argued, to maintain both affluence and leisure and to protect the country from following the example of advanced Western countries into luxurious and wasteful consumption.[41]

But at the same time, there was a growing chorus of voices insisting that it was a waste to work too much and pushing back against the conception of time only in productive terms. What was being challenged was the suggestion that even "time off" had to be used toward a purpose and that free time was wasted time. Leftist critics, like the General Council of Trade Unions of Japan (Nihon Rōdō Kumiai Sōhyō Gikai, or Sōhyō) and the Marxist scholar Watanabe Osamu, took issue with the increased consumption of leisure services and the commodification of free time.[42] More in the mainstream, in the newsweekly *Asahi jānaru* (Asahi Journal), an article titled "*Yasume! Yasume!*" (Rest! Rest!) opened with a note from the editors posing questions about whether lifestyles had become more affluent and how there could be more rest, pleasure, and enjoyment in daily life. What followed was a conversation between the sociologist Katō Hidetoshi and the illustrator, essayist, and manga artist Minami Shinbō in which the two men challenged and criticized the salaryman's way of thinking about time. They agreed that while only a minority of the population held such full-time white-collar jobs, the work hours of salarymen were viewed as natural and normal, and having free time (*hima*) was not considered cool. As a result, housewives who did have more time after they saw their husbands off to work and children off to school felt guilty, and others who did not keep such work schedules were seen as hanging about idly and at strange times of day. The government perpetuated these norms, they suggested, by implying in surveys that watching television, napping, or lying around was not a good use of time. For Katō and Minami, it was those who had a wealth of time, like housewives, who were affluent. Work should be interesting, work schedules more flexible, and play an important value.[43]

Children too, some argued, needed more free time. With the high percentages of people going on to high school and the increasing importance of the high school diploma, entrance examinations and cram schools for junior high and high schools had robbed students of time. The professor Katō Tsuchimi envisioned a typical family with the father coming home at an indeterminate time, the mother working part-time, and the child off at cram school, turning the home into a mere boardinghouse that was poor in its familial relationships.[44]

There were other such criticisms of an overly busy life that maximized the utilization of time, which generally tended to come from outside the halls of corporate Japan, business schools, and management associations. The art commentator and University of Tokyo professor Takashina Shūji, for one, took aim at the singular focus on increasing efficiency and eliminating waste because it treated human beings like robots and stifled innovation.[45] In a more sustained and self-conscious critique of advice literature on how to use time efficiently, Honda Shin'ichi argued that only robots eliminated the "three *mu*" and worked for the sake of being efficient, while people did not think in terms of not wasting anything. Honda himself had worked at Jiji Press (Jiji Tsūshinsha), but left the company to become an independent writer and consultant. In a book titled *Jinsei o yutaka ni suru tame no "jikan" no tsukaikata* (How to Use "Time" to Enrich Your Life), he described his own life as one like that of a "hippie" which he lived for himself, with time for himself. Having shed his wristwatch, he had freed himself from control by the clock to pay more attention to the natural rhythms of his own body. Honda did offer some concrete advice to his readers: to make more time, do not do things that you do not enjoy or are not in keeping with your beliefs and principles; do not put too much emphasis on perfection, for in the end you will do less work; and ease the transition from being a hippie on Sunday to a businessman on Monday by sitting in a coffee shop for an hour before work and reading a business magazine. But in another sign that a new way of thinking about time had not yet developed much less taken root as a norm, Honda's pace of life, much like that of fictional Kōsuke, was difficult to replicate for those who had not or could not opt out of more conventional labor structures. As Honda said himself, people were caught in a net of worshipping money and preserving a middle-class lifestyle. One entwined in the net could still have and be satisfied with their own time, but disentanglement would require living differently and holding values outside the norm.[46]

A Lifestyle Superpower?

In 1989 the Prime Minister's Office asked 7,735 people which they would prioritize in their lives going forward: affluence of the heart and *yutori*, or material affluence. This question had been posed in the annual survey of national lifestyles since 1972, and it was in 1979 that affluence of the heart irreversibly overtook the affluence of things by a paper-thin margin of less than 1 percent. Ten years later, the gap had widened to 16.6 percentage points. Also in 1989, the area of life into which the greatest number of people (33.7 percent) wanted to put effort from then on was leisure; consumer durables and clothing barely registered, at 4.0 and 1.4 percent, respectively.[47] This desire for affluence of the heart, *yutori*, and leisure was described at the time as part of a broader phenomenon—that despite national economic achievements, people were not feeling affluent in their daily lives.[48] This sentiment was partially about rising expectations, about what more could be pursued. And it was partially about the reality of high prices, steep housing costs, and long working hours. In a survey in 1989 of 7,610 people from seven developed countries around the world conducted by the Leisure Development Center (Yoka Kaihatsu Sentā), the percentage of Japanese respondents who said they had two-day weekends was low (19.7 percent), especially in comparison to Americans (68.4 percent). Also noted in a newspaper article about the survey was Japan's level of engagement in leisure, which for twenty-three of forty-three activities ranked at the very bottom.[49]

By the end of the decade, the need to realize an affluence beyond the purely financial and material was expressed from many and various corners of the country. Critical of a perceived gap between economic growth and lifestyles, the Japan Federation of Private Sector Trade Unions (Zen Nihon Minkan Rōdō Kumiai Rengōkai, or Rengō) declared as its aim the pursuit of a true affluence, meaning *yutori*, wealth, and justice appropriate for an economically advanced country. This would require a "lifestyle struggle" and economic reform that prioritized lifestyles and domestic demand over industry and foreign consumption.[50] A similar sentiment, albeit in not such leftist terms, was expressed by Prime Minister Kaifu Toshiki in 1989. In response to what he saw as the distortions and strains of material prosperity, the prime minister established an eleven-member group to consider what Japanese people and society should be, with an eye toward the twenty-first century. In his opening remarks, Kaifu noted that the era of seeking material affluence was over and that the watchwords for the future were the realization of a just society and an affluence of the heart.[51] In 1991, in his own response to acutely felt shortcomings and the need to define new national goals, Prime Minister Miyazawa Ki'ichi pronounced that Japan should become a "lifestyle superpower."[52]

The desire for an affluence of the heart was thus not born of a period of economic downturn as a response to the elusiveness of realizing any other kind of wealth, but a time of financial affluence and material plenty, even excess. It may not have been as prominent in this decade as it would become in later years. But this longing suggests that the 1980s, and the bubble years in particular, were characterized not just by exuberance but also by dissatisfaction, impatience, and unease. Embedded in expressions of disappointment, expectation, and displeasure were ideas about waste, about what should and should not be meaningful in people's daily lives.

At a time when issues of waste were not terribly remarkable or mainstream, connections between an affluence of the heart, lifestyles, and waste were sometimes forged quietly, inconspicuously, or implicitly. Waste consciousness was advocated, however modestly, as a way to make life better. And as much as waste was still understood largely through the logics of efficiency and productivity, its hold on conceptions of free time, leisure, and *yutori* began to show signs of loosening. Indeed, planted in this decade were the seeds of ideas about waste and an affluent heart that would take fuller form in subsequent years. Cultivated amidst financial prosperity and material abundance was a linguistic and conceptual vocabulary to suggest that the acquisition of material things did not guarantee gratification, that time which was truly free should not have to be productive, and that financial wealth did not promise happiness.

BATTLING THE TIME THIEVES

In August 1983, the *Asahi* newspaper published a cogent synopsis of a children's book that it said could make the hearts of adult readers pound, so captivating its story and so striking its questions about the very nature of their contemporary lives. Could people become truly happy with a lifestyle in which efficiency is everything, speed is a priority, and time is money? What was being lost in living this way? Highlighted in the succinct review were the book's key themes—that the mindset of being stingy with time, or not wasting time, came at the cost of being stingy with something much more important. And that the more people tried to save time, the more their lives would wither away. Through an entertaining story, it was explained, readers were being asked to consider the meaning of true affluence.[1]

This unusually sophisticated, penetrating, and popular book was *Momo: Jikan dorobō to nusumareta jikan o ningen ni torikaeshitekureta onnanoko no fushigi na monogatari* (Momo: The Mysterious Story of the Time Thieves and the Girl Who Brought the Stolen Time Back to the People).[2] Written by Michael Ende, the German original was translated into Japanese in 1976, making available to Japanese readers this tale of a young waif named Momo and her battle against insidious time thieves known as the men in gray. In a newspaper advertisement about its release, the book was promoted by its well-known publisher as a "unique fantasy that interrogates the true meaning of time." The first line of its short description cleverly teased, "Today's people, chased by time, restless, forgetting the intrinsically human way to live."[3] If one read on, it became clear that the line was referring to the fictional world of the book, but it was strategically worded to catch the attention of contemporary Japanese readers of a nonfictional world who felt that they had no time to waste.

Momo became not just a best seller in Japan but a "long seller" that, along with its author, enjoyed a popularity starting in the 1980s that endured into the 1990s and beyond. In 1986, Michael Ende delivered the keynote address at the World Congress on Children's Books in Tokyo, where he was flooded with requests for his autograph.[4] The author also gave numerous interviews and in 1989 was named, on the basis of unspecified criteria, one of the one hundred most influential people of the 1980s by the *Asahi* newspaper, making the list in the culture category just after Andy Warhol and right before Raymond Carver and Herbert von Karajan.[5] In 1999, four years after Ende's death, the public broadcaster NHK aired a one-hour documentary about him and his ideas titled *Ende no yuigon* (Ende's Last Words).[6] The story of Momo itself was so compelling that the film version, a joint West German and Italian production, made the rounds in Japan in the summer of 1988.[7] It also inspired a ballet as well as an opera by the avant-garde composer Ichiyanagi Toshi.[8] Sales of the book reached 350,000 by 1986 and the milestone of a million copies by 1992, the most of any of the thirty-three different translations of the work and outdone only by the German original.[9] By 1997, the Japanese version had gone through fifty-six printings and sold a million and a half copies.[10] It was given to children as a classic, excerpted in high school textbooks, used in college courses, and discussed by adults.[11]

Although *Momo* was initially marketed to children in the fifth grade and higher, the book of about 350 pages garnered attention from a much wider audience because it tapped into, crystallized, and expressed the dissatisfactions and yearnings of the time. For the general reader and scholar alike, the fantasy created an idealized world that resonated deeply with their own. There seemed to be enshrined in *Momo* the *yutori* so strongly desired—the relaxation and leisure pursued in the second half of the 1980s, and the truly free time sought in the 1990s and 2000s. As people grappled with questions about what constituted meaningful and wasteful time, and as there developed ways of thinking about valuable time outside the framework of productivity and efficiency, *Momo* not only gave voice to such reflections but also probed the causes of disappointment. In tackling the topics of time and money, the book addressed how underlying societal and economic assumptions operated, and provided much fodder for readers and critics to engage with those ideas they found most closely related to their own concerns, be it capitalism, progress, modernity, materialism, or consumption. The work's continued relevance has been due in no small measure to its substantive exploration of fundamental aspects of contemporary life and its resonance with abiding discontents. To examine *Momo* and its popularity is thus to appreciate how alternative conceptions of value have been imagined, and how the very longing for an affluence of the heart, however defined, has transcended economic booms and busts to endure from the 1980s well into the twenty-first century.

The World of Momo

In author Ende's rendering, "time is life itself, and life resides in the human heart."[12] This was not the objective time of Newton, the universal time of Kant, or any understanding of time as something outside of oneself that can be easily measured.[13] On the contrary, what was at stake in the book was a battle between an unforgivingly objective, external, quantifiable time and a subjective, internal, life-enriching time.[14] So profoundly personal was this subjective time that one Japanese literary scholar, echoed by other writers, suggested that Ende's equation of time with *Leben* in the original German was best expressed not by the Japanese *seikatsu*, as in the published translation, but by *inochi*.[15] While neither Japanese word was as broadly encompassing as *Leben*, the association of *seikatsu* with "living" hinted too much at the mundane as compared to the more transcendent *inochi*. The attention given to this particular linguistic issue and to this particular sentence was but one indication of how much the book was read as offering an ideal vision of life, set against its dehumanizing antithesis, through a competition between two fundamentally different conceptions of time.

The heroine in this struggle, and the embodiment of life-enriching time, was Momo—a girl of uncertain age and unknown origins. She purchased nothing, did not have or need money, or hold a job. She simply showed up one day on the outskirts of a nondescript but vaguely Italian city and made her home among the ruins of a small amphitheater.[16] In Momo, Ende created a character for his utopian fantasy who was free from the disciplining institutions of orphanage, school, and workplace, and from the entrapments of the money economy. So liberated, Momo understood clearly what was of real value. She appreciated what had been or might be discarded as waste by others: she dressed in worn clothes, ate scraps of food that had been brought to her, and lived in a forgotten wasteland. She embraced friendship, imagination, play, adventure, and fun. And she listened carefully and patiently to all who came and talked with her in a way that was for them emotionally and psychologically transformative.

Momo's lack of concern with financial affluence, Ende suggested, enabled her to experience this truly rich life. He described warmly, and romantically, the bricklayer, carpenter, and other neighbors who welcomed Momo to the amphitheater and with her "celebrated as zestfully as only the poor of the world know how."[17] In Momo's life, wealth was not monetary, time was not money, and both were beyond measure.

In distinct contrast, Momo's antagonists—the men in gray—sought to convince people that understanding time as a quantifiable commodity would improve their lives. Early on in their efforts to infiltrate the city, the men in gray explained this with stark clarity to one of their first victims, named Mr. Fūjī in the Japanese edition.[18] Mr. Fūjī enjoyed his work as a barber but occasionally felt as though he was not leading the "right kind of life." He did not know what this meant, only "vaguely pictured it as a distinguished and luxurious existence such as he was always reading about in weekly magazines."[19] Preying on Mr. Fūjī's inchoate unease, the men in gray dispatched to the barbershop an agent dressed in their characteristic gray suit and bowler hat with gray briefcase, notebook, and cigar. Agent No. X Y Q/384/b informed Mr. Fūjī, "You're wasting your life with scissors, chitchat, and lather." But Mr. Fūjī need not despair, because the "right kind of life" would be attainable if only he had more time, and he would have more time if he stopped "wasting it in an utterly irresponsible way."[20] Agent No. X Y Q/384/b then proceeded to calculate how much time, or "capital," Mr. Fūjī had at his disposal (2,207,520,000 seconds) and how much of it he had already wasted (1,324,512,000 seconds). This figure was derived from deeming the following activities wasteful: sleeping; working; eating; talking with his elderly mother; keeping a pet parakeet; doing housework; going to the movies, singing in a social club, going out drinking, reading, and talking with friends; seeing a woman named Miss Daria whom he did not intend to marry; and daydreaming.[21] A stunned Mr. Fūjī was thus convinced that he would be better off if he saved his time in an interest-bearing account at the Timesaving Bank, represented by the man in gray.[22] To maximize his savings, Agent No. X Y Q/384/b advised Mr. Fūjī to work hastily and stop doing unnecessary things, which meant putting his mother in a nursing home, no longer seeing Miss Daria, getting rid of his pet, and reducing time spent on leisure.[23] The men in gray not only epitomized the idea of time as money, but they also peddled the fallacy that time could be treated like money, that it could be stored up and saved. With this commodified view of time, together with waste elimination taken to the extreme, the men in gray gradually stripped Mr. Fūjī's life of meaningful work, companionship, and pleasure.

Unknown to the befuddled Mr. Fūjī, the men in gray were plundering the time being "saved" in the Timesaving Bank. As Agent No. B L W/553/c explained to the suspicious Momo: "The time saved by human beings does not remain in their hands. We steal it, store it, and use it for our own purposes."[24] Momo eventually came to learn from a character named Mr. Hora that he was the distributor of every individual's time in the form of hour-lilies and that the men in gray were robbing people of their hour-lilies, preserving and stockpiling the flowers, and plucking off petals to make the gray cigars on which they subsisted. Or to put it more succinctly, the men in gray survived on "dead human time."[25] People like Mr. Fūjī were being deceived into saving time, which only served to deplete his life and keep alive the very logic of saving time. This empty, nonsensical cycle could be broken only by Momo who, in her ultimate fight against the men in gray, sought to restore the stolen hour-lilies to their rightful owners.

Stolen Time

The idea of time as a quantifiable commodity and as a currency equivalent to money—what might be considered a modern, industrial, and capitalist conception of time—was not new to Japan in the decades of *Momo*'s popularity. If we look back to the early years of the Meiji period (1868–1912), we find that the understanding of time as something to be synchronized and measured precisely was assumed by the government's adoption of the Gregorian calendar and the twenty-four-hour clock as well as its promotion of a modern time consciousness.[26] Punctuality and not wasting time, for example, were important lessons to be taught to students. Both virtues were exemplified by a story in a fourth-grade ethics textbook about a Frenchman named Daguesseau, who arrived in the dining room for lunch every day precisely at noon. On those occasions when the meal was not yet ready, he used that time to write down ideas. After ten years, these notes became a "fine book" because "he did not waste time." Although the text went on to mention that "time is money," the moral of this particular tale was that punctuality and temporal thrift led not so much to financial wealth as to good work. In this emphasis on the virtue of hard and honest industry was an implied connection between valuable time and productivity, that not wasting time led to progress.[27] It was not just the government that cultivated a modern time consciousness. The story of Daguesseau was loosely taken from Samuel Smiles's *Self-Help*, originally published in Britain in 1859 and translated into Japanese in 1871.[28] The book not only provided many an anecdote for ethics textbooks but also became a best seller, with readers snatching up over a million copies. The popularity of this book, especially in the early Meiji years, has been attributed to its reinforcement of the belief that individual work and character paved the way to national progress and that a modern time consciousness, with its concomitant staving off of "idleness," was essential if Japan was to rise in the world.[29]

The phrase "rising in the world" (*risshin shusse*) became popular after the Sino-Japanese War in the 1890s, and the inclination to define not just national but also individual success in monetary terms became increasingly common in the early twentieth century. The conceptual vocabulary for this trend was provided by the phrase "time is money," credited to Benjamin Franklin and widely recognized as having been introduced to Japan by Smiles in *Self-Help*.[30] As the historian Kuriyama Shigehisa has pointed out, Franklin's expression emphasized money over time: wasted time was significant insofar as it was wasted money.[31] Close parallels between time and money also came to be underscored linguistically, as both could be "used," "saved," and "wasted."

When *Momo* was published, some of what it criticized—measuring time, eliminating the perceived waste of time, equating time and money—had long been familiar, even deep-seated, ideas in daily life. There were readers who thus understood *Momo* as depicting a world before the modernizing changes of the Meiji period, and interpreted the contrast drawn by Ende as one between modern time consciousness, represented by the men in gray, and a premodern understanding of time, represented by Momo.[32] Living in, and ultimately fighting for, a world uncorrupted by the logic of the men in gray, Momo was described by the book's Japanese translator, Ōshima Kaori, as pristinely natural and as a symbol of people not yet subject to the control and order of a civilized society.[33] Momo's home was, after all, an ancient ruin, as one literary scholar pointed out. And so, argued Shimauchi Keiji, the book was about the retrieval not just of the time stolen by the men in gray but also of an "ancient spirit"; about modern civilization adopting the desirable aspects of ancient civilization.[34]

But to interpret *Momo* simply as an allegory about modern civilization would shortchange both Ende and his readers and would not shed much light on its popularity at this historical moment. The book drew a rapt audience not because it was a commentary on a vague and sweeping notion of modernity, but because it spoke to the particular incarnations, perversions, and manifestations of modernity that readers saw as characterizing and shaping their daily lives. The idea of time being stolen, for example, very much resonated with the contemporary sense that there was not enough time, that the pace of life was too fast, and that people were too harried. The book, commented the journalist Hashimoto Toshio, tugged at the hearts of busy Japanese.[35] For one person, the thirty-five-year-old housewife Shimizu Aki from Fukuoka prefecture, *Momo* reached her through its illumination of her husband's all-consuming work schedule. Having reread the book after a fight with her husband, she became less annoyed with his absenteeism and became somewhat more sympathetic toward work-related demands on his time.[36] A woman named Kojima Akiko also looked at the lives of people around her through the lens of the book and lamented that they were so harried they did not have any time to spare, even to potentially prevent suicides by listening to young people reaching out to them. The thirty-one-year-old office worker from Fujisawa city urged in the *Asahi* newspaper a reclamation of "wasted time," or the valuable and ever scarcer free time that had come to be deemed wasteful.[37] Taking more of a bird's-eye view, the historian of science and technology Hashimoto Takehiko lamented how developments like the emergence of the information society had accelerated the workings of the world. With increasing speed and increasing demands for the management of segmented time, he worried that people's field of vision would become even more shortsighted and narrow. He welcomed projects like the Clock of the Long Now in the United States, designed to tick once a year for ten thousand years as a symbol of deep time and long-term thinking.[38] In all of this unease with speed and busyness were the echoes of Ende's description of Mr. Fūjī's experience of time after his encounter with Agent No. X Y Q/384/b: "Mysteriously, the time that he saved vanished. Although imperceptible at first, it gradually became clear that his days were getting shorter. In an instant, a week flew by, then a month, then a year and another and another."[39]

Related to the busyness of everyday life was concern about the pressure to work more quickly, to eliminate wasted time in a "frightful era" in which efficiency was everything.[40] The assumption that the faster one worked, the better, was worrisome to Umeda Masaaki, an unemployed former worker at a food company who published a book about time in the late 1990s. To Umeda, the fetishization of efficiency was encapsulated by a passage in Momo in which the men in gray posted notices that read, "TIME IS PRECIOUS—DON'T WASTE IT! TIME IS MONEY—SAVE IT!"[41] The men in gray, with their promotion of efficiency and rejection of anything seemingly useless as a waste, struck Umeda as even more like Franklin than Franklin himself. To value constant activity and efficiency and to disparage inactivity and idleness as wasteful was deemed a mistake. In Umeda's view, this seemingly useless time had meaning, like the realization of yutori. What had to be recovered in the book and in daily lives, he implied, was the pleasure of time spent living.[42]

Momo's life-enriching time spoke especially to those Japanese readers who yearned for more free time. On occasion, this was defined more narrowly in terms of vacation and leisure time. Hayabusa Nagaharu, a member of the Asahi newspaper editorial board, urged his readers on the cusp of summer vacation in 1985 to think carefully about what a humane lifestyle might be and to use their time away from work to recover their "human being-ness" or humanity. More specifically, Hayabusa presented the results of a survey conducted by the Ministry of Labor (Rōdōshō) in which one-third of the firms that participated said their summer vacation was only three days long, defined as a two-day weekend plus one additional day. If Ende examined such vacation policies, speculated Hayabusa, he would diagnose the Ministry of Labor as afflicted with "efficiency disease."[43] In more philosophical terms, the scholar Hashizume Taiki hoped in a Yokagaku *kenkyū* (Journal of Leisure Studies) article published in 2011 that Momo's conception of time might serve as the foundation for a new temporality of leisure.[44]

Other commentators interpreted Momo's internal and subjective time through their own particular lens, focused on the need in contemporary lives for truly and meaningfully free time. But this did not simply mean more opportunity for leisure, which was susceptible to being viewed, as it was by the men in gray, as something that "had to be used without the slightest waste" and "packed with as much amusement as possible."[45] People should not be expected to play purposefully and busily, but instead should experience a time of contentment, happiness, and meaning that was "free" in the sense of both freedom from work and liberation from a mindset of productivity and utility. Reflecting on this idea of free time, the economist Nakamura Tatsuya penned an essay published in a junior high school Japanese language textbook, approved in 1993 by the Ministry of Education (Monbushō), in which he argued that people did not have free and rich time. Already lost was much of what Momo represented, as people had become like Mr. Fūjī—handcuffed by their wristwatches, busy, and bereft of time. He explained that the country had become financially wealthy and that people were now able to consume and acquire things, but they did not feel enriched, in part because they did not have time for themselves. People might have more nonworking time in the 1990s than they did at the beginning of the century, he observed, but this was not to be mistaken for truly free time.[46]

Nakamura's thoughts were echoed and quoted in an *Asahi* newspaper editorial published in May 1994 which chronicled a postwar history in which an affluence of the heart proved elusive despite economic, technological, and material achievement. In the editorial board's recounting of the fairly recent past, the era of mass consumption had promised that a convenient and affluent lifestyle could be attained through the purchase of things, newly created through the wonders of technological progress. But as households brimmed over with stuff, people were not experiencing an affluence of the heart because they had become busier in order to buy the very things that were supposed to save them time. In wholehearted agreement with Nakamura's contention that time, rather than money or things, should become the measure of wealth, the editorial endorsed an increase in free time. This would mean a decrease in working hours, income, consumption, and production, all of which, they recognized, would translate into slowed economic growth. But it would also give rise to *yutori* in living. Imagined was a future when husbands would come home from work earlier and help out with household chores and the raising of children, and wives would experience true free time. To drive this point home, the editorial closed with the line from *Momo* that time is life itself, and the more people try to "save" time, the more life thins out and disappears.[47]

The emptiness of material acquisition alluded to in the *Asahi* editorial was a central point in other readings of *Momo*. For Ogose Tōru, a professor of education, the modern time consciousness embodied and promoted by the men in gray revealed the extent to which society was controlled by things. Or to put it another way, their perversion of temporality represented the modern consumption society. As with the men in gray, the culture of consumption was a system that ensnared people and blinded them to its problems. What Ende laid bare, in Ogose's view, was how a consumption society could be affluent but also create uneasiness and lethargy.[48]

Ende did indeed draw many connections between time and material consumption in *Momo*, perhaps most emblematically in the trial of Agent No. B L W/553/c by fellow men in gray for betraying too much about them to Momo. The spectacle, presided over by magistrates and witnessed by hordes of men in gray, unfolded at the municipal garbage dump far outside the city at the top of "a veritable mountain of ash, broken glass, aluminum cans, old futons, plastic rubbish, cardboard boxes, and all sorts of other junk discarded by the city's inhabitants, all waiting to be fed, little by little, into huge incinerators."[49] For the Waseda University professor Koyasu Michiko, the garbage symbolized material civilization, and the image of the agents atop this physical waste was a call to see the men in gray in the consumer goods and advertising posters with which people in Japan were inundated.[50] Indeed, together in this scene was the mound of garbage (fed by dead things, the material detritus of society) alongside the men in gray (fed by dead human time, the temporal detritus of society). Here was a visual representation of the costs and sacrifices of mass consumption.

The contemporary resonance of *Momo* was sometimes less thematic and more grounded in particular social issues. One such topic of concern was the nature of children's lives. Ende himself, in an interview on NHK television on New Year's Day 1990, spoke about how the casualties of the ongoing "war of time" were children.[51] That children should be spared time-related malaise was implied in the book itself. Momo was a child; her friends, most of whom were children, staged a protest against the men in gray; and ultimately the children were the last to fall under the influence of the time thieves. This was by design, for the men in gray themselves feared children as their "natural enemies" and knew that it would be more difficult to turn children than adults into time savers. Hence one of their strictest, and most sinister, laws: "Leave the children until last."[52] In the afterword to the Japanese version of *Momo*, the translator, Ōshima Kaori, hinted that the time thieves had already gotten to Japanese children who, like adults, were saying that they had no time.[53]

More specifically, there was a widely shared sense that the pressures of the education system were robbing children of their time and their childhood. Shortly after *Momo*'s publication, an editorial in the *Asahi* newspaper declared that the society described in the book—a desolate society in which children had forgotten how to play because of an unhealthy emphasis on education—was contemporary Japan itself. Japanese children, the editorial warned, were too preoccupied with exams, and society was too blind to the vulnerabilities of both children and the elderly as its weakest members.[54] Such criticism of entrance examinations and the culture around them was voiced quite often and vociferously, especially in the late 1980s and early 1990s. In 1988 the cartoonist Yanase Takashi speculated that children could understand well the idea behind the men in gray for they, like adults, had become pressed for time. Yanase went on to share an anecdote about being on a Tokyo train on a weeknight around 10.00 pm and seeing many children "taken in" by time thieves, returning home from cram schools at which they were preparing for exams.[55]

There was a distinct sense in Yanase's comments and those of others that the problem of time-obsessed children was getting worse. Matsuoka Kyōko, director of the Tokyo Children's Library at the time, recalled that when she opened her own library in the early 1970s, children had time for themselves and no one noticed that there was no clock. By 1977, when she moved the library into a new room of her rebuilt house, Matsuoka felt compelled to put in a clock because she was so irked by how often children asked her what time it was. By the 1980s, it had become common for children to tell her that that they could stay at the library for only so long because they had to go to cram school or other lessons or classes of some sort.[56] While Matsuoka noticed that the problem had abated somewhat and implied that the restlessness of children would continue to subside in a period of economic slowdown, others were not so optimistic. The economist Nakamura Tatsuya was unsettled by the convention of elementary and middle school students wearing wristwatches, inclined as he was to think that people were being surveilled by clocks and that wristwatches were thus akin to handcuffs. Comparing Japanese children with Mr. Fūjī, he described cram school goers as having their time stolen.[57] As recently as 2010, scholars were still likening the fate of children in Ende's book to that of children in contemporary Japanese society, whose time was consumed by attending cram schools and studying for exams. One article even suggested that it was children in wealthy countries, not those in poor countries, who should be pitied because they hardly ever saw their friends, played with video games and with computers rather than going outside, and spent much of their time preparing for exams.[58]

In the assessment of Sakai Takashi, who had dedicated his professional life to working with various nonprofit organizations, many of the social issues of millennial Japan could be traced back to the "deadly tedium" that afflicted victims of the men in gray. This disease was described in the book by the character Mr. Hora:

You don't notice it at first, but suddenly one day you don't feel like doing anything anymore. Nothing interests you, everything bores. This lethargy doesn't disappear, but gets worse day by day and week by week. You feel more and more depressed, your heart becomes more and more empty, you become more and more dissatisfied with yourself and the world in general. Then even that feeling wears off, and you don't feel anything any more . . . With a blank, gray face, you bustle around restlessly just like the men in gray.[59]

To Sakai, this condition provided a way of thinking about the phenomena of acute social withdrawal (*hikikomori*) and youth without permanent full-time employment (*furītā*). Offering his own variation on the manifestation of "deadly tedium," he commented that in Ende's book the disease affected only those individuals who had reached an agreement with the men in gray and thus were robbed of their time, but in contemporary Japan, it infected the entire society. So pervasive was this condition that it drove some people, so-called *hikikomori*, to retreat into their rooms to escape from the gaze of a society that characterized them as lazy. *Hikikomori* were not afflicted with the alienating illness, as one might expect, but were trying to liberate themselves from it. They could thus be understood as akin to those in *Momo*, like the eponymous main character, who did not open a savings account with the men in gray so had plenty of time and yet were quite lonely because they did not have any similarly inclined friends. To address this situation, Sakai proposed finding for *hikikomori* those with whom they could share their time and recommending to them types of work, known as "slow work," that did not involve saving time. Not entirely unlike *hikikomori*, *furītā* were seen by Sakai as having repudiated the temporal illness of full-time employment by virtue of moving from job to job. He also criticized government efforts to address the phenomenon of NEETs, or those "not in employment, education, or training," as simply encouraging people to reach agreements with the men in gray rather than grappling with them head-on. Sakai used the conceptual vocabulary of Ende's fantasy world to paint not *hikikomori* and *furītā* but the larger society as ill with "deadly tedium."[60]

Momo's Fantastic Heart

The interwoven themes and interpretations of *Momo* were encapsulated cogently in what was often described by its Japanese readership as the book's main concern: the pursuit, protection, and preservation of an affluence of the heart. This was a story of a girl who helped "recapture people's affluence of the heart," as the *Asahi* newspaper put it.[61] Momo's sense of time, her way of life, and the world she inhabited were understood as profoundly humane, deeply meaningful, and truly rich, characterized as they were by pleasure, enjoyment, community, empathy, friendship, and freedom. In contrast, the men in gray and their victims like Mr. Fūjī were seen as incapable of and indifferent to happiness. The world they sought to create was regimented, constraining, shallow, materialistic, uniform, impersonal, lethargic, desolate, purposeless, and cold—utterly bereft of an affluence of the heart.[62]

Associated with the dystopian vision of the men in gray was consciousness of waste. It was the time thieves who infected people with the idea that anything that was not useful or productive was a waste, and that waste had to be eliminated. It was the time thieves who embodied the heartless rationality of scientific management. It was the time thieves who tricked people into saving time without a clear sense of purpose. Momo, unlike the men in gray, was so thoroughly unconcerned about waste that the concepts of waste and wastefulness simply did not figure in to how she lived and how she saw her world.

In *Momo* and its popularity was a reaction against the fetishization of waste consciousness, its associated logics, and the kind of society it helped create, and against the continued embrace of productivity and efficiency for the sake of economic growth and prosperity. The book deftly captured the zeitgeist of the time, tapping into dissatisfaction with the poverty of meaning in people's lives and a desire for greater contentment, happiness, and humaneness in contemporary Japanese life. This sense of discontent with financial and material wealth which became palpable in the 1980s has since endured. In more recent years, there have been discussions of *Momo* in the context of redefining affluence and happiness after the triple disasters of March 2011, continued references to "time thieves" in advice literature about time management, and a review of the book in a June 2015 issue of the prominent weekly business magazine *Ekonomisuto* (Economist).[63]

For the utopian world of the book, Ende decided to write a utopian ending in which Momo returned to people their hour-lilies and freed the world of men in gray. This might have been a fitting closure for a fantasy, but it did not provide resolution for readers who did not live in a society so easily and neatly divided between Momo and the men in gray. The book offered alternative ways to think about purpose, meaning, and affluence, but readers had to define, create, and realize such ideas while navigating a complicated reality in which waste elimination, productivity, efficiency, economic growth, and financial prosperity were tenacious, powerful, important, and desirable. *Momo* was an attractive and utopian expression of aspirations for an affluence of the heart for readers of a world in which the actual men in gray were not unquestionable and irredeemable villains. The challenge was not in jettisoning the time thieves but in reconciling their existence with a purposeful, meaningful, and truly affluent way of life.

Part IV

AFFLUENCE OF THE HEART

Identities and Values in the Slow-Growth Era, 1991–Present

GREENING CONSCIOUSNESS

Under the title "Live in the Now with Spiritual Affluence," the *Asahi* newspaper published an editorial in January 1999 that questioned the values and priorities of those who had come of age in the several decades just past, in a prosperous Japan. The editorial held up as an encapsulation of these postwar aspirations one photograph, staged and shot by photojournalist Peter Menzel in 1992 as part of a United Nations–supported project to capture the material lives of average families in various countries around the world. The four-member Japanese family, the Ukitas of far western Tokyo, sat in front of their two-story wood-frame house surrounded by all of their physical possessions, which had been taken from within to be put on full display. In the words of the newspaper, "Piled up in front of the house was an abundance of stuff, stuff, stuff." There were the electric appliances and consumer electronics (washing machine and dryer, microwave oven, toaster oven, television set, rice cooker, refrigerator, video game console, and electronic keyboard), the furniture (bed, shelving units, chests of drawers, desk, bookcases), the row of shoes, the minivan in the carport, the family dog and his home, and more—posed before the 1,421-square-foot house with all of its lights aglow. The absurdity of the sight, a home's innards splayed out on the curb and displaced from the space that gave their functions meaning, underscored the incredulity of the editorial, which asked, "Is this the happiness that we have sought?"[1]

The unequivocal answer given by the newspaper was that the enduring pursuit of material acquisition had not made people happy. The generations that had

FIGURE 8.1.   Stuff and Happiness. The photograph of the Ukita family's possessions, discussed in the *Asahi* newspaper.

Reproduced by permission from Peter Menzel, *Material World: A Global Family Portrait* (San Francisco: Sierra Club Books, 1994) © Peter Menzel/menzelphoto.com.

experienced the proliferation of things since the high-growth era and through the bubble economy were still chasing a narrowly conceived affluence and paying the price. The prioritization of work had compromised family relationships, health, friendships, and time to cultivate the spirit. With more than a hint of envy, the younger generation was described as valuing more than work, appreciating and enjoying the here and now, and turning more toward an affluence of the heart.[2] The upsetting implication was that the idea of a happier future had proved to be an illusion, that the material things which people had worked so hard to acquire had not delivered the gratification they had promised, and that the time and effort spent and sacrifices made in the name of financial and material gain might very well have been a waste.

Expressions of doubt about a preoccupation with financial and material wealth and of desire for a more expansive conception of meaning dated back to the 1980s, when the Japanese economy seemed strong and a mood of financial confidence opened up questions about the relative importance of the material and the spiritual. In the 1990s, as the collapse of the bubble economy reverberated throughout various aspects of the country's life, there was more that was up for grabs—about the country's place in the world, its sense of identity and purpose, how people might live in a slow-growth environment, and what their values and priorities should be.

It took time for these questions to crystallize. The economic malaise that would come to define the decade was not a given in its early years, and was not caused by a single event. There was the fall in stock market prices in late 1989 and 1990, the burst of the real estate bubble, and, by 1992, a dip into recession. But gross domestic product returned to a positive trajectory in the middle of the decade and there were signs, however mixed, of possible recovery. When people were asked about their current lives in large nationwide surveys conducted by the Prime Minister's Office, there was no sudden and precipitous drop in satisfaction in the early 1990s. There was instead an upward trend, followed by a fall in 1994 and then a sharp rise in 1995; it was not until the second half of the decade that there was a steady decline.[3] Indeed, it was not until the late 1990s that the country fell into a prolonged recession and both the *Nihon keizai* newspaper (Japan Economic Journal) and *Newsweek* could define the preceding ten years, only in hindsight, as "the lost decade" (*ushinawareta jūnen*).[4] The complex economic and social troubles that came to be referred to in shorthand as "the collapse of the bubble" was thus not experienced like the Oil Shock of 1973, when the oil crisis provoked almost immediate revelations about the end of high-speed growth and the country's dangerous reliance on imports as well as concomitant calls to not waste things, money, resources, and energy. In the 1990s, the contours and realizations of the post-bubble years took shape over time, in a kind of slow burn that did not make itself fully felt until the decade was near its end.

During these unsettled years, values and commitments that had retreated into the background in the previous decade emerged again, this time framed by and configured for an era of both economic uncertainty and global environmental challenges. Concern with the global environment had burgeoned in the late 1980s, when issues like climate change flouted geographic boundaries. As international as the environmental awakening of the 1960s and 1970s had been, problems such as industrial pollution had largely been seen as local and thus had elicited relatively localized responses. But in these years, the scale of degradation of everything from stratospheric ozone to rainforests transcended borders. And in Japan, as elsewhere, the "global environment" entered the mainstream lexicon and captured public attention, so much so that some envisioned 1989 as "year one" in Japan of the "global environmental age."[5]

Attempts to rearticulate priorities in the age of the global environment came to link waste consciousness and environmental consciousness, which together became established and widespread norms. To be seen as aware of environmental issues, and therefore of waste, became an increasingly strong aspiration. And many wanted to think of themselves as committed to addressing issues of waste and the environment, even when their behavior might have suggested otherwise. It was not as though waste and wastefulness were understood in fundamentally different ways than in the recent past. Attention was still focused on the thoughtless use of things, resources, and energy, and the main antidotes were recycling and reuse. The reduction of waste was still not to mean the sacrifice of comfort, convenience, or consumption, in keeping with the spirit of bright stinginess conceived in the 1970s.

Yet, at the same time, these now customary ideas took on new meanings and additional purposes as the global environmental shift helped reframe waste consciousness in somewhat more global and somewhat less anthropocentric terms.[6] Local initiatives for waste reduction that had taken root in the 1970s were connected to translocal problems like global warming. Environmental preservation was talked about as more of a good or an end in itself than it had been in the past, when so much focus had been placed on resource conservation as an underwriter of economic growth. There were new, ecologically minded ways to think about consumption, or at least new, ecologically minded products to consume. And environmental commitments were looped into discussions about how a true affluence should be defined. As both the economy and the global environment seemed frail, environmental concerns assumed a solid and stable position as an important thread in regenerated conceptions of waste and wastefulness.

The Global Environment

An official narrative about waste, approved by the Ministry of Education (Monbushō) in 1993, told a fairly familiar story about mass production, mass consumption, and mass waste. Subtitled *Ningen to shite no yutaka na seikatsu o mezashite* (Aiming for an Affluent Lifestyle as Human Beings), a textbook adopted for use in high school home economics classes described how electric appliances, cars, and other consumer goods produced to make life convenient required a large amount of resources, and how mass production and daily living resulted in garbage. This had been the case since the era of high growth, it was explained, so the students as consumers were instructed to reexamine their consuming lives and familiarize themselves with cooperative associations, recycling movements, swap meets, and other practices that supposedly would not create garbage. The promotion of recycling and the reference to a more humane affluence were not new. And the connection drawn between mass production, mass consumption, and mass waste had a history that reached back to the 1970s, even if it had retreated from public attention in the 1980s.

But what was different was how prominently this narrative featured the environment. There was a section of the textbook titled "A Lifestyle That Protects the

Environment," in which mass production, mass consumption, and mass waste were directly tied to what was described as the serious problem of environmental destruction. Conservation of the environment was presented as the goal of practices such as reuse (e.g., buying things at recycling centers or flea markets) and recycling (e.g., properly discarding paper, milk cartons, cans, and bottles).[7] And readers were encouraged to care about environmental protection as an end in itself, more than as a way to attain or maintain financial wealth. To become a consumer who was thoroughly affluent, in a rather comprehensive sense that reached beyond the monetary and the material, was to be environmentally conscious.

The messages in this textbook echoed those of a report by the Economic Planning Agency (Keizai Kikakuchō) that had been released two years earlier. Looking ahead to 2010, the agency determined that two things were important in the long term: people and the earth. When it spoke of people, the report was referring specifically to fostering people's ability to pursue in their individual and diverse ways an affluence of the heart and a relaxed life. And caring for the earth meant sustaining the planet through the efforts of global citizens to deal with environmental, resource, energy, and population problems.[8] What the agency brought together was an expansive conception of affluence that had begun to be formulated in the previous decade, and an environmentalism stamped with contemporary global interests.

This reframing of long-held concerns in environmental terms that were more global and less anthropocentric than those of the late 1960s and 1970s took shape as the country was starting to participate in burgeoning discussions about newly recognized environmental problems, especially climate change, in the late 1980s and 1990s. This was a moment when there was an international shift in focus away from unfettered, intensive economic growth and toward the idea of sustainability, as studies about the negative environmental consequences of human activity and development culminated in the acknowledgment that the future was being mortgaged for the present. In 1987, the UN World Commission on Environment and Development issued its now famous report *Our Common Future*, in which it argued that "humanity has the ability to make development sustainable to ensure that it meets the needs of the present without compromising the ability of future generations to meet their own needs." And further, "Sustainable global development requires that those who are more affluent adopt life-styles within the planet's ecological means."[9]

In Japan, the environment was made an important political issue with the efforts of the Environment Agency (Kankyōchō) and a faction of the Liberal Democratic Party (Jiyū Minshutō, or LDP) that sought to bolster the country's standing and image abroad. In 1988, the Environment Agency articulated the need to deal with environmental issues such as global warming, and the country became a member of the International Panel on Climate Change created by the World Meteorological Organization and the UN Environment Program. On Prime Minister Takeshita Noboru's suggestion, an international conference on the environment was held the following year in Japan. The Tokyo Conference on Global Environmental Protection was chaired by Ōkita Saburō, the economist and politician who had served on the executive committee for the Club of Rome when it published its seminal report *The Limits to Growth* in 1972; almost two decades later, Ōkita adopted the language of sustainable development to promote slow growth for the Japanese economy, at a rate of about 3 percent, so that economic growth could be balanced with environmental protection.[10] In 1989, Prime Minister Takeshita's successor, Uno Sōsuke, managed in his brief two-month tenure to establish the position of global environmental minister and the Ministerial Council on Global Environmental Protection (Chikyū Kankyō Hozen ni Kansuru Kankei Kakuryō Kaigi), which set a goal of limiting carbon dioxide emissions. In 1992, Japan was a party to the Framework Convention on Climate Change signed at the UN Conference on Environment and Development in Rio de Janeiro. The framework set the stage for the Kyoto Protocol, adopted in 1997, which established targets for emissions reduction.[11]

Such concern about the global environment was reinforced in the late 1990s by local manifestations of a besieged earth in revolt which could not be contained within borders. In 1997, information came to light that revealed the degree to which an incinerator in the town of Nose, in Osaka prefecture, was contaminating the environment with dioxins, a toxic by-product of burning plastics which was known to cause cancer and disrupt hormones that regulate biological processes. Low-grade fears and citizens' movements against dioxins of earlier years became more urgent, and concerns about dioxins and so-called environmental hormones garnered further national attention two years later when a news program on TV Asahi reported that vegetables grown in Tokorozawa city, in Saitama prefecture, registered dangerously high levels of dioxins. The story transformed isolated and contained incidents of dioxin contamination into a danger that could seep into soil and food, and thereby be transported and spread anywhere across the country. Although it turned out that TV Asahi had greatly exaggerated its claims and was compelled to issue a retraction, its report helped ensure that dioxins would remain a national concern by reinforcing the link between incinerators and harm to both health and the environment, and by stoking serious reports as well as more spurious suspicions about dioxins as the cause of various ailments.[12] In response to the heightened attention from different sources to this health and environmental hazard in the late 1990s, the Ministry of Health and Welfare (Kōseishō) established new guidelines in 1997 to control and reduce dioxin emissions from incinerators.[13]

A more visible embodiment of nature perverted by waste was the crow. As the number of crows grew, they became a common sight in the streets of urban areas and a topic of increasing media interest in the late 1990s. A menace literally fed by raw garbage replete with food waste, crows were also proliferating because of the warming of cities, which decreased their death rates in the winter. And in certain places like the island of Kyūshū, the spread of residential construction forced birds out of the mountains and into cities. The crows thus were, in the determination of the *Yomiuri* newspaper, emblematic of an "era of satiation."[14] Not only did the population of jungle crows (*Corvus macrohynchos*, or *hashibutogarasu*) explode—as it did in the Tokyo area from an estimated 10,000 in 1990 to 20,000 in 1995, and then to somewhere between 80,000 and 100,000 in 2001—but also some of their number became aggressive.[15] Unlike the mosquitoes, flies, and rats that had accompanied the garbage of yesteryear, these birds seemed willful in their attacks on zoo animals (a marmot, a newborn wallaby, and a baby deer in Kita Kyūshū city), pets (such as cats and dogs), and even people (including elementary school children and housewives in the Setagaya ward of Tokyo).[16] The raven-like birds were also preternaturally crafty and smart. They scrounged up wire hangers to make nests on utility poles, causing shorts and power outages.[17] They pulled off or found their way through the nets that were thrown over piles of garbage in an effort to prevent their contents from being scattered by the crows.[18] They woke up early in the morning, before sunrise, necessitating garbage collection at night in busy commercial districts.[19] So bad was the crow problem by 2001 that Tokyo governor Ishihara Shintarō declared that crows were the "disgrace" of the capital and that they were to be "repelled." And the *Yomiuri* newspaper called the situation the "Tokyo Crow War."[20] Across the country, nests were removed, nets were tried, garbage containers with lids were recommended, garbage bags were coated on the inside with the capsaicin from chili peppers or were manufactured in yellow to interfere with the birds' vision, and residents were urged to reduce waste and handle their garbage properly.[21] Some combination of these efforts stemmed the tide of the population explosion, though calls have continued for vigilance in the battle against improperly discarded garbage and stubborn crows.

With an ever brighter spotlight on environmental issues, various connections were drawn between waste and its negative ecological consequences. The wasteful and excessive consumption of resources and energy was held to account for a host of environmental problems in a 1992 publication by the Economic Planning Agency's National Lifestyle Bureau (Keizai Kikakuchō Kokumin Seikatsukyoku). Explicitly, if broadly, the recent uptick in household energy consumption for such uses as heating, air conditioning, and lighting along with an increase in the disposal of plastics and large items like home appliances were linked to various environmental challenges from global warming and the destruction of the ozone layer to air pollution and dioxin emissions from ill-managed waste incineration.

What was called for was saving resources and saving energy (*shōshigen, shōenerugī*), by now a conventional prescription that was reformulated as an amalgam of ideas both familiar and new. The purpose of saving resources and energy became less about preserving limited inputs for economic growth, as it had been in previous decades, and more about valuing environmental conservation. And environmental conservation was deemed important for the realization of a "true affluence" that required, but transcended, financial prosperity. This true affluence presupposed wealth, but it entailed thinking about the total person, which meant ensuring health and safety, forming real human relationships, and creating a rich environment in which to live. There were echoes here of the bright stinginess of the 1970s, with its insistence that waste consciousness must not sacrifice standards of living; the bureau made clear that eliminating the wasting of resources and energy was not to mean the constant and pervasive saving characteristic of poverty, but rather an intentional, planned, and skillful way of living. In this incarnation, to save resources and energy was to practice environmental consciousness. And environmental consciousness, in turn, became a significant value that was not at odds with financial wealth, but was essential for a more capacious kind of affluence.[22]

This promotion of a true affluence with environmental awareness through saving resources and energy was echoed by others, including various groups that bridged the state and society. Among them were the Central Council of the National Movement to Value Resources and Energy (Shigen to Enerugī o Taisetsu ni Suru Kokumin Undō Chūō Kaigi), the New Life Movement Association (Shin Seikatsu Undō Kyōkai), and the Association to Build the Japan of Tomorrow (Ashita no Nihon o Tsukuru Kyōkai). These organizations emphasized how the consumption of resources and energy resulted in the emission of Freon gas and carbon dioxide, which harmed health, safety, and the environment. This environmental consciousness was tied to a "true affluence," though their definition contained a characteristic dose of conservative moralism. Their "true affluence" was distinguished from an "affluence of the heart," which they saw as encouraging the very self-centeredness and presentism that spawned environmental problems. To create what these groups considered a truly affluent life, each person would need to realize that they were but one living thing, one member of society, one global citizen. Presenting the saving of resources and energy in this way had a strategic dimension, for as the organizations themselves pointed out, their previous emphasis on limits to supply had only short-term effects. As soon as the immediate crisis of a shortage and high prices had passed, waste consciousness faded. It was hoped that nurturing a concern for the environment, from the local to the global, would encourage a more abiding dedication to not wasting resources and energy.[23]

Others also foregrounded environmental concerns as a way to more effectively promote changes to wasteful behavior that they had been advocating for decades. Ishige Takeshi, who had helped found the Recycling Movement Citizens' Association (Risaikuru Undō Shimin no Kai) in the mid-1970s, published a book in the early 1990s titled *Watashitachi ni dekiru gomi o herasu kurashi no kufū 101* (101 Lifestyle Strategies We Can Use to Reduce Garbage). The specific aspirations and suggestions in his book would have been familiar to anyone who was already concerned with physical waste and recycling. Sounding notes from 1970s-era refrains about the culture of disposability, Ishige called for a shift from a disposing lifestyle of convenience and comfort to one that valued things. And many of the concrete pieces of advice that he offered had become conventional, such as avoiding plastic containers, maintaining and repairing electric appliances, declining excessive wrapping, frequenting flea markets, composting, and walking or bicycling instead of using a car. But now he stressed the environmental damage inflicted by garbage. The book bore the subtitle *Kore ijō, chikyū o hakai shinai tame ni* (For Not Further Destroying the Earth), and argued that global environmental destruction was being wrought by the pursuit of convenience, economic development, and affluence. And the first, direct step toward protecting the environment, leading an earth-friendly lifestyle, and ensuring a future for children was to think about and reduce what was being thrown out as garbage.[24]

Consumption in a Circulatory Society

In some important ways, existing practices to minimize waste did indeed take greater hold and even expand in a time of heightened environmental awareness. Flea markets and secondhand shops, which could be anything from a small outfit specializing in brand-name clothing or electric appliances to a large enterprise that carried a variety of goods, increased in number and spread well beyond the country's big cities.[25] In addition to women's magazine articles about how to navigate such selling and purchasing opportunities, guidebooks were published that listed and described flea markets and recycling shops.[26] According to the Ministry of the Environment (Kankyōshō), the cabinet-level ministry created in 2001 by the promotion of what had been the subcabinet Environment Agency, there was a fourfold increase in retailers of used goods between 1997 and 1999, when they came to number about 10,500 stores. Flea markets had also become a regular, everyday phenomenon, with some six hundred to seven hundred held just in Tokyo in any given year, drawing a total attendance of more than 2 million people. The Internet also helped link consumers to recycling shops, and became a place for virtual flea markets and auctions.[27]

There were likely multiple reasons why flea markets and secondhand shops became more popular in the 1990s. The element of saving money played a part, especially as economic sluggishness became protracted. There were also changes in how people viewed goods, as resistance to used items started to give way to a willingness to purchase them secondhand, particularly when it came to games, music, and books. A product's newness on the market lost some of its luster as consumers became more attuned to its substance. Especially among a younger generation, acquiring old (or "vintage") clothes and furniture was considered not a sign of poverty but a fun hobby or a way to live the simple life. There was also an increasing awareness that what was no longer desirable to you could be useful to someone else, that it might be wasteful simply to throw away what you no longer needed, and that recycling a good in this way was preferable to banishing it to the trash heap.[28]

The extensive promotion of recycling as a way to reduce waste and address environmental problems was captured in the phrase *junkangata shakai*—usually translated as "recycling society," though it has connotations closer to something like "circulatory society." Used with greater frequency starting in the late 1990s, the term emphasized the circularity of flow in contrast to a one-way conception of production, consumption, and disposal, and it appeared with regularity in discussions about recycling. In 1997 the Tokyo Metropolitan Government and the United Nations agreed to cosponsor in May of the following year the World Conference on International Cooperation of Cities and Citizens, which aimed to bring together citizens, government administrators, and nongovernmental organizations to realize a "recycling society," or what was translated into English as an "eco-society." The three themes, taken up by almost a dozen working groups, were "establishment of regional recycling systems," "international cooperation for realization of a recycling society," and "the civilization of a recycling society, towards new patterns of consumption and production."[29] The extent to which an eco-friendly circulatory society came to be advanced as a desirable aim was reflected in a survey of over three thousand households conducted by the Tokyo Sanitation Bureau (Tokyo-to Seisōkyoku) in 1998, in which an overwhelming 92.8 percent of respondents expressed some degree of interest in creating a "recycling society."[30] By 2002, the Ministry of the Environment saw fit to declare boldly in its *Junkangata shakai hakusho* (White Paper on the Recycling Society) that "'the economy versus the environment' is now over." In this intentional twist on the famous 1956 statement by the Economic Planning Agency that the "'postwar' is now over," the ministry punctuated its argument that the era of economic growth fueled by the waste of resources had ended and that growth from here on out would be supported by circularity (*junkan*).[31]

The advancement of recycling was not just rhetorical, as multiple new laws were enacted to promote circulatory practices. In 1991 the Diet passed the Law to Promote the Use of Recycled Resources (Saisei Shigen no Riyō no Sokushin ni Kansuru Hōritsu) which, among other things, specified one category of products that were to be made more recyclable and another that were to indicate their contents so as to aid separate collection.[32] In 1995, the Law to Promote Separate Collection and Recycling of Containers and Packaging (Yōki Hōsō ni Kakaru Bunbetsu Shūshū Oyobi Saishōhinka no Sokushin Tō ni Kansuru Hōritsu) was intended to reduce the large proportion, about 60 percent, of total municipal solid waste that consisted of containers and packaging by targeting for recycling glass containers, plastic PET (polyethylene terephthalate) bottles, and most paper cartons.[33] In 1998, the Specified Home Appliance Recycling Law (Tokutei Kateiyō Kiki Saishōhinka Hō) designated four products that retailers were to collect, and manufacturers were to recycle, at consumers' expense: air conditioners, television sets, refrigerators, and washing machines.[34] And in 2000, the Diet approved the comprehensive Basic Law for Establishing a Recycling Society (Junkangata Shakai Keisei Suishin Kihon Hō), which spelled out the respective responsibilities of the federal government, municipalities, businesses, and the public in a recycling society, including attentiveness to the design of products, container materials, and the labeling of recyclables so as to facilitate separation by consumers.[35] Also passed that year was the Law to Promote the Recycling of Food Resources (Shokuhin Junkan Shigen no Saisei Riyō Tō no Sokushin ni Kansuru Hōritsu), followed in 2002 by the Law for the Recycling of End-of-Life Vehicles (Shiyōzumi Jidōsha no Saishigenka Tō ni Kansuru Hōritsu).[36]

For consumers, these laws had implications that kept issues of recycling and environmentalism within their view, regardless of how much they did or did not change their own waste-producing behavior. The laws encouraged changes in garbage-related practices, as in Nagoya city, where separate collection for containers and packaging made of plastic and paper was instituted to comply with the Containers and Packaging Recycling Law. This required residents to be more attuned to how they managed their garbage, which was explained to them in numerous meetings held by the city about the new system even as residents grumbled that it was troublesome and hard to understand.[37] In addition, consumers were presented with more information about the eco-friendliness of goods by manufacturers and marketers who were responding to the growing awareness about environmental conservation. Department stores and supermarkets sought to stock more items that were considerate of the environment, and established special sections (eco-goods corners, or *eko shōhin kōnā*) to highlight such offerings.[38] In the mid-1990s, the large Japan Federation of Economic Organizations (Nippon Keizai Dantai Rengōkai) adopted objectives for its member groups of reducing waste, lowering carbon dioxide emissions, and shifting from a disposing to a recycling economy through such measures as the simplification and recycling of packaging, restraint when it came to the frequent model changes of such goods as cars and home electric appliances, and the development of energy-saving products.[39]

On the purchasing side, the idea of the "green consumer" emerged in Japan as it did in other countries around this time. In 1988, *The Green Consumer Guide* was released in England, and in 1989, *Shopping for a Better World* in the United States. The Green Consumer Network (Gurīn Konshūmā Nettowāku) followed suit in 1994 with the publication of *Chikyū ni yasashī kaimono gaido* (A Guide to Earth-Friendly Shopping). The idea of the green consumer emphasized the consideration of waste at earlier stages of consumption and not just at the point of disposal as had been the focus in the past, particularly in Japan of the 1980s. This book suggested that while recycling things like cans or milk cartons and saving electricity by taking care to turn off switches was important, it seemed somehow insufficient. What was proposed was thinking about the environment, and about garbage as the end result of consumption, at the moment when purchasing decisions were made—about adopting an ecological lifestyle at the stage of consuming and using things. Consumers, it was believed, had the power to influence production and distribution and thus to change the economy and lifestyles through their choices about how and what to purchase. In this way, environmental problems could be solved and an affluence of the heart more considerate of the environment could be realized.[40]

The guide outlined various ways in which readers could become green consumers, including an articulation of ten principles such as: buy only what you need; choose items with minimal packaging or recyclable containers; eschew disposable products for those that you can use for a long time; select goods that have minimal environmental impact when they are made and when they are used; and buy things that do not waste resources or energy in their production, distribution, use, or disposal. Provided too was a description of the environmentally conscious practices, from policies about packaging to recycling of resources, of various stores from Daiei supermarkets to the sprawling 7-Eleven convenience store chain.[41] In subsequent years, similar publications followed suit, such as *Gurīn konshūmā nyūmon* (Green Consumer Manual), which dealt with the consumption of not just things but also energy, and *Ichioku nin no kankyō kakeibo* (An Environmental Account Book for a Hundred Million People). Putting a twist on a household's financial account book, this environmental account book tracked not monetary but environmental expenditures and savings.[42] Scorecards were provided for keeping track of the wasting and saving of electricity (by reducing time spent watching television, and by not overstuffing the refrigerator or keeping its door open), and the production and reduction of garbage (by planning consumption, not buying goods with excessive packaging, consuming food before its expiration date, and recycling newspapers and magazines).[43]

In addition to such books, institutional structures were also created around the idea of green consumption. The Green Consumer Tokyo Net (Gurīn Konshūma Tokyo Netto) was inaugurated in December 1997, a partnership of businesses, government administrators, and consumer groups like the Housewives Association (Shufu Rengōkai) and the Recycling Movement Citizens' Association. Concerned generally with lessening environmental burdens through changing consumer behavior, the organization took up specific issues such as encouraging the purchase of toilet paper made from 100 percent recycled materials, water-saving washing machines, and energy-saving air conditioners.[44] In 2002 the government sought to encourage the consumption of environmentally friendly goods and services through the Law on Promoting Green Purchasing (Gurīn Kōnyū Hō).[45] And such attentiveness was encouraged in the next generation of consumers with the approval in that same year of a textbook for use in high school home economics classes which included a discussion about environmentally friendly purchasing behavior that entailed reducing garbage, recycling, saving energy, and preventing environmental pollution. In the section titled "A Consuming Lifestyle, Resources, and the Environment," the term "green consumer" appeared in bold along with a list of ten key green consuming principles.[46]

By these early millennial years, there seems to have been a generally positive disposition toward green consumption. In a national survey about the recycling society conducted in 2001, about 83 percent of the more than three thousand respondents reported that they were engaging in green consumption to some degree—that when buying stuff, they were mindful of whether it was made of recycled materials, whether it was easy to recycle at the end of its life, and whether it was gentle to the environment.[47] Defined this way, green consuming behaviors did not mean rejecting or even significantly curtailing the purchasing of things. In keeping with the desire to maintain middle-class lifestyles which reached back to at least the 1970s, consumers were not to go without. They were instead to be more conscious of their consuming behavior so as to minimize waste and protect the environment.

That waste reduction and environmental preservation could be seen as congruent with the established practices of daily life like consumption was also evident in public acceptance of the government's Cool Biz and Warm Biz initiatives. Spearheaded by the Ministry of the Environment in the summer of 2005, the Cool Biz campaign urged workplaces to curtail their energy use through such measures as setting thermostats higher, at 28 degrees Celsius (about 82 degrees Fahrenheit) or above. This was part of the effort to stop global warming by meeting the target set by the Kyoto Protocol for Japan of a 6 percent reduction in greenhouse gas emissions. To make uncomfortably hot offices tolerable, workers were encouraged to wear lighter outfits to stay cool.[48] The winter counterpart suggested a temperature of 19 to 20 degrees Celsius (66 to 68 degrees Fahrenheit) or below for Warm Biz, the campaign's official name, which thankfully beat out Cool Biz Winter and Hot Biz. Government office workers were asked to turn off lights during lunch breaks, shut down their computers when they left their desks, use the stairs, and exercise self-restraint in driving official vehicles on certain days. Firms and households were encouraged to turn off outside lights at night, and people were advised not to idle their cars, and to use trains and buses for commuting and leisure.[49]

In content, Cool Biz and Warm Biz were reminiscent of the efforts in the late 1970s to cut down on the wasteful use of energy with the "energy-saving look" and "energy-saving suit." But they succeeded in taking root where the earlier attempt had failed because they tapped into positive associations with environmental consciousness that had not been so strong several decades earlier. They also did not rely on moral suasion, but recognized and embraced business and consumer interests. For businesses, the campaigns were very much in line with efforts to cut costs, so it was not surprising that many participated. According to the Japan Business Federation (a reincarnation of the Japan Federation of Economic Organizations), about 85 percent of the five hundred firms they surveyed were instituting Cool Biz in some way through such measures as reducing air conditioning, shutting off unnecessary lights, and wearing lighter clothes. Roughly half were changing over to energy-saving equipment or having employees turn off the engines of company vehicles when they were stopped.[50]

The government also made it a point to characterize the campaigns as enabling freedom rather than mandating restraint, with the explicit encouragement to develop new fashions in clothing. Saving energy was not to have a "negative image of self-denial," which might have carried the stench of past experiences with poverty and hardship, but was to establish a new lifestyle inclusive of fashion.[51] Retailers took full advantage of this opportunity to sell clothes and accessories. For the first year of Warm Biz, department stores in the city of Fukuoka devoted special areas to the campaign and offered items such as vests, cardigans, and ascots. A similar look was marketed at the Mitsukoshi department store in the Nihonbashi area of Tokyo, which put together a look for men—a suit with a zip-up cardigan underneath the jacket and an ascot. The Takashimaya department store came up with the theme "Spending (the Winter) Warmly in Today's Styles" and suggested clothes not just for men, but for women as well. The womenswear look consisted of a black pantsuit with a "narrow muffler" that could be worn in the office, or for those times when they had a date after work, a lace satin camisole layered with a thin knitted top and a soft jacket.[52]

For the fourth year of Cool Biz, in 2008, several groups including the Japan Department Store Association (Nihon Hyakkaten Kyōkai) and the Shōchiku movie studio and kabuki production company hosted a presentation at the upscale

Tokyo Midtown complex to promote "Cool Biz +" which added new suggestions to prevent global warming. Men modeled "my bottle" (*mai boteru*), to be used instead of PET bottles to reduce garbage, and a cloth wrapping (*furoshiki*) to take the place of disposable shopping bags. Also proposed as part of Cool Biz + were "my chopsticks" to replace the disposable variety; "my cup," presumably to discourage people from running water while brushing their teeth; participation in flea markets; and more.[53] To the delight of retailers, many consumers seem to have opened their wallets as the market for Cool Biz–related products grew from 88.7 billion yen in 2005 to 186 billion yen in 2006, and for Warm Biz from 151.8 billion yen in 2005 to 223.8 billion yen in 2006.[54] Entwined with business and consumer interests, Cool Biz and Warm Biz became perennial campaigns which served as a reminder in workplaces and in stores of energy saving and climate change, helping to make waste consciousness and environmental awareness mainstream values.

Competing Desires

Awareness of waste as well as the health of the global environment came to the foreground even as the results of waste reduction efforts were mixed and many people's actual behavior may have fallen short of, or even been out of step with, the emerging norm of professing their importance. It seems that many people wanted to see themselves as being conscious of waste and the environment, regardless of the more complicated picture of whether they were actually living in environmentally responsible ways. In the residential sector (as distinct from industry and transportation), there was an upward trend in energy consumption through the 1990s and into the early 2000s. And while the trajectory of energy consumption per household was less linear, that figure was markedly greater by 2000 than it had been ten years earlier. Total household electricity use ticked up over the course of the decade, with an increasing share consumed by televisions, lighting, and air conditioners. Though air conditioners had become more efficient, as required by strengthened energy-saving standards, more units were being sold, which drove up their overall consumption of electricity.[55] Household electricity consumption was trending upward, the *Asahi* newspaper determined, because an increasing number of people were putting a premium on comfort.[56]

That considerations such as comfort and convenience shaped decisions even as many expressed concern about the environment was also evident when it came to physical waste. In a modest survey of 150 housewives across three prefectures and Tokyo, an overwhelming percentage had negative impressions of disposable goods like diapers and chopsticks because they wasted resources and increased the output of garbage. But a majority of both the youngest and oldest respondents (twenty to thirty-five years old, and over sixty-five) admitted purchasing and using disposable goods because they were hygienic and convenient.[57] Tensions between values and behavior could also be seen in a much larger national survey about the "recycling society." Of the 3,467 respondents, a very high proportion (89.8 percent) said that they cared to some extent about the "garbage problem," which many (70.5 percent) attributed to the lifestyle pattern of mass production, mass consumption, and mass waste. And most (82.1 percent) did claim to be properly sorting their household garbage. At the same time, fewer than a third reported that they repaired and repeatedly used things that were broken, declined disposable bags at the store or asked for simplified packaging, refrained from buying disposable products, or actively purchased goods made of recycled materials.[58] Reflecting on similar results in their survey of 6,524 respondents, the lifestyle research division of the homebuilder Daiwa House Group (Daiwa Hausu Kōgyō Kabushiki Gaisha Seikatsu Kenkyūjo) concluded that convenience trumped ecological consciousness, and a gap existed between what people knew they should do and what they actually did. The researchers argued further that the focus on the separation of trash created the false impression that such recycling alone was sufficient to address the garbage problem and that it prevented people from thinking about how to avoid producing so much waste and consuming energy so wastefully.[59]

The desire to identify as a "recycling society" was strong enough not just to pave over behavior that suggested otherwise but also to quiet the relatively muted voices of those who expressed doubts about the efficacy of recycling and who sought more wholesale changes to the societal and economic structures that produced waste. In July 1993 the prominent physicist Tsuchida Atsushi made a case for the shortcomings of recycling in a debate with the political economist and recycling advocate Yorimoto Katsumi in the pages of the *Mainichi* newspaper. Tsuchida argued that it was a fallacy to think that recycling could reduce waste to zero, that the use of resources always and necessarily resulted in the creation of waste, and that the economics of recycling were not scalable, since the greater the amount of things collected, the lower their value would be, forcing recycling firms out of business. For his part, Yorimoto attributed the struggling financial situation of recycling firms to other causes and pushed back against the idea that recycling campaigns legitimized the use of such things as milk cartons and aluminum cans.[60] Several years later, a cautionary note about the potential of recycling appeared in the newsletter of the Association for Thinking about the Throwaway Age (Tsukaisute Jidai o Kangaeru Kai), a group that was founded in the early 1970s by Tsuchida's son Tsuchida Takashi. The piece suggested that recycling did not reduce garbage but simply extended the life of things, and that it distracted attention from the responsibility of businesses not to make things that would become garbage. To illustrate this point, the association presented data from the period between 1984 and 1994, when the recycling rate for aluminum cans increased from 40 to 61 percent, but the number of cans thrown away as trash increased from 2.5 to 5.8 billion because of the sheer number that were manufactured. To put it clearly, stated the group, "we don't want to promote recycling."[61]

A similar argument was made in a more sustained, rigorous way by Takatsuki Hiroshi, a professor and specialist in issues of waste and the environment who also published cartoons under the pen name High Moon. Much of Takatsuki's writing was for a specialist audience, but one of his books intended for the general reader, *Gomi mondai to raifusutairu* (The Garbage Problem and Lifestyles), was popular enough to go through multiple printings. This book opened with Peter Menzel's photograph of the Ukita family and all of their belongings. And its cover was graced with Takatsuki's cartoon of his so-called *mononoke hime*, the characters used to spell out the title of the well-known anime film *Princess Mononoke* changed to mean instead "Princess of Eliminating Things." Takatsuki's heroine was seen pushing away a vending machine, disposable bag, television set, PET bottle, tissue paper, and more, much to the delight of a smiling tree and animal in the background. Such cartoons dotted the book, which also presented much longitudinal data about how the production volume of things like aluminum cans and PET bottles (though not steel cans or glass bottles) increased over the same period that their recycling rates increased.[62] Takatsuki's larger point was that much more emphasis needed to be placed on reducing and reusing rather than recycling garbage, because an increasing recycling rate would have little meaning as long as the amount of garbage disposed did not decrease. Current lifestyles needed to be reexamined and transformed into a "simple life," he wrote, which might very well mean that the economy as it was currently structured might collapse. Though he left it up to economists to envision an alternative, Takatsuki was sympathetic to an agriculturally centered society not driven by production, sales, and profit.

Such views about a fundamentally different economy or the shortcomings of recycling gained little traction in the 1990s and early 2000s. Nor was much mention made of data that complicated the idealized vision of Japan as a recycling society. One might expect, for example, that with the substantial and increasing attention given to the proper sorting of garbage into categories, recycling rates in Japan would have been quite high. And indeed the recycling rates for steel and aluminum cans, glass bottles, and especially PET bottles rose through much of the 1990s. But the recycling rate for garbage, or the amount of garbage recycled as a percentage of the total collected and discarded, remained fairly flat.[63] In international comparisons, Japan's garbage recycling rate as a percentage of municipal solid waste was roughly 15 percent in the early 2000s, lower than that of many other countries such as Austria, Belgium, Germany, and the Netherlands (with rates in the 50 to 60 percent range) and the United States (around 31 percent).[64]

Overlooked in the promotion of a waste consciousness intertwined with environmental awareness was a potentially more complex picture of people's relationship to waste in their daily lives.

Looking Ahead

Concern for the global environment sank its roots into waste consciousness at a time when awareness of waste was being newly and slowly revived by uncertainty about both prosperity and the planet. The global environmental turn of the late 1980s and 1990s helped forge some of what would become the most substantial strands of conceptions about waste. The reduction of waste and the minimization of wastefulness came to be understood as serving the cause of global environmental conservation in ways that extended beyond safeguarding resources and economic growth to ensuring the health of the earth. To this end, consumers were to recycle and to make purchasing decisions befitting life in a circulatory society. An environmental consciousness also helped link waste to the desire for a more well-rounded kind of affluence, as concerns for the environment came to be defined as one characteristic of a "true affluence." Even when waste took on increasingly expansive meanings after the turn of the century, such attention to the environment would remain an important pillar of waste consciousness.

The prominence of environmental considerations in thinking about waste also influenced the spatial and temporal hues that waste consciousness assumed in the 1990s and carried into the new millennium. There was something of an opening outward as the minimization of waste and wastefulness was connected to the environment, the earth, or ecology however vaguely conceived. Despite the continued emphasis on the local in concrete responses to wastage, concerns about the climate, air quality, or the ozone layer impelled a broad geographical orientation that transcended manmade boundaries. And a sense of commitment to the global environment would feed later efforts to project and promote the virtues of waste consciousness beyond the country's borders. The forging of a more substantive connection between waste and the environment also adjusted temporal orientations, as waste dilemmas having to do with rubbish or resources were not just about the exigencies of the current moment but also about securing possibilities for generations yet to come. An anticipatory inclination had been a sustained undercurrent of waste reduction efforts since the 1960s, with both their anxiety about potential hardship and their promise of improvement and progress in daily life. In the 1990s, and even more in the millennial years, the interweaving of an environmental thread into waste consciousness strengthened this impulse not just to consider the present but also to imagine an ever-extending future.

WE ARE ALL WASTE CONSCIOUS NOW

As the case was made for waste consciousness and global environmental preservation in the 1990s, there were occasional expressions, nostalgic and wistful, about the supposedly lost virtue of *mottainai*. *Mottainai* in its postwar incarnation expressed attention to wastefulness, though the word has a long linguistic history of many and various definitions. In premodern times, it suggested trouble, harm, impropriety, regret, disappointment, or graciousness; in modern usage the word could mean unworthy or undeserving, as well as impious, irreverent, profane, or sacrilegious.[1] In postwar Japan, the predominant definition of *mottainai* was "waste" or "wasteful"—as in "What a waste!" or "How wasteful!"— and it would come to be invoked to promote waste consciousness and to criticize waste of various sorts. Many who would deploy the term simply assumed that *mottainai* had always been associated with wastefulness and an ideal of waste consciousness.

In the 1990s, what mentions there were of *mottainai* tended to imply that this ideal had been eroded by some postwar development related to prosperity. The *Mainichi* newspaper, for example, published in 1991 an editorial titled "The Rehabilitation of *Mottainai*" in which it observed how unusual it was to hear the word since lifestyles had become affluent. The word should be resurrected, the piece argued, to combat the garbage problem, nurture in children a heart that values things, and inspire people to think about what real affluence might be.[2] For the recycling advocate Honda Atsuhiro, the extinction of the idea of *mottainai* was a direct result of mass production and mass consumption.[3] Indeed, in this decade, appearances of *mottainai* were relatively few and far between. And at least for the young generation, the word had some negative connotations. When asked what they thought when they heard *mottainai*, a majority (62.2 percent) of 990 high school students surveyed did choose "valuing things." At the same time, roughly a quarter said "shabby or dingy" (27.8 percent) or "stingy" (23.6 percent).[4]

It was after the turn of the twenty-first century that *mottainai* became a prominent, oft-repeated idea. In the early 2000s, the years just past came to be understood as the "lost decade," and a feeling of economic vulnerability hardened into the realization that substantial economic growth would prove elusive for the foreseeable future. As the uncertainty of the 1990s yielded to reluctant certainty about a hobbled economy, *mottainai* emerged at the center of an astounding flood of attention to waste unprecedented since the early 1970s. Waste consciousness assumed a visible position in the mainstream as children's books, mass-market nonfiction, advice literature, magazines, newspapers, songs, government ministries, corporations, and nongovernmental organizations took up the question of what was to be deemed wasteful and, conversely, what was to be deemed meaningful.

In this sweeping engagement with wastefulness, *mottainai* became a convenient one-word encapsulation of an expansive waste consciousness comprising the many meanings of waste that had been made, remade, frayed, dropped, revived, and reframed over the preceding three decades. The proliferation of garbage, resource scarcity, and energy insecurity proved to be perennial concerns which were placed at the feet of a throwaway culture and a society of mass production, mass consumption, and mass waste, much as they had been in the 1970s. Present too was the desire for a wealth beyond the financial and material, for a "true affluence" or "affluence of the heart," which dated back to the 1980s. And the particular environmental consciousness forged in the late 1980s and 1990s continued to inform thinking about waste. In the new millennium, all of these threads were woven together to create a tangled and capacious understanding of waste consciousness.

More explicitly and enthusiastically than in past years, this waste consciousness was also infused with affective and vaguely spiritual meanings such as regret and shame for the loss of things; appreciation and respect for things as well as those who made them; and empathy and compassion. The idea that things were imbued with a life to be nurtured had been expressed in previous decades, but the frequency and sentimentality with which it was urged in these millennial years was distinctive. Another distinguishing characteristic of millennial waste consciousness was a future-oriented nostalgia: a simplistic remaking of the past to create values and meaning not just for the present but also for future generations.

Altogether, the redefinition and popularization of *mottainai* reflected a historical moment when there came to be an uneasy acceptance of an economically stagnant Japan that needed to construct new senses of self and nation. From the cold ashes of the country's economic juggernaut, *mottainai* emerged to offer a possible path forward—values, meanings, and identities around waste consciousness that would define how to live and how to be in an economically anemic, but still wealthy, Japan.

Repurposing the Past

In 2004 the children's book author Shinju Mariko introduced her readers to the character of Mottainai Bāsan, or No-Waste Grandma. Mottainai Bāsan wore her hair pulled into a tight bun, balanced her spectacles on the tip of her nose, and wielded a cane that seemed more like an accessory than a necessity for the sturdy and threatening woman. Of a generation that remembered the hardships of the World War II years, this grandma descended upon her young and fearful grandson to scrutinize his wasteful habits—leaving kernels of rice at the bottom of his bowl, letting the water run while he brushed his teeth, and discarding tangerine peels that could be put in bathwater to make it aromatic.[5] Mottainai Bāsan's lessons so captivated readers that 160,000 copies of the best seller were snatched up in its first year, inspiring a series of books, a song, and a card game that helped fuel the popular and widespread fascination with the concept of *mottainai*.[6]

As part of the generation that had experienced the war, the fictional Mottainai Bāsan personified nostalgia for an era before high economic growth with values untainted by mass consumption and affluence. At the same time, this was not the kind of nostalgia that sought a return to the past, but one that accepted what the cultural theorist Svetlana Boym has described as fundamental to all forms of modern nostalgia: "the modern conception of unrepeatable and irreversible time."[7] In this version, there was no desire to give up the advantages of affluence or to emulate completely the waste conscious practices of the wartime generation. What was sought instead was the affirmation of *mottainai* as a supposedly lapsed national virtue as well as a seemingly loose adaptation of certain practices and values from the country's past.

It was not unusual for the figure of the grandmother to mediate between the past and the present, to convey the purported lessons of the wartime generation to the generation that had known nothing other than an affluent Japan. In the first installment of a six-volume children's series titled *Mottainai kara hajimeyō!* (Let's Start with Mottainai!), it was the grandmother with her white hair pulled into a tight bun and glasses on her nose who had the most to say about the

「ぽっかぽかの　みかんぶろさ」

FIGURE 9.1.   No-Waste Grandma. Mottainai Bāsan taught her grandson how good it feels to put dried tangerine peels in bathwater.

Reproduced by permission from Shinju Mariko, *Mottainai bāsan* (Tokyo: Kōdansha, 2004) © Shinju Mariko.

concept to the children who asked about it: "Don't do things that are *mottainai*. If you waste things, something bad will happen to you."[8] In the Mottainai Bāsan series, the grandson was not educated by his postwar-born mother, who either was conspicuously absent or inadvertently fell into habits of wastefulness herself.

Even she needed to be taught how to salvage the yarn from an old sweater to knit something new and was scolded gently by the grandmother for taking more food at a buffet than she could eat.[9] In contrast, not being wasteful came naturally to Mottainai Bāsan because she grew up knowing how not to waste. That she was dubbed Miss No Waste in her younger days suggests that she did not discover the ills of wastefulness in her old age but had been well aware of them all along, perhaps with unusual zeal but otherwise not unlike the rest of her generation.[10]

With Mottainai Bāsan as the messenger, there was an implication that the virtues she extolled had to be reintroduced to a generation that had lost its sense of what was truly meaningful. One of the values most emphasized was appreciating the worth of things as well as the people who made them. Mottainai Bāsan thus paid particular attention to the waste of material objects, doling out tips on how to fix or repurpose things that were old, use things fully, and minimize food waste.[11] But wastefulness was not just defined in terms of the material; *mottainai* was also applied to the nonmaterial, such as emotions, time, and states of being, broadly conceived. To Mottainai Bāsan, it was wasteful to take photos or video of a sporting match and miss truly seeing the teamwork and hearing the cheers of support, or to look at the autumn leaves without picking them up and playing with them.[12] And the Mottainai Bāsan card game had one card each for the following incarnations of *mottainai*: being angry all the time, not learning, doing something without earnestness, not looking up at the night sky, not listening to the sound of insects, carelessly losing at the word game *shiritori*, and not valuing life. What is more, attention to all of these forms of wastefulness was infused with "love," which was what made *mottainai* different from the stinginess of *kechi*.[13] These virtues extolled by Mottainai Bāsan extended far beyond not wasting to encompass the importance of play, cooperation, happiness, education, earnestness, world peace, a vague sense of humanism, experiencing and living in the moment, not being thoughtlessly stupid, and appreciating nature.[14]

As much as Mottainai Bāsan proselytized to the younger generations about these values, there was no hint of a desire to return to the decades of her youth or to a time before Japan became affluent. In a 2008 book that tackled problems in the contemporary world, the author Shinju Mariko had Mottainai Bāsan offer vignettes about nine children from different countries who suffered from the effects of climate change, food and water shortages, war, and poverty. There was the young girl in India who had never been to school, did not know how to read and write, and worked twelve hours a day in a rug factory where the boss scolded and hit the workers; the child soldier in Sierra Leone who was given a shot of drugs before being sent off to the battlefield where children marched ahead of adults to set off land mines; and the homeless boy in Russia whose parents' drinking had driven him to the streets, where he begged in order to survive and sniffed glue to forget his sadness. In stark contrast, the Japanese girl, nine years old like all the other children in the book, was picky about what she ate and left food on her plate. It was explained that Japan imported 60 percent of its food and discarded 30 percent of its food uneaten, which an angry Mottainai Bāsan criticized as a lack of gratitude for nature's bounty.[15] There was a good dose of guilt here for the young Japanese reader who did not appreciate the privileges afforded by affluence, but the book did not begrudge those privileges. The message, however misleading in its implication that Japan was free of economic and social problems, was that Japanese were fortunate to live in an affluent country and should not waste the opportunities and lifestyles that wealth provided.

A nonfictional counterpart of Mottainai Bāsan for adult readers was Mottainai Jīsan, or No-Waste Grandpa, so dubbed in a book penned by his daughter-in-law Imai Misako. The book's subject was advertised on the dust jacket in large font: "the heart [kokoro] and lifestyle of 'mottainai' that Japanese people are trying to consign to oblivion." As in the Mottainai Bāsan series, mottainai was about material objects and more—in this case kokoro, meaning heart or spirit. And highlighting its allegedly imminent disappearance may have been intended as an appeal to potential readers' nostalgic desire to learn about something that had allegedly once been so vital. The historical mediator in this case, Mottainai Jīsan, was a man named Imai Shigefumi who was born in 1914 and spent thirty-three years living under the same roof with his son and daughter-in-law until he passed away in 2003. Mottainai Jīsan's lifestyle was full of lessons about how to make the most of things such as paper, water, food, clothes, and money, some of which (like drying tangerine skins to put in bathwater) were exactly the same as those taught by Mottainai Bāsan. He used newspaper as tissues, reused cellophane tape, eked four to five servings out of one teabag, and dried fish bones to make his own soup stock.[16] That these habits were influenced by the wartime years was only implied with Mottainai Bāsan, but stated explicitly by and about Mottainai Jīsan. Author Imai observed that her father-in-law was taught during the war that material things have lives and that he absorbed the oft-repeated wartime motto "Luxury is the enemy!" His experience of the scarcity of goods and a hunger that was sometimes debilitating profoundly affected his lifestyle and approach to everyday life well after he had the money to live differently. Mottainai Jīsan himself looked upon the postwar generation as having been raised at a time when consumption was considered a virtue and was promoted to increase production and earnings; those born after the war came of age in an era of disposability that was, he implied, alien to him.[17]

From the perspective of Imai Misako, it was her father-in-law's lifestyle that seemed somewhat alien to hers and to the times. Although she claimed that she respected Mottainai Jīsan's strong will to continue living as he always had without changing, there were hints that she found at least some aspects of his lifestyle strange and excessive. Imai suggested that there were times when Mottainai Jīsan crossed over the line from frugality into stinginess, especially when his seeming obsession with fully exhausting the life of things trumped any sensitivity to the feelings of other people. It was an invasion of privacy, in her view, when her father-in-law would rifle through her trash to see what could be reused or would recycle private letters as a memo pad that was kept next to the telephone.[18] As much as Imai endorsed the idea and spirit of *mottainai*, the gap between generations was undeniable, for while she could adopt some of her father-in-law's thrifty techniques, she did not want to embrace his lifestyle. She could incorporate lessons from his war-forged life, but she did not want to return to it.

Although Mottainai Jīsan might have exacerbated rather than narrowed the gap between past and present, the figure of the waste-conscious grandmother or grandfather in both fiction and nonfiction could resonate with contemporary readers who found such characters reminiscent of people in their own lives. In a feature column on *mottainai* in the February 2006 issue of the monthly magazine *Gendai* (The Present Age), well-known personalities from authors to entertainers to business executives were asked about what they considered to be wasteful and remembered grandparents and parents who had told them not to waste. The actress Muroi Shigeru, born in 1958, recalled her grandmother who embodied *mottainai*, the word rendered in the dialect of her native Toyama prefecture as *attaramon na*. Instilled by her own "Attaramon Bāsan" to not throw away things that could still be of use, Muroi kept supermarket bags, small boxes, and ribbons; repurposed film canisters to store hairpins or 500 yen coins; and salvaged day-old dried-up rice that had been sitting out as an offering on her home's Buddhist altar by softening it with hot tea for her to eat or putting it in miso soup for her cat. Muroi attributed her waste conscious ways to her grandmother, whose voice she could still hear saying, "Hey, this is wasteful [*attaramon na*]!"[19] In the same column, the professor and science commentator Kitano Masaru, born during the war in 1942, shared his earliest memory of *mottainai*, which was of the word coming out of his mother's mouth. During his childhood, it was a given that food would not be left on one's plate and that not eating all of one's rice, in particular, was seen as insulting to the labor of farmers. Kitano's mother warned him that children who did not eat all of the rice in their bowl would go blind, a threat that was also made by the mother of the comic storyteller Tatekawa Shiraku, who was born a couple of decades later, in 1963.[20] Through childhood memories of the figure of a grandparent or parent, or one's own experience for some, a connection could be fashioned between millennial Japan and the waste consciousness of the wartime generation.

It was not just the wartime years that were remade in an effort to illustrate how important a value wastefulness had been before the era of mass consumption and

FIGURE 9.2. From Tokyo.

affluence. The nostalgic evocation could hark back even farther in time—to the early modern Tokugawa or Edo period (1600–1868), when there was allegedly little to no waste.[21] "There was nothing *mottainai* in the Edo period," boldly claimed one of the Mottainai Bāsan playing cards.[22] "Japan through the Edo period was a nearly perfect recycling society," asserted a children's book on *mottainai* and Japanese "traditions."[23] That the lack of garbage in the streets of Tokugawa Japan was noticed by Westerners was commented on by the prize-winning writer and artist Akasegawa Genpei. To Akasegawa, this absence of waste stemmed from the valuing of things and of reuse, which came so naturally that people may not even have been aware of it, at least from the early modern years through the prewar period.[24]

The author Akiyama Hiroko drew on the conventional wisdom about this lack of waste in her three-volume children's book series on what could be learned about *mottainai* from life in the Tokugawa period. In the first installment, she

FIGURE 9.3.   To Edo. A brother and sister who traveled back in time from contemporary Tokyo to early modern Edo learned and conveyed lessons about waste consciousness.

Reproduced by permission from Akiyama Hiroko, *Gomi o herasu chie*, vol. 1 of *Edo no kurashi kara manabu "mottainai"* (Tokyo: Chōbunsha, 2009) © Ito Masaaki.

explained that the spirit of not wasting had already taken root in the lives of ordinary people in Tokugawa Japan and introduced to readers their guides to the past: a brother and sister, with a neighborhood cat, who traveled back in time from contemporary Tokyo to its early modern incarnation as Edo. On one page, the two children were on the dirty streets of Tokyo, pointing out the garbage in the river, the discarded cigarette butts on the sidewalks, the usable goods that had been thrown out as trash, and the household garbage deposited curbside that had been strewn about by scavenging crows. On the next page, the pair found themselves in Edo, where the sister exclaimed, "There are so many people in Edo, but the streets are clean!"[25]

In Akiyama's reimagination, the city of Edo became an idyllic place that had much wisdom to offer the young millennial Japanese children about how to live. These lessons were about particular values and principles that could be exported to the twenty-first century, not about the embrace of the early modern standard of living or lifestyle in its entirety. The two siblings learned that in the Tokugawa period, people did not have refrigerators so bought from itinerant vendors only what they needed for a given day so as not to have excess food that they could not store. The take-home lesson here was not to do away with the refrigerator, but to buy only what one really needed. The two siblings also learned that in a time without electricity and gas, people matched their lives to the rising and setting of the sun. The takeaway lesson here was not to do without electricity and gas, but to enjoy activities outside and, a bit more literally, take advantage of solar energy.[26]

Much was elided in the nostalgia for the waste consciousness of the early modern period or the wartime years. It can be convincingly argued that many people in the Tokugawa period used resources efficiently, but this must be considered in the context of a time when the country had limited interactions with the rest of the world and thus had to rely on and maximize domestic resources.[27] And it should be remembered that the mythical re-creations of historical figures of this time into paragons of thrift and frugality, like Ninomiya Sontoku, have been selective not just in terms of what about a person has been highlighted and adapted to the causes of the present, but also in ignoring examples of extravagance and excess, like those characteristic of the Genroku era (1688–1703).[28] When it comes to the wartime years, there has been inadequate acknowledgment of how attempts to not waste stemmed largely from necessity, from poverty and starvation. If there were any serious examination of this past, or even any real care given to history, then it would become much harder to speak of waste consciousness as an inherent, enduring, or particularly Japanese virtue.

Most obviously, and conveniently for the nostalgic construction of the past, both the early modern period and the wartime years preceded the flourishing of mass consumption in Japan. This meant that material life, and the resources and energy it required, were fundamentally different in the postwar period than in the 1930s and 1940s, much less the 1600s to mid-1800s. A parallel cannot be drawn between eras with and without, for example, electric appliances and the proliferation of plastics. People who lived in these earlier periods did not have to grapple with the difficult conundrum of how to dispose of material goods bought and used on a scale and with a frequency unprecedented in the country's history. The nostalgia for these previous eras glossed over these complexities to give weight to discrete lessons in the present and skirted the central dilemma of how to be waste conscious in a time of mass consumption, of how to both minimize waste and consume in the ways that people had come to desire.

The past may have been simplified and distorted in some instances because the audience was children and the temporal orientation was toward the future. The sheer number of books and educational efforts about *mottainai* geared toward the youngest in Japanese society was impressive. In addition to the Mottainai Bāsan franchise and the Akiyama Hiroko books, there was the seven-volume series called *Mottainai seikatsu daijiten* (Encyclopedia of *Mottainai* Living), which addressed topics such as waste consciousness and garbage, cooking, resources, energy, and nature.[29] In the same year, 2007, the six-volume series *Mottainai kara hajimeyō!* was published which included installments about garbage, water, greenery, food, and energy.[30] On a smaller scale, the Taitō ward in Tokyo published a handbook for children explaining how the Tokugawa period offered hints about ways to live in their present, from switching off lights (in the past, there was no electricity) to reusing what you can (in the past, there were no flush toilets and human waste was used as fertilizer), in order to save energy and prevent global warming.[31] Vague characterizations of a culture and society of some past in which there was appreciation for things and time and nature were a way to reinforce specific pieces of advice doled out about the present day, from eating all of your food to properly separating your garbage to cutting down on air conditioning. Such messages were presumably intended as much for parents as for the ostensible audience of children, but they also suggested an optimistic hope that this generation, unlike those shaped by high growth, the bubble economy, and the pursuit of prosperity, might somehow be able to reconcile a modern, consuming, affluent lifestyle and its production of mass waste.

Redefining Affluence and Identity

With its hopeful tenor, nostalgia for a waste conscious past was used not just to encourage reflection about how to live in a time of fragile affluence, but also to recast the economic downturn as an opportunity to think about the very meaning of affluence—about how it had been, and should be, defined. Looking back at the Tokugawa period, Akiyama Hiroko claimed that people then were "rich in heart" (*kokoro no yutaka*). Even though they did not have material things or present-day conveniences, they knew what "real wealth" (*hontō no yutakasa*) was because they did not just think about their own happiness, like people in contemporary Japan, but understood the importance of mutual support and gratitude.[32] In Akiyama's view, the kind of affluence that really mattered—that of heart and spirit—was rooted not in financial wealth but in values that could transcend and endure the country's economic ups and downs as they supposedly had for centuries. Using the same vocabulary as Akiyama, the professor Kitano Masaru too observed that the era of "material wealth" was ending, giving way to affluence of the heart and mind. Expanding on this idea, a storage consultant named Iida Hisae warned that people would continue their wasteful habits until they asked themselves, "What is real wealth?"[33]

Financial affluence itself was even bemoaned as wasteful. In several popular songs, the unthinking pursuit and acceptance of affluent lifestyles were described as leaving people indifferent and empty. In 2005 the folk-pop artist Sada Masashi released the song "MOTTAINAI," which opened with a verse about how those born into a prosperous era did not feel sad when leaving food uneaten and threw away things that could be repaired and used. In later verses, he implied that affluence had created a self-centered generation that was unaware of their parents' love and cared only about their own well-being. The chorus lamented, "The heart aches, divine favor is bad, *mottainai, mottainai, mottainai, mottainai*."[34] The actor and singer Kobayashi Akira went further in his 2006 song, in which he suggested that the mainstream lifestyles and goals of the recent past were themselves a waste. He called *mottainai* recent college graduates who became new employees only to busily run about, bowing here and there, with no time even to get drunk. In one verse, a new employee took out a loan for a house with a nice lawn and sunny garden only to have a tall building constructed in front of it, casting a shadow over all. After expressing his sadness about mountains of garbage and a marriage gone bad, the song ends with "Only one life . . . *mottainai*."[35] Others, too, echoed the theme of wasting one's life by devoting it to unappreciated work. One book commented that it was "*mottainai* to bury your talent in a workplace that wastes it."[36] In this vein of questioning the aspirations of an affluent Japan, some emphasized the striving for happiness unconnected to material or financial accumulation. Nishinari Katsuhiro, a mathematical physicist of emergent systems, mentioned in his study of waste the idea of "gross national happiness," pointing out that in one list of countries rated by this measure in 2006, Japan ranked ninetieth while Bhutan, even with its poverty rate of 30 percent, ranked ninth.[37]

In a more sophisticated articulation of post-bubble aspirations, Hiroi Yoshinori, a scholar of public policy and social security, declared that the era of single-minded obsession with growth had ended. Gone were the days when the abundance of goods and the desire for them, as measured by money, fueled the perpetual expansion of the economy. The singular focus on economic growth had succeeded, the affluence of goods had been achieved, but the emphasis on the speed of growth and on the closed nature of companies and families—what had, in short, been the dominant way of thinking about the country's postwar economic life—had to change. With the market economy now saturated, advised Hiroi, more attention had to be geared toward the proliferation of the kinds of human activities and desires that could not be measured by money. Writing in 2006, Hiroi envisioned in this way the end of one era and the beginning of another, one of "zero growth" in which economic expansion was not society's absolute and unconditional goal but in which there would be plenty of "affluence." Hiroi did not elaborate on how he defined this affluence, but he suggested a concern with equality of opportunity and treatment of the individual, rather than the company or the family, as the basic unit of policy making. For Hiroi, this broader understanding of affluence was tied to a conception of *mottainai* that was about much more than economizing or monetary savings and thus allowed for a more expansive consideration of value beyond mere efficiency. That *mottainai* was in the contemporary spotlight was one hopeful indication to him of a movement toward reexamining the meaning of affluence.[38]

The reconceptualization of affluence in more psychological or affective terms resonated with the endowing of *mottainai* with spiritual meaning. The spiritual could be construed quite broadly, in ways that dovetailed with rather secular values and that extended beyond what might be considered religious belief. A book titled *Mottainai* claimed that the idea gave form to the "unique spiritual world of the Japanese people" in which the nonmaterial and nonvisible life of an object was appreciated and mourned when dissipated through waste. *Mottainai* was defined as "not just about material loss, but also about the sense of respect and compassion for the story behind every material object."[39] Here, the values of gratitude and regret were endowed with spiritual overtones. Others spoke of specific spiritual beliefs related to wastefulness. In one of her children's books, Akiyama Hiroko shared with readers her simplified version of the history of *tsukumogami*, spirits that resided in tools that had been used for a long time. The Japanese characters for *tsukumo* were the same as those for "ninety-nine," she explained, which hinted at ninety-nine years of use or ninety-nine types of objects, thereby expressing the importance of an object's long life. Conversely, tools not cared for would become malevolent ghosts (*yōkai*).[40]

The spiritual was also sometimes tied to an established religion in Japan, typically Buddhism. Yamaori Tetsuo, a scholar of religious thought and culture, located the roots of *mottainai* far in the past and considered its 1,500-year history a testament to the concept as an expression of the heart or soul of the Japanese people; he also considered *mottainai* inseparable from Buddhist ideas about the transience and evanescence of life.[41] And the author Shinju Mariko revealed that she had modeled Mottainai Bāsan after the Buddha.[42] Such associations made between waste consciousness, the appreciation of things, and Buddhism served several purposes. The problematic assumption that there was a pure and unchanging Buddhist idea of *mottainai* which predated modern life reinforced both the nostalgia for a reimagined premodern past and the narrative of retrieving values that had been lost, in addition to endowing otherwise mundane acts of not wasting with a vaguely religious weight.[43]

This adaptation of Buddhist ideas tended to be reductionist in its treatment of a complex and dynamic religion with many schools, and of the syncretic nature of religion in Japan. This can be seen by examining one particular religious practice that was said to embody core tenets of *mottainai*: funeral rites (*kuyō*) for inanimate objects.[44] Though varied in practice, these rites have been a way for those with a connection to a thing, usually an everyday object like shoes or a clock or a doll, to express appreciation for and part with it. While some suggest that this ritual can be traced back to a Buddhist notion that the inanimate can attain enlightenment, Japanese ethnographers have contended instead that the origins can be found in animist beliefs that the spirit of an object could curse the human if not pacified before being thrown away. A more nuanced explanation has been offered by the scholar Angelika Kretschmer, who argues that *kuyō* developed as a hybrid of Buddhist and animist beliefs that cannot be easily decoupled and identified. In their performance, the rites themselves might be a Buddhist ceremony, but can also be held at Shinto shrines with Shinto priests. And it cannot be claimed that the rituals were contemporaneous with the introduction of Buddhism to Japan, because their earliest performance started centuries later, in the Tokugawa period.[45] Given these many and intermingled beliefs, the practice of *kuyō* and the idea of respecting the life of a thing cannot be considered solely and uniquely Buddhist.

At a ceremony for sewing needles that I attended in February 2016 on the temple grounds of Sensōji in Tokyo, a priest acknowledged these complexities in his view of appreciating things. He spoke at some length about the syncretic Shinto and Buddhist history of the Awashima Hall in which he was standing. The priest also discouraged people from assuming that the idea of a thing having a life or spirit was specific to religions in Japan. The conception of family as including not just people but also objects was not to be considered singularly characteristic of Japan, he said, but was a widely shared and commonly held value. Beyond the priest's sermon, it was difficult to get a sense of the various reasons that had brought the large crowd of people, overwhelmingly women, to the temple this Monday morning. For some, this was in part a social outing with a sewing group. It was also an opportunity to easily discard many needles. And there were also quite a few women who wished their used needles well but did not stay for the religious service or the priest's words.[46]

There have also been thoroughly pragmatic motivations behind these rites in the postwar period. Many new versions of *kuyō* were inaugurated only in the second half of the twentieth century through the initiative of professional associations that worked with a particular object, such as the retailers of clocks, jewelry, and eyeglasses who established rites for clocks and watches in 1961; representatives of the shoe trade who established rites for shoes in 1975; and the hairdresser who spearheaded rites for scissors in 1977. For professional groups, these annual events have been a public relations and community-building opportunity as they also have been for the temple or shrine at which they are held, and a moneymaking occasion for the local shopping district. While spiritual or religious reasons for organizing and participating in these rites should not be dismissed, neither should motives of obligation, community, and profit.[47] Given the many dimensions of even an ostensibly Buddhist ritual like *kuyō*, characterizations of *mottainai* as a purely Buddhist concept should invite scrutiny. Any selective and casual adaptation of Buddhism to *mottainai* could be said to reflect the contemporary reformulations of ideas and practice more than the resurrection of a supposedly fixed tradition.

Along with simplistic claims about the unique spiritual meaning of *mottainai*, tropes and anxieties about resource scarcity in Japan were also marshaled to promote the idea that *mottainai* might become the cornerstone of Japanese identities in the twenty-first century.[48] The country's resource vulnerability had helped forge desirable character traits and abilities, one narrative went. The book *Mottainai* explained in English: "Japan is known to have very few natural resources. How to effectively use these limited resources has been deeply ingrained in the Japanese mind. Japanese innovation has come from a long heritage of maximizing potential in a limited environment."[49] The notion that there is such a thing as a singular "Japanese mind" that has remained unchanged through time was irredeemably ahistorical, and the mention of "long heritage" too vague and general. But such reductionist glosses on the country's history resonated with the nostalgic harking back to the supposed *mottainai* spirit of the past and implied that the waste consciousness of *mottainai* might come more naturally to Japanese than to other people.

While such problematic comparisons were sometimes drawn obliquely, in other instances invidious distinctions were made quite explicitly. Akasegawa Genpei was the avant-garde artist and writer who had taken up the theme of waste in fairly radical ways in the 1960s with projects like "Cleaning Event," and even in the 1980s with his search for Thomassons. By the 2000s, he seemed to be peddling cultural essentialism as part of a now mainstream interest in *mottainai*. He distinguished Japan's attentiveness to food waste with the supposed custom in China and South Korea of leaving food on the plate. But the brunt of his disdain fell on the United States, which Akasegawa sardonically accused of being the source of a practice that epitomized wastefulness: the eating of a grapefruit with a knife and spoon so that edible fruit is left attached to the inside of the skin. That, said Akasegawa, was the kind of country the United States was, in contrast to Japan, where grapefruits did not appear until the postwar period. The implication was that wasteful American ways tainted Japan in the postwar decades, before which Japanese did not consume grapefruit but instead ate tangerines whose fruit could be eaten in their entirety and whose skin could be dried and used as mosquito-repelling incense. Akasegawa went so far as to suggest that Americans probably could not understand the "characteristically Japanese concept of *mottainai*" because they were so accustomed to ample space that everything, from people to cars, became unnecessarily and wastefully large.[50] Others pointed out the linguistic uniqueness of *mottainai*. Kitano Masaru, for example, made the oft-repeated claim that there was no clear English translation of or equivalent to the word *mottainai* so as to underscore its particularly Japanese character.[51] Although not all celebrations of the concept were so deeply rooted in cultural generalizations, essentialisms, and disdainful comparisons between countries, those who considered it an aspect of the country's identity did presuppose some degree of Japanese uniqueness to *mottainai*.

Marketing *Mottainai*, Branding Japan

The millennial concept of *mottainai*, and the notion that it was an expression of Japanese identity, catapulted to national and even global attention in early 2005 when the Kenyan activist, government minister, and Nobel laureate Wangari Maathai was invited to Japan by a reporter from the *Mainichi* newspaper and was introduced to *mottainai* which she embraced and then promoted as a keyword for the global environmental movement. "When I learned the concept of *mottainai*," explained Maathai, "I immediately knew it would be an important element of my message to the world. I liked the spiritual roots of *mottainai*. I also liked the fact that it captures in one term the '3Rs' [reduce, reuse, recycle] that we environmentalists have been campaigning for over many years."[52] Her visit to Japan inspired the establishment of the Mottainai Campaign, sponsored by the Mainichi Newspapers Company (Mainichi Shinbunsha) and the conglomerate Itōchū Corporation (Itōchū Shōji) with Maathai as honorary chair.

The Mottainai Campaign sought to internationalize *mottainai*, putting it forward as a Japanese idea that Japanese people could feel proud sharing with the world. The Itōchū Corporation conceived of MOTTAINAI as a brand, complete with a logo that was printed on products such as T-shirts and cloth bags.[53] The brand was intended to be global with a Japanese flavor, as was unequivocally announced at the top of the campaign's English-language website: "Mottainai. It is the message from Japan to the world." The Japanese version echoed this sentiment, if worded slightly differently: "*Mottainai* is the watchword of the world."[54] Expanding on this message, the official statement of the Second National Convention on Mottainai, sponsored by the campaign in the summer of 2008 for about four thousand participants, proclaimed, "On this occasion, we declare our commitment to promoting *MOTTAINAI*, the spirit we Japanese have cherished since ancient times, throughout Japan and subsequently throughout the world."[55] This spirit was defined as more than a synonym for the 3Rs, made unique by being Japanized at this moment of international presentation with the addition of a fourth "R" (respect) such that *mottainai* was said to equal "3R + R." Although the fourth "R" did not gain much traction beyond the Mottainai Campaign, it was intended to transcend the pragmatism of environmentally friendly practices to embody sentiments and values: "Mottainai is the painful longing for things that have been lost" and "Mottainai is a way to say thanks to someone who has helped you."[56]

In international forums, Wangari Maathai served as a spokesperson for the Mottainai Campaign, which was linked to her own Green Belt Movement. In March 2005, a month after her visit to Japan, she mentioned the term *mottainai* at a session of the United Nations Commission on the Status of Women and she would continue her publicizing efforts in the years to come.[57] In May of that year, she talked about *mottainai* at the National Press Club in Washington, D.C.[58] In September 2009, at a UN summit, she urged world leaders to arrive at a climate change agreement several months hence in Copenhagen and explained that individuals, too, could do their part in addressing the problem: "we can all reduce, re-use and recycle, what is embraced as Mottainai in Japan, a concept that also calls us to express gratitude, to respect and to avoid wastage."[59] Several months later at the UN Climate Change Conference in Copenhagen, she argued that values rather than science might be the key to concluding a meaningful and binding climate change agreement and mentioned *mottainai* in this context as one such compelling value. She explained hearing, at events organized by religious leaders, "words that express values like compassion, empathy and mottainai (encompassing respect, gratitude and not wasting)."[60] Other international promotion efforts included media coverage, such as national broadcaster NHK's special episode of its program *Radio Japan*, geared to some twenty foreign countries, on the theme "Reviving the *Mottainai* Heart." The Mottainai Bāsan series was to be discussed along with Maathai's message about the concept. The aim was to "spread to the world a time-honored Japanese word together with a heart that values resources."[61]

While there was a global dimension to the Mottainai Campaign, it was strongly rooted in a domestic movement to encourage waste consciousness driven by a well-oiled marketing machine. The *Mainichi* newspaper, as one of its sponsors, carried regular coverage of events, speeches, and advice. It shaped and promoted the concept, explaining, for example, that *mottainai* was not the stinginess of *kechi*. Attempting to distance this waste consciousness from any negative associations with an excessive or unpleasant frugality, *mottainai* was to be distinguished by tender loving care for things and the gentleness of using something until its very end. This might mean sewing aprons from old skirts, or making marmalade out of tangerine peels.[62] NHK was friendly to the campaign, airing a reading of the Mottainai Bāsan book, approved by the campaign, on its educational television station.[63] There were also events, as at the flagship Mitsukoshi department store in the Nihonbashi area of Tokyo, where a "Mottainai Fair" was held in the fall of 2006 to sell campaign-related books including the Mottainai Bāsan series.[64] Having been adopted by the Mottainai Campaign, Shinju Mariko's books sold over 500,000 copies by the fall of 2007.[65] Another book promoted by the campaign was *Watashi no, mottainai* (My *Mottainai*), consisting of a preface written by Maathai and prizewinning essays chosen from over two thousand submissions to a nationwide contest sponsored by the *Mainichi* newspaper and the publisher Magazine House (Magajin Hausu).[66] A Mottainai Flea Market kicked off in 2007, held every weekend in a suburb of the Kantō area, at which old clothes, books, and DVDs were collected and sold, and hard-to-dispose-of things like oil used for frying tempura were collected.[67] Also in 2007, the first multiday convention to promote the movement was held in the city of Utsunomiya, which had been promoting garbage reduction and reuse, and attracted roughly two thousand participants from across the country. There, the host city spoke of its "*mottainai* declaration," a pledge that families were to make in order to spread the spirit of *mottainai*, prevent global warming, and reduce garbage. The seven specific pledges to be made were to plan purchasing in order to not spend wastefully or have food left over; buy products in containers that can be refilled when it comes to things like shampoo and detergent; recycle resources in order to reduce garbage; take one's own bag for shopping and refuse excessive packaging; set air conditioners to 28 degrees Celsius (about 82 degrees Fahrenheit) in the summer and heaters to 20 degrees Celsius (68 degrees Fahrenheit) in the winter; not keep water running when brushing one's teeth or showering; and turn off the car's engine when stopped or parked.[68] There was also the changing and expanding line of Mottainai Campaign products, from "my bottles" to "my umbrellas," available at the brick-and-mortar store, events, and online, with some of the proceeds going to Maathai's afforestation initiative in Kenya.[69]

The business model of the Mottainai Campaign was one not of environmental volunteerism but of corporate sponsorship to establish a brand and develop goods whose profits would be used toward environmental conservation. The Itōchū Corporation had two people dedicated to working on the campaign whose job it was to seek corporate participants (from Toyota Motors, or Toyota Jidōsha, to the Nisshin Fire and Marine Insurance Company, or Nisshin Kasai Kaijō Hoken); to create tie-ins for the launch of initiatives such as the Mottainai

Café at 160 locations of the Pronto coffee shop chain, or the Mottainai card of the credit company Orient Corporation (Orico, or Oriento Kōporēshon); and to license the use of the Mottainai Campaign logo on products to establish MOTTAINAI as a "lifestyle brand." In its first year, the campaign had profits of roughly 100 million yen, of which 30 million yen was donated to Maathai's Green Belt Movement.[70]

The Mottainai Campaign became so prominent that it inspired references to *mottainai*, and sometimes to Maathai, even when ties to the formal campaign were seemingly loose or nonexistent. The word *mottainai* popped up with unusual frequency in the titles of books on subjects like disposable chopsticks or ecological living.[71] The nonprofit Mottainai Society (Mottainai Gakkai) was established in 2007 with the aim of building a post-oil, post-waste civilization that values *mottainai* and affluence of the heart more than unlimited growth in gross domestic product.[72] And local waste consciousness movements incorporated *mottainai* into their names, as in Yamagata city which dubbed its promotion of energy saving and Warm Biz the Yamagata "Mottainai" Movement.[73] The Mottainai Campaign was also infused into already existing initiatives, like the Mottainai Detectives (Mottainai Tanteidan). Begun in the mid-1990s by a ward in Yokohama city, the program mobilized elementary school students to seek out instances of wastefulness around them. Promoting the detectives in the mid-2000s, the head of the ward spoke about Maathai and how Japanese people from long ago valued *mottainai*, but that it had become hard for children and adults to have this consciousness in a time overflowing with things. Citizens were urged to develop a *mottainai* consciousness and reconsider their disposing lifestyles.[74]

While the Mottainai Campaign was a nongovernmental effort backed by media and corporate sponsorship, the Japanese government also promoted *mottainai* as a brand for environmentalism and, by extension, the nation. Prime Minister Koizumi Jun'ichirō repeatedly spoke of *mottainai* to domestic and international audiences after he met with Maathai during her initial visit to Japan in 2005, apparently struck by her embrace of the concept. Inspired by Maathai, he gave his own take on the origins of *mottainai*: an unspecified time of food shortages when parents told their children to eat their rice mindful of those people who had produced it.[75] As Koizumi retold the story of his meeting with Maathai in subsequent months, he imprinted *mottainai* with Japanese origins using Orientalist tropes as he sought its internationalization. The concept was "hard to understand," he initially claimed, by which he meant hard to understand for non-Japanese—all the more reason why he was surprised about its embrace by Maathai. What was implied in this early statement was explicitly spelled out in others, in which he expressed his desire for "foreigners" to understand the meaning of the word and pondered how difficult it would be to use in English, as well as in French, German, and other foreign languages.[76] By suggesting that *mottainai* had an inherently Japanese quality that was unknowable to foreigners, Koizumi preserved the allegedly unique Japanese nature of the concept so that it would still be branded as Japanese even as he was convinced that it could become a global word. Flipping the conventional conception of Japan as a liminal space in which foreign ideas become Japanized, Koizumi pushed outward a Japanese idea to be largely, if not thoroughly, internationalized.[77]

For Koizumi, *mottainai* was part of an articulation of national identity in a post bubble Japan. The era of mass production, mass consumption, and mass disposal was declared over. Economic growth, once a source of national pride, had come at the expense of environmental degradation. Now allegedly wise about environmental pollution and climate change, Japan was to seek both environmental protection and economic development. While the country would continue to strive for economic growth, its identity could no longer rest solely on such accomplishments. Koizumi presented himself as the prime minister of both economic reforms and Cool Biz. And in a press conference following the Gleneagles Summit of the G8 in July 2005, Koizumi put Japan forward as a country that sought to be a "zero waste, zero emission society" and ended by reporting that he had introduced at the summit the Japanese word *mottainai* as the encapsulation of the importance of environmental protection and the valuing of things.[78]

This theme was echoed by Minister of the Environment Koike Yuriko, who advocated education about the spirit of *mottainai* as a kind of character-building enterprise to construct a society that could both maintain affluence and reduce its environmental burden.[79] In an attempt to teach the Japanese public about the wastefulness of plastic bags, Koike created the *mottainai furoshiki*, a wrapping cloth made out of recycled plastic bottles that sported a painting by Tokugawa-era artist Itō Jakuchū so as to highlight the "*furoshiki* culture" of that period. *Furoshiki* were said to have a long history dating as far back as the eighth century, and to be a physical manifestation of the values of *mottainai*. This special *furoshiki*, a symbol of environmentally conscious techniques and heart of Japan, was put on display and sold as the embodiment of Japan's "traditional culture" of the wrapping cloth and of valuing things.[80] Prime Minister Koizumi, who went to one of the *mottainai furoshiki* exhibitions in Tokyo, hailed the wrapping cloth as a way to reduce garbage and to promote a recycling society that valued things, both of which were essential to a Japan that was to embrace both environmental protection and economic growth.[81]

Government interest in highlighting Japan's long-held "tradition" of waste consciousness as an aspect of national identity peaked during Koizumi's administration but continued with somewhat muted enthusiasm through the succession of one-year prime ministerships that followed. Though unfocused for a brief time during Abe Shinzō's first term, with his vague notion of building a "beautiful country, Japan," *mottainai* continued to be invoked in environmental conversations both domestically and in international forums like the UN. The term was also occasionally used by the government in non-environmental contexts. In June 2011, the Japan Patent Office (Tokkyochō, or JPO) collaborated with its counterparts in seven other countries to establish a pilot of what was dubbed PPH MOTTAINAI, a program intended to facilitate the consideration of patent requests in multiple countries. The name of the pilot program was born out of dissatisfaction with the existing patent application process, which was so inefficient as to be considered wasteful.[82]

The attention given to *mottainai* by the Japanese government was mirrored by quasi-governmental and nongovernmental organizations with global reach that aimed to introduce *mottainai* into the lexicon of countries around the world. In Latin America, Mottainai Brasil had been established in the mid-1990s by the Japan chapter of the nonprofit Junior Chamber International as part of its Global Mottainai Movement and continued to be active in the 2000s.[83] In Vietnam, the Japan International Cooperation Agency, an independent governmental entity, supported a "MOTTAINAI Fair" hosted by the 3R Hanoi Project in March 2008.[84] And in Malaysia, the Japanese consumer electronics corporation Panasonic launched a *mottainai* campaign in September 2009 to promote its eco-friendly products. As was explained by the company's general manager of communications and branding, "*mottainai* was a universal phrase now that the company wanted to 'popularise' to Malaysians." Efforts included an eco-ideas exhibition in Kuala Lumpur that showcased the concept, and outreach to preschool and kindergarten students through Mottainai Bāsan, who taught the children about not wasting through stories, songs, and activities.[85] Sony Computer Entertainment also brought the word some attention from English-speaking players with its spring 2009 release of "Trash Panic" ("Gomibako," or "Garbage Can," in the Japanese market), a vaguely "Tetris"-like game for the PlayStation 3 console in which trash must be destroyed but valuable items labeled *mottainai* must be saved.

The concept also popped up as an inspirational idea or brand name in various places without conscious and purposeful promotion by a Japanese organization. In 2007, recent graduates of the Fashion Institute of Technology in New York City established a Brooklyn-based brand of sustainable menswear called Mottainai New York. One of the co-founders, Luke McCann, took to the concept when it was introduced to him by the Japanese artist Yoshino Minako because it encapsulated his dissatisfaction with cheap, poor-quality, mass-produced, and mass-consumed clothes as well as his commitment to high-quality, stylish, and durable clothes made from organic and recycled materials. An explanation of the brand name was regularly asked for in media coverage and was provided on the company's website: "The word Mottainai (moe tie nie) roughly translates into 'what a waste,' and can be interpreted to sum up when people squander natural resources. Deeply embedded in Japanese folk tales, it is commonly used by parents to ensure children eat all of their rice. Children are taught that if they waste things, the 'mottainai ghost' will come."[86] The Mottainai New York brand and philosophy reverberated with a Japanese magazine about small- and medium-sized businesses which ran a story on how Japan could learn from this American company that had internalized and capitalized on Japanese ideas, ways of thinking, and business culture. While McCann was described as having taken some time to truly understand *mottainai*, his company was also credited with reminding Japanese of the several-hundred-year history of the concept. Japan, it was feared, needed this foreign prodding about the value of its "traditional culture" and "ancient ideas" at a time when mass production, mass consumption, and fast fashion were hastening the loss of this "Japanese virtue."[87]

Finding Hope

On a hot and humid Saturday afternoon in June 2016, I sat in the air-conditioned auditorium of the New Kōtō Incineration Plant (Shin Kōtō Seisō Kōjō). Completed in 1998, the large facility is adjacent to and generates electricity for the park and sports complex built atop the former Island of Dreams landfill in the Kōtō ward of Tokyo. As part of a public tour of the plant, I was taking an interactive video quiz about garbage and its fate hosted by this facility's mascot, Rui the dolphin. The plant incinerates 1,800 tons of garbage a day, the other participant and I answered correctly. Separation of garbage into categories is necessary because they are disposed of differently, we responded. We were also told to value things for the sake of reducing garbage and protecting the earth, to reuse things, and to take advantage of flea markets. The fifteen-minute video was clearly not aimed at adults, but was perfectly suited to its intended audience of elementary school students. There was also a brochure for kids and toys to hand out, like a kaleidoscope made out of recycled incinerator ash. Because such public tours had been conceived in the 1970s as a way to convince residents of the need to reduce garbage and the safety of incinerators, the focus on children was unexpected. The guide and plant employee explained that the Ministry of Education, Culture, Sports, Science and Technology (Monbu Kagakushō, or MEXT) now requires all students in the fourth grade to visit a sewage treatment plant and an incineration facility.[88]

The focus on teaching young people about waste and wastefulness can be seen not just in the formal education system, which requires field trips to incineration plants and includes curricula about garbage, but in the sheer number of children's books about wastefulness and *mottainai*, like the series by Shinju Mariko and Akiyama Hiroko. Waste-related topics have also appeared in works not specifically or centrally about waste, such as the award-winning manga series *Yotsubato!*, the first volume of which became a best seller when it was released in 2003 and had gone through forty-eight printings by 2015.[89] In a not so overtly didactic way, lessons about wastefulness were periodically woven into vignettes about daily life, starting on the day the rambunctious pigtailed young protagonist Yotsuba and her father moved into their new home at the very beginning of the series. The first interaction that the father had with anyone in the new neighborhood was about where he should dispose of cardboard boxes. One of the teenage girls who lived next door, Fūka, went on to explain which days were designated for burnable and nonburnable garbage pickup. Having received an orientation in the proper disposal of waste, Yotsuba's father was that much closer to becoming a full-fledged resident of the neighborhood. Several episodes later, Fūka's younger sister Ena taught Yotsuba about global warming, saying that she tried not to use the air conditioner very much because it caused the earth to get warmer, the ice at the North Pole to melt, and islands to sink. Thinking that air conditioners were the "enemy" of the earth, Yotsuba responded angrily when her father revealed that even though Grandma and Grandpa did not have them, he had bought two for their new home. She calmed down, not when mention was made of energy-saving models, but when lied to about how coolers actually cool the earth. A young reader of the manga could draw a number of lessons from this chapter, but it seems probable that the outright nature of the lie and Yotsuba's utter naïveté might at least sow the seeds of doubt about the careless use of air conditioners.[90] Such lessons about garbage and climate change in a manga not ostensibly about waste or wastefulness likely reinforced the more formal instruction encountered elsewhere, with its casual and incidental tone helping to normalize consciousness of waste for its young readers. In addition to books, some of which have been more intentionally and fully about waste than others, the Mottainai Campaign has made a concerted effort to encourage children's participation in its events. At the MOTTAINAI Festival (MOTTAINAI Fesuta) held in the Akihabara area of Tokyo in June 2016, except for the flea market, most of the activities were geared toward children, from the juggling show to the area inside castle gates where used toys and books could be traded.[91]

These efforts to teach children to be conscious of waste have been especially intense in the millennial years. It is difficult to say whether this stems from a perhaps natural turn to the next generation when trying to shape behavior, an attempt to reach parents through their children, or a certain impatience about the capacity of adults, particularly those who experienced Japan at peak economic growth and materialism, to change their lifestyles in substantial or fundamental ways. Whatever the various assumptions and motivations at work, there has been in the focus on children and in much of the content taught an optimism—an orientation toward the future and the hope that values and behaviors can change. And such optimism complicates, even challenges, the story of loss and despair that has often been told about the 2000s. If the 1990s were lost only in hindsight, perhaps the 2000s have not been lost at all.

Beyond the attention given to young people, the explorations of meaning and identities for which *mottainai* provided a conceptual vocabulary indicate a forward-looking, constructive, and hopeful impulse. At the level of the individual, *mottainai* raised questions about what affluence had meant for what was valued and desired, and what leading a rich life might and should mean. At the level of the nation, *mottainai* was a particular angle from which to consider, redefine, and express Japanese identity. In attempting to create a sense of national pride that was not tied to economic accomplishments, the discourse on *mottainai* resonated with the recently anointed "cool Japan," an idea given currency by the American writer Douglas McGray in his 2002 article titled "Japan's Gross National Cool." The prospect that Japan could be cool, and that this might help define the country in the new millennium, was excitedly taken up by Japanese politicians, bureaucrats, and businesspeople who championed the export of Japanese popular culture, in particular, as a means of branding Japan and expanding its global influence.[92] Adopting a variation of Joseph Nye's concept of "soft power," proponents of "cool Japan" hoped that national strength and recognition might be gained and measured by the export of Japanese-branded lifestyles and values at a time when it was felt that the country could not boast of military prowess or economic might. The idea that Japan might exert soft power in some form was not new, but the values that Japan was supposed to project to the world in the 2000s were intentionally framed and expressed in terms of a consciousness of wastefulness. As one example, an article published in the *Asahi* newspaper in March 2005 asserted that Japan's assumption of an honorable position in the twenty-first-century world would depend on international appreciation of the country's core values—one of which was *mottainai*. *Mottainai*, it was explained, foregrounded the values of not wasting things, not creating garbage, protecting the natural environment, and preventing global warming.[93]

What differentiated the millennial decade from the preceding one, then, was the fading of the trauma of rupture between the years of growth and the years of torpor. If the 1990s had revealed that the economic downturn was not temporary, the 2000s eradicated any remaining possibility of an economically ascendant Japan in the near future.[94] And this acceptance created an opening for constructive self-reflection about values, priorities, and identities. That worries, dilemmas, and challenges continued to hang over millennial Japan should not be understated. But the first decade of the twenty-first century was not itself lost or wasted, for embedded in the waste consciousness of these years was an environmentalism concerned about the future and a yearning for spiritual or psychological well-being which hinted at new ways of thinking about living in a time of stagnant affluence.

SORTING THINGS OUT

In December 2009, self-described "clutter consultant" Yamashita Hideko published the book *Shin, katazukejutsu danshari* (*Danshari*, A New Technique for Tidying), which promised in its subtitle, "Your Life Will Change with 'Tidying.'" The name she gave her method—*danshari*—consisted of three characters that were interpreted to mean: severing your relationship with incoming things you do not need (*dan*); throwing away the clutter that overruns your house (*sha*); and separating yourself from a deep attachment to things and existing in *yutori*, or a space of relaxed ease (*ri*). By practicing *danshari*, you could realize a kind of *yutori* similar in spirit to the one of leisure promoted in the 1980s, but with greater emphasis on a sense of freedom, mindfulness, and serenity. To clean your house of clutter, said Yamashita, was to clean your heart, mind, and spirit (*kokoro*) of clutter. And the very act of decluttering could change your heart. In its encouragement of a psychological or spiritual well-being, *danshari* was like the waste consciousness of *mottainai*. And the idea was similarly alluring, with the best seller surging into its thirty-ninth printing and sales reaching more than 300,000 copies in its first two years, launching a phenomenon with multiple books, articles, seminars, and media appearances.[1]

Danshari was only part of a veritable boom in books about how to throw things away. This genre had previously been of popular but clearly delineated interest, aimed at those who wanted to improve their organizing or cleaning skills. In the early twenty-first century, advice about decluttering came to enjoy widespread attention with its variations on the message that people should freely discard what they do not really need and keep only what brings them peace, happiness, or joy.

The tremendous appeal of both decluttering and *mottainai* has exemplified the heightened pursuit of an affluence of the heart in the millennial years, as people have searched for values and meaning beyond the financial. What had been a modest if healthy desire for a truly rich life in the 1980s evolved into an attempt to substantially redefine what a good life could and should be. And being conscious of waste was a way to figure out and express the commitments and priorities of lives well lived. Waste consciousness in millennial Japan was thus expansive in conception. There was room for *mottainai*, with its promotion of reducing garbage, conserving resources and energy, recycling, and protecting the environment. There was also room for decluttering, with its espousal of throwing things away, paying little mind to physical waste, and transcending an emotionally bankrupt materialism.

As much as decluttering and *mottainai* have both nurtured the ideal of an affluent heart, their visions of psychological and spiritual richness have diverged markedly in their approaches to material things, their temporal orientations, and their conceptions of the self. If *mottainai* has summoned an appreciation of things for the sake of societal or even global good, not just in the present but also in the future, then ideas like *danshari* have subordinated the material to the realization of one's own happiness in the present moment. For her part, Yamashita Hideko slighted *mottainai* and its focus on the act of keeping (as opposed to discarding) because it was centrally about things. In contrast, she argued, *danshari* was primarily about oneself, about knowing and liking the real you in the here and now.[2] Indeed, the decluttering literature appealed directly, explicitly, and unapologetically to an introspective, affective self.[3] Distinct from the waste consciousness efforts spearheaded by various kinds of organizations that served some communal interest, decluttering was promoted by personalities whose advice for finding happiness centered on the individual and his or her sense of self-fulfillment in the present.[4]

As illustrated by the almost simultaneous prominence of *mottainai* and decluttering, there has been a diversification as well as a broadening of waste consciousness in the early twenty-first century. Under the umbrella of an attention to waste, there has existed both a deemphasis on the material and an appreciation of things, the yearning for *yutori* and the embrace of productivity and efficiency, the questioning of prosperous lifestyles and the desire for financial and material comfort. These distinct threads in waste consciousness have appeared not just in the promotion of *mottainai* and decluttering but also in the advice literature about saving money and saving time. And they have been amplified by the gendered differences in the purposes of minimizing waste. While both women and men were to think about self-satisfaction, women much more than men were to look beyond the material and to seek happiness. And men much more than women were to define their individual goals in terms of work and career, thereby sustaining earlier logics of scientific management and rationalization.

These many and disparate elements of waste consciousness were perpetuated, not reconciled, diminished, or erased, by the Great Disaster of Eastern Japan (Higashi Nihon Daishinsai), or 3.11, the collective name for the devastating earthquake and tsunami of March 11, 2011, and the ensuing crisis at the Fukushima Daiichi nuclear power plant. The disaster has underscored the overarching and enduring need to find what is of true importance, but this might mean any number of things, from savoring the present moment because one's life could so quickly change or turning away from material things because all of one's physical possessions could be washed away in a matter of minutes, to ensuring that the environment has a long future. Both *mottainai* and decluttering have enjoyed popularity since 2011. And in the calls to save electricity can be heard familiar echoes with a longer past—the bright stinginess from the 1970s and a steadfast concern with productivity and profit. After March 2011, as in the years before it, people living in a time and place of stagnant affluence marked by both insecurity and privilege persist in their various attempts to determine how to give meaning to and make meaning of their possessions, their time, and themselves.

The Decluttered Self

For Yamashita Hideko, *danshari* was the antidote for a lifestyle overflowing with stuff. This condition was sometimes the fault of one's own decisions, like buying a larger bottle of mayonnaise than one needed because of a sale. But it was also the result of techniques used to induce people to buy things and of the untamable flood of goods that were not acquired by choice, like mid-year and year-end gifts, thick mail order catalogs, packaging, and advertising leaflets stuffed into mailboxes. With this incessant inflow of things, houses could easily become reservoirs of muck. What *danshari* provided, most concretely, was a method of discarding for those who struggled to do so. A fundamental step in the process was to determine why you were unable to throw things away, which could be distilled down to three main reasons, or three main types of people: those who were busy or were not at home much; those who were attached to the past and wanted to keep mementos; and those who stocked up on things because they were worried about the future, like people who hoarded toilet paper because they were concerned about the reoccurrence of an event like the Oil Shock. The discarding itself was to begin with throwing out things that were clearly garbage, first sorting them into three groups (general, resource, and non-resource) and then tackling further separation into however many other categories were mandated by one's municipality. Next, one was to decide whether to keep or to get rid of the things that were not obviously garbage. Finally, those things not discarded were to be organized.[5] *Danshari* was originally conceived for the home, and a readership of women, and then expanded its audience and applicability to include men and the workplace.[6] Yamashita herself wrote a book that transferred her strategies from the home to the office, which meant changing the examples to things like throwing out ballpoint pens that had run out of ink, discarding fancy Mont Blanc or Waterman pens that were not being used, and tidying around one's desk and inside drawers.[7]

With its encouragement of throwing things away, *danshari* had little concern for physical waste. On the contrary, the amount of garbage produced through decluttering was evidence of the success of both the person who undertook *danshari* and of the technique itself. One prominent *danshari* advocate was Kawabata Nobuko, a former management consultant turned psychotherapist who had read Yamashita's advice, attended the lectures, trained in the method, and even written books of her own. In one of her many works about *danshari*, edited by Yamashita, Kawabata boasted of the twenty large 45-liter bags full of stuff she had thrown away when she first embarked on decluttering.[8] Another *danshari* surrogate created, in conjunction with Yamashita, a manga version of the method's central tenets, its cover graced with a drawing of a woman in a yoga pose with four bags of garbage behind her. On the back of the book was an illustration of a smiling woman taking out two bags of garbage.[9] In another testimonial of sorts, one woman reported that she had paid 30,000 yen to attend a two-day *danshari* seminar after learning about Yamashita on television and reading her book. The woman was satisfied with her investment in decluttering, for the tidying of her desk at work had yielded four 45-liter garbage bags of stuff and one box of non-burnable refuse.[10]

Although mention was sometimes made of recycling or donating one's unwanted things, one of the central ideas of *danshari* was that a sense of responsibility to reuse or recycle (as would be encouraged by *mottainai* advocates) could be an obstacle in the quest to discard. Yamashita made it a point to criticize *mottainai* as indulging an attachment to the material and encouraging a guilty conscience that made it hard to dispose of things. *Mottainai* was thus deemed antithetical to *danshari*. The real meaning of not wasting, Yamashita explained, was to respect a thing when you bought or received it and then to simply say "sorry" or "thank you" when you threw it away.[11] This antipathy toward *mottainai* solidified as the number of *danshari* surrogates, books, and articles grew. In the psychotherapist Kawabata's book, a feeling of *mottainai* was listed first as a reason why people ended up keeping too many things. Readers were urged to do

FIGURE 10.1. *Danshari*. The front cover of *Danshari serapī* (*Danshari* Therapy).

Reproduced by permission from Aikawa Momoko with Yamashita Hideko, ed., *Danshari serapī* (Tokyo: Seishun Shuppansha, 2011).

away with the notion that it was a sin to throw things away, to focus instead on not taking in wasteful things, and to not keep things out of a sense of *mottainai*, for that would result in losing a space of *yutori*.[12] The *danshari* camp's criticism that *mottainai* was centered on things was somewhat unfair, considering that reuse and recycling were often framed in terms of environmental protection. But comparatively speaking, especially given the emphasis that *mottainai* placed on valuing and extending the lives of things, *danshari* did decenter the material and minimize concern with the materiality of waste.

    Danshari was but one decluttering method that encouraged people to throw away their things as garbage. Riding the wave of the *danshari* boom, the "tidying consultant" Kondō Marie launched a veritable empire of her own. Published in

2011, Kondō's inaugural book was titled *Jinsei ga tokimeku katazuke no mahō*, or as it was translated for the English version released a few years later, *The Life-Changing Magic of Tidying Up*. The book sold over a million copies in its first year, was in its sixty-first printing by the spring of 2015, and inspired media coverage, appearances by Kondō, and even a special television drama about a hapless client whose room was decluttered and life problems solved by a tidying consultant.[13] As a testament to the book's international popularity, in April 2015 *Time* magazine named Kondō one of the one hundred most influential people in the world. The only other Japanese person so designated that year was Murakami Haruki.[14] And in January 2016, the English version of the first book, which had already spent sixty weeks on the *USA Today* best-seller list, reached number one; Kondō's recently released second English book, *Spark Joy*, was number three.[15] Of both Yamashita Hideko's and Kondō Marie's books, the *Asahi* newspaper noted how well they were selling not just domestically but also internationally. Their success, it was explained, could be attributed to a common concern in advanced countries about excess possessions and a global desire for a simpler way of living.[16]

Like *danshari*, Kondō Marie's approach to decluttering, or the KonMari method, sought to cultivate the ability to throw things away with ease and with little concern about the materiality of waste. With the KonMari method, one was to begin by defining for oneself the purpose of tidying and by imagining a detailed picture of one's ideal way of living. That was to be followed by reflection about why that way of living was desirable or, in short, what would bring happiness. The heart of the tidying technique was about deciding what to keep and what to throw away, which was to be accomplished thus: Take a thing into your hands. If it brings you joy (if it enchants you, excites you, or gives you peace of mind), then keep it. If not, then throw it away.[17] What was most important was joy in the present, for as Kondō insisted, one cannot live in the past.

As with *danshari*, any feelings that prevented an unjoyful object's disposal were to be overcome. If a sense of *mottainai* kept you from throwing away a thing that did not elicit joy, then you were to imagine the role that it would play in your life if you were to keep it, and this exercise was to lead inevitably to the realization that the object had already fulfilled its purpose and could be tossed. An item of clothing, for example, that brought you joy when you bought it or showed you that its style did not suit you well had already served its function, and should be discarded. To throw away a lot of things was not, argued Kondō, a waste of things. The forgotten and forlorn stuff in the back of the closet or dresser was not being valued, so it was to be thanked and thrown out. According to a proud Kondō, the record for the amount of stuff discarded through her method was held by a couple who produced two hundred bags of garbage and more than ten items of large refuse.[18]

Both Kondō and Yamashita were offering their own variations on an approach to discarding stuff that had been articulated some years earlier. In 2000, the marketing planner Tatsumi Nagisa published her book *"Suteru!" gijutsu* ("Throw Away!" Techniques), a best seller that sold 800,000 copies during its first four months in print and has been credited with kicking off the popular and persistent trend of decluttering. Tatsumi too started with the premise that people's lives were overflowing with things, and encouraged discarding. But for her, throwing things away was not about minimizing one's material possessions but about making room for new purchases. Anticipating and rebuking the values of *mottainai* advocates, she argued that environmental commitments, a lifestyle of saving, the appreciation of things, and restraint from buying items you did not need were not the remedy for the proliferation of things. To stop consuming, to forgo the fun of having things you like, would be too sad. Keeping wasteful consumption to a minimum might be friendly to the environment and good for household finances, but doing so was impossible because it went against a fundamental human desire to possess things.[19] In Tatsumi's version of decluttering, there was little apology for, much less a disavowal of, embracing material things.

The *danshari* and KonMari methods constituted a new generation in the decluttering literature. This was in part because their end goal of discarding was not simply a well-organized space that was easy to manage, as Tatsumi would have it, but a full heart and an enriched self. As was remarked in media coverage, Yamashita and Kondō infused decluttering with a "spiritual element."[20] But what also distinguished *danshari* and the KonMari method from their predecessors was a more complicated attitude toward the material, at once quite indifferent to physical waste and very conscious of people's relationships with things. And the two authors differed in their conceptions of this relationship. For Kondō, as much as she advocated a release or liberation from the things that no longer evoked joy, she found that equating tidying with throwing things away was bound to create unhappiness and so put more emphasis on what was kept than on what was discarded. This was not a "ruthless war on stuff," as a *New York Times Magazine* headline might have us believe.[21] On the contrary, implicit in her detailed instructions for how to store and organize possessions, be it how to fold socks or how to file away warranties for electric appliances, was an obsessive concern with things and their proper place.[22] The idea that each thing has a home, a designated location to which it should always be returned, was reminiscent of the advice literature from the 1950s about rationalizing the household, but the aim in this incarnation was not efficiency or productivity. Rather, it was through material things—through the process of deciding what to discard and what to keep, of figuring out where and how items should be kept—that KonMari practitioners were to figure out what was important to them, find themselves, define their individual values, and experience joy. And all of this in the present, without attachment to the past or anxiety about the future.[23] That the KonMari method is at its core a way to tidy for the sake of realizing happiness is illustrated by its origin story. Kondō relayed in interviews that as a child, she had read her mother's magazines and tried the suggested techniques for saving money on water bills or storing things more efficiently. She then became a "discarding machine" upon reading Tatsumi's book. But having discarded and tidied to the point of exhaustion, Kondō developed her particular focus on the decision to keep in order to be happy.[24]

In contrast to Kondō's concern with what was not discarded, Yamashita conceived of *danshari* as a way to nurture one's heart through a detachment from material things, a philosophy informed by her practice of yoga. The origin story of *danshari* opens with Yamashita's experience of yoga in college, when she encountered the three characters that composed *danshari* and learned of parting with a sense of attachment. Her epiphany of sorts came during a pilgrimage to a temple at Mount Kōya where she saw the lodgings for pilgrims, a space that had achieved the richness of not containing unnecessary things. The purpose of cleansing one's life of material things, she determined, was to create a space of health, safety, security, energy, and openness—all matters of the mind, spirit, and heart.[25]

Intrinsic to the realization of a lighter heart was a focus on oneself. As Yamashita saw it, the decision about what to throw away or what to keep hinged not on the usefulness of a thing but on whether it was suitable or appropriate to you, which placed the self at the center of the discarding process.[26] The centrality of the self was also emphasized in the works about *danshari* authored by the advocate Kawabata, for whom the most important outcome of tidying was the liberation of oneself from negativity, from insecurities about one's ability to tidy, which could escalate into the belief that one is a bad person. To *danshari* was to be able to value yourself and to realize self-affirmation.[27] In a variation for businesspeople, penned by the management consultant and executive Tazaki Masami, *danshari* meant focusing your professional efforts in the field of your strengths and your likes, and discarding everything else. And out of that process would come satisfaction in your work. People were to throw away notions of economic growth and increased wealth, for what was important was that Japan had already become an affluent society in which individuals could freely choose for themselves the purpose of their life.[28]

The implications of the varied and sometimes contradictory attitudes that decluttering advocates assumed toward material things could be understood in two different ways. On the one hand, their indifference toward the disposal of physical waste seems to undermine the kind of waste consciousness that has been promoted for decades by those who have been concerned about the proliferation, management, and negative environmental effects of garbage. It would also be reasonable to interpret the KonMari method in particular as accepting and even legitimizing wasteful practices such as shortening the life span of goods, changing models frequently, and crafting marketing strategies that appeal to unthinking desires and impulse buying. After all, there seems to be little discouragement of purchasing something if it brings one joy at that moment and then throwing it out soon after when its emotional effect has waned. On the other hand, the rhetoric of detaching oneself from things, more prominent in Yamashita's thinking than in Kondō's, reinforces the notion that meaning and satisfaction cannot be found in things and, perhaps, that the accumulation of the material is therefore fundamentally a wasteful pursuit. Or as had been put in various ways over the past several decades, the abundance of stuff might not create a genuine sense of affluence.[29]

One phenomenon that has claimed the lineage of *danshari* and KonMari is a kind of minimalism that emerged in the 2010s. The central figure of the minimalists is Sasaki Fumio, an unmarried man in his thirties who worked at a publishing company.[30] In 2014 he launched the website "Minimal & ism less is future," and a year later he published the book *Bokutachi ni, mō mono wa hitsuyō nai* (We No Longer Need Things). The book sold 160,000 copies, was in its seventh printing in less than six months, and was later published in English as *Goodbye, Things*.[31] Interviews with Sasaki appeared in newspapers, the word "minimalist" was a candidate for first prize in a contest of new and fashionable terms, and blogs by people who identified themselves as minimalists became so common that one hosting site counted some seven hundred contributions in this recently established category.[32]

For Sasaki and other minimalists, throwing things away is only the first, albeit fundamental, step toward living with few things. In this philosophy, material things are antithetical to happiness; happiness is to be found not through things but outside of them. And minimalism is defined as a means for finding what is really important, not by figuring out what you might want but by determining what you really need. In the actual techniques recommended for throwing things away, there is overlap with the decluttering strategies, like starting by discarding things that are clearly garbage and being aware of what moves your heart when deciding what to keep and what to throw away. These strategies are to be applied not just to the home but to the office, where Sasaki follows three rules: throw away things that are clearly garbage (e.g., pens that have run out of ink); throw away those things for which you have multiples (e.g., scissors of different sizes); and throw away things that you have not used for a year (e.g., written materials).[33] And while he does try to resist throwing out something that can still be used, he argues that it is wasteful to hold on to things just because you think discarding them would be *mottainai*.

At the same time, Sasaki diverges from the declutterers in his clearer renunciation of material things. In his pursuit of well-being, Sasaki is relatively unconcerned with tidying or organizing and prioritizes instead reducing the number of things one owns. He insists, for example, that you must not buy one thing without first getting rid of another. He also offers more alternatives to purchasing or keeping things, such as taking full advantage of the sharing economy by renting and borrowing items. Another suggestion is to digitize those things that are hard to discard; taking a picture of an object you want to remember, for example, would help you throw it away. Sasaki also goes one step further than Kondō, pronouncing that there should come a time when one throws away even those things that bring joy. By jettisoning from his daily life as many things as possible, Sasaki says that he feels more free, can focus better, is healthier, saves money, has more time, is more ecologically minded, enjoys life, savors the here and now, and can be truly happy.[34]

Sasaki's minimalism has been especially attractive to those in their twenties and thirties, a demographic with which his book has sold particularly well.[35] This may say something about the values and aspirations of youth more than this particular generation, as other movements for thinking about things in decades past, like the Recycling Movement Citizens' Association (Risaikuru Undō Shimin no Kai), have also been driven by young people. And one could posit that it is easier for those in their twenties and thirties to lead a minimalist life, free as they may be from the commitments and responsibilities characteristic of mid-life. But it is also worth considering whether the attention to minimalism reflects something about this particular generation. Having come of age in the 1990s and beyond, young people of the 2010s in Japan are seeking to define the nature of their relationship to stuff having never experienced the high-growth era or the bubble years, and only ever knowing a time of both economic anemia and material plenty.

With minimalism, and occasionally with *danshari*, the philosophies have been loosely associated with Buddhism to give them more spiritual heft, to make more credible the promise of a psychologically and emotionally fulfilling life through the discarding of things. As presented by the *danshari* advocate Kawabata, attachment as torment was a Buddhist idea and material things rendered visible the heart's attachments.[36] The Buddhist dimension of the minimalist philosophy was articulated with particular clarity by Masuno Shunmyō, a Sōtō Zen Buddhist priest, chief priest at Kenkōji in Yokohama, and well-known landscape architect. Asked in a 2015 interview if he thought the recent attention to the spirit of Zen and Zen-like spaces free of waste was a reaction to an era overflowing with things, Masuno observed that the past equation of an affluence of things with an affluence of human beings fed a pursuit of one new thing after another and did not lead to happiness. As there came to be doubts about this way of living, he continued, what emerged was a Zen that valued affluence of the heart. Masuno went on to interpret the teachings of Zen as advocating the elimination of waste, the discarding of unnecessary things, the removal of dirt and dust, detachment, and freedom from greed and vanity. The very act of cleaning would make people's hearts shine, and living only with what was truly necessary was beautiful and rich. What Masuno did not address was how the emphasis of methods like *danshari* and minimalism on satisfaction of the self could be reconciled with Buddhist ideas of no self, of the self as illusory.

What the Sōtō Zen priest did imply was that the feeling of *mottainai*, described by some of its advocates as a Buddhist idea, should be overcome in pursuit of a decluttered space. When asked about what people should do if they were unable to put their things in order because of *mottainai*, Masuno offered some concrete, common strategies for pushing through this obstacle, like throwing out clothes that had not been worn in the past two years. And he echoed the decluttering line that there was nothing more *mottainai* than storing and keeping unused things in the house.[37] In the quiet struggle that pitted *mottainai* advocates against declutterers and minimalists, people from both camps claimed Buddhist inspiration, and this priest did not shy away from taking a side.

That Buddhism, often vaguely and simply conceived, was evoked to justify both keeping (as an act of appreciating things) and discarding (as an act of detaching oneself from things) reflects how it was flexibly, selectively, and purposefully used to reinforce whatever views one might have toward waste and wastefulness. In the particular case of Masuno, the head of a Buddhist institution who has written prolifically for lay audiences about everything from Winnie the Pooh's hints for happiness to Zen and business thinking, he seems to be reformulating Zen Buddhism to make it relevant to everyday life.[38] What his interpretation of Buddhism shares with other, conflicting invocations is the attempt to imbue values with religious meaning, to emphasize the spiritual and psychological in one's relationship with things, and to render more attainable an affluence of the heart.

There are hints in the minimalist philosophy of real changes in how material things are viewed, which could have implications for ideas of waste and wastefulness. The premise that things are not necessary forecloses a search for fulfillment or happiness through stuff, and shifts the focus of consumption away from the acquisition of things. It does not discourage the act of consumption itself; as Sasaki has explained, being a minimalist is not about refraining from consumption or saving money. He himself enjoys going on trips and attending live music concerts.[39] But there is a way in which money is disconnected from the material things it can buy. And this creates the possibility that a philosophy not centrally or explicitly about waste consciousness might challenge the desires and logics of mass consumption that have undergirded practices, from impulsive or excessive purchasing to creating large amounts of garbage, often criticized as wasteful. Or put more simply, a minimalist lifestyle could also very well be a waste-reducing lifestyle.

Variations on the motif of reconsidering one's relationship to things were also woven into advice literature that centrally and explicitly did recommend a consciousness of waste. Neither as popular nor as voluminous as the works about *danshari*, KonMari, minimalism, or *mottainai*, the books and articles about waste consciousness nonetheless shared the overarching purpose of seeking well-being and happiness. Under this banner was a loosely amalgamated jumble of various familiar ideas about waste and wastefulness. A book by the lifestyle essayist Yamazaki Eriko, for example, suggested saving as a way to realize a waste-free life of *yutori*. What Yamazaki meant by saving was not the stinginess of not spending money but rather the skillful use of money to make life rich and to feel a luxury of the heart. What this entailed in practice was valuing things, or keeping only those things that one really valued so as to create a space and thereby a heart of greater *yutori*. Yamazaki valued things through longevity of use (like her mother's rice cooker from the late 1960s in that era's vintage green), reuse (like turning old newspapers into containers for holding food in the refrigerator), or full use (like making tangerine peels into insect repellent, deodorizer, or a bathwater additive).[40] Here in Yamazaki's thinking were traces of bright stinginess, *mottainai*, decluttering, and minimalism.

Writing in the same genre, the interior architect Katō Emiko suggested that living without waste, richly and beautifully, was the key to realizing one's true affluence, real luxury, and happiness. Waste (*muda*) and unreasonableness (*muri*) were to be eliminated, and this process was not to entail either the kind of frugality or saving that would sap the fun out of buying things or the storing up of things because it would be wasteful to throw them away. Instead, readers were to think about waste rather than convenience when pursuing something, rid themselves of useless attachments, and live simply, seeking pleasure and beauty. Here in Katō's thinking were echoes of the Toyota Production System, bright stinginess, green consumption, and decluttering.[41] Encapsulated in works like those of Katō and Yamazaki was a formulation of waste consciousness in these years that threw together seemingly disparate views of waste drawn from a veritable postwar history of different and shifting ideas about wastefulness, informed and framed by an ambivalence toward the material and the search for meaning and happiness characteristic of this moment.

That people increasingly sought out advice about what they should do with all of their stuff or how they might think about their material possessions does not mean that they were actually living without wasteful things in minimalist spaces free of untidy clutter.[42] Instead, as with other self-help topics like dieting and weight loss, turning to guidance may very well be indicative of a lived experience very different from the ideal presented in advice literature. What the popularity of decluttering and minimalism does suggest is that people have concerns and yearnings about finding meaning and happiness not exclusively or firmly rooted in the material. This is not a theme peculiar to a few bestselling books, but the driving force of new categories of writing from which we have examined only the most well-known examples. In the genre of literature about throwing things away, there have also been issues of women's magazines dedicated to clearing one's room and one's heart, books by business publishers about discarding unneeded stuff, derivative methods for overcoming obstacles to casting off unwanted things, and much more.[43] There has been a steady stream of writing in the minimalist vein as well, which has also dovetailed with works about the "simple life."[44]

Much of this genre has been targeted to, and captivating for, an audience of women. *Danshari* has been more familiar among housewives than men, and the KonMari method has been particularly resonant with working women in their late twenties and early thirties as well as housewives in their late forties and fifties. This is in part because the decluttering advice, especially from Kondō, has been less about the workplace than about the home, which continues to be viewed largely as the domain of women whether they are full-time housewives or not. Yet the gendered dimension of this literature should not be viewed simply or solely as placing on the shoulders of women the responsibility of keeping the home free of clutter. This is not the immediate postwar period, when advice about the clean, organized, and efficiently managed home stressed duties and obligations without much mention of purpose. What *danshari* and KonMari did instead was gender not just the act of decluttering but also its goals, aspirations, and hopes. This rendered it normative for women, more than men, to openly and actively seek self-cultivation, fulfillment, and happiness in their daily lives.

Gendered Hearts

The pursuit of a more spiritual, psychological, and emotional affluence not so focused on the financial and the material was encouraged in other, more established genres of advice literature. Here, too, it was primarily women who were to strive for a good life through waste consciousness. And this theme appeared even in the most unintuitive of places, like articles and books about monetary savings.

The prudence of not wasting money assumed urgency and gravity in the late 1990s, as the country attempted to reckon with the severity of its economic challenges and the ripple effects of the Asian financial crisis. In this context, the household was to be attentive to saving money.[45] Sometimes the strategies presented were framed as making the most of a tight financial environment, as with one discussion published in the magazine *Fujin kōron* (Women's Review) which, though ostensibly about what it called a "bright stinginess" (*akarui kechikechi*), was less about brightness as its 1970s counterpart had been than about restraint as a means to weather the recession.[46]

But what emerged as a more prominent theme in advice about not wasting money in the household, directed mainly at women, was that while money should be saved, it was not critical for or even central to living a rich life. Money began to be decoupled from material acquisition, and luxury came to be conceived in less material terms. In a special series about the household budget in the magazine *Fujin no tomo* (Woman's Companion), a section about the "simple life" (*shinpuru raifu*) illustrated through example how everyday life could be rich without money. A certain Tanaka Kumiko, a thirty-three-year-old wife and mother in the western city of Niigata, explained that her family did save money, but they were not stingy. By repairing tools, making things, fishing, and picking seaweed at the seashore, they made their daily life fun and full without needing or spending much money.[47] A similar message was conveyed in a book published in 1999 about the elimination of wasteful expenses. While the advice was framed as a way to cope with recession and included savings targets for the purchase of things like a car or a home, one of the four "laws" of saving money established in the book was that money was not everything when it came to saving money. That is, curbing wasteful expenditures could be valuable not just because it saved money but also because it could lead to a more healthy and ecologically responsible way of living and could make time more *yutori*. And the purpose of saving money was deemed to be a life that was rich, defined in nonfinancial and nonmaterial terms.[48] In other works as well, daily lives of waste elimination and monetary saving were held up as a path to *yutori*, a truly affluent lifestyle, and the realization of dreams.[49]

This emphasis on seeking a kind of emotional affluence, even in literature about monetary savings, persisted into the millennial years. In one variation, advice was offered about how to live richly on a small income or in a state of self-chosen relative poverty. The novelist and politician Yamasaki Hisato related in his book on an "affluent, economizing lifestyle" how he did only those things that enriched his heart. As an example, he described the enjoyment he found in making his own food, like the yogurt he typically ate for breakfast along with a banana at a total cost of 40 yen.[50] In another variation, it was the idea not just of affluence but also of "luxury" (*zeitaku*) that was redefined. Popular advice books explained how to live luxuriously without spending money, with quite a few turning to European countries like France for inspiration.[51] Deemphasizing the material was especially explicit in the book *Kechi jōzu* (Skillful Stinginess), in which the author, Ogasawara Yōko, focused on monetary savings but also suggested that the acquisition of things should not be the barometer of one's life. Readers were to think about what was really necessary and throw away stuff they did not need, for those with fewer material things enjoyed more psychological and spiritual luxury.[52]

Even more than the literature about people's relationship with money or things, the advice about time has been starkly gendered in the reasons and purposes given for waste consciousness. What has transcended the writing for women and men is the shared sense that there is not enough time in daily life. If the surge of interest in decluttering has been about coping with an overabundance of material things, suggestions about how to save time have been about scarcity. There have been exceptions, like the occasional case made for savoring "slow time."[53] But on the whole, to use an oft-evoked reference to Michael Ende's *Momo*, there has been a feeling that minutes and hours are being stolen by "time thieves." It is the consequences of this theft that have been framed differently for home and workplace, women and men.

Influenced in part by the specific and well-defined niches for publications, those geared more toward women and the household have repeatedly emphasized time for oneself to enrich one's life and have used the vocabulary of one's heart with regularity. An article in the magazine *Fujin no tomo* about simple living, for example, discussed the responses on a questionnaire given to mothers of small children. Asked whether they felt in their daily lives "a relaxed and leisurely heart" (*kokoro no yutori*), the women revealed how they tried to enjoy their time. Some commented that they made time for small pleasures, like chatting over tea with a friend, watching television intentionally, or planning a dinner menu. Some also spoke of relaxing by growing herbs on the veranda or taking a long bath or working out to an exercise video.[54] The idea that time should be used efficiently so as to create opportunities for enjoyment and self-fulfillment was expressed quite often, as by the "time designer" Arakawa Nami. In her book, Arakawa advised that eliminating time lost to wavering and hesitation would increase time for whatever one might find meaningful. Women were to use time effectively so as to have a chance to relax, experience fulfilling days, and lead happy and enriched lives.[55] For the women readers of such writings, the goal of efficiency was defined not just as being able to do everything that needed to get done, but also as having the time to nurture one's spirit as one wanted.

For women who worked outside the home, emphasis was placed on efficiency on the job so as to create time for enjoyment and self-enrichment off the job. This idea that fulfillment was to be found outside of working hours was a fundamental assumption of a volume on time management published in 2009 by the magazine *Nikkei woman*, whose target readership was working women in their twenties and thirties. The goal of minimizing wasted time at work, according to the publication, was to maximize "off time." A specific schema for accomplishing this end was laid out by the economics commentator and working mother Katsuma Kazuya, who delineated four types of time that needed to be managed properly. The one type that could make your life full, rich, and happy and thus should be increased was "investment time," which could be spent learning new things, being with family or a lover, or playing sports. The three other types were to be shortened as much as possible. "Working time" was to be used more effectively so that the same results could be produced more quickly. "Wasted time" delivered little return, so was to be transformed into investment time by studying during a long commute or working out at the gym instead of going out for drinks by force of habit or inertia. And "wasteful time," spent smoking or mindlessly watching television or drinking too much, was to be decreased. For Katsuma, the central reason for eliminating the waste of time was to realize a happier and more spiritually affluent life.[56] And this approach was in keeping with the publication's general theme of managing time skillfully and minimizing overtime to be able to do whatever one might want, like seeing a movie, meeting up with friends, going to a restaurant, taking a trip, or reading a book.[57]

Rare was the woman executive who wrote about time management, but Wada Hiromi took up the task and infused happiness into her writing about work. While the theme of self-enjoyment was characteristic of advice literature for women, Wada made the unconventional argument, unusual for any readership regardless of gender, that pleasure could be found in one's working life. In her book *Shiawase o tsukamu!* (Seizing Happiness!), which had the English subtitle *Time Management for Happiness*, Wada was unapologetic about how much she liked her work, even if that meant not having much of a private life. Taking a very different approach from that of most time management literature about the workplace, Wada did not recapitulate the principles of scientific management. She asserted instead that specific techniques were not as important for working efficiently as considerations of the heart and mind, such as being positive and having motivation and energy. For Wada, the wasting of time was marked not so much by particular unproductive activities as by a lack of intentionality and meaning in whatever one was doing. Stressing individual choice and will, she defined luxury as time to reflect, feel, or replenish one's reservoir of determination and grit.[58]

Parallel to the advice literature for women that foregrounded themes of pleasure, happiness, and self-fulfillment, comparable publications for men featured more conventional concerns with efficiency and productivity in the workplace.

There have been some notable millennial modifications, but the logics of scientific management and rationalization persist as a mainstay of working life and continue to be projected onto male workers with particular intensity. This should not be too surprising, given that the assumptions, drivers, and goals of the economic system have not fundamentally changed, and that efficiency, productivity, and mass consumption have therefore remained important principles. Saving money in the workplace, gendered male, is thus still fundamentally and centrally about corporate and government bottom lines.

In the push for businesses to save money in the late 1990s and early 2000s, there was much that was reminiscent of advice and campaigns from the 1970s.[59] Especially in a corporate world struggling with recession, restructuring, and rationalization, many spoke of adopting "stinginess strategies" (kechikechi sakusen) in order to survive. Common measures taken, according to a survey of 350 companies conducted in May 1998, included reducing entertainment expenses and cutting the costs of office supplies, phone use, communications, photocopying, and printing. Specific examples abounded. At Tokyo Gas (Tokyo Gasu), ballpoint pens were to be used until they ran out of ink. At a business machine manufacturer in Fukuoka city, prepaid cards were issued for office phones so their use could be monitored. At the cosmetics company Shiseidō, approval was to be obtained from a manager to make color copies or send something via express delivery. To reduce electricity bills, employees of the Odakyū department store were urged to save electricity and water and cut the running time of escalators. To save on water bills, the Kirin brewery collected rainwater in a tank for use in toilets.[60]

Such "stinginess strategies" were also instituted by prefectural and municipal governments that were falling into debt due in part to sluggish tax revenues. In Kanagawa prefecture, employees were to turn off lights during the afternoon lunch break, not serve tea at meetings, and choose double-sided photocopying. Some municipalities were trying to save on electricity bills or were selling off their expensive official cars.[61] Echoing the rationale for stinginess measures that had been expressed in the early 1970s, a representative of the management consulting firm JMA Consultants (Nihon Nōritsu Kyōkai Konsaruchingu) explained that while the financial savings might be small, the purpose was to change employees' consciousness. The implication was that at this moment, the definition of waste had become lax and awareness of wastefulness needed to be instilled.[62]

Not wasting was also an imperative in the abundant literature about time management aimed at a readership of businesspeople. In these publications, the predominant theme was that wasted time had to be eliminated for efficiency, productivity, and financial gain—be it for one's firm or, increasingly, for oneself. This message, with its focus on career success and scant concern with self-fulfillment, was aimed more at working men than working women. The authors and advice givers were more frequently men than women, the photographs and illustrations more frequently of men than women, and the language of "businessman" more common than the more gender-neutral "businessperson." The audience for such publications could certainly include working women, but these female readers could also turn to the body of writing intended for women, housewives or not, about how to pursue enjoyment and enrichment in their daily lives. Such a genre of advice literature has not really existed for men, particularly of the sort that addresses how to not waste, and how to savor, time spent at home or in the household.

In advice for businesspeople about saving time, the well-worn values of efficiency, productivity, and profit were paramount, but translated into terms more befitting an individual worker than a corporation as a whole. As put plainly in the business magazine *Senken keizai* (Economic Foresight), the highest priority for both individuals and firms in a capitalist society was raising productivity by eliminating wasted time. Businessmen thus should, among other things, keep their desks clean, put their written documents in order, and use a planner to organize their time.[63] Similarly, the Japanese version of the Personal Efficiency Program (PEP), originally created by the American productivity guru Kerry Gleeson, established time management "rules" for increasing efficiency and productivity which included doing the same kind of work all at once and deciding on a time to deal with all of your e-mail.[64]

In the millennial years, when there has been a seeming upsurge in advice geared less toward managers and more toward a typical office worker, greater attention has been given to curtailing waste for the sake of one's own work performance, effectiveness as an employee, financial success, and career advancement. A salesman might have picked up a book like *Saikyō no jikan kanrijutsu* (The Best Time Management Techniques) with the clear goal of becoming a top seller. And he would have learned to do such things as arrive early for meetings and schedule appointments in a way that minimized time spent in transit.[65] Readers might also have financial ambitions, expressed as a desired salary. Playing to this objective, an article from 2008 in the business magazine *Purejidento* (President), which regularly took up the topic of time management, contrasted how people with an annual salary of 6 million yen (about $56,000) and of 20 million yen (about $187,000) thought about and used their time. It was determined that those in the higher income group lived the aphorism "time is money" by, for example, making more effective use of unexpected, unscheduled gaps of time. With an extra minute, those with the higher income were more likely than the lower earners to confirm their schedules and less likely to do nothing or take a break. With an extra five minutes, they were more likely to come up with ideas and, again, less likely to do nothing or take a break.[66] In addition to a higher salary, position and stature could be sought as well. Tapping into such aspirations, publications often asked company executives and presidents to provide their secrets to time management success.[67]

This genre of advice literature for businesspeople, in the vein of *The 7 Habits of Highly Effective People*, has been perpetuated by management consultants, personnel trainers, and executive coaches; fueled by business publishers; and voraciously consumed by readers. Reflecting the circumstances of their production and consumption, there has been relatively little attention in these publications to life outside of work. In one piece in *Purejidento*, Yamada Hitoshi, the president of the PEC Industrial Education Center (PEC Sangyō Kyōiku Sentā) and the author of books such as *Muda tori* (Waste Elimination), was primarily concerned with adapting the Toyota Production System to the office setting. He outlined a multistep process that involved setting clear goals, prioritizing, and analyzing the extent to which the plan had been executed. Mention was made of how any extra time could be spent drinking with colleagues or leaving work earlier than expected, but this "relaxation and leisure" (placed in scare quotes in the original text) was an afterthought tacked onto the article in its last paragraph.[68]

There have been some voices, however faint, that have emphasized the need for (male) workers to experience greater *yutori*. In 1995 the author Nomura Masaki published a book with the subtitle *"Jibun jikan" o yutaka ni suru 101 no hinto* (101 Hints for Making Your "Own Time" Rich), which went through three printings that year. Nomura suggested that time could be viewed not just as an outlay for the purpose of generating profits but also as an asset to make people's lifestyles and lives richer. What the reader was to accept was the book's theme of thinking about time in terms of "to be" (how one should live) rather than "to do" (what one should do). And this would enable businessmen to enjoy *yutori*.[69]

In recent years, and especially since the global financial crisis of 2008, there has been a greater sense of treating workers more as whole people than as mere employees. The words "work-life balance" can be heard, and not just in conversations by and about working women.[70] And even a human resource development consultant like Matsumoto Yukio could question why he had spent a career training people how to be efficient, shorten their work hours, and avoid overtime. In his 2009 book, one of more than one hundred that he has authored, Matsumoto shared his realization that he had been preaching the virtues of efficiency with such devotion that efficiency itself had become the goal. He, and his readers and trainees, had lost sight of why they were trying to become more efficient. Rather than filling the time created by his strategies with more work, he now advocated enjoying life—pursuing simple things, like spending time with people you love. Reworking the oft-repeated tenet that "time is money," Matsumoto argued that "time is life" and that life should be lived with will and intention. While the suggested time strategies themselves were very familiar, the focus on one's life as a whole as opposed to competitiveness, money, or efficiency for its own sake shifted the rationale for eliminating waste.[71] Advice like Matsumoto's notwithstanding, these more holistic strains in publications for businesspeople have not yet come close to being the norm in a genre dominated by the logics of scientific management and rationalization.

What has become starkly apparent in the larger body of advice literature about saving money and saving time are the distinct threads in waste consciousness, amplified by the gendered differences in the purposes of minimizing waste and how they map onto different realms of daily life. While both women and men were to think about self-satisfaction, women much more than men were encouraged to look beyond the material and to seek happiness, especially in the home. And men much more than women became the repositories of earlier logics of scientific management and rationalization, especially in the workplace. These gendered conceptions of waste were a change, realized over decades, from the earlier postwar years when rationalizing and eliminating waste in both the workplace and the home were seen as going hand in hand as part of a shared project of economic growth and betterment. In millennial Japan, what was to be sought differed by gender, with women encouraged more than men to pursue an affluence of the heart.

Keep Calm and Carry On

As people were engrossed in their daily routines and attempted to find meaning in the things and time of their day-to-day lives, the sudden and unexpected tumult of 3.11 was profoundly jarring. Roughly twenty thousand people lost their lives or were missing, and well over half a million residents were displaced in the immediate aftermath of the earthquake and tsunami. Even for those outside of the Tōhoku region, whose homes and livelihoods had not been swept away, the everyday had been upset. Just after the 9.0-magnitude earthquake, workers in Tokyo now without access to the sprawling transportation system walked for hours to return to their homes. In subsequent days and weeks, the vocabulary of "cesium" and "millisieverts" entered the mainstream lexicon as concern spread about irradiated soil and food. And a general sense of fragility seemed to persist in the years that followed.

For all of its destructive and disruptive power, 3.11 has not yet provoked substantial and fundamental shifts in thinking about waste. The triple disaster was quickly recognized as a crisis, with an immediacy not unlike the Oil Shock of the early 1970s. In a rough parallel to that time, the country faced an energy supply problem as nuclear reactors were taken offline, which promptly spurred calls to save electricity. When urging limits to electricity use in 2011, Tokyo governor Ishihara Shintarō made explicit reference to similar measures from 1973.[72] Yet at this writing there have not been the kinds of deep and far-reaching changes in conceptions of waste that characterized the early 1970s. Rather, the events and aftermath of 3.11 have given momentum to the diverse and disparate ways of conceiving of waste and wastefulness that already existed in millennial Japan. What has persisted is the overarching pursuit of an affluence of the heart as well as the different strands in waste consciousness that have taken shape over the past several decades—the *mottainai* movement; decluttering, minimalism, and an ambivalence about the material; and the bright stinginess of both conserving energy and consuming lifestyles of convenience and comfort.

The Mottainai Campaign, launched in 2005, remains vibrant. It continues to sell campaign books, disseminate literature, and organize activities and events, like its Mottainai Flea Markets. One such flea market was held in Miyagi prefecture, in the central Tōhoku area, to support reconstruction from 3.11. At the event in late November 2014, about seven thousand attendees including four hundred or so children came to donate and buy used toys, clothes, stationery, and more. The modest proceeds from the fair games, like ring toss and golf putting, were given to the Disaster Countermeasures Headquarters (Saigai Taisaiku Honbu) in the Miyagi city of Natori. And money made from selling old clothes at all of the campaign's flea markets was donated to this group.[73]

Even as the campaign has loosely associated itself with relief efforts in Tōhoku, the very concept of *mottainai* continues to enjoy broad recognition and resonance. That the decluttering advocates have found it necessary to explain their own philosophies and methods vis-à-vis *mottainai* suggests the idea's prominence. The word has also continued to pop up in local garbage reduction and recycling initiatives, as in Kawasaki city, where the R-shaped mascot, designed to symbolize the 3Rs and newly created to promote the inauguration of separate collection of plastic containers, has as its favorite phrase *mottainai*.[74] And echoes of constituent ideas of *mottainai*, from its nostalgia for the premodern period to its valuing of things and resources, can be heard in everything from the Mitsui real estate corporation's idea of an "Eco Edo" to the post-3.11 calls for saving energy.[75]

Parallel to and in tension with the promotion of *mottainai*, the disaster has been evoked to legitimize a decentering of the material. The popularity of declutterers and the emergence of minimalists coincided with 3.11 and its aftermath, which some of the advocates explicitly addressed. Yamashita Hideko's book on *danshari* for the workplace was in its final stages of production in March 2011, and she did wonder about forging ahead with its release when there were people who had lost so much. She ultimately decided that its publication was especially important at that moment, because she was discussing and encouraging the brightening of "one's societal life." Thinking of work not as labor but as an act that supports life and as an integral part of societal life, she maintained that practicing *danshari* in this context was about improving how one existed and lived in society.[76] Yamashita's focus was still on the emotional well-being of the self, but with some acknowledgment that the individual is not disconnected from societal structures and communities. While Yamashita treated 3.11 as a mere backdrop for her advice, Sasaki Fumio argued that the Great Disaster of Eastern Japan was one of the necessary conditions for the birth of minimalism. It influenced values and changed decisively how things were thought about, he asserted, for in the earthquake, things that had been treasured became deadly weapons, and in the tsunami, precious things were washed away and destroyed.[77] Expressing a more general and not unusual sentiment, the interior architect and waste elimination advocate Katō Emiko observed that even more than after the financial crisis of 2008, people were seeking new ways of living and redefining affluence and happiness.[78]

If a search for meaning and contentment was reinforced by 3.11, with its perpetuation of both *mottainai* and a reconsideration of things, it also sustained an equation of a good life with comfort that could be traced back to the desire for *yutori* in the 1980s or even further back to the idea of a bright stinginess in the 1970s. This theme was noticeable in the responses to electricity-saving measures enacted for the mitigation of the energy crisis. In the wake of the meltdown at the Fukushima Daiichi nuclear power plant, these reactors were rendered permanently inoperable and well over half of the country's other nuclear reactors were taken offline for inspection before the summer, as people braced for a sweltering season of rolling blackouts amidst a severe electricity shortage.[79] Newspapers, television and radio stations, and websites began to provide information about levels of electricity use in what were called "electricity forecasts" (*denki yohō*, something of a wordplay on "weather forecasts," or *tenki yohō*); and smartphone apps were developed to send notifications when an electricity outage was likely.[80] To alleviate as much strain as possible on an overburdened system, the national government urged households to reduce their electricity consumption by 15 to 20 percent between 10:00 am and 9:00 pm by refraining from using microwaves and dryers during those hours, raising the temperature settings on air conditioners and reducing their use, and shortening time spent watching television. Companies were to do their part as well, with the Tōkyū department store in the Shibuya area of Tokyo turning off lights and curtailing elevator use, Family Mart and Circle K Sunkus lowering lights and adjusting temperatures in their convenience stores, beverage makers reducing the lighting of their vending machines, Narita Airport dimming lights, and the East Japan Railway Company (JR Higashi Nihon) reducing service by 20 percent, cutting the cooling of train cars, and shutting down escalators in large stations.[81]

In the abundant advice about how to save electricity (*setsuden*), there was an enduring insistence that not wasting electricity was not to compromise happiness or comfort. In the summer of 2011, the national broadcaster NHK aired television programming and published a guide on how to cut back on the wasteful consumption of electricity. To help viewers and readers prevent prolonged outages, NHK offered specific advice, such as minimize electricity consumption at times of peak demand; find non-electric alternatives for household tasks, like using the gas fish grill to make toast; buy energy-saving home appliances; choose LED lightbulbs; do not leave the refrigerator door open; turn off switches when not needed; clean the air conditioner filter; and put up curtains and blinds to block sunlight. These strategies, it was made clear, were not about refraining from using electricity but about efficiency, not about self-denial but about saving power without experiencing difficulty. The argument was that electricity saving could be skillfully adapted to daily life and was perfectly compatible with the lifestyles that people assumed and expected.[82]

A similar note was struck by much of the advice given about how to save electricity in the household. The Smart Life Research Group (Sumāto Raifu Kenkyūkai), an organization of housewives who sought a simple, ecologically responsible, and healthful lifestyle, published a book in July 2011 insisting that the kind of saving they were advocating was not about going without or even just about saving money. Real saving meant spending money on the truly important things that enriched one's life, and was to be enjoyed. When it came to saving electricity, the subject of the book's first chapter, suggested techniques included using a toilet seat cover rather than the electric toilet seat heater; setting the washing machine to a shorter cycle; and swapping out the vacuum cleaner for a broom and dustpan when possible.[83] These strategies and others were repeated so often in advice literature that they became a kind of canon for electricity saving often framed, as they also were in the magazine *Kurashi no techō* (Notebook of Everyday Life), as an elimination of waste that was not unbearable or immoderate.[84]

One particular subgenre of energy-saving literature was about how to continue cooking delicious meals without using much electricity or gas. This was a variation on recipes suggested in the mid- to late 1990s and early 2000s about how to cook meals that saved money, wasted little, and minimized garbage.[85] In the post-3.11 literature, recipes were accompanied by some oft-repeated principles for saving energy: use canned foods that do not need to be cooked or ingredients that can be eaten raw; take full advantage of residual heat for carryover cooking; be skillful with the microwave; and more.[86] By using such techniques, suggested the cooking expert Ishizawa Kiyomi, dishes like shrimp pasta gratin or a Japanese meat and potato stew could be made with minimal energy. This was not about monetary saving, she explained, but about cutting down on the excessive use of energy in the home.[87]

On occasion, there was acknowledgment that an electricity-saving lifestyle might cause some inconvenience. The environmental writer and marketing planner Minowa Yayoi pointed out that there were costs to the convenience of creating cool air or moving the toilet lid with the flick of an electrical switch. But she also insisted that people could live comfortably by using a small amount of energy efficiently, that affluence need not be synonymous with the mass consumption of energy. While Minowa seemed to be suggesting that saving energy might entail meaningful changes to one's lifestyle, she ultimately used the language and reinforced the value of comfort. And her specific recommendations, from not overstuffing the refrigerator to cleaning the filters of electric appliances, were very much in line with the canonic advice about saving electricity.[88]

Being conscious about the waste of electricity was thus not to mean discomfort, nor was it to require curtailing the enjoyment of material consumption. On the contrary, for manufacturers and retailers, the electricity shortage, consciousness of saving electricity, and summer heat created an opportunity to develop and sell new products. Nissin realized that putting ice in its conventionally hot Cup Noodle was tastier than expected, a discovery that culminated in the introduction of its cold product Cup Noodle Light. In May and June 2011, sales of the Cup Noodle series were up two and a half times over the previous year. Asahi Beer launched its extra-cold BAR concept in four major cities, and retailer Aeon marketed its light cotton kimono as bringing fun and happiness to the summer.[89] There was also a mentholated spray for clothes, designed to do away with the unpleasantness of sweaty train commutes to work or school.[90]

Consumption also continued to be stimulated by the government's Cool Biz and Warm Biz campaigns. The exigencies of the summer of 2011 reinvigorated Cool Biz, begun in 2005 and ramped up in this year to Super Cool Biz. Starting on June 1, the list of acceptable office wear was expanded to include polo shirts, Hawaiian shirts, plain T-shirts, jeans, sneakers, and sandals. (Shorts, running pants, torn jeans, and beach sandals were still prohibited.)[91] Exemplifying the importance of consumption to the campaign, Super Cool Biz held its kickoff event at the Mitsukoshi department store in Nihonbashi with four generations of environmental ministers in attendance and male news broadcasters serving as models for casual business clothing.[92] In late 2011, earnings of the country's four leading department stores were up, with Warm Biz–related items selling well.[93] And in 2012, sales of Super Cool Biz styles and goods increased from the previous year, with electricity-saving consumption estimated at over 1.9 trillion yen.[94] New products were also rolled out for women, whether clothes like skirts and knits that could be hand-washed at home rather than dry-cleaned, bras and underwear made out of "touch cool" material, or body mist and facial lotion with a refreshing hint of baby mint.[95] By 2013, the "super" was sometimes dropped from the campaign's moniker, but the promotion of consuming the most recent fashions continued. That summer, the American classic look, preppy styles, blue, pink, stripes, and gingham check were in, as were, for women, "cool impression" hairstyles and makeup that could withstand sweat. Accessories included a cover for ice packs that could be worn around the neck.[96] In the winter of 2015, expensive cashmere-silk underwear was offered as part of Warm Biz at the Takashimaya department store, and the casual wear company Uniqlo had expanded its Heattech line to 320 products.[97] As of the summer of 2016, these government campaigns to save electricity, complete with their encouragement of material consumption, remained established annual rituals.[98]

In firms, the endurance of Cool Biz and Warm Biz reflects the perpetuation of energy-saving measures that began before March 2011 and were sustained as cost-cutting measures. In a June 2008 survey of 10,396 firms of all sizes, over three-quarters (77.9 percent) had already noted that they were making efforts with regard to environmental issues, and about 68 percent of respondents reported that they were taking energy-saving measures, such as cutting back on the use of electricity, in order to reduce costs.[99] The electricity shortages post-3.11 may have added urgency to such efforts and encouraged their diffusion. As short-term responses, some manufacturers shifted their hours of operation to non-peak hours and instituted wholesale vacations to shut down production for a period. And there was also greater pressure to cut overtime work.[100] But for the most part, electricity-saving measures have changed little if at all in substance and purpose, and firms seem to have generally continued practices begun previously. In a nationwide survey of fifty-two corporations of various sizes conducted in June 2011, a full 92.4 percent reported that they had instituted Cool Biz several years earlier; only 3.8 percent started the practice in the aftermath of 3.11. It seems likely that the high percentage (88.5 percent) of firms saving electricity through attention to the use of lighting also predated the post-3.11 shortages.[101]

Although there has not been a fundamental shift in values since 3.11, there is some evidence that consumption of electricity has declined since 2011. There had been an inconsistent downward trend in household energy consumption since 2000; after 2011, there was a clear drop. In the non-manufacturing sector, with the exception of 2014, there has been a decrease in energy consumption since around 2005.[102]

In addition, rare voices did urge or presage some kind of wholesale change in the wake of 3.11. There were errant comments from one conservative political figure or another about leveraging this moment to do away with greed or excessive materialism.[103] In this vein, the businessperson and writer Tsujii Takashi (or Tsutsumi Seiji) declared that the nuclear disaster had put an end to the mass-consuming civilization. The idea of "consumption is a virtue" was becoming a dangerous ideology, and what was necessary was an affluence of the heart and revaluation of tradition, said Tsujii, in a statement that was not just anachronistic in its reference to a phrase not much used since the 1960s but also hypocritical. After all, Tsujii was the director of the Saison Foundation (Sezon Bunka Zaidan) and former president of Seibu department stores (Seibu Hyakkaten), one of the corporate mainstays of consumerism.[104] Like Tsujii, the professor emeritus and author Suzuki Takao was optimistic that 3.11 would force people to reconsider mass consumption, not just of goods but also of electricity and other resources. He was unusual in suggesting that Japanese society needed to come to terms with a certain degree of trouble and inconvenience. There would be nothing more wonderful, Suzuki opined in his book *Shiawase setsuden* (Happy Electricity Saving), than Japan becoming a country that did not waste water, gas, or electricity.[105]

Yet such calls for change were few and far between, and the pragmatic responses to the electricity shortage after 3.11 do not seem to have evolved into a probing examination of various manifestations of waste in daily lives of convenience, comfort, and consumption. In one nationwide survey of one thousand people, responses suggested that electricity saving caused some undesirable strain. About 39.8 percent of respondents in 2011 and 32.5 percent in 2013 said that they felt stress because of their efforts to save electricity. In 2011, the cause of the stress most often cited (by 65.3 percent of respondents) was not being able to live comfortably; in 2013, that reason was the second-most commonly chosen (by 48.5 percent of respondents).[106] What seems to be reflected in these numbers is an ambivalence about not wasting energy shaped by competing forces: an understanding of the exigencies of electricity shortages and a desire for convenient and comfortable lifestyles.

The Dissonant Decades

In the aftermath of 3.11, as in all of the millennial years, the diversification of waste consciousness—with enduring strands as well as new developments in thinking about discarding, saving, and wasting—has been emblematic of a historical time marked by dissonances. The country remains financially affluent by many economic measures, but was unsettled by the recession of the late 1990s, to a lesser extent by the Lehman shock in 2008, and 3.11. The logics of industrial production endure in the white-collar offices of the postindustrial economy. Everyday life seems to be characterized by both overabundance and scarcity, to have both too much and not enough. It is not surprising, then, that assumptions about and desires for middle-class lifestyles afforded by financial affluence have persisted—the values of productivity, efficiency, consumption, and comfort. And that, at the very same time, the longing for an affluence of the heart, variously conceived, has grown.

Different conceptions of an "affluence of the heart" themselves illustrate the incongruities of contemporary Japan. When ideas about psychological, emotional, and spiritual well-being gained traction in the 1980s, they envisioned a good life and *yutori* that usually presumed, not criticized, material affluence. A supposed turn away from the material was largely rhetorical, as true affluence was seen as a supplement to, rather than a replacement for, financial and material plenty.[107] Then in the 1990s, and particularly in the 2000s, affluence of the heart took on divergent meanings: an environmental consciousness that valued things and spurned garbage as encapsulated in the concept of *mottainai*, and the pursuit of a self-fulfillment ambivalent about the material and unconcerned with physical waste, as articulated by declutterers and minimalists.

The recent popularity of decluttering, minimalism, and the theme of looking beyond money and things both reflect the dissonances of contemporary Japan and suggest ways in which people are attempting to work through them. And they may be a sign, among others, of a modest challenge both to the ubiquity of material acquisition and to the inhibition of material discard. There does seem to be a recent ebb in anxieties about material waste, especially in comparison to the 1970s and 1980s. While an overwhelming percentage of people say that the "garbage problem" is important when confronted about it directly, if asked more generally about concern for environmental problems, survey respondents have expressed much greater interest in global warming than in issues related to garbage.[108] This demonstrates how prominent an issue climate change has become, but also the extent to which the problem of proliferating rubbish has become less acute. In the years when the new generation of literature on decluttering and minimalism has enjoyed such popularity, per capita municipal solid waste disposal has steadily dropped.[109] And the shortage of landfill space has become somewhat less acute as new purposes, like the making of cement, have been found for the sludge ash created by the incineration process.[110] With recycling procedures and processes of various kinds firmly in place, there is no sense of crisis about the materiality of rubbish. It may be that the tremendous amount of radioactive waste produced by the Fukushima nuclear disaster in such forms as contaminated water, debris, and millions of bags of irradiated topsoil will assert themselves as a concern in daily life if temporary storage solutions fail and more long-term methods of disposal prove elusive. But as of now, neither garbage nor radioactive waste has thrust the material to the forefront of waste consciousness.

Along with different attitudes toward the material in a fundamentally materialist society, other tensions have assumed convoluted shape in the millennial years. At the same time that daily lives feel uncertain in an economically fragile Japan, the questions of self-fulfillment that they raise rest on a foundation of some privilege. To throw excess things away and to decide to live with fewer things is to be in a position of considerable security. Especially for young people, the minimalists in their twenties and thirties, for example, this may be in small part a privilege of age. They can choose, without imposing on others, to live without many things. A stark contrast that illustrates the relevance of age is another emergent phenomenon, one of elderly people who have been literally overwhelmed by things and garbage in their homes. They are described as living in *gomi yashiki*, or trash homes, a catchall term for the residences of everyone from the chronically messy to those with psychological conditions that manifest themselves in hoarding. Still inadequately studied and understood, the purported increase in *gomi yashiki* in recent years has been connected with the plight of the elderly who are unable to manage their garbage for reasons ranging from complicated trash separation systems to physical disabilities and dementia. Increasingly surrounded by stuff they cannot discard, these elderly people have sometimes been described unsympathetically as troublesome and sometimes sympathetically as prone to not receiving help, becoming isolated, neglecting themselves, and dying alone.[111]

Much more than age, the decentering of the material reflects the privilege of the very financial affluence under reconsideration. As has been pointed out by critics of the KonMari method in the United States, where decluttering along with related trends like the tiny house movement are currently enjoying popularity, there is a class dimension to having the choice to throw things away, to owning so much stuff that help is needed to discard it.[112] Echoes of this privilege can be heard in the popular book by the writer and literary critic Nakano Kōji who, not unlike the author of *Dai Tokyo binbō seikatsu manyuaru* (Manual for Poor Living in Greater Tokyo) from the 1980s, romanticized lives of "honorable poverty" in which choices could be made to be waste conscious in the extreme.[113] The various struggles with the abundance of things and the acutely felt scarcity of time assume as their base a way of life characteristic of an advanced, post-industrial, and wealthy country.

The search for values and meaning in twenty-first-century Japan has been informed by a particular coexistence of wealth and insecurity, comfort and anxiety, excess and insufficiency. What has taken shape are different ways of thinking about the importance of material things, the environment, the self, the present, and the future, as conceptions of waste and wastefulness have expanded and diversified. However these various ideas develop in the years to come, what has endured and become more acute in the recent period of frail affluence is the desire for a happiness, an affluence of the heart, that has seemed as yet elusive.

WASTE AND WELL-BEING

The fate of the tangerine peel, of the bitter rind left over after the fleshy fruit has been consumed, may seem like mere triviality in daily life and in history. We might not expect something so commonplace and so expendable to be worthy of much attention. But in the fall of 1945, what was done with a tangerine peel, corncob, or radish top was not a trifling matter. To toss out such things was to throw away a source of nutrients at a time when malnutrition imperiled health and even subsistence. These desperate exigencies abated and the logics for not wasting changed as the country ventured further into the postwar. A few decades after war's end, by the mid-1970s, eating all parts of a fruit or vegetable was advised as a strategy not to survive scarcity but to mitigate the costs and anxieties born of excess. Exhortations to value food and to value things sought to promote conservation of the finite resources that had fueled rapid economic growth and reduction of the garbage produced by a society of consumers. Frying, sautéing, or pickling these less desirable parts could help defend middle-class lifestyles, and in an enjoyable way that was virtually stripped of any stench of wartime poverty and any tinge of hardship or sacrifice. By the early 2000s, the use of dried tangerine peels as an aromatic in bathwater was often suggested for relaxation and rejuvenation. They could be cut and carved to make cute art. And recipes were divorced from caloric need, presented instead as a way to practice the virtue of using things fully. When No-Waste Grandma tweeted about making soup from corncobs, she simply deemed it wasteful to throw them away and described how a superb dish could be created from the umami-rich cores.[1] What had once been considered a necessity was transformed into an amenity in lifestyles of plenty.

Through the banality of the everyday, through the prescriptions about what to do with something as unremarkable as a tangerine peel, we can see how waste was implicated in shifting values and attitudes, and we can appreciate the extraordinary arc of life in postwar Japan as it assumed a place among the wealthy and consumptive countries of the modern world.

Over the course of this long postwar, the meanings of waste were reconfigured and rearticulated as people made sense of their contemporary lives. Waste could be variously understood as backward and retrogressive, an impediment to progress, a pervasive outgrowth of mass consumption, incontrovertible proof of societal excess, the embodiment of resources squandered, a hazard to the environment, and more. And waste consciousness could be variously encouraged as a civilizing and modernizing imperative, a moral good, an instrument for advancement, a path to self-satisfaction, an environmental commitment, an expression of identity, and more. There was nothing fixed or simple about ideas of wastefulness, no such thing as a singular and enduring Japanese waste consciousness. On the contrary, conceptions of waste were as dynamic and contradictory as the postwar world that fashioned them and to which they in turn gave shape.

Ubiquitous and multivalent, waste was constitutive of daily life in postwar Japan. Waste as a phenomenon was embedded in the practices, structures, norms, and relationships of the everyday, be it in the home or in the workplace. In its material form as rubbish, waste was a physical reminder of the dialectical relationship between consuming and discarding, of the impossibility of acquiring goods without disposing of them. Everything from pests feasting on piles of trash to household sorting of refuse by category insinuated themselves into the regular rhythms of daily life. More expansively, waste as an idea and as a subjective judgment created meaning and constructed the values and priorities of everyday life. To merely define something as a waste or as wasteful was to inscribe it with worthlessness. And calls to be conscious of, minimize, or eliminate waste were issued in the name of purposes presumed worthwhile. To urge the reduction of waste on the assembly line was to further productivity and profit; to offer advice on saving time with housework was to embrace relaxation; and to criticize frequent drives in the family car was to encourage environmental preservation. Most fundamentally, discussions ostensibly about waste were negotiations about how life should be lived.

The meanings created and the decisions made about waste were part of an economic story, of the security in achieving financial and material prosperity as well as the insecurity of weathering many ups and downs. But they were also inseparable from other central aspects of life in postwar Japan. What one was to do with one's time, money, and stuff could be different for women than for men, informed by gendered expectations. From the late 1940s into the early 1960s, a close parallel was drawn between the housewife as responsible for the home and the husband as responsible for the workplace. Both were to apply strategies of efficiency and rationalization in pursuit of economic recovery and growth. But a gap began to open up between waste management roles as men came to be associated more with production and women more with consumption. As consumption became ever more prominent in daily life, women were to take the reins of consuming and of discarding consumption's detritus. In the 1970s, men were to reduce waste in the workplace for the conventional purpose of maximizing financial profit, while women were to promote environmental conservation, make household frugality fun and bright, and model the moral virtue of minimizing waste. This more expansive conception of waste consciousness stuck to women in a way that it never did to men, as advice in the millennial years about everything from decluttering to enjoying free time was geared primarily toward women. Even as productivity and financial success continued to be the main goals for waste consciousness practiced by men, it was women who were encouraged to think more about an affluence of the heart.

Environmentalism also figured into waste consciousness in different ways at different times. In the 1970s, environmental concerns such as pollution and resource conservation were framed in rather anthropocentric terms, and were driven by the aims of ensuring basic health and assuring continued economic growth. It was in the late 1980s and 1990s that an environmental consciousness took firmer hold and environmental protection became more of an end in itself. Saving resources and energy, while certainly not without its financial benefits, was less about defending middle-class lifestyles as it had been in the 1970s and more about embracing a value in its own right. Though often vague and abstract in conception, caring for the earth became something that one was to simply do or profess, at least in principle.

Decidedly central to the history of waste, particularly since the 1960s, has been the pervasiveness of consumption. Even as their precise contours have changed over the years, the inescapability of marketing and advertising, the firm desire for the purchase of convenience and comfort, and the almost unwavering equation of the ability to buy with the achievement of a better life have been abiding features of middle-class lifestyles. Waste conscious practices from buying wisely to recycling and reusing were never to cause much inconvenience or fundamentally compromise consumption. The assumed identity of people, particularly women, as consumers was so hegemonic that even campaigns about waste consciousness encouraged consumption, be it by selling lunch boxes with the word *mottainai* printed on them or creating a demand for Cool Biz clothes. The Mottainai Campaign has turned waste consciousness, and Kondō Marie has turned decluttering, into products to be branded, marketed, advertised, and consumed.[2]

Residing at the nexus of these defining elements of the country's postwar experience, ideas about waste have been uniquely able to reflect and express a vital through line of this past: the enduring search for what might be called well-being, a good life, or a life well lived. This was a quintessentially middle-class pursuit that emerged in its postwar incarnation during the late 1950s, contemporaneous with economic growth and mass consumption. In the many decades since, the ways in which people responded to the questions of why, how, and even whether to be conscious of waste revealed much about their hopes and aspirations, frustrations, and disappointments. Once the basics of food and shelter had been secured, there could be a shift, uneasy at first, toward considering what more there might be. Consumption was one answer, especially the consumption of specific markers of a middle-class life, be it a particular good or form of leisure. As wallets were cracked open, one could begin to imagine liberation from the anxieties of wasting. But it turned out that consumption alone did not a good life make, as the desire for material things, convenience, and comfort proved to be, if not exactly insatiable, then persistent. A better life thus came to be conceived as one not just of more or improved things but also of more or improved time, which was to be the source of pleasure, relaxation, or well-being however defined. And during the most consumptive of times, there developed a yearning for a more spiritual, emotional, and psychological sense of well-being—an affluence measured not in yen but by the edification of the heart, mind, and spirit. Figuring out what might make for an affluent heart has become more individualized and the possibilities have diversified as people have grown increasingly mindful of what brings meaning to their daily lives. Throughout the entirety of this period, as the normative expectations and definitions of the good life have evolved, there has been an enduring struggle to understand and to deal with the insufficiencies of financial and material prosperity. Some, perhaps many, have realized over these years that economic growth and affluence have not brought all that had been envisioned—not an abundance of time to do with as one pleases, nor an abiding sense of self-fulfillment, contentedness, or happiness.

None of this is specific to postwar Japan. Neither the inextricability of waste and everyday life nor the elusiveness of an affluent heart has been a uniquely Japanese affliction. They are, after all, products not so much of postwar Japan but of its condition as an industrialized country of relative wealth, mass consumption, and material abundance. It would be too vague to describe this state more broadly as modern, because modernity has not necessarily been synonymous with pervasive consumerism and impressive wealth. And it would be too narrow to label it capitalist, because the phenomena that have left the heaviest imprints on waste—industrialization, development, mass production, and mass consumption—have taken particular forms and have perhaps been intensified in a capitalist society but are not unique to capitalism.[3] In the Japanese case, most people who concerned themselves with waste in the postwar did not speak of their situation as modern or capitalist but rather as shaped by prosperity, the proliferation of things, and the inescapability of consumption. Defined in these terms, this condition might be seen as one of a global first world, so for any country that is part of its ranks, a historical examination of waste could say much about its changing values and priorities—about attitudes toward consumption, views on the relationship between economic growth and the environment, meanings of work and leisure, gender and class dimensions of societal expectations, and conceptions of the good life. It also does not take much more than a glance at our current moment to recognize that this condition is not sequestered in the past. In Japan's unending postwar, the historical world that we have been exploring is also that of the present day, and not just in Japan but also in the United States and beyond. To see waste is thus to understand the hopes, expectations, disappointments, and contradictions of a condition both historical and contemporary.

On Happiness

To hear the envious speak of it, the Kingdom of Bhutan—a country about half the size of Indiana with a population about one-eighteenth that of Tokyo—is close to paradise on earth. Japanese newspapers have described its neighborly and communal spirit, embrace of peace, free medical care and education, and absence of homeless people in the streets.[4] Japanese researchers and tourists have traveled to Bhutan to learn and understand its secrets.[5] American media have spoken admiringly of its fresh air, absence of extreme poverty and crime, lack of overdevelopment, slow pace of life, abstinence from fast food, forest preservation, and educational curriculum that includes meditation and challenges consumerism and materialism.[6] *The Guardian* echoed many of these observations and added that a national waste management project requires everything material used in schools to be recycled. Never mind the drug use, unemployment, recent rise in violent crime, shortage of medical professionals, or history of political repression.[7] Never mind that the country's per capita gross national product was $160 in 1989, at a time when Japan's figure was 120 times larger; that in 2005, per capita salary was one-fiftieth that of Japan; that in 2015, GNP per capita at purchasing power parity was over four and a half times greater in Japan and over six and a half times greater in the United States than in Bhutan.[8] In fact, that is precisely the point for those who minimize the country's problems: that despite Bhutan being one of the poorest countries in the world, its people are reportedly happy.

The concept of "gross national happiness" (GNH) was conceived by the king of Bhutan in 1972 as a preferred alternative to GNP, signaling the prioritization of well-being over material production and financial growth. Its "four pillars" of good governance, sustainable socioeconomic development, preservation and promotion of culture, and environmental conservation became the foundation for a detailed index of happiness, and the very idea of GNH has been credited with attracting political and academic attention to a more holistic definition of well-being.[9] In July 2011 the United Nations adopted a resolution that declared the pursuit of happiness a "fundamental human goal" and acknowledged that "the gross domestic product indicator by nature was not designed to and does not adequately reflect the happiness and well-being of people in a country."[10] In April 2012, at UN headquarters in New York City, the government of Bhutan convened with eight hundred participants the High-Level Meeting on Wellbeing and Happiness: Defining a New Economic Paradigm.[11] And the UN Sustainable Development Solutions Network developed its own survey of well-being with results published annually in "world happiness reports."[12] Along with GNH and the world happiness survey, there has been a surge of scholarly studies by economists, psychologists, sociologists, and others about happiness, well-being, and life satisfaction.[13]

The appeal of GNH in Japan is but one expression of an ambivalence that has colored, in various ways and to various extents, feelings about and experiences with affluence for much of the postwar period. As the country emerged from the poverty of the immediate postwar years and the government set its sights on economic development, there was some uneasiness about what would happen to values and lifestyles forged in times of need and want as there dawned an era of material plenty and mass consumption. Inchoate concerns about the environmental implications of economic growth assumed full form with acknowledgment of the incontrovertible damage it wrought and the realization that the natural resources on which the country depended were finite. Economic growth, particularly of the high-speed variety, was revealed to undercut the very possibility of continued prosperity and to have costs in the harm inflicted on people's lives. Even as the country arrived, secure in its status among the wealthy of the world, there was a sense that the promises of affluence had been illusory, that people's daily lives were not as they were imagined or hoped to be.[14] The desire for an affluence of the heart, cultivated by economic achievement and nurtured by economic stagnation, was a clarion expression of the perceived insufficiencies and inadequacies of financial affluence.

The idea of a blissful Bhutan has been so seductive because it appears to be the apotheosis of an affluence of the heart, but it rests on the romanticization of poverty and an idealistic nostalgia for a premodern society. Its lifestyles have been likened to those of Japan several hundred years ago, and described as appearing today as Japanese lifestyles must have looked to Western eyes in the late nineteenth and early twentieth centuries. The introduction of television and the Internet to Bhutan in 1999 has been reported in a cautious tone, as the harbinger of modern change that will mar the country's premodern happiness.[15] What this nostalgia elides is the appeal of consumption and both the impossibility and the undesirability of a return to the lifestyles before the high growth of the 1960s, much less to those of an underdeveloped, poor, and somehow "traditional" Japan.

What it also tends to overlook is the enduring tension at the heart of ambivalence about affluence. On the one hand, there has been an abiding commitment to achieving, defending, and securing the middle-class lifestyles made possible by economic growth. At its base, this has meant a roof over one's head, a certain level of health and hygiene, education, and safety as well as convenience and comfort.[16] Expectations of comfort, and definitions of a middle-class life, could and did change. The purchase of a washing machine or a television set which had marked one's arrival into the middle class became over time the acquisition of many and sundry electric appliances and electronic goods. Possibilities for amusement came to include golf, skiing, drives in the family car, multiday vacations, and travel abroad. Creature comforts encompassed air conditioning and a dizzying array of foods. Consumers could expect to choose from many and diverse options the one that best suited their own tastes, and could covet the latest goods and occasional indulgence. On the other hand, there has been a discomfort and dissatisfaction with the logics, costs, and consequences of the very prosperity that made such middle-class lifestyles possible. The emphasis on productivity, expanding reach of commodification, abundance of material goods, importance of efficiency, and prioritization of utility have become for some the source of their unhappiness.

At any given moment in Japan's postwar history, there has not been just a single story of economic chauvinism, empty affluence, or economic precarity. Nor has there been a simple arc of financial success followed by failure. Rather, there has been a decades-long attempt to reconcile the many and changing desires and expectations of middle-class life with the forces and mechanisms that helped create it. This struggle was presaged, however imperfectly, by John Maynard Keynes, whose ideas informed macroeconomic policies of the earlier postwar decades.[17] In 1931, after several years of drafting and revising, Keynes published an essay in which he predicted that in one hundred years' time, the standard of living in "progressive countries" would be somewhere between four and eight times greater. The resulting world of plenty and leisure that Keynes envisioned was one in which people would work three hours a day, and more out of desire than need. This lifestyle obviously did not come to pass in Japan or elsewhere, even as the country's gross domestic product increased about elevenfold in real terms over the course of the postwar period.[18] But Keynes did suggest that the full realization and appreciation of such a life would require people to free themselves from the habits and assumptions that had made it possible. In his words, "It will be those people, who can keep alive, and cultivate into a fuller perfection, the art of life itself and do not sell themselves for the means of life, who will be able to enjoy the abundance when it comes." To live well, people would have to shed their ingrained concern with money, the accumulation of wealth, means rather than ends, economic incentives, and utility.[19] The challenge in postwar Japan was that the very habits and assumptions, the "means of life," that had created a lifestyle of abundance and affluence were thought necessary to perpetuate it and so endured in ways that came into tension with its enjoyment.[20]

The many and different ways of conceiving of waste were enmeshed in these challenges and tensions of affluence and have captured something not just about postwar Japan, but also about other industrialized, wealthy, and developed countries. A comparison of all such countries would be welcome and is beyond the scope of these reflections, but a glance at the United States might be illustrative. It also seems appropriate, given the extent to which the United States has served as a reference point for postwar Japan—at different times and in different eyes a forerunner of rationalization, efficiency, and productivity; a model of a middle-class life of plenty; and the embodiment of wasteful excess. While anxieties about prosperity and a desire for self-fulfillment have longer histories in both countries, in this contemporary moment, the sense of the aborted promises and continued allure of affluence seems closely shared in the United States and Japan, two of the wealthiest countries in the world.[21]

The idea that people have too much stuff, and that this material acquisition is causing stress more than it is bringing happiness, has been widely observed in the United States as in Japan. When the Center on Everyday Lives of Families sent anthropologists into the homes of thirty-two middle-class, dual-income families with school-age children, what they found across the occupationally and ethnically diverse group were spaces overflowing with material possessions. Among the things in one girl's bedroom were 165 Beanie Babies, 36 figurines, 22 Barbies, and 20 other dolls. And while these homes were all in the greater Los Angeles area, the media coverage of the findings presumed that they spoke to a broader middle-class phenomenon. A *Time* magazine article made this assumption and summarized the researchers' finding that "accumulating bigger piles of stuff may in fact decrease happiness and increase stress." Or put more colorfully in the *Washington Post*, "the very items that signify success, ease and comfort—say, a freezer jam-packed with pizzas and potpies and drumsticks—turn ugly on you . . . The more you have, the more stress they make."[22]

The emotional angst of material acquisition has provoked various responses, among them a veritable flood of advice literature about the practice of declutter-ing. And none of them has garnered as much attention in the past few years as the KonMari method. Kondō Marie's book *The Life-Changing Magic of Tidying Up*, published in October 2014, had sold 1.6 million copies in the United States by early 2016.[23] As of mid-August 2016, the book had been on the *USA Today* best-seller list for ninety weeks and on the *New York Times* best-seller list in the category of "Advice, How-To & Miscellaneous" for ninety-three weeks. At the time of writing, it occupied the number-two slot in the *New York Times* rank-ings, followed in third place by Kondō's other English-language book, *Spark Joy*. Kondō's books have been reviewed in a wide range of newspapers and magazines, and she has appeared on television shows, given a talk at Google, and been the subject of many articles.[24] Secondhand stores have reported an increase in inven-tory since the publication of the first book, positing a connection that is hard to confirm.[25] Kondō's approach to decluttering is so widely known as to have elicited both criticism and defense as well as parody.[26] On the now defunct femi-nist humor site *The Toast*, a piece about the method opened with the trenchant sentence "It's important to be very rich but have almost no items in your home."[27]

The overabundance of material things has encouraged in some a decision to take decluttering further, to live a minimalist life. The venture capitalist, for-mer hedge fund manager, and financial expert James Altucher was inspired by Kondō's book to discard almost all of his belongings. In a 2016 profile in the *New York Times*, he explained that he now owned only fifteen items because he had discovered that his "lavish lifestyle did not fill his emotional void."[28] Another self-avowed minimalist described in the same newspaper his small studio apart-ment with scant possessions, having concluded that things did not seem to be making anyone happier. His embrace of minimalism was a response to a previ-ous way of life funded by the lucrative sale of his technology start-up, and in the context of what he described as "a world of surfeit stuff, of big-box stores and 24-hour online shopping opportunities."[29] In the case of both of these minimal-ists, they decided to shed their stuff from a privileged position of financial secu-rity. They did not have to worry about housing, hunger, or health care. For them to extol the virtues of throwing things away was to overlook the sense of safety that the material, physical, and monetary can provide. They are not unlike the wealthy Japan, which can ignore the poverty of Bhutan and try to adopt only that which might bring happiness. For those not similarly fortunate, the appeal of this kind of minimalism may not just be a certain freedom from material things but the wealth that makes it possible.

Physical and material downsizing can also be seen in the popularity of the idea of tiny houses. The actual purchase of tiny houses, or those less than three hundred square feet, has been estimated to account for less than 1 percent of home sales.[30] But the so-called tiny-house movement has been covered in the media and has spawned several television series, all of which launched in 2014: *Tiny House Hunting* on FYI, *Tiny House Nation* on A&E, and *Tiny House Hunters* on HGTV. With minimalism as with the tiny-house movement, the imagined prospect of being happier with less material stuff or in a smaller physical space seems to be more attractive than an actual change in lifestyle. That similarly extreme lifestyle choices which reject material consumption have been of much more limited interest also reflects the unwillingness of most to resist the allure of consumption and material goods. Marginal have been "freegans" who spurn mass production, mass consumption, and mass waste in their daily lives by adopting such strategies as "urban foraging" or "dumpster diving."[31] Also unique have been people like "no impact man" Colin Beavan who changed his consuming habits, including giving up toilet paper for a year, to minimize his environmental impact and create little to no waste.[32]

In the United States, as in Japan, the concern with material overabundance has been accompanied by dissatisfaction with a lack of time. Busyness is the presumed condition of contemporary life, so much so that even children are said to have no time. As the sociologist Juliet Schor argued in her book *The Overworked American*, "The conventional wisdom that economic progress has given us more things *as well as* more leisure is difficult to sustain."[33] Many research hours and much ink have been spent explaining why people in an affluent country like the United States feel so poor in time and leisure. In a piece in the *New York Times*, the essayist and cartoonist Tim Kreider made a case for idleness and indolence, and suggested that people were addicted to being busy, that "busyness serves as a kind of existential reassurance, a hedge against emptiness."[34] In response to Kreider, the leadership consultant John Baldoni argued that businesspeople in particular would not feel so busy if they managed their time better, if they treated their time like money, delegated wasteful meetings, and carved out time to reflect.[35] Others have blamed the emphasis on time management and productivity for their woes, as in an article from *The Guardian* titled "Why Time Management Is Ruining Our Lives."[36] When the British historian Robert Skidelsky and the philosopher Edward Skidelsky proposed a social and economic organization that would encourage leisure and reduce work to twenty hours a week, one reviewer of their book pushed back by suggesting not just that productivity, national defense, and internal order would suffer, but also that Americans valued expensive leisure which they could afford only by working hard.[37] Economists have offered their own competing explanations for busyness, be it the insatiability of consumer desire, a lack of practice enjoying leisure, the meaning and pleasure found in work, or the value of improvement and progress.[38]

In contemporary Japan, an ambivalence about affluence continues to take different forms. There are ongoing debates about the desirability and necessity of robust economic growth. Governments and political administrations set the goal of, and are under pressure to, stimulate economic expansion and are judged by GDP growth rates. Some economists and many in the corporate world emphasize the importance of higher economic growth.[39] Others have argued that GDP should no longer be the measure of affluence, that the concern with economic growth should be replaced by a commitment to addressing poverty, economic inequality, and stability in employment. In the literature about gross national happiness, there has begun to be consideration of what a GNH suited to Japan might look like. The *Asahi* newspaper has published a series titled "Aiming to Become a Happiness Superpower," and there have been serious calls to look past affluence in the pursuit of happiness. The case has also been made for figuring out how to live richly in a zero-growth environment.[40]

If we are now in a low-growth world, if those who posit the irrevocable loss of high levels of economic growth and productivity prove to be right, then Japan may yet be a valuable model of how to navigate this condition of wealth and stagnation.[41] Unwittingly, the country has in many ways been at the vanguard of what may be a permanent transition for mature economies as it has experienced, in some cases early or severely, the collapse of a real estate bubble, financial crises, decline in manufacturing jobs, and an aging population.[42] The various and disparate efforts to make sense of and live in this world are but another chapter in a long postwar history of reflection about how to relate to things and time, work and leisure, consumption and disposal. In this present moment, as in decades now past, there abides the indispensable question of how to find meaning and define value in the decisions, routines, and commitments of affluent daily lives.

Notes

INTRODUCTION. MEANING AND VALUE IN THE EVERYDAY

1. "AC Japan CM mottainai," https://www.youtube.com/watch?v=GXODCN6rfTc (accessed August 19, 2016). This link to the AC Japan spot is no longer live, but the announcement can be found elsewhere online.

2. "NHK-AC kyōdō kyanpēn CM hōsō kaishi!" http://www.cwfilms.jp/news/20150701/ (accessed August 19, 2016).

3. The intended aim of the announcement was to suggest that quitting or not doing anything when life was not going as you might want was wasteful, though its message was actually much broader. "AC Japan kōkoku ākaibu," https://www.ad-c.or.jp/campaign/search.php?page=5&sort=businessyear_default&businessyear=2015 (accessed May 24, 2017).

4. On trash as the product of categorizing and sorting, see Susan Strasser, *Waste and Want* (New York: Henry Holt and Company, 1999), 3–12.

5. Michael Thompson made a similar argument, specifically about objects. Michael Thompson, *Rubbish Theory* (Oxford: Oxford University Press, 1979), 8–9.

6. About garbage, Gay Hawkins and Stephen Muecke have persuasively argued: "Changing relations to waste mean changing relations to self. These shifts in habits, conscience, and self-cultivation reveal the place of waste in historically variable forms of subjectivity." Gay Hawkins and Stephen Muecke, introduction to *Culture and Waste*, ed. Gay Hawkins and Stephen Muecke (New York: Rowman & Littlefield, 2003), xiv.

7. I am sympathetic to Harry Harootunian's assertion that a focus on "the conceptualization of the everyday in order to identify a unified experience of modernity" is one way "to relate this knowledge of an outside local experience [histories of societies outside Euro-America] to the inside of a larger, more familiar referent capable of explaining comparisons." Harry Harootunian, *History's Disquiet* (New York: Columbia University Press, 2000), 6.

8. Anthony Giddens, *Modernity and Self-Identity* (Cambridge: Polity, 2008), 14. My view of everyday life echoes that of Giddens, although I place more emphasis on the condition of affluence than on modernity.

9. On the history of human waste from the 1600s through the early 1900s, see David L. Howell, "Fecal Matters," in *Japan at Nature's Edge*, ed. Ian Jared Miller, Julia Adeney Thomas, and Brett L. Walker (Honolulu: University of Hawaii Press, 2013), 137–51.

10. Catriona Kelly, *Refining Russia* (Oxford: Oxford University Press, 2001), xxv.

11. Michel de Certeau, *The Practice of Everyday Life*, trans. Steven Rendall (Berkeley: University of California Press, 1984), xxii.

12. On how deeply surveys probed into aspects of twentieth-century American life and citizenship, see Sarah Elizabeth Igo, *The Averaged American* (Cambridge: Harvard University Press, 2007).

13. For example, *Christian Science Monitor*, August 6, 1980; *New York Times*, March 23, 1983, and May 12, 2005. On Kondō Marie's decluttering method, see chapter 10 and the afterword. See also the Reddit discussion "What We Can Learn about Frugality from Japan," https://www.reddit.com/r/Frugal/comments/4mkxb7/what_we_can_learn_about_frugality_from_japan/ (accessed August 24, 2016).

14. Sheldon Garon has written extensively about monetary saving in Japan, and has argued that Americans have been the outliers as spenders while Japanese and Europeans have been savers: "Entrenched cultures of thrift . . . continued to restrain [in Europe and Japan] the expansion of consumption and consumer credit in ways seldom seen in the United States." Sheldon Garon, *Beyond Our Means* (Princeton: Princeton University Press, 2012), 5. Note that the savings rate in Japan recently dipped into negative territory. Keiko Ujikane and Toru Fujioka, "Japan's Savings Rate Turns Negative in Challenge for Abe," Bloomberg, December 26, 2014, http://www.bloomberg.com/news/articles/2014-12-26/japan-s-real-wages-decline-most-since-2009-in-challenge-for-abe (accessed August 24, 2016).

15. Laura E. Hein, *Fueling Growth* (Cambridge: Council on East Asian Studies, Harvard University, 1990), 248–49, 285–88; Eric Gordon Dinmore, "A Small Island Nation Poor in Resources" (Ph.D. diss., Princeton University, 2006), 216.

16. The connection has loosened somewhat in recent decades, as technologies have been developed to harness the heat from garbage incineration for electricity generation.

17. Simon Partner, *Assembled in Japan* (Berkeley: University of California Press, 1999), 152; Mari Osawa, "Twelve Million Full-Time Housewives," in *Social Contracts Under Stress*, ed. Olivier Zunz, Leonard Schoppa, and Nobuhiro Hiwatari (New York: Russell Sage Foundation, 2002), 259–60.

18. Anne E. Imamura, *Urban Japanese Housewives* (Honolulu: University of Hawaii Press, 1987), 12; Robin M. LeBlanc, *Bicycle Citizens*, with a foreword by Saskia Sassen (Berkeley: University of California Press, 1999), 31.

19. Mary C. Brinton has argued that "Japanese women's roles are not . . . simply the product of a strong sex-role ideology in Japanese culture. Rather, they are closely tied to the development of social and economic institutions in postwar Japanese society." Mary C. Brinton, *Women and the Economic Miracle* (Berkeley: University of California Press, 1993), 2, 6, 10, 27–28; Organisation for Economic Co-operation and Development, "Labor Force Participation Rate," https://data.oecd.org/emp/labour-force-participation-rate.htm (accessed August 25, 2016). On part-time employment, see Kaye Broadbent, *Women's Employment in Japan* (London: RoutledgeCurzon, 2003), 3; International Labour Organization, "Part Time Employment, Female (% of Total Part Time Employment)," http://data.worldbank.org/indicator/SL.TLF.PART.TL.FE.ZS?locations=JP (accessed August 25, 2016). To take one example of expectations about women's management of the home, in the mid-2000s, husbands in Japan with children under age five averaged thirty minutes per day on housework, child care, and elder care regardless of whether their wives were stay-at-home mothers or worked part-time or full-time; when the children were older than five, the average time dropped to ten minutes per day; when the children were over ten years old, three minutes a day. This put Japan at the bottom of international comparisons. Scott North, "Negotiating What's 'Natural,'" *Social Science Japan Journal* 12, no. 1 (Summer 2009): 25; see also Broadbent, *Women's Employment in Japan*, 107. This general division of household labor was also seen with blue-collar workers. Glenda S. Roberts, *Staying on the Line* (Honolulu: University of Hawaii Press, 1994), 154–60.

20. On management of the household budget, see Brinton, *Women and the Economic Miracle*, 94.

21. LeBlanc spoke of "housewife citizens" and argued that "being a housewife paradoxically restricts the expansion of a Japanese woman's public life in many important ways while, at the same time, providing her with a unique vehicle for other sorts of public participation." LeBlanc, *Bicycle Citizens*, 7–8, 24.

22. The dynamic between some of these civil society groups and the government, even if it could not necessarily be characterized as "social management," was captured aptly in Sheldon Garon, *Molding Japanese Minds* (Princeton: Princeton University Press, 1997).

23. Andrew Gordon, "The Short Happy Life of the Japanese Middle Class," in Zunz, Schoppa, and Hiwatari, *Social Contracts Under Stress*, 117–21. On middle-classness in prewar Japan, see chapter 5 of Jordan Sand, *House and Home in Modern Japan* (Cambridge: Harvard University Asia Center, 2003).

24. William W. Kelly, "At the Limits of New Middle-Class Japan," in Zunz, Schoppa, and Hiwatari, *Social Contracts Under Stress*, 232–36.

25. Gordon, "Short Happy Life," 126.

26. Responses to the survey question have remained in the 90 percent range through the 2000s, with "middle" consistently the most common answer. Naikaku Sōri Daijin Kanbō Kōhōshitsu, *Kokumin seikatsu ni kansuru seron chōsa* (Tokyo: Naikaku Sōri Daijin Kanbō Kōhōshitsu, 2014), http://survey.gov-online.go.jp/h26/h26-life/zh/z29.html (accessed August 26, 2016).

27. On transwar Japan, see Andrew Gordon, "Consumption, Leisure and the Middle Class in Transwar Japan," *Social Science Japan Journal* 10, no. 1 (April 2007): 1–21; Hiromu Nagahara, *Tokyo Boogie-Woogie* (Cambridge: Harvard University Press, 2017).

28. Other defining aspects of the postwar period might include a largely defensive military, pacifism, and rural depopulation.

29. See Andrew Gordon, ed., *Postwar Japan as History* (Berkeley: University of California Press, 1993); Iwasaki Minoru et al., eds., *Sengo Nihon sutadīzu*, 3 vols. (Tokyo: Kinokuniya Shoten, 2008–9).

30. On precarity, see Anne Allison, *Precarious Japan* (Durham: Duke University Press, 2013); Frank Baldwin and Anne Allison, eds., *Japan* (New York: New York University Press, 2015).

31. See Claire Bond Potter and Renee C. Romano, eds., *Doing Recent History* (Athens: University of Georgia Press, 2012).

32. The phrase "financial affluence" may strike the ear of an economist as odd, but it is used to distinguish the financial from the more spiritual definitions of affluence.

CHAPTER 1. THE IMPERATIVES OF WASTE

1. Kobayashi Kan, "Fuyu ni sonaete kansō yasai, yasō no tsukurikata, takuwaekata, itadakikata," *Fujin kurabu* 26, no. 5 (August–September 1945): 17.

2. John W. Dower, *Embracing Defeat* (New York: W. W. Norton & Company, 1999), 45–48, 62–64.

3. Owen Griffiths, "Need, Greed, and Protest in Japan's Black Market, 1938–1949," *Journal of Social History* 35, no. 4 (Summer 2002): 827–28.

4. Samuel Hideo Yamashita, *Daily Life in Wartime Japan, 1940–1945* (Lawrence: University Press of Kansas, 2015), 39–57.

5. Quoted in George Solt, *The Untold History of Ramen* (Berkeley: University of California Press, 2014), 48.

6. Katō Keiko, "Shō kaisetsu," in Yamamoto Taketoshi and Nagai Yoshikazu, *Haisen to kurashi*, vol. 1 of *Senryōki seikatsu sesōshi shiryō* (Tokyo: Shinyōsha, 2014), 222; Howard F. Smith, "Food Controls in Occupied Japan," *Agricultural History* 23, no. 3 (July 1949): 220.

7. Dower, *Embracing Defeat*, 96.

8. Ibid., 93; Solt, *Untold History*, 56; Smith, "Food Controls," 220. On the minority of Japanese people who ate "relatively well" even in the worst years of the food crisis, see Katarzyna Cwiertka and Miho Yasuhara, "Beyond Hunger," in *Japanese Foodways, Past and Present*, ed. Eric C. Rath and Stephanie Assmann (Urbana: University of Illinois Press, 2010), 166–67.

9. Dower, *Embracing Defeat*, 96–97.

10. Kobayashi, "Fuyu ni sonaete," 17; Kuroda Yoneko, "Muda nashi ryōrihō no tettei," *Fujin gahō* 495 (November 1945): 20–21; Inoue Kaneo, *Eiyō no jōshiki* (Tokyo: Ryūbunsha, 1946), 51; "Omoitsuki de muda o nakushimashō," *Josei raifu* 2, no. 10 (October 1947): 48.

11. "Kō sureba muda naku dekiru," *Fujin no tomo* 42, no. 4 (April 1948): 21–25.

12. Sakai Shōhei, "Shoku seikatsu no gōrika no tame ni (2)," *Kaitaku* 21 (December 1949): 37–38.

13. Inoue, *Eiyō no jōshiki*, 50–51.

14. Shoko Higashiyotsuyanagi, "The History of Domestic Cookbooks in Modern Japan," in Rath and Assmann, *Japanese Foodways, Past and Present*, 138–42.

15. Cwiertka and Yasuhara, "Beyond Hunger," 173.

16. Sheldon Garon, "Japan's Post-war 'Consumer Revolution,' or Striking a 'Balance' between Consumption and Saving," in *Consuming Cultures, Global Perspectives*, ed. John Brewer and Frank Trentmann (Oxford: Berg, 2006), 193.

17. Higashiyotsuyanagi, "History of Domestic Cookbooks," 140–41.

18. Sheldon Garon, "Luxury Is the Enemy," *Journal of Japanese Studies* 26, no. 1 (Winter 2000): 42.

19. Griffiths, "Need, Greed, and Protest," 830; Cwiertka and Yasuhara, "Beyond Hunger," 173–75.

20. Shunya Yoshimi, "'America' as Desire and Violence," trans. David Buist, *Inter-Asia Cultural Studies* 4, no. 3 (2003): 443.

21. My thanks to Wiebke Denecke for the idea of reference cultures. See Wiebke Denecke, *Classical World Literatures* (Oxford: Oxford University Press, 2014), 4–10.

22. Harada Hiroshi, *MP no jīpu kara mita senryōka no Tokyo* (Tokyo: Sōshisha, 1994), 23–26.

23. Quote from Dower, *Embracing Defeat*, 93–94.

24. Harada, *MP no jīpu*, 121–24.

25. Katō, "Shō kaisetsu," 223.

26. Ishikawa Hiroyoshi, *Yokubō no sengoshi* (Tokyo: Kōsaidō Shuppan, 1989), 16–18.

27. Dower, *Embracing Defeat*, 209.

28. Lucy Herndon Crockett, *Popcorn on the Ginza* (New York: William Sloane Associates, 1949), 55.

29. "To Depot Commanders, All Branch Exchanges, Subject: Amendment to Section I, Operational Memorandum 24, Dated June 6, 1947" (October 4, 1947); SCAP; ESS; DPU; ID; IPCB; Topical File, 1940–1950; Record Group 331; box 7186; folder 19; NACP.

30. "Reconditioning, Inspection and Salvage Section, Headquarters Eighth Army, Eighth Army Exchange, APO 343, Sub-standard Merchandise to be Sold to the Japanese Government"; SCAP; ESS; DPU; ID; IPCB; Topical File, 1940–1950; Record Group 331; box 7186; folder 19; NACP.

31. "Amendment to Section I, Operational Memorandum 24"; "Army Canteens Service, B.C.O.F. Detachment, Kure, Japan" (June 14, 1949); SCAP; ESS; DPU; ID; IPCB; Topical File, 1940–1950; Record Group 331; box 7186; folder 19; NACP. On the Sangyō Fukkō Kōdan, see Ikeo Katsumi, "Sangyō fukkō kōdan o meguru sho mondai," *Keizai antei shiryō* 5 (November 1948): 35–39; Sangyō Fukkō Kōdan Shi Hensan Iinkai, ed., *Sangyō fukkō kōdan shi* (Tokyo: Sangyō Fukkō Kōdan Shi Hensan Iinkai, 1952), 7–9.

32. "Disposal of Surplus Exchange Merchandise, April 12, 1949," "To Industry Div., ESS, GHQ, SCAP, From Sangyo Fukko Kodan, Subject: Application for Release of 8th Army Exchange Surplus Merchandise to Sangyo Fukko Kodan" (August 6, 1949); "Informational Memorandum for Economic Stabilization Board, Subject: Purchase and Disposition of Eighth Army Exchange Surplus Merchandise" (August 9, 1949); "Estimated Income and Expenditure Regarding Sale of Merchandise to be Released from 8th Army Exchange Tokyo Yokohama Area"; SCAP; ESS; DPU; ID; IPCB; Topical File, 1940–1950; Record Group 331; box 7186; folder 19; NACP.

33. "Memo for Record" (September 5, 1950); "From SCAP Tokyo Japan to BCOF Kure Japan" (September 7, 1950); SCAP; ESS; DPU; ID; IPCB; Topical File, 1940–1950; Record Group 331; box 7186; folder 19; NACP.

34. "General Headquarters, Supreme Commander for the Allied Powers, Memorandum for the Imperial Japanese Government, Subject: Disposition of Garbage and Waste, AG 720, SCAPIN 1548" (February 27, 1947); SCAP; CAS; KCAR; Public Health Activities File, 1946–1951; Record Group 331; box 2821; folder 8; NACP.

35. "Disposal Sub-Div., Cleansing Operation Dep., T.M.O., Designation of Contractors on Disposal of Wastes from the Occupation Forces Installations for Fiscal 1951" (January 1951); SCAP; CAS; KCAR; Public Health Activities File, 1946–1951; Record Group 331; box 2821; folder 8; NACP.

36. "General Headquarters, Supreme Commander for the Allied Powers, APO 500, Memorandum for Japanese Government, Subject: Disposition of Garbage and Waste, AG 720, SCAPIN 1915" (July 1, 1948); SCAP; Civil Property Custodian; Executive Division; Decimal File, 1946–1952; Record Group 331; box 4895; folder 7; NACP; "From Ota En, Chief of the Sanitation Operations Department, To Chief of the Kanto Civil Affairs Region, Subject: Prescribed Sign-board Put on Trucks Being Operated by the Agencies for T.M.O. in Collection and Disposal of Garbage and Trash from the Occupation Forces Installations" (April 22, 1950); SCAP; CAS; KCAR; Public Health & Disease Control, 1947–1951; Record Group 331; box 2817; folder 5; NACP. Problems with unauthorized "scavengers" were also noted in Yokohama. See "Headquarters Yokohama Command, APO 503, Subject: Unauthorized Disposal of Tin Cans and Bottles" (April 12, 1949); SCAP; CAS; TCAR; Miscellaneous File, 1946–1951; Record Group 331; box 2607; folder 18; NACP.

37. "Santama Waste Disposing for Occupation Forces Installation Company, Tachikawa, Tokyo-to, To The Supreme Commander, Subject: Petition for Disposition of Garbage and Waste" (February 12, 1951); SCAP; CAS; KCAR; Public Health & Disease Control, 1947–1951; Record Group 331; box 2817; folder 5; NACP.

38. "From Shoji Akiyama, Representative Director, Shinyu Shokai, Ltd., No. 8 Shiba-Takahamacho, Minato-ku, Tokyo, To Colonel Kegley, Petition" (March 31, 1951); SCAP; CAS; KCAR; Public Health Activities File, 1946–1951; Record Group 331; box 2821; folder 8; NACP.

39. In the early years of the Meiji period (1868–1912), garbage was considered anything—dirt, small stones, broken tiles—that was out of its proper place in a way that impeded how things should work. The state was primarily concerned about maintaining order in decidedly public spaces such as roads, ditches, and rivers. Regulations of the late 1860s and early 1870s, for example, sought to prevent obstructions of traffic. See Mizoiri Shigeru, *Meiji Nihon no gomi taisaku* (Tokyo: Risaikuru Bunkasha, 2007), 29–31; Dajōkan, Dōro sōji jōmoku (October 28, 1872).

40. Mizoiri, *Meiji Nihon*, 41–47, 53, 81–83. Making a slightly different point about dumps, Gay Hawkins categorized together "prisons, madhouses, hospitals, dumps, *drains*." Gay Hawkins, "Down the Drain," in *Culture and Waste*, ed. Gay Hawkins and Stephen Muecke (Lanham, MD: Rowman & Littlefield, 2003), 41.

41. Obutsu sōji hō shikō kisoku, Naimushō rei dai go gō (March 1900), Articles 1, 3, 5–6, 8–10, 12, in *Gyōsei sho hōki*, vol. 6 (1928), 643–44.

42. "Kyoto City Garbage and Refuse Collection, Report No. 2-s, USSBS Index Section 8" (November 16, 1945); Records of the U.S. Strategic Bombing Survey; Entry 43; USSBS Transcriptions of Interrogations and Interrogation Reports of Japanese Industrial, Military, and Political Leaders, 1945–1946; Record Group 243; "Sewage, Garbage and Night Soil Disposal, Kyoto: Data on Garbage and Refuse Disposal, Kyoto, Report No. 12c(9)(f), USSBS Index Section 2"; Records of the USSBS; Entry 41; Pacific Survey Reports and Supporting Records, 1928–1947; Record Group 243.

43. "Sewage, Garbage and Refuse, and Night Soil Disposal, Nagasaki, Yokohama, Kobe, Hiroshima, Sasebo Shi: Interview on Garbage and Refuse Disposal, Yokohama, Report No. 12c(11)(e)," USSBS Index Section 2; Records of the USSBS; Entry 41; Pacific Survey Reports and Supporting Records, 1928–1947; Record Group 243.

44. "Sewage, Garbage and Refuse, and Night Soil Disposal, Nagasaki, Yokohama, Kobe, Hiro-shima, Sasebo Shi: Data on Sewage, Hiroshima, Report No. 12c(11)(h), USSBS Index Section 2," Records of the USSBS; Entry 41; Pacific Survey Reports and Supporting Records, 1928–1947; Record Group 243.

45. "Garbage and Refuse Disposal in Nagasaki, Serial No. 13, Report No. 2-c(11), USSBS Index Section 8"; Records of the USSBS; Entry 43; USSBS Transcripts of Interrogations and Interrogation Reports of Japanese Industrial, Military, and Political Leaders, 1945–1946; Record Group 243.

46. Imamura Mitsuo, *Gomi to Nihonjin* (Kyoto: Mineruva Shobō, 2015), 271–78. Throughout the book, "ton" usually refers to a metric ton or 1,000 kilograms.

47. Tokyo-to Seisōkyoku Sōmubu Sōmuka, ed., *Tokyo-to seisō jigyō hyakunen shi* (Tokyo: Tokyo-to, 2000), 126.

48. Dower, *Embracing Defeat*, 103.

49. "For the Press Conference: August 24, 1948"; SCAP; CAS; TCAR; Public Health & Welfare Activities, 1946–1951; Record Group 331; box 2583; folder 5; NACP.

50. "School Sanitation Association, General Meeting, November 12–13, 1948, School Sanitation Problems" (November 12, 1948); SCAP; CAS; TCAR; Public Health & Welfare Activities, 1946–1951; Record Group 331; box 2583; folder 5; NACP.

51. "Depends Upon the Intention of Dwellers, Lets [*sic*] Cooperate and Make Clean, MG Too[?] Inspection Tour Group, Housing Area, from *Yukan Tohoku*, August 27, 1948"; SCAP; CAS; TCAR; Public Health & Welfare Activities, 1946–1951; Record Group 331; box 2583; folder 5; NACP.

52. *Kyoto shinbun*, April 21, 1949.

53. *Hokkaidō shinbun*, June 1, 1949.

54. Ishikawa Tomoyoshi, *Shō eiseigaku* (Tokyo: Tōhōdō, 1947), 47.

55. "Current Japanese Public Opinion Surveys, no. 19" (March 17, 1949); SCAP; Civil Information and Education Section; Public Opinion and Sociological Research Division; General Subject File, 1946–1951; Record Group 331; box 5876; folder 20; NACP.

56. "From All Inhabitants of 4 Minamishinagawa, Onegai" (June 24, 1948); SCAP; CAS; KCAR; Public Health Activities File, 1946–1951; Record Group 331; box 2823; folder 10; NACP.

57. *Kyoto shinbun*, July 28, 1948.

58. "Register of Complaints"; SCAP; CAS; KCAR; Public Health Activities File, 1946–1951; Record Group 331; box 2823; folder 10; NACP.

59. Crockett, *Popcorn on the Ginza*, 87.

60. *Pittsburgh Courier*, September 15, 1951.

61. *Yomiuri shinbun*, November 6, 1951.

62. *Saga shinbun*, July 6, 1948.

63. *Jiji shinbun*, November 21, 1948.

64. See Mary Douglas, *Purity and Danger* (London: Routledge & Kegan Paul, 1976).

65. William M. Tsutsui, "The Way of Efficiency," *Modern Asian Studies* 35, no. 2 (2001): 441–42, 448–51; William M. Tsutsui, *Manufacturing Ideology* (Princeton: Princeton University Press, 1998), 8, 58–71.

66. Matsumoto Masanobu, "Hansei shiryō," *Jitsumu techō* 3, no. 5 (May 1949): 52–57.

67. Ishikawa Tadashi, "Shitsumu no muda haijo 80-kajō," *Jimu nōritsu* 1, no. 4 (July 1949): 26–27, and 1, no. 5 (August 1949): 24.

68. "Dai-ichiji kenkyū jū mokuhyō" (November 3, 1946), reprinted in Matsushita Kōnosuke, *PHP no kotoba* (Tokyo: PHP Kenkyūjo, 1975), 15.

69. Matsushita Kōnosuke, "Tenyo no tokushitsu o ikashite (August 18, 1961)," in *Matsushita Kōnosuke hatsugen shū*, ed. PHP Sōgō Kenkyūjo Kenkyū Honbu "Matsushita

Kōnosuke Hatsugen Shū" Hensanshitsu Henshū Seisaku, vol. 42 (Kyoto: PHP Kenkyūjo, 1992), 70.

70. Ueno Yōichi, *Nōritsugaku genron* (Tokyo: Nihon Nōritsu Gakkō, 1948), 97–100.

71. "Keihi no setsuyaku wa kokka no kyūmu," *Jitsumu techō* 3, no. 8 (June 1949): 2–5.

72. Tsutsui, "Way of Efficiency," 441–44; Tsutsui, *Manufacturing Ideology*, 18–24. Ueno Yōichi quoted in Tsutsui, *Manufacturing Ideology*, 23.

73. Ishimori Chiyo, "Hataraku fujin no jikan no kufū," *Izumi* 1, no. 2 (February 1949): 28–29.

74. Henshūbu, "Haha no seikatsu jikan," *Seikatsu kagaku* 6, no. 3 (March 1948): 13–15.

75. Ōmoto Moichirō, *Katei seikatsu no kagaku* (Tokyo: Chikyū Shuppan, 1949), 22–28, 44–48, 85–86.

76. Ueno Shige, "Seikatsu ni wa konna muda ga aru," *Fujin gahō* 533 (February 1949): [21–22].

77. Furugaki Tetsurō, foreword to Sakai Yoneo, *Shin Amerika dayori* (Tokyo: Meikyokudō, 1949), 2; Ishikawa, *Yokubō no sengoshi*, 33–34.

78. Sakai, *Shin Amerika dayori*, 17–19, 225.

79. Nakano Gorō, *Amerika ni manabu* (Tokyo: Nihon Kōhōsha, 1949), 91–92. In the view of Ueno Yōichi, his own country would have to not just emulate but also exceed the waste consciousness of the United States. Ueno remarked that there was some encouragement of frugality and thrift in the United States, but also suggested that a country with so much land and an abundance of things was not, and did not have to be, so attuned to eliminating waste. Japan, in contrast, with much less land and inadequate goods and materials, simply could not waste things. Ueno, *Nōritsugaku genron*, 145.

80. Iwamoto Shigeki, *Akogare no burondi* (Tokyo: Shinyōsha, 2007), 1–3.

81. Reprinted ibid., 103.

82. *Asahi shinbun*, November 8 and 9, 1950.

83. Reprinted in Iwamoto, *Akogare no burondi*, 49.

84. Matsushita Kōnosuke, "Ningensei ni motozuku seiji, kyōiku o (September 28, 1947)," in *Matsushita Kōnosuke hatsugen shū*, ed. PHP Sōgō Kenkyūjo Kenkyū Honbu "Matsushita Kōnosuke Hatsugen Shū" Hensanshitsu Henshū Seisaku, vol. 36 (Kyoto: PHP Kenkyūjo, 1992), 224–26.

85. Konosuke Matsushita, *Quest for Prosperity* (Tokyo: PHP Institute, 1988), 259.

86. Ibid., 259–60.

87. Simon Partner, *Assembled in Japan* (Berkeley: University of California Press, 1999), 64.

88. Dower, *Embracing Defeat*, 541–44; Griffiths, "Need, Greed, and Protest," 849–50.

89. Okuda Junko, "Shokuhin o muda naku katsuyō suru ni wa," *Shoku seikatsu* 47, no. 6 (June 1953): 10, 12–13.

90. "Muda naku jōzu ni taberu ni wa," *Shufu to seikatsu* 8, no. 5 (April 1953): 366–71.

91. "Zeitaku wa teki da!," *Josei kōron* (June 1946): 59.

92. Suzuki Koshirō, "Zeitaku wa hatashite teki ka," *Meiboku* 2, no. 9 (September 1948): 13–14.

93. Inokuma Gen'ichirō, Fukushima Keiko, and Hanamori Yasuji, "Zeitaku ni tsuite," *Geijutsu shinchō* 2, no. 2 (February 1951): 76–83.

CHAPTER 2. BETTER LIVING THROUGH CONSUMPTION

1. Iue Toshio, "Zeitaku wa teki de wa nai," *Bungei shunjū* 33, no. 11 (June 1955): 286–89.

2. John Dower, *Embracing Defeat* (New York: W. W. Norton & Company, 1999), 172–80.

3. Keizai Kikakuchō, ed., *Shōwa 31 nendo keizai hakusho* (Tokyo: Shiseidō, 1956), 1–4, 42.

4. *Yomiuri shinbun*, July 17, 1956.

5. Keizai Kikakuchō, *Shōwa 31 nendo*, 14–17.

6. Scott O'Bryan, *The Growth Idea* (Honolulu: University of Hawaii Press, 2009), 162–63.

7. Ibid., 160–63; Simon Partner, *Assembled in Japan* (Berkeley: University of California Press, 1999), 5.

8. *Shin seikatsu undō kyōkai* (Tokyo: Shin Seikatsu Undō Kyōkai, 1982), 8; Sheldon Garon, *Molding Japanese Minds* (Princeton: Princeton University Press, 1997), 167–69; Partner, *Assembled in Japan*, 146–47.

9. Quoted in Tanaka Sen'ichi, "Shin seikatsu undō to Shin Seikatsu Undō Kyōkai," *Seijō bungei* 181 (January 2003): 22–23.

10. Partner, *Assembled in Japan*, 145–47; Garon, *Molding Japanese Minds*, 162–67.

11. Quoted in Andrew Gordon, "Managing the Japanese Household," *Social Politics* 4, no. 2 (Summer 1997): 253.

12. *Yomiuri shinbun*, January 16, 1953.

13. *Mainichi shinbun*, October 11, 1957.

14. Garon, *Molding Japanese Minds*, 171; Gordon, "Managing the Japanese Household," 255.

15. "Nihon no shio," *Sekai* 122 (February 1956): 148.

16. *Mainichi shinbun*, June 12, 1956.

17. *Mainichi shinbun*, April 28, 1957.

18. The number was, however, not very high at 11.1 percent. *Shin seikatsu undō kyōkai*, 8.

19. Quoted in Gordon, "Managing the Japanese Household," 260.

20. Ibid., 259–61.

21. "Buppin no setsuyaku katsuyō," *Nōritsu* 5, no. 6 (June 1954): 14–16.

22. Kurata Chikara, "Yottsu no muda ari," *Jimu to keiei* 7, no. 74 (November 1955): 8–9.

23. Miyanaga Susumu, *Muda monogatari* (Tokyo: Daiyamondosha, 1954), i, 48–56, 87–98.

24. William M. Tsutsui, *Manufacturing Ideology* (Princeton: Princeton University Press, 1998), 178.

25. Ibid., 178–79.

26. Andrew Gordon, *The Wages of Affluence* (Cambridge: Harvard University Press, 1998), 64–65.

27. Quoted ibid., 75.

28. Hongō Takanobu, "Tōshiba 'jōzu na kurashi no undō' no ikikata," *Rōmu kenkyū* 10, no. 12 (December 1957): 30–32.

29. Ibid., 33–34; Gordon, *Wages of Affluence*, 75–76.

30. Ueno Yōichi, "Seikatsu jikan no gōrika," *Nōritsudō* 22, no. 11 (November 1955): 2–7.

31. On prewar rural improvement campaigns, see Kerry Smith, *A Time of Crisis* (Cambridge: Harvard University Asia Center, 2001).

32. Nōrinshō Nōgyō Kairyōkyoku Seikatsu Kaizenka, ed., *Zusetsu nōka no seikatsu kaizen* (Tokyo: Asakura Shoten, 1954), 13–14, 18, 22–23; Tsuji Mieko, "Nōka no seikatsu kaizen," *Fujin to nenshōsha* 28 (September 1955): 9; Kondō Tadashi, "Nōgyō keiei to seikatsu kaizen," *Fumin* 22, no. 8 (August 1950): 54–56; Yamaguchi Mutsumi, "Kankonsōsai no kansoka wa kanō ka," in *Kurashi no kakumei*, ed. Tanaka Sen'ichi (Tokyo: Nōsangyoson Bunka Kyōkai, 2011), 360; Simon Partner, "Taming the Wilderness," *Monumenta Nipponica* 56, no. 4 (Winter 2001): 508–13.

33. *Asahi shinbun*, January 5, 1953.

34. Masuda Kinroku, "Muda to shippai o shinai seikatsu kufū," *Fujin kurabu* 33, no. 9 (September 1952): 244–45.

35. *Mainichi shinbun*, June 20, 1956.

36. *Asahi shinbun*, January 26, 1956.

37. Wada Kenji, "Kodomo o tsukuru mae ni kane o tsukure," *Bessatsu jitsugyō no Nihon* 16 (June 1951): 78.

38. Miya Rihei, "Sararīman de mo kane wa tamaru," *Bessatsu jitsugyō no Nihon* 29 (December 1953): 131.

39. Minobe Ryōkichi, Uno Masao, and Uji'ie Hisako, *Kakei to seikatsu* (Tokyo: Dōbun Shoin, 1958), i–ii, 71–76.

40. Ibid., 3.

41. Masuda, "Muda to shippai," 243. See also *Asahi shinbun*, January 5, 1953, and June 20, 1956.

42. "Nihon no shio," 148.

43. Nakano Gorō, "Muda naku muri naku," *Ōru seikatsu* 10, no. 12 (December 1955): 50.

44. Katō Yoshio, "Kojin seikatsu ni miru Amerika no gōrika to Nihon no muda," *Jitsugyō no Nihon* 58, no. 12 (May 1955): 38–39.

45. "Nihon no shio," 148–51.

46. Hongō, "Tōshiba," 30–31.

47. Ibid.

48. Gordon, "Managing the Japanese Household," 267.

49. Quoted in Partner, *Assembled in Japan*, 148.

50. Kaneko Hiroshi, "Muda no kōyō," *Seikai ōrai* 22, no. 5 (May 1956): 124–29.

51. Yamakawa Hiroji et al., eds., *Shōwa kōkoku 60-nen shi* (Tokyo: Kōdansha, 1987), 212–13, 228–29, 236.

52. Partner, *Assembled in Japan*, 149–56.

53. Ibid., 157.

54. Ibid., 166.

55. Ibid., 157–58, 162–66.

56. Ishikawa Hiroyoshi, *Yokubō no sengoshi* (Tokyo: Kōsaidō Shuppan, 1989), 116–17; Yamakawa, *Shōwa kōkoku*, 280–81.

57. George Solt, *The Untold History of Ramen* (Berkeley: University of California Press, 2014), 104. Starting in 1960, Nissin Foods was allowed to market the deep-fried noodles as a "government certified 'special health food'" because of vitamin B_1 and B_2 additives in the noodles. The earlier ventures of Andō Momofuku, the inventor of instant ramen, similarly involved using inexpensive ingredients to create "nutritious" foods. A case in point was Andō's *furikake*, a condiment "which was manufactured from leftover fish parts . . . [and] marketed as a good source of protein and calcium." As explained by the historian George Solt, "Andō's food-processing ventures brought him in close contact with officials from the Ministry of Health and Welfare, who were enthusiastic supporters of his attempts to create alimentary matter from waste." Solt, *Untold History of Ramen*, 96.

58. Ishikawa, *Yokubō no sengoshi*, 116–17.

59. Kazuo Usui, *Marketing and Consumption in Modern Japan* (London: Routledge, 2014), 117–18; Sakoi Sadayuki, "Shōhi no rōhi kōzō to shōhisha shinri," *Aichi kyōiku daigaku kenkyū hōkoku* 50 (March 2001): 181. There is disagreement about what should be considered the first supermarket in Japan. Marilyn Ivy named Daiei, opened in 1957. See Marilyn Ivy, "Formations of Mass Culture," in *Postwar Japan as History*, ed. Andrew Gordon (Berkeley: University of California Press, 1993), 247.

60. Kōdō Seichōki o Kangaeru Kai, ed., *Kazoku no seikatsu*, vol. 2 of *Kōdō seichō to Nihonjin* (Tokyo: Nihon Editāsukūru Shuppanbu, 2005), 109, 111.

61. Yamakawa, *Shōwa kōkoku*, 348–49; *Kōdo seichō no kiseki*, vol. 7 of *Ichioku nin no Shōwa shi* (Tokyo: Mainichi Shinbunsha, 1976), 178; Giles Slade, *Made to Break* (Cambridge: Harvard University Press, 2006), 117–18.

62. Keizai Kikakuchō, ed., *Keizai hakusho* (Tokyo: Ōkurashō Insatsukyoku, 1960), 27.

63. Ivy, "Formations of Mass Culture," 242–43.

64. In 1959, households with higher incomes tended to have higher rates of ownership of electric fans, television sets, and electric refrigerators. (This was not the case in the very highest income brackets for sewing machines.) As one illustration of variation in consumption by occupation, take the rates of ownership of a washing machine: households of company executives, 67.6 percent; non-executive workers, 40.2 percent; and laborers, 14.4 percent. The gap between cities and rural areas was also stark, with ownership rates of 33 versus 6.8 percent. Keizai Kikakuchō Chōseikyoku, *Kokumin seikatsu hakusho* (Tokyo: Ōkurashō Insatsukyoku, 1959), 149–50.

65. Keizai Kikakuchō, *Keizai hakusho*, 10–11, 31–32; Keizai Kikakuchō Chōseikyoku, *Kokumin seikatsu hakusho*, 150.

66. Miyamoto Ken'ichi, *Keizai taikoku*, vol. 10 of *Shōwa no rekishi* (Tokyo: Shōgakkan, 1983), 71.

67. Ibid.

68. Simonetta Falasca-Zamponi, *Waste and Consumption* (New York: Routledge, 2011), 13.

69. Carol Gluck, "The Past in the Present," in Gordon, *Postwar Japan as History*, 75; William W. Kelly, "Finding a Place in Metropolitan Japan," ibid., 195.

70. "Kechi wa bitoku, mudazukai mo tanoshī," *Shufu to seikatsu* (February 1961): 134–35, 137.

71. *Mainichi shinbun*, January 19, 1964.

72. "Hikōki de rāmen o kui ni iu 'rōhi no bitoku,'" *Shūkan shinchō* 13, no. 47 (November 23, 1968): 41.

73. Ozawa Tadashi, "Mottainai, mottainai," *Haha no tomo* 183 (August 1968): 88–91.

74. *Shufu no jiyū jikan ni kansuru ishiki chōsa* (Tokyo: Rōdōshō Fujin Shōnenkyoku, 1959), i.

75. *Nijūgonen go no rekuriēshon no bijon* (Tokyo: Nihon Rekuriēshon Bijon Iinkai, 1968), 8.

76. Ibid., 6.

77. David W. Plath, *The After Hours* (Berkeley: University of California Press, 1964), 109–16.

78. For data on working hours, see Nippon Hōsō Kyōkai Hōsō Bunka Kenkyūjo, ed., *Nihonjin no seikatsu jikan* (Tokyo: Nippon Hōsō Shuppan Kyōkai, 1963), 208; Tamura Kazuhiko, "Rejā shōhigaku to jiyū jikan," *Doshisha shōgaku* 29, no. 4–5–6 (March 1978): 304, 306.

79. Nippon Hōsō Kyōkai Hōsō Bunka Kenkyūjo, *Nihonjin no seikatsu jikan*, 204; Tamura, "Rejā shōhigaku," 295.

80. The list was rounded out by hobbies such as photography and music (169 billion yen), sports supplies (157.1 billion), and performances (103.5 billion). *Nijūgonen go no rekuriēshon*, 9.

81. For such photographs, see *Kōdo seichō no kiseki*, 174–77.

82. Seikatsu Kagaku Chōsakai, ed., *Yoka* (Tokyo: Ishiyaku Shuppan, 1961), i–ii, 20–21; Kitazawa Masakuni, "Fujiyū na 'jiyū jikan,'" *Asahi jānaru* 9, no. 46 (November 5, 1967): 14.

83. J. K. Galbraith, *Yutaka na shakai*, trans. Suzuki Tetsutarō (Tokyo: Iwanami Shoten, 1960), ii.

84. John Kenneth Galbraith, *The Affluent Society* (Boston: Houghton Mifflin Company, 1958), 2, 147; Galbraith, *Yutaka na shakai*, 4, 140.

85. Galbraith, *Yutaka na shakai*, ii.

86. Shinozaki Hiromi, "Hirakeyuku 'rōhi wa bitoku' jidai," *Kinzoku* 30, no. 19 (October 1, 1960): 91.

87. *Yomiuri shinbun*, July 28, 1960.

88. *Yomiuri shinbun*, June 18, 1964.

89. G. Katona, *Taishū shōhi shakai*, trans. Shakai Kōdō Kenkyūjo (Tokyo: Daiyamondosha, 1966), 431; *New York Times*, June 19, 1981; George Katona, *The Mass Consumption Society* (New York: McGraw-Hill Book Company, 1964), 4, 333.

90. Katona, *Mass Consumption Society*, 49; Katona, *Taishū shōhi shakai*, 67.

91. Katona, *Mass Consumption Society*, 6; Katona, *Taishū shōhi shakai*, 9.

92. Katona, *Taishū shōhi shakai*, i.

93. Ishii Kinnosuke, *Shōhi wa bitoku de aru* (Tokyo: Tōyō Keizai Shinpōsha, 1960), i–ii.

94. For more on Packard and an analysis of these three books, see Daniel Horowitz, *Vance Packard and American Social Criticism* (Chapel Hill: University of North Carolina Press, 1994).

95. Vance Packard, *The Hidden Persuaders* (New York: David McKay Company, 1957), 162, 258; Vance Packard, *Kakureta settokusha*, trans. Hayashi Shūji (Tokyo: Daiyamondosha, 1958), 191–92, 286.

96. Vance Packard, *The Waste Makers* (New York: David McKay Company, 1960), 7; Vance Packard, *Rōhi o tsukuridasu hitobito*, trans. Minami Hiroshi and Ishikawa Hiroyoshi (Tokyo: Daiyamondosha, 1961), 8. In 1961, translators Minami and Ishikawa did not use the Japanese phrase for "throwaway age" that would become widely used in the 1970s; they spoke of a *nagesute no jidai* rather than a *tsukaisute jidai*.

97. Packard, *Waste Makers*, 8, 233; Packard, *Rōhi o tsukuridasu hitobito*, 9, 267.

98. Packard, *Waste Makers*, 29–31, 146–58; Packard, *Rōhi o tsukuridasu hitobito*, 31–34, 166–80.

99. Packard, *Waste Makers*, 41–47; Packard, *Rōhi o tsukuridasu hitobito*, 44–51.

100. Packard, *Waste Makers*, 53–127; Packard, *Rōhi o tsukuridasu hitobito*, 57–144.

101. Vance Packard, "Muda o tsukuru hitobito," trans. Ishikawa Hiroyoshi, *Chūō kōron* 76, no. 4 (April 1961): 119.

102. Iizuka Takeo, "Shōhisha wa baka de wa nai," *Hon no hon* 226 (December 1961): 20; *Yomiuri shinbun*, September 26, 1962.

103. *Yomiuri shinbun*, December 17, 1962.

104. *Yomiuri shinbun*, May 25, 1964.

105. Ishikawa, *Yokubō no sengoshi*, 89–91.

106. The psychologist Ernest Dichter, a Viennese émigré to the United States, pioneered the focus group and the "depth interview." Founder of the Institute for Motivational Research, he consulted for companies such as Procter & Gamble, Exxon, General Foods, Chrysler, General Mills, and DuPont. In 1959, Dichter traveled to Japan and was received warmly by those familiar with his work. Around that time, a division of Dentsū had established an institute for motivational research that used various methods developed by Dichter. "Retail Therapy," *The Economist* (December 17, 2011): 119–23; E. Dichter, *Yokubō o tsukuridasu senryaku*, trans. Tako Akira (Tokyo: Daiyamondosha, 1964), i–ii. Hayashi Shūji was a prolific writer whose many works during these years included *Mākechingu risāchi* (Tokyo: Daiyamondosha, 1958); *Kigyō no imēji senryaku* (Tokyo: Daiyamondosha, 1961); and *Ryūtsū kakumei* (Tokyo: Chūō Kōronsha, 1962).

107. Ishikawa, *Yokubō no sengoshi*, 92–95, 100–101.

108. *Yomiuri shinbun*, October 31, 1961.

109. Uno Masao, "Shōhi kakumei to rōhi kakumei," *Jitsugyō no Nihon* 64, no. 9 (May 1, 1961): 60.

110. Ōhara's series spanned twelve issues of the journal *Mingei* from March 1962 to October 1964. The first was Ōhara Sōichirō, "'Rōhi o tsukuridasu hitobito,'" *Mingei* 111 (March 1962): 33–35.

111. Household or personal saving rates are an imperfect barometer for the rationalization of finances, given that they are, as Charles Yuji Horioka has argued, "the result not of cultural factors but of economic, institutional, and demographic factors." Nonetheless, insofar as the propensity to save reflects a rational approach to personal finances to some degree, it is worth mentioning that the household saving rate in Japan was generally higher than in the United States during the 1960s. See Charles Yuji Horioka, "Consuming and Saving," in Gordon, *Postwar Japan as History*, 285–87. See also Sheldon Garon, *Beyond Our Means* (Princeton: Princeton University Press, 2012), 325.

112. *Yomiuri shinbun*, December 15, 1962. Several months later Packard offered a very different impression of Japan to an American audience. In an article in the *Saturday Evening Post*, Packard made no mention of Japanese wastefulness and was surprisingly complimentary toward the Japanese advertising industry: "To the extent that it [advertising] has, by reasonable appeals, helped an impoverished people attain those things that are widely assumed to be desirable in modern, well-balanced societies, advertising has been at its best as a social force." Vance Packard, "This Is the New Japan," *Saturday Evening Post* 236, no. 15 (April 1963): 36.

113. Packard, *Rōhi o tsukuridasu hitobito*, 375–76.

114. Uno, "Shōhi kakumei to rōhi kakumei," 59–60.

115. *Yomiuri shinbun*, September 26, 1962.

116. *Yomiuri shinbun*, December 17, 1962.

117. *Mainichi shinbun*, January 5, 1961. In 1961, the question of whether consumption was a virtue was posed directly in interviews conducted by the National Lifestyles Research Institute (Kokumin Seikatsu Kenkyūjo) with 1,377 people between the ages of twenty and thirty-nine in Tokyo and Osaka. Of the respondents in Tokyo, more than half (50.4 percent) said "absolutely not" (*tondemonai*), while 34.2 percent agreed or strongly agreed, and 15.5 percent did not know. Reflecting at least some degree of ambivalence about consumption, a majority of those interviewed did not think, or did not think they could say, that "consumption is a virtue." *Yomiuri shinbun*, September 21, 1962.

118. *Yomiuri shinbun*, May 29, 1961.

119. *Yomiuri shinbun*, March 12, 1959.

120. *Yomiuri shinbun*, June 28, 1966.

121. Terai Minako, "Mottainai to iu koto," *Shisō no kagaku* 39 (June 1965): 111–12.

122. Yasuoka Masahiro, "Osomatsu to mottainai," *Shi to tomo* 12, no. 3 (March 1960): 2–3, 8; Eddy Dufourmont, "Yasuoka Masahiro," in *Japan's Postwar*, ed. Michael Lucken et al., trans. J. A. A. Stockwin (New York: Routledge, 2011), 99–100; Roger H. Brown, "A Confucian Nationalist for Modern Japan" (Ph.D. diss., University of Southern California, 2004), 262–66.

123. *Yomiuri shinbun*, December 11, 1960.

124. "Hikōki de rāmen," 40–41.

125. Daimon Ichiju, "Rōhi jidai no Nihon," *Shoku seikatsu* 63, no. 3 (March 1969): 130–33.

126. Ueyama Kazuo, "Tokyo orinpikku to Shibuya, Tokyo," in *Tokyo orinpikku no shakai keizai shi*, ed. Oikawa Yoshinobu (Tokyo: Nihon Keizai Hyōronsha, 2009), 67–69; Kawamoto Saburō and Jinnai Hidenobu, "Kawatta no wa machi dake ja nakatta!," *Tokyo jin* 206 (September 2004): 64; *Mainichi shinbun*, August 11, 1961; "Tokyo no hyakunen," *Tokyo o utsukushiku* 35 (July 25, 1968): 7.

127. Tokyo-to Eiga Kyōkai To Kōhōshitsu, *Tokyo nyūsu* (Tokyo: May 1954). See also *Mainichi shinbun*, August 10, 1955, and October 18, 1955.

128. *Yomiuri shinbun*, June 27, 1956.

129. *Yomiuri shinbun*, September 12, 1956; April 24, 1957; and June 30, 1957.

130. *Yomiuri shinbun*, April 16, 1958, and July 3, 1958.

131. Kang Sangjung, *Zainichi* (Tokyo: Kōdansha, 2004), 37–38, 43.

132. Shibata Tokue, *Nihon no seisō mondai* (Tokyo: Tokyo Daigaku Shuppankai, 1961), 166–69.

133. *Yomiuri shinbun*, May 31, 1959.

134. Ibid.

135. In a 1961 report, the amount budgeted for the Hygiene Bureau (Eiseikyoku) to do this work was 202,170,573 yen; for the Sanitation Bureau, 6,695,292 yen. Individual wards also had their own budgets for the elimination of mosquitoes and flies. Tokyo-to Kōhōshitsu Kōhōbu, ed., *"Ka to hae o nakusu tomin undō"* (Tokyo: Tokyo-to Kōhōshitsu Kōhōbu, 1961), 1–7.

136. *Yomiuri shinbun*, August 11, 1963.

137. The association claimed that at 15,000 tons, New York City disposed of twice as much garbage per day as Tokyo, but was beautiful not just because of its methods of garbage collection but also because every person had the desire and the morals to keep the city clean. It was pointed out too that New York was the headquarters of Keep America Beautiful, which had 70 million members. *Machi o minna de utsukushiku*, no. 4 of *Shin seikatsu shirīzu* (Tokyo: Shin Seikatsu Undō Kyōkai, [1962–63]), 5–8, 13, 16. The New Life Movement in Tokyo was especially well funded in the years around the Olympics. In 1962 it had a budget of 20 million yen; in 1965 the budget reached its peak of 25 million yen. Segawa Dai, "Chihō soshiki kara mita shin seikatsu undō," in *Shin seikatsu undō to Nihon no sengo*, ed. Ōkado Masakatsu (Tokyo: Nihon Keizai Hyōronsha, 2012), 242.

138. See, for example, *Yomiuri shinbun*, April 13, 1955.

139. *Yomiuri shinbun*, April 11, 1958.

140. *Yomiuri shinbun*, April 4, 1960.

141. *Yomiuri shinbun*, July 29, 1961.

142. *Yomiuri shinbun*, June 21, 1962.

143. Tokyo-to Seisōkyoku Sōmubu Sōmuka, ed., *Tokyo-to seisō jigyō hyakunen shi* (Tokyo: Tokyo-to, 2000), 171–72.

144. *Yomiuri shinbun*, July 12, 1962. The English title provided in the advertisement read "Olympic in Cleaner Tokyo." The same advertisement was published in the *Asahi shinbun* on July 24; see Yamakawa, *Shōwa kōkoku*, 296–97.

145. *Yomiuri shinbun*, August 27, 1962.

146. One housewife, thirty-year-old Tomiko from Tokyo's Minato ward, expressed her displeasure with having been coerced into buying a new garbage container for 1,000 yen. The garbage boxes, she said, were lined up properly, while the garbage containers rolled about. *Yomiuri shinbun*, November 29, 1962.

147. *Yomiuri shinbun*, December 29, 1962.

148. *Yomiuri shinbun*, June 12, 1963. Another company that advertised its garbage container was the Shin-Etsu Polymer Company (Shin Etsu Porimā). See, for example, *Yomiuri shinbun*, July 30, 1963.

149. *Yomiuri shinbun*, February 10, 1962.

150. Ueyama, "Tokyo orinpikku," 71. Additional personnel were recruited to clean up litter at the four major Olympic venues; the garbage-related etiquette of attendees was described in one newspaper article as "passable." *Asahi shinbun*, October 26, 1964.

151. Ishizaka Yuji, "Tokyo orinpikku to kōdo seichō no jidai," *Nenpō, Nihon gendai shi* 14 (2009): 167.

152. According to Ishiwata Yūsuke, by 1964, more human waste was being dumped into the ocean than was used on farmland. See Ishiwata Yūsuke, "Mirai no toshi, mirai

no toshiteki seikatsu yōshiki," in *Orinpikku sutadīzu*, ed. Shimizu Satoshi (Tokyo: Serika Shobō, 2004), 164–65.

153. Ueyama, "Tokyo orinpikku," 67–68.

154. *Yomiuri shinbun*, August 2, 1962.

155. *Yomiuri shinbun*, December 6, 1962.

156. Ueyama, "Tokyo orinpikku," 70.

157. *Yomiuri shinbun*, April 4, 1962.

158. *Yomiuri shinbun*, February 15, 1964.

159. William Marotti, "Political Aesthetics," *Inter-Asia Cultural Studies* 7, no. 4 (2006): 606, 610–11; William Marotti, "Creative Destruction," *Artforum International* 51, no. 6 (February 2013): 194–96, 201; Reiko Tomii, "State v. (Anti-)Art," *positions* 10, no. 1 (Spring 2002): 147.

160. Akasegawa Genpei, *Tokyo mikisā keikaku* (Tokyo: Paruko Shuppankyoku, 1984), 172–74.

161. Akasegawa, *Tokyo mikisā*, 174–83; Tomii, "State v. (Anti-)Art," 158.

162. *Asahi shinbun*, July 16, 1965; *Yomiuri shinbun*, July 17, 1965. The incident was considered serious enough to make the international press. See *New York Times*, July 17, 1965.

163. *Gendai no eizō* (Nippon Hōsō Kyōkai, August 27, 1965).

164. *Yomiuri shinbun*, July 29, 1965.

165. *Yomiuri shinbun*, October 20, 1965; Tokue Shibata, "Land, Waste and Pollution," in *Sustainable Cities*, ed. Hidenori Tamagawa (Tokyo: United Nations University Press, 2006), 101.

166. *Yomiuri shinbun*, October 20, 1965; *Mainichi shinbun*, November 18, 1965.

167. Tokyo-to Eiseikyoku Yobōbu Bōekika, ed., *Ka to hae kujo no kyakkan chōsa* (Tokyo: Tokyo-to Eiseikyoku Yobōbu, 1967), 32, 39.

168. *Yomiuri shinbun*, August 27, 1965.

169. Particularly challenging was the diffusion of flush toilets. In the designated areas to which the plan applied, about 35 percent of the population of 77,680,000 had flush toilets, compared to 89.5 percent in the United States and 92.3 percent in England. *Mainichi shinbun*, February 21, 1969.

170. *Mainichi shinbun*, May 12, 1966.

171. *Yomiuri shinbun*, August 5, 1966.

172. Shōji Hikaru and Miyamoto Ken'ichi, *Osorubeki kōgai* (Tokyo: Iwanami Shoten, 1964).

173. *Gendai no eizō*; *Yomiuri shinbun*, July 30, 1966; August 10, 1966; and July 17, 1968.

174. Shibata Tokue, *Gomi* (Osaka: Rokugatsusha, 1964), 2, 34–35.

175. *Gendai no eizō*; *Yomiuri shinbun*, August 5, 1966.

176. Kurīn Japan Sentā, ed., *Kurīn Japan Sentā 10-nen no ayumi* (Tokyo: Kurīn Japan Sentā, 1986), 14.

177. *Yomiuri shinbun*, August 5, 1967, and November 8, 1968; *Mainichi shinbun*, April 19, 1969.

178. *Yomiuri shinbun*, August 5, 1967.

179. *Mainichi shinbun*, April 19, 1969.

180. Seisō hō, Hōritsu dai nanajūni gō (April 1954).

181. *Mainichi shinbun*, April 22, 1969.

CHAPTER 3. WARS AGAINST WASTE

1. The Tokyo Sanitation Bureau (Tokyo-to Seisōkyoku) noted that population growth was negligible during those ten years, and observed that the increase in garbage output more closely tracked income than population. Tokyo-to Seisōkyoku, ed., *Tokyo no*

gomi (Tokyo: Tokyo-to Seisōkyoku, 1971), 1, 3. A similar relationship between garbage output and income could be seen in Osaka as well. See Ogino Jirō, "Seisō jigyō no genkyō to mondai ten," *Toshi mondai kenkyū* 24, no. 4 (April 1972): 86.

2. Between 1966 and 1970, plastic as a percentage of garbage increased from 5.4 to 10.3 percent. Tokyo-to Seisōkyoku, *Tokyo no gomi*, 17.

3. Asked at a later session of the Tokyo Metropolitan Assembly about whom the Garbage War was being waged against, Minobe explicitly named garbage as the enemy. *Mainichi shinbun*, October 10, 1971.

4. The Garbage War was also sometimes called the Tokyo Garbage War, to distinguish it from battles against rubbish fought later in other places.

5. "'Gomi sensō' ni kansuru chiji hatsugen," *Tosei* 18, no. 8 (August 1973): 18–19.

6. Yorimoto Katsumi, for one, commented on the use of such a "sensational" word. See Yorimoto Katsumi, "Gomi ni hikari o ateyō," in *Gomi ni hikari o ateyō*, ed. Yorimoto Katsumi (Tokyo: Nippō, 1975), 14.

7. "'Gomi sensō' ni kansuru chiji hatsugen," 19.

8. See *Mainichi shinbun*, April 6, 1970.

9. See Karen R. Merrill, *The Oil Crisis of 1973–1974* (Boston: Bedford/St. Martin's, 2007).

10. Chalmers Johnson, *MITI and the Japanese Miracle* (Stanford: Stanford University Press, 1982), 298; Nakamura Takafusa, "An Economy in Search of Stable Growth," *Journal of Japanese Studies* 6, no. 1 (Winter 1980): 156–57.

11. Kokumin Seikatsu Sentā, ed., *Monobusoku sawagi* (Tokyo: Kokumin Seikatsu Sentā Kikaku Chōseishitsu, 1975), 1; Keizai Kikakuchō Kokumin Seikatsukyoku and Kokumin Seikatsu Seisakuka, eds., *Shōshigen, shōenerugī to korekara no kurashi* (Tokyo: Ōkurashō Insatsukyoku, 1979), 1; Nakamura, "Economy in Search of Stable Growth," 156.

12. See Eric Gordon Dinmore, "A Small Island Nation Poor in Resources" (Ph.D. diss., Princeton University, 2006).

13. Ōno Osamu, "Minobe to the Rescue," *Japan Quarterly* 16, no. 3 (July–September 1969): 268; Laura Hein, *Reasonable Men, Powerful Words* (Berkeley: University of California Press, 2004), 191.

14. Shibata Tokue, *Nihon no seisō mondai* (Tokyo: Tokyo Daigaku Shuppankai, 1961).

15. In April 1957, the Tokyo Sanitation Bureau had replaced the term "garbage incinerator" (*jinkai shōkyakujō*) with "incineration plant" or "sanitary treatment plant" (*seisō kōjō*) to underscore its technological capabilities. Tokyo-to Seisōkyoku Sōmubu Sōmuka, ed., *Tokyo-to seisō jigyō hyakunen shi* (Tokyo: Tokyo-to, 2000), 149.

16. David L. Howell, "Fecal Matters," in *Japan at Nature's Edge*, ed. Ian Jared Miller, Julia Adeney Thomas, and Brett L. Walker (Honolulu: University of Hawaii Press, 2013), 137.

17. Tokyo-to Seisōkyoku Sōmubu Sōmuka, *Tokyo-to seisō jigyō*, 249–50; Tokue Shibata, "Land, Waste and Pollution," in *Sustainable Cities*, ed. Tamagawa Hidenori (Tokyo: United Nations University Press, 2006), 103–4.

18. This area of the capital had, in fact, been a dumping ground in the prewar period when residents of what was then Fukagawa ward "had been suffering from fumes, offensive odor, and swarms of flies originating in the open trash landfills." Indeed, Fukagawa had an "association with waste" as early as the 1700s. Mariko Asano Tamanoi, "Suffragist Women, Corrupt Officials, and Waste Control in Prewar Japan," *Journal of Asian Studies* 68, no. 3 (August 2009): 805–7.

19. The original Island of Dreams was Landfill Number Fourteen, which was in use from 1957 to 1967. The (new/second) Island of Dreams was Landfill Number Fifteen, which was in use from 1965 to 1974. Multiple generations of the Island of Dreams would follow.

20. Tokyo-to Seisōkyoku Sōmubu Sōmuka, *Tokyo-to seisō jigyō*, 233; Nakamura Masa-nori, *Ōraru hisutorī no kanōsei* (Tokyo: Ochanomizu Shobō, 2011), 9; Shibata, "Land, Waste and Pollution," 101.

21. Tokyo-to Seisōkyoku Sōmubu Sōmuka, *Tokyo-to seisō jigyō*, 238–39; Shibata, "Land, Waste and Pollution," 101–2; "Gomi sensō, sono sengen kara Suginami no kaiketsu made," *Gomi sensō shūhō* 135 (December 27, 1974): 2–4.

22. *Yomiuri shinbun*, May 22 and 23, 1973; *Asahi shinbun*, May 23 and 24, 1973; *Mainichi shinbun*, May 22 and 23, 1973; Tokyo-to Seisōkyoku Sōmubu Sōmuka, *Tokyo-to seisō jigyō*, 243; Nakamura, *Ōraru hisutorī*, 2, 34.

23. *Yomiuri shinbun*, May 24, 1973; *Asahi shinbun*, May 25, 1973; *Mainichi shinbun*, May 26, 1973.

24. An exhibit titled "Let's Shine a Light on Garbage," displayed in the metropolitan government building in the fall of 1971, sought to "shine a light on" and "make mag-nificent" what was in the shadows: the kitchen, the garbage bin, and the privy. Yorimoto, "Gomi ni hikari o ateyō," 14.

25. *Gomi to tokonoma* (Nippon Hōsō Kyōkai, October 5, 1973).

26. Nakamura, *Ōraru hisutorī*, 40–44; Tokyo-to Seisōkyoku Sōmubu Sōmuka, *Tokyo-to seisō jigyō*, 252–54; Shibata, "Land, Waste and Pollution," 104–5; Margaret A. McKean, *Environmental Protest and Citizen Politics in Japan* (Berkeley: University of California Press, 1981), 105.

27. Tokyo-to Seisōkyoku Sōmubu Sōmuka, *Tokyo-to seisō jigyō*, 614–15.

28. The percentage of respondents who required conditions was 69.6 percent; those who did not, 5.5 percent. Tokyo-to Tominshitsu, ed., *Gomi mondai ni kansuru seron chōsa hōkokusho* (Tokyo: Tokyo-to Tominshitsu, 1971), 31.

29. In the 1971 survey, only 5.5 percent of the respondents did not require conditions; in 1973, 18.6 percent. Also, note that the wording of the multiple-choice answer changed from "absolutely opposed" in 1971 to "opposed" in 1973. Tokyo-to Tominshitsu, ed., *Gomi mondai ni kansuru seron chōsa* (Tokyo: Tokyo-to Tominshitsu, 1973), 18. For those who agreed to the construction of an incineration plant with conditions, the most commonly cited condition by far was no emission of pollution (64.1 percent), followed by cleanliness (22.5 percent), and no pollution by garbage trucks (20.7 percent). For those who were opposed, the top reason by far was emission of pollution (70.9 percent).

30. On the question of whether each area should dispose of its own garbage, the per-centage who were opposed or somewhat opposed in 1971 was 20.3; in 1973, it was 4.9. Tokyo-to Tominshitsu, *Gomi mondai ni kansuru seron chōsa hōkokusho*, 27; Tokyo-to Tominshitsu, *Gomi mondai ni kansuru seron chōsa*, 19.

31. On the question of building a sanitary treatment plant in Suginami ward, 44.1 per-cent agreed or agreed somewhat; 31 percent were opposed or somewhat opposed. Tokyo-to Tominshitsu, *Gomi mondai ni kansuru seron chōsa hōkokusho*, 25. At the same time, there was empathy (72.9 percent in support) for the stance of Kōtō residents against the transporting of others' garbage into their ward. Tokyo-to Tominshitsu, *Gomi mondai ni kansuru seron chōsa hōkokusho*, 23.

32. Tokyo-to Seisōkyoku, *Tokyo no gomi*, 44–46.

33. On citizen activism and antipollution movements, see McKean, *Environmental Pro-test and Citizen Politics*; Timothy S. George, *Minamata* (Cambridge: Harvard University Asia Center, 2001); Simon Andrew Avenell, *Making Japanese Citizens* (Berkeley: University of California Press, 2010); Simon Avenell, *Transnational Japan in the Global Environmental Movement* (Honolulu: University of Hawaii Press, 2017); and Brett L. Walker, *Toxic Archi-pelago* (Seattle: University of Washington Press, 2010).

34. Jeffrey Broadbent, *Environmental Politics in Japan* (Cambridge: Cambridge Univer-sity Press, 1998), 120–28.

35. Tokyo-to Seisōkyoku, *Tokyo no gomi*, 46.

36. This phrase was published by the Tokyo Metropolitan Government in a weekly report on the Garbage War. Oshida Isao, "'Suteru' to wa (2)," *Gomi sensō shūhō* 80 (July 13, 1973): 4–6; "Gomi kara mono o kangaeyō," *Gomi sensō shūhō* 41 (September 29, 1972): 2.

37. *Asahi shinbun*, May 17, 1970; Asahi Shinbun Keizaibu, ed., *Kutabare GNP* (Tokyo: Asahi Shinbunsha, 1971), iv.

38. John Kenneth Galbraith, "The GNP as Status Symbol and Success Story," in Asahi Shinbun Keizaibu, *Kutabare GNP*, vii.

39. Tsuru Shigeto, "In Place of GNP," *Social Science Information* 10 (August 1971): 8. See also Hein, *Reasonable Men, Powerful Words*, 206.

40. Scientist Ui Jun, for example, argued that "understanding pollution as a distortion or a consequence was a mistake. On the contrary . . . pollution made high-speed growth possible; it was the third pillar [*daisan no hashira*] of the miracle." Avenell, *Making Japanese Citizens*, 155.

41. Yorimoto, "Gomi ni hikari o ateyō," 13–14.

42. Shibata Tokue quoted in Nakamura, *Ōraru hisutorī*, 25.

43. Tokyo-to Seisōkyoku Sōmubu Sōmuka, *Tokyo-to seisō jigyō*, 246–47. See also *Yomiuri shinbun*, December 16, 1974.

44. Each year from 1972 to 1976, the bureau received well over four thousand entries from over one hundred elementary schools. Tokyo-to Seisōkyoku, ed., *Minna de gomi mondai o kangaeru* (Tokyo: Tokyo-to Seisōkyoku, 1977), 4–5, 30–32, 35.

45. Tokyo-to Tominshitsu, *Gomi mondai ni kansuru seron chōsa hōkokusho*, 13.

46. On the question about the amount of garbage discarded, 70.2 percent responded that it had increased "very much" and 24.8 percent said "somewhat." Ibid., 5–7.

47. Ōhashi Tomoko, "Gomi sensō to Suginami Shōhisha no Kai," *Shimin* 7 (March 1972): 135.

48. "Ankēto," *Toseijin* 362 (February 1972): 48–49.

49. *Keizai taikoku to sekiyu shokku*, vol. 12 of *Shōwa shi* (Tokyo: Mainichi Shinbunsha, 1985), 114; *Zen Chifuren 30-nen no ayumi* (Tokyo: Zenkoku Chiiki Fujin Dantai Renraku Kyōgikai, 1986), 122.

50. See Laura E. Hein, *Fueling Growth* (Cambridge: Council on East Asian Studies, Harvard University, 1990).

51. Donella H. Meadows et al., *The Limits to Growth* (New York: Universe Books, 1972), 9–10, 12, 23, 185. The translation of the book into Japanese was supervised by Ōkita Saburō, a member of the six-person executive committee for the Club of Rome and head of the Japan Economic Research Center. The Japanese version of the report was published as Donella H. Meadows et al., *Seichō no genkai*, translation supervised by Ōkita Saburō (Tokyo: Daiyamondosha, 1972).

52. Kunio Gotō, "The Oil Crisis and Energy Saving Policies," in *A Social History of Science and Technology in Contemporary Japan*, vol. 4, ed. Shigeru Nakayama and Hitoshi Yoshioka (Melbourne: Trans Pacific Press, 2006), 171–72. This roundtable about the throwaway age began with a discussion about consumers' perspectives on the Club of Rome's report. See Fujiwara Fusako, Seo Michiko, and Wakamori Tamae, "Tsukaisute jidai no hansei," *Gekkan kokumin seikatsu* 3, no. 6 (June 1973): 10–11.

53. Kokumin Seikatsu Sentā, *Monobusoku sawagi*, 5.

54. "Senri nyū taun," *Chūō kōron keiei mondai* 13, no. 1 (March 1974): 198.

55. *Keizai taikoku to sekiyu shokku*, 116; *Asahi shinbun*, October 31, 1973.

56. *Yomiuri shinbun*, November 2, 1973; *Keizai taikoku to sekiyu shokku*, 116; Kokumin Seikatsu Sentā, *Monobusoku sawagi*, 4–5, 8, 10–12; "Senri nyū taun," 198; Yamakawa Katsumi, "Senri nyū taun no panikku," *Kansai daigaku hōgaku ronshū* 29, no. 4 (December 1979): 76–78.

57. Komatsu Yūgorō, *Gekidō no tsūsan gyōsei* (Tokyo: Jihyōsha, 1978), 153.

58. *Yomiuri shinbun*, November 19, 1973; *Mainichi shinbun*, November 19, 1973.

59. Sekiyu shokku, gen'ei ni obieta 69 nichikan; Kokutetsu rōshi funsō, suto ken dakkan suto no shōgeki, vol. 5 of *Sengo 50-nen sono toki Nihon wa* (Tokyo: Nippon Hōsō Shuppan Kyōkai, 1996), 53–54; Komatsu, *Gekidō no tsūsan gyōsei*, 153.

60. *Yomiuri shinbun*, November 3 and 19, 1973; *Broadcasting in Japan* (Tokyo: NHK, 2002), 214–15. See also Johnson, *MITI*, 298.

61. *Yomiuri shinbun*, December 16, 1973.

62. "Senri nyū taun," 198; Miyamoto Ken'ichi, *Keizai taikoku*, vol. 10 of *Shōwa no rekishi* (Tokyo: Shōgakkan, 1983), 64; André Sorensen, *The Making of Urban Japan* (London: Routledge, 2002), 183–85.

63. *Asahi shinbun*, December 28, 1973.

64. *Nishi Nihon shinbun*, January 4, 1974.

65. *Yomiuri shinbun*, November 25, 1973.

66. "Dai 72-kai kokkai ni okeru Tanaka naikaku sōridaijin shoshi hyōmei enzetsu (December 1, 1973)," http://www.mofa.go.jp/mofaj/gaiko/bluebook/1974_2/s49-shiryou-1-3.htm (accessed March 25, 2016).

67. *Asahi shinbun*, December 2, 1973.

68. See chapters 5 and 7 of Yoichi Nakano, "Negotiating Modern Landscapes" (Ph.D. diss., Harvard University, 2007); Kakuei Tanaka, *Building a New Japan*, trans. Simul International (Tokyo: Simul Press, 1973). Tanaka identified as one of the problems of urban life the "disposal difficulties" posed by "plastic containers and discarded household durables such as refrigerators and television sets." In his vision of "more livable cities," Tanaka imagined that garbage would be "collected by chutes which connect to these [multipurpose underground] tunnels to facilitate the collection and disposal of our ever-increasing garbage and waste." Tanaka, *Building a New Japan*, 38, 197.

69. Tokyo-to Seisōkyoku, *Tokyo no gomi*, 6.

70. *Mainichi shinbun*, November 8, 1971; *Asahi shinbun*, March 25, 1973; *Yomiuri shinbun*, August 18, 1973.

71. Ichikawa Tetsu, "Shigen no yūkō riyō o kangaeru," *Shōhi to seikatsu* 9, no. 5 (July 1974): 18; Kishimoto Eitarō, "Rōhi to kankyō hakai no kōdo seichō seisaku," *Nihon rōdō kyōkai zasshi* 16, no. 3 (March 1974): 2–5; *Yomiuri shinbun*, September 22, 1974.

72. See, for example, *Asahi shinbun*, November 16, 1973; *Mainichi shinbun*, November 19, 1973; Kuga Saburō, *Mama no kechikechi bukku* (Tokyo: Keisei, 1974), 8.

73. "Gonin no shufu ga jikkō shiteiru taikenteki kechikechi seikatsu," *Fujin seikatsu* (June 1974): 190.

74. "Osorubeki 'tsukaisute jidai,'" *Gomi sensō shūhō* 5 (January 14, 1972): 2.

75. Ishikawa Teizō, "Kono yo wa 'tsukaisute jidai,'" *Keizai ōrai* 23, no. 7 (July 1971): 296–97, 299.

76. *Asahi shinbun*, January 3, 1970.

77. *Yomiuri shinbun*, November 16, 1973.

78. Tokyo-to Seisōkyoku, *Tokyo no gomi*, 13–15.

79. *Yomiuri shinbun*, November 16, 1973.

80. Of the 90 percent of respondents who thought that there was a strong move toward throwing things away, 80 percent reported that this was not a good development, 3 percent that it was good. The top two reasons that this trend was viewed negatively: concern that the feeling of valuing things would be lost (58.3 percent) and that it promoted waste (*rōhi*) (21.9 percent). *Nishi Nihon shinbun*, January 4, 1974.

81. Haruno Tsuruko, "Seikatsu to gomi," in *Shufu no samā sukūru no kiroku*, ed. Tokyo-to Seisōkyoku (Tokyo: Tokyo-to Seisōkyoku, 1970), 19.

82. The Consumer Association of Bunkyō Ward was a group "founded primarily as an off-shoot of the Metropolitan Government consumer problems administration programs." See Maurine A. Kirkpatrick, "Consumerism and Japan's New Citizen Politics," *Asian Survey* 15, no. 3 (March 1975): 241.

83. Fujiwara, Seo, and Wakamori, "Tsukaisute jidai no hansei," 12.

84. Ichihashi Takashi, *Gomi to kurashi no sengo gojūnen shi* (Tokyo: Risaikuru Bunka-sha, 2000), 54; Shibata, "Land, Waste and Pollution," 105.

85. On the use of the language of "garbage reduction movements" and the "Garbage War," see *Asahi shinbun*, November 21, 1971, and December 1, 1971; *Yomiuri shinbun*, December 14, 1971, and January 30, 1972.

86. For example, the No Packaging Movement sprouted up in the Tokyo wards of Suginami, Shinjuku, and Minato; the cities of Musashino and Machida; and beyond the capital in prefectures like Ibaraki, Kanagawa, Yamanashi, Hyōgo, and Ōita. *Asahi shinbun*, November 22, 1971; *Yomiuri shinbun*, December 14, 1971; February 2 and 18, 1972; and October 7, 1977; Tabuse Mitsuko, "Genryō, sairiyō e no kyōryoku to shisei," in Yorimoto, *Gomi ni hikari o ateyō*, 127–28. Both Shinjuku and Minato organized "no packaging days" (*nō hōsō dē*) in their wards. *Yomiuri shinbun*, February 2 and 18, 1972. There was also an attempt to turn *furoshiki* into fashionable items. *Yomiuri shinbun*, December 4, 1971.

87. *Asahi shinbun*, November 3 and 6, 1971. On similar activities in the Suginami ward, see Ōhashi, "Gomi sensō," 134.

88. *Asahi shinbun*, May 24, 1972.

89. "Muda na hōsō tsuihō," *Gomi sensō shūhō* 46 (November 3, 1972): 2. On the activities of one daily life school in the city of Kunitachi, see the publication of the Tokyo New Life Movement Association, *Kurashi o yutaka ni* 55 (January 21, 1972): 6.

90. *Asahi shinbun*, November 21, 1971.

91. *Asahi shinbun*, November 3, 6, 19, and 22, 1971; December 1, 1971; November 23, 1973; and February 5, 1979; Yamanouchi Shōgo, "Eko mākechingu e no apurōchi," *Sērusu manejā* 8, no. 5 (May 1972): 76; Kyoto Shinbunsha, ed., *Ima nara kateru gomi sensō* (Kyoto: Kyoto Shinbunsha, 1973), 267–68.

92. Yamanouchi, "Eko mākechingu," 77.

93. Saitō Yoshio et al., "Haikibutsu no shori, sairiyō," *Jurisuto* 571 (October 1, 1974): 28.

94. *Yomiuri shinbun*, January 30, 1972; *Asahi shinbun*, December 1, 1971.

95. *Asahi shinbun*, November 19, 1971.

96. *Asahi shinbun*, November 21, 1971; May 24, 1972; and February 5, 1979.

97. Several dozen consumer and women's groups reported that from October 1973 to March 1974, at the height of the Oil Shock, they were especially active. And in a survey of forty-six such organizations, 73.3 percent said that they were arranging swap meets, and 66.7 percent that they had undertaken movements against excessive packaging. Kokumin Seikatsu Sentā, *Monobusoku sawagi*, 170–71.

98. *Asahi shinbun*, May 24, 1972, and November 29, 1974; *Yomiuri shinbun*, July 4, 1974.

99. In a survey of 1,291 Tokyo housewives conducted in January 1975, not many (13.9 percent) had yet been to a swap meet. But almost half (48.6 percent) said that if there was a swap meet held near them, they would sell (48.6 percent) or purchase (38.6 percent) items. *Shufu no ishiki chōsa, Shōwa 49 nendo* (Tokyo: Shufu Rengōkai, 1975), 14, 17–18.

100. Satō Tomio, "Shimin undō ni sasaerareta atarashī ryūtsū jigyō tai no tenkai" (Ph.D. diss., 1997), 10.

101. *Yomiuri shinbun*, November 19, 1977. On another swap meet held in Suginami ward, a well-attended affair that had about three thousand items for sale, see Ōkubo Motosaburō, "Gomi to toshi to ningen to," *Keizai hyōron* 23, no. 2 (February 1974): 110.

102. Nagoya-shi Kankyō Jigyōkyoku, *Shufu no gomi kōgengaku* (Mainichi Eigasha, 1978), 14–15.

103. *Yomiuri shinbun*, October 16, 1976.

104. *Yomiuri shinbun*, March 9, 1974.

105. *Yomiuri shinbun*, May 3, 1975.

106. Of the housewives surveyed, 62 percent said they knew of a repair corner, 35 percent did not. Fourteen percent had actually made use of the service. *Shufu no ishiki chōsa*, 11.

107. *Asahi shinbun*, December 8, 1977.

108. "Tsukaisute jidai o kangaenaosu (July 14, 1973)," in *Korekara dō suru shakai to kurashi*, ed. "Tsukaisute Jidai o Kangaeru Kai" Jūshūnen Shinpo Jikkō Iinkai (Tokyo: Hakujusha, 1984), 202; Tsuchida Takashi, "Tanoshiku nakayoku samazama ni," ibid., ii–iii.

109. "Tsukaisute Jidai o Kangaeru Kai kiyaku," ibid., 205.

110. Zukeran Kaoru, "Tsukaisute Jidai o Kangaeru Kai," *Gendai no me* 16, no. 1 (November 1975): 198–99.

111. Tsuchida Takashi and Yamada Harumi in discussion with author, October 11, 2015.

112. Ibid.

113. On Niijima Atsuyoshi, see Yoshihiro Kuriyama, "A Japanese 'Maoist,'" *Asian Survey* 16, no. 9 (September 1976): 846–54. On the Yamagishikai, see John Spiri, "Whatever Happened to Yamagishi?" *Asia-Pacific Journal* 6, no. 2 (February 2008).

114. Tsuchida Takashi and Yamada Harumi in discussion with author, October 11 and 13, 2015.

115. "Tsukaisute jidai o kangaenaosu," 200–201; Zukeran, "Tsukaisute Jidai o Kangaeru Kai," 198; Tsuchida Takashi and Yamada Harumi in discussion with author, October 11, 2015.

116. Tsuchida Takashi and Yamada Harumi in discussion with author, October 11 and 13, 2015.

117. Zukeran, "Tsukaisute Jidai o Kangaeru Kai," 198; "Tsukaisute Jidai o Kangaeru Kai" Jūshūnen Shinpo Jikkō Iinkai, 207; Tsuchida Takashi and Yamada Harumi in discussion with author, October 11, 2015.

118. "Tsukaisute jidai o kangaenaosu," 202.

119. Akiyama Hanako, "'Tsukaisute Jidai o Kangaeru Kai' de sugoshita sanjūnen," *Karin* 76 (November 2003): 14.

120. "Tomin wa gomi mondai o dō miru ka (sono 6)," *Gomi sensō shūhō* 111 (March 1, 1974): 8.

121. Ishimaru Yoshitomi, "'Zero seichō' no higenjitsusei," *Asahi jānaru* 15, no. 47 (November 30, 1973): 13. Note that Ishimaru was presenting, not promoting, this narrative.

122. *Yomiuri shinbun*, September 22, 1974.

123. Numazu Shiyakusho Kōseika, ed., *Shōshigen jidai no shōhi seikatsu* ([Numazu]: Numazu-shi, 1977), i, 159.

124. Shimizu Keihachirō, "Nihonteki shigen o kangaeru," in *Shōshigen Nihon no kōzu*, ed. Nihon Seinen Kaigisho (Tokyo: Daiyamondosha, 1974), 13–15.

125. Matsushita Kōnosuke, "Shigen wa mugen ni aru (May 17, 1977)," in *Matsushita Kōnosuke hatsugen shū*, ed. PHP Sōgō Kenkyūjo Kenkyū Honbu "Matsushita Kōnosuke Hatsugen Shū" Hensanshitsu Henshū Seisaku, vol. 5 (Kyoto: PHP Kenkyūjo, 1991), 21–23.

126. *Asahi shinbun*, March 25, 1973.

127. *Shōhisha undō sanjūnen* (Osaka: Kansai Shufu Rengōkai, 1976), 155. On the postwar history of the National Federation of Regional Women's Associations and the Kansai Housewives Association, see Patricia L. Maclachlan, *Consumer Politics in Postwar Japan* (New York: Columbia University Press, 2002), 62, 65–67.

128. *Mono no seimei futatabi* (Tokyo: Shin Seikatsu Undō Kyōkai, 1975), 2–3.

129. Asano Junji, of Tokyo's Sanitation Bureau, articulated the hope that the Oil Shock would precipitate such a societal shift, which would also help the people of Tokyo win the battle against garbage. See *Kurashi o yutaka ni* 66 (February 25, 1974): 3.

130. Honda Atsuhiro, *Gomi monogatari* (Tokyo: Shōenerugī Sentā, 1978), 44–45.

131. Ōkubo, "Gomi to toshi to ningen to," 111.

132. Yanagisawa Takashi, "Gomi no sairiyō," *Jurisuto* 571 (October 1, 1974): 48; Tokyo-to Seisōkyoku Sōmubu Sōmuka, *Tokyo-to seisō jigyō*, 276–78. On one such system in the city of Chiba, see *Yomiuri shinbun*, October 19, 1976.

133. On plastics, see Harada Yoshishige, "Gomi sensō no shuyaku," *Kagaku* 28, no. 2 (February 1973): 44–52.

134. According to Yanagisawa Takashi, there were 20,872 collection firms in Japan in 1974. Yanagisawa, "Gomi no sairiyō," 47.

135. In 1971, a system for the collection of large refuse had been established in all twenty-three wards of Tokyo. Tokyo-to Seisōkyoku Sōmubu Sōmuka, *Tokyo-to seisō jigyō*, 262, 266. In April 1979, the city of Naha in Okinawa prefecture began to make a distinction between combustible and noncombustible garbage. Nihon Keizai Shinbunsha, ed., *Gomyunichī* (Tokyo: Nihon Keizai Shinbunsha, 1979), 114.

136. Plastic was added as a fourth category in April 1999. Mano Morihiro, "'Wakereba shigen, mazereba gomi' o aikotoba ni hajimatta san bunbetsu shūshū 'Numazu hōshiki' no kaishi kara 40-nen no ayumi," *Toshi seisō* 68, no. 325 (May 2015): 26–27.

137. Ōkubo, "Gomi to toshi to ningen to," 108; *Apāto no gomi mondai* ([Tokyo]: Tokyo-to Seisōkyoku, 1976), 3–6.

138. The city of Osaka resisted separate collection, arguing that complicating the process of collecting and transporting garbage would undo recently attained progress in the rationalization of waste management. There was concern, too, that the effects of recycling would be compromised by the number of goods that were made of a mix of materials like plastic, metal, and wood. Nihon Keizai Shinbunsha, *Gomyunichī*, 1, 49, 133.

139. *Asahi shinbun*, March 25, 1973.

140. *Asahi shinbun*, October 28, 1974. The Federation of Housewives also seemed to discourage the purchase of disposable chopsticks. Tabuse, "Genryō, sairiyō," 128.

141. *Asahi shinbun*, September 18, 1974; *Mono no seimei*, 40–43, 55–59.

142. *Yomiuri shinbun*, November 10, 1974.

143. *Yomiuri shinbun*, December 16, 1974, and February 13, 1975.

144. *Tabemono o taisetsu ni suru dokuhon* (Tokyo: Betā Hōmu Kyōkai, 1976), 1–2.

145. Shigen to Enerugī o Taisetsu ni Suru Kokumin Undō Chūō Renraku Kaigi, Shōshigen Shōenerugī Kokumin Undō Chihō Suishin Kaigi, and Shin Seikatsu Undō Kyōkai, eds., *Shōenerugī undō suishin kinyū zenkoku shūkai* ([Tokyo]: Shigen to Enerugī o Taisetsu ni Suru Kokumin Undō Chūō Renraku Kaigi, Shōshigen Shōenerugī Kokumin Undō Chihō Suishin Kaigi, and Shin Seikatsu Undō Kyōkai, 1979), 41–42.

146. *Tabemono o taisetsu ni*, 1–2. A survey conducted by the Life Study Group (Kurashi no Kenkyūkai), a housewives' association in the Kansai area, revealed that even when people thought that they were being mindful of waste, they were throwing away substantial amounts of food. *Asahi shinbun*, February 12, 1974.

147. *Yomiuri shinbun*, September 22, 1974.

148. Keizai Kikakuchō Kokumin Seikatsukyoku and Kokumin Seikatsu Seisakuka, *Shōshigen, shōenerugī*, i, 1–3, 7–10.

149. *Asahi shinbun*, November 16, 18, and 20, 1973.

150. *Asahi shinbun*, October 28, 1974.

151. *Yomiuri shinbun*, October 21, 1973.

152. *Nagasaki shinbun*, January 9, 1974.

153. *Asahi shinbun,* November 12, 19, and 30, 1973.

154. *Yomiuri shinbun,* January 1, 1974.

155. *Asahi shinbun,* November 1, 4, 16, and 27, 1973.

156. These energy-saving measures were reportedly taken by respondents to a survey of 610 housewives conducted in the summer of 1974. Matsui Shizuko, Kawai Keiko, and Matsui Matsunaga, "Shufu no shōenerugī ni kansuru ishiki ni tsuite," *Kaseigaku kenkyū* 22, no. 1 (September 1975): 54, 57.

157. Shigen to Enerugī o Taisetsu ni Suru Kokumin Undō Chūō Renraku Kaigi, Shōshigen Shōenerugī Kokumin Undō Chihō Suishin Kaigi, and Shin Seikatsu Undō Kyōkai, *Shōenerugī undō,* 56–58.

158. Matsui, Kawai, and Matsui, "Shufu no shōenerugī," 54, 57.

159. *Yomiuri shinbun,* October 21, 1973.

160. Banmo Yoshimitsu, *Gojira tai hedora* (Tōhō, 1971). Many thanks to Sharona Bol linger for bringing this film to my attention. For an analysis of other films about disaster from this period, see Susan J. Napier, "Panic Sites," *Journal of Japanese Studies* 19, no. 2 (Summer 1993): 327–51.

161. For example, Shibata Tokue argued that the conventional wisdom of thinking serially about production, consumption, then disposal needed to be challenged. He proposed that disposal should be the starting point, and that production should be limited to the amount of goods that could be disposed of easily. Nakamura, *Ōraru hisutorī,* 25.

162. Sangyō Keikaku Kondankai, ed., *Sangyō kōzō no kaikaku* (Tokyo: Taisei Shuppansha, 1973), 202–5; Shibata Tokue, "Gomi mondai no tenkai," *Toshi mondai kenkyū* 28, no. 12 (December 1976): 25.

CHAPTER 4. A BRIGHT STINGINESS

1. "Dai ichibu, Osaka," *Fujin kurabu* (January 1974): 348.

2. Yamataka Shigeru, "Kechikechi undō to ningensei kaifuku," *Gekkan kokumin seikatsu* 4, no. 4 (April 1974): 1; *Yomiuri shinbun,* December 12, 1973.

3. Yamataka, "Kechikechi undō," 1.

4. Sumitomo Shintaku Ginkō Kurashi no Shiryōshitsu, ed., *Konna ni muda ga atta no ka* (Tokyo: Mainichi Shinbunsha, 1974), 222; Yamataka, "Kechikechi undō," 1.

5. *Yomiuri shinbun,* September 17, 1973.

6. *Tabemono o taisetsu ni suru dokuhon* (Tokyo: Betā Hōmu Kyōkai, 1976), 2.

7. *Katei shūri dokuhon* (Tokyo: Betā Hōmu Kyōkai, 1975), 1–2. Wakamiya Akitsugu wove a similar version of a past in which people had a heart that valued the life of things. See Wakamiya Akitsugu, "Mono ga 'aru' kedo 'nai' toki no seikatsu tekunikku," *Ōru seikatsu* 29, no. 4 (March 1974): 76.

8. "Dai ichibu," 348–49.

9. Akabane Shūichi, *Kechi seikatsu no chie* (Tokyo: Ēru Shuppansha, 1975), 78, 80, 92.

10. Sumitomo Shintaku Ginkō Kurashi no Shiryōshitsu, *Konna ni muda,* 73, 76.

11. "Dai ichibu," 347.

12. "Yo no naka zeitaku ni narimashita," *Fujin seikatsu* (September 1973): 214.

13. "Dai ichibu," 347.

14. Sumitomo Shintaku Ginkō Kurashi no Shiryōshitsu, *Konna ni muda,* 167–68.

15. *Tabemono o taisetsu ni,* 2, 4–8.

16. "Dai ichibu," 347.

17. Ibid., 347–48; *Yomiuri shinbun,* April 21, 1973.

18. Sumitomo Shintaku Ginkō Kurashi no Shiryōshitsu, *Konna ni muda,* 88–89, 92–95; *Yomiuri shinbun,* April 21, 1973, and September 17, 1973; "Gonin no shufu ga jikkō shiteiru taikenteki kechikechi seikatsu," *Fujin seikatsu* (June 1974): 191.

19. "Yo no naka zeitaku," 213.

20. See Lauren Weber, *In Cheap We Trust* (New York: Little, Brown and Company, 2009).

21. Yamato Yūzō, "'Setsuyaku' to 'kechi' to wa chigau," *Shufu to seikatsu* 28, no. 13 (November 1973): 270.

22. "Watashitachi ga shiawase ni naru 'setsuyaku' to wa donna koto?" *Shufu to seikatsu* 28, no. 13 (November 1973): 271–73.

23. Ihara Ryūichi, "Kechi wa bitoku ka akuto ka," *Ōru seikatsu* 29, no. 2 (February 1974): 48–50; "Gonin no shufu," 186–87.

24. Bandō Eriko, *Āra mottainai!* (Tokyo: Shūeisha, 1975), 7–9.

25. Ibid., 11.

26. Ibid., 10–11, 13–14, 32–33.

27. Ibid., 45, 51–58.

28. "Madamada yareru shanai 'kechikechi' dai sakusen," *Kindai chūshō kigyō* 15, no. 7 (June 1980): 54; "Tsukaisute jidai to monobusoku," *Gekkan sekai keizai* 2, no. 22 (November 1973): 225.

29. Yoshida Sei, "Kechikechi undō no susume," *PPM* 4, no. 10 (October 1973): 1.

30. Takafusa Nakamura, *The Postwar Japanese Economy* (Tokyo: University of Tokyo Press, 1995), 205–7; Seiyama Takurō, "A Radical Interpretation of Postwar Economic Policies," in *Japanese Capitalism since 1945*, ed. Tessa Morris-Suzuki and Takuro Seiyama (New York: M. E. Sharpe, 1989), 60–63.

31. "Ichiryū kaisha de wa yaru 'kechikechi undō' no kazeatari," *Keizai tenbō* 43, no. 6 (April 1, 1971): 78–79.

32. "Kigyō no 'kechikechi undō' dai sakusen no imi wa?" *Shūkan yomiuri*, March 5, 1971, 139–41.

33. "Ichiryū kaisha," 79; "Kigyō no 'kechikechi undō,'" 139.

34. *Yomiuri shinbun*, November 13, 1970.

35. *Asahi shinbun*, September 24, 1971.

36. The saying in the original Japanese was "Chiri mo tsumoreba yama to naru." "Ichiryū kaisha," 78.

37. Ibid., 78–79.

38. Japanese National Railways was not alone in economizing on pencils. Tombow Pencil (Tonbo Enpitsu) estimated a drop in orders of about 20 percent as clients reduced or temporarily ceased their purchasing of pencils. "Kigyō no 'kechikechi undō,'" 138–39, 141.

39. *Asahi shinbun*, September 24, 1971.

40. "Kigyō no 'kechikechi undō,'" 141.

41. "Tsukaisute jidai to monobusoku," 225.

42. "Kechikechi setsuyaku," *Shūkan daiyamondo* (June 25, 1977): 10–12.

43. "Madamada yareru," 55–59. After the Oil Shock, the phrase "stinginess movements" also came to be used in non-corporate workplaces, such as government offices, mainly to describe energy-saving efforts. See, for example, *Nagasaki shinbun*, January 9, 1974.

44. "Kechikechi setsuyaku," 10.

45. Satake Hiroaki, "Toyota seisan hōshiki to 'muda' gainen no ganchiku," *Fukui kenritsu daigaku keizai keiei kenkyū* 6 (March 1999): 29–30.

46. Ōno Tai'ichi, *Toyota seisan hōshiki* (Tokyo: Daiyamondosha, 1978), i, 97, 106.

47. Ibid., 36–38, 75, 97.

48. As explained by the historian William Tsutsui: "In his attempts to slash 'non-value-added work' . . . Ōno applied job routines far stricter than the standards recommended by American Taylorites or the experts of Japan's efficiency movement. Under the Toyota regime, standard times for workshop tasks were based on the abilities of the most skilled

workers, rather than being pegged at an average level or set in accordance with scientifically determined optimal times." William M. Tsutsui, *Manufacturing Ideology* (Princeton: Princeton University Press, 1998), 187.

49. Sasaki Tōru, *MCON Report No. 109* (Tokyo: Mākechingu Kondankai, 1979), i.

50. *Kokumin seikatsu hakusho, Shōwa gojū nendo* (Tokyo: Keizai Kikakuchō, 1975), 11–13.

51. Naikaku Sōri Daijin Kanbō Kōhōshitsu, *Kokumin seikatsu ni kansuru seron chōsa* (Tokyo: Naikaku Sōri Daijin Kanbō Kōhōshitsu, 1974), 28.

52. *Kokumin seikatsu hakusho*, 9–10.

53. Naikaku Sōri Daijin Kanbō Kōhōshitsu, *Kokumin seikatsu*, 26–27.

54. *Kokumin seikatsu hakusho*, 7–8.

55. Tokyo-to Tominshitsu, ed., *Gomi mondai ni kansuru seron chōsa* (Tokyo: Tokyo-to Tominshitsu, 1975), 44.

56. Honda Atsuhiro, *Gomi monogatari* (Tokyo: Shōenerugī Sentā, 1978), 21.

57. *Kokumin seikatsu hakusho*, 8–9.

58. The head of the Economic Planning Agency claimed, in 1975, that the attitude toward saving was not a temporary response to changes in the economic environment. *Kokumin seikatsu hakusho*, i.

59. Kankyō Sangyō Shinbunsha, *Haikibutsu nenkan, 1981-nen ban* (Tokyo: Kankyō Sangyō Shinbunsha, 1980), 28; Kankyō Sangyō Shinbunsha, *Haikibutsu nenkan, 1986-nen ban* (Tokyo: Kankyō Sangyō Shinbunsha, 1985), 43.

60. Shibata Tokue, "Gomi mondai ni tenkai," *Toshi mondai kenkyū* 28, no. 12 (December 1976): 25.

61. Keizai Kikakuchō, ed., *Shōwa 52 nendo kokumin seikatsu hakusho* (Tokyo: Ōkurashō Insatsukyoku, 1977), 23–24, 94–95.

62. Sōgō Kenkyū Kaihatsu Kikō, ed., *Shōenerugī no jittai to hyōka* (Tokyo: Sōgō Kenkyū Kaihatsu Kikō, 1979), 15.

63. Naikaku Sōri Daijin Kanbō Kōhōshitsu, *Shōenerugī, shōshigen ni kansuru seron chōsa* (Tokyo: Naikaku Sōri Daijin Kanbō Kōhōshitsu, 1978), 3–5, 195.

64. *Yomiuri shinbun*, April 21, 1973.

65. Sōgō Kenkyū Kaihatsu Kikō, *Shōenerugī no jittai*, 81–83.

66. *Asahi shinbun*, July 27, 1976.

67. *Asahi shinbun*, March 8, 1978.

68. Nakamura, *Postwar Japanese Economy*, 237–40.

69. *Yomiuri shinbun*, June 15, 1979.

70. Sasaki, *MCON Report*, 11; *Yomiuri shinbun*, June 27, 1979.

71. *Asahi shinbun*, July 5, 1979.

72. *Mainichi shinbun*, August 24, 1979.

73. *Yomiuri shinbun*, April 15, 1979.

74. *Yomiuri shinbun*, June 10, 1979.

75. "Kore ga enerugī setsuyaku daihonzan 'Esaki tsūsan daijin' no katta 'natsufuku,'" *Shūkan shinchō* 24, no. 17 (April 26, 1979): 152–54; *Yomiuri shinbun*, May 1 and 24, 1979, and June 6 and 10, 1979; *Asahi shinbun*, May 30, 1979; "Shōene rukku," *Ōru seikatsu* (July 1979): 11.

76. *Asahi shinbun*, May 30, 1979.

77. *Asahi shinbun*, March 16, 1979, and May 29, 1979; "Shōene rukku," *Tosei kenkyū* 13, no. 8 (August 1980): 36.

78. "Shōene rukku no honmei wa jinbei," *Ōru taishū* 33, no. 14 (August 1980): 42–43.

79. *Yomiuri shinbun*, June 20, 1979; "Shōene rukku no honmei," 43.

80. "Kore zo! Konka no shōene rukku," *Ōru taishū* 32, no. 10 (June 1979): 46–47; Naitō Hideo, "Shōene rukku no yukue," *Gekkan seifu shiryō* 63 (August 1979): 1.

81. "Shōene rukku no honmei," 42.

82. For a rare mention of energy-saving fashions for women, see *Asahi shinbun*, July 24, 1979; *Mainichi shinbun*, October 26, 1979.

83. "Shōene rukku no honmei," 43; Shinoda Yūjiro, "Shōene rukku to Nihonjin," *Keizai ōrai* 32, no. 7 (July 1980): 106–7.

84. *Asahi shinbun*, May 30, 1979; *Yomiuri shinbun*, June 13 and 16, 1979.

85. *Yomiuri shinbun*, June 15, 1979.

86. "Kore ga enerugī setsuyaku," 153; *Yomiuri shinbun*, May 1, 1979, and June 6, 1979.

87. *Yomiuri shinbun*, January 1, 1979. For another description of this trend, see Sakano Shigenobu, *Ikigai to yutakasa o motomete* (Tokyo: Sankaidō, 1979).

88. Keizai Kikakuchō, *Shōwa 52 nendo kokumin seikatsu hakusho*, 15.

89. Naikaku Sōri Daijin Kanbō Kōhōshitsu, *Kokumin seikatsu ni kansuru seron chōsa* (Tokyo: Naikaku Sōri Daijin Kanbō Kōhōshitsu, 1979), 14, 100.

90. Nakamura, *Postwar Japanese Economy*, 213–18.

CHAPTER 5. CONSUMING DESIRES

1. *Yomiuri shinbun*, March 21, 1984.

2. Tanaka Yasuo, *Nantonaku, kurisutaru* (Tokyo: Kawade Shobō Shinsha, 1981); *Japan Times*, September 4, 2005; Masao Miyoshi, "Against the Native Grain," in *Postmodernism and Japan*, ed. Masao Miyoshi and H. D. Harootunian (Durham: Duke University Press, 1989), 157; Norma Field, "*Somehow*," in *Postmodernism and Japan*, 170–71; Anne Allison, *Millennial Monsters* (Berkeley: University of California Press, 2006), 74. For a less knowledgeable discussion of *Somehow, Crystal*, see Morris Berman, *Neurotic Beauty* (Portland, OR: One Spirit Press, 2015).

3. GDP Data from the World Bank, http://data.worldbank.org/indicator/NY.GDP. PCAP.CD?end=2000&locations=JP-US&start=1980 (accessed August 18, 2015).

4. Toshiaki Tachibanaki, *Confronting Income Inequality in Japan* (Cambridge: MIT Press, 2005), 15–16, 32.

5. The exact number of survey respondents was 3,506. Naikaku Sōri Daijin Kanbō Kōhōshitsu, *Kurashi no ishiki ni kansuru seron chōsa* (Tokyo: Naikaku Sōri Daijin Kanbō Kōhōshitsu, 1984), 18, 289.

6. For household savings data, see Charles Yuji Horioka, "Are the Japanese Unique?" in *The Ambivalent Consumer*, ed. Sheldon Garon and Patricia L. Maclachlan (Ithaca: Cornell University Press, 2006), 114–16, 135–36. The first question in a survey about life and saving conducted by the Prime Minister's Office in 1989 asked people how they thought about saving. Of the 3,787 respondents, more said that they were not wasting money and saving as much as they could (52.2 percent) than emphasizing their own capabilities or an affluent lifestyle and not fixating on saving (40.9 percent). But the latter answer was given more than the former by women in their twenties and men in their twenties, thirties, and forties. Naikaku Sōri Daijin Kanbō Kōhōshitsu, *Kurashi to chochiku ni kansuru seron chōsa* ([Tokyo]: Naikaku Sōri Daijin Kanbō Kōhōshitsu, 1989), 1, 18–19, 73. For more on saving during an affluent time, see Chochiku Keizai Kenkyū Sentā, ed., *Yutaka na jidai no kurashi to chochiku* (Tokyo: Gyōsei, 1989).

7. Gay Hawkins, *The Ethics of Waste* (Lanham, MD: Rowman & Littlefield, 2006), vii.

8. "'Mono banare' sesō no naka de no sararīman katei no mochimono chōsa," *Rōdō to keizai* 626 (February 1983): 24–25.

9. Kōseishō, ed., *Kōsei hakusho* (Tokyo: Gyōsei, 1991), 6.

10. Saitō Sei'ichirō, "Shōhi bunkaron no kaitō," *Voice* 3 (March 1986): 109, 111.

11. *Asahi shinbun*, November 10, 1989.

12. Awata Fusaho, "Kono mama de wa ikenai," *Sekai* 529 (July 1989): 92–93.

13. *Nikkei ryūtsū shinbun*, November 11, 1989.

14. Naikaku Sōri Daijin Kanbō Kōhōshitsu, *Kokumin seikatsu ni kansuru seron chōsa* (Tokyo: Naikaku Sōri Daijin Kanbō Kōhōshitsu, [1992]), 3, 85; Naikaku Sōri Daijin Kanbō Kōhōshitsu, *Kokumin seikatsu ni kansuru seron chōsa* (Tokyo: Naikaku Sōri Daijin Kanbō Kōhōshitsu, [1986]), 49; Naikaku Sōri Daijin Kanbō Kōhōshitsu, *Kokumin seikatsu ni kansuru seron chōsa* (Tokyo: Naikaku Sōri Daijin Kanbō Kōhōshitsu, [1989]), 91.

15. Keizai Kikakuchō Kokumin Seikatsukyoku, ed., *Shōenerugī seikatsu no suishin no tame ni* (Tokyo: Ōkurashō Insatsukyoku, 1981), 4, 16–19. The Research Group on Energy-Saving Lifestyles was established by the bureaucratic consultative body known as the Council on National Lifestyles (Kokumin Seikatsu Shingikai).

16. Keizai Kikakuchō Kokumin Seikatsukyoku, *Shōenerugī seikatsu*, 133–35.

17. *Asahi shinbun*, September 4, 1981.

18. Hashimoto Takashi, *Shōenerugī no chie* (Tokyo: Kōdansha, 1980), 6, 298–301.

19. Sugihara Yasuo et al., *Gendai shakai* (Tokyo: Jiyū Shobō, 1985), 166, 169–70. The original version of the textbook was authorized for use in high school social studies classes by the Ministry of Education (Monbushō) in 1981; this revised version was approved in 1984.

20. Keizai Kikakuchō Kokumin Seikatsukyoku, *Shōenerugī seikatsu*, 16–17.

21. The exact number of respondents was 3,889. *1980-nen ichiman setai no shōene sōtenken hakusho* (Tokyo: Shin Seikatsu Undō Kyōkai, 1980), 1–3, 9–11, 143.

22. Tokyo Denryoku Eigyōbu and Shōenerugī Sentā, *Okyakusama no shōenerugī ishiki to kōdō* (Tokyo: Tokyo Denryoku Eigyōbu and Shōenerugī Sentā, 1980), 8–9, 11.

23. Furukawa Denki Kōgyō Kabushiki Gaisha, Netsu Shisutemu Jigyōbu, *Enerugī, shigen mondai ni kansuru shufu no ishiki* (Furukawa Denki Kōgyō Kabushiki Gaisha, 1981), 1–2, 5.

24. The exact number of respondents was 7,878. Naikaku Sōri Daijin Kanbō Kōhōshitsu, *Kurashi to shigen ni kansuru seron chōsa* (Tokyo: Naikaku Sōri Daijin Kanbō Kōhōshitsu, 1985), 1, 10–11, 122.

25. Keizai Kikakuchō Kokumin Seikatsukyoku, ed., *Yutakasa to risaikuru* (Tokyo: Ōkurashō Insatsukyoku, 1989), ii, v.

26. Kishimoto Shigenobu, "'Yutakasa' no gensō to kankyō mondai," *Risaikuru bunka* 24 (Spring–Summer 1989): 11–12.

27. "Sengen," *Chūō kaigi kaihō* 12 (March 1983): 1.

28. Shigen Enerugīchō and Shōenerugī Sekiyu Daitai Enerugī Taisakuka, *Shōenerugī sōran, 1990* (Tokyo: Tsūsan Shiryō Chōsakai, 1989), 72.

29. *Asahi shinbun*, September 9, 1985.

30. For the February 1980 survey, n = 4085; for May 1985, n = 7,878. Naikaku Sōri Daijin Kanbō Kōhōshitsu, *Shōenerugī ni kansuru seron chōsa* (Tokyo: Naikaku Sōri Daijin Kanbō Kōhōshitsu, [1990]), 11.

31. Kankyōshō Daijin Kanbō Haikibutsu, Risaikuru Taisakubu Haikibutsu Taisakuka, *Nihon no haikibutsu shori* (Tokyo: Kankyōshō, 2001), 4, http://www.env.go.jp/recycle/waste_tech/ippan/h10/index.html (accessed July 21, 2016); Kōseishō, *Kōsei hakusho*, 14–19.

32. Kurīn Japan Sentā, ed., *Sodai gomi no yūkō riyō manyuaru* (Tokyo: Kurīn Japan Sentā, 1985), 121, 130.

33. *Yomiuri shinbun*, August 14, 1989.

34. *Yomiuri shinbun*, July 2, 1983.

35. *Haikibutsu no genryō to sairiyō, shigenka tokushū*, no. 67 of *Chōsa shiryō* (Tokyo: Tokyo-to Gikai Gikaikyoku Chōsabu, 1991), 118–19, 128.

36. Ichihashi Takashi, *Gomi to kurashi no sengo gojūnen shi* (Tokyo: Risaikuru Bunka-sha, 2000), 92.

37. Kōseishō, *Kōsei hakusho*, 8, 21.

38. *Yomiuri shinbun*, July 12, 1982.

39. Kōseishō, *Kōsei hakusho*, 8.

40. *Nihon keizai shinbun*, June 14, 1985.

41. "Purasuchikku gomi sensō," *Kagaku asahi* 49, no. 10 (October 1989): 106.

42. Murata Tokuji, "Sekiyu bunka to purasuchikku mondai kara tsukaisute shakai o kangaeru," *Risaikuru bunka* 30 (April–June 1991): 21.

43. *Haikibutsu no genryō*, 130–32.

44. Ichihashi, *Gomi to kurashi*, 84, 94, 102.

45. Yamamoto Isao, "Tsukaisute yōki o kangaeru," *Chūō kaigi kaihō* 26 (December 1986): 15–16. In 1983, 730 million glass bottles were returned for reuse; by 1988, that figure was 210 million. Ishizawa Kiyoshi, "Gomi o dasanai atarashī ikikata," *Chishiki* 106 (September 1990): 147.

46. Kōseishō, *Kōsei hakusho*, 21–23; *Haikibutsu no genryō*, 140.

47. In Tokyo, paper grew from 38.3 percent of burnable waste in 1984 to 45.6 percent in 1988. Takahashi Takayuki, "TOKYO SLIM '89," *Toseijin* 53, no. 7 (July 1989): 16–20.

48. "Gomi mondai o kiru," *Keidanren geppō* 38, no. 12 (December 1990): 28.

49. Katsumi Yorimoto, "Tokyo's Serious Waste Problem," *Japan Quarterly* 37, no. 3 (July 1990): 331; Ishizawa, "Gomi o dasanai," 145.

50. Gotō Sukehiro, *Gendai no gomi mondai* (Tokyo: Chūō Hōki Shuppan, 1983), 166.

51. Ide Toshihiko, "Gomi 'shori' no sakkaku," *Sekai* 532 (September 1989): 195, 197, 200–201.

52. *Yomiuri shinbun*, October 31, 1984.

53. *Asahi shinbun*, June 14, 1985.

54. Kōseishō, *Kōsei hakusho*, 9–10, 18, 34–35.

55. Tsuji Kiyoaki et al., *Gendai shakai* (Tokyo: Jiyū Shobō, 1991), 171–72. This textbook was originally approved for use in high school social studies classes by the Ministry of Education in 1981; revised versions were subsequently authorized in 1984, 1987, and 1990.

56. Allen Hershkowitz and Eugene Salerni, *Garbage Management in Japan* (New York: INFORM, 1987), 39.

57. Gotō, *Gendai no gomi mondai*, 152; Monna Kimiyuki, *Seikatsu no saikōchiku* (Tokyo: Shin Jidaisha, 1982), 154–55.

58. *Yomiuri shinbun*, June 28, 1980, and July 9, 1980.

59. Shigen to Enerugī o Taisetsu ni Suru Kokumin Undō Chūō Kaigi, ed., *Shōshigen, shōenerugī undō jissen jirei shū* (Tokyo: Shigen to Enerugī o Taisetsu ni Suru Kokumin Undō Chūō Kaigi, 1982), 16–18.

60. *Asahi shinbun*, January 1, 1981; *Yomiuri shinbun*, June 21, 1981; "Tokyo-to no gomi shi'nyō shori no genkyō to kadai," *Tokyo raifu* 21, no. 2 (February 1983): 18.

61. Henshūbu, "'Asobi gokoro' de hirogeru chiiki o mamoru 'kokorozashi,'" *Asahi jānaru* 25, no. 28 (July 1, 1983): 18–23.

62. Nishimura Ichirō, *Ikasō mono no inochi* (Tokyo: Rengō Shuppan, 1986), 158–59.

63. Yomiuri Shinbunsha, ed., *Daisan no shigen* (Tokyo: Risaikuru Bunkasha, 1987), 27–28.

64. "Risaikuru-tte nan da?" *Gekkan risaikuru* (March 15, 1980): 1; *Asahi shinbun*, April 8, 1984. On the activities of the various branches of the Recycling Movement Citizens' Association, see Shōhin Kagaku Kenkyūjo and CDI, ed., *Seikatsuzai no shobun to sairyūtsū* (Tokyo: Shōhin Kagaku Kenkyūjo, 1987), 82–93.

65. *Asahi shinbun*, June 25, 1987.

66. Yomiuri Shinbunsha, *Daisan no shigen*, 29.

67. *Asahi shinbun*, May 1, 1988.

68. "Risaikuru shoppu gaido," *Asahi jānaru* 25, no. 28 (July 1, 1983): 24–29; Nishimura, *Ikasō mono no inochi*, 159.

69. *Yomiuri shinbun*, July 2, 1983.

70. *Yomiuri shinbun*, August 14, 1980.

71. *Asahi shinbun*, October 27, 1989; Koyama Sonoko, "Gomi no hirogari," *Tosei kenkyū* 23, no. 3 (March 1990): 61.

72. *Risaikuru nōto* (Kyoto: Mono o Taisetsu ni Suru Undō Kyoto-fu Suishin Kaigi, Kyoto-fu Shōkōbu Shōhi Seikatsuka, 1989).

73. Itō Kiyoe et al., *Katei ippan* (Tokyo: Tokyo Shoseki Kabushiki Gaisha, 1988). This textbook was authorized for use in high school home economics courses by the Ministry of Education in 1987.

74. *Yomiuri shinbun*, June 7, 1980.

75. Kōkyō Hōkoku Kikō, "Mottainai obake" (1982), http://www.youtube.com/ watch?v=6be2IvKKdo4 (accessed July 20, 2016).

76. "*Risaikuru ondo*," *Chūō kaigi kaihō* 8 (March 1982): 68–69.

77. *Asahi shinbun*, August 24, 1979.

78. *Yomiuri shinbun*, August 14, 1980.

79. Kishimoto, "'Yutakasa' no gensō," 15.

80. Naikaku Sōri Daijin Kanbō Kōhōshitsu, *Kurashi to shigen*, 1–3, 121.

81. Tokyo-to Seisōkyoku Sōmubu Fukyū Chōsaka, ed., *Tokyo no gomi ni tsuite kangaeru fōramu* (Tokyo: Tokyo-to Seisōkyoku Sōmubu Fukyū Chōsaka, 1989), 4, 31.

82. Ishizawa, "Gomi o dasanai," 144.

83. *Yomiuri shinbun*, September 28, 1989, and November 8, 1989; *Asahi shinbun*, November 8, 1989; Taguchi Masami, *Gomi mondai hyakka* (Tokyo: Shin Nihon Shuppansha, 1991), 20.

84. Mori Kento, "'Suteru gawa' to 'suterareru gawa' o aruku," *Sekai* 532 (September 1989): 178–92; Kanari Yūzō, "'Tōhoku gomi sensō' no shūhen," *Shinbun kenkyū* 468 (July 1990): 37–38. Chiba itself was dealing with the illegal dumping of industrial waste in the prefecture, a problem made more difficult by threats and intimidation from yakuza or yakuza types. Ueno Hideo, "'Yutaka' na Nihon no uragawa 'sanpai Ginza o iku,'" *Gekkan jichiken* 31, no. 6 (June 1989): 36, 39; Taguchi, *Gomi mondai hyakka*, 16–20.

85. *Asahi shinbun*, August 3, 1989; "Gomi no naka kara konna mono ten," *Shūkan gendai* 31, no. 44 (October 1989): unpaginated.

86. Tokyo-to Seisōkyoku Sōmubu Fukyū Chōsaka, *Tokyo no gomi*, i–ii, 1.

87. "TOKYO SLIM IN DOME," *Gekkan haikibutsu* 16, no. 5 (May 1990): 66–73.

88. *Nihon keizai shinbun*, August 25, 1989; Takahashi, "TOKYO SLIM '89," 18–20, 22; Yorimoto Katsumi, "Tokyo no gomi sensō to surimu '89," *Ashita* 8, no. 12 (December 1989): 123, 127.

89. Fujiwara Toshikazu, "Konnichi no gomi mondai to shimin no kadai," *Risaikuru bunka* (Autumn–Winter 1989): 14.

90. Many anthropologists and garbologists consider garbage a reflection of the society that produced it. Barry Allen, "The Ethical Artifact," in *Trash*, ed. John Knechtel (Cambridge: MIT Press, 2007), 198. For a classic work on garbology, see William L. Rathje, *Rubbish! The Archaeology of Garbage* (New York: HarperCollins Publishers, 1992).

91. Kōseishō, *Kōsei hakusho*, 5, 8.

92. Henshūbu, "'Asobi gokoro,'" 19–20, 22–23.

93. "Tsukaisute Jidai o Kangaeru Kai" Jūshūnen Shinpo Jikkō Iinkai, ed., *Korekara dō suru shakai to kurashi* (Tokyo: Hakujusha, 1984), 9, 14–15.

94. Tsuchida Takashi, "'Shi' no sekai kara 'sei' no sekai e," *80 nendai* 4 (July 1980), in *Kyōsei no jidai* (Tokyo: Jushinsha, 1981), 108–11; Tsuchida Takashi, "'Tsukaisute jidai' no hakyoku wa chikai," *Asahi jānaru* 25, no. 28 (July 1983): 4; Tsuchida, *Kyōsei no jidai*, 21.

95. "Tsukaisute Jidai o Kangaeru Kai," *Asahi jānaru* 27, no. 51 (December 1985): 40; Hanafusa Hiroko, "Tsukaisute Jidai o Kangaeru Kai," *Risaikuru bunka* 26 (March 1990): 23.

96. Hai Mūn, *Gomikku "haikibutsu,"* vol. 1 (Tokyo: Nippō Shuppan, 1986), 20, 42.

97. Akasegawa Genpei with Ni'imi Yasuaki and Tsukaisute Kōgen Gakkai, eds., *Tsukaisute kōgengaku* (Tokyo: Jitsugyō no Nihonsha, 1987), 3–5, 34.

98. *Asahi shinbun,* September 16, 1987.

99. Akasegawa et al., *Tsukaisute kōgengaku,* 12–28.

100. Ibid., 50–128.

101. Genpei Akasegawa, *Hyperart,* trans. Matthew Fargo (New York: Kaya Press, 2009), 6.

102. On the idea of the "afterlife" of objects, see Raiford Guins, *Game After* (Cambridge: MIT Press, 2014), 7.

103. Akasegawa, *Hyperart,* 17, 19. The term "Thomasson" spread beyond Japan. It was used by William Gibson in his 1993 novel *Virtual Light,* and gained more attention in 2009 when Akasegawa's book was published in English translation. "There's a Name for Architectural Relics That Serve No Purpose," http://www.slate.com/blogs/the_eye/2014/08/27/roman_mars_99_percent_invisible_on_thomassons_architectural_relics_that.html (accessed September 19, 2016).

104. Jordan Sand, "Open Letter to Gary Thomasson," in Akasegawa, *Hyperart,* 397–400. See also chapter 3 of Jordan Sand, *Tokyo Vernacular* (Berkeley: University of California Press, 2013).

105. Miyajima Nobuo, *Tairyō rōhi shakai,* rev. ed. (1990; repr., Tokyo: Gijutsu to Ningen, 1994), 13, 21, 79–87.

106. Yorimoto, "Tokyo's Serious Waste Problem," 330.

107. *Asahi shinbun,* August 24, 1979; Monna, *Seikatsu no saikōchiku,* 134–36, 223.

108. Monna, *Seikatsu no saikōchiku,* 1, 220–23, 285–86.

109. *Yomiuri shinbun,* January 12, 1980.

110. *Yomiuri shinbun,* August 14, 1980; Gotō, *Gendai no gomi mondai,* 140; Ishizawa, "Gomi o dasanai," 148.

111. Gotō, *Gendai no gomi mondai,* 24–26.

112. *Asahi shinbun,* August 24, 1979; *Los Angeles Times,* November 15, 1987.

113. *Yomiuri shinbun,* July 2, 1983.

114. *Yomiuri shinbun,* May 27, 1985.

115. *Yomiuri shinbun,* November 15, 1980.

116. Ishizawa, "Gomi o dasanai," 144–45.

117. The exact number of survey respondents was 2,443. Naikaku Sōri Daijin Kanbō Kōhōshitsu, *Gomi shori ni kansuru seron chōsa* (Tokyo: Naikaku Sōri Daijin Kanbō Kōhōshitsu, [1988]), 6–7, 39.

118. "Konna mono made!," *Shūkan hōseki* 10, no. 36 (September 27, 1990): unpaginated.

119. Naikaku Sōri Daijin Kanbō Kōhōshitsu, *Gomi shori,* 29, 42.

120. Ishizawa Kiyofumi, *Gaborojī* (Tokyo: Risaikuru Bunkasha, 1983), 20–23.

121. Henshūbu, "'Asobi gokoro,'" 22–23.

122. Eyal Ben-Ari, "A Bureaucrat in Every Japanese Kitchen?" *Administration & Society* 21, no. 4 (February 1990): 476.

CHAPTER 6. LIVING THE GOOD LIFE?

1. Arakawa Ichirō, "Yume no shima kōen," *Ekonomisuto* 56, no. 45 (November 7, 1978): 64–66; *Mainichi shinbun,* March 3, 1979.

2. For one presentation of this narrative, see Tateishi Yoshio, "Seikatsu taikoku e no kigyō no yakuwari," *Keizaijin* 45, no. 10 (October 1991): 16.

3. Gavan McCormack translated *yutori* as "leisure, or time and space to do their own thing." Gavan McCormack, *The Emptiness of Japanese Affluence* (Armonk, NY: M. E.

Sharpe, 1996), 85. For an optimistic take on affluence, *yutori*, and happiness, see the work of economist Iida Tsuneo, including Iida Tsuneo, *"Yutakasa" no ato ni* (Tokyo: Kōdansha, 1984).

4. Hakuhōdō Seikatsu Sōgō Kenkyūjo, ed., *Sofuto wēbu* (Tokyo: Nihon Nōritsu Kyōkai, 1984), 1, 8, 41–42.

5. *Yomiuri shinbun*, December 28, 1989.

6. *Yomiuri shinbun*, January 5, 1990.

7. "Hontō no yutakasa to wa nani ka," *Shōhi to seikatsu* 168 (July 1989): 20.

8. *Yomiuri shinbun*, January 5, 1990.

9. Kamada Masaru, *Muda, mura, muri o nakuse* (Tokyo: Nihon Nōritsu Kyōkai, 1988), 34–39, 54–84, 107–9, 156–57.

10. Kurokawa Yasumasa, *"Kurokawa shiki"* (Tokyo: HBJ Shuppan, 1991), 2–4, 15–17, 19, 23–26, 28 31, 138–39, 157–59, 171–72.

11. Suda Hiroshi, "'Yoka' kō," *Keizaijin* 45, no. 10 (October 1991): 6–7.

12. Kanba Wataru, *Jikan kanrijutsu* (Tokyo: Tokuma Shoten, 1990), 17–20, 32, 51, 61–63, 93–95. On another aspect of the push for leisure, see Gavan McCormack on how the so-called Resort Law (Sōgō Hoyō Chiiki Seibi Hō) of 1987 set off a supply-side-driven boom in resort and golf course construction. Gavan McCormack, "The Price of Affluence," *New Left Review* 1, no. 188 (July–August 1991): 123–25.

13. Kishimoto Shigenobu, "'Yutakasa' no gensō to kankyō mondai," *Risaikuru bunka* 24 (Spring–Summer 1989): 10, 14–15.

14. Ishizawa Kiyoshi, "Gomi o dasanai atarashī ikikata," *Chishiki* 106 (September 1990): 150.

15. Shimane-ken Shakai Fukushibu Kenmin Seikatsuka, "Shin no yutakasa motome 'setsuyaku' kara 'sōzō' e," *Chūō kaigi kaihō* 17 (July 1984): 26–27.

16. Teruoka Itsuko, *Yutakasa to wa nani ka* (Tokyo: Iwanami Shoten, 1989); Ōhira Ken, *Yutakasa no seishin byōri* (Tokyo: Iwanami Shoten, 1990); Iwanami Shoten Henshūbu, ed., *Hontō no yutakasa to wa* (Tokyo: Iwanami Shoten, 1991); Kagawa Yoshiko et al., *Katei ippan* (Tokyo: Chūkyō Shuppan Kabushiki Gaisha, 1991), 1. The textbook was approved by the Ministry of Education (Monbushō) in 1987 for use in high school home economics classes; this revised version was authorized in 1990.

17. Teruoka, *Yutakasa to wa nani ka*, 2, 7, 16, 92–93. Galbraith's work also resonated with Monna Kimiyuki, who became interested in garbage when he encountered a quote from the economist about how the limit to growth was not the depletion of resources but the exhaustion of space for garbage. Monna Kimiyuki, *Seikatsu no saikōchiku* (Tokyo: Shin Jidaisha, 1982), 7.

18. Maekawa Tsukasa, *Dai Tokyo binbō seikatsu manyuaru*, vol. 1 (Tokyo: Kōdansha, 1988), 2.

19. Reiko Kosugi, "Youth Employment in Japan's Economic Recovery," *Asia-Pacific Journal* 4, no. 5 (May 2006): 1.

20. Maekawa Tsukasa, *Dai Tokyo binbō seikatsu manyuaru*, vol. 2 (Tokyo: Kōdansha, 1988), 55; ibid., 1:2–3.

21. Ibid., 1:11, 16, 32; 2:12–13; Maekawa Tsukasa, *Dai Tokyo binbō seikatsu manyuaru*, vol. 3 (Tokyo: Kōdansha, 1988), 63–64; Maekawa Tsukasa, *Dai Tokyo binbō seikatsu manyuaru*, vol. 4 (Tokyo: Kōdansha, 1989), 91–94.

22. Ibid., 1:19, 24; 3:49.

23. Ibid., 1:45; 3:63–66; 4:38.

24. *Yomiuri shinbun*, April 9, 1987.

25. Maekawa, *Dai Tokyo binbō*, 3:67–70; Maekawa Tsukasa, *Dai Tokyo binbō seikatsu manyuaru*, vol. 5 (Tokyo: Kōdansha, 1989), 35–38.

26. See Yoshino Shōji, *Atarashī yutakasa* (Tokyo: Rengō Shuppan, 1984).

27. Forty-five percent of the respondents described themselves as "new rich," or not being poor and having *yutori*. *Yomiuri shinbun*, September 10, 1988.

28. Hakuhōdō Seikatsu Sōgō Kenkyūjo, ed., *"Bunshū" no tanjō* (Tokyo: Nihon Keizai Shinbunsha, 1985), 3–4, 60–61, 145–48, 151, 161, 167, 172. On the idea of the "fragmented masses" or "micromasses" in the context of the postwar history of "class and mass," see William W. Kelly, "Regional Japan," in *Showa*, ed. Carol Gluck and Stephen R. Graubard (New York: W. W. Norton & Company, 1992), 227n12.

29. Suda, "'Yoka' kō," 4–5. Murai Masamori, "Yutori no kaifuku ni mukete," *Keizaijin* 45, no. 10 (October 1991): 10–11.

30. The exact number of respondents was 4,065. Naikaku Sōri Daijin Kanbō Kōhōshitsu, *Jiyū jikan ni okeru kōdō ishiki ni kansuru seron chōsa* (Tokyo: Naikaku Sōri Daijin Kanbō Kōhōshitsu, 1982), 2, 229.

31. Ōkita Saburō, "Seichō no genkai to shigen mondai," *Chūō kaigi kaihō* 16 (March 1984): 5, 8, 12.

32. Akuto Hiroshi, *Shōhi bunka ron* (Tokyo: Chūō Keizaisha, 1985), 54–55.

33. The exact number of respondents was 14,400. Nippon Hōsō Kyōkai Hōsō Seron Chōsajo, *Nihonjin no seikatsu jikan, zusetsu* (Tokyo: Nippon Hōsō Shuppan Kyōkai, 1987), 21. The figures declined in the 1990 survey; see Nippon Hōsō Kyōkai Hōsō Seron Chōsajo, *Nihonjin no seikatsu jikan, zusetsu* (Tokyo: Nippon Hōsō Shuppan Kyōkai, 1992), 51.

34. In 1990, 18 percent of workers had workdays of ten hours or more. Nippon Hōsō Kyōkai Seron Chōsajo, *Nihonjin no seikatsu jikan* (1992), 51.

35. Daniel H. Foote, "Law as an Agent of Change?" in *Japan, Economic Success and Legal System*, ed. Harald Baum (Berlin: Walter de Gruyter, 1997), 290–91.

36. The figures for free time did tick up in 1990, to four hours and seven minutes on weekdays, five hours and eight minutes on Saturdays, and six hours and twenty-two minutes on Sundays. Nippon Hōsō Kyōkai Hōsō Seron Chōsajo, *Nihonjin no seikatsu jikan* (1992), 43.

37. Koishikawa Zenji, *Nihonjin wa itsu kara hatarakisugi ni natta no ka* (Tokyo: Heibonsha, 2014), 10, 15; Watanabe Osamu, *"Yutaka na shakai" Nihon no kōzō* (Tokyo: Rōdō Junpōsha, 1990), 32–37; Ronald E. Yates, "Japanese Live . . . and Die . . . for Their Work," *Chicago Tribune*, November 13, 1988.

38. David Leheny, *The Rules of Play* (Ithaca: Cornell University Press, 2003), 107.

39. For an example of the contrarian view, see Iida Tsuneo, *"Yutakasa" to wa nani ka* (Tokyo: Kōdansha Gendai Shinsho, 1980).

40. Foote, "Law as an Agent," 263–64, 269–70, 295.

41. Toyama Shigeru, *Nihonjin no kinben, chochikukan* (Tokyo: Tōyō Keizai Shinpōsha, 1987), 161, 173, 185, 209–10, 215–16; Sheldon Garon, "Japan's Post-war 'Consumer Revolution,' or Striking a 'Balance' between Consumption and Saving," in *Consuming Cultures, Global Perspectives*, ed. John Brewer and Frank Trentmann (Oxford: Berg, 2006), 211.

42. "Asobi to seikatsu to jiyū jikan o kangaeru," *Gekkan sōhyō* 376 (April 1989): 18; Leheny, *Rules of Play*, 110.

43. Katō Hidetoshi and Minami Shinbō, "'Hima' mo 'iikagen' mo kakko ii," *Asahi jānaru* 29, no. 1 (January 2–9, 1987): 6–11.

44. Katō Tsuchimi, "'Mono yori kokoro' no jidai o mukaete," *Aiiku* 50, no. 1 (January 1985): 6–7.

45. Takashina Shūji, "Nōritsu to muda," *Kōkoku* 25, no. 4 (July–August 1984): 3.

46. Honda Shin'ichi, *Jinsei o yutaka ni suru tame no "jikan" no tsukaikata* (Tokyo: Besuto Bukku, 1990), 3, 56–57, 64–66, 90–94, 112–15, 216–20, 222–23.

47. Naikaku Sōri Daijin Kanbō Kōhōshitsu, *Kokumin seikatsu ni kansuru seron chōsa* (Tokyo: Naikaku Sōri Daijin Kanbō Kōhōshitsu, [1989]), 1, 68, 94–95. Note that spending on passenger cars and consumer durables increased during this time. Koino Shigeru, "Yoka to rizōto kaihatsu," *Keizaijin* 44, no. 5 (May 1990): 40.

48. For one version of this observation, see Ichiki Shigeo, "Shōhisha no tachiba ni tatta kaikaku o," *Keizaijin* 44, no. 5 (May 1990): 5.

49. *Mainichi shinbun*, December 1, 1989.

50. Watanabe, *"Yutaka na shakai,"* 13.

51. *Mainichi shinbun*, November 9, 1989.

52. Leheny, *Rules of Play*, 4–6.

CHAPTER 7. BATTLING THE TIME THIEVES

1. *Asahi shinbun*, August 2, 1983.

2. Michael Ende, *Momo*, trans. Ōshima Kaori (Tokyo: Iwanami Shoten, 1976).

3. *Yomiuri shinbun*, September 30, 1976.

4. *Asahi shinbun*, August 20, 1986.

5. *Asahi shinbun*, December 26, 1989.

6. The documentary can be viewed at https://www.youtube.com/watch?v=Hh3vfM XAPJQ.

7. *Asahi shinbun*, June 6, 1988; July 4 and 13, 1988; and August 3, 1988.

8. *Yomiuri shinbun*, June 26, 1992; *Asahi shinbun*, October 12, 1995; *Daily Yomiuri*, December 15, 1998.

9. *Asahi shinbun*, July 28, 1986, and December 3, 1992; *Yomiuri shinbun*, November 17, 1992.

10. *Yomiuri shinbun*, May 10, 1997.

11. Sakai Takeshi, *"Momo" to kangaeru jikan to okane no himitsu* (Tokyo: Shoshi Shinsui, 2005), 273; *Asahi shinbun*, July 28, 1986, and July 1, 1989; *Yomiuri shinbun*, November 17, 1992.

12. Ende, *Momo*, 75; Michael J. Ende, *Momo*, trans. J. Maxwell Brownjohn (London: Penguin, 1984), 55. I have quoted the published English translation of the original German book only when it captures effectively the meaning and nuances of the Japanese text.

13. On conceptualizations of time, see chapter 1 of Stephen Kern, *The Culture of Time and Space, 1880–1918* (Cambridge: Harvard University Press, 1983).

14. On internal and external time, see Mihyaeru Ende et al., *Mittsu no kagami*, ed. Koyasu Michiko (Tokyo: Asahi Shinbunsha, 1989), 144–45.

15. Koyasu Michiko, *"Momo" o yomu* (Tokyo: Gakuyō Shobō, 1987), 83; Sakai, *"Momo" to kangaeru*, 32, 87.

16. Ende, *Momo*, trans. Ōshima, 13–14; Ende, *Momo*, trans. Brownjohn, 12–13.

17. Ende, *Momo*, trans. Ōshima, 19; Ende, *Momo*, trans. Brownjohn, 16.

18. Mr. Fūjī is Mr. Figaro in the English translation. Ende, *Momo*, trans. Brownjohn, 55.

19. Ende, *Momo*, trans. Ōshima, 77. The translation is my own, only slightly different from the published English version. For the published English version, see Ende, *Momo*, trans. Brownjohn, 56.

20. Ende, *Momo*, trans. Ōshima, 79; Ende, *Momo*, trans. Brownjohn, 57.

21. Ende, *Momo*, trans. Ōshima, 79–84; Ende, *Momo*, trans. Brownjohn, 58–61.

22. For an interpretation of Ende's portrayal of money as something that existed primarily to be saved and accumulated, see Kitano Shū and Izumisawa Kanako, "Mihyaeru Ende 'Momo' no kijutsu ni miru gendai keizai shakai hihan," *Sangyō keizai kenkyū* 50, no. 4 (March 2010): 77–79.

23. Ende, *Momo*, trans. Ōshima, 86–91; Ende, *Momo*, trans. Brownjohn, 62–65.

24. Ende, *Momo*, trans. Ōshima, 129; Ende, *Momo*, trans. Brownjohn, 89.

25. Ende, *Momo*, trans. Ōshima, 319–21; Ende, *Momo*, trans. Brownjohn, 214.

26. Nishimoto Ikuko, "The 'Civilization' of Time," *Time & Society* 6, no. 2/3 (1997): 244; Stefan Tanaka, *New Times in Modern Japan* (Princeton: Princeton University Press, 2004), 3–5, 8–9.

27. Nishimoto, "'Civilization' of Time," 251; Nishimoto Ikuko, "Kodomo ni jikan genshu o oshieru," in *Chikoku no tanjō*, ed. Hashimoto Takehiko and Kuriyama Shigehisa (Tokyo: Sangensha, 2006), 172, 174–75.

28. Samuel Smiles, *Self-Help*, new ed. (London: John Murray, 1884), 130.

29. Nishimoto, "Kodomo ni jikan," 168; Nishimoto, "'Civilization' of Time," 251.

30. Nishimoto, "Kodomo ni jikan," 168; Nishimoto, "'Civilization' of Time," 251–52. For a fascinating social history on the idea of "time is money," see Nishimoto Ikuko, *Jikan ishiki no kindai* (Tokyo: Hōsei Daigaku Shuppankyoku, 2006). See also Earl H. Kinmonth, *The Self-Made Man in Meiji Japanese Thought* (Berkeley: University of California Press, 1981), 40. Franklin himself did not shun the goal of financial wealth: "In short, the way to wealth, if you desire it, is as plain as the way to market. It depends chiefly on two words, *industry* and *frugality*; that is, waste neither *time* nor *money*, but make the best use of both." Benjamin Franklin, "Advice to a Young Tradesman, 1748," in Benjamin Franklin, *The Writings of Benjamin Franklin*, vol. 2, ed. Albert Henry Smyth (New York: Macmillan Company, 1907), 372.

31. Kuriyama Shigehisa, "'Toki wa kane nari' no nazo," in Hashimoto and Kuriyama, *Chikoku no tanjō*, 331–32.

32. Hashimoto Takehiko, foreword to Hashimoto and Kuriyama, *Chikoku no tanjō*, 8; Ogose Tōru, "Mihyaeru Ende 'Momo' ni okeru kiku koto," *Ibaraki daigaku kyōiku gakubu kiyō (Kyōiku kagaku)* 55 (March 2006): 247.

33. Ōshima Kaori, afterword to Ende, *Momo*, trans. Ōshima, 357–58.

34. Shimauchi Keiji, *Ende no kureta takaramono* (Tokyo: Fukutake Shoten, 1990), 72–73.

35. *Yomiuri shinbun*, August 21, 1986.

36. *Yomiuri shinbun*, August 9, 1999.

37. *Asahi shinbun*, July 12, 1992.

38. Hashimoto, foreword to Hashimoto and Kuriyama, *Chikoku no tanjō*, 8–9.

39. Ende, *Momo*, trans. Ōshima, 91; Ende, *Momo*, trans. Brownjohn, 65–66.

40. *Asahi shinbun*, July 4, 1988.

41. Ende, *Momo*, trans. Ōshima, 94; Ende, *Momo*, trans. Brownjohn, 67.

42. Umeda Masaaki, *Jikan to jinsei ni tsuite* (Tokyo: Nihon Tosho Kankōkai, 1998), 143–47, 250–53.

43. *Asahi shinbun*, July 21, 1985.

44. Hashizume Taiki, "Yoka no jikansei," *Yokagaku kenkyū* 14 (March 2011): 27–38.

45. Ende, *Momo*, trans. Ōshima, 93; Ende, *Momo*, trans. Brownjohn, 67.

46. Nakamura Tatsuya, "'Yutakasa' saikō," in Kinoshita Junji et al., *Chūgaku kokugo* (Tokyo: Kyōiku Shuppan, 1993), 226–30.

47. *Asahi shinbun*, May 29, 1994.

48. Ogose, "Mihyaeru Ende," 247, 250–51, 265.

49. Ende, *Momo*, trans. Ōshima, 150–52; Ende, *Momo*, trans. Brownjohn, 104–5.

50. Koyasu, "*Momo*" o yomu, 112–13.

51. Shimauchi, *Ende*, 180.

52. Ende, *Momo*, trans. Ōshima, 154–55; Ende, *Momo*, trans. Brownjohn, 106–7.

53. Ōshima, afterword to Ende, *Momo*, 357.

54. *Asahi shinbun*, February 26, 1977.

55. *Asahi shinbun*, July 4, 1988.

56. Kyoko Matsuoka, "The Japanese Child in a Changing World," in *Window on Japan*, ed. Sybille A. Jagusch (Washington, DC: Library of Congress, 1990), 16.

57. Nakamura, "'Yutakasa' saikō," 226–29.

58. Kitano and Izumisawa, "Mihyaeru Ende," 89, 92.

59. Ende, *Momo*, trans. Ōshima, 321–22; Ende, *Momo*, trans. Brownjohn, 215.

60. Sakai, *"Momo" to kangaeru*, 113–17.

61. *Asahi shinbun*, December 3, 1992.

62. Ōshima, afterword to Ende, *Momo*, 360; Ogose, "Mihyaeru Ende," 257–58; *Yomiuri shinbun*, April 29, 2003; Shimauchi, *Ende*, 80, 96–97, 181; *Asahi shinbun*, July 12, 1992.

63. Myōjin Isao, "3.11 'Fukushima'-go no ningen to shakai," *Hokkaidō keizai* 546 (October 2012): 1–31; Koyasu Michiko, "Jikan to kinri," *Ekonomisuto* 93, no. 22 (June 2, 2015): 37.

CHAPTER 8. GREENING CONSCIOUSNESS

1. *Asahi shinbun*, January 15, 1999. The photograph was published in a section titled "Japan: Paradoxical Affluence" in Peter Menzel, *Material World* (San Francisco: Sierra Club Books, 1994), 48–55.

2. *Asahi shinbun*, January 15, 1999.

3. Naikaku Sori Daijin Kanbō Kōhōshitsu, *Kokumin seikatsu ni kansuru seron chōsa* (Tokyo: Naikaku Sōri Daijin Kanbō Kōhōshitsu, [1999]), http://survey.gov-online.go.jp/h11/kokumin/images/zu05.gif (accessed July 13, 2016).

4. See the introduction to *Examining Japan's Lost Decades*, ed. Yoichi Funabashi and Barak Kushner (London: Routledge, 2015); *Nihon keizai shinbun*, July 21, 1998, cited in Andrew Gordon, "Making Sense of the Lost Decades," ibid., 97; Bill Powell and Velisarios Kattoulas with Hideko Takayama, "The Lost Decade," *Newsweek*, July 27, 1998, 28–31.

5. Simon Avenell, *Transnational Japan in the Global Environmental Movement* (Honolulu: University of Hawaii Press, 2017), 2, 4, 7, 22, 178.

6. On the "decidedly anthropocentric and 'situated' approach to environmental problems" that was "a distinctive feature of contemporary Japanese environmentalism" as a result of the history of postwar industrial pollution, see ibid., 213.

7. Abe Akashi et al., *Katei ippan* (Tokyo: Tokyo Shoseki, 1994), 13–14, 54.

8. Keizai Kikakuchō Sōgō Keikakukyoku, ed., *2010-nen e no sentaku* (Tokyo: Ōkurashō Insatsukyoku, 1991), 1–2, 23, 30, 69–70.

9. World Commission on Environment and Development, *Report of the World Commission on Environment and Development* (1987), 16.

10. Saburo Okita, "Outgrowing Catch-Up Capitalism," in *Tackling the Waste Problem*, ed. Koya Ishino et al. (Tokyo: Foreign Press Center Japan, 1992), 50–51.

11. Shinichi Nakamura and Atsushi Toyonaga, *Making Environmental Policy in the United States and Japan* (Cambridge: Program on U.S.-Japan Relations, Harvard University, 1991), 3, 11–14; Shizuka Oshitani, *Global Warming Policy in Japan and Britain* (Manchester: Manchester University Press, 2006), 1–2; Miranda A. Schreurs, *Environmental Politics in Japan, Germany, and the United States* (Cambridge: Cambridge University Press, 2002), 162–64.

12. Peter Wynn Kirby, *Troubled Natures* (Honolulu: University of Hawaii Press, 2011), 38–42, 54–57, 62–65; Watanabe Misuzu, "Sutoppu za daiokishin," *Rekishi chiri kyōiku* 584 (October 1998): 28–30.

13. Kōgai Chikyū Kankyō Mondai Kondankai, ed., *Daiokishin wa nakuseru* (Tokyo: Gōdō Shuppan, 1998), 6–7, 12–22, 62–67; Miyata Hideaki and Yasuda Yukuo, *Daiokishin no genjitsu* (Tokyo: Iwanami Shoten, 1999), 50–51. Dioxin emissions from incinerators did decline after 1997. See Ōsawa Masaaki, "Gomi kinenbi," *Seikatsu to kankyō* 52, no. 5 (May 2007): 70–71.

14. *Asahi shinbun*, May 28, 1991; *Yomiuri shinbun*, June 9, 1992.

15. Kankyōshō Shizen Kankyōkyoku, *Jichitai tantōsha no tame no karasu taisaku manyuaru* (Tokyo: Kankyōshō Shizen Kankyōkyoku, 2001), 18–19; *Yomiuri shinbun*, August 16, 2001. In Kanagawa prefecture, the crow population increased an estimated

3.7-fold between the mid-1980s and 2001; in cities like Yokohama, Kawasaki, and Fujisawa, the increase was about sixfold. *Asahi shinbun*, June 2, 2001.

16. Kankyōshō Shizen Kankyōkyoku, *Jichitai tantōsha*, 22–23, 36; *Yomiuri shinbun*, June 9, 1992, and April 12, 1995; *Sankei shinbun*, May 16, 1995.

17. *Yomiuri shinbun*, June 9, 1992; Kankyōshō Shizen Kankyōkyoku, *Jichitai tantōsha*, 36.

18. *Asahi shinbun*, January 22, 1998; *Yomiuri shinbun*, November 21, 2012.

19. *Asahi shinbun*, January 16, 1999, and August 31, 1999; Kankyōshō Shizen Kankyōkyoku, *Jichitai tantōsha*, 61–62.

20. *Yomiuri shinbun*, August 16, 2001, and November 7, 2001; *Sankei shinbun*, November 8, 2001.

21. *Sankei shinbun*, January 16, 1999; *Mainichi shinbun*, May 16, 2000; *Yomiuri shinbun*, August 16, 2001; November 27, 2004; and October 25, 2007; *Asahi shinbun*, June 25, 2005; April 26, 2006; October 25, 2007; and October 1, 2014; Suginami-ku Kankyō Seisōbu Seisō Kanrika, ed., *Karasu taisaku gomi shūsekijo jittai chōsa hōkokusho, Heisei 14 nendo ban* (Tokyo: Suginami-ku Kankyō Seisōbu Seisō Kanrika, 2003), 59; Suginami-ku Kankyō Seisōbu Seisō Kanrika, ed., *Karasu taisaku gomi shūsekijo jittai chōsa hōkokusho, Heisei 20 nendo ban* (Tokyo: Suginami-ku Kankyō Seisōbu Seisō Kanrika, 2009), 1, 19, 30–31.

22. Keizai Kikakuchō Kokumin Seikatsukyoku, ed., *Chie no aru yutakasa o* (Tokyo: Ōkurashō Insatsukyoku, 1992), i–ii, 1–4, 9–14.

23. "Chie no aru yutakasa o," *Chūō kaigi kaihō* 48 (June 1992): 2, 5–10.

24. Ishige Takeshi, *Watashitachi ni dekiru gomi o herasu kurashi no kufū 101* (Tokyo: Ōizumi Shoten, 1992), 7, 16–19, 23, 40–42, 62–63, 72–73, 84–85, 174–75.

25. Kokumin Seikatsu Sentā, *Furī māketto risaikuru shoppu risaikuru kōnā o riyō suru* (Tokyo: Kokumin Seikatsu Sentā, 1998), i, 7–8; Kitamura Akiko, "'Mottainai' o taisetsu ni," *LDI Report* 102 (May 1999): 58–59.

26. "Kashikoi misesu wa risaikuru jōzu," *Shufu to seikatsu* 45, no. 3 (March 1990): 179–87; Risaikuru Bunka Henshū Gurūpu, ed., *Risaikuru zenseikatsu gaido* (Tokyo: Risaikuru Bunka-sha, 1991); *Shutoken furī māketto & risaikuru shoppu* (Tokyo: Nihon Kōtsū Kōsha Shuppan Jigyōkyoku, 1996); LIPS Kyoto, ed., *Kansai furī māketto tengoku* (Kyoto: Yunipuran, 1996).

27. Kankyōshō Daijin Kanbō Haikibutsu Risaikuru Taisakubu Junkangata Shakai Suishinshitsu, ed., *Junkangata shakai hakusho* (Tokyo: Gyōsei, 2002), 14–15.

28. Kokumin Seikatsu Sentā, *Furī māketto*, 6; Kitamura, "'Mottainai' o taisetsu ni," 58–59; Taniguchi Masakazu, "Mono no mochisugi ya muda no kakko warusa, yutakasa no naimen de dai henka ga okite iru," *Keieisha* 55, no. 3 (March 2001): 60.

29. *Mainichi shinbun*, October 14, 1997; press release, June 3, 1998, http://www.un.org/press/en/1998/19980603.eco5.html (accessed June 22, 2016).

30. The number of households surveyed was around 3,287. *Mainichi shinbun*, August 6, 1998.

31. Kankyōshō Daijin Kanbō Haikibutsu Risaikuru Taisakubu Junkangata Shakai Suishinshitsu, *Junkangata shakai hakusho*, 3.

32. Shigen no yūkō na riyō no sokushin ni kansuru hōritsu, Hōritsu dai yonjūhachi gō (April 26, 1991), http://law.e-gov.go.jp/htmldata/H03/H03HO048.html (accessed June 22, 2016).

33. Yōki hōsō ni kakaru bunbetsu shūshū oyobi saishōhinka no sokushin tō ni kansuru hōritsu, Hōritsu dai hyakujūni gō, June 16, 1995, http://law.e-gov.go.jp/htmldata/H07/H07HO112.html (accessed June 22, 2016). See also Yōki hōsō risaikuru hō, http://www.meti.go.jp/policy/recycle/main/admin_info/law/04/ (accessed June 22, 2016,).

34. Tokutei kateiyō kiki saishōhinka hō, Hōritsu dai kyūjūnana gō, June 5, 1998, http://law.e-gov.go.jp/htmldata/H10/H10HO097html (accessed June 22, 2016). See also Kaden

risaikuru hō, http://www.meti.go.jp/policy/it_policy/kaden_recycle/index.html (accessed June 22, 2016).

35. Junkangata shakai keisei suishin kihon hō, Hōritsu dai hyakujū gō, June 2, 2000, http://law-e.gov.go.jp/htmldata/H12/H12HO110.html (accessed June 22, 2016). To bring them into line with the Basic Law, the Waste Management and Cleaning Law of 1970 (Haikibutsu no Shori Oyobi Seisō ni Kansuru Hōritsu) and the Law to Promote the Use of Recycled Resources were amended that same year.

36. Shokuhin junkan shigen no saisei riyō tō no sokushin ni kansuru hōritsu, Hōritsu dai hyakujūroku gō, June 7, 2000, http://law.e-gov.go.jp/htmldata/H12/H12HO116.html (accessed June 23, 2016); Shiyōzumi jidōsha no saishigenka tō ni kansuru hōritsu, Hōritsu dai hachijūnana gō, July 12, 2002, http://law.e-gov.go.jp/htmldata/H14/H14HO087.html (accessed June 23, 2016).

37. *Mainichi shinbun*, August 7, 2000. The number of municipalities that separately collected PET bottles increased from 1,082 to 2,286 from 2000 to 2001, although there were only 864 that separately collected plastic containers, like the trays used by supermarkets for packaging. *Mainichi shinbun*, April 17, 2001. The city of Numazu, at the forefront of separate collection in the 1970s, began separate collection of "plastic garbage" in 1999; in 2003 that category was further differentiated into "plastic containers and packaging" and "other plastics." See Takahashi Sei'ichi and Ota Ichirō, "Numazu-shi no purasuchikku gomi no bunbetsu to sono kōka ni tsuite," *Haikibutsu gakkai shi* 16, no. 5 (2005): 20–24.

38. *Mainichi shinbun*, December 4, 1993.

39. Keizai Dantai Rengōkai, "Keidanren kankyō apīru," July 16, 1996, https://www.keidanren.or.jp/japanese/policy/pol094.html (accessed June 23, 2016); *Mainichi shinbun*, July 17, 1996.

40. Gurīn Konshūmā Nettowāku, *Chikyū ni yasashī kaimono gaido* (Tokyo: Kōdansha, 1994), 3–7.

41. Ibid., 17–19, 100–236.

42. Honma Miyako, *Gurīn konshūmā nyūmon* (Tokyo: Hokuto Shuppan, 1997).

43. Yamada Kunihiro, *Ichioku nin no kankyō kakeibo* (Tokyo: Fujiwara Shoten, 1996), 106–7, 114, 136, 146. The book went through six printings between its original publication in 1996 and 2002.

44. "Junkangata shakai no jitsugen ni wa, tomin, NPO, jigyōsha, gyōsei no kyōdō ga hitsuyō desu," *Tokyo slim* 8 (January 1999): 2.

45. "Gurīn kōnyū hō ni tsuite," https://www.env.go.jp/policy/hozen/green/g-law/ (accessed September 25, 2016).

46. Kagawa Yoshiko et al., *Katei sōgō* (Tokyo: Dai'ichi Gakushūsha, 2003), frontispiece 2, 86–89, 92.

47. The precise number of respondents was 3,476. Naikakufu Daijin Kanbō Seifu Kōhōshitsu, *Junkangata shakai no keisei ni kansuru seron chōsa* (Tokyo: Naikakufu Daijin Kanbō Seifu Kōhōshitsu, [2001]), 3, 66, 91.

48. Kankyōshō, ed., *Kankyō hakusho* (Tokyo: Gyōsei, 2005), i.

49. *Asahi shinbun*, August 23, 2005; *Mainichi shinbun*, August 23, 2005, and November 6, 2005.

50. *Sankei shinbun*, September 1, 2005; *Mainichi shinbun*, September 4, 2005. According to the Energy Conservation Center (Shōenerugī Sentā), Cool Biz was carried out in its early years by 95.1 percent of local governments, 73.7 percent of manufacturers, 68.2 percent of the service industry, 66.2 percent of wholesalers and retailers, 62.7 percent of the finance and insurance industry, and 46.8 percent of the transportation industry. Orii Takahiro, "Kūru bizu, wōmu bizu o kokumin undō ni," *Enerugī* 39, no. 7 (July 2006): 95–96.

51. *Mainichi shinbun*, November 6, 2005.

52. *Asahi shinbun*, September 22, 2005; *Sankei shinbun*, October 2, 2005.

53. Henshūbu, "Yonenme o mukaeta kūru bizu to wōmu bizu," *SC Japan Today* 413 (November 2008): 36, 39.

54. Nagahama Toshihiro, "Kūru bizu, wōmu bizu no shōene to keizai kōka," *Re: Building Maintenance and Management* 30, no. 1 (July 2008): 37. The figure reported, presumably for sales, in the first year of Cool Biz by the *Mainichi shinbun* was 100.8 billion yen. *Mainichi shinbun*, August 26, 2005.

55. Keizei Sangyōshō, Shigen Enerugīchō, "Minsei bumon no enerugī shōhī kōdō ni tsuite" (n.d.), 1–3, 5–7, 10, 12, http://www.meti.go.jp/report/downloadfiles/g40324d20j. pdf (accessed June 24, 2016).

56. *Asahi shinbun*, January 30, 1997.

57. *Mainichi shinbun*, November 8, 1994.

58. Naikakufu Daijin Kanbō Seifu Kohōshitsu, *Junkangata shakai*, 5, 12, 24, 28.

59. Daiwa Hausu Kōgyō Kabushiki Gaisha Seikatsu Kenkyūjo, ed., *Katei nai no gomi ni kansuru chōsa kekka hōkokusho* (Osaka: Daiwa Hausu Kōgyō Kabushiki Gaisha Seikatsu Kenkyūjo, 1999), 2, 10, 14, 16.

60. *Mainichi shinbun*, July 25, 1993.

61. "Risaikuru wa gomi herashi ni naranai," *Karin* 65 (December 1997): 15.

62. Takatsuki Hiroshi, *Gomi mondai to raifusutairu* (Tokyo: Nihon Hyōronsha, 2004), 49–58, 155, 181–84.

63. Kankyōshō, ed., *Kankyō hakusho* (Tokyo: Gyōsei, 2002), chap. 1, sec. 4, http://www. env.go.jp/policy/hakusyo/hakusyo.php3?kid=215 (accessed June 23, 2016).

64. Organisation for Economic Co-operation and Development, *Environment at a Glance* (Paris: OECD Publishing, 2005), 63–70. According to the Ministry of the Environment, the recycling rate in Japan was 15.9 percent in FY 2002 and 16.8 percent in FY 2003. Ministry of the Environment, "State of Discharge and Treatment of Municipal Solid Waste in FY 2003," November 4, 2005, https://www.env.go.jp/en/press/2005/1104a.html (accessed June 23, 2016). It should be noted that the per capita amount of household garbage discarded in Japan was lower than in Austria, Belgium, Germany, the Netherlands, and the United States in 2000. "Kakkoku no ippan haikibutsu hassei ryō," http://www.env. go.jp/doc/toukei/data/2015_2.38.xls (accessed June 24, 2016).

CHAPTER 9. WE ARE ALL WASTE CONSCIOUS NOW

1. Matsumura Akira, Yamaguchi Akio, and Wada Toshimasa, eds., *Ōbunsha kogo jiten*, 8th ed. (Tokyo: Ōbunsha, 1994), 1174.

2. *Mainichi shinbun*, March 30, 1991.

3. Honda Atsuhiro, *E de miru shōhi to risaikuru* (Tokyo: Kurīn Japan Sentā, 1995), 10. There were other books that evoked *mottainai*, such as Satō Yumi and Doi Chizuru, *Mottainai* (Tokyo: Fūtōsha, 1992); Uotsuka Junnosuke, *Ā! Mottainai* (Tokyo: Kōbunsha, 1995); and Sakata Ryūichi, *"Mottainai" no fukkatsu* (Tokyo: Bunkōsha, 1997).

4. *Mainichi shinbun*, July 28, 1994.

5. Shinju Mariko, *Mottainai bāsan* (Tokyo: Kōdansha, 2004).

6. "Koramu tokushū," *Gendai* 40, no. 2 (2006): 234.

7. Svetlana Boym, *The Future of Nostalgia* (New York: Basic Books, 2001), 13.

8. La Zoo, *Mottainai-tte nan darō?* ed. Kankyō Jōhō Fukyū Sentā, vol. 1 of *Mottainai kara hajimeyō!* (Tokyo: Gakushū Kenkyūsha, 2007), 2–3.

9. Shinju Mariko, *Mottainai koto shite nai kai?* (Tokyo: Kōdansha, 2007), 21, 23.

10. Shinju Mariko, *Mottainai bāsan karuta* (Tokyo: Kōdansha, 2006).

11. Shinju Mariko, *Mottainai bāsan to kangaeyō sekai no koto* (Tokyo: Kōdansha, 2008), 2.

12. Shinju, *Mottainai koto*, 3–4.

13. Shinju, *Mottainai bāsan karuta*.

14. For a lesson in cooperation and working with others, see Shinju Mariko, *Mottainai bāsan no tengoku to jigoku no hanashi* (Tokyo: Kōdansha, 2014). In another children's book, *mottainai* was defined as the waste of one's heart, body, and life, and therefore the waste of one's potential. Okamoto Masashi, *Mottainai to Nihon no dentō*, vol. 7 of *Mottainai seikatsu daijiten* (Tokyo: Gakushū Kenkyūsha, 2007), 45.

15. Shinju, *Mottainai bāsan to kangaeyō*, 9–11, 33–35, 37–39, 45–47.

16. Imai Misako, *Mottainai jīsan* (Tokyo: Sakuhinsha, 2005), 7, 15, 35, 56–57, 88–89, 92, 209.

17. Ibid., 15, 19–20, 153–54.

18. Ibid., 43–44.

19. "Koramu tokushū," 229.

20. Ibid., 245, 247–48.

21. Occasionally there was a harking back to an even earlier time. Author Ishida Yutaka wrote of returning to the state of "primitive man," though what he sought was a kind of self-determination and self-awareness (thinking and doing things for and by oneself) that had the distinct stamp of the modern. In more mundane terms, Ishida called for a return to 1980, before the subsequent rise in energy consumption. Ishida Yutaka, *Mottainai kokoro* (Tokyo: WAVE Shuppan, 2003), 2–3, 124–25, 238–39.

22. Shinju, *Mottainai bāsan karuta*.

23. Okamoto, *Mottainai*, 22–23.

24. Akasegawa Genpei, *Mottainai hanashi desu* (Tokyo: Chikuma Shobō, 2007), 7, 25.

25. Akiyama Hiroko, *Gomi o herasu chie*, vol. 1 of *Edo no kurashi kara manabu "mottainai"* (Tokyo: Chōbunsha, 2009), 4–5.

26. Akiyama, *Gomi*, 8–11; Akiyama Hiroko, *Kaiteki ni sugosu kufū*, vol. 2 of *Edo no kurashi kara manabu "mottainai,"* 12–13, 18; Akiyama Hiroko, *Muda o dasanai shakai*, vol. 3 of *Edo no kurashi kara manabu "mottainai,"* 14, 26.

27. On this subject, see chapter 3 of Susan Hanley, *Everyday Things in Premodern Japan* (Berkeley: University of California Press, 1997), 51–76.

28. On the uses to which Ninomiya Sontoku was put, see Sheldon Garon, *Beyond Our Means* (Princeton: Princeton University Press, 2012), 134–42.

29. All seven volumes were published in 2007. For the first in the series, see Okamoto Masashi, *Mottainai o mitsukeyō*, vol. 1 of *Mottainai seikatsu daijiten*.

30. All six volumes were published in 2007. For the first in the series, see La Zoo, *Mottainai-tte nan darō*.

31. Taitō-ku Kankyō Seisōbu Kankyō Hozenka, *Edo kara manabu watashitachi no kurashi* (Tokyo: Taitō-ku Kankyō Seisōbu Kankyō Hozenka, 2007), 1, 6–7, 18–19.

32. Akiyama, *Gomi*, 2; Akiyama, *Kaiteki ni sugosu*, 2; Akiyama, *Muda*, 2, 30.

33. "Koramu tokushū," 246, 248.

34. Sada Masashi, "MOTTAINAI," 2005.

35. Kobayashi Akira, "Akira no mottainai ondo" (Tokuma Japan Komyunikēshonzu, compact disc, 2006).

36. Puranetto Rinku, ed., *Mottainai* (Tokyo: Magajin Hausu, 2006), 9.

37. Nishinari Katsuhiro, *Mudagaku* (Tokyo: Shinchō Sensho, 2008), 189–91.

38. Hiroi Yoshinori, "'Keizai seichō ni yoru kaiketsu' kara dassuru tame ni," *Bōsei* 37, no. 7 (2006): 25–30.

39. Puranetto Rinku, *Mottainai*, 7–9.

40. Akiyama, *Gomi*, 15. A similar point was made by Okamoto Masashi in *Mottainai to Nihon*, 24–25. *Tsukumogami* have typically been understood as residing not just in tools but more generally in or as "common household objects." See Michael Dylan Foster, *Pandemonium and Parade* (Berkeley: University of California Press, 2009), 7–8.

41. Yamaori Tetsuo, "Nihonjin wa ima, donna kachi o shinrai subeki ka," *Bōsei* 37, no. 7 (2006): 12, 18.

42. "Koramu tokushū," 234.

43. For a related point on the idea of "originally pure doctrine," see Stephen G. Covell and Mark Rowe, "Editors' Introduction," *Japanese Journal of Religious Studies* 31, no. 2 (2004): 246–47.

44. On the claim that these rituals were part of a "tradition" of *mottainai*, see Okamoto, *Mottainai to Nihon*, 26–27.

45. Angelika Kretschmer, *Kuyō in Contemporary Japan* (Göttingen: Cuvillier Verlag, 2000), 145–46, 148, 193, 196.

46. Field notes of observation by author, *hari kuyō* at Awashimadō in Tokyo, February 8, 2016. According to Angelika Kretschmer: "We should . . . beware of seeing sentimental feelings as the motivation to perform *kuyō* rites for objects. In most cases, these feelings of gratitude and estimation are much rationalized, and in my opinion they are more of an expression of duty than sentimental attachment." Kretschmer, *Kuyō*, 195.

47. Angelika Kretschmer, "Mortuary Rites for Inanimate Objects," *Japanese Journal of Religious Studies* 28, no. 3/4 (Fall 2000): 379–80, 382, 384, 401–2; Kretschmer, *Kuyō*, 200–204, 207.

48. On this trope, see Eric Gordon Dinmore, "A Small Island Nation Poor in Resources" (Ph.D. diss., Princeton University, 2006).

49. Puranetto Rinku, *Mottainai*, 8–9.

50. Akasegawa, *Mottainai hanashi*, 36–40, 42–43, 90–91.

51. "Koramu tokushū," 247.

52. Puranetto Rinku, *Mottainai*, 3–5.

53. "Itōchū to Create 'Mottainai' Brand for Environment Conservation," *Kyōdō News International*, July 26, 2005.

54. "MOTTAINAI," http://www.mottainai.info/english/ and http://www.mottainai.info/jp/ (accessed July 2, 2010).

55. "Second National Convention on Mottainai," http://mottainai.info/english/topics/2008/07/000705.php; *Mainichi shinbun*, June 20, 2008 (accessed August 9, 2011).

56. http://www.mottainai.info/english/ and http://www.mottainai.info/jp/.

57. Kankyōshō, ed., *Kankyō hakusho* (Tokyo: Gyōsei, 2005), http://www.env.go.jp/policy/hakusyo/zu/h17/ (accessed June 28, 2016); *Mainichi shinbun*, March 5, 2005.

58. *Mainichi shinbun*, May 14, 2005.

59. Wangari Maathai, "Statement by Prof. W. Maathai, Nobel Peace Laureate, on Behalf of Civil Society," speech presented at the United Nations Summit on Climate Change, New York City, New York, September 22, 2009.

60. Wangari Maathai, "Statement by Prof. Wangari Maathai, Nobel Peace Laureate, Goodwill Ambassador for the Congo Basin Forest Ecosystem, and UN Messenger of Peace," speech presented at the Opening of the High-Level Segment of the United Nations Framework Convention on Climate Change, Copenhagen, Denmark, December 15, 2009.

61. *Mainichi shinbun*, April 22, 2005.

62. *Mainichi shinbun*, April 29, 2005.

63. *Mainichi shinbun*, November 7, 2005.

64. *Mainichi shinbun*, September 18, 2006.

65. *Mainichi shinbun*, January 5, 2008.

66. Magajin Hausu, ed., *Watashi no, mottainai* (Tokyo: Magajin Hausu, 2006).

67. Anbo Fumiko, "'MOTTAINAI kyanpēn' no katsudō ni tsuite," *Re: Building Maintenance and Management* 33, no. 2 (October 2011): 13.

68. *Yomiuri shinbun*, August 29, 2007; *Mainichi shinbun*, September 3, 2007; *Mottainai zenkoku taikai in Utsunomiya hōkokusho*, vol. 1 (Utsunomiya: Mottainai Zenkoku Taikai Jikkō Iinkai Jimukyoku, 2007), 37.

69. On the umbrellas, see *Mainichi shinbun*, June 10, 2009; on the bottles, *Mainichi shinbun*, January 5, 2011.

70. Ishiwata Masayoshi, "Kankyō benchā saizensen 20," *Gabanansu* 68 (December 2006): 90–92.

71. See Tanaka Atsuo, *Waribashi wa mottainai?* (Tokyo: Chikuma Shobō, 2007); Mihara Keiko, *"Mottainai!" o kurashi no naka ni kufū o kasanete eko seikatsu* (Kyoto: Bunrikaku, 2008).

72. "Mottainai Gakkai," http://mottainaisociety.org/society-overview/greeting/ (accessed May 27, 2016).

73. *Mainichi shinbun*, December 11, 2005.

74. *Mottainai tanteidan* (Yokohama: Mottainai Tanteidan, 2006), 1–2.

75. Koizumi Jun'ichirō, "Dai nijūyon-kai," radio address, February 19, 2005; "Kenia kankyō fukudaijin to kaidan, February 18, 2005," Shushō Kantei, http://www.kantei.go.jp/jp/koizumiphoto/2005/02/18kenya.html (accessed August 12, 2011).

76. "'Mottainai' no kokoro," *Koizumi naikaku mēru magajin* 177 (February 24, 2005); Koizumi Jun'ichirō, "Dai nijūgo-kai," radio address, March 19, 2005; Koizumi Jun'ichirō, "Gurenīguruzu samitto," press conference, July 8, 2005.

77. On the idea of Japan as a "liminal space" that has transcended various binaries, see David Leheny, "The Samurai Ride to Huntington's Rescue," in *Civilizations in World Politics*, ed. Peter J. Katzenstein (London: Routledge, 2009), 115.

78. Koizumi, "Gurenīguruzu samitto"; Koizumi Jun'ichirō, "Kagaku gijutsu to jinrui no mirai ni kansuru kokusai fōramu kaikaishiki Koizumi naikaku sōri daijin kichō kōen," speech presented at the Science and Technology in Society Forum, Kyoto, September 11, 2005.

79. Kankyōshō, *Kankyō hakusho*, i–ii.

80. Kankyōshō, ed., *Kankyō hakusho* (Tokyo: Gyōsei, 2006); "Mottainai furoshiki, April 2006," Kankyōshō, http://www.env.go.jp/recycle/info/furoshiki (accessed August 12, 2011).

81. "Mottainai furoshiki," *Koizumi naikaku mēru magajin* 231 (April 20, 2006).

82. Keizai Sangyōshō Tokkyochō, "Shinsei yōken o kanwa shita tokkyo shinsa haiwei shikō puroguramu shichigatsu jūgonichi kara kaishi," June 17, 2011.

83. For more on the history of Mottainai Brasil, see http://www.mottainai.org.br/movimento/historico.

84. See "Japan International Cooperation Agency," http://www.jica.go.jp/vietnam/english/office/topics/events03.html.

85. Abby Lu, "Mottainai!," *New Straits Times*, October 23, 2009; Alycia Lim, "Mottainai's the Word," *The Star*, October 4, 2009; Jade Chan, "Grandma Teaches Kids Not to Waste," *The Star*, October 30, 2009.

86. "Mottainai New York," http://www.mottainainy.com/ (accessed August 23, 2011).

87. "'Mottainai seishin' ni motozuita NY-hatsu no fasshon burando," *Decide* 47, no. 20 (October 2010): unpaginated. Many thanks to Luke McCann for bringing this article to my attention. On a more local level, the Mottainai Ramen noodle shop in Gardena, California, and the "Mottainai" LEED-certified residential building project in Cincinnati, Ohio, also used the concept as a convenient brand that encapsulated environmental consciousness and quality. "3CDC," http://www.3cdc.org/follow-our-projects/mottainai/ (accessed August 30, 2011). Mottainai could also be a philosophy, as in the "Share Your Food" project in Berlin, in which people exchanged ideas over a communal meal prepared by a chef who embraced the vegetarian version of head-to-hoof cooking. Monika Meuller-Kroll, "The 'Mottainai' Concept: A Buddhist Style of Cooking in Neukoelln," National Public Radio, April 18, 2011.

88. Author's field notes, June 11, 2016.

89. *Asahi shinbun*, October 31, 2003; *Yomiuri shinbun*, April 27, 2016.

90. Azuma Kiyohiko, *Yotsubato!*, vol. 1 (Tokyo: Kadokawa, 2003), 16–17, 102–14.

91. Author's field notes, June 12, 2016.

92. Douglas McGray, "Japan's Gross National Cool," *Foreign Policy,* May–June 2002, 44–54. On the popularity of "cool Japan" as a form of soft power, see David Leheny, "A Narrow Place to Cross Swords," in *Beyond Japan,* ed. Peter J. Katzenstein and Takashi Shiraishi (Ithaca: Cornell University Press, 2006), 211–33.

93. *Asahi shinbun*, March 20, 2005.

94. See Harry Harootunian and Tomiko Yoda, introduction to *Japan after Japan,* ed. Tomiko Yoda and Harry Harootunian (Durham: Duke University Press, 2006), 1.

CHAPTER 10. SORTING THINGS OUT

1. Yamashita Hideko, *Shin, katazukejutsu danshari* (Tokyo: Magajin Hausu, 2009), 4–6, 8. On media appearances, see "Danshari," http://www.yamashitahideko.com (accessed April 18, 2016).

2. Yamashita, *Shin, katazukejutsu danshari*, 25, 63, 174.

3. Many thanks to Chris Waters for his insights about the introspective self.

4. Gordon Mathews has made a similar argument about how recent advice books have "shifted towards the self." Gordon Mathews, "Happiness in Neoliberal Japan," in *Happiness and the Good Life in Japan,* ed. Wolfram Manzenreiter and Barbara Holthus (London: Routledge, 2009), 235.

5. Yamashita, *Shin, katazukejutsu danshari*, 48–53, 56–57, 61, 137–39.

6. See the series "Muri, muda, mura o nakushite, atama no naka o sukkiri kaishō!," *Za nijūichi* 28, no. 6 (June 2011): 49–57.

7. Yamashita Hideko, *Shigoto ni kiku "danshari"* (Tokyo: Kadokawa Mākechingu, 2011), 18–19, 109–17.

8. Kawabata Nobuko with Yamashita Hideko, ed., *Mono o sutereba umaku iku danshari no susume* (Tokyo: Dōbunkan Shuppan, 2009), 17.

9. Aikawa Momoko with Yamashita Hideko, ed., *Danshari serapī* (Tokyo: Seishun Shuppansha, 2011).

10. Fukumitsu Megumi, "'Danshari seminā' taikenki," *Nikkei bijinesu associé* 9, no. 19 (December 7, 2010): 45, 47.

11. Yamashita, *Shin, katazukejutsu danshari*, 120–21, 140–43.

12. Kawabata with Yamashita, *Mono o sutereba*, 50–51.

13. Kondō Marie, *Jinsei ga tokimeku katazuke no mahō* (Tokyo: Sanmāku Shuppan, 2011); *Sankei shinbun*, October 3, 2011; *Yomiuri shinbun*, December 26, 2012; *Tokyo shinbun*, September 25, 2013. For the English version, see Marie Kondo, *The Life-Changing Magic of Tidying Up*, trans. Cathy Hirano (Berkeley: Ten Speed Press, 2014).

14. *Mainichi shinbun*, April 17, 2015; "'Sekai de mottomo eikyōryoku no aru 100 nin' Kondō Marie wa ōbeijin kirā," *Shūkan bunshun* 57, no. 17 (April 30, 2015): 145.

15. *Asahi shinbun*, January 15, 2016.

16. *Asahi shinbun*, October 23, 2015.

17. Kondō, *Jinsei ga tokimeku*, 54–59, 62–63. On the meanings of *tokimeku*, translated into English as "joy," see Kondō Marie, *Jinsei ga tokimeku katazuke no mahō 2* (Tokyo: Sanmāku Shuppan, 2012), 28–29.

18. Kondō, *Jinsei ga tokimeku*, 85–88, 154, 242–43.

19. Tatsumi Nagisa, *"Suteru!" gijutsu* (Tokyo: Takarajimasha Shinsho, 2000), 6–7, 17–18; *Asahi shinbun*, September 8, 2000. That Tatsumi's method did not help with the accumulation of garbage was pointed out around the time of the book's publication. "Gomi rettō 'suteru' gijutsu," *Sandē mainichi* 79, no. 53 (November 12, 2000): 131.

20. "Kajō na kinō yori dezainsei o jūshi 'katazuke būmu' de shōhin sentaku kōdō ga kawaru?" *Senden kaigi* 855 (February 15, 2013): 71.

21. Taffy Brodesser-Akner, "Marie Kondo and the Ruthless War on Stuff," *New York Times Magazine*, July 6, 2016.

22. Kondō, *Jinsei ga tokimeku* (2011), 62, 88, 111–15, 138–40.

23. Ibid., 7, 238, 240; Kondō, *Jinsei ga tokimeku* (2012), 277.

24. "Intabyū," *Shinchō* 34, no. 7 (July 2015): 314; Kondō, *Jinsei ga tokimeku* (2011), 60–62.

25. Yamashita Hideko, "Besuto serā no chosha ga, katazuke heta ni mo wakariyasuku pointo o kaisetsu 'danshari' nyūmon," *Purejidento* 49, no. 34 (October 29, 2011): 6–7, 13; "Naze, ima 'danshari' na no ka?" *Za nijūichi* 28, no. 6 (June 2011): 53. Together with an author of books about yoga, Yamashita applied *danshari* to dieting. See Yamashita Hideko and Tatsumura Osamu, *Kokoro to karada o jōka suru danshari daietto* (Tokyo: Sekai Bunkasha, 2011).

26. "Naze, ima 'danshari,'" 53.

27. Kawabata Nobuko, "'Danshari' ni manabu mono to no kakawarikata," *Jidō shinri* 65, no. 14 (October 2011): 32–34

28. Tazaki Masami, *Bijinesu pāson no tame no danshari shikō no susume* (Tokyo: Dōbunkan Shuppan, 2010), 216–23; Tazaki Masami, "Kyaria keisei mo 'danshari shikō' de umaku iku," *Za nijūichi* 28, no. 6 (June 2011): 56–57.

29. For example, Katō Hidetoshi, "Sumai to kazai," *Chūō kōron* 115, no. 11 (October 2000): 308–19.

30. Sasaki's minimalism was considered by some to fit into this family of books about finding pleasure in throwing things out. See *Asahi shinbun*, August 2, 2015.

31. Fumio Sasaki, *Goodbye, Things*, trans. Eriko Sugita (New York: W. W. Norton, 2017).

32. Sasaki Fumio, *Bokutachi ni, mō mono wa hitsuyō nai* (Tokyo: Wani Bukkusu, 2015), 51; "Minimal & ism less is future," http://minimalism.jp (accessed April 20, 2016); *Asahi shinbun*, September 24, 2015; *Yomiuri shinbun*, November 17, 2015.

33. "Wadai no minimarisuto ga kataru 'Mono o sutete eta "shigoto no meritto,"'" *Nikkei bijinesu associé* (January 2016): 40.

34. Sasaki, *Bokutachi ni*, 34, 47–49, 108, 113, 125, 139–40, 145, 153, 162, 172–204, 225–50, 266–73, 283–93.

35. "Naze, ima 'danshari,'" 50; "Kajō na kinō," 70; *Mainichi shinbun*, September 9, 2015; *Yomiuri shinbun*, November 17, 2015.

36. Kawabata, "'Danshari' ni manabu," 38.

37. Hirabayashi Rie, "'Minimarisuto' no kiwami?!," *Nikkei otona no off* (December 2015): 70–73.

38. On the "contemporary struggle to define Buddhism and to justify its societal role," see Stephen G. Covell and Mark Rowe, "Editors' Introduction," *Japanese Journal of Religious Studies* 31, no. 2 (2004): 247.

39. "Mono o shoyū shinai ikikata minimarisuto ga zōshoku chū," *Shūkan daiyamondo* 104, no. 1 (December 26, 2015–January 2, 2016): 146.

40. Yamazaki Eriko, *Yamazaki Eriko no shinpuru setsuyaku seikatsu e yōkoso* (Tokyo: Shufu no Tomosha, 2005), 6–7, 24–25.

41. Katō Emiko, *Muda naku, yutaka ni, utsukushiku ikiru 30 no koto* (Tokyo: Disukabā Tōenchiwan, 2011), 3–4, 14, 22, 55, 255.

42. In the observation of the anthropologist Inge Daniels, "The ideology of tidiness might be prominent but in practice homes vary enormously in degrees of orderliness." Inge Daniels, *The Japanese House*, photography by Susan Andrews (Oxford: Berg, 2010), 132.

43. See Kawakami Takuya, *Binbō to iu ikikata* (Tokyo: WAVE Shuppan, 2010); "Heya to kokoro o sukkiri!," *Nikkei woman* 348 (January 2013): upaginated; *Iranai mono o sukkiri suteru!*, no. 52 of *PHP kurashi rakūru* (December 2014); Nakayama Mayumi, *Suterarezu ni iru fuyōhin no "sutedoki" ga wakaru hon* (Tokyo: Fusōsha, 2015).

44. See Arakawa Nami, *Mono no tame ni yachin harau na!* (Tokyo: WAVE Shuppan, 2008); Azuma Kanako, *Motanai, sutenai, tamekomanai* (Tokyo: Shufu no Tomo Infosu

Jōhōsha, 2015); Kudō Hanae, "Mono de yutaka ni kurasu hōhō," *Nikkei woman* (December 2015): 26–27.

45. The household savings rate generally declined through the second half of the 1990s and 2000s. Organisation for Economic Co-operation and Development, "Household Savings (Indicator)," https://data.oecd.org/hha/household-savings.htm (accessed on September 30, 2016).

46. Tamaru Misuzu, Mikanagi Rika, and Yamazaki Eriko, "Fujin kōron itobata kaigi," *Fujin kōron* 83, no. 21 (December 7, 1998): 164–69. Other advice put more emphasis on the importance of saving not being stinginess in the sense of doing without what you need, nor being unreasonable (*muri*). See Yamamoto Tazu, *Setsuyaku seikatsu nyūmon* (Osaka: Sōgensha, 1999).

47. "Kakei tokushū," *Fujin no tomo* 90, no. 12 (December 1996): 78, 80.

48. Seikatsu Jōhō Kenkyūkai, ed., *Muda na shuppi o nakushitara setsuyaku dekichatta* (Tokyo: Goma Shobō, 1999), 3–5.

49. See, for example, Setsuyaku Seikatsu Kenkyū Gurūpu, *Setsuyaku seikatsu o tokoton tanoshimu 700 no chie* (Tokyo: Chūkei Shuppan, 1999).

50. Yamasaki Hisato, *Nenshū 100-man en no yutaka na setsuyaku seikatsu jutsu* (Tokyo: Bungei Shunjū, 2011), 35, 42, 62, 85–87.

51. See Duran Reiko, *Furansuryū kechi ni mienai zeitaku na setsuyaku seikatsu* (Tokyo: PHP Kenkyūjo, 2011); Satō Eko, *Furansujin no zeitaku no setsuyaku seikatsu* (Tokyo: Shōdensha, 2002).

52. Ogasawara Yōko, *Kechi jōzu* (Tokyo: Bijinesusha, 2003), 20–23.

53. For Tsuji Shin'ichi, "slow time" did not just refer to speed and pace but also meant ecological and sustainable. See Tsuji Shin'ichi, *Surō izu byūchifuru* (Tokyo: Heibonsha, 2001).

54. "Purasu arufa no jikan o umidasu 77 no chie," *Fujin no tomo* 95, no. 5 (May 2001): 64–65.

55. Arakawa Nami, *Sōmei na josei no jikan setsuyaku seikatsu* (Tokyo: Mikasa Shobō, 2002), 4, 55–58, 202–3.

56. Nikkei Woman, ed., *Jinsei o kaeru jikan kanrijutsu* (Tokyo: Nikkei BPsha, 2009), 10–13.

57. Ibid., 7, 70–73, 76–77.

58. Wada Hiromi, *Shiawase o tsukamu!* (Tokyo: Daiyamondosha, 2005), 17–18, 32–34, 100–101, 108, 110, 179–82.

59. Advice for cutting communications expenses was offered in Fujinaga Shin'ichi, "Motto motto setsuyaku dekiru!," *Kindai chūshō kigyō* 37, no. 13 (December 2002): 104–12. A more expansive list of one hundred ideas for saving in the workplace could be found in the special series Auto Pātonā Kyōkai Keihi Setsugen Kenkyū Gurūpu, "Hisaku, myōan, tokusaku o dai kōkai!," *Kigyō jitsumu* 42, no. 8 (July 2003): 22–31.

60. *Mainichi shinbun*, September 5, 1998.

61. *Yomiuri shinbun*, November 12, 1998; *Mainichi shinbun*, October 16, 2000.

62. *Mainichi shinbun*, September 5, 1998.

63. Matsu Masaoki, "Sagyō kōritsu o ageru dai ichi te wa, 'mijika na koto' no kaizen kara," *Senken keizai* 591 (March 7, 2005): 14–16.

64. "Jikan wa shisan, dakara mudazukai shinai seisansei takameta nōhau o kōkai," *Nikkei jōhō sutoratejī* 16, no. 8 (September 2007): 146–47.

65. Aoki Satoshi, *Saikyō no jikan kanrijutsu* (Tokyo: Kōdansha, 2002), 1–3, 97–98, 110–11.

66. "Nenshū 2000-man no jikanjutsu," *Purejidento* (February 18, 2008): 25, 35, 43. A similar point about income and time consciousness, with a focus on managers of small and medium-sized companies, was made in "'Jikan ga nai!' to wa iwasenai," *Nikkei benchā*

249 (June 2005): 121. For other articles about time management from *Purejidento*, see Ōmae Ken'ichi et al., *Jikan to muda no kagaku* (Tokyo: Purejidento, 2006).

67. Shigoto Kōritsu Kenkyūkai, ed., *Tabo shachō no "kekka o daseru" jikanjutsu* (Tokyo: Seibidō Shuppan, 2009).

68. Yamada Hitoshi, "Anata wa mainichi roku jikan mo mudazukai shite iru," *Purejidento* 44, no. 13 (June 12, 2006): 50–53.

69. Nomura Masaki, *Bijinesuman no tame no chiteki jikanjutsu* (Tokyo: PHP Kenkyūjo, 1995), 3–5.

70. See, for example, Yoshikoshi Kōichirō, *Muda na shigoto wa mō, yameyō!* (Tokyo: Kanki Shuppan, 2008); Mizoguchi Kazuhiko, "Setsuden taisaku de mietekita taimu manejimento no hitsuyōsei," *Risonāre* 9, no. 10 (October 2011): 11. Earlier works had made passing references to enjoying life or achieving "balance"; see Saitō Shigeta, *Jikan no tsukaikata* (Tokyo: Mikasa Shobō, 2001).

71. Matsumoto Yukio, *Ichinichi o nibai ni tsukau!* (Tokyo: Dōbunkan Shuppan, 2009), i–iii, 13, 21, 220–22.

72. *Sankei shinbun*, March 19, 2011.

73. *Mainichi shinbun*, December 26, 2014; Anbo Fumiko, "'MOTTAINAI kyanpēn' no katsudō ni tsuite," *Re: Building Maintenance and Management* 32, no. 2 (October 2011): 14–15; "MOTTAINAI furī māketto to wa," http://www.mottainai.info/jp/event/fleama (accessed July 9, 2016).

74. *Tokyo shinbun*, December 28, 2012.

75. "ECO EDO Nihonbashi 2012," http://www.mitsuifudosan.co.jp/corporate/news/2012/0615_01/download/20120615.pdf (accessed October 26, 2012). On business ideas that could be born of the philosophy of *mottainai*, see Mitamura Fukiko, "Sozai, kūkan, jikan . . . minomawari no muda o ikasu 'mottainai' ga bijinesu ni naru!," *Nyūtoppu L.* 6, no. 2 (February 2014): 32–37.

76. Yamashita, *Shigoto ni kiku*, 3–5.

77. Sasaki, *Bokutachi ni*, 51, 59.

78. Katō, *Muda naku*, 259.

79. Genshiryoku Anzen Kiban Kikō, ed., *Genshiryoku shisetsu unten kanri nenpō* (Tokyo: Genshiryoku Anzen Kiban Kikō, 2012), 27, 30, 32, 38–39.

80. *Mainichi shinbun*, May 2, 2011. The idea of "electricity forecasts" was not new in 2011; see Shinoda Masahiro, "'Setsuden no onegai' chūshin ni hatsudensho no genkyō mo kimekomakaku," *Kōken repōto* 252 (May 2008): 9.

81. *Sankei shinbun*, March 30, 2011, and April 9, 2011.

82. Nippon Hōsō Kyōkai, *Kurashi o minaosu natsu no setsuden taisaku* (Tokyo: NHK Shuppan, 2011), 1–3, 6–7, 15, 20–21, 30, 46–47, 68–69.

83. Sumāto Raifu Kenkyūkai, *Ikka de kyōryoku suru setsuden, setsuyaku seikatsu no hōhō 150* (Tokyo: Shin Jinbutsu Ōraisha, 2011), 2–4, 24–25, 32–33.

84. Yamakawa Ayako, ed., "Shōene seikatsu 100 no kotsu," *Kurashi no techō* 57 (April–May 2012): 60.

85. See, for example, *Kechi wa kashikoi!* (Tokyo: Kōdansha, 1999).

86. ABC Cooking Studio Reshipi Ryōri Seisaku, *ABC Cooking Studio no setsuden eko okazu* (Tokyo: Shufu to Seikatsusha, 2011), i, 4–7; *Sankei shinbun*, March 22, 2011. See also Nojiri Masato, "Shōene seikatsu," *Eiyō to ryōri* 77, no. 8 (August 2011): 8–15; Honda Akiko and Tanaka Kanako, "Suzushiku, oishiku shōene kukkingu," *Eiyō to ryōri* 88, no. 8 (August 2011): 17–37.

87. Ishizawa Kiyomi, *Setsuden, setsugasu, sessui kashikoi reshipi* (Tokyo: Shufu no Tomosha, 2011), 2, 10, 20.

88. Minowa Yayoi, *Setsuden, shōene no chie 123* (Tokyo: Asuka Shinsha 2011), 2–3, 75, 88.

89. "Atsui natsu o suzushiku sugosu teian kappatsuka," *Kigyō to kōkoku* 38, no. 8 (August 2012): 39–41.

90. "Doraggu sutoa shōhin torendo kīwādo de miru shōhin bunseki," *Drug magazine* 54, no. 8 (July 2011): 55.

91. *Mainichi shinbun*, May 13, 2011; *Sankei shinbun*, May 13, 2011; "T shatsu, tanpan mo kaikin?" *Shūkan daiyamondo* 99, no. 22 (June 4, 2011): 56.

92. "Raifusutairu ga kawaru?!," *Kōhō kaigi* 31 (August 2011): 9.

93. *Asahi shinbun*, November 2, 2011.

94. *Nihon keizai shinbun*, June 2, 2012.

95. *Sankei shinbun*, July 4, 2012.

96. *Sankei shinbun*, May 24, 2013; *Mainichi shinbun*, May 21, 2013; "2013 imadoki no kūru bizu," *Mono magajin* 32, no. 10 (June 2, 2013): 119.

97. *Sankei shinbun*, November 24, 2015.

98. The Cool Biz period, which had extended from May through October since 2011, was shortened by one month to September in 2016 because only a few days in October were above 25 degrees Celsius (77 degrees Fahrenheit). *Yomiuri shinbun*, May 2, 2016. For the Cool Biz fashion trends for 2016, see *Asahi shinbun*, May 12, 2016.

99. Nihon Nōritsu Kyōkai Sōgō Kenkyūjo Mākechingu Dēta Banku, ed., *Kankyō ishiki, eko raifu kanren mākechingu dēta hakusho, 2009-nen ban* (Tokyo: Nihon Nōritsu Kyōkai Sōgō Kenkyūjo, 2008), 187.

100. Mizobuchi Ken'ichi and Takeuchi Kenji, *Katei ni okeru setsuden o dō susumeru ka* (Kobe: Graduate School of Economics, Kobe University, 2011), 2; Mizoguchi, "Setsuden taisaku," 11; *Asahi shinbun*, December 11, 2012.

101. Kagaku Keiei Kenkyūkai, "Setsuden taisaku ni kansuru ankēto chōsa ni tsuite," *Kagaku keiei* 437 (July 2011): 71, 73.

102. Note that in 2014, roughly half (50.9 percent) of household energy consumption was of electricity. That number was virtually the same in 2011 (51 percent). Keizai Sangyōshō Shigen Enerugīchō, *Heisei 27 nendo enerugī hakusho* ([Tokyo]: Shigen Enerugīchō, 2016), 148, 150–51, http://www.enecho.meti.go.jp/about/whitepaper/2016pdf/whitepaper2016 pdf_2_1.pdf (accessed July 12, 2016); Keizai Sangyōshō Shigen Enerugīchō, *Heisei 23 nendo enerugī hakusho* ([Tokyo]: Shigen Enerugīchō, 2012), 102, http://www.enecho.meti. go.jp/about/whitepaper/2012pdf/whitepaper2012pdf_2_1.pdf (accessed July 12, 2016).

103. On the remarks of conservatives, see Richard J. Samuels, *3.11* (Ithaca: Cornell University Press, 2013), 30; Peter Duus, "Dealing with Disaster," in *Natural Disaster and Nuclear Crisis in Japan*, ed. Jeff Kingston (New York: Routledge, 2012), 176.

104. *Chūnichi shinbun*, April 24, 2011.

105. Suzuki Takao, *Shiawase setsuden* (Tokyo: Bungei Shunju, 2011), 19–20, 125.

106. For the question about reasons for feeling stress, n = 329 for the July 2011 survey and n = 229 for June 2013. "Kontō no setsuden riyū 'denkidai agarisō' 6 warijaku," *Nikkei shōhi insaito* 5 (August 2013): 74.

107. The characterization of a "heaver emphasis on belonging, self-expression, and the quality of life" as "postmaterial" does not quite capture the extent to which the material was, and to some extent still continues to be, valued. For a comparative examination of "postmaterialist values" in the 1970s and 1980s, see chapter 2 of Ronald Inglehart, *Culture Shift in Advanced Industrial Society* (Princeton: Princeton University Press, 1990).

108. On garbage, see Naikakufu Daijin Kanbō Seifu Kōhōshitsu Seron Chōsa Tantō, *Kankyō mondai ni kansuru seron chōsa* ([2012]), http://survey.gov-online.go.jp/h24/ h24-kankyou/2-1.html (accessed July 13, 2016). See the results of two surveys on environmental issues in Nihon Nōritsu Kyōkai Sōgō Kenkyūjo Mākechingu Dēta Banku, *Kankyō ishiki*, 56, 100.

109. In 2004, per capita solid waste disposal was 1,146 grams; in 2014, 963 grams per person. Kankyōshō Daijin Kanbō Haikibutsu Risaikuru Taisakubu Haikibutsu Taisakuka, "Ippan haikibutsu no haishutsu oyobi shori jōkyō tō (Heisei 26 nendo) ni tsuite," February 22, 2016, 3, http://www.env.go.jp/recycle/waste_tech/ippan/h26/data/env_press.pdf (accessed July 13, 2016).

110. Author's field notes, June 11, 2016.

111. *Sankei shinbun*, April 8, 2009; Furukawa Miho, "Gomi yashiki, sukebē, rōhi guse . . . kyōgaku no jittai to wa," *Fujin kōron* 95, no. 15 (July 22, 2010): 128–29; *Asahi shinbun*, August 14, 2012, and September 10, 2014.

112. *New York Times*, July 18, 2016; Arielle Bernstein, "Marie Kondo and the Privilege of Clutter," *The Atlantic*, March 25, 2016.

113. Nakano Kōji, *Seihin no shisō* (Tokyo: Bungei Shunjū, 1996).

AFTERWORD: WASTE AND WELL-BEING

1. Mottainai Bāsan, Twitter post, July 1, 2017, https://twitter.com/mottainaibaasan.

2. Many thanks to Christopher Bolton for his observations about the production of decluttering.

3. On the limitations of foregrounding the distinctions between capitalism and non-capitalism, pre-capitalism, or semi-capitalism, especially when thinking in global terms, see Julia Adeney Thomas, "Using Japan to Think Globally," in *Japan at Nature's Edge*, ed. Ian Jared Miller, Julia Adeney Thomas, and Brett L. Walker (Honolulu: University of Hawaii Press, 2013), 293–95.

4. *Yomiuri shinbun*, October 25, 1989, and November 21, 2014; *Sankei shinbun*, June 20, 2005.

5. *Yomiuri shinbun*, March 8, 2013, and June 19, 2014.

6. *New York Times*, January 9, 2005; Meg Lowman, "Gross National Happiness," *Huffington Post,* January 25, 2016, http://www.huffingtonpost.com/meg-lowman/gross-national-happinessb_b_9062856.html (accessed August 15, 2016); Barry Petersen and T. Sean Herbert, "Bhutan's Secret of Happiness," *CBS News*, April 17, 2016, http://www.cbsnews.com/news/bhutans-secret-of-happiness/ (accessed August 15, 2016).

7. *The Guardian*, December 1, 2012; *New York Times*, June 29, 2013; *Yomiuri shinbun*, November 21, 2014.

8. *Yomiuri shinbun*, October 25, 1989; *Sankei shinbun*, June 20, 2005.

9. On GNH, see http://www.gnhcentrebhutan.org/what-is-gnh/four-pillars-and-nine-domains/.

10. General Assembly Resolution 65/309, *Happiness*, A/65/L.86, July 19, 2011, http://www.un.org/ga/search/view_doc.asp?symbol=A/RES/65/309 (accessed August 15, 2016).

11. Royal Government of Bhutan, *The Report of the High-Level Meeting on Wellbeing and Happiness* (Thimphu: Office of the Prime Minister, 2012).

12. In the World Happiness Report published in 2017, which averaged rankings for 2014 to 2016, Japan was number 51, just after Belize and above Lithuania. Bhutan was number 97. John Helliwell, Richard Layard, and Jeffrey Sachs, eds., *World Happiness Report 2017* (New York: Sustainable Development Solutions Network, 2017), 12, http://worldhappiness.report/wp-content/uploads/sites/2/2017/03/HR17.pdf (accessed June 7, 2017).

13. Happiness has become a topic of interest to Japan specialists as well. See Wolfram Manzenreiter and Barbara Holthus, eds., *Happiness and the Good Life in Japan* (New York: Routledge, 2017).

14. The "emptiness" of affluence was observed by scholars of Japan, particularly in the 1990s. See Gavan McCormack, *The Emptiness of Japanese Affluence* (Armonk, NY: M. E. Sharpe, 1996).

15. *Yomiuri shinbun*, October 25, 1989, and February 7, 2000; *Sankei shinbun*, June 20, 2005.

16. Historian Jordan Sand has argued that "the foundation of the promise [of postwar industrial development] was not (as in the United States) that anyone might become rich, it was that all would be comfortable." Jordan Sand, "Living with Uncertainty after March 11, 2011," *Journal of Asian Studies* 71, no. 2 (May 2012): 316–17.

17. Tessa Morris-Suzuki, *A History of Japanese Economic Thought* (London: Routledge, 1989), 136–37.

18. Between 1955 and 2014, GDP in real terms increased about elevenfold; GDP per capita grew about eightfold. Takahashi Nobuaki, "Seichō wa yutaka na shakai o motarasu no ka?" *DIO* (December 2015): 4.

19. John Maynard Keynes, "Economic Possibilities for Our Grandchildren" (1930), in *Revisiting Keynes*, ed. Lorenzo Pecchi and Gustavo Piga (Cambridge: MIT Press, 2008), 21, 23–25; Lorenzo Pecchi and Gustavo Piga, "*Economic Possibilities for Our Grandchildren*," ibid., 2.

20. Put in a slightly different way by the historian and Keynes biographer Robert Skidelsky and the philosopher Edward Skidelsky, "the irony is . . . that now that we have at least achieved abundance, the habits bred into us by capitalism have left us incapable of enjoying it properly." Robert Skidelsky and Edward Skidelsky, *How Much Is Enough?* (New York: Other Press, 2012), 7.

21. For a longer history of American thoughts on affluence and consumer culture, see Daniel Horowitz, *The Anxieties of Affluence* (Amherst: University of Massachusetts Press, 2004).

22. Brad Tuttle, "Got Stuff?" *Time*, July 19, 2012, http://business.time.com/2012/07/19/got-stuff-typical-american-home-cluttered-with-possessions-and-stressing-us-out/ (accessed June 20, 2012); Jack Feuer, "The Clutter Culture," *UCLA Magazine*, July 1, 2012, http://magazine.ucla.edu/features/the-clutter-culture/ (accessed June 20, 2012); *Washington Post*, July 3, 2012.

23. *USA Today*, January 14, 2016.

24. For a small sample, see Molly Young, "Domestic Purging with Japanese Tidying Guru Marie Kondo," *New York Magazine*, February 10, 2015; Bourree Lam, "The Economics of Tidying Up," *The Atlantic*, May 13, 2015; Barry Yourgrau, "The Origin Story of Marie Kondo's Decluttering Empire," *The New Yorker*, December 8, 2015; *New York Times*, January 23, 2016, and June 6, 2016; Chloe Malle, "A *Vogue* Editor Learns the Art of Closet-Cleaning from Marie Kondo," *Vogue*, February 2, 2016; Kate Storey, "Marie Kondo Told Us Her Secret Clutter Vice," *Good Housekeeping*, April 29, 2016; "Talks at Google," https://www.youtube.com/watch?v=w1-HMMX_NR8; *The Ellen DeGeneres Show*, https://www.youtube.com/watch?v=KdUAUQT8E9g.

25. Lauren Sherman, "The KonMari Method Is a Boon to Secondhand Stores and E-tailers," *Fashionista*, April 6, 2015, http://fashionista.com/2015/04/konmari-method-goodwill (accessed August 17, 2016).

26. Arielle Bernstein, "Marie Kondo and the Privilege of Clutter," *The Atlantic*, March 25, 2016; *New York Times*, July 18, 2016; Sarah Knight, *The Life-Changing Magic of Not Giving a F*ck* (New York: Little, Brown and Company, 2015).

27. Mallory Ortberg, "How to Get Rid of Clutter and Live Abundantly," *The Toast*, February 24, 2015, http://the-toast.net/2015/02/24/get-rid-clutter-live-abundantly/ (accessed August 17, 2016).

28. "June Reading List," http://www.jamesaltucher.com/june-reading-list/ (accessed August 17, 2016); *New York Times*, August 6, 2016.

29. *New York Times*, March 9, 2013.

30. Ann Brenoff, "Downsizing: Could You Live in a Tiny Home in Retirement?" *Huffington Post*, October 22, 2012, http://www.huffingtonpost.com/2012/10/22/downsizing-for-

retirement_n_1961961.html (accessed August 17, 2016). The "tiny-house movement" has not been popular in Japan, where the average home size has been much smaller than in the United States. One issue of a general goods magazine geared toward men included a series of articles about tiny houses (called *tainī hausu*, or *koya*), but the definition of a tiny house was quite broad and included various kinds of temporary, mobile, or makeshift shelter (e.g., campers, tents, and tree houses) as well as small residences. See *Mono magajin* 35, no. 11 (June 2016).

31. On the freegan philosophy, see "Freeganifo," http://freegan.info/.

32. *No Impact Man* (Oscilloscope, 2009); Colin Beavan, *No Impact Man* (New York: Farrar, Straus and Giroux, 2010).

33. Juliet B. Schor, *The Overworked American* (New York: BasicBooks, 1991), 11.

34. *New York Times*, June 30, 2012.

35. John Baldoni, "Stop Wasting Time Being Busy," *Forbes*, July 2, 2012, http://www.forbes.com/sites/johnbaldoni/2012/07/02/stop-wasting-time/#39fd1e345e5b (accessed August 17, 2016).

36. *The Guardian*, December 22, 2016, https://www.theguardian.com/technology/2016/dec/22/why-time-management-is-ruining-our-lives (accessed June 7, 2017).

37. Skidelsky and Skidelsky, *How Much Is Enough*, 180–218; *New York Times*, August 17, 2012.

38. See the essays in Pecchi and Piga, *Revisiting Keynes*, especially Joseph E. Stiglitz, "Toward a General Theory of Consumerism," 41–85; Richard B. Freeman, "Why Do We Work More Than Keynes Expected?" 135–42; Gary S. Becker and Luis Rayo, "Why Keynes Underestimated Consumption and Overestimated Leisure for the Long Run," 179–84. For a cogent synopsis of various views on busyness, see Elizabeth Kolbert, "No Time," *The New Yorker*, May 26, 2014, http://www.newyorker.com/magazine/2014/05/26/no-time (accessed August 17, 2016).

39. See Yoichi Funabashi and Barak Kushner, eds., *Examining Japan's Lost Decades* (London: Routledge, 2015); Seiyama Kazuo, "'Atarashī yutakasa' ni tsuite," *DIO* 269 (March 2012): 11–13.

40. Takahashi, "Seichō wa yutaka na shakai o motarasu no ka?" 7; Ichikawa Tomoko, "Nihonrashī GNH to wa nani ka," *GNH kokumin sō kōfukudo kenkyū* (February 2014): 43–66; Shibuya Yukio et al., "'Yutakasa ron' no hensen," *Mitsubishi sōgō kenkyūjo shohō* 47 (2006): 42; Tsuji Shin'ichi, *Shiawase-tte, nan dakke* (Tokyo: Sofuto Banku Kurieichibu, 2008); Takahashi Nobuaki, *Yasashī keizaigaku* (Tokyo: Chikuma Shobō, 2003).

41. Robert J. Gordon, *The Rise and Fall of American Growth* (Princeton: Princeton University Press, 2016); *New York Times*, August 6, 2016.

42. Stephen Vlastos, "Bookending Postwar Japan," in *Japan since 1945*, ed. Christopher Gerteis and Timothy S. George (New York: Bloomsbury, 2013), 259.

Bibliography

DOCUMENTS OF THE SUPREME COMMANDER FOR THE ALLIED POWERS (SCAP)

CAS = Civil Affairs Section
DPU = Director of Production and Utilities
ESS = Economic and Scientific Section
ID = Industry Division
IPCB = Industrial Production and Construction Branch
KCAR = Kanto Civil Affairs Region
NACP = National Archives at College Park, MD
TCAR = Tohoku Civil Affairs Region

"Amendment to Section I, Operational Memorandum 24, Dated June 6, 1947"; "Army Canteens Service, B.C.O.F. Detachment, Kure, Japan" (June 14, 1949); SCAP; ESS; DPU; ID; IPCB; Topical File, 1940–1950; Record Group 331; box 7186; folder 19; NACP.

"Current Japanese Public Opinion Surveys, no. 19" (March 17, 1949); SCAP; Civil Information and Education Section; Public Opinion and Sociological Research Division; General Subject File, 1946–1951; Record Group 331; box 5876; folder 20; NACP.

"Depends Upon the Intention of Dwellers, Lets [sic] Cooperate and Make Clean, MG Too[?] Inspection Tour Group, Housing Area, from *Yukan Tohoku*, August 27, 1948"; SCAP; CAS; TCAR; Public Health & Welfare Activities, 1946–1951; Record Group 331; box 2583; folder 5; NACP.

"Disposal of Surplus Exchange Merchandise, April 12, 1949," "To Industry Div., ESS, GHQ, SCAP, From Sangyo Fukko Kodan, Subject: Application for Release of 8th Army Exchange Surplus Merchandise to Sangyo Fukko Kodan" (August 6, 1949); "Informational Memorandum for Economic Stabilization Board, Subject: Purchase and Disposition of Eighth Army Exchange Surplus Merchandise" (August 9, 1949); "Estimated Income and Expenditure Regarding Sale of Merchandise to be Released from 8th Army Exchange Tokyo Yokohama Area"; SCAP; ESS; DPU; ID; IPCB; Topical File, 1940–1950; Record Group 331; box 7186; folder 19; NACP.

"Disposal Sub-Div., Cleansing Operation Dep., T.M.O., Designation of Contractors on Disposal of Wastes from the Occupation Forces Installations for Fiscal 1951" (January 1951); SCAP; CAS; KCAR; Public Health Activities File, 1946–1951; Record Group 331; box 2821; folder 8; NACP.

"For the Press Conference: August 24, 1948"; SCAP; CAS; TCAR; Public Health & Welfare Activities, 1946–1951; Record Group 331; box 2583; folder 5; NACP.

"From All Inhabitants of 4 Minamishinagawa, Onegai" (June 24, 1948); SCAP; CAS; KCAR; Public Health Activities File, 1946–1951; Record Group 331; box 2823; folder 10; NACP.

"From Ota En, Chief of the Sanitation Operations Department, To Chief of the Kanto Civil Affairs Region, Subject: Prescribed Sign-board Put on Trucks Being Operated by the Agencies for T.M.O. in Collection and Disposal of Garbage and Trash from the Occupation Forces Installations" (April 22, 1950); SCAP; CAS; KCAR; Public Health & Disease Control, 1947–1951; Record Group 331; box 2817; folder 5; NACP.

"From Shoji Akiyama, Representative Director, Shinyu Shokai, Ltd., No. 8 Shiba-Takahamacho, Minato-ku, Tokyo, To Colonel Kegley, Petition" (March 31, 1951); SCAP; CAS; KCAR; Public Health Activities File, 1946–1951; Record Group 331; box 2821; folder 8; NACP.

"General Headquarters, Supreme Commander for the Allied Powers, APO 500, Memorandum for Japanese Government, Subject: Disposition of Garbage and Waste, AG 720, SCAPIN 1915" (July 1, 1948); SCAP, Civil Property Custodian; Executive Division; Decimal File, 1946–1952; Record Group 331; box 4895; folder 7; NACP.

"General Headquarters, Supreme Commander for the Allied Powers, Memorandum for the Imperial Japanese Government, Subject: Disposition of Garbage and Waste, AG 720, SCAPIN 1548" (February 27, 1947); SCAP; CAS; KCAR; Public Health Activities File, 1946–1951; Record Group 331; box 2821; folder 8; NACP.

"Headquarters Yokohama Command, APO 503, Subject: Unauthorized Disposal of Tin Cans and Bottles" (April 12, 1949); SCAP; CAS; TCAR; Miscellaneous File, 1946–1951; Record Group 331; box 2607; folder 18; NACP.

"Memo for Record" (September 5, 1950); "From SCAP Tokyo Japan to BCOF Kure Japan" (September 7, 1950); SCAP; ESS; DPU; ID; IPCB; Topical File, 1940–1950; Record Group 331; box 7186; folder 19; NACP.

"Reconditioning, Inspection and Salvage Section, Headquarters Eighth Army, Eighth Army Exchange, APO 343, Sub-standard Merchandise to be Sold to the Japanese Government"; SCAP; ESS; DPU; ID; IPCB; Topical File, 1940–1950; Record Group 331; box 7186; folder 19; NACP.

"Register of Complaints"; SCAP; CAS; KCAR; Public Health Activities File, 1946–1951; Record Group 331; box 2823; folder 10; NACP.

"Santama Waste Disposing for Occupation Forces Installation Company, Tachikawa, Tokyo-to, To The Supreme Commander, Subject: Petition for Disposition of Garbage and Waste" (February 12, 1951); SCAP; CAS; KCAR; Public Health & Disease Control, 1947–1951; Record Group 331; box 2817; folder 5; NACP.

"School Sanitation Association, General Meeting, November 12–13, 1948, School Sanitation Problems" (November 12, 1948); SCAP; CAS; TCAR; Public Health & Welfare Activities, 1946–1951; Record Group 331; box 2583; folder 5; NACP.

"To Depot Commanders, All Branch Exchanges, Subject: Amendment to Section I, Operational Memorandum 24, Dated June 6, 1947" (October 4, 1947); SCAP; ESS; DPU; ID; IPCB; Topical File, 1940–1950; Record Group 331; box 7186; folder 19; NACP.

RECORDS OF THE UNITED STATES STRATEGIC BOMBING SURVEY (USSBS)

"Garbage and Refuse Disposal in Nagasaki, Serial No. 13, Report No. 2-c(11), USSBS Index Section 8"; Records of the USSBS; Entry 43; USSBS Transcripts of Interrogations and Interrogation Reports of Japanese Industrial, Military, and Political Leaders, 1945–1946; Record Group 243.

"Kyoto City Garbage and Refuse Collection, Report No. 2-s, USSBS Index Section 8" (November 16, 1945); Records of the USSBS; Entry 43; USSBS Transcriptions of

Interrogations and Interrogation Reports of Japanese Industrial, Military, and Political Leaders, 1945–1946; Record Group 243.

"Sewage, Garbage and Night Soil Disposal, Kyoto: Data on Garbage and Refuse Disposal, Kyoto, Report No. 12c(9)(f), USSBS Index Section 2"; Records of the USSBS; Entry 41; Pacific Survey Reports and Supporting Records, 1928–1947; Record Group 243.

"Sewage, Garbage and Refuse, and Night Soil Disposal, Nagasaki, Yokohama, Kobe, Hiroshima, Sasebo Shi: Data on Sewage, Hiroshima, Report No. 12c(11)(h), USSBS Index Section 2," Records of the USSBS; Entry 41; Pacific Survey Reports and Supporting Records, 1928–1947; Record Group 243.

"Sewage, Garbage and Refuse, and Night Soil Disposal, Nagasaki, Yokohama, Kobe, Hiroshima, Sasebo Shi: Interview on Garbage and Refuse Disposal, Yokohama, Report No. 12c(11)(e)," USSBS Index Section 2; Records of the USSBS; Entry 41; Pacific Survey Reports and Supporting Records, 1928–1947; Record Group 243.

TEXTBOOKS

Abe Akashi et al. *Katei ippan: Ningen to shite no yutaka na seikatsu o mezashite.* Tokyo: Tokyo Shoseki, 1994.

Itō Kiyoe et al. *Katei ippan.* Tokyo: Tokyo Shoseki Kabushiki Gaisha, 1988.

Kagawa Yoshiko et al. *Katei ippan.* Tokyo: Chūkyō Shuppan Kabushiki Gaisha, 1991.

———. *Katei sōgō: Seikatsu ni yutakasa o motomete.* Tokyo: Dai'ichi Gakushūsha, 2003.

Nakamura Tatsuya. "'Yutakasa' saikō." In *Chūgaku kokugo,* by Kinoshita Junji et al. Tokyo: Kyōiku Shuppan, 1993.

Sugihara Yasuo et al. *Gendai shakai.* Tokyo: Jiyū Shobō, 1985.

Tsuji Kiyoaki et al. *Gendai shakai.* Tokyo: Jiyū Shobō, 1991.

INTERVIEWS AND OBSERVATIONS

Observation by author. *Hari kuyō* at Awashimadō, Tokyo. February 8, 2016.

Observation by author. MOTTAINAI Festival, Tokyo. June 12, 2016.

Observation by author. Tour of New Kōtō Incineration Plant, Tokyo. June 11, 2016.

Tsuchida Takashi and Yamada Harumi. October 11 and 13, 2015.

NEWSPAPERS AND NEWS SITES

Asahi shinbun, Bloomberg, CBS News, *Chicago Tribune, Christian Science Monitor, Chūnichi shinbun, Daily Yomiuri, The Guardian, Hokkaidō shinbun, Huffington Post, Japan Times, Jiji shinbun,* Kyōdō News International, *Kyoto shinbun, Los Angeles Times, Mainichi shinbun, Nagasaki shinbun,* National Public Radio, *New Straits Times, New York Times, New York Times Magazine, Nihon keizai shinbun, Nikkei ryūtsū shinbun, Nishi Nihon shinbun, Pittsburgh Courier, Saga shinbun, Sankei shinbun, The Star, Tokyo shinbun, USA Today, Washington Post, Yomiuri shinbun*

WORKS CITED

"3CDC." http://www.3cdc.org/follow-our-projects/mottainai/.

1980-nen ichiman setai no shōene sōtenken hakusho: Shōene jidai no atarashī seikatsu yōshiki to chiiki shakai no kōchiku: Shōshigen shōene tenken katsudō shūkei hōkokusho. Tokyo: Shin Seikatsu Undō Kyōkai, 1980.

"2013 imadoki no kūru bizu." *Mono magajin* 32, no. 10 (June 2, 2013): 111–20.

ABC Cooking Studio Reshipi Ryōri Seisaku. *ABC Cooking Studio no setsuden eko okazu.* Tokyo: Shufu to Seikatsusha, 2011.

"AC Japan CM mottainai." https://www.youtube.com/watch?v=GXODCN6rfTc.

"AC Japan kōkoku ākaibu: Mottainai de ashita wa kawaru." https://www.ad-c.or.jp/campaign/search.php?page=5&sort=businessyear_default&businessyear=2015.

Aikawa Momoko with Yamashita Hideko, ed. *Danshari serapī: Iron na koto ga raku ni naru!* Tokyo: Seishun Shuppansha, 2011.

Akabane Shūichi. *Kechi seikatsu no chie: Setsuyaku jidai o tanoshiku kurasu aidea shū.* Tokyo: Ēru Shuppansha, 1975.

Akasegawa Genpei. *Mottainai hanashi desu.* Tokyo: Chikuma Shobō, 2007.

———. *Tokyo mikisā keikaku: Haireddo sentā chokusetsu kōdō no kiroku.* Tokyo: Paruko Shuppankyoku, 1984.

Akasegawa, Genpei. *Hyperart: Thomasson.* Translated by Matthew Fargo. New York: Kaya Press, 2009.

Akasegawa Genpei, with Ni'imi Yasuaki and Tsukaisute Kōgen Gakkai, eds. *Tsukaisute kōgengaku.* Tokyo: Jitsugyō no Nihonsha, 1987.

Akiyama Hanako. "'Tsukaisute Jidai o Kangaeru Kai' de sugoshita sanjūnen." *Karin* 76 (November 2003): 12–14.

Akiyama Hiroko. *Gomi o herasu chie.* Vol. 1 of *Edo no kurashi kara manabu "mottainai."* Tokyo: Chōbunsha, 2009.

———. *Kaiteki ni sugosu kufū.* Vol. 2 of *Edo no kurashi kara manabu "mottainai."* Tokyo: Chōbunsha, 2009.

———. *Muda o dasanai shakai.* Vol. 3 of *Edo no kurashi kara manabu "mottainai."* Tokyo: Chōbunsha, 2009.

Akuto Hiroshi. *Shōhi bunka ron: Atarashī raifusutairu kara no hassō.* Tokyo: Chūō Keizaisha, 1985.

Allen, Barry. "The Ethical Artifact: On Trash." In *Trash,* edited by John Knechtel, 196–213. Cambridge: MIT Press, 2007.

Allison, Anne. *Millennial Monsters: Japanese Toys and the Global Imagination.* Berkeley: University of California Press, 2006.

———. *Precarious Japan.* Durham: Duke University Press, 2013.

Anbo Fumiko. "'MOTTAINAI kyanpēn' no katsudō ni tsuite." *Re: Building Maintenance and Management* 33, no. 2 (October 2011): 12–15. Part of a series titled "Mottainai."

"Ankēto: Genba kara no koe: Gomi sensō: Seisōsagyōin wa dō uketometa ka." *Toseijin* 362 (February 1972): 46–52.

Aoki Satoshi. *Saikyō no jikan kanrijutsu.* Tokyo: Kōdansha, 2002.

Apāto no gomi mondai: Shōwa 50-nendo taiwa shūkai jisshi hōkokusho. Tokyo-to Seisōkyoku, 1976.

Arakawa Ichirō. "Yume no shima kōen: Gomi no shima kara midori no shima e." *Ekonomisuto* 56, no. 45 (November 7, 1978): 64–71.

Arakawa Nami. *Mono no tame ni yachin harau na! Kaeba kau hodo fusai ni naru!* Tokyo: WAVE Shuppan, 2008.

———. *Sōmei na josei no jikan no setsuyaku seikatsu.* Tokyo: Mikasa Shobō, 2002.

Asahi Shinbun Keizaibu, ed. *Kutabare GNP: Kōdō seichō no uchimaku.* Tokyo: Asahi Shinbunsha, 1971.

"Asobi to seikatsu to jiyū jikan o kangaeru." *Gekkan sōhyō* 376 (April 1989): 16–18.

"Atsui natsu o suzushiku sugosu teian kappatsuka: Setsuden de seikatsusha no ishiki mo kawari." *Kigyō to kōkoku* 38, no. 8 (August 2012): 38–43.

Auto Pātonā Kyōkai Keihi Setsugen Kenkyū Gurūpu. "Hisaku, myōan, tokusaku o dai kōkai! Madamada konna ni atta 'setsuyaku aidea' 100 renpatsu." *Kigyō jitsumu* 42, no. 8 (July 2003): 22–31.

Avenell, Simon. *Transnational Japan in the Global Environmental Movement*. Honolulu: University of Hawaii Press, 2017.

Avenell, Simon Andrew. *Making Japanese Citizens: Civil Society and the Mythology of the Shimin in Postwar Japan*. Berkeley: University of California Press, 2010.

Awata Fusaho. "Kono mama de wa ikenai: Zeitaku shōhi shakai wa doko e." *Sekai* 529 (July 1989): 92–94.

Azuma Kanako. *Motanai, sutenai, tamekomanai: Minotake seikatsu*. Tokyo: Shufu no Tomo Infosu Jōhōsha, 2015.

Azuma Kiyohiko. *Yotsubato!* Vol. 1. Tokyo: Kadokawa, 2003.

Baldoni, John. "Stop Wasting Time Being Busy." *Forbes*, July 2, 2012. http://www.forbes.com/sites/johnbaldoni/2012/07/02/stop-wasting-time/#39fd1e345e5b.

Baldwin, Frank, and Anne Allison, eds. *Japan: The Precarious Future*. New York: New York University Press, 2015.

Bandō Eriko. *Āra mottainai!* Tokyo: Shūeisha, 1975.

Banno Yoshimitsu. *Gojira tai hedora*. Tōhō, 1971.

Beavan, Colin. *No Impact Man: The Adventures of a Guilty Liberal Who Attempts to Save the Planet and the Discoveries He Makes about Himself and Our Way of Life in the Process*. New York: Farrar, Straus and Giroux, 2010.

Ben-Ari, Eyal. "A Bureaucrat in Every Japanese Kitchen? On Cultural Assumptions and Coproduction." *Administration & Society* 21, no. 4 (February 1990): 472–92.

Berman, Morris. *Neurotic Beauty: An Outsider Looks at Japan*. Portland, OR: One Spirit Press, 2015.

Bernstein, Arielle. "Marie Kondo and the Privilege of Clutter." *The Atlantic*, March 25, 2016.

Boym, Svetlana. *The Future of Nostalgia*. New York: Basic Books, 2001.

Brinton, Mary C. *Women and the Economic Miracle: Gender and Work in Postwar Japan*. Berkeley: University of California Press, 1993.

Broadbent, Jeffrey. *Environmental Politics in Japan: Networks of Power and Protest*. Cambridge: Cambridge University Press, 1998.

Broadbent, Kaye. *Women's Employment in Japan: The Experience of Part-Time Workers*. London: RoutledgeCurzon, 2003.

Broadcasting in Japan: The Twentieth Century Journey from Radio to Multimedia. Tokyo: NHK, 2002.

Brown, Roger H. "A Confucian Nationalist for Modern Japan: Yasuoka Masahiro, the Nation-State, and Moral Self-Cultivation, 1898–1983." Ph.D. dissertation. University of Southern California, 2004.

"Buppin no setsuyaku katsuyō." *Nōritsu* 5, no. 6 (June 1954): 14–16.

Certeau, Michel de. *The Practice of Everyday Life*. Translated by Steven F. Rendall. Berkeley: University of California Press, 1984.

"Chie no aru yutakasa o: Atarashī shiten to hassō ni yoru shōshigen, shōenerugī o mezashite." *Chūō kaigi kaihō* 48 (June 1992): 2–13.

Chochiku Keizai Kenkyū Sentā, ed. *Yutaka na jidai no kurashi to chochiku*. Tokyo: Gyōsei, 1989.

Covell, Stephen G., and Mark Rowe. "Editors' Introduction: Traditional Buddhism in Contemporary Japan." *Japanese Journal of Religious Studies* 31, no. 2 (2004): 245–54.

Crockett, Lucy Herndon. *Popcorn on the Ginza: An Informal Portrait of Postwar Japan*. New York: William Sloane Associates, 1949.

Cwiertka, Katarzyna, and Miho Yasuhara. "Beyond Hunger: Grocery Shopping, Cooking, and Eating in 1940s Japan." In *Japanese Foodways, Past and Present*, edited by Eric C. Rath and Stephanie Assmann, 166–85. Urbana: University of Illinois Press, 2010.

"Dai 72-kai kokkai ni okeru Tanaka naikaku sōridaijin shoshi hyōmei enzetsu." December 1, 1973. http://www.mofa.go.jp/mofaj/gaiko/bluebook/1974_2/s49-shiryou-1-3.htm.

"Dai ichibu, Osaka: Yarikuri jōzu de hyōban misesu no zadankai: Kechikechi shugi o tsuranuki tōshimasu!" *Fujin kurabu* (January 1974): 346–49.

Daimon Ichiju. "Rōhi jidai no Nihon." *Shoku seikatsu* 63, no. 3 (March 1969): 130–33.

Daiwa Hausu Kōgyō Kabushiki Gaisha Seikatsu Kenkyūjo, ed. *Katei nai no gomi ni kansuru chōsa kekka hōkokusho: Gomi ni taisuru ishiki to jittai.* Osaka: Daiwa Hausu Kōgyō Kabushiki Gaisha Seikatsu Kenkyūjo, 1999.

Dajōkan. *Dōro sōji jōmoku.* October 28, 1872.

Daniels, Inge. *Photography by Susan Andrews. The Japanese House: Material Culture in the Modern Home.* Oxford: Berg, 2010.

"Danshari." http://www.yamashitahideko.com.

Denecke, Wiebke. *Classical World Literatures: Sino-Japanese and Greco-Roman Comparisons.* Oxford: Oxford University Press, 2014.

Dichter, E. *Yokubō o tsukuridasu senryaku.* Translated by Tako Akira. Tokyo: Daiyamondosha, 1964.

Dinmore, Eric Gordon. "A Small Island Nation Poor in Resources: Natural and Human Resource Anxieties in Trans–World War II Japan." Ph.D. dissertation. Princeton University, 2006.

"Doraggu sutoa shōhin torendo, kīwādo de miru shōhin bunseki: Takamaru setsuden ishiki ni kotaeru seihin: Baiyā no shisen wa sude ni 'wōmu bizu' e." *Drug Magazine* 54, no. 8 (July 2011): 54–56.

Douglas, Mary. *Purity and Danger: An Analysis of Concepts of Pollution and Taboo.* London: Routledge and Kegan Paul, 1976.

Dower, John W. *Embracing Defeat: Japan in the Wake of World War II.* New York: W. W. Norton & Company, 1999.

Dufourmont, Eddy. "Yasuoka Masahiro: A Conservative Vision of the Postwar." In *Japan's Postwar,* edited by Michael Lucken et al., 98–118. Translated by J. A. A. Stockwin. New York: Routledge, 2011.

Duran Reiko. *Furansuryū kechi ni mienai zeitaku na setsuyaku seikatsu.* Tokyo: PHP Kenkyūjo, 2011.

Duus, Peter. "Dealing with Disaster." In *Natural Disaster and Nuclear Crisis in Japan: Response and Recovery after Japan's 3/11,* edited by Jeff Kingston, 175–87. New York: Routledge, 2012.

"ECO EDO Nihonbashi 2012." http://www.mitsuifudosan.co.jp/corporate/news/2012/0615_01/download/20120615.pdf.

The Ellen DeGeneres Show. https://www.youtube.com/watch?v=KdUAUQT8E9g.

Ende, Michael. *Momo.* Translated by J. Maxwell Brownjohn. London: Penguin, 1984.

———. *Momo: Jikan dorobō to nusumareta jikan o ningen ni torikaeshitekureta onna no ko no fushigi na monogatari.* Translated by Ōshima Kaori. Tokyo: Iwanami Shoten, 1976.

Ende Mihyaeru, et al. *Mittsu no kagami: Mihyaeru Ende to no taiwa,* edited by Koyasu Michiko. Tokyo: Asahi Shinbunsha, 1989.

Ende no yuigon: Kongen kara okane o tou. https://www.youtube.com/watch?v=Hh3vfMXAPJQ.

Falasca-Zamponi, Simonetta. *Waste and Consumption: Capitalism, the Environment, and the Life of Things.* New York: Routledge, 2011.

Feuer, Jack. "The Clutter Culture," *UCLA Magazine,* July 1, 2012. http://magazine.ucla. edu/features/the-clutter-culture/.

Field, Norma. "*Somehow*: The Postmodern as Atmosphere." In *Postmodernism and Japan,* edited by Masao Miyoshi and H. D. Harootunian, 169–88. Durham: Duke University Press, 1989.

Foote, Daniel H. "Law as an Agent of Change? Governmental Efforts to Reduce Working Hours in Japan." In *Japan, Economic Success and Legal System,* edited by Harald Baum, 251–302. Berlin: Walter de Gruyter, 1997.

Foster, Michael Dylan. *Pandemonium and Parade: Japanese Monsters and the Culture of Yōkai.* Berkeley: University of California Press, 2009.

Franklin, Benjamin. "Advice to a Young Tradesman, 1748." In *The Writings of Benjamin Franklin: Collected and Edited with a Life and Introduction by Albert Henry Smyth.* Vol. 2. New York: Macmillan Company, 1907.

"Freeganinfo: Strategies for Sustainable Living beyond Capitalism." http://freegan.info/.

Fujinaga Shin'ichi. "Motto motto setsuyaku dekiru! Tsūshinhi no tettei 'muda tori' tekunikku." *Kindai chūshō kigyō* 37, no. 13 (December 2002): 104–12.

Fujiwara Fusako, Seo Michiko, and Wakamori Tamae. "Tsukaisute jidai no hansei: Zadankai." *Gekkan kokumin seikatsu* 3, no. 6 (June 1973): 10–26.

Fujiwara Toshikazu. "Konnichi no gomi mondai to shimin no kadai." *Risaikuru bunka* (Autumn–Winter 1989): 12–22. Part of the series "Gomi repōto '90."

Fukumitsu Megumi. "'Danshari seminā' taikenki: Mono o sutereba jinsei ga kawaru?" *Nikkei bijinesu associé* 9, no. 19 (December 7, 2010): 45–47.

Funabashi, Yoichi, and Barak Kushner, eds. *Examining Japan's Lost Decades.* New York: Routledge, 2015.

Furugaki Tetsurō. Foreword to *Shin Amerika dayori,* by Sakai Yoneo. Tokyo: Meikyokudō, 1949.

Furukawa Denki Kōgyō Kabushiki Gaisha, Netsu Shisutemu Jigyōbu. *Enerugī, shigen mondai ni kansuru shufu no ishiki.* Furukawa Denki Kōgyō Kabushiki Gaisha, Netsu Shisutemu Jigyōbu, 1981.

Furukawa Miho. "Gomi yashiki, sukebē, rōhi guse . . . kyōgaku no jittai to wa: Hyōhen shita rōjin ni furimawasarete." *Fujin kōron* 95, no. 15 (July 22, 2010): 128–31.

Galbraith, J. K. *Yutaka na shakai.* Translated by Suzuki Tetsutarō. Tokyo: Iwanami Shoten, 1960.

Galbraith, John Kenneth. *The Affluent Society.* Boston: Houghton Mifflin Company, 1958.

——. "The GNP as Status Symbol and Success Story." In *Kutabare GNP: Kōdō seichō no uchimaku,* edited by Asahi Shinbun Keizaibu, ii–xi. Tokyo: Asahi Shinbunsha, 1971.

Garon, Sheldon. *Beyond Our Means: Why America Spends While the World Saves.* Princeton: Princeton University Press, 2012.

——. "Japan's Post-war 'Consumer Revolution,' or Striking a 'Balance' between Consumption and Saving." In *Consuming Cultures, Global Perspectives: Historical Trajectories, Transnational Exchanges,* edited by John Brewer and Frank Trentmann, 189–217. Oxford: Berg, 2006.

——. "Luxury Is the Enemy: Mobilizing Savings and Popularizing Thrift in Wartime Japan." *Journal of Japanese Studies* 26, no. 1 (Winter 2000): 41–78.

——. *Molding Japanese Minds: The State in Everyday Life.* Princeton: Princeton University Press, 1997.

GDP Data from the World Bank. http://data.worldbank.org/indicator/NY.GDP.PCAP. CD?end=2000&locations=JP-US&start=1980.

Gendai no eizō: Jinkai toshi. Nippon Hōsō Kyōkai: August 27, 1965.

General Assembly Resolution 65/309. *Happiness: Towards a Holistic Approach to Development*, A/65/L.86. July 19, 2011. http://www.un.org/ga/search/view_doc.asp?symbol=A/RES/65/309.

Genshiryoku Anzen Kiban Kikō, ed. *Genshiryoku shisetsu unten kanri nenpō: Heisei 24-nen ban*. Tokyo: Genshiryoku Anzen Kiban Kikō, 2012.

George, Timothy S. *Minamata: Pollution and the Struggle for Democracy in Postwar Japan*. Cambridge: Harvard University Asia Center, 2001.

Giddens, Anthony. *Modernity and Self-Identity: Self and Society in the Late Modern Age*. Cambridge: Polity, 2008.

Gluck, Carol. "The Past in the Present." In *Postwar Japan as History*, edited by Andrew Gordon, 64–95. Berkeley: University of California Press, 1993.

"Gomi kara mono o kangaeyō." *Gomi sensō shūhō* 41 (September 29, 1972): 2–3.

"Gomi mondai o kiru." *Keidanren geppō* 38, no. 12 (December 1990): 24–31. Part of the special issue "Haikibutsu taisaku no shigen risaikuru no suishin."

"Gomi no naka kara konna mono ten: Kore mo 'Tokyo gomi sensō' no okage desu." *Shūkan gendai* 31, no. 44 (October 1989): unpaginated.

"Gomi rettō 'suteru' gijutsu." *Sandē mainichi* 79, no. 53 (November 12, 2000): 131–36.

"'Gomi sensō' ni kansuru chiji hatsugen." *Tosei* 18, no. 8 (August 1973): 18–34.

"Gomi sensō, sono sengen kara Suginami no kaiketsu made: Gomi sensō nikki." *Gomi sensō shūhō* 135 (December 27, 1974): 2–16.

Gomi to tokonoma: Dokyumentarī. Nippon Hōsō Kyōkai: October 5, 1973.

"Gonin no shufu ga jikkō shiteiru taikenteki kechikechi seikatsu." *Fujin seikatsu* (June 1974): 186–91.

Gordon, Andrew. "Consumption, Leisure and the Middle Class in Transwar Japan." *Social Science Japan Journal* 10, no. 1 (April 2007): 1–21.

——. "Making Sense of the Lost Decades: Workplaces and Schools, Men and Women, Young and Old, Rich and Poor." In *Examining Japan's Lost Decades*, edited by Funabashi Yoichi and Barak Kushner, 77–100. New York: Routledge, 2015.

——. "Managing the Japanese Household: The New Life Movement in Postwar Japan." *Social Politics* 4, no. 2 (Summer 1997): 245–83.

——, ed. *Postwar Japan as History*. Berkeley: University of California Press, 1993.

——. "The Short Happy Life of the Japanese Middle Class." In *Social Contracts Under Stress: The Middle Classes of America, Europe, and Japan at the Turn of the Century*, edited by Olivier Zunz, Leonard Schoppa, and Nobuhiro Hiwatari, 108–29. New York: Russell Sage Foundation, 2002.

——. *The Wages of Affluence: Labor and Management in Postwar Japan*. Cambridge: Harvard University Press, 1998.

Gordon, Robert J. *The Rise and Fall of American Growth: The U.S. Standard of Living since the Civil War*. Princeton: Princeton University Press, 2016.

Gotō, Kunio. "The Oil Crisis and Energy Saving Policies." In *A Social History of Science and Technology in Contemporary Japan*, edited by Shigeru Nakayama and Hitoshi Yoshioka, 169–88. Vol. 4. Melbourne: Trans Pacific Press, 2006.

Gotō Sukehiro. *Gendai no gomi mondai: Bunka hen*. Tokyo: Chūō Hōki Shuppan, 1983.

Griffiths, Owen. "Need, Greed, and Protest in Japan's Black Market, 1938–1949." *Journal of Social History* 35, no. 4 (Summer 2002): 825–58.

Guins, Raiford. *Game After: A Cultural Study of Video Game Afterlife*. Cambridge: MIT Press, 2014.

Gurīn Konshūmā Nettowāku. *Chikyū ni yasashī kaimono gaido: Shizen o mamori, jibun o mamoru*. Tokyo: Kōdansha, 1994.

"Gurīn kōnyū hō ni tsuite." https://www.env.go.jp/policy/hozen/green/g-law/.

Hai Mūn. *Gomikku "haikibutsu": Manga*. Vol. 1. Tokyo: Nippō Shuppan, 1986.

Haikibutsu no genryō to sairiyō, shigenka tokushū. No. 67 of *Chōsa shiryō*. Tokyo: Tokyo-to Gikai Gikaikyoku Chōsabu, 1991.

Hakuhōdō Seikatsu Sōgō Kenkyūjo, ed. *"Bunshū" no tanjō: Nyūpīpuru o tsukamu shijō senryaku to wa*. Tokyo: Nihon Keizai Shinbunsha, 1985.

———. *Sofuto wēbu: Mirai chōryū to sendō shūdan*. Tokyo: Nihon Nōritsu Kyōkai, 1984.

Hanafusa Hiroko. "Tsukaisute Jidai o Kangaeru Kai: Tsukaisute jidai ni kangaerubeki koto wa ippai aru, dakara, sorezore suki na koto o yaru." *Risaikuru bunka* 26 (March 1990): 22–23.

Hanley, Susan B. *Everyday Things in Premodern Japan: The Hidden Legacy of Material Culture*. Berkeley: University of California Press, 1997.

Harada Hiroshi. *MP no jīpu kara mita senryōka no Tokyo: Dōjō keisatsukan no kansatsuki*. Tokyo: Sōshisha, 1994.

Harada Yoshishige. "Gomi sensō no shuyaku: Purasuchikku haikibutsu no shori to sairiyō." *Kagaku* 28, no. 2 (February 1973): 44–52.

Harootunian, Harry. *History's Disquiet: Modernity, Cultural Practice, and the Question of Everyday Life*. New York: Columbia University Press, 2000.

Harootunian, Harry, and Tomiko Yoda. Introduction to *Japan after Japan: Social and Cultural Life from the Recessionary 1990s to the Present*, edited by Tomiko Yoda and Harry Harootunian, 1–15. Durham: Duke University Press, 2006.

Haruno Tsuruko. "Seikatsu to gomi." In *Shufu no samā sukūru no kiroku: Tokyo no gomi o kangaeru*, edited by Tokyo-to Seisōkyoku, 13–19. Tokyo: Tokyo-to Seisōkyoku, 1970.

Hashimoto Takashi. *Shōenerugī no chie: Ken'yaku no kagaku*. Tokyo: Kōdansha, 1980.

Hashimoto Takehiko. Foreword to *Chikoku no tanjō: Kindai Nihon ni okeru jikan ishiki no keisei*, edited by Hashimoto Takehiko and Kuriyama Shigehisa, 3–10. Tokyo: Sangensha, 2006.

Hashizume Taiki. "Yoka no jikansei: M. Ende *Momo* kara." *Yokagaku kenkyū* 14 (March 2011): 27–38.

Hawkins, Gay. "Down the Drain: Shit and the Politics of Disturbance." In *Culture and Waste: The Creation and Destruction of Value*, edited by Gay Hawkins and Stephen Muecke, 51–63. Lanham, MD: Rowman & Littlefield, 2003.

———. *The Ethics of Waste: How We Relate to Rubbish*. Lanham, MD: Rowman & Littlefield, 2006.

Hawkins, Gay, and Stephen Muecke. "Introduction: Cultural Economies of Waste." In *Culture and Waste: The Creation and Destruction of Value*, edited by Gay Hawkins and Stephen Muecke, 9–17. New York: Rowman & Littlefield, 2003.

Hayashi Shūji. *Kigyō no imēji senryaku*. Tokyo: Daiyamondosha, 1961.

———. *Mākechingu risāchi*. Tokyo: Daiyamondosha, 1958.

———. *Ryūtsū kakumei: Seihin, keiro oyobi shōhisha*. Tokyo: Chūō Kōronsha, 1962.

Hein, Laura E. *Fueling Growth: The Energy Revolution and Economic Policy in Postwar Japan*. Cambridge: Council on East Asian Studies, Harvard University, 1990.

———. *Reasonable Men, Powerful Words: Political Culture and Expertise in Twentieth-Century Japan*. Berkeley: University of California Press, 2004.

Helliwell, John, Richard Layard, and Jeffrey Sachs, eds. *World Happiness Report 2017*. New York: Sustainable Development Solutions Network, 2017. http://worldhappiness.report/wp-content/uploads/sites/2/2017/03/HR17.pdf.

Henshūbu. "'Asobi gokoro' de hirogeru chiiki o mamoru 'kokorozashi.'" *Asahi jānaru* 25, no. 28 (July 1, 1983): 18–23. Part of the series "Wakamono ga mezasu risaikuru raifu."

Henshūbu. "Haha no seikatsu jikan." *Seikatsu kagaku* 6, no. 3 (March 1948): 13–15.

Henshūbu. "Yonenme o mukaeta kūru bizu to wōmu bizu." *SC Japan Today* 413 (November 2008): 36–41.

Hershkowitz, Allen, and Eugene Salerni. *Garbage Management in Japan: Leading the Way*. Preface by Maurice D. Hinchey. New York: INFORM, 1987.

"Heya to kokoro o sukkiri! Suteru gijutsu." *Nikkei woman* 348 (January 2013): unpaginated.

Higashiyotsuyanagi, Shoko. "The History of Domestic Cookbooks in Modern Japan." In *Japanese Foodways, Past and Present*, edited by Eric C. Rath and Stephanie Assmann, 129–44. Urbana: University of Illinois Press, 2010.

"Hikōki de rāmen o kui ni iku 'rōhi no bitoku.'" *Shūkan shinchō* 13, no. 47 (November 23, 1968): 40–42.

Hirabayashi Rie. "'Minimarisuto' no kiwami?! Zensō ni manabu motanai kurashi o tanoshimu 'Zenteki' mesoddo." *Nikkei otona no off* (December 2015): 70–73.

Hiroi Yoshinori. "'Keizai seichō ni yoru kaiketsu' kara dassuru tame ni: 'Mottainai' kara mietekita shakai no kizashi." *Bōsei* 37, no. 7 (July 2006): 25–30.

Honda Akiko and Tanaka Kanako. "Suzushiku, oishiku shōene kukkingu." *Eiyō to ryōri* 88, no. 8 (August 2011): 17–37. Part of the series "Dekiru koto kara hajimeyō shōene ressun."

Honda Atsuhiro. *E de miru shōhi to risaikuru*. Tokyo: Kurīn Japan Sentā, 1995.

——. *Gomi monogatari: Gomi nashi shakai no sōzō*. Tokyo: Shōenerugī Sentā, 1978.

Honda Shin'ichi. *Jinsei o yutaka ni suru tame no "jikan" no tsukaikata: Ima kono isshun o dō jūjitsu saseru ka*. Tokyo: Besuto Bukku, 1990.

Hongō Takanobu. "Tōshiba 'jōzu na kurashi no undō' no ikikata." *Rōmu kenkyū* 10, no. 12 (December 1957): 30–34.

Honma Miyako. *Gurīn konshūmā nyūmon*. Tokyo: Hokuto Shuppan, 1997.

"Hontō no yutakasa to wa nani ka: Keikichō, kokumin kaigi kaisai." *Shōhi to seikatsu* 168 (July 1989): 20.

Horioka, Charles Yuji. "Are the Japanese Unique? An Analysis of Consumption and Saving Behavior in Japan." In *The Ambivalent Consumer: Questioning Consumption in East Asia and the West*, edited by Sheldon Garon and Patricia L. Maclachlan, 113–36. Ithaca: Cornell University Press, 2006.

——. "Consuming and Saving." In *Postwar Japan as History*, edited by Andrew Gordon, 259–92. Berkeley: University of California Press, 1993.

Horowitz, Daniel. *The Anxieties of Affluence: Critiques of American Consumer Culture, 1939–1979*. Amherst: University of Massachusetts Press, 2004.

——. *Vance Packard and American Social Criticism*. Chapel Hill: University of North Carolina Press, 1994.

Howell, David L. "Fecal Matters: Prolegomenon to a History of Shit in Japan." In *Japan at Nature's Edge: The Environmental Context of a Global Power*, edited by Ian Jared Miller, Julia Adeney Thomas, and Brett L. Walker, 137–51. Honolulu: University of Hawaii Press, 2013.

Ichihashi Takashi. *Gomi to kurashi no sengo gojūnen shi*. Tokyo: Risaikuru Bunkasha, 2000.

Ichikawa Tetsu. "Shigen no yūkō riyō o kangaeru: Rōhi kara setsuyaku jidai e no tenkan e." *Shōhi to seikatsu* 9, no 5 (July 1974): 16–21.

Ichikawa Tomoko. "Nihonrashī GNH to wa nani ka: Higashi Nihon daishinsai fukkō shien katsudō no torikumi kara." *GNH kokumin sō kōfukudo kenkyū* (February 2014): 43–66. Part of the series "GNH o dō ikasu ka."

Ichiki Shigeo. "Shōhisha no tachiba ni tatta kaikaku o." *Keizaijin* 44, no. 5 (May 1990): 4–8. Part of the series "Ima, shin no yutakasa o tou."

"Ichiryū kaisha de wa yaru 'kechikechi undō' no kazeatari." *Keizei tenbō* 43, no. 6 (April 1, 1971): 78–79.

Ide Toshihiko. "Gomi 'shori' no sakkaku: Moto Numazu shichō ni kiku intabyū." *Sekai* 532 (September 1989): 193–201. Part of the special issue "Gomi mondai o kangaeru."

Igo, Sarah Elizabeth. *The Averaged American: Surveys, Citizens, and the Making of a Mass Public.* Cambridge: Harvard University Press, 2007.

Ihara Ryūichi. "Kechi wa bitoku ka akutoku ka." *Ōru seikatsu* 29, no. 2 (February 1974): 48–50.

Iida Tsuneo. *"Yutakasa" no ato ni: Shiawase to wa nani ka.* Tokyo: Kōdansha, 1984.

——. *"Yutakasa" to wa nani ka: Gendai shakai no shiten.* Tokyo: Kōdansha Gendai Shinsho, 1980.

Iizuka Takeo. "Shōhisha wa baka de wa nai: Yameru Amerika keizai no jittai." *Hon no hon* 226 (December 1961): 20–21.

Ikeo Katsumi. "Sangyō fukkō kōdan o meguru sho mondai." *Keizai antei shiryō* 5 (November 1948): 35–39.

Imai Misako. *Mottainai jīsan.* Tokyo: Sakuhinsha, 2005.

Imamura, Anne E. *Urban Japanese Housewives: At Home and in the Community.* Honolulu: University of Hawaii Press, 1987.

Imamura Mitsuo. *Gomi to Nihonjin: Eisei, kinken risaikuru kara miru kindaishi.* Kyoto: Mineruva Shobō, 2015.

Inglehart, Ronald. *Culture Shift in Advanced Industrial Society.* Princeton: Princeton University Press, 1990.

Inokuma Gen'ichirō, Fukushima Keiko, and Hanamori Yasuji. "Zeitaku ni tsuite." *Geijutsu shinchō* 2, no. 2 (February 1951): 75–87.

Inoue Kaneo. *Eiyō no jōshiki.* Tokyo: Ryūbunsha, 1946.

"Intabyū: Kondō Marie-san: 'Konmari mesoddo' hitto no riyū." *Shinchō* 34, no. 7 (July 2015): 314–15.

International Labour Organization. "Part Time Employment, Female (% of Total Part Time Employment)." http://data.worldbank.org/indicator/SL.TLF.PART.TL.FE. ZS?locations=JP.

Iranai mono o sukkiri suteru! No. 52 of *PHP kurashi rakūru.* December 2014.

Ishida Yutaka. *Mottainai no kokoro.* Tokyo: WAVE Shuppan, 2003.

Ishige Takeshi. *Watashitachi ni dekiru gomi o herasu kurashi no kufū 101: Kore ijō, chikyū o hakai shinai tame ni.* Tokyo: Ōizumi Shoten, 1992.

Ishii Kinnosuke. *Shōhi wa bitoku de aru.* Tokyo: Tōyō Keizai Shinpōsha, 1960.

Ishikawa Hiroyoshi. *Yokubō no sengoshi: 'Takōshō' Nihonjin no purofīru.* Tokyo: Kōsaidō Shuppan, 1989.

Ishikawa Tadashi. "Shitsumu no muda haijo 80-kajō." *Jimu nōritsu* 1, no. 4 (July 1949): 24–27.

——. "Shitsumu no muda haijo 80-kajō." *Jimu nōritsu* 1, no. 5 (August 1949): 24–25.

Ishikawa Teizō. "Kono yo wa 'tsukaisute jidai': Sengo nijūrokunen, sedai to tomo ni seikatsu wa henka shita." *Keizai ōrai* 23, no. 7 (July 1971): 296–99.

Ishikawa Tomoyoshi. *Shō eiseigaku.* Tokyo: Tōhōdō, 1947.

Ishimaru Yoshitomi. "'Zero seichō' no higenjitsusei." *Asahi jānaru* 15, no. 47 (November 30, 1973): 13–17.

Ishimori Chiyo. "Hataraku fujin no jikan no kufū." *Izumi* 1, no. 2 (February 1949): 28–29.

Ishiwata Masayoshi. "Kankyō benchā saizensen 20: Mottainai kyanpēn: Kankyō hozen undō no burandoka." *Gabanansu* 68 (December 2006): 90–92.

Ishiwata Yūsuke. "Mirai no toshi, mirai no toshiteki seikatsu yōshiki: Orinpikku 60-nendai Tokyo." In *Orinpikku sutadīzu: Fukusū no keiken, fukusū no seiji*, edited by Shimizu Satoshi, 154–72. Tokyo: Serika Shobō, 2004.

Ishizaka Yuji. "Tokyo orinpikku to kōdo seichō no jidai." *Nenpō, Nihon gendai shi* 14 (2009): 143–85.

Ishizawa Kiyofumi. *Gaborojī: Gomigaku.* Tokyo: Risaikuru Bunkasha, 1983.

Ishizawa Kiyomi. *Setsuden, setsugasu, sessui kashikoi reshipi: Kaku reshipi ni setsuyaku dekiru meyasu ryō tsuki.* Tokyo: Shufu no Tomosha, 2011.

Ishizawa Kiyoshi. "Gomi o dasanai atarshī ikikata." *Chishiki* 106 (September 1990): 142–50.

Iue Toshio. "Zeitaku wa teki da wa nai: Akarui katei wa denka kara." *Bungei shunjū* 33, no. 11 (June 1955): 286–89.

Ivy, Marilyn. "Formations of Mass Culture." In *Postwar Japan as History*, edited by Andrew Gordon, 239–58. Berkeley: University of California Press, 1993.

Iwamoto Shigeki. *Akogare no burondi: Sengo Nihon no Amerikanizēshon.* Tokyo: Shinyōsha, 2007.

Iwanami Shoten Henshūbu, ed. *Hontō no yutakasa to wa: Shinpojiumu.* Tokyo: Iwanami Shoten, 1991.

Iwasaki Minoru et al., eds. *Sengo Nihon sutadīzu.* 3 vols. Tokyo: Kinokuniya Shoten, 2008–9.

"Japan International Cooperation Agency." http://www.jica.go.jp/vietnam/english/office/topics/events03.html.

"'Jikan ga nai!' to wa iwasenai." *Nikkei benchā* 249 (June 2005): 120–27.

"Jikan wa shisan, dakara mudazukai shinai seisansei takameta nōhau o kōkai." *Nikkei jōhō sutoratejī* 16, no. 8 (September 2007): 146–52.

Johnson, Chalmers. *MITI and the Japanese Miracle: The Growth of Industrial Policy, 1925–1975.* Stanford: Stanford University Press, 1982.

"June Reading List." August 17, 2016. http://www.jamesaltucher.com/june-reading-list/.

Junkangata shakai keisei suishin kihon hō. Hōritsu dai hyakujū gō. June 2, 2000. http://law-e.gov.go.jp/htmldata/H12/H12HO110.html.

"Junkangata shakai no jitsugen ni wa, tomin, NPO, jigyōsha, gyōsei no kyōdō ga hitsuyō desu." *Tokyo Slim* 8 (January 1999): 2.

Kaden risaikuru hō. http://www.meti.go.jp/policy/it_policy/kaden_recycle/index.html.

Kagaku Keiei Kenkyūkai. "Setsuden taisaku ni kansuru ankēto chōsa ni tsuite." *Kagaku keiei* 437 (July 2011): 71–77.

"Kajō na kinō yori dezainsei o jūshi 'katazuke būmu' de shōhin sentaku kōdō ga kawaru? Katazuke konsarutanto Kondō Marie." *Senden kaigi* 855 (February 15, 2013): 70–71.

"Kakei tokushū: Seikatsu wa shinpuru ni yume wa yutaka ni." *Fujin no tomo* 90, no. 12 (December 1996): 47–109.

"Kakkoku no ippan haikibutsu hassei ryō." http://www.env.go.jp/doc/toukei/data/2015_2.38.xls.

Kamada Masaru. *Muda, mura, muri o nakuse: Myōnichi kara dekiru kaizen dokuhon.* Tokyo: Nihon Nōritsu Kyōkai, 1988.

Kanari Yūzō. "'Tōhoku gomi sensō' no shūhen." *Shinbun kenkyū* 468 (July 1990): 37–39. Part of the series "'Yutakasa' no honshitsu o saguru, yutakasa no kage ni."

Kanba Wataru. *Jikan kanrijutsu: 24 jikan no tsukaikata ga subete o kimeru.* Tokyo: Tokuma Shoten, 1990.

Kaneko Hiroshi. "Muda no kōyō: Katsute no nōritsu kyokuchō ga Amerika ni atte kataru." *Seikai ōrai* 22, no. 5 (May 1956): 124–29.

Kang Sangjung. *Zainichi*. Tokyo: Kōdansha, 2004.

Kankyō Sangyō Shinbunsha. *Haikibutsu nenkan, 1981-nen ban*. Tokyo: Kankyō Sangyō Shinbunsha, 1980.

———. *Haikibutsu nenkan, 1986-nen ban*. Tokyo: Kankyō Sangyō Shinbunsha, 1985.

Kankyōshō, ed. *Kankyō hakusho*. Tokyo: Gyōsei, 2006.

———, ed. *Kankyō hakusho: Datsu ondanka—"hito" to "shikumi" zukuri de kizuku shinjidai*. Tokyo: Gyōsei, 2005.

———, ed. *Kankyō hakusho: Ugokihajimeta jizoku kanō na shakai zukuri*. Tokyo: Gyōsei, 2002. http://www.env.go.jp/policy/hakusyo/hakusyo.php3?kid=215.

Kankyōshō Daijin Kanbō Haikibutsu Risaikuru Taisakubu Haikibutsu Taisakuka. "Ippan haikibutsu no haishutsu oyobi shori jōkyō tō (Heisei 26 nendo) ni tsuite." February 22, 2016. http://www.env.go.jp/recycle/waste_tech/ippan/h26/data/env_press.pdf.

———. *Nihon no haikibutsu shori: Heisei 10 nendo ban*. Tokyo: Kankyōshō, 2001. http://www.env.go.jp/recycle/waste_tech/ippan/h10/index.html.

Kankyōshō Daijin Kanbō Haikibutsu Risaikuru Taisakubu Junkangata Shakai Suishinshitsu, ed. *Junkangata shakai hakusho: Junkangata shakai ni okeru raifu sutairu, bijinesu sutairu*. Tokyo: Gyōsei, 2002.

Kankyōshō Shizen Kankyōkyoku. *Jichitai tantōsha no tame no karasu taisaku manyuaru*. Tokyo: Kankyōshō Shizen Kankyōkyoku, 2001.

"Kashikoi misesu wa risaikuru jōzu: Furī māketto katsuyō jutsu & risaikuru shoppu jōhō." *Shufu to seikatsu* 45, no. 3 (March 1990): 179–87.

Katei shūri dokuhon. Tokyo: Betā Hōmu Kyōkai, 1975.

Katō Emiko. *Muda naku, yutaka ni, utsukushiku ikiru 30 no koto*. Tokyo: Disukabā Tōenchiwan, 2011.

Katō Hidetoshi. "Sumai to kazai: 'Mono mochi' no henbō." *Chūō kōron* 115, no. 11 (October 2000): 308–19.

Katō Hidetoshi and Minami Shinbō. "'Hima' mo 'iikagen' mo kakko ii." *Asahi jānaru* 29, no. 1 (January 2–9, 1987): 6–11.

Katō Keiko. "Shō kaisetsu." In *Haisen to kurashi*, by Yamamoto Taketoshi and Nagai Yoshikazu, 222–26. Vol. 1 of *Senryōki seikatsu sesōshi shiryō*. Tokyo: Shinyōsha, 2014.

Katō Tsuchimi. "'Mono yori kokoro' no jidai o mukaete: 'Mono no yutakasa' kara 'kokoro no yutakasa' e." *Aiiku* 50, no. 1 (January 1985): 4–7.

Katō Yoshio. "Kojin seikatsu ni miru Amerika no gōrika to Nihon no muda." *Jitsugyō no Nihon* 58, no. 12 (May 1955): 38–40.

Katona, G. *Taishū shōhi shakai*. Translated by Shakai Kōdō Kenkyūjo. Tokyo: Daiyamondosha, 1966.

Katona, George. *The Mass Consumption Society*. New York: McGraw-Hill Book Company, 1964.

Kawabata Nobuko. "'Danshari' ni manabu mono o te kakawarikata." *Jidō shinri* 65, no. 14 (October 2011): 32–38.

Kawabata Nobuko with Yamashita Hideko, ed. *Mono o sutereba umaku iku danshari no susume*. Tokyo: Dōbunkan Shuppan, 2009.

Kawakami Takuya. *Binbō to iu ikikata*. Tokyo: WAVE Shuppan, 2010.

Kawamoto Saburō and Jinnai Hidenobu. "Kawatta no wa machi dake ja nakatta!" *Tokyo jin* 206 (September 2004): 67–73.

"Kechi wa bitoku, mudazukai mo tanoshī: Zadankai." *Shufu to seikatsu* (February 1961): 132–37.

Kechi wa kashikoi! Setsuyaku kukkingu juku: Okane o kakenai, muda o dasanai, mono o sutenai. Tokyo: Kōdansha, 1999.

"Kechikechi setsuyaku: Kono gōrika no wakiyaku tachi: 'Isshūkan 27 do ijō' ga reibō no jōken etc." *Shūkan daiyamondo* (June 25, 1977): 10–12.

"Keihi no setsuyaku wa kokka no kyūmu." *Jitsumu techō* 3, no. 8 (June 1949): 2–5.

Keizai Dantai Rengōkai. "Keidanren kankyō apīru: 21 seiki no kankyō hozen ni muketa keizaikai no jishu kōdō sengen." July 16, 1996. https://www.keidanren. or.jp/japanese/policy/pol094.html.

Keizai Kikakuchō, ed. *Keizai hakusho: Nihon keizai no seichōryoku to kyōsōryoku.* Tokyo: Ōkurashō Insatsukyoku, 1960.

——, ed. *Shōwa 31 nendo keizai hakusho.* Tokyo: Shiseidō, 1956.

——, ed. *Shōwa 52 nendo kokumin seikatsu hakusho: Kurashi o minaoshi, atarashī yutakasa o motomete.* Tokyo: Ōkurashō Insatsukyoku, 1977.

Keizai Kikakuchō Chōseikyoku. *Kokumin seikatsu hakusho: Sengo kokumin seikatsu no kōzōteki henka.* Tokyo: Ōkurashō Insatsukyoku, 1959.

Keizai Kikakuchō Kokumin Seikatsukyoku, ed. *Chie no aru yutakasa o: Atarashī shiten to hassō ni yoru shōshigen shōenerugī o mezashite.* Tokyo: Ōkurashō Insatsukyoku, 1992.

——, ed. *Shōenerugī seikatsu no suishin no tame ni.* Tokyo: Ōkurashō Insatsukyoku, 1981.

——, ed. *Yutakasa to risaikuru: Shōshigen, shōenerugī seikatsu suishin kenkyūkai hōkoku.* Tokyo: Ōkurashō Insatsukyoku, 1989.

Keizai Kikakuchō Kokumin Seikatsukyoku and Kokumin Seikatsu Seisakuka, eds. *Shōshigen, shōenerugī to korekara no kurashi.* Tokyo: Ōkurashō Insatsukyoku, 1979.

Keizai Kikakuchō Sōgō Keikakukyoku, ed. *2010-nen e no sentaku: Messējī "chikyū" to "ningen."* Tokyo: Ōkurashō Insatsukyoku, 1991.

Keizai Sangyōshō Shigen Enerugīchō. *Heisei 23 nendo enerugī hakusho.* [Tokyo]: Shigen Enerugīchō, 2012. http://www.enecho.meti.go.jp/about/ whitepaper/2012pdf/whitepaper2012pdf_2_1.pdf.

——. *Heisei 27 nendo enerugī hakusho.* [Tokyo]: Shigen Enerugīchō, 2016. http://www. enecho.meti.go.jp/about/whitepaper/2016pdf/whitepaper2016pdf_2_1.pdf.

——. "Minsei bumon no enerugī shōhī kōdō ni tsuite." N.d. http://www.meti.go.jp/ report/downloadfiles/g40324d20j.pdf.

Keizai Sangyōshō Tokkyochō. "Shinsei yōken o kanwa shita tokkyo shinsa haiwei shikō puroguramu shichigatsu jūgonichi kara kaishi: 'PPH MOTTAINAI' shikō puroguramu." June 17, 2011.

Keizai taikoku to sekiyu shokku: Shōwa 46–52 nen. Vol. 17 of *Shōwa shi.* Tokyo: Mainichi Shinbunsha, 1985.

Kelly, Catriona. *Refining Russia: Advice Literature, Polite Culture, and Gender from Catherine to Yeltsin.* Oxford: Oxford University Press, 2001.

Kelly, William W. "At the Limits of New Middle-Class Japan." In *Social Contracts Under Stress: The Middle Classes of America, Europe, and Japan at the Turn of the Century,* edited by Olivier Zunz, Leonard Schoppa, and Nobuhiro Hiwatari, 232–54. New York: Russell Sage Foundation, 2002.

——. "Finding a Place in Metropolitan Japan: Ideologies, Institutions, and Everyday Life." In *Postwar Japan as History,* edited by Andrew Gordon, 189–216. Berkeley: University of California Press, 1993.

——. "Regional Japan: The Price of Prosperity and the Benefits of Dependency." In *Showa: The Japan of Hirohito,* edited by Carol Gluck and Stephen R. Graubard, 209–27. New York: W. W. Norton & Company, 1992.

"Kenia kankyō fukudaijin to kaidan, February 18, 2005." Shushō Kantei. http://www. kantei.go.jp/jp/koizumiphoto/2005/02/18kenya.html.

Kern, Stephen. *The Culture of Time and Space, 1880–1918*. Cambridge: Harvard University Press, 1983.

Keynes, John Maynard. "Economic Possibilities for Our Grandchildren." 1930. In *Revisiting Keynes: Economic Possibilities for Our Grandchildren*, edited by Lorenzo Pecchi and Gustavo Piga, 17–26. Cambridge: MIT Press, 2008.

"Kigyō no 'kechikechi undō' dai sakusen no imi wa?" *Shūkan yomiuri* (March 5, 1971): 138–41.

Kinmonth, Earl H. *The Self-Made Man in Meiji Japanese Thought: From Samurai to Salary Man*. Berkeley: University of California Press, 1981.

Kirby, Peter Wynn. *Troubled Natures: Waste, Environment, Japan*. Honolulu: University of Hawaii Press, 2011.

Kirkpatrick, Maurine A. "Consumerism and Japan's New Citizen Politics," *Asian Survey* 15, no. 3 (March 1975): 234–46.

Kishimoto Eitarō. "Rōhi to kankyō hakai no kōdo seichō seisaku: 'Kōgai to jūmin undō' jo." *Nihon rōdō kyōkai zasshi* 16, no. 3 (March 1974): 2–12.

Kishimoto Shigenobu. "'Yutakasa' no gensō to kankyō mondai." *Risaikuru bunka* 24 (Spring–Summer 1989): 10–16.

Kitamura Akiko. "'Mottainai' o taisetsu ni." *LDI Report* 102 (May 1999): 58–59.

Kitano Shū and Izumisawa Kanako. "Mihyaeru Ende 'Momo' no kijutsu ni miru gendai keizai shakai hihan." *Sangyō keizai kenkyū* 50, no. 4 (March 2010): 63–97.

Kitazawa Masakuni. "Fujiyū na 'jiyū jikan': Rejā ni moteasobareru seishin no kōzō." *Asahi jānaru* 9, no. 46 (November 5, 1967): 12–16.

Knight, Sarah. *The Life-Changing Magic of Not Giving a F*ck: How to Stop Spending Time You Don't Have with People You Don't Like Doing Things You Don't Want to Do*. New York: Little, Brown and Company, 2015.

Kobayashi Akira. "Akira no mottainai ondo." Tokuma Japan Komyunikēshonzu. Compact disc. 2006.

Kobayashi Kan. "Fuyu ni sonaete kansō yasai, yasō no tsukurikata, takuwaekata, itadakikata." *Fujin kurabu* 26, no. 5 (August–September 1945): 15–17.

Kōdo Seichōki o Kangaeru Kai, ed. *Kazoku no seikatsu*. Vol. 2 of *Kōdo seichō to Nihonjin*. Tokyo: Nihon Editāsukūru Shuppanbu, 2005.

Kōdo seichō no kiseki. Vol. 7 of *Ichioku nin no Shōwa shi*. Tokyo: Mainichi Shinbunsha, 1976.

Kōgai Chikyū Kankyō Mondai Kondankai, ed. *Daiokishin wa nakuseru: Nakuse kōgai, mamorō chikyū kankyō!* Tokyo: Gōdō Shuppan, 1998.

Koino Shigeru. "Yoka to rizōto kaihatsu." *Keizaijin* 44, no. 5 (May 1990): 40–43. Part of the series "Ima, shin no yutakasa o tou."

Koishikawa Zenji. *Nihonjin wa itsu kara hatarakisugi ni natta no ka*. Tokyo: Heibonsha, 2014.

Koizumi Jun'ichirō. "Dai nijūgo-kai: Ai, chikyūhaku." Radio address. March 19, 2005.

———. "Dai nijūyon-kai: Kyoto giteishō hakkō." Radio address. February 19, 2005.

———. "Gurenīguruzu samitto: Koizumi sōri naigai kisha kaiken (*yōshi*)." Press conference. July 8, 2005.

———. "Kagaku gijutsu to jinrui no mirai ni kansuru kokusai fōramu kaikaishiki Koizumi naikaku sōri daijin kichō kōen." Speech presented at the Science and Technology in Society Forum. September 11, 2005.

Kokumin seikatsu hakusho, Shōwa gojū nendo: Kawaru seikatsu, kawaru jidai. Tokyo: Keizai Kikakuchō, 1975.

Kokumin Seikatsu Sentā. *Furī māketto risaikuru shoppu risaikuru kōnā o riyō suru: Risaikuru, riyūsu jidai no fuyōhin katsuyō hō.* Tokyo: Kokumin Seikatsu Sentā, 1998.

——, ed. *Monobusoku sawagi.* Tokyo: Kokumin Seikatsu Sentā Kikaku Chōseishitsu, 1975.

Kōkyō Hōkoku Kikō. "Mottainai obake." 1982. http://www.youtube.com/watch?v=6be2IvKKdo4.

Kolbert, Elizabeth. "No Time: How Did We Get So Busy?" *The New Yorker,* May 26, 2014. http://www.newyorker.com/magazine/2014/05/26/no-time.

Komatsu Yūgorō. *Gekidō no tsūsan gyōsei: Kaiko to tenbō.* Tokyo: Jihyōsha, 1978.

Kondō Marie. *Jinsei ga tokimeku katazuke no mahō.* Tokyo: Sanmāku Shuppan, 2011.

——. *Jinsei ga tokimeku katazuke no mahō 2.* Tokyo: Sanmāku Shuppan, 2012.

Kondo, Marie. *The Life-Changing Magic of Tidying Up: The Japanese Art of Decluttering and Organizing.* Translated by Cathy Hirano. Berkeley: Ten Speed Press, 2014.

Kondō Tadashi. "Nōgyō keiei to seikatsu kaizen." *Fumin* 22, no. 8 (August 1950): 54–56.

"Konna mono made! Tsukaisute guzzu." *Shūkan hōseki* 10, no. 36 (September 27, 1990): unpaginated.

"Kontō no setsuden riyū 'denkidai agarisō' 6 warijaku: Setsuden ni kansuru chōsa." *Nikkei shōhi insaito* 5 (August 2013): 74–75.

"Koramu tokushū: Mottainai!" *Gendai* 40, no. 2 (February 2006): 228–50.

"Kore ga enerugī setsuyaku daihonzan 'Esaki tsūsan daijin' no katta 'natsufuku.'" *Shūkan shinchō* 24, no. 17 (April 26, 1979): 152–55.

"Kore zo! Konka no shōene rukku." *Ōru taishū* 32, no. 10 (June 1979): 46–47.

Kōseishō, ed. *Kōsei hakusho: Shin no yutakasa ni mukatte no shakai shisutemu no saikōchiku, yutakasa no kosuto, haikibutsu mondai o kangaeru.* Tokyo: Gyōsei, 1991.

"Kō sureba muda naku dekiru: 'Bunryō no katagami' o goran kudasai." *Fujin no tomo* 42, no. 4 (April 1948): 21–25.

Kosugi, Reiko. "Youth Employment in Japan's Economic Recovery: 'Freeters' and 'NEETs.'" *Asia-Pacific Journal* 4, no. 5 (May 2006): 1–5.

Koyama Sonoko. "Gomi no hirogari: TOKYO SLIM kyanpēn." *Tosei kenkyū* 23, no. 3 (March 1990): 60–61.

Koyasu Michiko. "Jikan to kinri: Mihyaeru Ende no 'jikan dorobō' *Momo* ni komerareta keiku." *Ekonomisuto* 93, no. 22 (June 2, 2015): 37.

——. *"Momo" o yomu: Shutainā no seikaikan o chikasui to shite.* Tokyo: Gakuyō Shobō, 1987.

Kretschmer, Angelika. *Kuyō in Contemporary Japan: Religious Rites in the Lives of Laypeople.* Göttingen: Cuvillier Verlag, 2000.

——. "Mortuary Rites for Inanimate Objects: The Case of *Hari Kuyō.*" *Japanese Journal of Religious Studies* 27, no. 3/4 (Fall 2000): 379–404.

Kudō Hanae. "Mono de yutaka ni kurasu hōhō." *Nikkei woman* (December 2015): 26–27.

Kuga Saburō. *Mama no kechikechi bukku: Kakei o nijū pāsento setsuyaku suru hiketsu shū.* Tokyo: Keisei, 1974.

Kurashi o yutaka ni 55 (January 21, 1972): 6.

Kurashi o yutaka ni 66 (February 25, 1974): 3.

Kurata Chikara. "Yottsu no muda ari." *Jimu to keiei* 7, no. 74 (November 1955): 8–9.

Kurīn Japan Sentā, ed. *Kurīn Japan Sentā 10-nen no ayumi.* Tokyo: Kurīn Japan Sentā, 1986.

——, ed. *Sodai gomi no yūkō riyō manyuaru.* Tokyo: Kurīn Japan Sentā, 1985.

Kuriyama Shigehisa. "'Toki wa kane nari' no nazo." In *Chikoku no tanjō: Kindai Nihon ni okeru jikan ishiki no keisei*, edited by Hashimoto Takehiko and Kuriyama Shigehisa, 321–43. Tokyo: Sangensha, 2006.

Kuriyama, Yoshihiro. "A Japanese 'Maoist': Niijima Atsuyoshi." *Asian Survey* 16, no. 9 (September 1976): 846–54.

Kuroda Yoneko. "Muda nashi ryōrihō no tettei." *Fujin gahō* 495 (November 1945): 20–21.

Kurokawa Yasumasa. *"Kurokawa shiki": Nijūyojikan no chiteki jikanjutsu: Jibun no naimen o migaku nōryoku kaihatsu no hōhō*. Tokyo: HBJ Shuppan, 1991.

Kyoto Shinbunsha, ed. *Ima nara kateru gomi sensō*. Kyoto: Kyoto Shinbunsha, 1973.

La Zoo. *Mottainai-tte nan darō? Kansha no kimochi o sodateru hon*. Edited by Kankyō Jōhō Fukyū Sentā. Illustrations by Sugawara Keiko. Vol. 1 of *Mottainai kara hajimeyō!* Tokyo: Gakken, 2007.

Lam, Bourree. "The Economics of Tidying Up." *The Atlantic*, May 13, 2015.

LeBlanc, Robin M. *Bicycle Citizens: The Political World of the Japanese Housewife*. Foreword by Saskia Sassen. Berkeley: University of California Press, 1999.

Leheny, David. "A Narrow Place to Cross Swords: Soft Power and the Politics of Japanese Popular Culture in East Asia." In *Beyond Japan: The Dynamics of East Asian Regionalism*, edited by Peter J. Katzenstein and Takashi Shiraishi, 211–33. Ithaca: Cornell University Press, 2006.

——. *The Rules of Play: National Identity and the Shaping of Japanese Leisure*. Ithaca: Cornell University Press, 2003.

——. "The Samurai Ride to Huntington's Rescue: Japan Ponders Its Global and Regional Roles." In *Civilizations in World Politics: Plural and Pluralist Perspectives*, edited by Peter J. Katzenstein, 114–36. London: Routledge, 2009.

LIPS Kyoto, ed. *Kansai furī māketto tengoku: Furima jōhō ban*. Kyoto: Yunipuran, 1996.

Machi o minna de utsukushiku. No. 4 of *Shin seikatsu shirīzu*. Tokyo: Shin Seikatsu Undō Kyōkai, [1962–63].

Maclachlan, Patricia L. *Consumer Politics in Postwar Japan: The Institutional Boundaries of Citizen Activism*. New York: Columbia University Press, 2002.

"Madamada yareru shanai 'kechikechi' dai sakusen: Kyō kara tsuihō 10 no pointo 51 no muda." *Kindai chūshō kigyō* 15, no. 7 (June 1980): 54–59.

Maekawa Tsukasa. *Dai Tokyo binbō seikatsu manyuaru*. Vols. 1–5. Tokyo: Kōdansha, 1988–89.

Magajin Hausu, ed. *Watashi no, mottainai*. Tokyo: Magajin Hausu, 2006.

Malle, Chloe. "A *Vogue* Editor Learns the Art of Closet-Cleaning from Marie Kondo." *Vogue*, February 2, 2016.

Mano Morihiro. "'Wakereba shigen, mazereba gomi' o aikotoba ni hajimatta san bunbetsu shūshū 'Numazu hōshiki' no kaishi kara 40-nen no ayumi." *Toshi seisō* 68, no. 325 (May 2015): 26–29.

Manzenreiter, Wolfram, and Barbara Holthus, eds. *Happiness and the Good Life in Japan*. New York: Routledge, 2017.

Marotti, William. "Creative Destruction: The Art of Akasegawa Genpei and Hi-Red Center." *Artforum International* 51, no. 6 (February 2013): 192–96, 198–201, 268.

——. "Political Aesthetics: Activism, Everyday Life, and Art's Object in 1960s' Japan." *Inter-Asia Cultural Studies* 7, no. 4 (2006): 606–18.

Masuda Kinroku. "Muda to shippai o shinai seikatsu kufū." *Fujin kurabu* 33, no. 9 (September 1952): 242–45.

Mathews, Gordon. "Happiness in Neoliberal Japan." In *Happiness and the Good Life in Japan*, edited by Wolfram Manzenreiter and Barbara Holthus, 227–42. London: Routledge, 2009.

Matsu Masaoki. "Sagyō kōritsu o ageru dai ichi te wa, 'mijika na koto' no kaizen kara." *Senken keizai* 591 (March 7, 2005): 14–16.

Matsui Shizuko, Kawai Keiko, and Matsui Matsunaga. "Shufu no shōenerugī ni kansuru ishiki ni tsuite." *Kaseigaku kenkyū* 22, no. 1 (September 1975): 54–59.

Matsumoto Masanobu. "Hansei shiryō: Koko ni muda ari." *Jitsumu techō* 3, no. 5 (May 1949): 52–57.

Matsumoto Yukio. *Ichinichi o nibai ni tsukau! Sugoi jikanjutsu: Itsumo "yutori" no nai anata no shigoto o kōritsuka suru hōhō.* Tokyo: Dōbunkan Shuppan, 2009.

Matsumura Akira, Yamaguchi Akio, and Wada Toshimasa, eds. *Ōbunsha kogo jiten.* 8th ed. Tokyo: Ōbunsha, 1994.

Matsuoka, Kyōko. "The Japanese Child in a Changing World." In *Window on Japan: Japanese Children's Books and Television Today,* edited by Sybille A. Jagusch, 11–18. Washington, DC: Library of Congress, 1990.

Matsushita Kōnosuke. "Ningensei ni motozuku seiji kyōiku o (September 28, 1947)." In *Matsushita Kōnosuke hatsugen shū,* edited by PHP Sōgō Kenkyūjo Kenkyū Honbu "Matsushita Kōnosuke Hatsugen Shū" Hensanshitsu Henshū Seisaku, 203–52. Vol. 36. Kyoto: PHP Kenkyūjo, 1992.

——. *PHP no kotoba.* Tokyo: PHP Kenkyūjo, 1975.

——. "Shigen wa mugen ni aru (May 17, 1977)." In *Matsushita Kōnosuke hatsugen shū,* edited by PHP Sōgō Kenkyūjo Kenkyū Honbu "Matsushita Kōnosuke Hatsugen Shū" Hensanshitsu Henshū Seisaku, 13–46. Vol. 5. Kyoto: PHP Kenkyūjo, 1991.

——. "Tenyo no tokushitsu o ikashite (August 18, 1961)." In *Matsushita Kōnosuke hatsugen shū,* edited by PHP Sōgō Kenkyūjo Kenkyū Honbu "Matsushita Kōnosuke Hatsugen Shū" Hensanshitsu Henshū Seisaku, 67–107. Vol. 42. Kyoto: PHP Kenkyūjo, 1992.

Matsushita, Konosuke. *Quest for Prosperity: The Life of a Japanese Industrialist.* Tokyo: PHP Institute, 1988.

McCormack, Gavan. *The Emptiness of Japanese Affluence.* Foreword by Norma Field. Armonk, NY: M. E. Sharpe, 1996.

——. "The Price of Affluence: The Political Economy of Japanese Leisure." *New Left Review* 1, no. 188 (July–August 1991): 121–36.

McGray, Douglas. "Japan's Gross National Cool." *Foreign Policy* (May–June 2002): 44–54.

McKean, Margaret A. *Environmental Protest and Citizen Politics in Japan.* Berkeley: University of California Press, 1981.

Meadows, Donella H., et al. *The Limits to Growth: A Report for the Club of Rome's Project on the Predicament of Mankind.* New York: Universe Books, 1972.

——. *Seichō no genkai: Rōma kurabu 'jinrui no kiki' repōto.* Translation supervised by Ōkita Saburō. Tokyo: Daiyamondosha, 1972.

Menzel, Peter. *Material World: A Global Family Portrait.* San Francisco: Sierra Club Books, 1994.

Merrill, Karen R. *The Oil Crisis of 1973–1974: A Brief History with Documents.* Boston: Bedford/St. Martin's, 2007.

Mihara Keiko. *"Mottainai!" o kurashi no naka ni kufū o kasanete eko seikatsu.* Kyoto: Bunrikaku, 2008.

"Minimal & ism less is future." http://minimalism.jp.

Ministry of the Environment. "State of Discharge and Treatment of Municipal Solid Waste in FY 2003." November 4, 2005. https://www.env.go.jp/en/press/2005/1104a.html.

Minobe Ryōkichi, Uno Masao, and Uji'ie Hisako. *Kakei to seikatsu.* Tokyo: Dōbun Shoin, 1958.

Minowa Yayoi. *Setsuden, shōene no chie 123: 'Enerugī shifuto' ni mukete.* Tokyo: Asuka Shinsha, 2011.

Mitamura Fukiko. "Sozai, kūkan, jikan . . . minomawari no muda o ikasu 'mottainai' ga bijinesu ni naru!" *Nyūtoppu L.* 6, no. 2 (February 2014): 32–37.

Miya Rihei. "Sararīman de mo kane wa tamaru." *Bessatsu jitsugyō no Nihon* 29 (December 1953): 130–45.

Miyajima Nobuo. *Tairyō rōhi shakai: Tairyō seisan, tairyō hanbai, tairyō haiki no shikumi.* 1990. Revised edition. Tokyo: Gijutsu to Ningen, 1994.

Miyamoto Ken'ichi. *Keizai taikoku.* Vol. 10 of *Shōwa no rekishi.* Tokyo: Shōgakkan, 1983.

Miyanaga Susumu. *Muda monogatari.* Tokyo: Daiyamondosha, 1954.

Miyata Hideaki and Yasuda Yukuo. *Daiokishin no genjitsu.* Tokyo: Iwanami Shoten, 1999.

Miyoshi, Masao. "Against the Native Grain: The Japanese Novel and the 'Postmodern' West." In *Postmodernism and Japan,* edited by Masao Miyoshi and H. D. Harootunian, 143–68. Durham: Duke University Press, 1989.

Mizobuchi Ken'ichi and Takeuchi Kenji. *Katei ni okeru setsuden o dō susumeru ka: Higashi Nihon daishinsai go no setsuden seisaku.* Kobe: Graduate School of Economics, Kobe University, 2011.

Mizoguchi Kazuhiko. "Setsuden taisaku de mietekita taimu manejimento no hitsuyōsei: Zangyō o shinai, sasenai shigoto jutsu." *Risonāre* 9, no. 10 (October 2011): 11–14.

Mizoiri Shigeru. *Meiji Nihon no gomi taisaku: Obutsu sōji hō wa dono yō ni shite seiritsu shita ka.* Tokyo: Risaikuru Bunkasha, 2007.

Monna Kimiyuki. *Seikatsu no saikōchiku: Haiki kara no hassō.* Tokyo: Shin Jidaisha, 1982.

"'Mono banare' sesō no naka de no sararīman katei no mochimono chōsa." *Rōdō to keizai* 626 (February 1983): 24–32.

Mono magajin 35, no. 11 (June 2016).

Mono no seimei futatabi: "Risaikuringu undō" ronbun, sakuhin boshū nyūsen ronbunshū. Tokyo: Shin Seikatsu Undō Kyōkai, 1975.

"Mono o shoyū shinai ikikata minimarisuto ga zōshoku chū." *Shūkan daiyamondo* 104, no. 1 (December 26, 2015–January 2, 2016): 146.

Mori Kento. "'Suteru gawa' to 'suterareru gawa' o aruku: Gomi tōki jiken kara kangaeru." *Sekai* 532 (September 1989): 178–92. Part of the special issue "Gomi mondai o kangaeru."

Morris-Suzuki, Tessa. *A History of Japanese Economic Thought.* London: Routledge, 1989.

"MOTTAINAI." http://www.mottainai.info/english/ and http://www.mottainai. info/jp/.

Mottainai Bāsan. Twitter post. July 1, 2017. https://twitter.com/mottainaibaasan.

"Mottainai Brasil." http://www.mottainai.org.br/movimento/historico.

"MOTTAINAI furī māketto to wa." http://www.mottainai.info/jp/event/fleama.

"Mottainai furoshiki." *Koizumi naikaku mēru magajin* 231 (April 20, 2006).

"Mottainai furoshiki, April 2006." http://www.env.go.jp/recycle/info/furoshiki.

"Mottainai Gakkai." http://mottainaisociety.org/society-overview/greeting/.

"Mottainai New York." http://www.mottainainy.com/.

"'Mottainai' no kokoro." *Koizumi naikaku mēru magajin* 177 (February 24, 2005).

"'Mottainai seishin' ni motozuita NY-hatsu no fasshon burando." *Decide* 47, no. 20 (October 2010): unpaginated.

Mottainai tanteidan: An Advertisement of the MOTTAINAI Detectives. Yokohama: Mottainai Tanteidan, 2006.

Mottainai zenkoku taikai in Utsunomiya hōkokusho. Vol. 1. Utsunomiya: Mottainai Zenkoku Taikai Jikkō Iinkai Jimukyoku, 2007.

"Muda na hōsō tsuihō: Gomi genryō tomin no tsudoi." *Gomi sensō shūhō* 46 (November 3, 1972): 2.

"Muda naku jōzu ni taberu ni wa." *Shufu to seikatsu* 8, no. 5 (April 1953): 366–71.

Murai Masamori. "Yutori no kaifuku ni mukete." *Keizaijin* 45, no. 10 (October 1991): 8–11. Part of the series "Nihon wa seikatsu taikoku tariuru ka."

Murata Tokuji. "Sekiyu bunka to purasuchikku mondai kara tsukaisute shakai o kangaeru." *Risaikuru bunka* 30 (April–June 1991): 14–23. Part of the series "Tsukaisute shakai, kajō hōsō shōkōgun."

"Muri, muda, mura o nakushite, atama no naka o sukkiri kaishō! Sutoresu zero no 'danshari' shigoto jutsu." *Za nijūichi* 28, no. 6 (June 2011): 49–57.

Myōjin Isao. "3.11 'Fukushima'-go no ningen to shakai: Mō hitotsu no yutakasa, mō hitotsu no shiawase." *Hokkaidō keizai* 546 (October 2012): 1–31.

Nagahama Toshihiro. "Kūru bizu, wōmu bizu no shōene to keizai kōka." *Re: Building Maintenance and Management* 30, no. 1 (July 2008): 37–40.

Nagahara, Hiromu. *Tokyo Boogie-Woogie: Japan's Pop Era and Its Discontents.* Cambridge: Harvard University Press, 2017.

Nagoya-shi Kankyō Jigyōkyoku. *Shufu no gomi kōgengaku.* Mainichi Eigasha, 1978.

Naikaku Sōri Daijin Kanbō Kōhōshitsu. *Gomi shori ni kansuru seron chōsa: Shōwa 63-nen 10-gatsu chōsa.* Tokyo: Naikaku Sōri Daijin Kanbō Kōhōshitsu, [1988].

——. *Jiyū jikan ni okeru kōdō ishiki ni kansuru seron chōsa: Shōwa 56-nen 10-gatsu chōsa.* Tokyo: Naikaku Sōri Daijin Kanbō Kōhōshitsu, 1982.

——. *Kokumin seikatsu ni kansuru seron chōsa: Heisei 4-nen 5-gatsu chōsa.* Tokyo: Naikaku Sōri Daijin Kanbō Kōhōshitsu, [1992].

——. *Kokumin seikatsu ni kansuru seron chōsa: Heisei 11-nen 12-gatsu chōsa.* Tokyo: Naikaku Sōri Daijin Kanbō Kōhōshitsu, [1999]. http://survey.gov-online.go.jp/h11/kokumin/images/zu05.gif.

——. *Kokumin seikatsu ni kansuru seron chōsa: Heisei gannen 5-gatsu chōsa.* Tokyo: Naikaku Sōri Daijin Kanbō Kōhōshitsu, [1989].

——. *Kokumin seikatsu ni kansuru seron chōsa: Shōwa 26-nen 6-gatsu chōsa.* Tokyo: Naikaku Sōri Daijin Kanbō Kōhōshitsu, 2014. http://survey.gov-online.go.jp/h26/h26-life/zh/z29.html.

——. *Kokumin seikatsu ni kansuru seron chōsa: Shōwa 49-nen 1-gatsu chōsa.* Tokyo: Naikaku Sōri Daijin Kanbō Kōhōshitsu, 1974.

——. *Kokumin seikatsu ni kansuru seron chōsa: Shōwa 54-nen 5-gatsu chōsa.* Tokyo: Naikaku Sōri Daijin Kanbō Kōhōshitsu, 1979.

——. *Kokumin seikatsu ni kansuru seron chōsa: Shōwa 61-nen 5-gatsu chōsa.* Tokyo: Naikaku Sōri Daijin Kanbō Kōhōshitsu, [1986].

——. *Kurashi no ishiki ni kansuru seron chōsa: Shōwa 59-nen 3-gatsu chōsa.* Tokyo: Naikaku Sōri Daijin Kanbō Kōhōshitsu, 1984.

——. *Kurashi to chochiku ni kansuru seron chōsa: Shōwa 60-nen 5-gatsu chōsa.* Tokyo: Naikaku Sōri Daijin Kanbō Kōhōshitsu, [1989].

——. *Kurashi to shigen ni kansuru seron chōsa: Shōwa 60-nen 5-gatsu chōsa.* Tokyo: Naikaku Sōri Daijin Kanbō Kōhōshitsu, 1985.

——. *Shōenerugī ni kansuru seron chōsa: Heisei 2-nen 12-gatsu chōsa.* Tokyo: Naikaku Sōri Daijin Kanbō Kōhōshitsu, [1990].

——. *Shōenerugī, shōshigen ni kansuru seron chōsa: Shōwa 53-nen 2-gatsu chōsa.* Tokyo: Naikaku Sōri Daijin Kanbō Kōhōshitsu, 1978.

Naikakufu Daijin Kanbō Seifu Kōhōshitsu. *Junkangata shakai no keisei ni kansuru seron chōsa: Heisei 13-nen 7-gatsu chōsa.* Tokyo: Naikakufu Daijin Kanbō Seifu Kōhōshitsu, [2001].

Naikakufu Daijin Kanbō Seifu Kōhōshitsu Seron Chōsa Tantō. *Kankyō mondai ni kansuru seron chōsa: Heisei 24-nen 6-gatsu chōsa.* [2012]. http://survey. gov-online.go.jp/h24/h24-kankyou/2-1.html.

Naitō Hideo. "Shōene rukku no yukue." *Gekkan seifu shiryō* 63 (August 1979): 1.

Nakamura Masanori. *Ōraru hisutorī no kanōsei: Tokyo gomi sensō to Minobe tosei.* Tokyo: Ochanomizu Shobō, 2011.

Nakamura, Shinichi, and Atsushi Toyonaga. *Making Environmental Policy in the United States and Japan: The Case of Global Warming.* Cambridge: Program on U.S.-Japan Relations, Harvard University, 1991.

Nakamura Takafusa. "An Economy in Search of Stable Growth: Japan since the Oil Crisis." *Journal of Japanese Studies* 6, no. 1 (Winter 1980): 155–78.

Nakamura, Takafusa. *The Postwar Japanese Economy: Its Development and Structure, 1937–1994.* Tokyo: University of Tokyo Press, 1995.

Nakano Gorō. *Amerika ni manabu: Minshūteki na shakai to seikatsu no arikata.* Tokyo: Nihon Kōhōsha, 1949.

———. "Muda naku muri naku: Beikokujin no seikatsu kan." *Ōru seikatsu* 10, no. 12 (December 1955): 48–50.

Nakano Kōji. *Seihin no shisō.* Tokyo: Bungei Shunjū, 1996.

Nakano, Yoichi. "Negotiating Modern Landscapes: The Politics of Infrastructure Development in Modern Japan." Ph.D. dissertation. Harvard University, 2007.

Nakayama Mayumi. *Suterarezu ni iru fuyōhin no "sutedoki" ga wakaru hon.* Tokyo: Fusōsha, 2015.

Napier, Susan J. "Panic Sites: The Japanese Imagination of Disaster from *Godzilla* to *Akira.*" *Journal of Japanese Studies* 19, no. 2 (Summer 1993): 327–51.

"Naze, ima 'danshari' na no ka?" *Za nijūichi* 28, no. 6 (June 2011): 50–53. Part of the series "Muri, muda, mura o nakushite, atama no naka o sukkiri kaishō! Sutoresu zero no 'danshari' shigoto jutsu."

"Nenshū 2000-man no jikanjutsu." *Purejidento* (February 18, 2008): 25–85.

"NHK-AC kyōdō kyanpēn CM hōsō kaishi!" http://www.cwfilms.jp/news/20150701/.

Nihon Keizai Shinbunsha, ed. *Gomyunichī: Saishigenka ni idomu chiiki shakai.* Tokyo: Nihon Keizai Shinbunsha, 1979.

"Nihon no shio: 'Shin seikatsu undō' gojūgonen tenmatsu ki." *Sekai* 122 (February 1956): 148–54.

Nihon Nōritsu Kyōkai Sōgō Kenkyūjo Mākechingu Dēta Banku, ed. *Kankyō ishiki, eko raifu kanren mākechingu dēta hakusho, 2009-nen ban.* Tokyo: Nihon Nōritsu Kyōkai Sōgō Kenkyūjo, 2008.

Nijūnen go no rekuriēshon no bijon: Yutaka na shakai to jiyū jikan o motomete. Tokyo: Nihon Rekuriēshon Bijon Iinkai, 1968.

Nikkei Woman, ed. *Jinsei o kaeru jikan kanrijutsu: Shigoto o supīdo appu! OFF taimu o motto jūjitsu!* Tokyo: Nikkei BPsha, 2009.

Nippon Hōsō Kyōkai. *Kurashi o minaosu natsu no setsuden taisaku: NHK terebi tekisuto.* Tokyo: NHK Shuppan, 2011.

Nippon Hōsō Kyōkai Hōsō Bunka Kenkyūjo, ed. *Nihonjin no seikatsu jikan: Kokumin seikatsu jikan chōsa, kaisetsu hen.* Tokyo: Nippon Hōsō Shuppan Kyōkai, 1963.

Nippon Hōsō Kyōkai Hōsō Seron Chōsajo. *Nihonjin no seikatsu jikan, zusetsu: 1985.* Tokyo: Nippon Hōsō Shuppan Kyōkai, 1987.

———. *Nihonjin no seikatsu jikan, zusetsu: 1990.* Tokyo: Nippon Hōsō Shuppan Kyōkai, 1992.

Nishimoto Ikuko. "The 'Civilization' of Time: Japan and the Adoption of the Western Time System." *Time & Society* 6, no. 2/3 (1997): 237–59.

———. *Jikan ishiki no kindai: "Toki wa kane nari" no shakaishi*. Tokyo: Hōsei Daigaku Shuppankyoku, 2006.

———. "Kodomo ni jikan genshu o oshieru: Shōgakkō no uchi to soto." In *Chikoku no tanjō: Kindai Nihon ni okeru jikan ishiki no keisei*, edited by Hashimoto Takehiko and Kuriyama Shigehisa, 157–87. Tokyo: Sangensha, 2006.

Nishimura Ichirō. *Ikasō mono no inochi: Risaikuru shakai o mezashite*. Tokyo: Rengō Shuppan, 1986.

Nishinari Katsuhiro. *Mudagaku*. Tokyo: Shinchō Sensho, 2008.

No Impact Man. Oscilloscope, 2009.

Nojiri Masato. "Shōene seikatsu: Setsuden seikatsu no tsubo." *Eiyō to ryōri* 77, no. 8 (August 2011): 8–15. Part of the series "Dekiru koto kara hajimeyō shōene ressun."

Nomura Masaki. *Bijinesuman no tame no chiteki jikanjutsu: "Jibun jikan" o yutaka ni suru 101 no hinto*. Tokyo: PHP Kenkyūjo, 1995.

Nōrinshō Nōgyō Kairyōkyoku Seikatsu Kaizenka, ed. *Zusetsu nōka no seikatsu kaizen*. Tokyo: Asakura Shoten, 1954.

North, Scott. "Negotiating What's 'Natural': Persistent Domestic Gender Role Inequality in Japan." *Social Science Japan Journal* 12, no. 1 (Summer 2009): 23–44.

Numazu Shiyakusho Kōseika, ed. *Shōshigen jidai no shōhi seikatsu: Shōhisha mondai shinpojiumu hōkokusho*. [Numazu]: Numazu-shi, 1977.

O'Bryan, Scott. *The Growth Idea: Purpose and Prosperity in Postwar Japan*. Honolulu: University of Hawaii Press, 2009.

Obutsu sōji hō shikō kisoku. Naimushō rei dai go gō. March 1900. In *Gyōsei sho hōki*. Vol. 6. 1928.

Ogasawara Yōko. *Kechi jōzu: Biteki ken'yaku kurashi*. Tokyo: Bijinesusha, 2003.

Ogino Jirō. "Seisō jigyō no genkyō to mondai ten." *Toshi mondai kenkyū* 24, no. 4 (April 1972): 80–98.

Ogose Tōru. "Mihyaeru Ende 'Momo' ni okeru kikukoto: Gendai shōhi shakai no jikansei kara jiyū ni naru koto." *Ibaraki daigaku kyōiku gakubu kiyō (Kyōiku kagaku)* 55 (March 2006): 247–66.

Ōhara Sōichirō. "'Rōhi o tsukuridasu hitobito.'" *Mingei* 111 (March 1962): 33–35.

Ōhashi Tomoko. "Gomi sensō to Suginami Shōhisha no Kai." *Shimin* 7 (March 1972): 133–36.

Ōhira Ken. *Yutakasa no seishin byōri*. Tokyo: Iwanami Shoten, 1990.

Okamoto Masashi. *Mottainai o mitsukeyō*. Vol. 1 of *Mottainai seikatsu daijiten*. Tokyo: Gakushū Kenkyūsha, 2007.

———. *Mottainai to Nihon no dentō*. Vol. 7 of *Mottainai seikatsu daijiten*. Tokyo: Gakushū Kenkyūsha, 2007.

Ōkita Saburō. "Seichō no genkai to shigen mondai." *Chūō kaigi kaihō* 16 (March 1984): 5–15.

Okita, Saburo. "Outgrowing Catch-Up Capitalism." In *Tackling the Waste Problem: Environmental Concerns and Recycling Efforts*, edited by Koya Ishino et al., 49–51. Tokyo: Foreign Press Center Japan, 1992.

Ōkubo Motosaburō. "Gomi to toshi to ningen to." *Keizai hyōron* 23, no. 2 (February 1974): 104–12.

Okuda Junko. "Shokuhin o muda naku katsuyō suru ni wa." *Shoku seikatsu* 47, no. 6 (June 1953): 10–13.

Ōmae Ken'ichi et al. *Jikan to muda no kagaku: Shigoto no hanbun wa "misekake"! Naze ka kekka ga deru hito no 24 jikan*. Tokyo: Purejidento, 2006.

"Omoitsuki de muda o nakushimashō." *Josei raifu* 2, no. 10 (October 1947): 48.

Ōmoto Moichirō. *Katei seikatsu no kagakuka*. Tokyo: Chikyū Shuppan, 1949.

Ōno Osamu. "Minobe to the Rescue." *Japan Quarterly* 16, no. 3 (July–September 1969): 268–75.

Ōno Tai'ichi. *Toyota seisan hōshiki: Datsu kibo no keiei o mezashite*. Tokyo: Daiyamondosha, 1978.

Organisation for Economic Co-operation and Development. *Environment at a Glance: OECD Environmental Indicators*. Paris: OECD Publishing, 2005.

——. "Household Savings (Indicator)." https://data.oecd.org/hha/household-savings. htm.

——. "Labor Force Participation Rate." https://data.oecd.org/emp/ labour-force-participation-rate.htm.

Orii Takahiro. "Kūru bizu, wōmu bizu o kokumin undō ni: Doramukan 155 man bon bun no gen'yu sakugen kōka." *Enerugī* 39, no. 7 (July 2006): 95–98.

Ortberg, Molly. "How to Get Rid of Clutter and Live Abundantly." *The Toast*, February 24, 2015. http://the-toast.net/2015/02/24/get-rid-clutter-live-abundantly/.

Osawa, Mari. "Twelve Million Full-Time Housewives: The Gender Consequences of Japan's Postwar Social Contract." In *Social Contracts Under Stress: The Middle Classes of America, Europe, and Japan at the Turn of the Century*, edited by Olivier Zunz, Leonard Schoppa, and Nobuhiro Hiwatari, 255–78. New York: Russell Sage Foundation, 2002.

Ōsawa Masaaki. "Gomi kinenbi: Obutsu to gomi to haikibutsu no naritachi to watashitachi no seikatsu." *Seikatsu to kankyō* 52, no. 5 (May 2007): 69–73.

Oshida Isao. "'Suteru' to wa (2)." *Gomi sensō shūhō* 80 (July 13, 1973): 4–8.

Ōshima Kaori. Afterword to *Momo: Jikan dorobō to nusumareta jikan o ningen ni torikaeshitekureta onna no ko no fushigi na monogatari*, by Michael Ende, 357–60. Translated by Ōshima Kaori. Tokyo: Iwanami Shoten, 1976.

Oshitani, Shizuka. *Global Warming Policy in Japan and Britain: Interactions between Institutions and Issue Characteristics*. Manchester: Manchester University Press, 2006.

"Osorubeki 'tsukaisute jidai': Hirogaru ka disupōzaburu māketto." *Gomi sensō shūhō* 5 (January 14, 1972): 2–3.

Ozawa Tadashi. "Mottainai, mottainai." *Haha no tomo* 183 (August 1968): 88–91.

Packard, Vance. *The Hidden Persuaders*. New York: David McKay Company, 1957.

——. *Kakureta settokusha*. Translated by Hayashi Shūji. Tokyo: Daiyamondosha, 1962.

——. "Muda o tsukuru hitobito." Translated by Ishikawa Hiroyoshi. *Chūō kōron* 76, no. 4 (April 1961): 116–27.

——. *Rōhi o tsukuridasu hitobito*. Translated by Minami Hiroshi and Ishikawa Hiroyoshi. Tokyo: Daiyamondosha, 1961.

——. "This Is the New Japan." *Saturday Evening Post* 236, no. 15 (April 1963): 28–36.

——. *The Waste Makers*. New York: David McKay Company, 1960.

Partner, Simon. *Assembled in Japan: Electrical Goods and the Making of the Japanese Consumer*. Berkeley: University of California Press, 1999.

——. "Taming the Wilderness: The Lifestyle Improvement Movement in Rural Japan, 1925–1965." *Monumenta Nipponica* 56, no. 4 (Winter 2001): 487–520.

Pecchi, Lorenzo, and Gustavo Piga. "*Economic Possibilities for Our Grandchildren*: A Twenty-First Century Perspective." In *Revisiting Keynes: Economic Possibilities for Our Grandchildren*, edited by Lorenzo Pecchi and Gustavo Piga, 1-16. Cambridge: MIT Press, 2008.

——. *Revisiting Keynes: Economic Possibilities for Our Grandchildren*. Cambridge: MIT Press, 2008.

Plath, David W. *The After Hours: Modern Japan and the Search for Enjoyment.* Berkeley: University of California Press, 1964.

Potter, Claire Bond, and Renee C. Romano, eds. *Doing Recent History: On Privacy, Copyright, Video Games, Institutional Review Boards, Activist Scholarship, and History That Talks Back.* Athens: University of Georgia Press, 2012.

Powell, Bill, and Velisarios Kattoulas, with Hideko Takayama. "The Lost Decade." *Newsweek,* July 27, 1998, 28–31.

"Press Release: Tokyo Declaration Breaks New Ground in International Efforts to Cultivate 'Eco-Society' at Local Level." June 3, 1998. http://www.un.org/press/en/1998/19980603.eco5.html.

Puranetto Rinku, ed. *Mottainai.* Tokyo: Magajin Hausu, 2006.

"Purasu arufa no jikan o umidasu 77 no chie." *Fujin no tomo* 95, no. 5 (May 2001): 5 49, 53 91.

"Purasuchikku gomi sensō." *Kagaku asahi* 49, no. 10 (October 1989): 104–8. Part of the series "Gomi junkan shakai e."

"Raifusutairu ga kawaru?! 'Sūpā kūru bizu' hajimaru." *Kōhō kaigi* 31 (August 2011): 9.

Rathje, William L. *Rubbish! The Archaeology of Garbage.* New York: HarperCollins Publishers, 1992.

"Retail Therapy." *The Economist,* December 17, 2011.

Risaikuru Bunka Henshū Gurūpu, ed. *Risaikuru zenseikatsu gaido: Zenkoku risaikuru shoppu gaido.* Tokyo: Risaikuru Bunkasha, 1991.

Risaikuru nōto: Mono o taisetsu ni suru undō. Kyoto: Mono o Taisetsu ni Suru Undō Kyoto-fu Suishin Kaigi (Kyoto-fu Shōkōbu Shōhi Seikatsuka), 1989.

"*Risaikuru ondo.*" *Chūō kaigi kaihō* 8 (March 1982): 68–69.

"Risaikuru shoppu gaido: Tokyo kinkō hen, Chūkyō hen, Keihanshin hen." *Asahi jānaru* 25, no. 28 (July 1, 1983): 24–29. Part of the series "Wakamono ga mezasu risaikuru raifu."

"Risaikuru-tte nan da?" *Gekkan risaikuru* (March 15, 1980): 1.

"Risaikuru wa gomi herashi ni naranai." *Karin* 65 (December 1997): 15.

Roberts, Glenda S. *Staying on the Line: Blue-Collar Women in Contemporary Japan.* Honolulu: University of Hawaii Press, 1994.

Royal Government of Bhutan. *The Report of the High-Level Meeting on Wellbeing and Happiness: Defining a New Economic Paradigm.* Thimphu: Office of the Prime Minister, 2012.

Sada Masashi. "MOTTAINAI." 2005.

Saitō Sei'ichirō. "Shōhi bunkaron no kaitō: Shōhi, kaisō soshite yutakasa." *Voice* 3 (March 1986): 88–113.

Saitō Shigeta. *Jikan no tsukaikata: Umai hito, heta na hito.* Tokyo: Mikasa Shobō, 2001.

Saitō Yoshio et al. "Haikibutsu no shori, sairiyō." *Jurisuto* 571 (October 1, 1974): 15–30.

Sakai Shōhei. "Shoku seikatsu no gōrika no tame ni (2): Ryōri no chishiki." *Kaitaku* 21 (December 1949): 34–39.

Sakai Takeshi. "*Momo*" *to kangaeru jikan to okane no himitsu.* Tokyo: Shoshi Shinsui, 2005.

Sakano Shigenobu. *Ikigai to yutakasa o motomete: Korekara no kokudo to seikatsu.* Tokyo: Sankaidō, 1979.

Sakata Ryūichi. "*Mottainai*" *no fukkatsu: Mono afure shakai ni ikiru Nihonjin e.* Tokyo: Bunkōsha, 1997.

Sakoi Sadayuki. "Shōhi no rōhi kōzō to shōhisha shinri." *Aichi kyōiku daigaku kenkyū hōkoku* 50 (March 2001): 177–89.

Samuels, Richard J. *3.11: Disaster and Change in Japan.* Ithaca: Cornell University Press, 2013.

Sand, Jordan. *House and Home in Modern Japan: Architecture, Domestic Space, and Bourgeois Culture, 1880-1930*. Cambridge: Harvard University Asia Center, 2003.

——. "Living with Uncertainty after March 11, 2011." *Journal of Asian Studies* 71, no. 2 (May 2012): 313–18.

——. "Open Letter to Gary Thomasson." In Genpei Akasegawa, *Hyperart: Thomasson*, 391–401. Translated by Matthew Fargo. New York: Kaya Press, 2009.

——. *Tokyo Vernacular: Common Spaces, Local Histories, Found Objects*. Berkeley: University of California Press, 2013.

Sangyō Fukkō Kōdan Shi Hensan Iinkai, ed. *Sangyō fukkō kōdan shi*. Tokyo: Sangyō Fukkō Kōdan Shi Hensan Iinkai, 1952.

Sangyō Keikaku Kondankai, ed. *Sangyō kōzō no kaikaku: Kōkai to shigen o chūshin ni*. Tokyo: Taisei Shuppansha, 1973.

Sasaki Fumio. *Bokutachi ni, mō mono wa hitsuyō nai*. Tokyo: Wani Bukkusu, 2015.

Sasaki, Fumio. *Goodbye, Things: The New Japanese Minimalism*. Translated by Eriko Sugita. New York: W. W. Norton, 2017.

Sasaki Tōru. *MCON Report 109: Shōenerugī jidai no mākechingu senryaku*. Tokyo: Mākechingu Kondankai, 1979.

Satake Hiroaki. "'Toyota seisan hōshiki to 'muda' gainen no ganchiku: Keizai gakusetsu jō no 'kūhi' gainen ni motozuku kentō." *Fukui kenritsu daigaku keizai keiei kenkyū* 6 (March 1999): 29–44.

Satō Eko. *Furansujin no zeitaku no setsuyaku seikatsu*. Tokyo: Shōdensha, 2002.

Satō Tomio. "Shimin undō ni sasaerareta atarashī ryūtsū jigyō tai no tenkai: Kankyō hogo dantai 'Nihon Risaikuru Undō Shimin no Kai' no jirei bunseki o chūshin ni." Ph.D. dissertation. 1997.

Satō Yumi and Doi Chizuru. *Mottainai*. Tokyo: Fūtōsha, 1992.

Schor, Juliet B. *The Overworked American: The Unexpected Decline of Leisure*. New York: Basic Books, 1991.

Schreurs, Miranda A. *Environmental Politics in Japan, Germany, and the United States*. Cambridge: Cambridge University Press, 2002.

"Second National Convention on Mottainai." http://mottainai.info/english/topics/2008/07/000705.php.

Segawa Dai. "Chihō soshiki kara mita shin seikatsu undō: Tokyo no jirei." In *Shin seikatsu undō to Nihon no sengo: Haisen kara 1970 nendai*, edited by Ōkado Masakatsu, 235–67. Tokyo: Nihon Keizai Hyōronsha, 2012.

Seikatsu Jōhō Kenkyūkai, ed. *Muda na shuppi o nakushitara setsuyaku dekichatta*. Tokyo: Goma Shobō, 1999.

Seikatsu Kagaku Chōsakai, ed. *Yoka: Nihonjin no seikatsu shisō*. Tokyo: Ishiyaku Shuppan, 1961.

Seisō hō. Hōritsu dai nanajūni gō. April 1954.

Seiyama Kazuo. "'Atarashī yutakasa' ni tsuite." *DIO: Rengō sōken repōto* 269 (March 2012): 11–13.

Seiyama Takurō. "A Radical Interpretation of Postwar Economic Policies." In *Japanese Capitalism since 1945: Critical Perspectives*, edited by Tessa Morris-Suzuki and Takuro Seiyama, 28–73. New York: M. E. Sharpe, 1989.

"'Sekai de mottomo eikyōryoku no aru 100 nin' Kondō Marie wa ōbeijin kirā." *Shūkan bunshun* 57, no. 17 (April 30, 2015): 145–46.

Sekiyu shokku, gen'ei ni obieta 69 nichikan; Kokutetsu rōshi funsō, suto ken dakkan suto no shōgeki. Vol. 5 of *Sengo 50-nen sono toki Nihon wa*. Tokyo: Nippon Hōsō Shuppan Kyōkai, 1996.

"Sengen." *Chūō kaigi kaihō* 12 (March 1983): 1.

"Senri nyū taun: Toiretto pēpā sōdō tenmatsuki." *Chūō kōron keiei mondai* 13, no. 1 (March 1974): 196–99.

Setsuyaku Seikatsu Kenkyū Gurūpu. *Setsuyaku seikatsu o tokoton tanoshimu 700 no chie.* Tokyo: Chūkei Shuppan, 1999.

Sherman, Lauren. "The KonMari Method Is a Boon to Secondhand Stores and E-tailers." *Fashionista,* April 6, 2015. http://fashionista.com/2015/04/konmari-method-goodwill.

Shibata Tokue. "Gomi mondai no tenkai: Kako, genzai, kongo no hōkō." *Toshi mondai kenkyū* 28, no. 12 (December 1976): 20–32.

———. *Gomi: Seisō kakumei wa hajimatte iru.* Osaka: Rokugatsusha, 1964.

———. *Nihon no seisō mondai: Gomi to benjo no keizaigaku.* Tokyo: Tokyo Daigaku Shuppankai, 1961.

Shibata, Tokue. "Land, Waste and Pollution: Challenging History in Creating a Sustainable Tokyo Metropolis." In *Sustainable Cities: Japanese Perspectives on Physical and Social Structures,* edited by Tamagawa Hidenori, 96–124. Tokyo: United Nations University Press, 2006.

Shibuya Yukio et al. "'Yutakasa ron' no hensen: Yutakasa tsuikyū kara shiawase tsuikyū e no katoki." *Mitsubishi sōgō kenkyūjo shohō* 47 (2006): 30–44.

Shigen Enerugīchō and Shōenerugī Sekiyu Daitai Enerugī Taisakuka. *Shōenerugī sōran, 1990.* Tokyo: Tsūsan Shiryō Chōsakai, 1989.

Shigen no yūkō na riyō no sokushin ni kansuru hōritsu. Hōritsu dai yonjūhachi gō. April 26, 1991. http://law.e-gov.go.jp/htmldata/H03/H03HO048.html.

Shigen to Enerugī o Taisetsu ni Suru Kokumin Undō Chūō Kaigi, ed. *Shōshigen, shōenerugī undō jissen jirei shū: Shōwa 56 nendo.* Tokyo: Shigen to Enerugī o Taisetsu ni Suru Kokumin Undō Chūō Kaigi, 1982.

Shigen to Enerugī o Taisetsu ni Suru Kokumin Undō Chūō Renraku Kaigi, Shōshigen Shōenerugī Kokumin Undō Chihō Suishin Kaigi, and Shin Seikatsu Undō Kyōkai, eds. *Shōenerugī undō suishin kinkyū zenkoku shūkai.* [Tokyo]: Shigen to Enerugī o Taisetsu ni Suru Kokumin Undō Chūō Renraku Kaigi, Shōshigen Shōenerugī Kokumin Undō Chihō Suishin Kaigi, and Shin Seikatsu Undō Kyōkai, 1979.

Shigoto Kōritsu Kenkyūkai, ed. *Tabo shachō no "kekka o daseru" jikanjutsu.* Tokyo: Seibidō Shuppan, 2009.

Shimane-ken Shakai Fukushibu Kenmin Seikatsuka. "Shin no yutakasa motome 'setsuyaku' kara 'sōzō' e: Shimane-ken no shōshigen, shōenerugī suishin undō." *Chūō kaigi kaihō* 17 (July 1984): 26–27.

Shimauchi Keiji. *Ende no kureta takaramono: "Momo" no sekai kōzō o yomu.* Tokyo: Fukutake Shoten, 1990.

Shimizu Keihachirō. "Nihonteki shigen o kangaeru: Hikari to mizu to tsuchi e no kaiki." In *Shōshigen Nihon no kōzu,* edited by Nihon Seinen Kaigisho, 4–37. Tokyo: Daiyamondosha, 1974.

Shin seikatsu undō kyōkai: 25-nen no ayumi. Tokyo: Shin Seikatsu Undō Kyōkai, 1982.

Shinju Mariko. *Mottainai bāsan.* Tokyo: Kōdansha, 2004.

———. *Mottainai bāsan karuta.* Tokyo: Kōdansha, 2006.

———. *Mottainai bāsan no tengoku to jigoku no hanashi.* Tokyo: Kōdansha, 2014.

———. *Mottainai bāsan to kangaeyō sekai no koto.* Tokyo: Kōdansha, 2008.

———. *Mottainai koto shite nai kai?* Tokyo: Kōdansha, 2007.

Shinoda Masahiro. "'Setsuden no onegai' chūshin ni hatsudensho no genkyō mo kimekomakaku: Kashiwazaki-Kariwa hatsudensho no unten teishi." *Kōken repōto* 252 (May 2008): 9.

Shinoda Yūjirō. "Shōene rukku to Nihonjin: Bunmei no mae ni bunka ga nakasareru kuni." *Keizai ōrai* 32, no. 7 (July 1980): 106–12.

Shinozaki Hiromi. "Hirakeyuku 'rōhi wa bitoku' jidai: 1960 nendai no shōhi seikatsu." *Kinzoku* 30, no. 19 (October 1, 1960): 89–95.

Shiyōzumi jidōsha no saishigenka tō ni kansuru hōritsu. Hōritsu dai hachijūnana gō. July 12, 2002. http://law.e-gov.go.jp/htmldata/H14/H14HO087.html.

"Shōene rukku." *Ōru seikatsu* 34, no. 7 (July 1979): 11.

"Shōene rukku." *Tosei kenkyū* 13, no. 8 (August 1980): 36–37.

"Shōene rukku no honmei wa jinbei: Suzushikute choppiri kofū na tokoro mo ukeru." *Ōru taishū* 33, no. 14 (August 1980): 42–43.

Shōhin Kagaku Kenkyūjo and CDI, ed. *Seikatsuzai no shobun to sairyūtsū*. Tokyo: Shōhin Kagaku Kenkyūjo, 1987.

Shōhisha undō sanjūnen: Kansai shufuren no ayumi, 1945–1975. Osaka: Kansai Shufu Rengōkai, 1976.

Shōji Hikaru and Miyamoto Ken'ichi. *Osorubeki kōgai.* Tokyo: Iwanami Shoten, 1964.

Shokuhin junkan shigen no saisei riyō tō no sokushin ni kansuru hōritsu. Hōritsu dai hyaku jūroku gō. June 7, 2000. http://law.e-gov.go.jp/htmldata/H12/H12HO116.html.

Shufu no ishiki chōsa, Shōwa 49 nendo: Fuyōhin kōkankai ni tsuite: Keizai Kikakuchō itaku chōsa. Tokyo: Shufu Rengōkai, 1975.

Shufu no jiyū jikan ni kansuru ishiki chōsa. Tokyo: Rōdōshō Fujin Shōnenkyoku, 1959.

Shutoken furī māketto & risaikuru shoppu. Tokyo: Nihon Kōtsū Kōsha Shuppan Jigyōkyoku, 1996.

Skidelsky, Robert, and Edward Skidelsky. *How Much Is Enough? Money and the Good Life.* New York: Other Press, 2012.

Slade, Giles. *Made to Break: Technology and Obsolescence in America.* Cambridge: Harvard University Press, 2006.

Smiles, Samuel. *Self-Help.* New edition. London: John Murray, 1884.

Smith, Howard F. "Food Controls in Occupied Japan." *Agricultural History* 23, no. 3 (July 1949): 220–23.

Smith, Kerry. *A Time of Crisis: Japan, the Great Depression, and Rural Revitalization.* Cambridge: Harvard University Asia Center, 2001.

Sōgō Kenkyū Kaihatsu Kikō, ed. *Shōenerugī no jittai to hyōka: Enerugī shōhi shutai no shōenerugī kōdō ni kansuru kenkyū.* Tokyo: Sōgō Kenkyū Kaihatsu Kikō, 1979.

Solt, George. *The Untold History of Ramen: How Political Crisis in Japan Spawned a Global Food Craze.* Berkeley: University of California Press, 2014.

Sorensen, André. *The Making of Urban Japan: Cities and Planning from Edo to the Twenty-First Century.* London: Routledge, 2002.

Spiri, John. "Whatever Happened to Yamagishi? Idealism, Nature and the Environment in Japan's Cooperative Agrarian Community." *Asia-Pacific Journal* 6, no. 2 (February 2008).

"Statement by Prof. Wangari Maathai, Nobel Peace Laureate, Goodwill Ambassador for the Congo Basin Forest Ecosystem, and UN Messenger of Peace." Opening of the High Level Segment of the United Nations Framework Convention on Climate Change. December 15, 2009.

"Statement by Prof. W. Maathai, Nobel Peace Laureate, on Behalf of Civil Society." United Nations Summit on Climate Change. September 22, 2009.

Storey, Kate. "Marie Kondo Told Us Her Secret Clutter Vice." *Good Housekeeping,* April 29, 2016.

Strasser, Susan. *Waste and Want: A Social History of Trash.* New York: Henry Holt and Company, 1999.

Suda Hiroshi. "'Yoka' kō: Yutaka na shakai o mezashite." *Keizaijin* 45, no. 10 (October 1991): 4–7.

Suginami-ku Kankyō Seisōbu Seisō Kanrika, ed. *Karasu taisaku gomi shūsekijo jittai chōsa hōkokusho, Heisei 14 nendo ban.* Tokyo: Suginami-ku, 2003.

——, ed. *Karasu taisaku gomi shūsekijo jittai chōsa hōkokusho, Heisei 20 nendo ban.* Tokyo: Suginami-ku Kankyō Seisōbu Seisō Kanrika, 2009.

Sumāto Raifu Kenkyūkai. *Ikka de kyōryoku suru setsuden, setsuyaku seikatsu no hōhō 150.* Tokyo: Shin Jinbutsu Ōraisha, 2011.

Sumitomo Shintaku Ginkō Kurashi no Shiryōshitsu, ed. *Konna ni muda ga atta no ka: Kurashi no aidea kettei han.* Tokyo: Mainichi Shinbunsha, 1974.

Suzuki Koshirō. "Zeitaku wa hatashite teki ka." *Meiboku* 2, no. 9 (September 1948): 13–14.

Suzuki Takao. *Shiawase setsuden.* Tokyo: Bungei Shunjū, 2011.

"T shatsu, tanpan mo kaikin? Konka wa sūpā kūru bizu." *Shūkan daiyamondo* 99, no. 22 (June 4, 2011): 56.

Tabemono o taisetsu ni suru dokuhon. Tokyo: Betā Hōmu Kyōkai, 1976.

Tabuse Mitsuko. "Genryō, sairiyō e no kyōryoku to shisei." In *Gomi ni hikari o ateyō: Sono tekisei shori, shigenka e no michi,* edited by Yorimoto Katsumi, 124–32. Tokyo: Nippō, 1975.

Tachibanaki, Toshiaki. *Confronting Income Inequality in Japan: A Comparative Analysis of Causes, Consequences, and Reform.* Cambridge: MIT Press, 2005.

Taguchi Masami. *Gomi mondai hyakka: Genjō to taisaku.* Tokyo: Shin Nihon Shuppansha, 1991.

Taitō-ku Kankyō Seisōbu Kankyō Hozenka. *Edo kara manabu watashitachi no kurashi: Kodomo no tame no shōene dokuhon.* Tokyo: Taitō-ku Kankyō Seisōbu Kankyō Hozenka, 2007.

Takahashi Nobuaki. "Seichō wa yutaka na shakai o motarasu no ka?" *DIO: Rengō sōken repōto* (December 2015): 4–7.

——. *Yasashī keizaigaku: Zero seichō o yutaka ni ikiru.* Tokyo: Chikuma Shobō, 2003.

Takahashi Sei'ichi and Ota Ichirō. "Numazu-shi no purasuchikku gomi no bunbetsu to sono kōka ni tsuite." *Haikibutsu gakkai shi* 16, no. 5 (2005): 20–24.

Takahashi Takayuki. "TOKYO SLIM '89: Gomi genryō no tame ni." *Toseijin* 53, no. 7 (July 1989): 16–22.

Takashina Shūji. "Nōritsu to muda." *Kōkoku* 25, no. 4 (July–August 1984): 2–3.

Takatsuki Hiroshi. *Gomi mondai to raifusutairu: Konna kurashi wa tsuzukanai.* Tokyo: Nihon Hyōronsha, 2004.

"Talks at Google." https://www.youtube.com/watch?v=w1-HMMX_NR8.

Tamanoi, Mariko Asano. "Suffragist Women, Corrupt Officials, and Waste Control in Prewar Japan: Two Plays by Kaneko Shigeri." *Journal of Asian Studies* 68, no. 3 (August 2009): 805–34.

Tamaru Misuzu, Mikanagi Rika, and Yamazaki Eriko. "Fujin kōron itobata kaigi: Akarui kechikechi de fukyō o norikiru." *Fujin kōron* 83, no. 21 (December 7, 1998): 164–69.

Tamura Kazuhiko. "Rejā shōhigaku to jiyū jikan." *Doshisha shōgaku* 29, no. 4–5–6 (March 1978): 290–311.

Tanaka Atsuo. *Waribashi wa mottainai? Shokutaku kara mita shinrin mondai.* Tokyo: Chikuma Shobō, 2007.

Tanaka Kakuei. *Building a New Japan: A Plan for Remodeling the Japanese Archipelago.* Translated by Simul International. Tokyo: Simul Press, 1973.

Tanaka Sen'ichi. "Shin seikatsu undō to Shin Seikatsu Undō Kyōkai." *Seijō bungei* 181 (January 2003): 16–54.

Tanaka, Stefan. *New Times in Modern Japan*. Princeton: Princeton University Press, 2004.

Tanaka Yasuo. *Nantonaku, kurisutaru*. Tokyo: Kawade Shobō Shinsha, 1981.

Taniguchi Masakazu. "Mono no mochisugi ya muda no kakko warusa, yutakasa no naimen de dai henka ga okite iru." *Keieisha* 55, no. 3 (March 2001): 58–61.

Tateishi Yoshio. "Seikatsu taikoku e no kigyō no yakuwari." *Keizaijin* 45, no. 10 (October 1991): 16–19. Part of the series "Nihon wa seikatsu taikoku tariuru ka."

Tatsumi Nagisa. *"Suteru!" gijutsu*. Tokyo: Takarajimasha Shinsho, 2000.

Tazaki Masami. *Bijinesu pāson no tame no danshari shikō no susume*. Tokyo: Dōbunkan Shuppan, 2010.

——. "Kyaria keisei mo 'danshari shikō' de umaku iku." *Za nijūichi* 28, no. 6 (June 2011): 56–57. Part of the series "Muri, muda, mura o nakushite, atama no naka o sukkiri kaishō! Sutoresu zero no 'danshari' shigoto jutsu."

Terai Minako. "Mottainai to iu koto: Dō jidai kan." *Shisō no kagaku* 39 (June 1965): 111–12.

Teruoka Itsuko. *Yutakasa to wa nani ka*. Tokyo: Iwanami Shoten, 1989.

"There's a Name for Architectural Relics That Serve No Purpose." http://www.slate. com/blogs/the_eye/2014/08/27/roman_mars_99_percent_invisible_on_ thomassons_architectural_relics_that.html.

Thomas, Julia Adeney. "Using Japan to Think Globally: The Natural Subject of History and Its Hopes." In *Japan at Nature's Edge: The Environmental Context of a Global Power*, edited by Ian Jared Miller, Julia Adeney Thomas, and Brett L. Walker, 293–310. Honolulu: University of Hawaii Press, 2013.

Thompson, Michael. *Rubbish Theory: The Creation and Destruction of Value*. New York: Oxford University Press, 1979.

Tokutei kateiyō kiki saishōhinka hō. Hōritsu dai kyūjūnana gō. June 5, 1998. http:// law.e-gov.go.jp/htmldata/H10/H10HO097html.

Tokyo Denryoku Eigyōbu and Shōenerugī Sentā. *Okyakusama no shōenerugī ishiki to kōdō: 'Shōenerugī ankēto' no bunseki kekka ni tsuite*. Tokyo: Tokyo Denryoku Eigyōbu and Shōenerugī Sentā, 1980.

"Tokyo no hyakunen: Sumidagawa." *Tokyo o utsukushiku* 35 (July 25, 1968): 7.

"TOKYO SLIM IN DOME: Sekai de hajimete gomi o tanoshiku shiru." *Gekkan haikibutsu* 16, no. 5 (May 1990): 66–73.

Tokyo-to Eiga Kyōkai To Kōhōshitsu. *Tokyo nyūsu: Tokyo no gomi*. Tokyo: May 1954.

Tokyo-to Eiseikyoku Yobōbu Bōekika, ed. *Ka to hae kujo no kyakkan chōsa*. Tokyo: Tokyo-to Eiseikyoku Yobōbu, 1967.

Tokyo-to Kōhōshitsu Kōhōbu, ed. *"Ka to hae o nakusu tomin undō": Tokyo-to Chūō Jissen Honbu jisshi hōkokusho*. Tokyo: Tokyo-to Kōhōshitsu Kōhōbu, 1961.

"Tokyo-to no gomi shinyō shori no genkyō to kadai." *Tokyo raifu* 21, no. 2 (February 1983): 8–35.

Tokyo-to Seisōkyoku, ed. *Minna de gomi mondai o kangaeru: Shōwa 51 nendo gomi gekkan jisshi hōkokusho*. Tokyo: Tokyo-to Seisōkyoku, 1977.

——, ed. *Tokyo no gomi: Sono genkyō to mondai*. Tokyo: Tokyo-to Seisōkyoku, 1971.

Tokyo-to Seisōkyoku Sōmubu Fukyū Chōsaka, ed. *Tokyo no gomi ni tsuite kangaeru fōramu: Tokyo Slim '89*. Tokyo: Tokyo-to Seisōkyoku Sōmubu Fukyū Chōsaka, 1989.

Tokyo-to Seisōkyoku Sōmubu Sōmuka, ed. *Tokyo-to seisō jigyō hyakunen shi*. Tokyo: Tokyo-to, 2000.

Tokyo-to Tominshitsu, ed. *Gomi mondai ni kansuru seron chōsa*. Tokyo: Tokyo-to Tominshitsu, 1973.

———, ed. *Gomi mondai ni kansuru seron chōsa hōkokusho*. Tokyo: Tokyo-to Tominshitsu, 1971.

Tomii, Reiko. "State v. (Anti-)Art: *Model 1,000-Yen Note Incident* by Akasegawa Genpei and Company." *positions* 10, no. 1 (Spring 2002): 141–72.

"Tomin wa gomi mondai o dō miru ka (sono 6): Gomi mondai ni kansuru seron chōsa." *Gomi sensō shūhō* 111 (March 1, 1974): 8–12.

Toyama Shigeru. *Nihonjin no kinben, chochikukan: Asu no keizai o sasaeru mono*. Tokyo: Tōyō Keizai Shinpōsha, 1987.

Tsuchida Takashi. *Kyōsei no jidai: Tsukaisute jidai o koete*. Tokyo: Jushinsha, 1981.

———. "'Shi' no sekai kara 'sei' no sekai e." *80 nendai* 4 (July 1980). In *Kyōsei no jidai: Tsukaisute jidai o koete*, 108–16. Tokyo: Jushinsha, 1981.

———. "Tanoshiku nakayoku samazama ni: 'Tsukaisute Jidai o Kangaeru Kai' no jūnen to korekara." In *Korekara dō suru shakai to kurashi: "Tsukaisute Jidai o Kangaeru Kai" sōritsu jūshūnen kinen shinpojiumu*, edited by "Tsukaisute Jidai o Kangaeru Kai" Jūshūnen Shinpo Jikkō Iinkai, i–xii. Tokyo: Hakujusha, 1984.

———. "'Tsukaisute jidai' no hakyoku wa chikai: Ningen no ikikata o kaenakute wa." *Asahi jānaru* 25, no. 28 (July 1983): 3–4.

Tsuji Mieko. "Nōka no seikatsu kaizen: Nōrinshō no shidō no nerai." *Fujin to nenshōsha* 28 (September 1955): 9–10.

Tsuji Shin'ichi. *Shiawase-tte, nan dakke: "Yutakasa" to iu gensō o koete*. Tokyo: Sofuto Banku Kurieichibu, 2008.

———. *Surō izu byūchifuru: Ososa to shite no bunka*. Tokyo: Heibonsha, 2001.

"Tsukaisute jidai o kangaenaosu (July 14, 1973)." In *Korekara dō suru shakai to kurashi: "Tsukaisute Jidai o Kangaeru Kai" sōritsu jūshūnen kinen shinpojiumu*, edited by "Tsukaisute Jidai o Kangaeru Kai" Jūshūnen Shinpo Jikkō Iinkai, 200–202. Tokyo: Hakujusha, 1984.

"Tsukaisute Jidai o Kangaeru Kai" Jūshūnen Shinpo Jikkō Iinkai, ed. *Korekara dō suru shakai to kurashi: "Tsukaisute Jidai o Kangaeru Kai" sōritsu jūshūnen kinen shinpojiumu*. Tokyo: Hakujusha, 1984.

"Tsukaisute Jidai o Kangaeru Kai kiyaku." In *Korekara dō suru shakai to kurashi: "Tsukaisute Jidai o Kangaeru Kai" sōritsu jūshūnen kinen shinpojiumu*, edited by "Tsukaisute Jidai o Kangaeru Kai" Jūshūnen Shinpo Jikkō Iinkai, 205–6. Tokyo: Hakujusha, 1984.

"Tsukaisute Jidai o Kangaeru Kai: Munōyaku yasai nado o 'kangaeru sozai' to shite ima no 'benri de yutaka na shakai' o toinaosu." *Asahi jānaru* 27, no. 51 (December 1985): 40–41.

"Tsukaisute jidai to monobusoku." *Gekkan sekai keizai* 2, no. 22 (November 1973): 224–25.

Tsuru Shigeto. "In Place of GNP." *Social Science Information* 10 (August 1971): 7–21.

Tsutsui, William M. *Manufacturing Ideology: Scientific Management in Twentieth-Century Japan*. Princeton: Princeton University Press, 1998.

———. "The Way of Efficiency: Ueno Yōichi and Scientific Management in Twentieth-Century Japan." *Modern Asian Studies* 35, no. 2 (2001): 441–67.

Tuttle, Brad. "Got Stuff? Typical American Home Is Cluttered with Possessions—and Stressing Us Out." *Time*, July 19, 2012. http://business.time.com/2012/07/19/got-stuff-typical-american-home-cluttered-with-possessions-and-stressing-us-out/.

Ueno Hideo. "'Yutaka' na Nihon no uragawa 'sanpai Ginza o iku.'" *Gekkan jichiken* 31, no. 6 (June 1989): 35–44. Part of the series "Futatabi, gomi sensō ka?"

Ueno Shige. "Seikatsu ni wa konna muda ga aru." *Fujin gahō* 533 (February 1949): [21–22].

Ueno Yōichi. *Nōritsugaku genron.* Tokyo: Nihon Nōritsu Gakkō, 1948.

——. "Seikatsu jikan no gōrika." *Nōritsudō* 22, no. 11 (November 1955): 2–8.

Ueyama Kazuo. "Tokyo orinpikku to Shibuya, Tokyo." In *Tokyo orinpikku no shakai keizai shi,* edited by Oikawa Yoshinobu, 39–74. Tokyo: Nihon Keizai Hyōronsha, 2009.

Umeda Masaaki. *Jikan to jinsei ni tsuite: Saigetsu no kūhi to sei no jūjitsu.* Tokyo: Nihon Tosho Kankōkai, 1998.

Uno Masao. "Shōhi kakumei to rōhi kakumei: Amerika to Nihon." *Jitsugyō no Nihon* 64, no. 9 (May 1, 1961): 58–60.

Uotsuka Junnosuke. *Ā! Mottainai: Uotsuka Junnosuke no ryōri jō, isshoku hyakuen, kyūkyoku no menyū.* Tokyo: Kōbunsha, 1995.

Usui, Kazuo. *Marketing and Consumption in Modern Japan.* London: Routledge, 2014.

Vlastos, Stephen. "Bookending Postwar Japan: Seeing a Whole Greater Than the Sum of Its Parts." In *Japan since 1945: From Postwar to Post-Bubble,* edited by Christopher Gerteis and Timothy S. George, 236–40. New York: Bloomsbury, 2013.

Wada Hiromi. *Shiawase o tsukamu! Jikan no tsukaikata: Bukiyō na hito no tame no taimu manejimento.* Tokyo: Daiyamondosha, 2005.

Wada Kenji. "Kodomo o tsukuru mae ni kane o tsukure." *Bessatsu jitsugyō no Nihon* 16 (June 1951): 69–81.

"Wadai no minimarisuto ga kataru 'Mono o sutete eta "shigoto no meritto."'" *Nikkei bijinesu associé* (January 2016): 38–40.

Wakamiya Akitsugu. "Mono ga 'aru' kedo 'nai' toki no seikatsu tekunikku: Mono o ikasu mottainai no kokoro." *Ōru seikatsu* 29, no. 4 (March 1974): 74–76.

Walker, Brett L. *Toxic Archipelago: A History of Industrial Disease in Japan.* Seattle: University of Washington Press, 2010.

Watanabe Misuzu. "Sutoppu za daiokishin: Shufu no funtōki." *Rekishi chiri kyōiku* 584 (October 1998): 28–33. Part of the series "Daiokishin osen."

Watanabe Osamu. "*Yutaka na shakai*" *Nihon no kōzō.* Tokyo: Rōdō Junpōsha, 1990.

"Watashitachi ga shiawase ni naru 'setsuyaku' to wa donna koto?" *Shufu to seikatsu* 28, no. 13 (November 1973): 271–73.

Weber, Lauren. *In Cheap We Trust: The Story of a Misunderstood American Virtue.* New York: Little, Brown and Company, 2009.

"What We Can Learn about Frugality from Japan." https://www.reddit.com/r/Frugal/comments/4mkxb7/what_we_can_learn_about_frugality_from_japan/.

World Commission on Environment and Development. *Report of the World Commission on Environment and Development: Our Common Future.* 1987.

Yamada Hitoshi. "Anata wa mainichi roku jikan mo mudazukai shite iru: 'Gyakusan no yoteihyō' ichinichi o koku tsukau hō." *Purejidento* 44, no. 13 (June 12, 2006): 50–53.

Yamada Kunihiro. *Ichioku nin no kankyō kakeibo: Risaikuru jidai no seikatsu kakumei.* Tokyo: Fujiwara Shoten, 1996.

Yamaguchi Mutsumi. "Kankonsōsai no kansoka wa kanō ka: Yamagata-ken Nanyō-shi no zōtō kiroku o chūshin ni." In *Kurashi no kakumei: Sengo nōson no seikatsu kaizen jigyō to shin seikatsu undō,* edited by Tanaka Sen'ichi, 352–72. Tokyo: Nōsangyoson Bunka Kyōkai, 2011.

Yamakawa Ayako, ed. "Shōene seikatsu 100 no kotsu." *Kurashi no techō* 57 (April–May 2012): 60–69.

Yamakawa Hiroji et al., eds. *Shōwa kōkoku 60-nen shi.* Tokyo: Kōdansha, 1987.

Yamakawa Katsumi. "Senri nyū taun no panikku." *Kansai daigaku hōgaku ronshū* 29, no. 4 (December 1979): 73–99.

Yamamoto Isao. "Tsukaisute yōki o kangaeru." *Chūō kaigi kaihō* 26 (December 1986): 15–17.

Yamamoto Tazu. *Setsuyaku seikatsu nyūmon: Rakuraku dekiru 63 no chie.* Osaka: Sōgensha, 1999.

Yamanouchi Shōgo. "Eko mākechingu e no apurōchi: 'Gomi sensō' ka no mākechingu o kangaeru." *Sērusu manejā* 8, no. 5 (May 1972): 74–78.

Yamaori Tetsuo. "Nihonjin wa ima, donna kachi o shinrai subeki ka." *Bōsei* 37, no. 7 (July 2006): 11–18.

Yamasaki Hisato. *Nenshū 100-man en no yutaka na setsuyaku seikatsu jutsu.* Tokyo: Bungei Shunjū, 2011.

Yamashita Hideko. "Besuto serā no chosha ga, katazuke heta ni mo wakariyasuku pointo o kaisetsu 'danshari' nyūmon." *Purejidento* 49, no. 34 (October 29, 2011). 4–13.

———. *Shigoto ni kiku "danshari".* Tokyo: Kadokawa Mākechingu, 2011.

———. *Shin, katazukejutsu danshari: "Katazuke" de jinsei ga kawaru.* Tokyo: Magajin Hausu, 2009.

Yamashita Hideko and Tatsumura Osamu. *Kokoro to karada o jōka suru danshari daietto.* Tokyo: Sekai Bunkasha, 2011.

Yamashita, Samuel Hideo. *Daily Life in Wartime Japan, 1940–1945.* Lawrence: University Press of Kansas, 2015.

Yamataka Shigeru. "Kechikechi undō to ningensei kaifuku." *Gekkan kokumin seikatsu* 4, no. 4 (April 1974): 1.

Yamato Yūzō. "'Setsuyaku' to 'kechi' to wa chigau." *Shufu to seikatsu* 28, no. 13 (November 1973): 268–70. Part of the series "Shin setsuyaku jidai."

Yamazaki Eriko. *Yamazaki Eriko no shinpuru setsuyaku seikatsu e yōkoso: Muda naku, yutori aru kurashi o tsukuru 200 aidia.* Tokyo: Shufu no Tomosha, 2005.

Yanagisawa Takashi. "Gomi no sairiyō." *Jurisuto* 571 (October 1, 1974): 46–49.

Yasuoka Masahiro. "Osomatsu to mottainai." *Shi to tomo* 12, no. 3 (March 1960): 2–8.

Yōki hōsō ni kakaru bunbetsu shūshū oyobi saishōhinka no sokushin tō ni kansuru hōritsu. Hōritsu dai hyakujūni gō. June 16, 1995. http://law.e-gov.go.jp/htmldata/H07/H07HO112.html.

Yōki hōsō risaikuru hō. http://www.meti.go.jp/policy/recycle/main/admin_info/law/04/.

Yomiuri Shinbunsha, ed. *Daisan no shigen: Gaborojī saizensen.* Tokyo: Risaikuru Bunkasha, 1987.

"Yo no naka zeitaku ni narimashita: Taikenteki kechikechi no susume." *Fujin seikatsu* (September 1973): 212–15.

Yorimoto Katsumi. "Gomi ni hikari o ateyō." In *Gomi ni hikari o ateyō: Sono tekisei shori, shigenka e no michi,* edited by Yorimoto Katsumi, 13–43. Tokyo: Nippō, 1975.

———. "Tokyo no gomi sensō to surimu '89." *Ashita* 8, no. 12 (December 1989): 123–27.

Yorimoto, Katsumi. "Tokyo's Serious Waste Problem." *Japan Quarterly* 37, no. 3 (July–September 1990): 328–33.

Yoshida Sei. "Kechikechi undō no susume." *PPM* 4, no. 10 (October 1973): 1.

Yoshikoshi Kōichirō. *Muda na shigoto wa mō, yameyō! Zangyō suru hodo hima ja nai.* Tokyo: Kanki Shuppan, 2008.

Yoshimi, Shunya. "'America' as Desire and Violence: Americanization in Postwar Japan and Asia during the Cold War." Translated by David Buist. *Inter-Asia Cultural Studies* 4, no. 3 (2003): 433–50.

Yoshino Shōji. *Atarashī yutakasa: Gendai seikatsu yōshiki no tenkan.* Tokyo: Rengō Shuppan, 1984.

Young, Molly. "Domestic Purging with Japanese Tidying Guru Marie Kondo." *New York Magazine,* February 10, 2015.

Yourgrau, Barry. "The Origin Story of Marie Kondo's Decluttering Empire." *The New Yorker,* December 8, 2015.

"Zeitaku wa teki da!" *Josei kōron* (June 1946): 59.

Zen Chifuren 30-nen no ayumi. Tokyo: Zenkoku Chiiki Fujin Dantai Renraku Kyōgikai, 1986.

Zukeran Kaoru. "Tsukaisute Jidai o Kangaeru Kai." *Gendai no me* 16, no. 1 (November 1975): 198–203.

Index

CPSIA information can be obtained
at www.ICGtesting.com
Printed in the USA
LVHW111310250522
719727LV00011B/67/J